ECONOMIC$ FOR BANKER$

EDMOND J. SEIFRIED

EDUCATION POLICY & DEVELOPMENT

AMERICAN BANKERS ASSOCIATION

1120 Connecticut Avenue, N.W.
Washington, D.C. 20036

Library of Congress Cataloging-in-Publication Data

Seifried, Edmond J.
  Economics for bankers.

  Includes index.
  1. Economics. I. Title.
HB171.5.S456 1987   330′.024332   87-27003
ISBN 0-89982-150-2

© 1987 by the American Bankers Association
All rights reserved
Printed in the United States of America

This book is dedicated to my friend, Dan Ettinger.

CONTENTS

Chapter 1

An Introduction to Economics	1
Objectives	1
Why Study Economics?	3
Economics: The Dismal Science	4
Microeconomics vs. Macroeconomics	5
Tools of the Trade	6
Misconceptions and Half-Truths	12
Economic Goals	15
Summary	16
Key Words	17
Questions for Review	18
Economics in the News	21

Chapter 2

Mathematics and Statistics	23
Objectives	23
Expressing Linear Relationships with Equations	25
Statistics and Economics	46
Data Conversions	55
Statistics and Economic Forecasts	58
Summary	60
Key Words	61
Questions for Review	62
Economics in the News	65

Chapter 3

Economic Problems, Systems, and Resources	67
Objectives	67
Scarcity and Unlimited Wants	69
Resource Payments	70
The Essence of Economics	71
Consumption and Investment Choice	72
The Command System and the Market System	84
Foundations of the Market Economy	87
Summary	93
Key Words	94

    Questions for Review 95
    Economics in the News 97

Chapter 4

The Concepts of Demand and Supply 101
    Objectives 101
    The Concept of Demand 103
    The Concept of Supply 115
    Supply, Demand, and the Market System 121
    Summary 130
    Key Words 131
    Questions for Review 131
    Economics in the News 135

Chapter 5

Demand and Supply in the Marketplace 139
    Objectives 139
    Market Equilibrium 141
    Applications of Supply and Demand 141
    Market Intervention 147
    The Concept of Elasticity 151
    Determinants of Elasticity of Demand 164
    Elasticity of Supply 166
    Determinants of Elasticity of Supply 167
    Other Measures of Elasticity 169
    Summary 171
    Key Words 172
    Questions for Review 172
    Economics in the News 175

Chapter 6

Government and the Mixed Economy 177
    Objectives 177
    The Private Sector and the Role of Government 179
    Revenues and Expenditures in the Public Sector 185
    Summary 197
    Key Words 198
    Questions for Review 198
    Economics in the News 201

Chapter 7

Business Organization 203
    Objectives 203

Types of Business Organization 205
The Evolution of American Industry 209
Bigness vs. Economic Efficiency 210
Barriers to Market Entry 219
The Health of American Business 220
Summary 221
Key Words 222
Questions for Review 222
Economics in the News 225

Chapter 8
Individuals in the U.S. Economy 227
    Objectives 227
    Population Trends 229
    The Labor Force 234
    U.S. Income Statistics 234
    History of Collective Bargaining 240
    Summary 249
    Key Words 250
    Questions for Review 250
    Economics in the News 253

Chapter 9
National Income Accounting 255
    Objectives 255
    National Income Accounting 257
    Gross National Product 258
    Other National Income Accounts 267
    Adjusting GNP for Price Changes 270
    Inflating and Deflating the GNP 274
    Summary 275
    Key Words 276
    Questions for Review 276
    Economics in the News 279

Chapter 10
The Business Cycle 281
    Objectives 281
    The Business Cycle 283
    Economic Indicators and Econometric Models 291
    Tracking the Composite Leading Index 306
    High-Tech Economic Forecasts 309
    Summary 312
    Key Words 313

    Questions for Review 313
    Economics in the News 315

Chapter 11

Unemployment 319
    Objectives 319
    Definition of Unemployment 321
    Discouraged Workers 327
    Underemployment 328
    Types of Unemployment 329
    Summary 335
    Key Words 336
    Questions for Review 336
    Economics in the News 339

Chapter 12

Inflation 341
    Objectives 341
    Definition of Inflation 343
    The Effects of Inflation 354
    The Sources of Inflation 358
    Inflation and Real Output 360
    Summary 367
    Key Words 368
    Questions for Review 368
    Economics in the News 371

Chapter 13

Classical vs. Keynesian Economics 373
    Objectives 373
    The Circular Flow of the U.S. Economy 375
    The Classical Doctrine 377
    Modern Classical Economics 381
    Keynesian Economics 384
    Summary 390
    Key Words 391
    Questions for Review 391
    Economics in the News 393

Chapter 14

Fundamentals of Keynesian Economics 395
    Objectives 395

Aggregate Demand 397
Aggregate Supply 413
The Equilibrium Level of National Income 413
The Multiplier Effect 417
The Paradox of Thrift 420
Inflationary and Recessionary Gaps 420
Summary 423
Key Words 424
Questions for Review 424
Economics in the News 427

Chapter 15

Keynesian Fiscal Policy in Action 429
   Objectives 429
   The Theory Behind Fiscal Policy 431
   The Nuts and Bolts of Fiscal Policy 435
   The Mathematics of Fiscal Policy 439
   Automatic vs. Discretionary Fiscal Policy 439
   Fiscal Policy Issues and Problems 442
   Federal Budget Policy 446
   Critiques of Keynesian Fiscal Policy 449
   Summary 453
   Key Words 454
   Questions for Review 454
   Economics in the News 457

Chapter 16

Current Macroeconomic Issues: The National Debt 459
   Objectives 459
   Definition of the Public Debt 461
   Public Debt Issues 464
   Summary 474
   Key Words 474
   Questions for Review 475
   Economics in the News 477

Appendixes

   I. Money 479
   II. Money Creation, Commercial Banks, and the Federal Reserve ... 489
   III. Federal Reserve Policy 503

Index 515

Figures

2.1	The Quadrant Coordinate System	30
2.2	Graph of Linear Equation	31
2.3	Graph of Linear Equation	32
2.4	Graph of Linear Equation	33
2.5	Graph of Linear Equation	34
2.6	Graph of Linear Equation	35
2.7	Graph of Linear Equation	36
2.8	Graph of Linear Equation	37
2.9	Graph of Linear Equation	38
2.10	Graph of Nonlinear Equation	40
2.11	Graph of Linear Equation	41
2.12	Five Ordered Pairs	42
2.13	Graph of Linear Equation	44
2.14	Graph of Linear Equation	45
3.1	Production Possibilities Curve	75
3.2	Resource Availability Changes and the Production Possibilities Curve	76
3.3	Technological Changes and the Production Possibilities Curve	77
3.4	Depreciation and the Production Possibilities Curve	79
3.5	Production Possibilities Curve for an Underdeveloped Economy	80
3.6	Output Possibilities, First National Bank	91
4.1	Consumer Demand Curve, Good X	108
4.2	Market Demand Curve	110
4.3	Change in Demand and Demand Curve Shifts	112
4.4	Change in Quantity Demanded and Movement Along the Curve	113
4.5	Change in Demand and Change in Quantity Demanded	114
4.6	Supply Curve	119
4.7	Change in Supply and Change in Quantity Supplied	120
4.8	Market Supply and Demand Curves, Good X	122
4.9	Increase in Demand with Supply Constant	123
4.10	Decrease in Demand with Supply Constant	124
4.11	Increase in Supply with Demand Constant	125
4.12	Decrease in Supply with Demand Constant	126
4.13	Increase in Demand with Decrease in Supply	127
4.14	Increase in Supply with Increase in Demand	128
5.1	Supply and Demand Curves, Good X	142
5.2	Supply and Demand Curves, Loanable Funds	143
5.3	Supply and Demand for Gasoline, 1977 and 1981	146
5.4	Minimum Wage and the Market for Unskilled Labor	150
5.5	Elasticity of Demand: Special Cases	155
5.6	Elasticity and the Demand Curve	158

5.7	Measurement of Elasticity from a Linear Demand Curve	160
5.8	Estimate of Elasticity from a Nonlinear Demand Curve	161
5.9	Time and Elasticity of Supply	168
6.1	Spillover Costs in a Competitive Market	183
6.2	Spillover Benefits in a Competitive Market	184
6.3	Proportional, Regressive, and Progressive Taxes	190
6.4	Sales Tax Incidence and Elasticity of Demand	194
6.5	Sales Tax Incidence and Completely Inelastic Demand	195
6.6	Sales Tax Incidence and Infinitely Elastic Demand	196
8.1	Components of Population Change, 1960–85	229
8.2	Educational Attainment of Americans 25 Years and Over	232
8.3	Educational Attainment of Black Americans 25 Years and Over	233
8.4	Union Membership in the United States, 1900–85	241
8.5	Percent Change in Wages and Salaries, by Union Status	246
8.6	Average Union Wage Rates, Skilled vs. Unskilled Workers	247
8.7	Percentage of Workers Covered by COLA	248
10.1	Phases of the Business Cycle	283
10.2	The Business Cycle	286
10.3	Leading, Coincidental, and Lagging Indicators and the Business Cycle	305
11.1	Unemployment by Duration, Selected Quarters, 1979 and 1983	326
11.2	Unemployment Rate and Average Duration of Unemployment, 1953–83	326
11.3	Unemployment Rate and the Business Cycle, 1948–83	330
11.4	Unemployment Rates in Selected Industries, Selected Months and Years	331
11.5	Unemployment Rates for Major Industry Divisions, Selected Quarters and Years	332
11.6	Characteristics of the Unemployed, 1985	333
11.7	Unemployment Rates by Education, 1982	334
12.1	Phillips Curve for Great Britain, 1861–1913	362
12.2	Phillips Curves for the United States, 1960s and 1970s	363
12.3	Phillips Curve Data, 1961–86	365
12.4	Phillips Curves, 1961–86	366
13.1	Circular Flow Model	376
13.2	Savings and Investment in the Classical Model	379
13.3	An Aggregate Demand Curve for an Economy	381
13.4	Two Aggregate Supply Curves	382
13.5	Modern Classical Theory: Aggregate Demand and Aggregate Supply	383
13.6	Keynesian Liquidity-Preference Curve	388
14.1	Planned Consumption and Planned Savings Schedules	400
14.2	An Autonomous Change in Consumption	407

14.3	Induced Change in Consumption and the Marginal Propensity to Consume	408
14.4	Investment Demand, Autonomous $I = I_0$	410
14.5	Building the Aggregate Demand Function: Investment Demand	411
14.6	Aggregate Demand (Consumption, Investment, Government Expenditures, and Net Exports)	412
14.7	Aggregate Supply Curve	414
14.8	Equilibrium National Income	415
14.9	Multiplier Effect for an Increase and Decrease in Investment Spending	421
14.10	Recessionary and Inflationary Gaps	422
15.1	Inflationary and Deflationary Gaps	432
15.2	Fiscal Policy Removal of an Inflationary Gap	433
15.3	Fiscal Policy Removal of a Recessionary Gap	434
15.4	Actual and Full Employment Budgets, 1960–84	448
16.1	The Crowding-Out Effect	467
16.2	The Crowding-Out Effect and Deficit Spending	468

Tables

1.1	Balance Sheet, Pat's Pizza Parlor	8
1.2	Stamping Machine Performance, ACME Products	9
1.3	Danger of Inflation	11
2.1	Time and Distance Equation	25
2.2	Cost of Account by Checks Written	27
2.3	Ordered Pairs, $y = 3 + .5x$	44
2.4	Ordered Pairs, $y = 5 - .5x$	45
2.5	Daily Balances, Account X	47
2.6	Balances Occurring in Account X	47
2.7	Adjacent Balances	48
2.8	Nonadjacent Balances	48
2.9	Ranked Balances, Odd Number	49
2.10	Ranked Balances, Even Number	50
2.11	Daily Balances, Account Y	51
2.12	Student Examination Scores	52
2.13	Deviation of Scores, Student Set A	53
2.14	Squared Deviation Scores, Student Set A	53
2.15	Standard Deviation of Profits vs. Rates of Return, 1926–78	55
2.16	Total Cash Assets of Commercial Banking Institutions, 1986	56
2.17	U.S. Unemployment Rates for 1981–85 Compared with Forecasts by Three Leading Economic Forecasters	59
3.1	Production Possibilities: "Guns" vs. "Butter"	73
3.2	Two Economic Systems	86
3.3	Consumer Items in the United States and the Soviet Union, 1984	86
3.4	Productivity Evaluation	90
4.1	Demand Schedule, Good X	107
4.2	Market Demand Curve, Good X and Four Consumers	109
4.3	Market Demand Equation	110
4.4	Unit Price and Quantity Supplied, Good X	118
5.1	Changes to Prime Rate, 1929–86	144
5.2	Average Prime Rate, 1947–86	145
5.3	Price and Consumption of Gasoline	147
5.4	Bank Credit Card Finance Charges: Maximum Allowed by Law for Selected States, 1985	148
5.5	Teenage Unemployment, 1979–86	150
5.6	Unit Price and Quantity Demanded, Good X	155
5.7	Price, Quantity, Revenues, and Elasticity	162
5.8	Revenue Test for Elasticity	163
5.9	Demand Elasticity Estimates	165

5.10	Unit Price and Quantity Supplied, Good X	167
6.1	Growth in Government Size	180
6.2	Government Revenues, 1975 and 1984	186
6.3	Government Expenditures, 1975 and 1984	187
6.4	Hypothetical Income Tax Schedule	189
6.5	Two Progressive Tax Schemes	190
6.6	Federal Income Tax for a Single Person, 1986	191
6.7	Tax Revenues as a Percentage of Gross Domestic Product (GDP)	197
7.1	Types of Businesses in the United States	205
7.2	Receipts by Type of Business	205
7.3	Top 10 American Businesses, Selected Years	209
7.4	Major Antitrust Laws	211
7.5	Merger and Acquisition Transactions	212
7.6	Four-Firm Concentration Ratios for Selected U.S. Manufacturing Industries	213
7.7	Annual Sales: Major Petroleum Firms, 1985	214
7.8	Herfindahl Index for Four Hypothetical Markets	215
7.9	Herfindahl Calculations of Oil and Gas Industry, 1985	216
7.10	Herfindahl Index for Selected U.S. Manufacturing Industries	217
7.11	Justice Department Merger Guidelines	218
7.12	Industrial and Commercial Failures: Number and Liabilities	220
7.13	Business Failures by Industry Sector, 1985 and 1986	221
8.1	U.S. Resident Population, Median Age for Selected Years	230
8.2	Bank Customer Growth Pattern: Population Projection by Age Bracket, 1980–90	231
8.3	Mobility of Americans	231
8.4	Civilian Labor Force Participation	235
8.5	Functional Distribution of Income, 1985	235
8.6	Labor's Share vs. Owner's Share, National Income	236
8.7	Income Distribution by Households, 1985	236
8.8	Current- and Constant-Dollar Median Family Income for Selected Years	237
8.9	Family Income Distribution by Quintile, 1985	237
8.10	Weighted Average Poverty Levels	238
8.11	Persons Below the Poverty Level, by Race and Family Status, 1985	239
8.12	Median Hourly Earnings, by Job Category	239
8.13	Median Weekly Earnings, White-Collar Jobs	240
9.1	U.S. Gross National Product and Components, 1985	261
9.2	U.S. Gross National Product and Components, Selected Years, 1940–85	262
9.3	Average Weekly Hours of Production Workers	265
9.4	The Underground Economy	267
9.5	National Income Accounts, 1985	268

9.6	Comparison of Savings Rates	270
9.7	Computation of Adjusted Hypothetical GNP	271
9.8	Current-Dollar vs. Constant-Dollar GNP, Selected Years	274
10.1	Peaks and Troughs of Business Cycles in the United States, 1854–1982	285
10.2	Specific Peak and Trough Dates, Leading Indicators	298
10.3	Specific Peak and Trough Dates for Selected Coincidental Indicators	301
10.4	Specific Peak and Trough Dates for Selected Lagging Indicators	304
10.5	Historical Variability of Forecast Errors	311
11.1	Unemployed Persons and Unemployment Rates, by Reason for Unemployment, 1973–83	324
11.2	Duration of Unemployment, 1984–86	327
11.3	Estimate of Unemployment, Including the Discouraged Worker, 1982	328
12.1	Consumer Price Indexes, Selected Years	344
12.2	Changes in Consumer Prices, All Urban Consumers	345
12.3	Consumer Price Index: Relative Importance of Major Groups, 1982–84	349
12.4	Consumer Price Index, All Urban Consumers, Selected Areas	351
12.5	Consumer Price Index, 1965–86	353
12.6	Consumer Price Index and the Value of a Dollar	356
12.7	Phillips Curve Data for the 1980s	364
13.1	Interest Rates and Investment Expenditures, 1929–41	387
14.1	Planned Consumption and Savings at Various Disposable Income Levels	399
14.2	Consumption, Savings, and Disposable Income: Marginal and Average Propensities	403
14.3	History of APC and APS: Selected Years, 1930–85	405
14.4	National Income Determination, Hypothetical Economy	416
14.5	The Multiplier Process	418
15.1	Hypothetical Economy without Government Spending	436
15.2	Hypothetical Economy with Government Spending	436
15.3	Hypothetical Economy: Impact of Taxes and Government Spending	437
15.4	Fiscal Policy in Action	440
16.1	Government Tax Receipts, Spending, Deficits, and Total Public Debt, 1929–87	461
16.2	Public Debt Relative to GNP, 1940–87	462
16.3	Interest on National Debt and its Relation to GNP and Federal Expenditures	463
16.4	Ownership Share of Public Debt, 1984	464
16.5	Recent Increases in Public Debt	470

PREFACE

Economics for Bankers has been written to meet the educational and professional development needs of bankers. Bankers must have an understanding of basic economic principles. Therefore, special efforts have been made in producing this book to tie economic concepts, theories, principles, and techniques to the banking industry. Banking statistics and examples are used whenever possible to show the reader that the subject of economics is very relevant to the business of banking.

This text is not a comprehensive study of the principles of economics. It is not set in the mold of the typical college economics text. Instead, it emphasizes those economic concepts and issues important to today's banker. It is intended to serve as a prerequisite to the American Bankers Association's *Money and Banking* textbook. Thus, money and banking topics are merely introduced in the appendixes to this text. *Economics for Bankers* contains elements of both macro- and microeconomics, with a definite emphasis on macroeconomic policy issues.

It is the author's hope that you will apply the concepts and principles of economics in your work as bankers and in your daily lives. An understanding of our economic system requires constant effort. Studying this text is not enough. If you search actively for economic news, follow economic trends, and track the movements of the business cycle, a better understanding of the motives of individuals, businesses, and government will be your reward. In the process, you will become a wiser consumer, citizen, and banker.

CHAPTER ONE

AN INTRODUCTION TO ECONOMICS

Objectives

After reading this chapter, you should be able to

•

explain how an understanding of economics can help you
be a better consumer, citizen, and banker

•

explain why economics is no longer called "the dismal science"

•

describe the differences between
micro- and macroeconomics

•

define some of the more common and most valuable
economic concepts and techniques

•

discuss some of the misconceptions and errors of
reasoning that can cloud proper economic thinking

•

list and define the four fundamental goals of
all economic systems

•

explain why attaining the fundamental economic goals
means making trade-offs

WHY STUDY ECONOMICS?

Many economics textbooks begin with the question, "Why study economics?" Several answers may be offered to this question. For example, many students who take economics classes are enrolled in preprofessional programs at school. For some students, the reasons for studying economics may relate to class aspirations. Their rationale might be expressed in the following terms: "By majoring in 'economics' I am really majoring in 'pre-wealth.' I must understand economics if I am going to make money, and a knowledge of economics will help me to enjoy 'the good life': luxury cars, designer clothes, gourmet restaurants, and condominium living." Such a viewpoint assumes that to benefit from the economy you must understand how the system works.

A second rationale stresses the importance of economic literacy to American politics. The proponents of this view insist that to be a well-informed citizen you must be able to understand the farm problem, Federal Reserve policy, or the significance of a decrease in the consumer price index. They contend that educated Americans should know whether the M1 is a rifle, a cold remedy, or a money supply measurement. If balanced budgets, deficit spending, right-to-work laws, farm parity programs, and recent antitrust decisions are meaningless words to you, your ability to understand and judge the platforms of politicians will be seriously hampered; placing an intelligent vote, based on the facts and issues, will be impossible. Moreover, if economic principles are inadequately taught at the secondary school level, it is the responsibility of higher education to remedy this deficiency; and while economic literacy benefits all citizens, it is especially important for persons who work in the financial fields.

Another reason for studying economics is its value as consumer protection. Caveat emptor—let the buyer beware—is a warning that challenges all participants in a free market economy to take responsibility for making educated, well-informed decisions. The study of economics can provide many of the tools you need to make wise choices as you encounter the laws of supply and demand, the forces of competition, and the consequences of economic activity throughout your life. If you are unable to cope with the economic system, you may be consumed by it. Understanding the workings of the economy is an important survival skill.

There is one more important reason for you to study economics: to become a better banker. You will be able to serve your customer better, improve the performance of your bank, and grow professionally. Economics is not easy to master; but if you persist and learn the concepts explained in this book, you will become a better-informed, more enlightened banker, and your deeper understanding of our economic system should position you for growth and prosperity in your profession.

ECONOMICS:
THE DISMAL SCIENCE

In 1798, a philosopher named Thomas Malthus published a gloomy prediction for humanity. He compared the normal reproductive rate of a human being with the rate at which the amount of land available to cultivate food can be increased. Inevitably, he claimed, the human population will outstrip the amount of food available:

> Taking the whole earth . . . and supposing the present population to be equal to a thousand millions, the human species would increase as the numbers 1,2,4,8,16,32,64,128,256, and subsistence as 1,2,3,4,5,6,7,8,9. In two centuries the population would be to the means of subsistence as 256 to 9; in three centuries as 4,096 to 13, and in two thousand years the difference would be incalculable.[1]

Believing that an imbalance between food and population was inescapable, Malthus concluded that such human misfortunes as infanticide, war, disease, and poverty were unavoidable:

> Famine seems to be the last, the most dreadful resource of nature. The power of population is so superior to the power of the earth to provide subsistence . . .that premature death must in some shape or other visit the human race. The vices of mankind are active and able ministers of depopulation. . . . But should they fail in this war of extermination, sickly seasons, epidemics, pestilence, and plague advance in terrific array and sweep off their thousands and tens of thousands. Should success still be incomplete, gigantic inevitable famine stalks in the rear, and with one mighty blow, levels the population with the food of the world.[2]

After reading Malthus's pessimistic forecast for humanity, Thomas Carlyle understandably called economics "a dismal science."[3]

Famines in Bangladesh and Ethiopia are recent examples of the stark realities of underdeveloped economic systems; and, indeed, developmental economists still search for solutions to the problems described by Malthus. The problem of hunger has not been eliminated. However, the pattern of relatively stable economic growth that has accompanied technological advancement in many countries during the twentieth century has led economists away from issues of subsistence and toward other, newer concerns. Today, U.S. agricultural economists debate the efficacy of a land bank program that pays farmers *not* to produce. Most western economists concern themselves with the modern problems of developed economies.

Many economists toil at gathering, analyzing, and disseminating statistics about the local, regional, national, or world economy. These statistics include total output or gross national product (GNP) figures, price movements, unemployment levels, interest rate levels, employee wages, retail sales, housing starts, trade levels, and many more. The compilation of this information is vital for corporate and financial planning, domestic policy decision making, and governmental and academic research. Perhaps the most exciting of all economic duties are those of the Council of Economic Advisers. This select group of individuals advises the president of the United States on policy-making issues regarding the U.S. economy.

Is economics a dismal science? Not any more. As our economy matures and the basic necessities of life are met for most individuals, economists strive to fine tune this magnificent economic engine that supports us all.

MICROECONOMICS VS. MACROECONOMICS

The words "micro" and "macro" are Greek words meaning small and large, respectively. Microeconomics deals with the behavior of consumers, producers, and markets, whereas macroeconomics involves the economy at large. Microeconomics addresses questions such as the following: How can a small business owner maximize his or her profits? How should a consumer spend income in order to receive the highest level of satisfaction? Should a particular bridge have a toll? If so, how much should the toll be? Should the toll be seen as a means of maximizing revenue for the bridge authority or minimizing traffic on the bridge? These are just a few of the issues that the microeconomist would consider.

Microeconomics is also known as price theory, and macroeconomics is sometimes called income theory. Economists D.S. Watson and M.A. Holman differentiate these terms as follows:

> Price theory explains the composition, or allocation, of total production—why more of some things are produced than of others. Income theory [macroeconomics] explains the level of total production and why the level rises and falls.... For two centuries, price theory has been the center of attention of economists. In the eighteenth and nineteenth centuries, it was known as the theory of value. The theory of value played a leading role as one of the intellectual foundations of the new freedoms that came after 1776.[4]

Modern readers may be more familiar with macroeconomic issues. These topics include the fluctuations in total national output, the unemployment rate for the labor force, price increases and inflation information, the capacity utilization of U.S. businesses, and the industrial production of our nation. Macroeconomic topics such as the Federal Reserve's actions regarding the U.S. money supply and interest rates are often found on the front pages of newspapers and heard in daily newscasts.

ECONOMICS FOR BANKERS

What makes macroeconomics such a challenging subject is well stated by economist Gary Smith:*

> Macroeconomics, because it deals with the behavior of millions of very different people, each following his or her own logic, intuition, and emotions, cannot be conveniently summarized in concise, immutable laws. Moreover, economists cannot make the world stand still while they run economic experiments under controlled laboratory conditions. Instead, they must make do with "nature's experiments," trying to unravel the effects of ongoing policies in a world in which many things are happening at once: Did the policy cause this, or was it caused by something else? And there is *always* something else.[5]

However, a well-rounded education about our economic system requires an understanding of both micro- and macroeconomic principles. In fact, it is almost impossible to study one without the other. For example, your understanding of the microeconomic concept of supply and demand must incorporate macroeconomic concepts regarding international trade and finance.

TOOLS OF THE TRADE: METHODOLOGY AND RULES

Bankers use mortgage amortization tables, physicians use CAT scan devices, and lawyers use law libraries. Economists also have specific tools: key concepts, rules, and a methodology for applying them. The economist's tools can be used by anyone in making sound decisions about financial matters. However, these ideas are best learned by practice. Reading them will not be enough. You must make a conscious attempt to use them in your life.

Opportunity Cost

Perhaps the most important contribution economics has made to the process of analytical thinking is the concept of opportunity cost. Opportunity cost establishes the real value of any resource. The mathematics of calculating opportunity cost are discussed in chapter 3. Here it is sufficient to understand what opportunity cost is: the value of a resource in its next best alternate use. It is the value of a resource that is forgone when the resource is used elsewhere. For example, the decision to attend college results in a financial cost and an

---

*Excerpted from *Macroeconomics* by Gary Smith. Copyright © 1985. Reprinted with the permission of W.H. Freeman and Company.

opportunity cost. The financial cost refers to the dollar value, or the price tag, of the resources used to attend college—tuition, the cost of books and supplies, room and board charges, and so on. The opportunity cost, often referred to as the hidden cost, may be difficult to quantify. In this example, the opportunity cost can be determined by considering how you would use the necessary resources if they were not used as payment for college attendance. In other words, if you decided not to go to college, the money and labor required could be used elsewhere. You might get a job instead, and the salary you would receive from that job would become part of the opportunity cost of attending college. Borrowing a phrase from Robert Frost, opportunity cost is the value of the road not taken.

A bank incurs opportunity cost when it sends an employee to a professional development program held during work time. This is more costly than management may realize. The true cost of the decision includes both the financial costs—the registration fee, travel expenses, and meal charges—and the real, or opportunity cost, of the lost productivity to the bank. The value of the work not done because the employee is absent is the opportunity cost to the bank. Ideally, the long-term productivity gain from professional development exceeds the opportunity cost. When a friend asks for a personal loan, you should consider the opportunity cost. What is the opportunity cost of lending money to friends? The answer depends upon the value of the money in its next best use. For example, if the money is in an interest-bearing account, the opportunity cost of lending it is the dollar value of the interest you would earn if the money were kept in the account. Of course, you must also consider the opportunity cost of *not* loaning the money to the friend! It may, in some cases, be of much greater value than lost interest.

In making decisions about the bank's portfolio, bank managers must consider opportunity cost. A bank's assets include investment securities, loans, cash, and premises. When a bank gives a certain portion of its assets to the government by purchasing government securities, it forgoes the opportunity to make the same funds available as loans to a new, small business in the community or to consumers for the purchase of autos and homes. Because greater risks are involved in lending to new, small businesses and consumers than in purchasing government securities, interest rates are higher for the loans. Thus, when bank funds are used to purchase government securities, the opportunity cost is the amount of the higher interest the bank would have earned had it loaned the money to the small business or consumer. The opportunity cost of lending to the businessperson or consumer is the value of the lower risk provided by the safer government securities.

Opportunity cost has played a role in your life from the first time you made a decision regarding the use of a resource. Decisions to save or spend your allowance, to study or play baseball, to go to college or go to work—all have opportunity costs associated with them. People who do not learn to consider opportunity costs are more likely to make decisions they later regret. For example, the real cost of not studying for an exam may be much higher than simply earning a failing grade on that exam. It may result in failing the entire course and having to repeat the course next year. A failure to recognize and pay the opportunity costs of pursuing an education can have a lifelong effect on a person's job prospects.

Opportunity cost often goes unrecognized by small business owners. They tend to ignore this important concept and, as a result, overestimate the vitality of their concern. Small business owners have opportunity cost in two very important areas: (1) the value of their lost wages and (2) the lost interest on their financial investment in the small business.

Table 1.1 shows a typical balance sheet of a small business. Sales revenues of $100,000 are seemingly balanced against material expenses of $50,000, taxes of $15,000, utilities of $10,000, and miscellaneous expenses of $15,000, for a total operating expense of $90,000. The bottom line shows an apparent profit of $10,000. However, two vital parts are missing from this picture. Had the owner not opened up this business, he or she would probably be working elsewhere. The value of the wages the owner gave up by making the decision to have the business is an opportunity cost. Second, if the owner has made a personal investment in the business, he or she has lost the value of the next best use of the money, or the interest that would have been received had the money been invested in an interest-bearing account.

Table 1.1 Balance Sheet, Pat's Pizza Parlor

Pizza sales		$100,000
Costs		
Raw materials	$ 50,000	
Taxes	15,000	
Utilities	10,000	
Other expenses	15,000	
Total costs	$ 90,000	$ 90,000
"Profit"		$ 10,000
Hidden opportunity costs		
Owner's labor (estimated lost wages)	$ 15,000	
Owner's investment (estimated lost interest)	$ 5,000	

As you can see, inclusion of opportunity cost in this simple example has turned the $10,000 profit into a $10,000 loss!

In many cases, the spouse or children of the small business owner may work in the business for little or no pay. The value of wages they might have received elsewhere is an additional opportunity cost.

Sunk Cost

A second very powerful economic tool is the concept of sunk cost. It can save you, as a consumer and a banker, a great deal of heartaches and money.

Sunk costs are expenses that have dollar values and were made at some past moment in time. These costs are still kept on the books and in one's memory, yet have no real economic significance and should be discounted in the economic decision-making process.

Table 1.2 Stamping Machine Performance, ACME Products

Fully allocated costs	
Labor expenses per period	$100,000
Material expenses per period	50,000
Depreciation expense per period	75,000
Use tax, utilities	10,000
Maintenance expense	25,000
Miscellaneous expenses	5,000
Total costs	$265,000
Total sales revenue	$220,000
Net profit (loss)	($ 45,000)

Consider a sampling of costs related to stamping machine performance at ACME Products (table 1.2). At first glance, it appears that ACME Products did not make the right decision in purchasing the stamping machine. The sales revenue it generated is less than the cost of running the machine, resulting in a $45,000 loss for the company.

However, a mistake has been made in calculating the costs of using the machine. Note the $75,000 depreciation expense. Depreciation expense is an accounting term used to indicate the dollar value of a piece of equipment or a parcel of land that is being used up. Its primary function is in calculating taxes owed. Depreciation expense is certainly a financial cost—it has a price tag. However, it is not a true cost in an economic sense. It is an example of a sunk cost. Depreciation expenses are historical in nature: they are charged against property, plants, and equipment purchased in the past. A decision to purchase this equipment was made, and a budget developed.

The depreciation expense has nothing to do with current operating income or cash flow (except for the current tax applications of depreciation expense) and should not be included in the current profit-and-loss statement. If we subtract the $75,000 from the costs column, the net loss of $45,000 turns into a profit of $30,000—a fair return indeed.

Bankers must consider sunk cost when making decisions regarding bad loans. Loan officers may extend troubled loans or increase the bank's exposure in the hope of recovering the money the customer has already borrowed. But a loan is sunk cost. It has been made. It is on the books. The often-used expression about the foolishness of throwing good money after bad applies here. When you view a loan as sunk cost, it becomes clear that the proper economic decision is to write off unrecoverable loans.

Sunk cost can also be illustrated in branch offices of banks. Management may perceive the original cost of brick and mortar as a reason not to close unproductive branches. This is faulty economic logic. The expense of building the branch facility is past. It is historical, sunk cost, and should not be used in present economic decision making.

A bank may continue to offer products and services that are not profitable in the belief that historical start-up costs must somehow be recovered. This is another clear case of throwing good money after bad.

Finally, the game of poker offers ready examples of sunk cost. Perhaps you have agonized over deciding whether to continue betting on your hand or to drop out of the game. If you drop from the game, you have no chance of winning the pot. Only by continuing to bet do you have a chance of winning. Players often decide to continue playing even when they know they have very little chance of winning. Why? Because they have already made sizable contributions to the pot. However, as you now can see, all past contributions are nothing more than sunk cost and should not be used as reasons for adding more money to the pile. The decision to stick with a given hand should be based on probability and statistics and not the urge to recover previous bets.

Check Your Understanding

Sunk cost is a major economic principle. Check your understanding of it by completing the following exercise. It involves a decision that frequently faces many American consumers—the decision of whether to scrap or to repair an automobile. If you can answer the questions that follow, you understand the concept of sunk cost and should go on to the next section. However, if you are confused or make the improper decision after reading the following problem, please review the sections on opportunity cost and sunk cost.

> Mr. Smith purchases a used car for $1,000 on June 1. This car comes with a 30-day used-car warranty supplied by the dealer. On July 1, the engine fails. Mr. Smith proceeds to a repair shop, where he is given an estimate of $600 to repair the broken engine. Mr. Smith goes ahead with the repairs and is given a 90-day warranty on the repair. On October 15, the repaired engine expires. A return to the repair shop finds Mr. Smith facing a second $600 engine overhaul bill.

What should Mr. Smith do? Should he repair the car or sell it for its scrap value?

Answer: Mr. Smith should fix the car only if the resale value of the car repaired is greater than the $600 repair bill plus the value of the car as scrap. What is important to note is that both the $1,000 purchase price and the initial $600 repair bill should *in no way* influence Mr. Smith's decision in this matter. Those expenses are sunk costs.

TANSTAAFL:
"There ain't no such thing as a free lunch."

TANSTAAFL is a meaningful acronym to economists. It is a reminder that when a resource is used, a cost is always incurred. For a good to have value, by definition it cannot be free. One way to discover hidden costs is to ask the question, "Free to whom?" For example, before the era of environmental awareness, air and water were considered to be "free" for anyone to use. We have, however, become increasingly aware of the cost of this fallacy. Pollution has damaged and destroyed animal and plant life, ruined recreational and residential areas, and cost us millions of dollars in recovery efforts. Breathable air and drinkable water are resources that have environmental, social, and financial costs.

The use of any resource has a cost attached. Sooner or later, someone pays for it. Remember, the concept of opportunity cost forces one to include the "total" costs of a resource in economic decision making. To consider only financial or surface costs can distort efficient resource use drastically.

Simple 70 Formula

Not all the tools of the economist are as ephemeral and difficult to grasp as the ones just discussed. Here's a simple tool that you may find useful. Banking, as well as economics, deals with interest rates, growth rates, and other statistics growing at a fixed percentage. It is often necessary to estimate the doubling time of such statistics. The simple 70 formula can be used to generate a good approximation of the doubling time of any statistic growing at a fixed rate. The formula is as follows:

$$\text{Years to double (or to halve)} = 70/g.$$
$$g = \text{constant growth rate}$$

Table 1.3 shows the power of compound growth rates and the usefulness of the simple 70 rule.

Table 1.3 Danger of Inflation

Inflation Rate (percent) (g)	Approximate Years for Prices to Double ($70/g$)
2%	35
5%	14
7%	10
10%	7
14%	5

You may also use this formula to calculate the amount of time it takes to reduce a figure by half. For example, if an employee retires at age 65 with a fixed pension and inflation is growing at 10 percent, it is easy to calculate how many years it will take for the retiree's real earning power to be cut in half. Dividing the inflation rate of 10 percent into 70 equals 7 years. In other words, when the retiree is 72, the purchasing power of his fixed pension will be half what it was at the start. If inflation continues at 10 percent, at age 79 the retiree's purchasing power will be halved again—now, only 25 percent of its original value.

These are just a few of the tools that are useful to students of economics. You will learn about others in later chapters. Now, we turn our attention to some commonly believed misconceptions and half-truths about economics.

MISCONCEPTIONS AND HALF-TRUTHS

Students must be forewarned of certain problems that may arise in their study of economics. The function of such warnings is similar to that of highway warning signs: the problem does not always occur, but the economist—or driver—should be alerted to its possibility. A road sign depicting a sharp, impending bend in the road is obviously important. So, too, are signs warning drivers about deer crossings and falling rock zones. Many drivers pass these signs without ever seeing deer crossing the road or an avalanche of rocks crashing down about them. But these events could and do happen, and the signs remind drivers of that fact. The pitfalls and fallacies about to be described can and do creep into our economic thinking. Becoming familiar with them will help you avoid their hazards.

Many terms familiar to bankers (such as variable rate loans, amortization, the rule of 78s, and compensating balances) are confusing to consumers. Economics also has a unique language that has developed over time. It has been said that learning any science is 90 percent understanding the terminology. This is undoubtedly the case in the study of economics. Many of the principles and concepts you will learn are, in fact, quite simple and straightforward. Not knowing the terminology, however, can cloud your understanding of these topics.

The Fallacy of Composition

The fallacy of composition is a common pitfall in economic understanding. This fallacy states that what is good for some must be good for all. The noted nineteenth-century economist John Stuart Mill even contributed to this fallacy by noting: "Each person's happiness is a good to that person, and the general happiness, therefore, a good to the aggregate of all persons."[6]

There are many cases in which this simply is not so. What is good for an individual firm or a group of firms in a certain region may not be good for the economy as a whole, and applying a decision made on the basis of individual benefit to a larger group can be a dangerous mistake. For example, if spring rains and record sunshine lead to bumper crops for farmers in Iowa, the climatic conditions would seem to have been advantageous to these individuals. Yet, if this weather prevailed everywhere in the United States, the result would be an extraordinarily large supply of farm products at harvest time. This overabundance would yield lower prices for the farmers' products. Thus, applied universally, the weather conditions would prove to have been disadvantageous to all farmers.

Check Your Understanding

Check your understanding of the fallacy of composition by considering what you would do in the following situation:

> You are in a crowded theater, and the performance is interrupted by a fire alarm. You are near a major exit, and there are smaller, secondary exits nearby.

What would be your best course of action?

Answer: If only a few patrons are seeking to use the nearby exit, you should use that exit. However, if the exit nearest to you is also the nearest exit for the entire crowd, you might be able to leave faster if you go to a more distant, less congested exit. In this case, what benefits the individual (you) cannot equate to what benefits the entire group; in other words, what is good for some is not necessarily what is good for all.

There is a similar fallacy of division, which contends that something true of the whole is also necessarily true of its parts. In other words, what is good for the large group is good for all individuals in that group. Of course, this is not the case. What is prudent economic policy for a country may not be so for an individual consumer. For example, a tax increase may help the country cut its budget deficit and thus is good for the whole. But most individuals paying the increased tax are unlikely to agree that it helps them personally.

The Fallacy of False Conclusions

The next pitfall is the fallacy of false conclusions. In Latin, this problem is described as believing that *post hoc ergo propter hoc*—or, "after this, therefore because of this." In essence, this problem results from judging an event (B) that occurs after another event (A) to be a result of the first event (A). The results of such conclusions can be disastrous. For example, consider a bank branch whose profits fall after an individual is promoted to branch manager. Event A is that a new manager is installed. Event B is that the branch's profits fall. Does it necessarily follow that the manager did a poor job of running the branch and caused the decline in profits? No. The manager may have caused the loss, or contributed to it, but many other factors could also have caused the loss. A nearby factory employing many of the branch's depositors may have closed down, or new competition may have entered the branch's territory. It is simply the case that sequential relationships are not of themselves causal relationships.[7]

Positive and Normative Statements

Considerable debate results from the failure to understand the difference between positive and normative economic statements. Positive economic statements are objective in nature. They explain that if particular conditions hold, certain results can be expected. The following is a positive economic statement: "Personal savings levels may increase as a result of revisions to the tax laws." Normative economic statements involve value judgments. For example, "The tax laws should be revised so that personal savings levels increase." Normative statements represent opinions and, as such, may be refuted by those with conflicting opinions.

Economists make both types of statements. Because economics is at heart a study of human behavior, economists cannot escape the need to make value judgments. As economist Robert A. Carson notes,

> economists, however, cannot evade making some determinations about optimal prices, optimal income distribution and so forth. Their decisions, while perhaps based upon a genuine effort at neutrality, detachment, and honest evaluation of the available evidence, finally must be a matter of interpretation, a value judgment based upon their own particular world views. . . . Struggle as it may, economics as a discipline is never free from ideology.[8]

Dual Terminology and Yellow Journalism

Finally, the use of dual terminology and emotional "yellow journalism" can confuse the student of economics. One economist may blame a recession on too much saving by consumers while another blames it on too little spending. "Oversaving" and "underspending" may sound like different terms, but they describe essentially the same phenomenon.

Mass media-generated misconceptions arise when the public reads inflammatory newspaper headlines such as "Inflation Rate Climbs to 18.5% in One Month." What has occurred is a 1.5 percent increase during one month, which translates to an *annual* increase of 18.5 percent if inflation continues to rise 1.5 percent a month for the next 11 months. Statistics are frequently misquoted in this way.[9]

ECONOMIC GOALS

Every economic system seeks to achieve a variety of goals, not all of which are compatible with each other or with other goals in the society. Every decision involves opportunity cost; and priorities often differ among economists, who vary in their political philosophies. Four major goals, however, drive all economies. They are stability, efficiency, fairness, and growth.

Stability

All economic systems strive to keep the business cycle stable. The business cycle reflects the fluctuations in economic activity that recur over a period of years. An ideal business cycle produces a gradual, steady rise in output. In reality, there are periods of decreasing as well as increasing activity, which can be dramatically sharp. The practical goal of an economic system is to keep these fluctuations from being too severe. In the process, it seeks to maintain steady average wage and price levels. You will learn more about how economic systems pursue this goal in chapter 12.

Efficiency

The second fundamental goal of economic systems is efficiency. A society must make the best use of its limited store of resources. Two types of efficiency are important. Technical efficiency refers to "full employment" of resources or the production of maximum output using available inputs in the most efficient manner. Economic, or allocative, efficiency refers to the match between individual preferences and the economy's products. When an economy is economically efficient, the goods and services it is producing match closely the purchasing preferences of its consumers. In a market system, this implies an unrestricted balance between supply and demand. Note that an economic system may be technically efficient, yet economically inefficient. The inverse, however, does not hold true. An economically efficient society must also be technically efficient.

Fairness

A society's efficiency has no relation to the fairness with which it distributes its wealth. The third major goal of an economic system is fair distribution of income. In other words, it seeks a means of distributing its output that is equitable. This does not necessarily mean equal distribution. A society's approach to this economic goal will be strongly influenced by its philosophical outlook and moral views.

Growth

Economic systems continually seek to improve the standard of living of their members. In other words, production levels, measured on a per person basis, should keep rising.

Of course, implementing these goals means using resources, thus incurring opportunity and other costs. Moreover, economic goals may conflict with other goals in a society. Our democratic society, for example, is committed to the concept of individual rights, including the freedom to choose one's profession. You have chosen to enter the banking profession. If the country needed more scientists than bankers, in order to achieve technical efficiency society would have to choose your profession for you. Yet this is not the way of a democratic nation.

The economic goals of fairness, growth, stability, and efficiency compete for priority with each other and with other, noneconomic goals. The Soviet Union and several of the Eastern bloc countries have emphasized the goals of military preparedness and rapid economic growth, while downplaying allocative efficiency and fairness. Their economies, for example, concentrate on heavy industry, while the production and distribution of consumer goods is considered a lower priority. Moreover, because such countries follow communist or socialist ideologies, their economic goals are set by considering the welfare of the state rather than that of the individual. In democratic capitalistic states, on the other hand, individual political and economic freedom plays a more important role; consequently, the economic policies of such countries are dominated by different goals.[10]

Individuals and firms have the same economic goals as do societies. Individuals seek to maximize their own welfare by making the best use of their resources. Businesses strive to increase their profitability. In all cases, achieving these goals involves trade-offs. Individuals, firms, and societies must make hard decisions as to the compromises they are willing to make to achieve their goals.

SUMMARY

An understanding of economics can help you be a better citizen, a wiser consumer, and a smarter, more effective banker. Economic systems involve individuals as well as societies.

When beginning the study of economics, it is essential to learn to use certain terms correctly. Several of the terms presented in this chapter are summarized below.

Microeconomics, or price theory, is the study of specific economic units in an economic system, while macroeconomics deals with the economy as a whole (or with large subdivisions of it).

Opportunity cost is the value of a resource (or benefit) forgone when a person chooses to use it one way rather than another. It is the value of the resource in its next best alternate use.

Sunk costs are actual historical expenses that are still kept on the books or in one's memory, but that have no real economic significance and should be discounted in the economic decision-making process.

The use of a resource always generates a cost to someone. In other words, TANSTAAFL: There ain't no such thing as a free lunch.

Economic terminology can be very confusing. Students of economics should beware of misinterpretations, misconceptions, and half-truths. The following stumbling blocks often create problems in economic reasoning.

It is important to distinguish between positive and normative economic statements. Positive economic statements describe "what is." Normative economic statements describe "what should be." While the latter are often controversial, the former are objective statements of fact.

It is also important to detect and avoid defects in logic. For example, the fallacy of composition wrongly states that what is good for one is necessarily good for all. The fallacy of division states that what is good for all is necessarily good for each individual. The fallacy of false conclusions states that because event B follows event A, A caused B.

Finally, economic systems do not operate independently of other factors in society. While all economic systems share certain goals, these goals compete and conflict—sometimes with each other and sometimes with other goals in the society. All economic systems struggle to achieve business cycle stability, technical and economic efficiency, fair distribution of income, and continued growth in quality of life. Achieving each of these goals requires costs and compromises. The political philosophies of different societies profoundly affect their economic priorities and policies.

KEY WORDS

allocative efficiency
business cycle
macroeconomics
microeconomics
normative statements
opportunity cost

positive statements
simple 70 formula
sunk cost
TANSTAAFL
technical efficiency

Questions for Review

1. How may an understanding of economics help you become a better consumer? A better citizen? A better banker?

2. Malthus's theory that population grows geometrically while the amount of arable land grows arithmetically led to predictions of famine in England and the Western world. Yet the population did not grow at nearly the rate he predicted. Average family size grew at a much slower pace. What factors may have slowed the growth rate?

3. The other half of Malthus's prediction (that the amount of arable land grows only arithmetically) was also faulty. He did not foresee the impact of advances in agricultural technology. Describe how these advances affect land use and food production.

4. A U.S. senator is concerned about the effects of a drought on the nation's wheat crop. She visits a farmer in Nebraska to discuss his crop yield. Identify the macroeconomic and the microeconomic issues.

5. What is the opportunity cost of investing part of your salary in a tax-sheltered annuity?

6. Ann impulsively buys an unframed painting from a neighborhood garage sale. When she gets home, she decides she does not like it very much. However, since she has already paid for it, she goes to the store and purchases a frame for it. Has Ann made an economic mistake? Describe the economic situation in which Ann's action would be appropriate. A mistake.

7. You can fish in federally owned waters without a fishing license. That means fish are available for free (at no cost). Agree or disagree. Explain your answer.

8. What hidden costs apply to "free" checking accounts?

9. A particular type of tree increases its height at a rate of 4 percent per year. How many years will it take for the tree to double its height?

10. Identify at least one fallacy in each statement below:

    a) A study finds that, 70 percent of the time, the Federal Reserve's decisions to increase the money supply are made within 10 days of a full moon. Therefore, the changes in the moon's phases lead to changes in the money supply.

b) All profitable banks have microcomputers. If the newly opened Worth Bank wants to be profitable, it should quickly purchase some microcomputers.

c) The Market Bank decides to increase its auto loan rate by 2 percent. All banks in the community would be smart to follow its lead and do the same.

11. Identify these statements as positive or normative.

a) We should keep the American automobile industry strong by limiting imports of foreign cars.

b) One way to decrease the federal deficit is to add a tax on all purchases and devote the earnings to deficit reduction.

c) The best way to decrease the federal deficit is to add a tax on all purchases and devote the earnings to deficit reduction.

12. Describe how wage and price ceilings may help achieve a goal of an economic system. What is the trade-off?

13. Describe the trade-off involved when import quotas are imposed.

14. At a concert, a single member of the crowded audience rises to get a better view of the musicians, thus improving his or her position. Yet if all members of the audience rise, everyone's position will not be improved. What fallacy does this example illustrate?

ENDNOTES

1. Thomas Robert Malthus, *An Essay on the Principle of Population; or, A View of Its Past and Present Effects on Human Happiness*, as quoted in Robert L. Heilbroner, *The Worldly Philosophers* (New York: Simon and Schuster, 1972), pp. 87, 88.

2. Ibid., p. 88.

3. For an interesting look at the perspectives of Malthus and other influential economic philosophers, see Robert L. Heilbroner, *The Worldly Philosophers* (New York: Simon and Schuster, 1972).

4. D.S. Watson and M.A. Holman, *Price Theory and Its Uses* (Boston: Houghton Mifflin Company, 1977), p. 2.

5. Gary Smith, *Macroeconomics* (New York: Freeman and Company, 1985), p. 4.

6. John Stuart Mill, *Utilitarianism*, ed. Samuel Gorovitz (Indianapolis: Bobbs-Merrill, 1971), p. 34.

7. See Martin Gardner, *Fads and Fallacies in the Name of Science*, 2d ed. (New York: Dover, 1957).

8. Robert A. Carson, "Alternative Economic Philosophies: A Survey of Conservative, Liberal, and Radical Critiques," in *Economic Issues Today: Alternative Approaches*, ed. Robert A. Carson, 3d. ed. (New York: St. Martin's Press, 1983), p. 17. Copyright © 1983 by St. Martin's Press, Inc. Used with permission.

9. A still relevant look at the manipulation of statistics can be found in Darrell Huff, *How to Lie With Statistics* (New York: W.W. Norton & Co., Inc., 1954).

10. For additional commentary on how political and social philosophies influence economic policy, see Milton H. Spencer, *Contemporary Economics* (New York: Worth Publishers, Inc., 1986), p. 16.

ECONOMICS IN THE NEWS

How Economists Think About World Trade

Charles N. Stabler   New York

Rightly or wrongly, non-economists often regard economists as a contentious bunch. The jibe about their inability to reach a conclusion even when laid end-to-end is always good for a chuckle when practical people discuss economists' pronouncements. But there are principles on which the professionals agree and high among these is that trade is mutually beneficial.

For 200 years economists of every stripe have maintained with unassailable logic that tariffs, quotas, subsidies and more imaginative restraints on trade mug the perpetrator as well as the victim. The proof is in any elementary text on the subject. It ranges from Adam Smith's sensible "maxim of every prudent household never to attempt to make at home what it will cost him more to make than to buy" to mathematical models of resources, weather and productivity.

The concept is readily understood. As it was stated long ago, even if Portugal could produce both wines and textiles at less cost than England, both countries gain if England specializes in textiles, where its disadvantage is least, and trades cloth for port. If both countries try to produce both products, then both Portuguese and English will work longer hours and have less of either good.

Most people, with perhaps a little thought, accept this, but only as an economic theory. In the real world, they say, imports cost domestic jobs because foreigners will work for less, we must encourage infant industries, free trade works only if it is fair trade and certain home industries, usually the speaker's, are vital to national defense.

Whatever political appeal these practical arguments have, economists maintain they overlook the costs of protection in higher consumer prices, inferior or less-diverse products and lower real wages.

Despite the economists, the "practical" view is clearly gaining. After decades of whittling down tariffs and expanding world trade, new and more effective forms of protectionism now are popping up everywhere. Often with some lip-service to the goal of free trade, political leaders, business executives and labor leaders in the U.S. and elsewhere reject it as Utopian.

The world has greatly changed, it is argued, from the static, competitive society of 18th Century England. The free market ideal has eroded everywhere. A nation can through intervention and industrial policy create advantages over other nations that can be countered only by more of the same. We should pursue free trade, of course, but it must be "fair" and reciprocal.

There is enough in this view to make it politically appealing, especially when it is accompanied by the very real anguish of steel and auto workers in America or marginal farmers in Japan. But the economists' argument for free markets doesn't depend on a static environment in a competitive society of small shopkeepers. For both workers and consumers, choices are enhanced and costs lowered as the market becomes more free, even if it never attains the ultimate.

What difference does it make to Americans if Japanese cars are cheap because of some natural advantage over Detroit or because of artificial intervention by the Ministry of International Trade and Industry? Our autoworkers will be in difficulty either way while consumers will benefit. Retaliatory intervention by the U.S., even in the relatively mild form of seeking voluntary import quotas isn't going to help the autoworker much, if the steel industry is a guide, but it clearly hurts consumers.

Why, if all this seems so apparent to economists, is their advocacy of free trade so often dismissed as a fantasy suitable only for textbooks and the ivory tower? The answer in large part is that the self-interest of particular groups hit by changes in international trade is more poignant than the lofty logic of improving the general well-being.

There may also be a more subtle difficulty. It involves the differences in what certain words mean to economists and non-economists. These are differences not only in definitions but in philosophy and they cause persistent misunderstanding and poor communications.

Ronald A. Krieger, vice president and director of economic publications for Chase Manhattan Bank, has given some thought to this as both an economist and a communicator. What he has concluded can be illustrated by a short, multiple-choice quiz. How would you answer the following:

Q. *The purpose of economic activity is?*
A. (1) to improve consumer well-being or (2) to create jobs and growth.
Q. *Work is a?*
A. (1) cost or (2) benefit.
Q. *Imports are a?*
A. (1) benefit or (2) cost.
Q. *Exports are a?*
A. (1) cost or (2) benefit.
Q. *The objective of trade is to?*
A. (1) get goods cheaply or (2) create jobs.

If you selected (1) as each answer, you are thinking like an economist. If you selected the alternative you have plenty of company, including the head of the United Auto Workers, the head of Chrysler Corp. and the leading Democratic candidate for president.

Mr. Krieger concludes: "Given this major divergence in perceptions and premises, it isn't surprising that economists have won few converts by preaching the consumptionist gospel of Adam Smith, valid as it may be. If the case for free trade is to be heard, economists will have to join the debate on the terms set by the protectionists and speak to the issues that have captured public attention: the trade balance, jobs and economic growth."

Reprinted by permission of *The Wall Street Journal*, © Dow Jones & Company, Inc., 1983. All Rights Reserved.

CHAPTER TWO

MATHEMATICS AND STATISTICS

Objectives

After reading this chapter, you should be able to

•

use a formula to express functional relationships between two variables

•

express the general form of a linear equation: $y = a + bx$

•

describe the quadrant coordinate system and explain how it can be used to represent linear equations graphically

•

list, define, and calculate three measures of central tendency

•

list, define, and calculate three measures of dispersion

•

convert economic data for a particular time period to work for other time periods

•

describe statistical measures useful in evaluating the success of economic forecasts

EXPRESSING LINEAR RELATIONSHIPS WITH EQUATIONS

Two people, Sam and Pat, were standing on the roof of a tall building and discussing the ways in which they could determine the height of the building. Sam pulled a stopwatch from his pocket and produced a balloon filled with chalk dust. He dropped the balloon and started his stopwatch at the same moment. When the balloon burst on the street below, he stopped the watch and exclaimed, "This building is 6 seconds tall." Pat thought for a moment and then said, "That means that, if we ignore the air resistance on the surface of the balloon and assume your eye-hand coordination is reliable, this building is 576 feet in height." "How did you figure that out?" asked Sam. "A gift from Galileo," Pat replied.

Galileo is credited with introducing to mathematics the concept of a function—the idea that a mathematical relationship between variables can be expressed as a formula. There is a relationship between the time an object takes to fall and the distance that object travels in its descent. The relationship between the variables of time (t) and distance (d) can be described in a formula that expresses distance as a *function* of time:

$$d = f(t).$$

In other words, distance traveled, to some extent, depends on time elapsed. Experiments have produced data such as that presented in table 2.1.

For every positive value of t, there exists a unique, corresponding value of d. Each relationship can be written as an ordered pair of variables (t, d), in which the first variable represents the time and the second the corresponding value for the distance.

By establishing a formula that describes the relationship between the numbers in these ordered pairs, we can calculate any distance, given the time an object takes to fall that distance. Likewise, we can calculate the falling time if we know the distance. Thus, a function is a set of ordered pairs (x, y) of values, for which there is a unique value of y for each value of x. The formula for calculating x, given y, or calculating y, given x, shows the precise mathematical relationship between x and y. The data in table 2.1 can be expressed as $(1,16)$, $(2,64)$, $(3,144)$, $(4,256)$, $(5,400)$, and $(6,576)$.

Table 2.1 Time and Distance Equation

Time (seconds)	Distance (feet)
1	16
2	64
3	144
4	256
5	400
6	576

The formula showing the relationship between distance and time is:

$$d = 16(t)^2.$$

Pat knew this formula and, substituting the value of 6 for the variable time (t), calculated the height of the building (the distance, d) to be 576 feet.

In summary, a formula expresses the functional relationship between two or more variables. We will use Galileo's concept of a function extensively in the chapters that follow.

Linear Equations—Two Variables

The general formulation for linear equations is:

$$y = a + bx.$$

The variable y is known as the dependent variable and the variable x is labeled the independent variable. This classification is a convention that was developed for use in research—the experimenter manipulates the independent variable (x) and measures its effects on the dependent variable (y).

The terms a and b in the linear equation signify constants. The solution to a linear equation with two variables is a set of ordered pairs (x, y). The set of ordered pairs that solves a linear equation is usually expressed in a graph. The expression of linear equations in graphs will be discussed later in this chapter. The structure and components of linear equations can be explained by example.

Suppose the cost accounting department of the First National Bank has determined that it costs the bank approximately $0.18 to process a check and an additional $30 per year to maintain a demand deposit account. In other words, the estimate of the variable cost is $0.18 per transaction. (It is a variable cost because the total number of transactions occurring in one year differs from account to account.) The fixed cost estimate is $30. A relationship can be shown between the total cost of an account (c) and the number of checks written against the account in one year (k). (See table 2.2.)

In our example, c is the dependent variable, corresponding to y in the general formula—and k is the independent variable, corresponding to x. We can describe this relationship as a function, using the following general equation:

$$c = f(k).$$

The specific linear relationship between the number of checks written per year and the total cost can be written as $c = a + bk$. The a term is a constant value in the equation. It remains the same, regardless of the value of the independent variable k. In the example above, the constant term a equals the fixed cost of maintaining the account, or $30.

Table 2.2 Cost of Account by Checks Written

Checks Written Annually	Total Annual Cost (dollars)
0	30
100	48
200	66
300	74
400	102
500	120
600	138
700	156
800	174
900	192
1000	210

When the value of the independent variable equals 0, the a term will have the same value as the dependent variable c. If no checks are written on our sample account, $k = 0$. Given the formula $c = a + bk$, when $k = 0$, $bk = 0$; therefore, $c = a$.

In our equation, the parameter b is another constant, called the slope or coefficient. It indicates how much the dependent variable changes when the independent variable changes by one unit. If the dependent variable increases when the independent variable increases, the value of b is positive. If the dependent variable decreases when the independent variable increases, the value of b is negative. If the dependent variable does not change as a function of the independent variable, the value of b equals 0. Thus, in our equation $c = a + bk$, if $b = 0$, then $bk = 0$, and, therefore, $c = a$.

Substituting the fixed cost of $30 for the constant a and the transaction cost of $0.18 for the slope parameter b, we get:

$$c = \$30 + (\$0.18)k.$$

Now the annual cost of maintaining a particular customer's account (c) can be determined by replacing the k with the number of transactions occurring in one year. If we are calculating historical cost, k will be an actual number; if we are projecting into the future, k will be an estimated number.

Let's say the customer wrote 2,000 checks last year. Substituting the number 2,000 for k, we calculate as follows:

$$c = \$30 + (\$0.18)\,2{,}000$$
$$c = \$30 + \$360$$
$$c = \$390.$$

Thus, it cost First National Bank $390 to maintain the customer's account last year.

Remember, the values of parameters a and b can be positive, negative, or zero.

Here's another example. A small bank with 2,500 demand deposit accounts estimates that for every $1 increase in return-check charges, 20 customers decide to take their business elsewhere. Management is considering a $5 increase and wants to determine its effect on the bank's total number of accounts. This relationship can be written as an equation:

$$n = a + br,$$

where n = the number of accounts *after* the change in the return-check charge,
a = the number of accounts *before* the change in the return-check charge,
b = the number of accounts *lost* in the process, and
r = the change in the return-check charge.

In our example $a = 2,500$, $b = -20$, and $r = 5$. Substituting the known information, we get:

$$n = 2,500 + [-20(5)]$$
$$n = 2,500 - 100$$
$$n = 2,400.$$

Thus, a $5 increase in the return-check charge will reduce the bank's total number of accounts to 2,400.

What if the bank decreases the return-check charge by $5? If the bank estimates that 20 customers will open accounts for each $1 reduction in the charge, the formula now reads:

$$n = 2,500 + [(-20)(-5)]$$
$$n = 2,500 + 100$$
$$n = 2,600.$$

Thus, a $5 decrease in the return-check charge yields a new total of 2,600 accounts. In other words, the bank can estimate that 100 customers would open accounts as a result of the decrease in return-check charges.

Many economic relationships can be expressed in linear equations. These equations can also be graphed using the quadrant coordinate system described below.

The Quadrant Coordinate System

Figure 2.1 illustrates the four zones, or quadrants, that represent the set of possibilities for any ordered pair (x, y) described by the linear equation $y = a + bx$.

The x value is known as the abscissa and the y value is called the ordinate. The vertical line separating Quadrants II and III from Quadrants I and IV is the y-axis. The horizontal line separating Quadrants I and II from Quadrants III and IV is the x-axis. The origin is the point at which the x- and y-axes intersect. At the origin, $x = 0$ and $y = 0$.

Quadrant I contains all ordered pairs with x and y values greater than zero. Quadrant II contains ordered pairs with x values less than zero and y values greater than zero. Quadrant III's ordered pairs have x and y values less than zero. Quadrant IV has ordered pairs with negative y values and positive x values.

Since economic variables are almost always positive, most economic equations appear in Quadrant I. The following graphs (figures 2.2 through 2.9) illustrate typical configurations of linear equations.

In figure 2.2, the graphed line begins at point a, where the value of a, or the y intercept, is positive, and the value of x equals zero. Note that the value of y increases as the value of x increases. The b term (the slope) in the equation is positive, indicating that when x increases by one unit, y *increases* by the product of x and b. The graphed line remains in Quadrant I for all positive values of x. In this example, x and y are said to be directly related because an increase in x leads to an increase in y and a decrease in x is accompanied by a decrease in y.

In figure 2.3, the graphed line begins in Quadrant IV where the value of a (the y intercept) is negative ($-a$), when x equals zero. However, like the equation in figure 2.2, the slope is positive and x and y have a direct, positive relationship. As x increases, the value of y increases and eventually becomes a positive number.

In figure 2.4, the value of the y intercept (a) is positive. Thus, the graphed line begins at $x = 0$, in Quadrant I, and moves downward to the right as the value of x increases. Note that this downward path means that as x increases, y decreases. This is called an inverse relationship: the direction of y is the opposite of the direction of x. At point c, the value of y is zero. At points below c (in Quadrant IV), x continues to increase and remains a positive value while y values become negative.

In figure 2.5, the graph of the linear equation begins in Quadrant IV. The y-intercept (a) is negative, and y values remain negative for all positive values of x. The variables (x,y) are inversely related.

In figure 2.6, the y-intercept (a) is positive, but the slope (b) is equal to zero. In other words, a change in x has no effect on y and for all values of x, y equals a. Since the value of a is positive, the graphed equation remains in Quadrant I. Note that when the slope of the line is zero, the line runs parallel to the x-axis.

Figure 2.7 is similar to figure 2.6 except that the location of the horizontal line is in Quadrant IV, rather than Quadrant I. In this case, the value of a, or the y-intercept, is negative. For all positive values of x, the straight-line graph remains in Quadrant IV. As in figure 2.6, such a graph indicates the absence of a linear relationship between x and y.

When the constant a is zero, the x- and y-intercepts are located at the origin (0,0). Since the slope in figure 2.8 is positive, the graphed equation rises to the right for all positive values of x.

ECONOMICS FOR BANKERS

Figure 2.1 The Quadrant Coordinate System

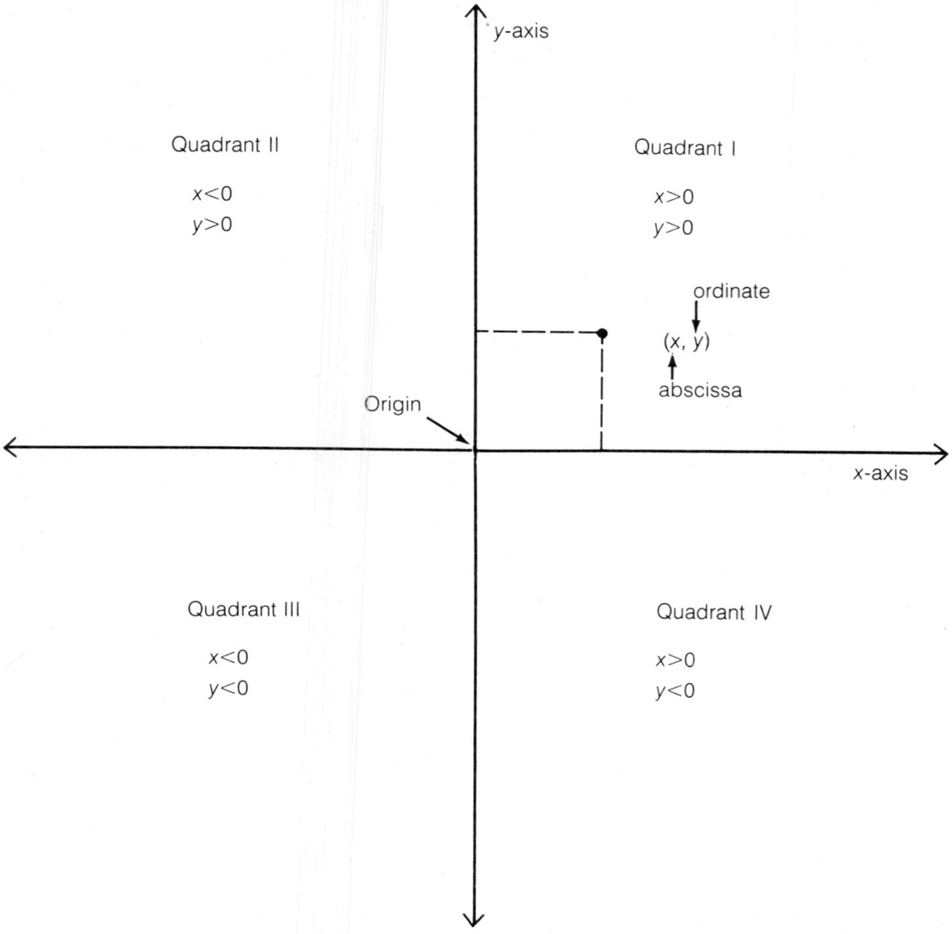

Quadrant II
$x<0$
$y>0$

Quadrant I
$x>0$
$y>0$

ordinate
(x, y)
abscissa

Origin

x-axis

y-axis

Quadrant III
$x<0$
$y<0$

Quadrant IV
$x>0$
$y<0$

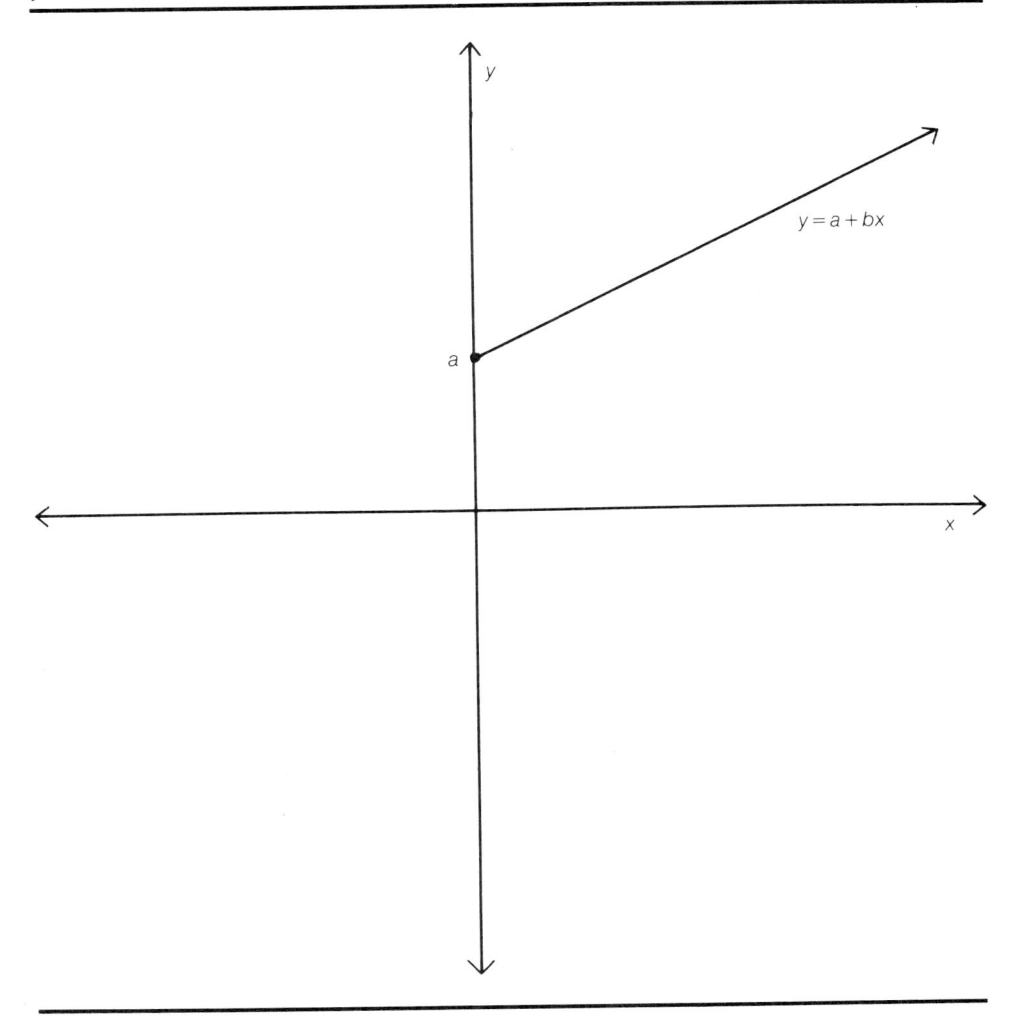

Figure 2.2 Graph of Linear Equation
$y = a + bx$, when $a>0$ and $b>0$

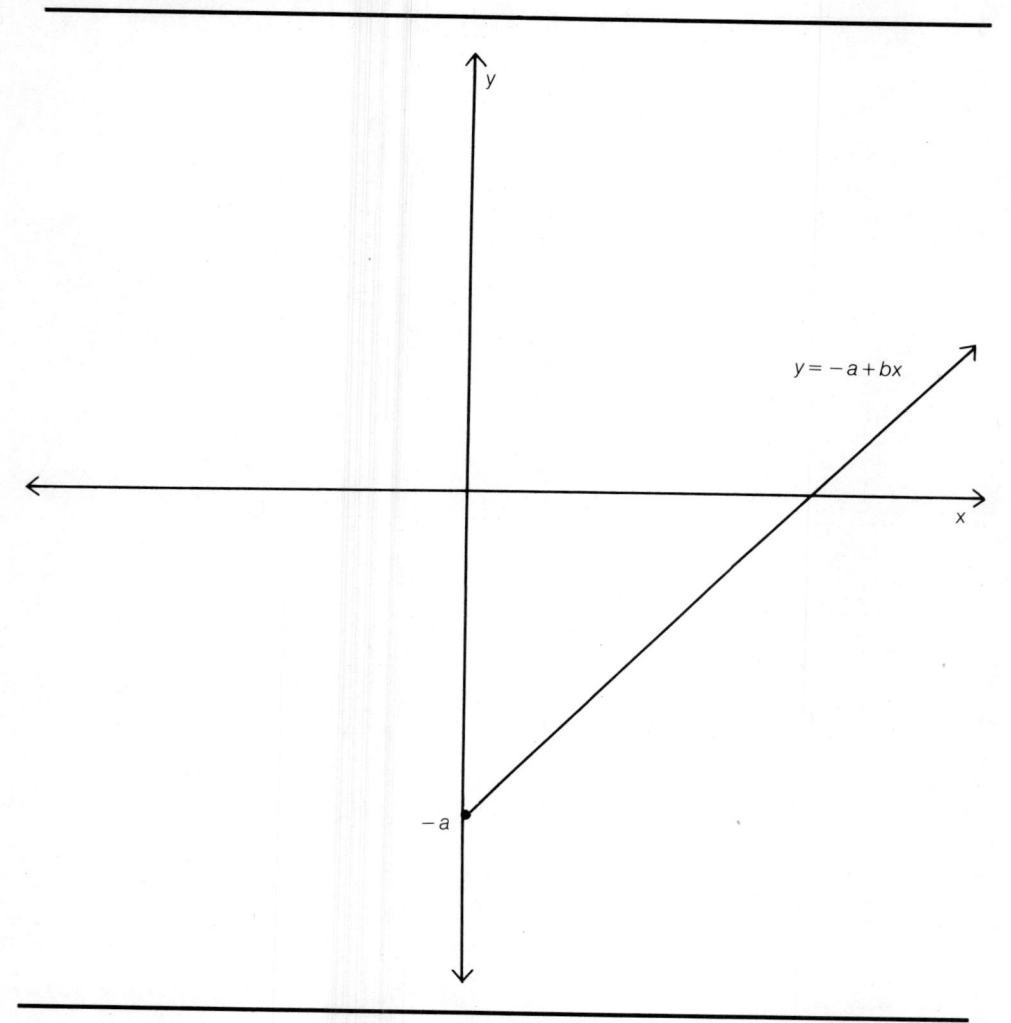

Figure 2.3 Graph of Linear Equation
$y = -a + bx$, when $a < 0$ and $b > 0$

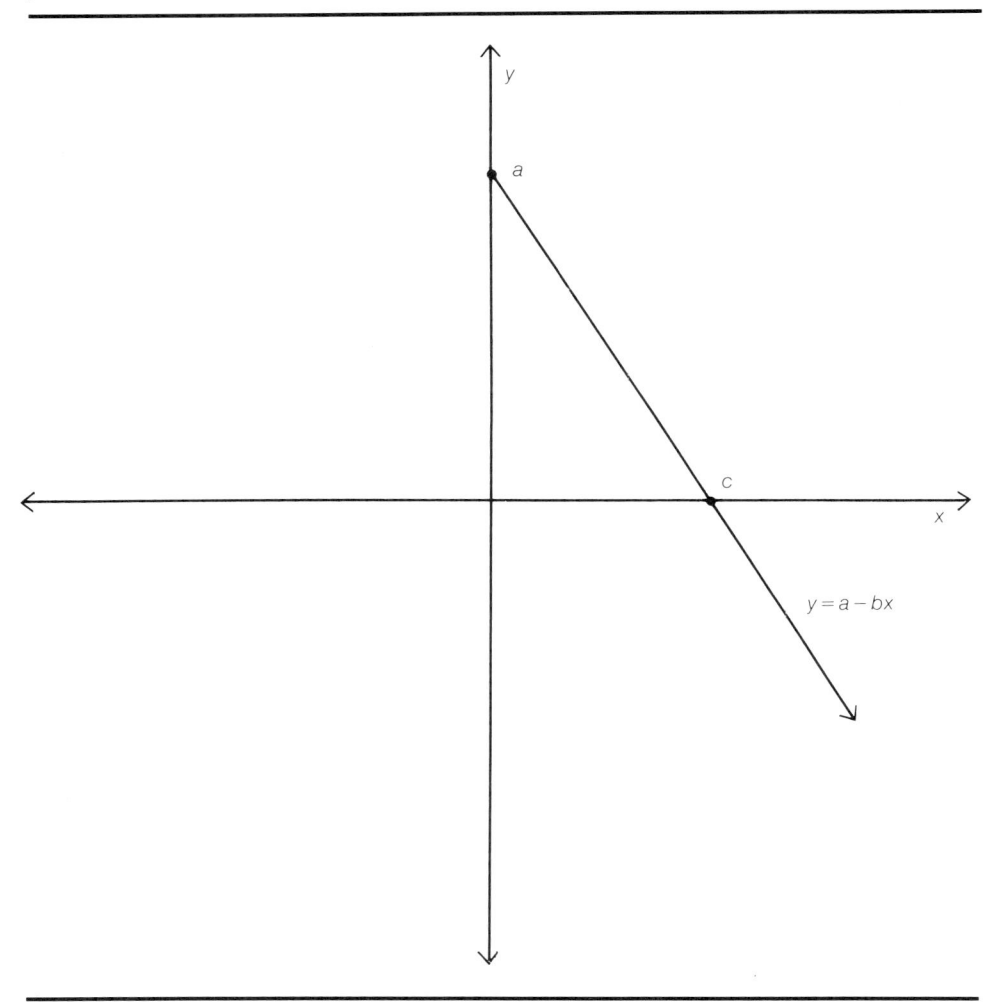

Figure 2.4 Graph of Linear Equation
$y = a - bx$, when $a > 0$ and $b < 0$

$y = a - bx$

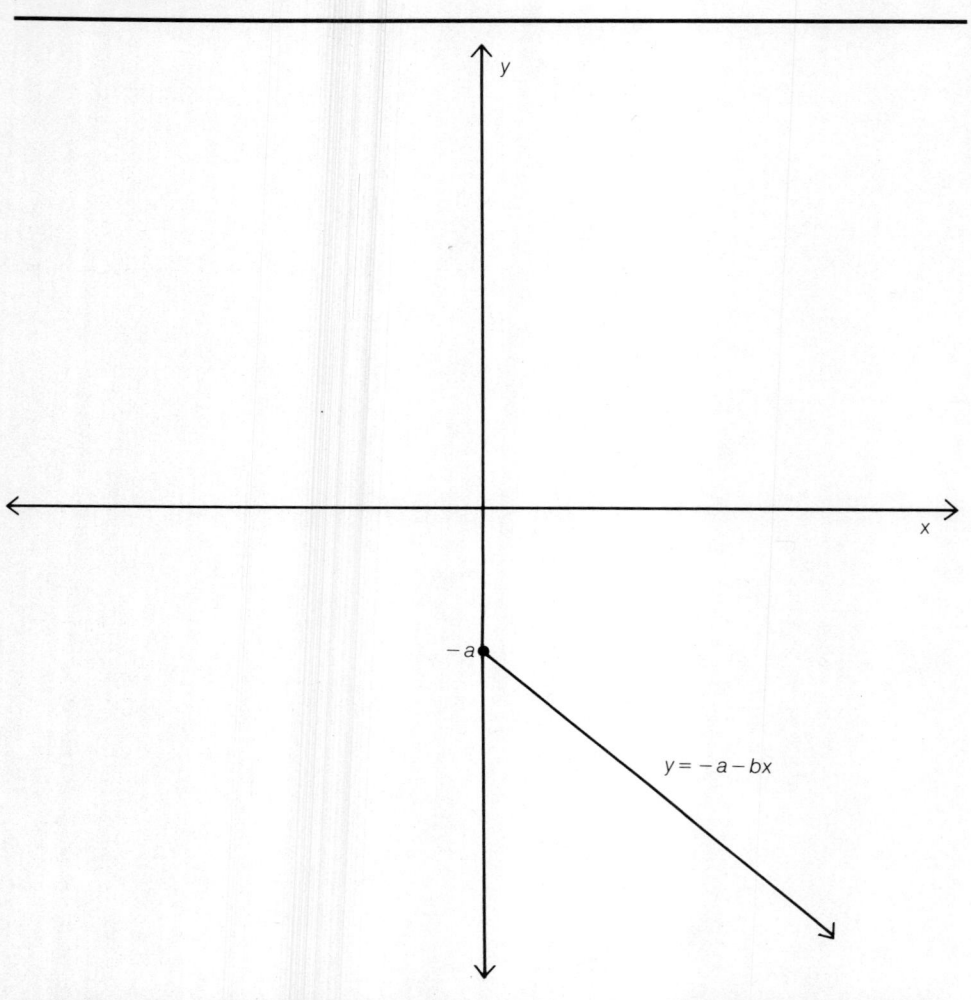

Figure 2.5 Graph of Linear Equation
$y = -a - bx$, when $a<0$ and $b<0$

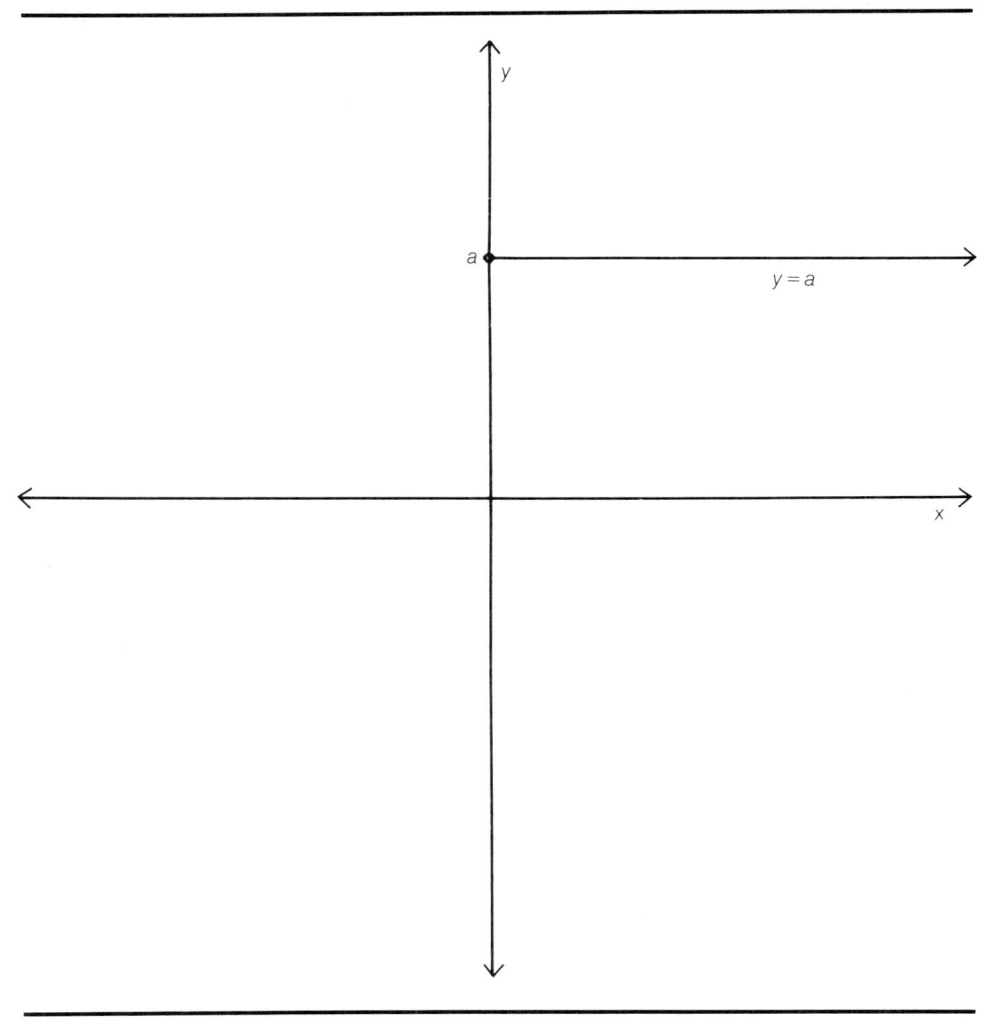

Figure 2.6 Graph of Linear Equation
$y = a + bx$, when $a > 0$ and $b = 0$ and $\therefore y = a$

ECONOMICS FOR BANKERS

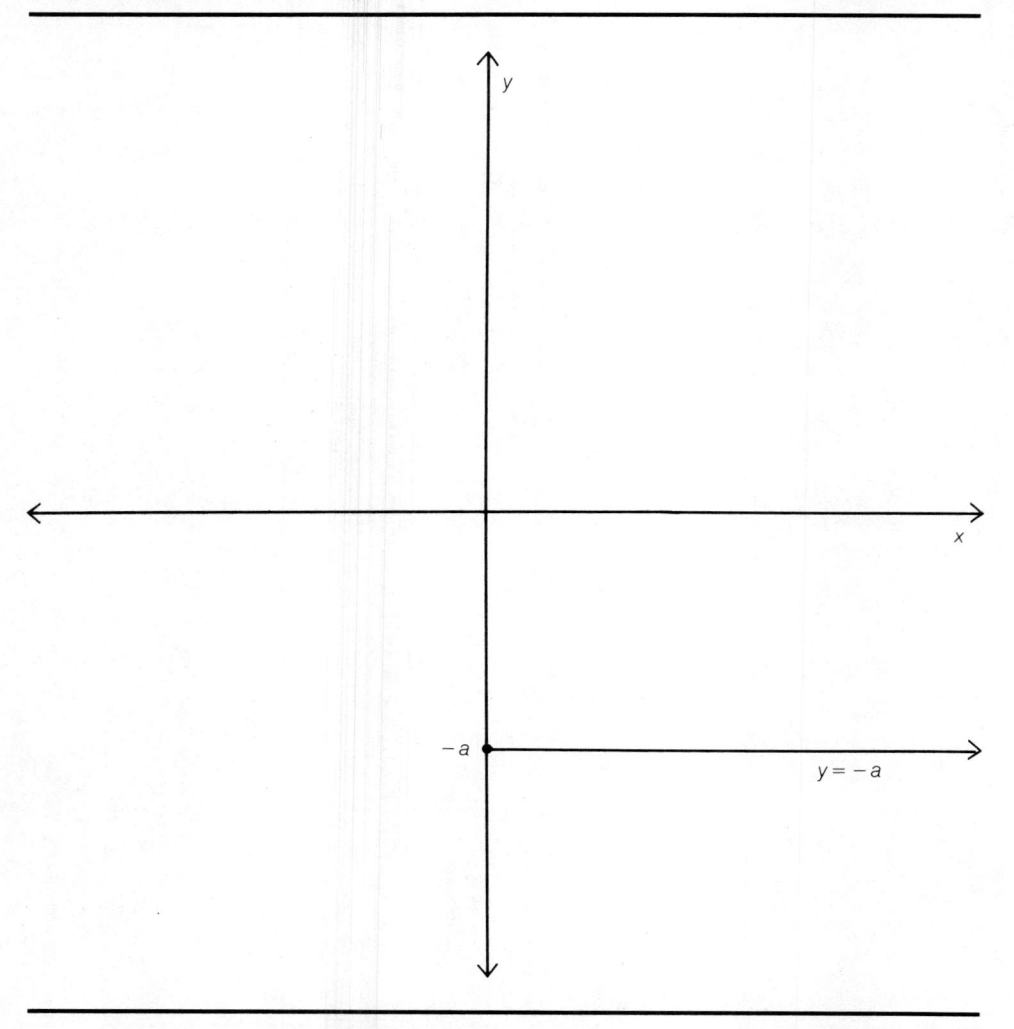

Figure 2.7 Graph of Linear Equation
$y = -a + bx$, when $a<0$ and $b=0$ and $\therefore y = -a$

36

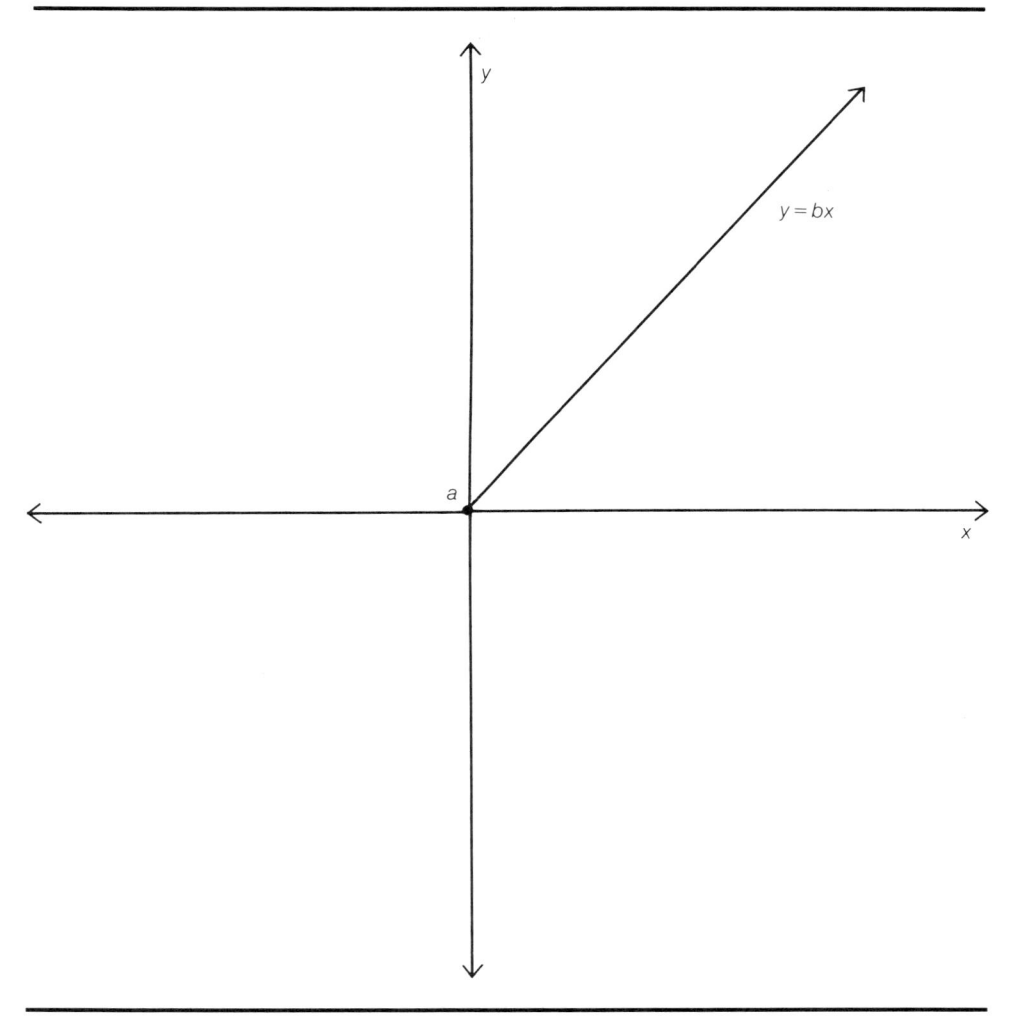

Figure 2.8 Graph of Linear Equation
$y = a + bx$, when $a = 0$ and $b > 0$ and $\therefore y = bx$

Figure 2.9 Graph of Linear Equation
$y = a + (-b)x$, when $a = 0$ and $b < 0$ and $\therefore y = -bx$

$y = -bx$

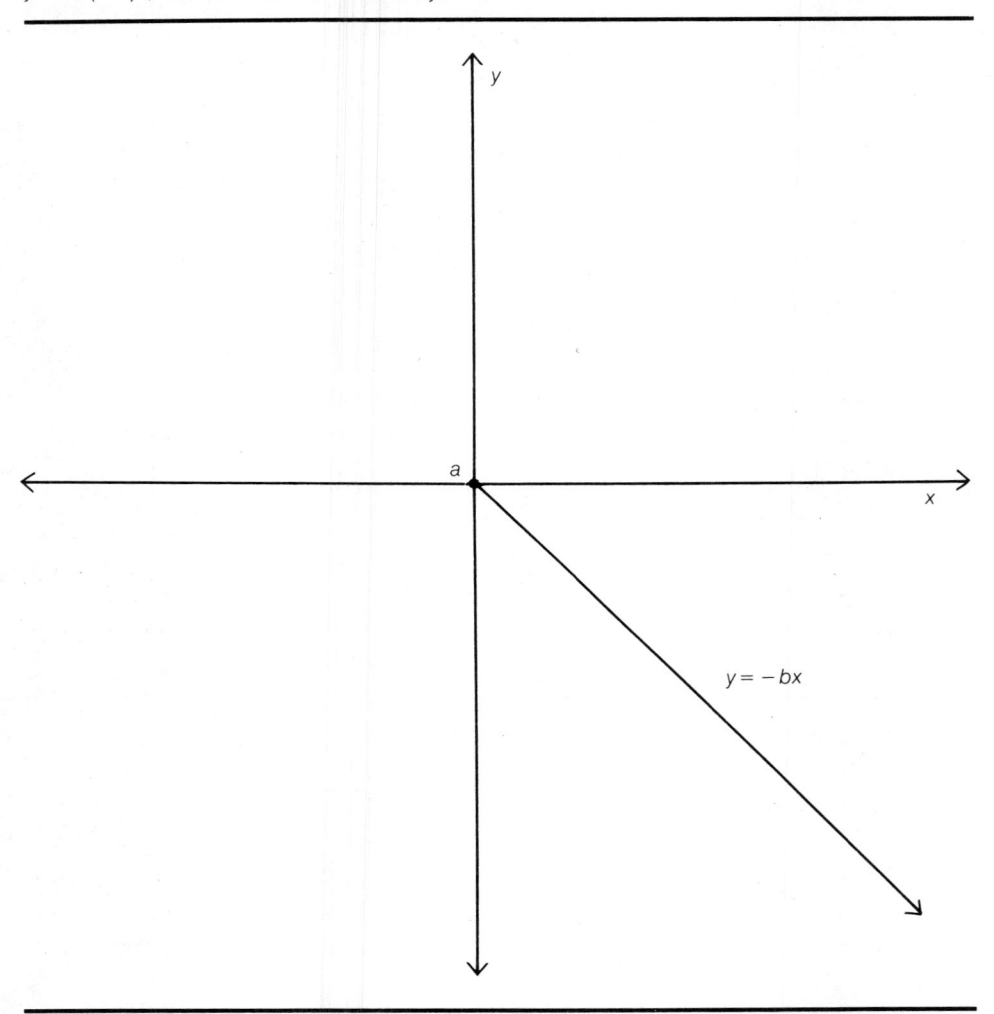

Figure 2.9 shows another case in which the intercepts are (0,0). The difference between figure 2.8 and figure 2.9 is the slope. The line in figure 2.9 moves downward, to the right, reflecting the negative value of b.

Special Cases

The examples given in figures 2.2–2.9 exhaust the possible configurations for linear equations commonly used in economics. However, the following nonlinear equation is also common to economic analysis:

$$a = xy.$$

This equation implies that the product of the values of x and y always yields a constant value, a. For positive values of x and y, this equation will always graph in Quadrant I as a downward curve that slopes to the right (see figure 2.10). This curve is called a rectangular hyperbola.

Note that while the graph approaches the x- and y-axes, it will never touch either axis. Such relationships are called asymptotic—the values of x and y approach, but never reach, zero.

Finally, instances occasionally arise in which you cannot solve for y (see figure 2.11). While this graph is actually quite common in economics, it still merits the label of a special case. The line has no slope ($b = 0$) and the value of x is constant. As in figures 2.6 and 2.7, no functional relationship between x and y is indicated. Regardless of the value of y, x remains constant at x_0.

Numerical Examples

In figure 2.12, the coordinate plane is shown to consist of four quadrants. Every ordered pair corresponds to a unique point on the coordinate plane. Point A in Quadrant I shows the value of the abscissa (x) to equal 9, and the value of the ordinate (y) to equal 2. Thus, point A can be written as the ordered pair (9,2). Note that (9,2) and (2,9) do *not* represent the same point on the graph. The first value is always the value of x and the second, the value of y.

Also note the locations of ordered pairs ($-6,9$), or point C, and ($-6, -9$), or point D. Point E in Quadrant IV represents the ordered pair $(4, -7)$.

Figure 2.10 Graph of Nonlinear Equation
$a = xy$

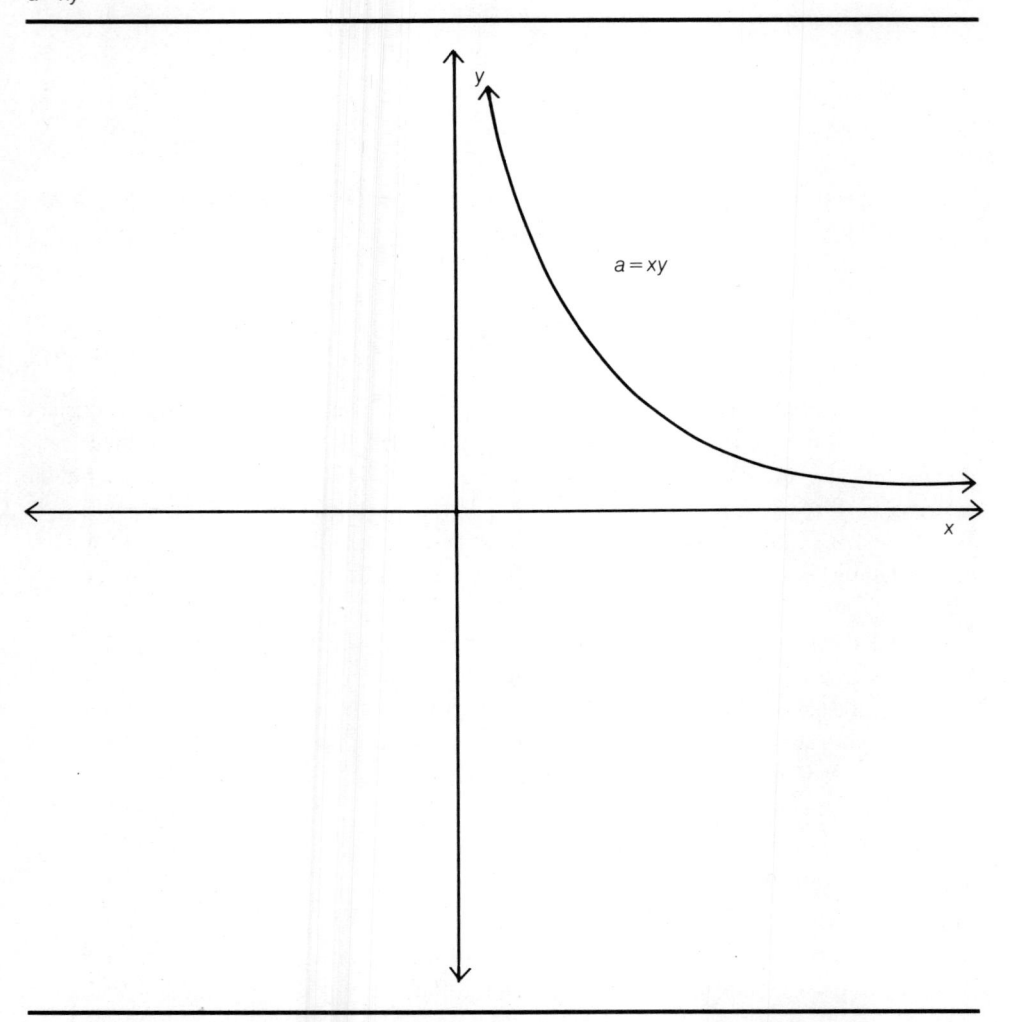

Figure 2.11 Graph of Linear Equation
$x = x_0$ (no functional relationship between x and y)

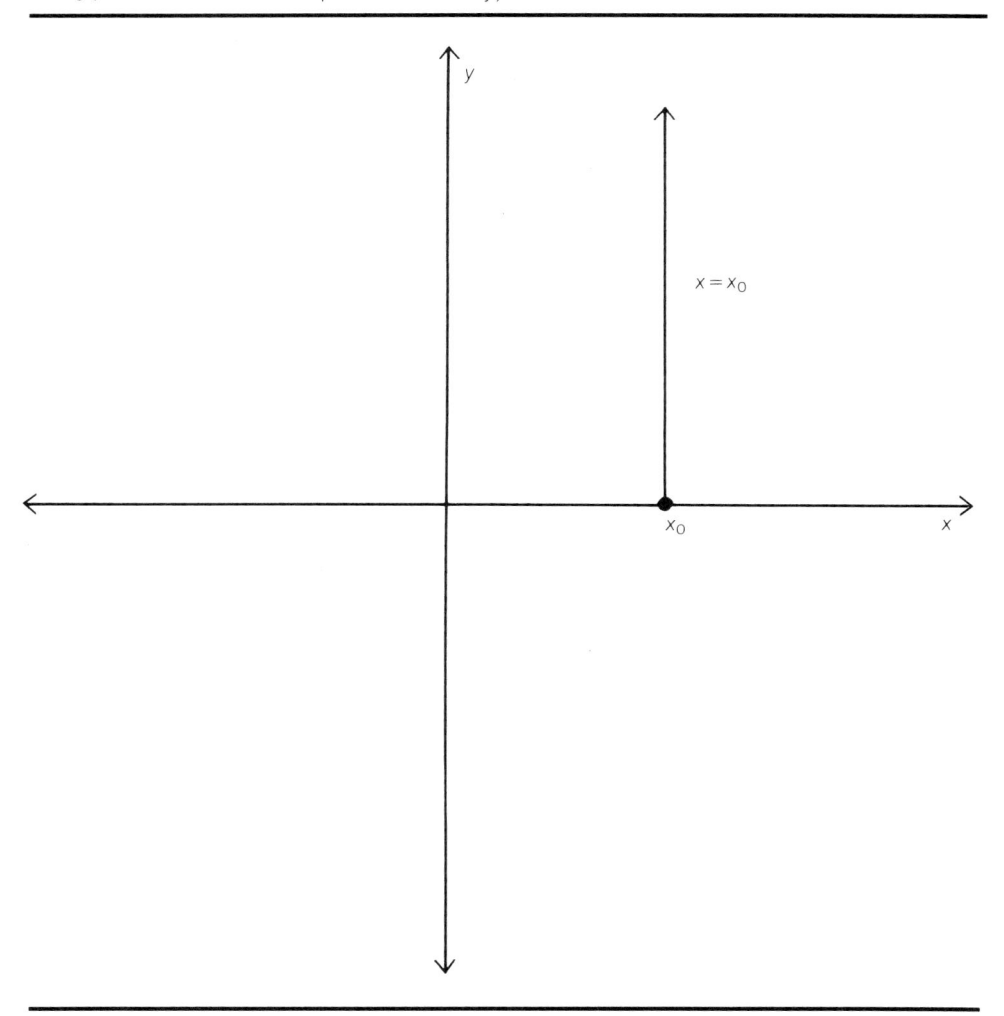

ECONOMICS FOR BANKERS

Figure 2.12 Five Ordered Pairs

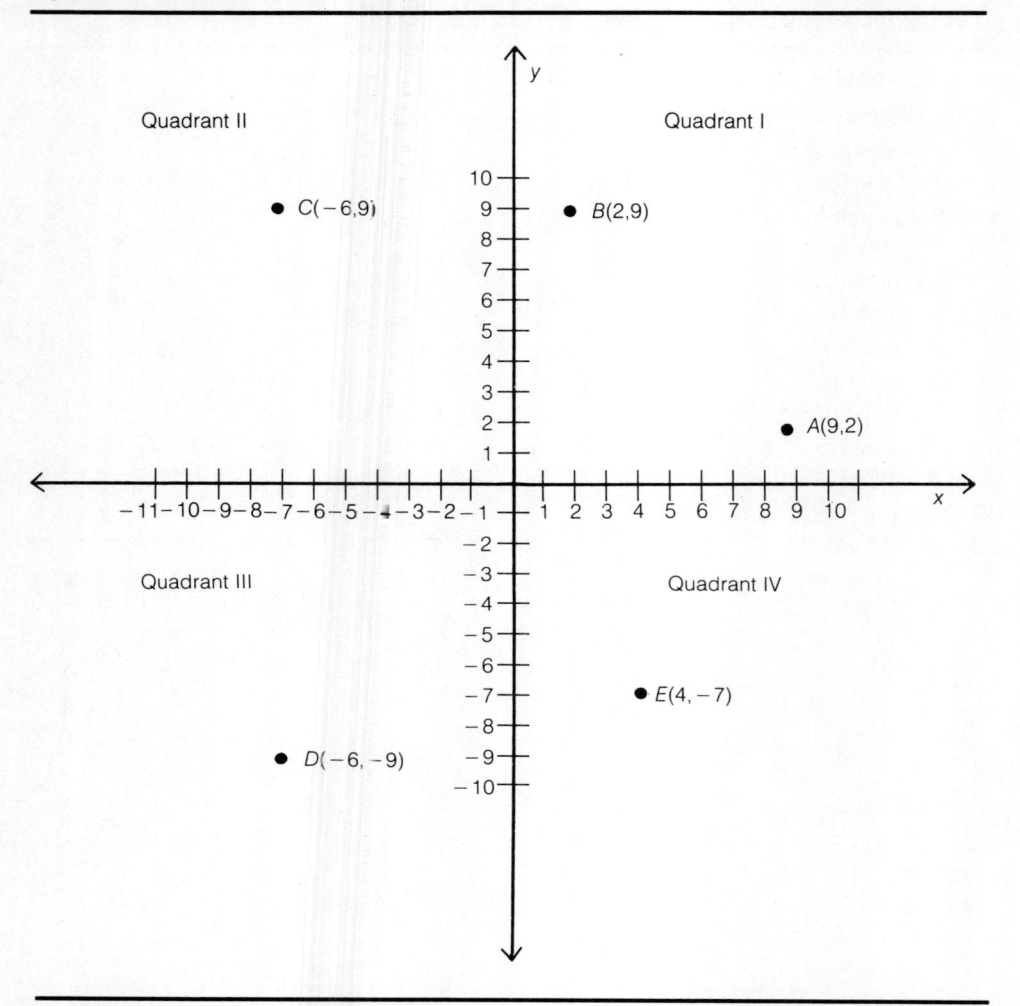

MATHEMATICS AND STATISTICS

Graphing Linear Equations

We can construct a graph for the linear equation $y = 3 + .5x$. To graph this equation, it is necessary to construct a table of ordered pairs that reflects the specific mathematical relationship between the independent variable (x) and the dependent variable (y). This is the same formula that appeared as a general equation in figure 2.2 and before that in our cost estimates for the First National Bank. Here, the value of the constant (a) is positive, signifying a y-intercept greater than zero. The slope term (b) equals .5, which indicates that for every one unit increase in x, the value of y rises by .5. The slope of the graph will be positive, moving upward to the right. Beginning with $x = 0$ and moving up to $x = 5$, a set of ordered pairs can be constructed for all values of x when $y = 3 + .5x$ (see table 2.3).

It is now quite simple to plot these ordered pairs onto a graph (figure 2.13). Note that the y-intercept is equal to 3.

The slope of any straight line can be calculated by measuring the "legs" of the right triangle created by connecting any two points on the line as shown in figure 2.13. Recall that the slope indicates the amount of change in y, given a unit change in x. In the triangle RST, the change in y is represented by the line ST and the change in x by the line RT. The slope is calculated by dividing the change in y (the length of ST) by the change in x (the length of RT). In the example, the change in y equals 1 unit and the change in x equals 2 units. The slope of the line equals:

$$\frac{\Delta y}{\Delta x} = \frac{1}{2} = .5.$$

In other words, every time x increases by one unit, y increases by .5, or one-half unit.

The slope can also be calculated by measurements from any triangle constructed from two points on the line. For example, using triangle QUV, QU, or Δx, equals 4 units and UV, or Δy, equals 2 units. Putting these values into the formula, the slope is the same: .5.

A set of ordered pairs can be constructed for a linear equation with a negative slope: $y = 5 - .5x$ (see table 2.4).

The corresponding graph (figure 2.14) shows a line with a y-intercept of 5 and a slope of $-.5$. In other words, as the value of x increases, the value of y decreases, resulting in a negative slope.

Knowing how to work with linear equations not only will help you later in this text, but also will make it easier for you to study financial information. To practice, you may want to look for mathematical relationships between and among the financial variables at your bank: for example, by plotting the number of customers or average deposit size by customer class, or by plotting income levels against loan defaults.

ECONOMICS FOR BANKERS

Table 2.3 Ordered Pairs, $y = 3 + .5x$

x	y
0	3.0
1	3.5
2	4.0
3	4.5
4	5.0
5	5.5

Figure 2.13 Graph of Linear Equation $y = a + bx$, when $a = 3$ and $b = .5$

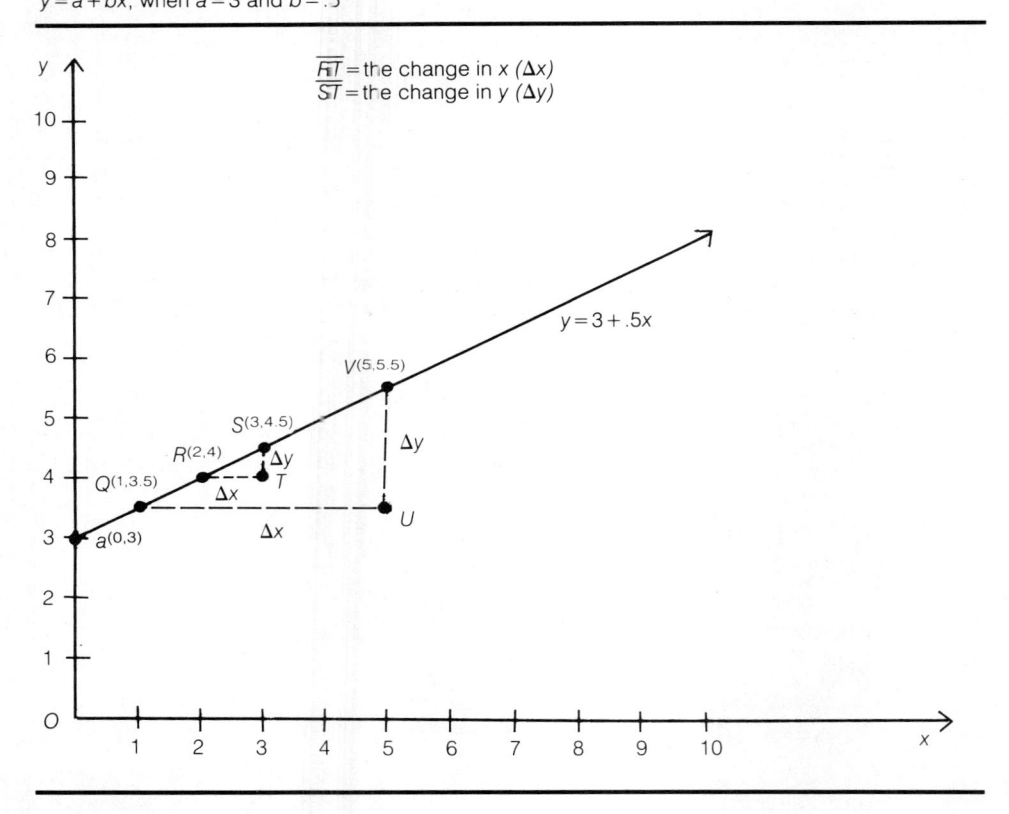

$\overline{RT}$ = the change in x (Δx)
$\overline{ST}$ = the change in y (Δy)

Points on graph: $a(0,3)$, $Q(1,3.5)$, $R(2,4)$, $S(3,4.5)$, $V(5,5.5)$

$y = 3 + .5x$

MATHEMATICS AND STATISTICS

Table 2.4 Ordered Pairs, $y = 5 - .5x$

x	y
0	5.0
1	4.5
2	4.0
3	3.5
4	3.0
5	2.5
6	2.0
7	1.5
8	1.0
9	0.5
10	0.0

Figure 2.14 Graph of Linear Equation $y = a + bx$, when $a = 5$ and $b = (-.5)$

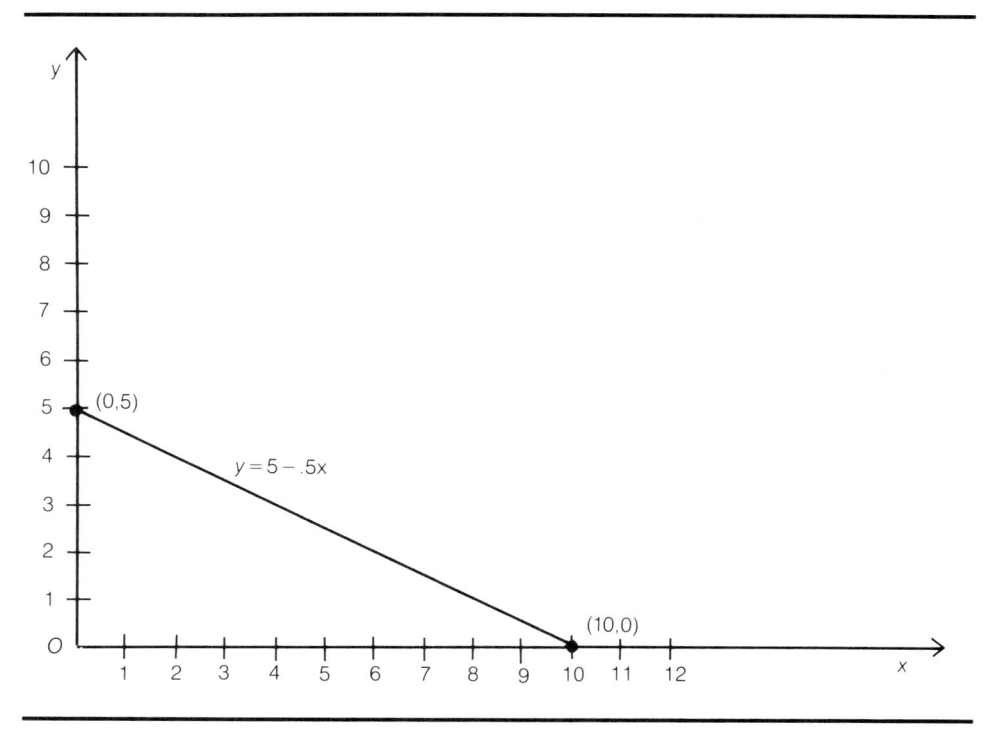

45

STATISTICS AND ECONOMICS

As noted in chapter 1, statistics are very powerful tools that, if misused or misunderstood, can lead to false conclusions. The processes involved in assessing the health of the economy generate a wide, potentially confusing array of numbers. Interpreting the data, uncovering relationships, and determining the significance of the relationships can only be accomplished if statistics are used correctly.

Improper handling of statistics obscures our understanding of a situation. For example, suppose a certain town has three banks. Bank A has $900 million in assets, Bank B has $100 million, and the newest bank in town, Bank C, has $50 million. A business development brochure implies that the town has a healthy, competitive banking environment by stating that the town's three local banks "average $350 million in assets." This statement is statistically correct. Averages are found by summing the individual figures and dividing by the total number of figures. Adding the banks' assets and dividing the total by 3 does yield an average of $350 million. Such an average, however, hardly reflects a healthy and competitive banking environment when one bank (Bank A) controls 90 percent of the market.

Mastery of a few general statistical concepts will enable you to avoid many of the traps into which many individuals fall when interpreting statistics. These concepts are the measures of central tendency (mean, median, and mode) and the measures of dispersion (range, average absolute deviation, variance, and standard deviation).

Measures of Central Tendency

Measures of central tendency are statistics that represent a "typical" value in a set of numbers, or data set. Three commonly used measures of central tendency are (1) the mode (the value that occurs most frequently in the data set); (2) the median (the value that separates all values in the data set into one of two groups, the lower 50 percent and the upper 50 percent); and (3) the mean (the "center of gravity" of the set, at which the values above exactly balance the values below).

Suppose we want to determine the typical balance in a particular customer's checking account over a 15-day period (see table 2.5, Daily Balances, Account X). We can begin by calculating the mode, the median, and the mean of this set of numbers.

The Mode

The mode is the value recorded most often. To find it, you count how many times each value is given. It is helpful to organize the data into sequential order, either lowest to highest or highest to lowest. The balances in Account X are organized from lowest to highest in table

Table 2.5 Daily Balances, Account X

Day	Balance (dollars)
1	580
2	340
3	340
4	425
5	200
6	825
7	460
8	500
9	310
10	500
11	760
12	480
13	630
14	580
15	580

Table 2.6 Balances Occurring in Account X

Daily Balance (dollars)	Instances
200	1
310	1
340	2
425	1
460	1
480	1
500	2
580	3
630	1
760	1
825	1
Total	15

2.6. The daily balance recorded most frequently is $580. Thus, $580 is the mode of this data set.

If the data set contains two or more values occurring with the highest frequency, two scenarios are possible. The values may be adjacent (table 2.7) or not adjacent (table 2.8).

If the values are adjacent, to obtain the mode you may sum the values that are tied and divide by the number of values added. In table 2.7 the adjacent values $500 and $580 each are listed as occurring three times. The mode of this set is calculated as:

$$(\$500 + \$580)/2 = \$540.$$

Table 2.7 Adjacent Balances

Daily Balance (dollars)	Instances
200	1
310	1
340	2
425	1
460	1
500	3
580	3
630	1
760	1
Total	14

Table 2.8 Nonadjacent Balances

Daily Balance (dollars)	Instances
200	1
310	3
340	2
480	1
500	2
580	3
630	1
760	1
825	1
Total	15

If the most frequently noted values are not adjacent, the set may have more than one mode. In table 2.8 the nonadjacent values $310 and $580 each are listed as occurring three times. This set is bimodal: it has two modes, $310 and $580.

Knowing how to calculate the mode will help you answer such questions as: What is the best-selling commercial loan product? On what day of the month does the bank see the most customers? Which of the bank's automatic teller machines (ATMs) leads in transaction volume?

The Median

The median is the value below or above which 50 percent of the remaining values fall. The median represents the 50th percentile of a data set. It is the middle value of a set of values ranked either from highest to lowest or vice versa. To locate the median value, first organize the list of values from highest to lowest, or vice versa. When the total number of individual values is an odd number, the location of the median value can be found by dividing the total number of values in the set by 2, rounding down to the nearest whole number, and then adding 1:

$$\text{Location of Median} = (n/2) + 1,$$
where n = number of values,
and $(n/2)$ is rounded down.

Given a set of 15 values (table 2.9), we can use the formula above to locate the median:

$$(15/2) + 1 = 7.5 + 1$$
$$= 7 + 1$$
$$= 8.$$

The median value of the data set represented by table 2.9 is the eighth value in the list, or $500.

With an even number of values (table 2.10), the median will lie between the values of the middle two positions. To find the first position, divide the total number of values by 2. If you are counting from the bottom of the list, the second position will be the value directly above the first position. If you are counting down from the top, the second position will be directly below the first position. Add the values in the two positions and divide the sum by 2 to find the median value.

$$\text{Location of Median} = [(n/2) + x]/2,$$
where x = the value of the number in the list represented by $(n/2) + 1$.

Given a set of 14 values, we can calculate $14/2 = 7$. The value in the seventh position of this set is $480. The value in the next (eighth) position is $500. The median value is the sum of these two values divided by 2, or $(\$480 + \$500)/2 = \$490$.

Table 2.9 Ranked Balances, Odd Number

Daily Balance (dollars)	Rank
200	1
310	2
340	3
340	4
425	5
460	6
480	7
500	8
500	9
580	10
580	11
580	12
630	13
760	14
825	15

ECONOMICS FOR BANKERS

Where there are vast disparities in values, the median can be more representative of the set than the mean. The median can also be useful to bankers evaluating relatively small data sets.

Table 2.10 Ranked Balances, Even Number

Daily Balance (dollars)	Rank
200	1
310	2
340	3
340	4
425	5
460	6
480	7
500	8
500	9
580	10
580	11
580	12
630	13
760	14

The Mean

The mean of a set of values is the arithmetic average of the data. To find the mean, add all of the individual values in the data set and divide the total by the number of values (n) in the set.

$$\text{Mean} = (x_1 + x_2 + x_3 + \ldots + x_n)/n$$

The mean is frequently written in the conventional symbols of the statistician as:

$$\bar{x} = \Sigma x_i,$$

where $\bar{x}$, called "x bar" is the mean, and the Greek symbol Σ, or "sigma," is defined as "the sum of what follows." The subscript attached to x signifies that all values of x (called x_i) from $x_1 = 1$ through x_n should be aggregated. Frequently, the range of values is obvious and the specific notation is dropped. Then, the mean of x can be written as:

$$\bar{x} = \frac{\Sigma x_i}{n},$$

where n = the number of values of x.

Given a set of 15 values (table 2.9), we can calculate the mean, or arithmetic average, by dividing the sum of the values by 15. In this example, the sum of the values (Σx) equals

$7,510. The number of values (n) equals 15. Thus, $\bar{x} = \$7,510/15 = \$500.67$ (rounded to the nearest hundredth).

While the mean is an important measure of central tendency, it can be biased by a few extreme values. For example, let us examine daily balances for 10 days in Account Y (table 2.11).

For the first 5-day period, Account Y's mean balance is ($100 + $120 + $90 + $110 + $80) /5, or $100.

During the second 5-day period, only one value, the last, differs from those in the first set. The sum of the balances for days 6 through 10 is $1,000, however, so the mean for this period is $200—twice the mean of the first 5 days. This average does not represent the typical balance in the account.

Indeed, the $580 balance on day 10 skews the average balance of Account Y for the entire 10-day period. The sum of the balances for days 1 through 10 is $1,500. Thus, the mean is $150—less reflective of the typical balance than the $100 mean derived from the first 5-day period.

Just as an exceptionally high value can pull the mean upward, so can an exceptionally low value bring the mean down to a misleadingly low number. Nonetheless, for a banker who understands its limitations, the mean can be of considerable use; it is easily calculated and understood by many people, and for sets of data that are sufficiently large, the mean can be used to show typical values.

In summary, the mean, median, and mode are commonly used measures of central tendency. All three measures provide useful information about data sets. Each measure, however, has its own special limitations. More importantly, the measures of central tendency do not reveal much about the spread of values in the data set. To find out about these characteristics, we turn to the measures of dispersion: the range, the standard deviation, and the variance.

Table 2.11 Daily Balances, Account Y

Day	Balance (dollars)
1	100
2	120
3	90
4	110
5	80
6	100
7	120
8	90
9	110
10	580

Measures of Dispersion

The spread of values refers to the degree to which the values differ from the mean of the data set. When the differences among the values are greater, the spread is greater. The more tightly the values cluster together, the smaller the spread.

The Range

The measure of dispersion simplest to compute is the range. The range is the difference between the highest and lowest value in a data set. We can, for example, compute the range of exam scores for three sets of economics students (table 2.12).

Table 2.12 Student Examination Scores

Set A Student	Score	Set B Student	Score	Set C Student	Score
1	100	1	100	1	100
2	85	2	75	2	100
3	70	3	75	3	100
4	70	4	75	4	100
5	75	5	75	5	75
6	75	6	75	6	75
7	85	7	75	7	50
8	75	8	75	8	50
9	50	9	75	9	50
10	65	10	50	10	50

The highest value in the data for Student Set A is 100; the lowest is 50. Therefore, the range for these scores is 100 − 50, or 50 points. For this set of scores the mean, median, and mode are each equal to 75 points.

The range is rarely used as the only measure of variability. It is relatively uninformative because it is based on the two most extreme values in the set. A banker might find the range useful in determining patterns of customer activity: for example, he or she might ascertain that the number of transactions at a particular ATM location typically ranges from 25 on a Sunday morning to 150 on a Friday night.

The Variance

The variance is another statistic that gives us information about the differences in data sets. To determine the variance of a set, you must first determine the deviation values in the set. A deviation value is the difference between an actual value and the mean: it measures the distance between the actual value and the mean. The deviation value also shows direction:

MATHEMATICS AND STATISTICS

a positive deviation value indicates that the actual value given is greater than the mean, while a negative deviation value indicates that the actual value is less than the mean. When the positive and negative deviation values are added together, their sum always equals zero.

Given the set of examination scores for Student Set A (table 2.12), we can calculate and list the deviation of each score, or value, from the mean (table 2.13). To eliminate the problem of negative and positive scores canceling each other out, we can square the deviation scores (table 2.14). The square of a negative number is always positive, as is the square of a positive number.

Table 2.13 Deviation of Scores, Student Set A

Student	Score	Mean	Deviation Score (Score − Mean)
1	100	75	25
2	85	75	10
3	70	75	−5
4	70	75	−5
5	75	75	0
6	75	75	0
7	85	75	10
8	75	75	0
9	50	75	−25
10	65	75	−10

Table 2.14 Squared Deviation Scores, Student Set A

Student	Score	Deviation Score	Squared Deviation Score
1	100	25	625
2	85	10	100
3	70	−5	25
4	70	−5	25
5	75	0	0
6	75	0	0
7	85	10	100
8	75	0	0
9	50	−25	625
10	65	−10	100

The variance equals the average of the squared deviation scores. For Student Set A, the variance is 1,600/10, or 160. The formula is written as follows:

$$\text{Variance:} \quad \frac{\Sigma\,(\bar{x} - x_i)^2}{n}.$$

While the variance is more informative than the range as a measure of dispersion, it creates a problem of scale: the squaring of the deviation scores solves the problem of signs, but it also increases the scale of the values. By taking the square root of the variance, we can return to the scale of the original values in the set. The square root of the variance is called the standard deviation.

The Standard Deviation

The standard deviation is the most commonly used measure of dispersion. It provides an index of the spread of values about the mean of a data set. The standard deviation is defined formally as the square root of the average squared deviation of values from the mean—in other words, the square root of the variance. The formula for the standard deviation is written as follows:

$$\text{Standard deviation: } \sqrt{\frac{\Sigma (\bar{x} - x_i)^2}{n}}.$$

This is the proper formula to use when you have all of the values from the data set. The average squared deviation of values from the mean for Student Set A was calculated as 160. The standard deviation for this set is $\sqrt{160}$, or 12.65. This means that the 10 actual scores in the data set are spread about the mean of 75 by an average value of 12.65.

When you have only a portion of the data set—as frequently happens to economists analyzing macroeconomic issues—the formula for standard deviation must be adjusted. This is necessary because the mean can only be estimated from incomplete data. In such cases, the denominator becomes n-1 rather than n.[1]

The usefulness of the standard deviation as a measure of dispersion can be illustrated by comparing the scores in Student Set A with those in Sets B and C (see tables 2.12 through 2.14). The range of scores—50 points—is identical for all three sets. Moreover, the mean, median, and mode of all three sets are the same: each equals 75. Yet, the distribution of scores in Set A is obviously different from Set B, and both of these differ from Set C.

If we add together the absolute values of the deviation values, we obtain the average deviation of each set. The average deviation of scores for Student Set A is 90. For Set B, the average deviation of scores is 50, and for Set C it is 200. The standard deviation, however, will give us the most precise indication of the degree to which the scores are scattered between the lowest and highest values of each set. The standard deviation for Set A, as previously noted, is 12.65. The standard deviation of the scores in Set B is 11.18; for Set C, it is 22.36.

Standard Deviation and Risk

Bankers often use the standard deviation as a measurement of risk. For example, the standard deviations of annual profit rates from average profit rates can be used to measure risk. The higher the standard deviation, the more a given year's profits deviate from the mean and the greater the risk in predicting a given year's average profits. Investments with large fluctuations in anticipated rates of return are riskier than those with moderate fluctuations. A higher return is required for investments with greater risk, while, on the other hand, safe, relatively risk-free investments require lower rates of return.

Researchers R.G. Ibbotson and R.A. Sinquefield found that for the period 1926–78 the annual rates of return for various investment instruments varied directly with the standard deviation of such returns (table 2.15).

Investment securities with relatively higher risks (that is, a high standard deviation of rates of return) paid higher yields, and those securities with lower risks (and a lower standard deviation of rates of return) paid lower yields.

Table 2.15 Standard Deviation of Profits vs. Rates of Return, 1926–78

Type of Security	Average Yield (percent)	Standard Deviation of Yield
Short-term U.S. government securities	2.5	2.2
Long-term U.S. government securities	3.4	5.7
Long-term corporate securities	4.1	5.6
Common stocks	11.2	22.2

Source: Ibbotson, Roger G., and Rex A. Sinquefield, *Stocks, Bonds, Bills and Inflation* (SBBI) 1982, updated in *SBBI 1983 Yearbook* and in the fourth quarter 1983 update, Ibbotson Associates, Chicago.

DATA CONVERSIONS

Economic data on such topics as production and national income accounts, prices, employment, and money and credit can be tracked and announced daily, weekly, monthly, quarterly, or yearly. Some economic statistics are given in terms of growth rates or rates of change over 3- and 6-month intervals. The multitude of numbers can be very confusing, especially when you are trying to compare statistics calculated on different bases. There are, however, ways to convert, or mathematically manipulate, data so that you can fully interpret their significance. Learning the following methods will enable you to convert monthly data to quarterly data, compute differences between periods, calculate percentage differences between periods, find percentage differences at annual rates, and determine 12-month moving averages.

Monthly Data to Quarterly

Consider an array of data on total cash assets of commercial banks (table 2.16). Total cash assets are composed of reserves with Federal Reserve banks, cash in vault, cash items in process of collection, demand balances at U.S. depository institutions, and "other" cash assets. To figure out what portion of the commercial banks' cash assets consisted of cash in vault, you must compare monthly data with quarterly data.

Table 2.16 Total Cash Assets of Commercial Banking Institutions, 1986

Month	Assets (billions of dollars)	Quarter	Cash in Vault (billions of dollars)
January	187.3	First	22.5
February	193.7		
March	198.1		
April	209.9	Second	23.7
May	221.0		
June	196.0		
July	206.2	Third	23.3
August	205.8		
September	196.6		
October	200.4	Fourth	23.8
November	223.9		
December	270.7		

Source: Federal Reserve *Bulletin,* May 1987, Table 1.25, p. A18.

It is fairly simple to change monthly figures to quarterly figures: add the data for the 3 months that correspond to each quarter and divide the total by 3. This is the same procedure used to find the mean of a data set. Total cash assets for the first quarter of 1986 averaged $193.03 billion. Dividing the cash in vault ($22.5 billion) by the total cash assets ($193.03 billion) for the first quarter gives us the proportion of cash in vault to total cash assets: 0.12, or 12 percent. The same steps apply when converting data for the second, third, and fourth quarters.

Converting data reported in 12 values per year to 4 values per year is helpful when you want to condense monthly data into a more compact format or when you want to make a direct comparison of data published monthly with data published quarterly.

This method is also used to convert weekly data into monthly data: add the data for each week in the corresponding month and divide the total by the number of weeks. To convert quarterly data into annual data, add the data for each quarter in the corresponding year and divide by 4.

Difference Between Periods

The difference between periods for a data series is the present value of the series minus the previous value of the series. This calculation is used to determine how much the data has changed from one period to the next. For example, in March 1986, the estimated daily average balance for gross demand deposits at commercial banks (individuals, partnerships, and corporations) was $307.4 billion. In April 1986, the figure was $322.4 billion. To determine the change from March to April, subtract $307.4 billion from $322.4 billion. The difference between these months is $15 billion.

Percentage Difference Between Periods

You may want to convert the change measured in the calculation above into a percentage difference. To transform a difference between periods into a percentage difference, divide it by the value of the first series, then multiply the result by 100 percent. Using the example above, you would divide $15 billion by $307.4 billion to get 0.05. Multipling 0.05 by 100 percent, we find that gross demand deposits increased by 5 percent between March and April.

Percentage Difference at Annual Rate

In the first quarter of 1986, total gross public debt of the U.S. Treasury was $1,986.8 billion. In the second quarter of 1986, the debt increased to $2,059.3 billion. If this increase had been replicated every quarter for the next year, what would be the annual rate of change? In other words, if the same quarter-to-quarter rate of change continued over an entire year, how much total change would occur?

To determine the rate of change in a monthly statistic in terms of its growth rate on an annual basis, you must (1) divide the more recent month's value by the earlier month's value; (2) multiply this value by itself 12 times; (3) subtract 1 from the product; and (4) multiply by 100 to change the proportion into a percent. The process is identical for determining the rate of change in a quarterly statistic except that in step 2 you multiply the value by itself 4 times.

Applying these steps to the example above, you would calculate:

$$
\begin{aligned}
2059.3/1986.8 &= 1.03649 \\
(1.03649)^4 &= 1.15414 \\
1.15414 - 1 &= 0.15414 \\
0.15414 \times 100 &= 15.414\%.
\end{aligned}
$$

The 15.414 percent rate is called the annualized growth rate.

12-Month Moving Average

A 12-month moving average is simply the arithmetic average or mean value of a data series over the preceding 12 months. The average of the series over the 12 months up to and including that time period can be calculated. There are 12 such averages per year for monthly data and 4 for quarterly data. The 12-month moving average for December (a monthly series) or the fourth quarter (a quarterly series) is the value of the series for the calendar year. You may use this conversion to consolidate data, express period data in the more common annual form, and smooth out short-term or seasonal variations in the data. To calculate the 12-month moving average, add the current quarter value to the values for the preceding 3 quarters and divide the total by 4.

For example, in the first quarter of 1986, corporate profits (after tax) were $126.9 billion. Corporate profits for the fourth quarter of 1985 were $139.4 billion. Third-quarter profits for 1985 were $133.4 billion and second-quarter profits were $126.7 billion. The 12-month moving average for this data is calculated as follows:

$$126.9 + 139.4 + 133.4 + 126.7 = 526.4$$
$$526.4/4 = 131.6.$$

The procedure is the same for monthly data: you would add the value for the current month to the values for the 11 months preceding it, then divide the total by 12 to obtain the moving average.

Many other data conversion techniques are used in comparing statistics. However, the five methods explained above will enable you to perform the more common and useful conversions.[2]

STATISTICS AND ECONOMIC FORECASTS

Every year, economists use high-powered econometric models to make predictions about the economy for the following year. These forecasts can be useful planning tools for bankers; but, as with any prediction, they should be viewed with caution. A number of the concepts you have learned in this chapter can help you evaluate economic predictions.

Table 2.17 contains forecasts of the U.S. unemployment rate for 1981–85 by three leading econometric forecasters. The table also shows the actual unemployment rate for the years forecasted.

It would be grossly unfair to judge the overall ability of these or other forecasters by the results of this exercise. The number of observations has been limited in this table for ease of understanding. Moreover, the sample size is far too small to be statistically significant. You should bear in mind that the forecasts made by these and other forecasters include many more economic variables than the ones shown here.[3]

There are two commonly used measures of error in economic forecasts. The first is the average absolute error, and it is very similar to the average absolute deviation score you

Table 2.17 U.S. Unemployment Rates for 1981–85 Compared with Forecasts by Three Leading Economic Forecasters

Forecasted Rates and Absolute Errors of Forecasts

		Chase Econometrics[a]			UCLA Business Forecast			Standard & Poors		
Year	Actual Rate	Forecast Rate	Absolute Error	Absolute Error Squared	Forecast Rate	Absolute Error	Absolute Error Squared	Forecast Rate	Absolute Error	Absolute Error Squared
1981	7.6	8.1	0.5	0.25	7.8	0.2	0.04	7.8	0.2	0.04
1982	9.7	7.3	2.4	5.76	8.9	0.8	0.64	8.5	1.2	1.44
1983	9.6	10.3	0.7	0.49	10.9	1.3	1.69	10.4	0.8	0.64
1984	7.5	8.0	0.5	0.25	8.2	0.7	0.49	8.2	0.7	0.49
1985	7.2	7.1	0.1	0.01	7.4	0.2	0.04	7.5	0.3	0.09
		Sum	4.2	6.76		3.2	2.90		3.2	2.70
		Average	0.84	1.352		0.64	0.58		0.64	0.54
Standard Error			$\sqrt{1.352} = 1.163$			$\sqrt{0.58} = 0.7616$			$\sqrt{0.54} = 0.7348$	

Source: Federal Reserve Bank of Richmond, *Business Forecasts*, February 1981, 1982, 1983, 1984, and 1985.
a. Chase Econometrics and Wharton Econometrics merged in 1987. The new forecasting agency is known as Wharton Econometrics.

MATHEMATICS AND STATISTICS

learned about earlier in this chapter. Rather than measure the difference between an actual value and the mean of the data set, however, the average absolute error measures the difference between the predicted value and the actual value. This difference is measured using absolute values—that is, without regard to sign.

For example, Chase Econometrics overestimated the unemployment rate for 1981: the forecast rate was 8.1 percent and the actual rate was 7.6 percent. Chase underestimated the rate in 1982—7.3 percent was forecast and 9.7 percent was the actual rate. The absolute errors for these forecasts are denoted as $|0.5|$ and $|-2.4|$, respectively. If you add the absolute errors for the years 1981–85, remembering to disregard sign, the sum is $|4.2|$. The average absolute error for the period was 0.84.

The second measure, the standard error, is the most important measure of forecasting accuracy. Standard error is similar in concept to standard deviation. It uses the same formula with one difference: instead of using squared average deviation scores, the standard error uses squared average absolute error values. The formula is given below:

$$\text{Standard error: } \frac{\sqrt{[(V_{f_1} - V_{a_1})^2 + (V_{f_2} - V_{a_2})^2 + \ldots + (V_{f_n} - V_{a_n})]}}{n},$$

where V_f = forecast value in period t,
V_a = actual value in period t, and
n = number of individual forecasts.

The average standard error for the UCLA forecast is 0.7616. This compares favorably with the relatively high average standard error of 1.163 for Chase Econometrics. Note that the absolute average error for both forecasts (0.84 for Chase and 0.64 for UCLA) provides a much smaller gap between the forecasts. Remember that squaring the error (the deviation score) gives more weight to these values and, consequently, highlights large errors very clearly. The large error in the 1982 Chase unemployment forecast is very damaging to the final error score.

SUMMARY

The mathematical relationship between two variables is called a function and describes a set of ordered pairs of values. The notation (x,y) represents the set of ordered pairs in which there is a unique value of y for each value of x. A mathematical formula expresses the functional relationships that exist between two or more variables.

Within a formula, variables are classified as independent or dependent. Formulas may also contain constants: terms that remain the same regardless of the value of the independent variable.

Linear and nonlinear equations are examples of formulas that can be depicted graphically using the quadrant coordinate system. The quadrants in this system are defined by a horizontal *x*-axis and a vertical *y*-axis. The *x*-intercept is the value at which the line described by the equation will intersect the *x*-axis. The *y*-intercept is the value at which the line will intersect the *y*-axis. The slope of the equation, also called the coefficient, is a constant that determines the direction of the line within the quadrant. The general formula for a linear equation is $y = a + bx$, where *x* is the independent variable, *y* is the dependent variable, *a* is the *y*-intercept value, and *b* is the slope. Many economic relationships can be graphed as linear equations in the quadrant coordinate system.

Statistical analysis is another mathematical tool for interpreting economic data. Measures of central tendency inform us about the "average" or "typical" value in a set of numbers. Three commonly used measures of central tendency are the mode (the value that occurs most frequently in the set), the median (the value that separates the lower 50 percent of values from the upper 50 percent), and the mean (the arithmetic average).

Measures of dispersion reveal information about the spread of values around the mean of a set. Measures of dispersion include the range (the difference between the highest and lowest value), the variance (the average of the squared deviation values), and the standard deviation (the average spread of values around the mean). The standard deviation is the most commonly used measure of dispersion.

When economic statistics are presented in different formats or for time periods of different lengths, the data must be converted mathematically to a common format for comparison. Moreover, the value of all statistics depends on the accuracy and validity of the data used to calculate them.

Statistics may be used not only to depict past or present situations but also to forecast future trends. Economic predictions are based on specific models which, by their nature, cannot incorporate all of the factors that influence the economy. Nevertheless, such predictions can be useful planning tools for bankers who evaluate them using the proper mathematical techniques.

KEY WORDS

abscissa
asymptotic relationship
average absolute error
constant
dependent variable
direct relationship
independent variable
inverse relationship
linear equation
mean
measures of central tendency
measures of dispersion

median
mode
ordered pair
ordinate
parameters
quadrant coordinate system
range
slope
spread
standard deviation
variance

Questions for Review

1. Graph the following equations:

   a) $y = 15 + 6x$
   b) $y = -23 + .3x$
   c) $y = 3x$
   d) $y = 10 - 4x$
   e) $y = 25$
   f) $x = 25$

2. Calculate the mode, median, and mean for the following set of test scores: 90, 85, 65, 75, 40, 100, 98, 78, 84, 90.

3. Calculate for yourself the standard deviations and the variances for the examination scores of Student Sets B and C in table 2.12. Consult page 54 for the correct answer.

4. The following data show rates of return on net assets for two firms. Which firm offers the greater risk to an investor and why?

	Rates of Return (percentages)	
Year	Firm A	Firm B
1980	10.0	15.0
1981	8.6	3.1
1982	9.3	4.1
1983	8.7	10.1
1984	10.1	8.1
1985	12.1	9.2
1986	8.5	16.0

5. Convert the total cash assets in table 2.16 from monthly to quarterly for quarters I, II, III, and IV.

6. Convert the production index data given below into
   a) the November 1986 12-month moving average
   b) differences between periods for July and August
   c) percentage differences between periods for November and December 1985
   d) percentage differences between periods at annual rates for Quarters I and II in 1986

Period	Industrial Production Index (1977 = 100)
1985	
November	124.8
December	125.6
1986	
January	126.2
February	125.3
March	123.6
April	124.7
May	124.2
June	124.2
July	124.9
August	125.1
September	125.1
October	125.2
November	125.9

7. Find the average absolute error and average standard error for the following interest rate forecast.

	Prime Rate (annual average percentage)	
Year	Forecast Rate	Actual Rate
1979	11.15	12.67
1980	13.12	15.27
1981	20.05	18.87
1982	17.16	14.86
1983	13.11	10.79
1984	14.18	12.04
1985	12.50	10.00

ENDNOTES

1. When you must estimate a statistic (in this case, the mean) based on incomplete data, you lose a "degree of freedom." For a thorough explanation of degrees of freedom, see Gary Smith, *Statistical Reasoning* (Boston: Allyn and Bacon, Inc., 1985).

2. Converting data into interpretable forms is one problem; extracting meaning from statistics is another. One concise guide to interpreting economic statistics is Albert T. Sommers, *The U.S. Economy Demystified* (Lexington, MA: D.C. Heath and Company, 1985).

3. For additional reading on economic forecasting, see Howard Keen, Jr., "Economists and Their Forecasts: Have the Projections Been That Bad?" *Business Economics*, vol. xxii, no. 1 (January 1987), pp. 37–40, and John Greenwald, "The Forecasters Flunk," *Time*, August 27, 1984, pp. 42–44.

ECONOMICS IN THE NEWS

While the mathematical and statistical tools explored in this chapter are valuable, reliable methods, their results are only as trustworthy and meaningful as the actual data used in the calculations. Consumers, businesses, and governments, who want a clear picture of the past, present and potential shifts in the economy, rely heavily upon the statistics we call economic indicators. The following article points out some concerns about economic indicators.

Mis-Leading Indicators?

Business Patterns Lead Index Astray

By Randall W. Forsyth

The government's index of leading economic indicators is supposed to do for economists what barometers and radar do for meteorologists: identify clues that tend to precede changes. Thus, they're called "leading" indicators because they point the way, not for any preeminence. Indeed, some analysts contend that the indicators have become more misleading than leading.

Be that as it may, the leading indicators have been signaling a strengthening of the economy, especially over the past three months. The reading for December, reported last week, recorded a robust 2.1% gain, the largest since the 3.1% rise in January 1983.

The leading-indicators index, compiled by the Commerce Department, consists of 12 component data series. Two of them measure labor market conditions: the workweek, which tends to increase before employment as employers boost workers' overtime before adding to job rolls, and initial claims for unemployment, which tend to fall as jobs become more plentiful.

Three are financial indicators: the money supply (the broad M2 measure, adjusted for inflation) and credit outstanding, which tend to move up or down ahead of spending, and stock prices, which tend to forecast corporate earnings.

The remaining seven are gauges of the industrial sector: building permits (which must be obtained before new construction begins); orders for consumer goods and plant and equipment (which would move up or down ahead of production); prices of materials (they'd react quickly to changes in demand); inventories (if low, they'd point to higher production for restocking, and vice versa); vendor performance (slower deliveries usually reflect strong business, faster usually means backlogs are being run down). . . .

In the meantime, the Commerce Department has announced that it will be scuttling one of the components, net business formations, beginning with March's leading indicators. That component has gone awry for a number of reasons, according to Joseph Duncan, economist and chief statistician at Dun & Bradstreet.

It should come as no surprise that Duncan remains confident in D&B's weekly figures on business failures, but he views the data on new businesses [a]s less reliable.

State governments' numbers on new incorporations are reported with a lag of as much as four months. Statistics on telephone installations, once a good indicator of business start-ups, haven't been as reliable since the break-up of AT&T, he adds.

Some analysts also argue that the financial components of the leading indicators have led them astray. The money supply in recent years has borne no relationship to spending. . . .

The last revision of the leading indicators was undertaken in 1975 to make the index less susceptible to inflation's distortions. Those changes, Duncan hypothesizes, may have made the index less useful since a measure of price stability has taken hold in recent years.

Finally, foreign trade looms larger over the economy than ever before and has become the crucial swing factor, but the leading indicators all but ignore that, Duncan adds. Inventories, previously the key and still the critical variable to the business cycle, haven't acted as they once did. Four years into the expansion, corporations have kept their inventories lean, although there have been mini-cycles along the way.

Reprinted by permission of *Barron's*. © Dow Jones & Company, Inc., 1987. All rights reserved.

CHAPTER THREE

ECONOMIC PROBLEMS, SYSTEMS, AND RESOURCES

Objectives

After reading this chapter, you should be able to

- explain the concept of unlimited wants

- define the resources that economies use to produce goods and services

- explain how economics seeks to reconcile the scarcity of resources with the unlimited wants of society

- describe the choice that must be made between producing and consuming goods now or investing in the future

- list the basic principles of production possibility theory

- construct a production possibilities curve

- define the law of increasing cost

- explain how changes in resource availability, technology, and depreciation can affect the production possibilities curve

- define the law of diminishing returns

- state the five questions that all economies must answer

- compare and contrast the ways the command system and the market system answer the five economic questions

-

describe how self-interest, consumer sovereignty,
the profit and loss system, and competition affect the market system

•

define the law of comparative advantage

•

state some shortcomings of the market system

SCARCITY AND UNLIMITED WANTS

Two powerful economic forces affect all economies—scarcity of resources and unlimited wants. Resources, defined as the "factors of production," are in constant demand. The four factors of production are land, labor, capital, and entrepreneurial ability. Periodically, a shortage of one or more of these factors will provoke an economic crisis. Many modern businesses have staffs whose major function is to plan for the efficient use of available resources.

The definition of "unlimited wants" is more subjective. Everyone has wants that he or she cannot satisfy. However, the economic wants of a millionaire are likely to be quite different from those of a person living in poverty.

Businesses, governments, and consumers each have economic desires. A business might want a larger factory, modernized production methods, the latest in computer hardware, new channels of distribution, and stronger marketing services. A government might like to increase or improve services to its citizens; build modern highways, bridges, and tunnels; provide better police and fire protection; and maintain a powerful and impressive system of national defense. The unlimited wants of the consumer stretch far beyond basic subsistence; but, even at this level, an individual's desires may change frequently. Low-calorie foods, "natural" foods, and high-fiber, low-fat products have become popular with U.S. consumers in recent years. The increasing numbers of prepackaged meals reflect shifts in social patterns and priorities.

The desire to be fashionable is another want that can be satisfied only temporarily. In developed economies, advertising and promotion play a big part in manipulating the unlimited desires of consumers by providing the major conduit for information on new and tempting products.

The history of the digital watch in the United States provides an excellent example of a product life cycle (introduction, growth, maturation, and decline) and the impact of new products on unlimited wants. The mechanical timepieces that Americans used before the digital watch were both reliable and inexpensive. Then, in the early 1970s, the first commercially successful electronic digital display watch appeared. Marketed to the upper-income segments of the population, it sold at an astonishingly high price of $1,500. As the technology evolved, however, the prices for such watches dropped. Decreasing prices and mass marketing by the watch industry created a desire for the digital watch in the middle- and lower-income segments of the market. Today, the once-expensive and coveted digital watch is ubiquitous. The purchase price now is often less than $10, and such watches are even given away as gifts in sales drives.

If consumer wants are often transient, they also can be quite contagious. Recent fads include home exercise equipment and videotape recorders. The life cycles of these products are fascinating to observe: purchasing patterns move across the population like waves, growing until a critical percentage of the market has satisfied its desire to obtain the product.

The concept of unlimited wants includes the idea that a particular desire, once satisfied, may return in another form. A purchase of a moderately priced stereo may be the result of weeks of study and evaluation. However, soon after the purchase has been made and the equipment used, the consumer often tires of the recent purchase and begins to seek more sophisticated equipment. This "drive for the state-of-the-art" influences businesses as well as individual consumers: a business owner may scrap a still-operable data processing system simply because it is not a state-of-the-art system.

The regeneration of wants is related to the drive for status. For social and psychological reasons, consumers may want to be associated with or set apart from a certain group. A particular make of car, a certain brand of apparel—these are examples of products with status value. The demand to own symbols of wealth and status fuels the market for illegal reproductions of "designer" products.

While some of the reasons for the constant turnover of products and services may seem frivolous, it is extremely important that they do turn over. Many modern economies are vitally affected by this concept of unlimited desires and wants. Indeed, some economists even postulate that the diminishing of consumer desire to replenish goods and services actually worsens periods of recession and depression.

In recessions, rising unemployment increases consumers' fears of loss of employment and income. This fear causes a sublimation of the unlimited wants drive. Consumers decrease their spending in order to increase savings, and the resultant constriction of spending may prolong and deepen the recession or depression.[1]

RESOURCE PAYMENTS

The four resources that economies use to produce goods and services are land, labor, capital, and entrepreneurial ability. These resources are limited in availability, or "scarce," and participants in an economy pay for their use. These payments are called resource payments, and specific types of payments are made for the use of each resource. Resource payments made to the owners of land are called rents. Premiums paid to the contributors of labor are wages and salaries. Interest income, in a strict economic sense, is the resource payment for the use of capital. The resource payment made for the use of entrepreneurial ability is known as profit.

The first category, land, refers to more than just acreage. As a resource, the term "land" includes the qualities and materials above, on, and below the surface: warm, sunny climates needed for food production, mineral and ore deposits, oil supplies, and even plant and animal life. Some components of the land resource hardly seem scarce. For instance, power derived from the light and heat of the sun seems inexhaustible. Other land resources are renewable: we can replant trees cut down for wood products, clean and recycle water polluted in manufacturing processes, and restock fish taken from our lakes and rivers. Other resources, however, such as minerals, are nonrenewable.

The second scarce resource is labor. Labor includes both mental and physical exertion. When a banker extends a line of credit to a small business, approves an automobile loan, or opens up a new account, the banker's actions constitute labor. When a professor gives a lecture or grades an exam, when a carpenter builds a home or a contractor paves a new highway, or when a songwriter writes a song and a singer sings it—all of these events are included in the calculation of labor. The only activity commonly considered labor that economists exclude from their definition is the managerial function of a business. Management is usually considered part of the entrepreneurial resource.

The third scarce resource is capital. Economists use this term in a different fashion from bankers. By capital, economists do not mean money, but the goods and services used to produce articles of consumption. When economists discuss capital goods, they mean products such as tools or machinery, and delivery channels such as bridges or roads—products that are used to generate other products or facilitate consumption. The premium paid to the owner of capital goods is called interest income. You should be careful *not* to confuse the economic meaning of this term with the banking definition of interest income as a return for certain types of deposits at assigned maturities.

The fourth factor of production is entrepreneurial ability. Some authors include entrepreneurial ability in the labor category. However, the entrepreneurial function in business is so important that it deserves separate study. Of the four scarce resources, entrepreneurial skill may be the most important. Entrepreneurial ability is the driving force behind all business ventures. The entrepreneur must identify a need and seek an opportunity to fill it. The entrepreneur must obtain and combine the other factors of production in a way that produces a good or service. The entrepreneur must market and sell this product or service to the consumer. Above all, the entrepreneur must risk money, time, and reputation on the success of his or her venture.

There is an ongoing debate as to whether entrepreneurial ability is a renewable factor of production. In the United States, we spend millions of dollars annually on business colleges, business administration programs, and graduate business programs, attempting to "manufacture" entrepreneurs. Some argue that the ability cannot be cultivated—that entrepreneurs are born, not made. Others say that individual entrepreneurial ability is an anachronism—that modern production methods require a corporate form of enterprise. It should also be pointed out that entrepreneurial ventures always involve the potential for loss rather than profit. In our market system there is no guarantee that a business venture will be profitable. If it is unprofitable, the original investment evaporates and the entrepreneur suffers an economic loss. Yet ongoing invention and innovation by high-spirited entrepreneurs continue unabated.

THE ESSENCE OF ECONOMICS

The tension between these two powerful forces—unlimited wants and scarcity of resources—makes the social science of economics an important tool in finding ways to maximize the returns or output from these scarce resources. As described in chapter 1, efficiency in the use of scarce resources is a major goal of economics. This is the essence of economics—how to maximize the welfare of society in terms of satisfying as many of the wants that exist with the given amount of resources.

Technical and Allocative Efficiency

Getting the most from society's resources is the goal of the economist. As discussed in chapter 1, the concept of efficiency includes both technical and allocative efficiency. Technical efficiency involves maximizing the output while conserving limited resources. Technical efficiency is essentially a problem of engineering. It is a hard rather than a soft science and deals with minimizing the waste generated in the production process.

Allocative efficiency means assigning scarce resources to their most highly valued uses, so that production is achieved at the lowest possible cost given current technical efficiency. Remember that the term cost, used in the economic sense, refers to more than the financial cost. In determining the real cost of using a resource, economists include the opportunity cost: the value of the resource in its next best alternative use. (To review the concept of opportunity cost, see chapter 1.)

CONSUMPTION AND INVESTMENT CHOICE

All economies must deal with scarcity of resources, and the method they select to do so influences their future ability to cope with this problem. Economies may choose to consume resources rapidly, stringently save for the future, or strive for a balance between consumption and conservation. The impact of these consumption and investment decisions can be shown graphically using production possibilities curves.

Production Possibility Theory

The production possibilities curve attempts to show the mechanism and results of one choice that all economies face: to produce and consume goods and services now or to invest for the future. To create a production possibilities curve, we must make four hypothetical assumptions about a hypothetical economy: (1) the availability of resources at any given moment is fixed; (2) the technology used to convert these resources into goods and services also is fixed; (3) the economy currently operates at full employment and all available resources are being used at a normal rate (that is, there is no voluntary unemployment, all capital equipment is being used, and no factories are idle); and (4) all of the economy's goods and services can be placed into one of two symbolic categories: "guns" or "butter."

ECONOMIC PROBLEMS, SYSTEMS, AND RESOURCES

Guns symbolize investment goods and represent the future, while butter represents consumer products used in the present.

A diagram of production possibilities can be an extremely useful device. President John F. Kennedy was a "hobby" economist of some renown. When asked what his favorite subject in economics was, he replied that, in his opinion, the "guns" and "butter" diagram was one of the most insightful pieces of pedagogy ever invented. Bankers can use this device for long-term strategy planning. For example, current earnings can either be distributed to owners or plowed back into the bank in the form of new branches, modernized computer equipment, additional ATMs, or other investments.

Table 3.1 Production Possibilities: "Guns" vs. "Butter"

Commodity	Production Choices (number of units per year)				
	A	B	C	D	E
Guns[a]	20	18	14	8	0
Butter[b]	0	2	4	6	8

a. measured in investment units.
b. measured in consumption units.

Table 3.1 lists five production choices that our hypothetical economy can make. Note that gun production is measured in investment units per year and butter production is measured in consumption units per year. (These units are used strictly for illustrative reasons. No such units exist in real economies.) Choice A represents a situation in which the economy produces 20 units of guns and 0 units of butter. In other words, the economy devotes its entire production in that particular year to future investments and ignores consumption completely. In reality, this would be a very difficult, if not impossible, situation because the economy depends upon the consumption of products to survive. Choice E represents the opposite extreme: here, the economy produces no guns (that is, makes no investments for the future) and allocates its entire year's production to butter (consumer products).

Choices B, C, and D represent alternatives in which some guns are produced and some butter is produced. Choice B shows production of 18 units of guns and 2 units of butter. To produce 2 units of butter, our economy has given up 2 units of gun production. In other words, a unit of butter can be produced only if a unit of guns is not produced. This is a statement of opportunity cost.

Alternative C presents 14 units of gun production and 4 units of butter production. Here, the opportunity cost of additional butter production increases. In order to obtain the second 2 units of butter production, that is, to move from point B to point C, the economy must forgo 4 units of gun production. Now, an additional unit of butter production can be obtained only if 2 units of guns are given up. Thus, the opportunity cost of butter production

73

for choice C is twice the amount as in choice B. Alternatively, we can calculate the cost of gun production in terms of forgone butter consumption. This phenomenon is called the law of increasing cost.

Law of Increasing Cost

The law of increasing cost can be stated as follows: as an economy devotes more of its resources to the production of one good and less resources to other goods, the opportunity cost to produce the first good, expressed in terms of all other goods, rises. This occurs because the factors of economic production are not completely flexible between uses. For example, it requires considerable time and effort to retrain a steelworker to become a computer programmer. Great cost is involved in converting the steel mill into a floppy disk factory. Whenever an economy shifts its resources from the production of one good to another, certain costs are incurred. The required resources are rarely exact matches. Workers must be retrained. Factory sites must be refitted. These adaptations cost money, time, and labor.

We can construct a production possibilities curve (figure 3.1) that graphically represents the choices given in table 3.1. The shape of the production possibilities curve is a reflection of the law of increasing cost. The production possibilities curve is concave to the origin, revealing that increased production of butter can only be accomplished by greater and greater sacrifices of guns. The opposite is also true. Look at points X and Y in figure 3.1.

Point X lies within the production possibilities curve, or production frontier. At point X, the economy is producing fewer units of guns and butter than it could produce at point C. This is a violation of the assumption of full efficiency and production. Therefore, point X represents an underemployment of resources. Point Y is equally troublesome. Point Y is beyond the production frontier. At point Y the economy is producing theoretically implausible amounts of guns and butter, given the current state of technology and resource availability. It may be possible to reach point Y by stretching (overutilizing) available resources. However, this would only work for a short time because the constant overutilization of resources would accelerate the depreciation of factories, erode the economy's industrial base, and eventually shrink its total production capabilities.

Changes in availability levels of resources also have a very important relationship to economic growth. Figure 3.2 shows how the production possibilities curve can shift when resource availability or resource delivery fluctuates.

Curve I represents the current state of resource availability and technology. If delivery of needed resources is curtailed and the supply is depleted, the production possibilities curve shifts inward, toward the origin, as in curve II. Here, the economy's ability to produce both investment goods and consumption goods is reduced. If resource availability or supply are brought back to normal levels, the curve automatically shifts back to its

ECONOMIC PROBLEMS, SYSTEMS, AND RESOURCES

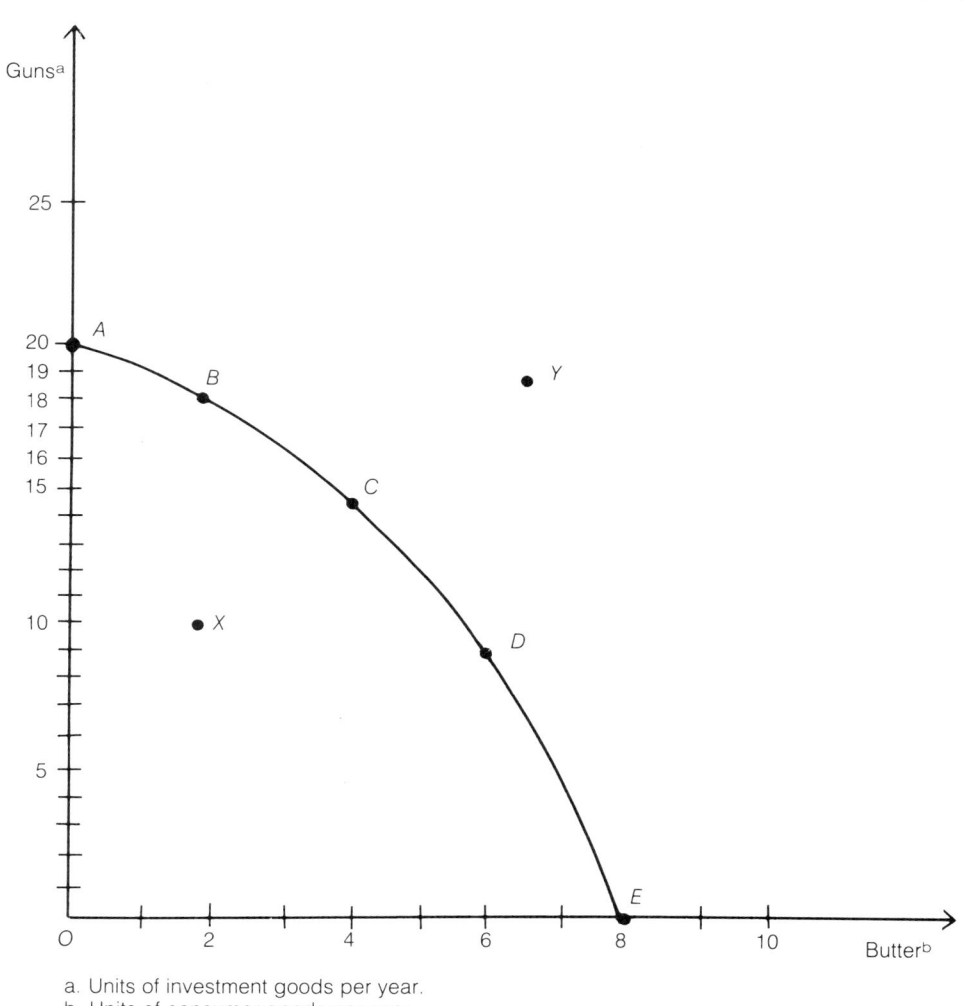

Figure 3.1 Production Possibilities Curve "Guns" vs. "Butter"

a. Units of investment goods per year.
b. Units of consumer goods per year.

original position. In the event of increased resource availability, the production frontier shifts outward, away from the origin, as in curve *III*. Such a shift in production possibilities may be brought about by an improvement in the flow of resources, new oil discoveries, mineral deposit discoveries, or an influx of skilled labor.

75

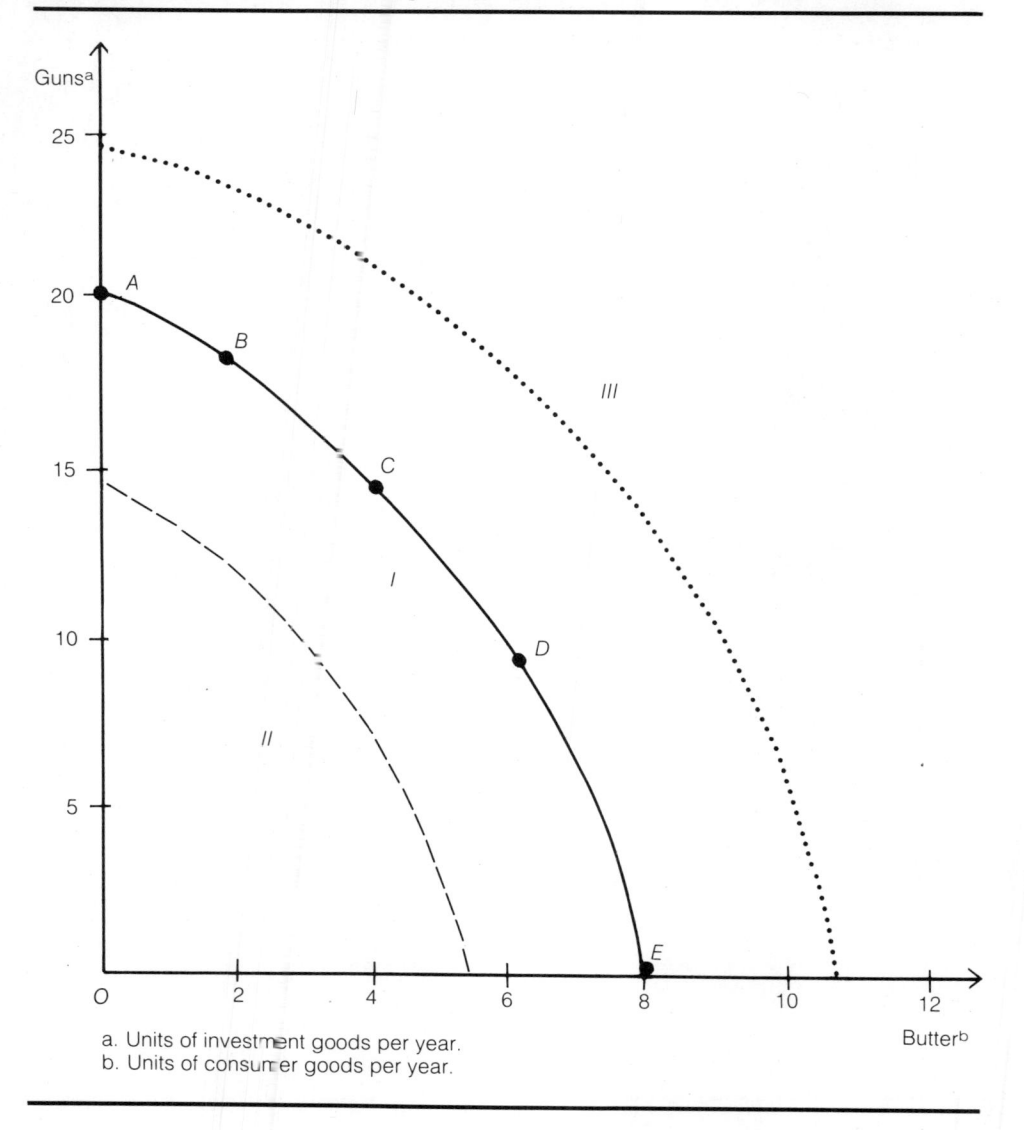

Figure 3.2 Resource Availability Changes and the Production Possibilities Curve

a. Units of investment goods per year.
b. Units of consumer goods per year.

Changes in technology also influence the economy. Figure 3.3 demonstrates the shift in the production possibilities curve when technological advances occur.

Curve *I* represents the production frontier given the current state of technology. If the technology to produce investment goods improves and the technology to produce consumer goods remains constant, then the production possibilities curve will, over time, change its

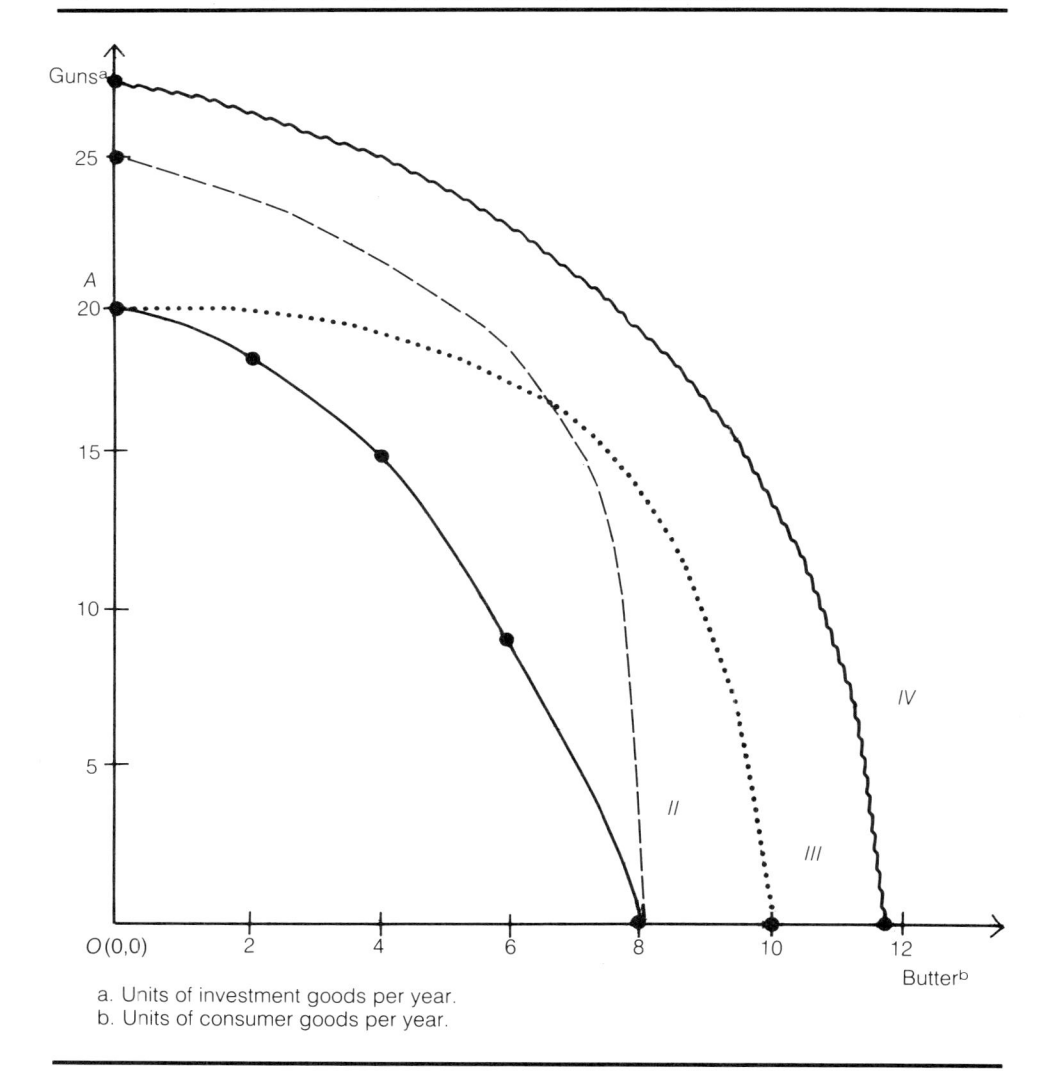

Figure 3.3 Technological Changes and the Production Possibilities Curve

a. Units of investment goods per year.
b. Units of consumer goods per year.

shape to that of curve *II*. Curve *III* represents a situation in which the ability to produce investment goods has not changed but there has been an improvement in the technology to produce consumer goods.

Point *A* on the guns (investment) axis has the coordinates (20,0) and shows the production possibility when no consumer goods are produced and the level of investment goods production is unchanged from curve *I*. However, the consumer goods (butter) axis

77

ECONOMICS FOR BANKERS

shows a definite increase. A more likely event is an improvement in technology that benefits production of goods of both types. The effect of such a change is depicted by curve *IV*.

The daily use of machinery in factories to produce both investment and consumer goods takes its toll. This toll is called the capital consumption allowance or depreciation. If depreciation is not taken into account and equipment replaced periodically, the economy's ability to sustain production is diminished. Figure 3.4 illustrates how depreciation can erode the production possibilities curve.

In figure 3.4, today's production possibilities frontier is represented by curve *AE*. The origin (0,0) is symbolized by *O*. The ray emanating from the origin, *ORF*, shows the engineering estimates of the depreciation-induced replacement that is required at any given production possibility level. For example, on production possibilities curve *AE*, the depreciation-replacement requirement ray strikes the curve at production possibility point *R*. This means that the minimum investment required to replace depreciated equipment is OI_0.

If the economy chooses to produce at the level indicated by point *R* on today's production possibilities curve, its future production possibilities curve will not change unless any of the assumptions regarding technology and resources change. The reason for this is that production possibility alternative *R* involves a large amount of consumption expenditure for butter and a small amount of resource commitment to investment. The minimum amount that must be committed to investment in order to maintain the current production possibilities frontier is represented by I_0. If the economy chooses to produce at a level between points *R* and *E* on today's production possibilities curve, in other words, to pick a point that corresponds to an investment output below level I_0, the economy will shrink. It will not be replacing worn-out equipment and the resulting curve with reduced production possibilities might look like $A''E''$.

On the other hand, if the economy picks a point on the production possibilities frontier between points *A* and *R* on today's curve, the resulting balance of guns and butter production requires an investment component larger than I_0 (the minimum necessary to maintain current production). The future curve would expand, becoming similar to $A'E'$. For future production possibilities curve $A'E'$, the minimum investment required to maintain that curve now becomes R', or investment level OI_1.

The production possibilities curve is useful in examining the plight of underdeveloped nations. Figure 3.5 depicts an underdeveloped economy. Point *R* on the production possibilities curve represents the minimum investment level required for this meager economy to sustain itself. In other words, for the economy not to shrink, but to maintain current levels, the production possibility choices must be OC_1 consumption and OI_0 investment. This choice leads to no further growth, but at least allows replacement of worn-out plant equipment. For growth to be sustained, a choice above point *R* on the production possibility frontier must be made. At point *A*, for example, investment has been raised to OI_1—a level well above the minimum necessary for replacement. Production of consumer goods has

78

ECONOMIC PROBLEMS, SYSTEMS, AND RESOURCES

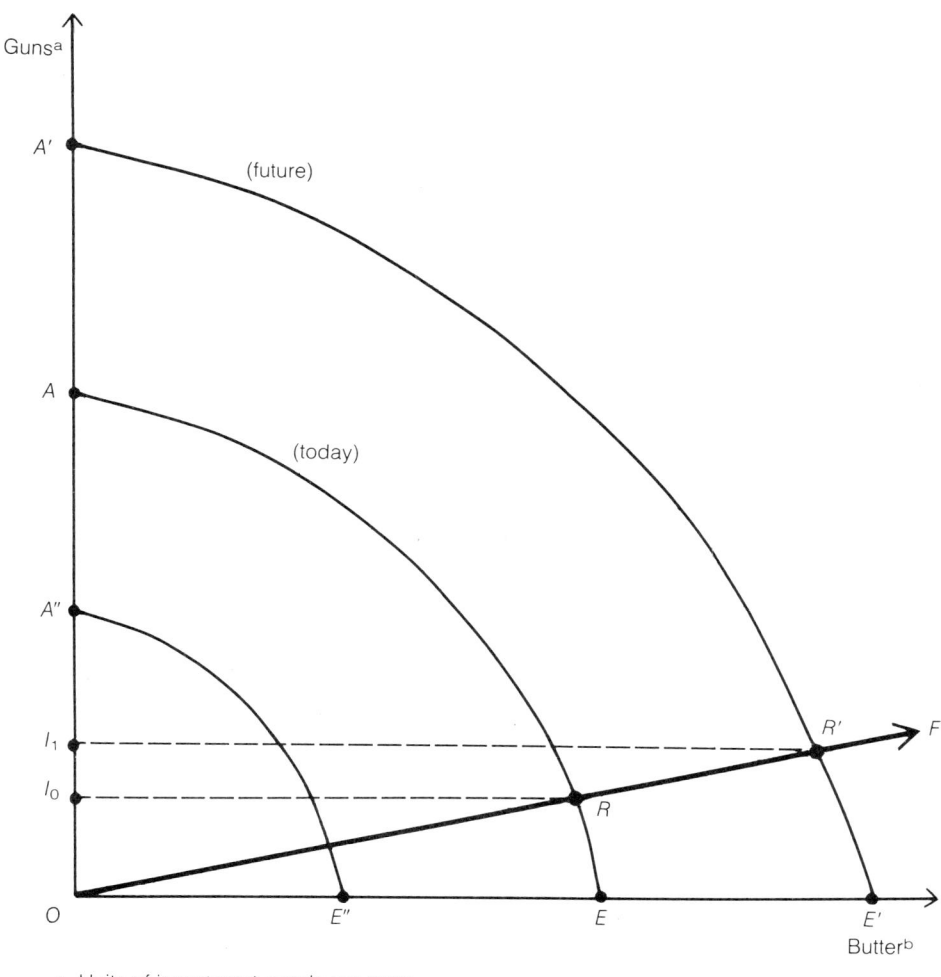

Figure 3.4 Depreciation and the Production Possibilities Curve

a. Units of investment goods per year.
b. Units of consumer goods per year.
Line 0F = Depreciation-replacement requirement.

moved from OC_1 to OC_0. But this increase in investment carries with it an opportunity cost. The cost of moving from point R to point A is a reduction in current consumption from point C_1 to C_0. In many cases, it is virtually impossible for poor nations to pay the opportunity cost required to increase investments and expand production.

79

Figure 3.5 Production Possibilities Curve for an Underdeveloped Economy

[Graph: Production possibilities curve with Investments on vertical axis (showing I_2, I_1, I_0) and Consumer Goods on horizontal axis (showing C_0, C_1, C_2). Point A is on the curve at (C_1, I_1), point R marks the "Minimum investment level for replacement" at I_0.]

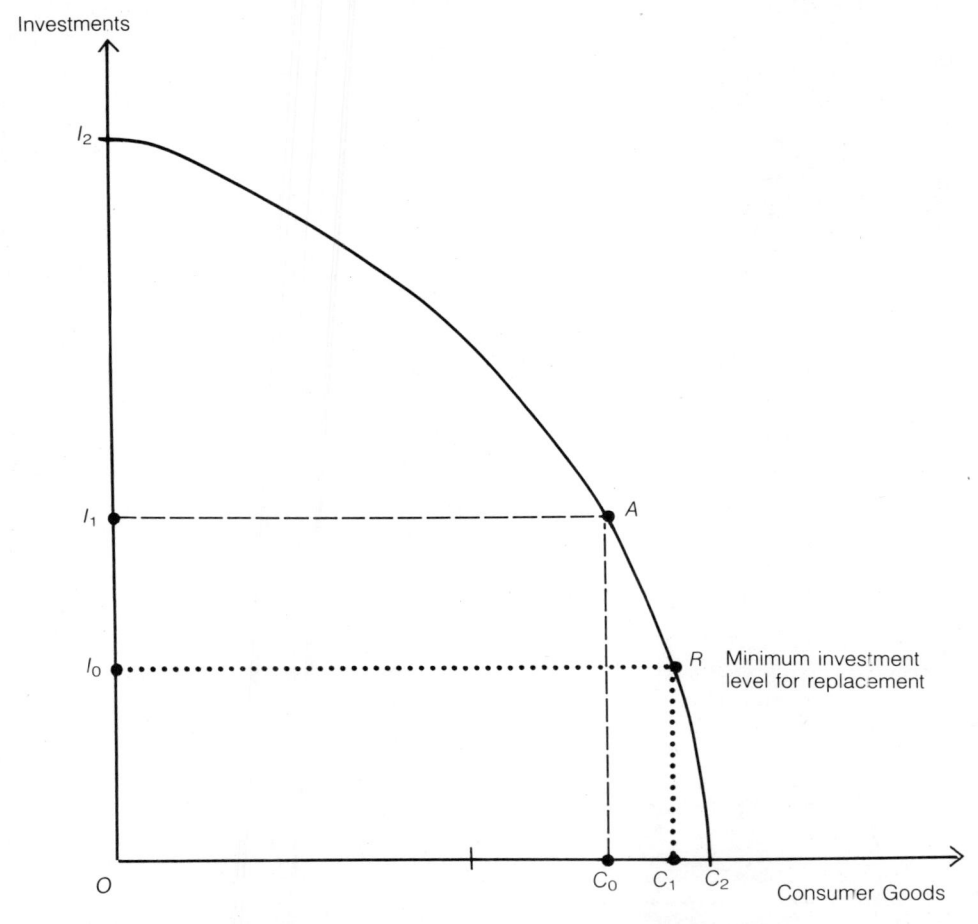

Not all investment costs are tied to physical items such as machinery and plant facilities. Investments are also made in human capital. Most investment in human capital comes in the form of education. However, as important as education is for the development of underdeveloped countries, the production curve in figure 3.5 can be used to illustrate how expensive it can be to provide education for the populace. Graphically, the investment in human capital is shown by $I_0 I_1$. The resulting cost in lost food production is measured by $C_1 C_0$. A poor economy cannot afford for its young people to be in classrooms when they could be in the labor force producing foodstuffs. Of course, without an educated work force, it is extremely difficult to improve technology of any sort and shift the production possibility curve outward.

Unfortunately, economic growth is not simply a matter of using more resources. It may seem logical to assume that increasing resource allocation by a certain percentage will increase total output by a proportionate amount. However, it is often difficult to increase all the necessary factors of production by the same proportion at the same time. It is more likely that some resources will be increased while others are held constant. This imbalance inhibits economic growth and is embodied in the law of diminishing returns.

The Law of Diminishing Returns

To illustrate the law of diminishing returns, let's look inside a small branch of a bank located in a busy neighborhood. The branch has four teller stations. The manager finds that even with four tellers there are still long lines of customers in the lobby. So a fifth teller is added to assist the others. This is an instance in which one resource—labor—is a variable factor of production (it can be changed), while another resource—capital (the size of the branch and the number of teller windows)—is a fixed factor of production. By adding a fifth teller, it is possible that the increase in the branch's total productivity (the output) may be greater than the increase in the cost of the additional labor. This is an example of increasing marginal returns. The word "marginal" refers to an additional unit of labor being added to the total amount of labor and the additional output compared to the total output. In other words, the margin is the additional output that results from an additional unit of labor.

What if the manager adds a sixth or seventh teller to assist the other five tellers? Obviously, at some point, the amount of the addition to the bank's total output or productivity will begin to diminish. The productivity added by the sixth worker will be slightly less than that contributed by the fifth worker. A seventh teller's contribution to total productivity will be even less than that of the sixth worker. In fact, one can envision the possibility of the additional productivity of the nth worker being negative. A point will be reached at which there are too many employees in the small branch. Total output decreases if for no other reason than the traffic behind the windows begins to reduce the productivity of all employees.

The law of diminishing returns is a universal law of economics. It affects all businesses and nations and is a real handicap to growth. The law of diminishing returns applies in cases of overuse of the fixed factor of production or underuse of the variable factor of production.

The law of diminishing returns helps explain why it is extremely difficult for underdeveloped nations to grow and prosper. While additions to the labor force may not be difficult to obtain, it is very hard for underdeveloped nations to expand their capital base. As the law of diminishing returns states, an increase in a single factor of production without increasing all necessary factors results, at some point, in a return in productivity that is less than the value of the increased input. For a poor country to increase the supply of *all* necessary factors of production requires hard choices along its production possibilities curves. It must constantly concern itself with the effects of the reduction of current consumption goods required to increase investment levels. A reduction in current consumption levels may be impossible when the people's standard of living is at subsistence level.

Questions All Economies Face

In attempting to resolve the problem of scarcity versus unlimited wants through the efficient use of resources, all economies must answer the following questions:

- What is to be produced?
- How much is to be produced?
- How is it to be manufactured or produced?
- To whom should the output be distributed?
- How should the product be distributed to consumers?

What Is To Be Produced?

Society must, through either collective market action or the decisions of a powerful few, determine what the production mix of consumption goods and investment goods will be. After determining what proportion of total output will go to consumption goods and what proportion will go to investment goods, society must decide what particular products will be produced under each general category. Should we produce automobiles with large, powerful engines that use a lot of gasoline, or less-powerful automobiles that are thrifty in their consumption of petroleum reserves? Should we build large four-bedroom houses on one-acre lots or should we construct high-rise condominiums? Should we invest in more interstate highways or upgrade our rail system? Should we widen streets and subsidize bus transportation or build rapid transit systems? These questions are representative of the first decision that all economies face: what is to be produced?

How Is It To Be Produced?

This question involves allocative rather than technical efficiency. The theories behind manufacturing cars or the mysteries of aluminum production are not of concern here. What is at issue is the mix of resources to be used in the production process. Producers often have options. For example, many workers may be needed in a particular manufacturing process. Another process may call for the purchase and use of robots. In other words, the production process can be labor or capital intensive. This kind of question must be answered in order for an economy to produce the greatest possible output with the minimum input. Under an economic system driven by the marketplace, the results of these decisions can be painful. For example, decisions must be made regarding exactly where, geographically, production will occur. In the U.S. during the 1970s and early 1980s, many industries moved from northern states to southern states. One major reason for the move was the lower labor cost of nonunion workers in the South. These often-abrupt moves left employees stunned, without hope, and in a state of utter confusion. Many small towns in the central Atlantic and New England states have large numbers of unemployed individuals who are the victims of the hard economic choices made by their previous employers. For a discussion on how displaced workers attempt to put their lives together, see the "Economics in the News" article at the end of chapter 8.

How Much Is To Be Produced?

This question is really a matter of resource utilization. For example, many manufacturing plants are scheduled for two 8-hour shifts per day. One begins at 8:00 a.m. and ends at 4:00 p.m. The second begins at 4:00 p.m. and ends at midnight. If conditions demand it, a third shift can be scheduled from midnight to 8:00 a.m., and many manufacturing concerns are open around the clock. Individual laborers normally work a standard 40-hour week. Some individuals seek to work overtime if they receive a premium for their labor above 40 hours per week. Not long ago, however, the 60-hour work week was the standard. Then, the 48-hour work week became the standard. Recently, there has been considerable discussion about having a 32-hour standard work week. The question boils down to a measure of the trade-offs between work and leisure. A society and its individuals must decide what percentage of the 24-hour day will be devoted to work and what percentage will be devoted to other activities, including child-rearing duties, educational and professional development, and leisure. Of course, the industry of leisure itself creates jobs for many people. In addition, as a society becomes more sophisticated technologically, it is likely to produce more products and services with fewer and fewer working hours. Increases in technology often make this question much easier to answer.

In addition, societal values may also influence production amounts. For example, the political process determines production quotas for various agricultural products. Laws governing the minimum age requirement for alcohol consumption influence the production of the brewery and distilled spirits industries.

To Whom Should Goods and Services Produced Be Distributed?

Answering this question is far more difficult than it appears because of the multitude of issues at stake. For example, what part of total output will be held for government services and what part for private consumption? Will goods and services be distributed to individuals on the basis of ability to pay, on some sort of equity basis, or on a system of rewards (wages) for work done? How will people be paid for their labor? Will all people earn the same wage regardless of variations in experience, education, and the difficulty of their job? If income is to be allotted by profession, how much should a banker make as compared with a rock star or a prize-fighter?

How To Ration Output?

This question assumes that the total quantity of goods and services produced by any given economy is scarce relative to the demand for it. In other words, all goods and services by definition have value (a price). How are the prices for goods and services set in the economy? Are the prices established by committee decision or through the bidding of consumers for the products available to them? Even more basic, are prices set in terms of the relative values of goods (barter) or in terms of some common unit of currency?

From the simplest to the most complex economy, these five questions must be answered. Societies have developed several ways to answer these questions. The following section discusses the two dominant socioeconomic and political systems that have evolved to address these fundamental economic questions.

THE COMMAND SYSTEM AND THE MARKET SYSTEM

Any attempt to delineate the various political and economic systems that have been developed to meet these basic economic challenges is fraught with danger. It is virtually impossible to assign these systems to clear categories. However, economic systems can be differentiated by the answers they give to the five fundamental economic questions. We will look at two extremes: the command system, which emphasizes social decision-making power, and the market system, which emphasizes individual decision-making power. Then we will look at reality, which is most often a blend of the two extremes.

The Command System

Small, select groups of individuals serve as economic planners and decision makers in the command economic system. The country as a whole, usually represented by the government, owns virtually all property resources: land, factories, equipment, roads, bridges, and so on. A central planning organization makes all of the important economic decisions about what to produce, the mix between investment goods and consumption goods, the type of consumption goods, and the methods and organization of production. The distribution of goods and services in a command system tends to be egalitarian; basic human needs generally are met first. Very little, if any, inequality of income is permitted, and goods and services are, at least in theory, distributed on the basis of need rather than on the basis of ability to pay. There is no individual profit motive as such because all profit returns to the state or to the people. Command economies orient themselves to group accomplishment—the maximization of production and returns for the good of the group rather than the individual. The U.S.S.R. is a good example of a country with a command economy.[2]

The Market System

In the market system, private individuals own the vast majority of the factors of production. These individuals are entitled to the rewards that come from use of the resources they own. The government plays a very limited role in the basic decision-making process. In fact, in its purest form, the market system allots government virtually no role in economic decision making. This is called *laissez-faire* economics. While the various levels of government provide some public services (such as a legal system, roads, schools, and national defense), the fundamental economic questions are answered not by a select group but through the participation of many individuals in the marketplace.

The cumulative result of individual decisions in a competitive environment drives resource allocation decisions. Goods and services are distributed on the basis of income and productivity, with no automatic provision for helping those who are unable to compete effectively. Questions about what goods to produce and how to produce them are answered through market forces, and decisions about how to use resources are made on the basis of price. The United States is a good example of a country that has a market economy.

The choice of which system to adopt provides an interesting study. Most economic systems lie along the continuum between a pure, free market economy at one end and a strict command system on the other. Very few countries use a system that can be placed at either extreme. The United States has a relatively strong free market economy in which virtually all of the factors of production are owned by private individuals, free markets are permitted, and free trade is fostered whenever possible. The laws of supply and demand are very active in the marketplace, and resources are free to shift from one use to another without encumbrance. However, the U.S. has also sought to erect "safety nets" so that the minimum needs of those individuals unable to function in a free market economy are met. At the other end of the spectrum is the Soviet system with virtually every factor of production owned by the state, very little free enterprise, and very little reliance on the free market system. The mobility of the factors of production is sharply curtailed and output is very carefully planned.

Obviously, the U.S. economic system is not strictly a free market system. Nor is the Soviet system a pure command system. In fact, over time, each economy has adopted some of the characteristics of the other. This merging of extremes is described by the convergence

Table 3.2 Two Economic Systems

Decision to be Made	Who Makes the Decision	
	Market System	Command System
What goods and services are to be produced?	Consumers in the marketplace; some public decision making	A central planning agency
How to produce goods and services?	Producers, guided by resource prices	Central planning agency, guided by prices and income
How to distribute goods and services?	Consumers in the marketplace, with some influence from government regulators	A central authority

hypothesis. The convergence hypothesis states that in the struggle to answer the fundamental problems of scarcity, economic systems begin to adopt the characteristics of one another. Capitalistic (market) economies adopt certain characteristics of command systems and command economies adopt certain characteristics of the market system. In the U.S., government ownership of land for purposes of resource conservation represents a divergence from the pure market economy. In the U.S.S.R., a relaxation of the restrictions against private enterprise reflects a shift away from a pure command economy. The key to remembering the differences between market and command economies lies in who makes the economic decisions (table 3.2). The different priorities assigned by these systems to consumer products is reflected in the access to and ownership of certain goods by consumers (see table 3.3).

Table 3.3 Consumer Items in the United States and the Soviet Union, 1984

	U.S.	U.S.S.R.
Percentage of households owning[a]		
clothes washing machines	73	55
refrigerators	100	65
televisions	88	38
Number of persons per automobile[b]	1.8	26.0
Number of[c]		
telephones per 100 persons	76	9.8
televisions per 1,000 persons	790	308
radios per 1,000 persons	2,043	514

Source: *Statistical Abstract of the United States*, 1987, U.S. Department of Commerce, Bureau of the Census, pp. 826, 827.
a. From Table no. 1449, "Percent of Households Owning Selected Appliances—Selected Countries, 1984."
b. From Table no. 1450, "World Motor Vehicle Registrations—Selected Countries, 1984."
c. From Table no. 1451, "Communications—Telephones, Newspapers, Television, and Radio, by Country."

FOUNDATIONS OF THE MARKET ECONOMY

> Every individual . . . neither intends to promote the public interest, nor knows how much he is promoting it. He intends only his own security, only his own gain. And he is in this led by an invisible hand to promote an end which was no part of his intention. By pursuing his own interest he frequently promotes that of society more effectually than when he really intends to promote it.—Adam Smith[3]

Adam Smith's "invisible hand" underlies the importance given individuals and individual decision making in a free market economy. Smith contended that individuals, operating alone and without government intervention, could seek fulfillment of personal needs and, at the same time, assist in satisfying the goals of the economy. The idea that self-interest adds to the good of society is a fundamental tenet of all market-driven economic systems.

Self-Interest

In *The Wealth of Nations,* Adam Smith hints that of all possible economic systems, the market system has the highest potential. He knew, in the late 1700s, that the driving force behind the free market economy would be individual self-interest. To praise self-interest in 1776, as Smith did, was revolutionary. The idea that self-interest could be a noble or acceptable virtue had only recently emerged. During the Middle Ages, self-interest was considered synonymous with greed and, thus, improper and immoral. There were usury laws against charging interest because it was thought sinful for a lender to extract interest from a borrower. It was not until the late 1700s, when the economist Jeremy Bentham described his pleasure-pain calculus, that self-interest began to be seen in a more positive light.

The theory behind the pleasure-pain calculus holds that if individuals seek their own satisfaction, society as a whole prospers. Bentham's idea is subject to the fallacy of composition: For example, a rock music fan who is pursuing the maximization of his or her pleasure may easily disturb the peace and tranquility of a neighbor who prefers classical music. What is good for one is not necessarily good for all. However, on the more basic issues of self-interest and societal welfare, most free market economists agree that Bentham's pleasure-pain calculus escapes the fallacy of composition. Adam Smith refined Bentham's idea with his concept of the invisible hand. Self-fulfillment, individual motivation, or the desire for profit, if controlled by the forces of competition, could create a better world for all. This belief is the foundation of the market system.

Within the market system, individual self-interest motivates the labor force—workers "trade" their labor for money they can use to purchase food, shelter, clothing, and other consumer goods. This is hardly altruistic. Nonetheless, the products and services generated by this labor benefit other people as well. For example, an airline pilot flies a commercial plane in order to earn a salary; however, the fact that the pilot performs his or her job enables many passengers to travel on the plane. Their purposes—whether business or pleasure—are also served by the pilot's self-interest in flying the plane.

Consumer Sovereignty

The second important principle of the market system is the idea of consumer sovereignty. Consumer sovereignty means that the individual consumer decides what is to be produced in the economy. In the United States, the executives of large corporations who decide what will be produced base their decisions on what they perceive to be the wishes of the marketplace. Thus, the sum total of individual consumer wants ultimately determines what is to be produced. A daily election of goods and services takes place in the marketplace of capitalism. That portion of a consumer's income that is available for spending in the marketplace is often referred to by economists as the consumer's "dollar votes." On a daily basis, consumers cast their ballots for those products that they believe are reliable, safe, and of good quality. Consumers reject products that do not perform well, are too highly priced, and seem to be bad bargains.

Store owners watch what is being sold on a daily basis. Items that are big sellers are reordered, while items that accumulate on store shelves are not reordered. Such products are not in great demand: they have "failed" the market test, lost the consumer election, and soon disappear from the market.

In the market system, producers must react quickly to capitalize on consumer interest, and they stand ready to reallocate resources at a moment's notice. Some products can be created almost instantaneously in response to consumer demand. Books are written, printed, and made available to the public remarkably soon after a major event of great concern or interest occurs. A particular song becomes a hit on the radio and, almost immediately, abundant supplies of the record appear in the stores. A popular professional football player appears on national television wearing an obscure brand of sunglasses and, suddenly, every budding athlete wants a pair. Almost overnight, retailers all over town are advertising the product's availability.

Profit and Loss

A third fundamental component of the market economy is the profit and loss system. Since the Arab oil embargo in the 1970s and the subsequent increases in oil prices, a growing awareness of the large profits enjoyed by American oil companies has led many Americans to become cynical about the idea of profit. Yet, profits are absolutely essential for the functioning of a market system. The profit and loss system is one of the major strengths of capitalism. Profits are the direct result of the dollar-voting system. Consumers reward companies for their efforts and good work by buying their products. Once a company's expenses are covered, the rest of the money it receives is considered profit.

Profit allows the business to grow and signals the opportunity for new businesses to start up, either in competition with or as a support to that particular business. Thus, profit spurs the economy to allot more resources to this particular enterprise. Greater competition often lowers prices and improves the quality of the product or service. In short, profit spurs competition, and competition, in turn, increases and improves consumer choices.

Losses, on the other hand, signify a failure in the market system. Ultimately, resources are withheld from those firms that lose in the competition for dollar votes. Other entrepreneurs are discouraged from entering a failing industry. Losses and bankruptcies may be harsh but are an unavoidable fact of life in the market system.

Profit plays a crucial role in our economy. It is the reward for success in the marketplace and the lifeblood of our economic system. Without the profit motive, new and better-quality products are unlikely to appear. It is the vital fuel of future economic growth.

Competition

The final major concept of the market system is that of competition. If firms must compete with one another for dollar votes, no one firm can set prices and earn supernormal or monopolistic profits. If this phenomenon should occur, it would only last for a short time because new firms would quickly enter the market and compete the price advantage away. While the goal of the market economy is to produce an environment of "pure" competition where many sellers and many buyers enter the market fray, no one firm can control prices, and all firms produce only a small part of the total output of each industry. The amount of actual competition and control varies among firms in different industries. At the opposite extreme is the monopoly in which one firm has complete control of the market for its product. It is probably safe to say that most U.S. industries fall somewhere between the extremes of pure competition and monopoly. The economist's goal is to make markets as competitive as possible. In the center of market system competition are the forces of supply and demand. These concepts are discussed in the following chapter.

Specialization and Comparative Advantage

The market economy forces efficiency upon all economic agents. Members of the labor force are compelled to specialize in order to compete with other individuals and other factors of production. The resulting division of labor increases the skills of individual laborers and raises productivity throughout the economy. Specialization is nurtured as the market system guides the factors of production into those occupations and uses in which their productive values are maximized. Specialization and division of labor require that each factor of production be funneled into work processes in which it has a comparative advantage over the other factors.

The Law of Comparative Advantage

The law of comparative advantage states that economic agents (for example, entrepreneurs) should specialize in those activities in which they have the greatest productive advantage over all other competing factors (or in which they have the fewest disadvantages). Moreover, resources—the factors of production—should also be so concentrated. Production advantage is measured in terms of opportunity cost. The concept of comparative advantage can be illustrated by examining the productivity of a bank manager and manager's assistant before and after specialization (table 3.4 and figure 3.6).

Figure 3.6 is a graph of the output possibilities of the manager and assistant manager at First National Bank for their two main duties, new account development and loan closings. Notice that the manager can increase the number of loan closings by 5 (moving from point A to B) by sacrificing 5 new accounts. Conversely, the opportunity cost of 1 loan closing for the manager is 1 new account. The assistant manager can increase loan closings by 5 (moving from point C to point D) only by giving up 10 new accounts. The opportunity cost of the assistant manager for 1 loan closing is 2 new accounts.

Assume the manager is currently operating at point A, producing 20 new accounts and 10 loan closings per week, while the assistant manager is operating at point E, producing 10 new accounts and 5 loan closings per week. These data correspond to the "before specialization" column in table 3.4.

Table 3.4 Productivity Evaluation

	Before Specialization	After Specialization	Combined Change
New Accounts			
Manager	20	0	
Assistant	10	20	
Combined	30	20	−10
Loan Closings			
Manager	10	30	
Assistant	5	0	
Combined	15	30	+15
		Net Gain	+5

ECONOMIC PROBLEMS, SYSTEMS, AND RESOURCES

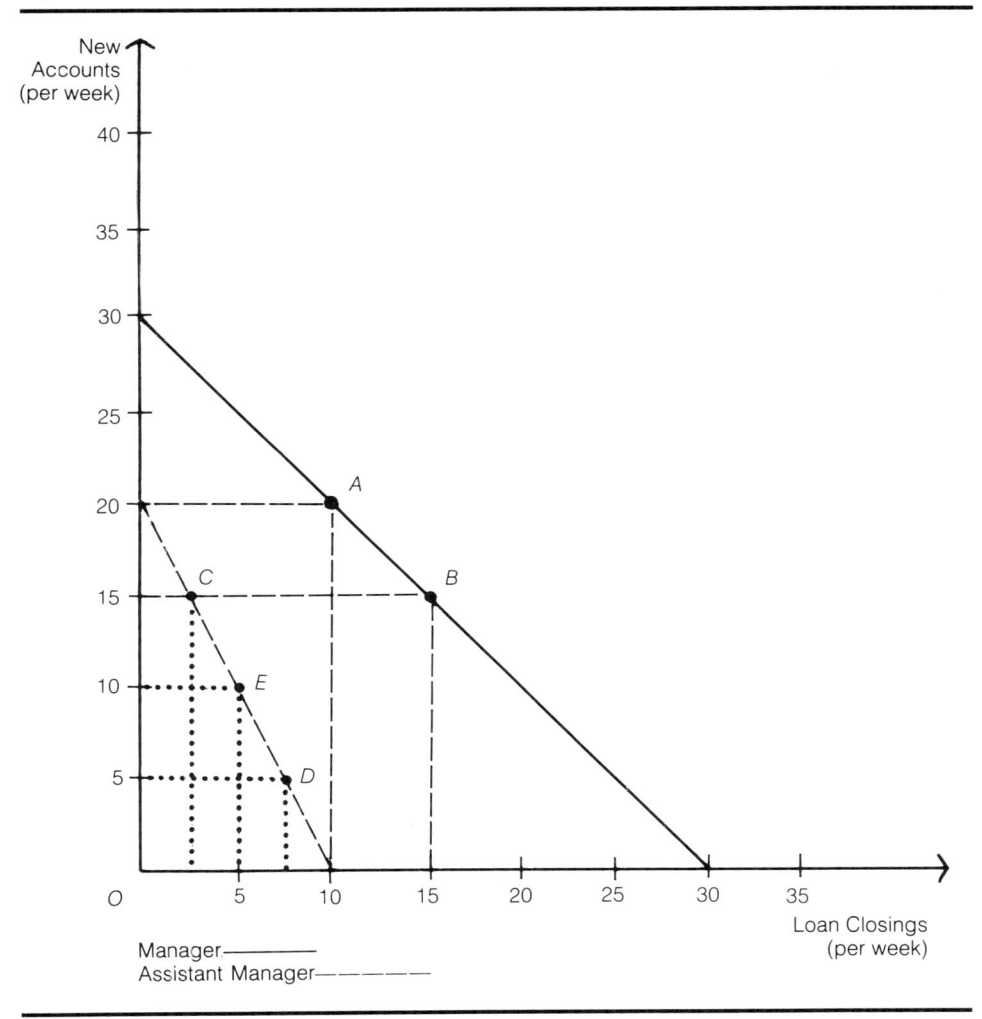

Figure 3.6 Output Possibilities, First National Bank

Manager ———
Assistant Manager — — — —

Note that the manager can open 20 new accounts and close 10 loans while the assistant manager can only handle 10 and 5, respectively. The manager is said to have an absolute advantage in both new accounts and loan closings. However, an analysis of comparative advantage reveals a different story.

The opportunity cost of developing 1 new account is 1 loan closing for the manager, while the opportunity cost of 1 new account is only half of a loan closing for the assistant manager. The assistant possesses a lower opportunity cost in terms of new accounts. This means the assistant possesses a comparative advantage in new account development.

91

However, the manager has a better opportunity cost in loan closings: 1-to-1 versus 1-to-2 closings to new accounts, respectively. Therefore, the manager has a comparative advantage in loan closings.

The law of comparative advantage calls for specialization at this point. Each individual should specialize to perform that function in which a comparative advantage exists. This means that the manager should specialize in loan closings exclusively, and the assistant should be responsible for new accounts. Performance data for the manager and assistant manager after specialization also appear in table 3.4.

The "combined change" column in table 3.4 shows the gain in productivity in loan closings that can be achieved from such specialization. After specialization occurs, there are fewer new accounts. However, the bank enjoys a net increase in activity of 5 additional loan closings.

Shortcomings of the Market System

The "invisible hand" of Adam Smith is said to be the beacon that guides the market economy to the most efficient heights. Yet the "invisible hand" is not an infallible one. There are some problems yet unresolved.

One problem is that inequitable income distribution may concentrate the consumption and accumulation of the economy's goods and services among certain consumer groups. Special interest groups, laws, and institutions may evolve that skew the income distribution toward favored groups or individuals.[4]

Although laissez-faire economics mandates a minimal level of government intervention, it may be harmful if certain legitimate governmental functions are ignored or assigned a low priority. If these important governmental services are underfinanced, the needs of the citizens may go unmet. This could undermine the very structure of the economy. On the other hand, when a large commitment to the public sector draws resources away from the private sector and government grows beyond the limits of necessity, the principles of laissez-faire are compromised. Economists disagree about the proper size and scope of government activities in a market economy.

The market system requirement of healthy competition may not be met for a variety of reasons. Technical, production-centered factors may reduce the size of an industry to only a few producers. Illegal, coercive, and predatory practices on the part of one or more firms may reduce the ranks of rivals to the point where the conspirator(s) may dominate the market, thereby side-stepping the forces of competition. Society must maintain a constant industry-by-industry vigil to enforce the rules of competition. Antitrust officials at the state and federal level seek to preserve competition by investigating certain mergers and acquisitions to determine if the competitiveness of U.S. industries has been injured. These regulators occasionally bring suit to stop or reverse corporate activity that is perceived as damaging to the competitive environment.

SUMMARY

Resources, or factors of production, include land, labor, capital, and entrepreneurial ability. These resources are in constant demand; they are called scarce resources because they have limited availability.

Consumers, businesses, and governments, however, have unlimited wants. An economic system seeks to satisfy as many of its members' wants as possible, given the resources available to it. Economies therefore strive to achieve both technical and allocative efficiency.

Technical efficiency involves maximizing output from a given amount of input or minimizing input for a given amount of output—preventing or eliminating waste of resources. Allocative efficiency involves making sure that resources are put to their best possible use.

Production possibility theory enables economists to evaluate the benefits and costs of different options in using resources. "Guns" symbolize investment goods or capital goods and represent saving resources for future use. "Butter" represents consumer goods and indicates consumption, or the use of resources today. Production possibilities can be shown graphically using a production possibilities curve. Changes in resource availability, technological advances, and depreciation of equipment are some things that affect the shape of the production possibilities curve.

Two economic laws that help us interpret production possibilities are the law of increasing cost and the law of diminishing returns. The law of increasing cost states that as increasing amounts of one good and decreasing amounts of a second good are produced, the amount of the second good that must be sacrificed in return for one more unit of the first good (the opportunity cost) will increase. The law of diminishing returns states that an increase in one factor of production without an increase in all other necessary factors of production eventually leads to an increase in output that is smaller than the value of the increased input.

All economic systems must decide what, how, and how much to produce. Also, they must decide how and to whom the resulting goods and services will be distributed. In the ideal command system, all economic decisions are made by a small group of planners, the government owns all property resources, and the emphasis is placed on the common good. In the ideal market system, private individuals own most factors of production, the government plays no role in economic decision making, and the forces in the marketplace determine answers to the economic questions described earlier. Almost every country in the world uses a form of either the command or the market system. In practice, market economies often adopt some of the characteristics of command economies. Similarly, countries using the command system will adopt some practices of the market system.

Four important concepts form the basis of the market system:

- Self-interest: the desire for self-improvement, when controlled by competitive forces, leads to a better life for everyone.
- Consumer sovereignty: the consumer is "king." Individual consumers decide, through participation in the marketplace, what is to be produced. Consumers cast "dollar votes" for the products they want and need.
- profit and loss: profit is the reward for success in the marketplace. Profits enable businesses to grow and encourage others to join the fray. Losses mark failures in the marketplace. Businesses that lose the election for dollar votes do not survive in the marketplace.
- Competition: competition improves consumer choices and prevents monopolistic practices.

Specialization is a requirement for efficient resource use in the market system. The law of comparative advantage states that economic agents and factors of production should specialize in that part of the production process in which they have the greatest advantage over all other factors.

The market system does have its faults. For example, inequitable income distribution is one problem that has not been resolved. Nonetheless, to a remarkable extent, the "invisible hand" described by Adam Smith in the late 1700s succeeds in guiding the market system.

KEY WORDS

absolute advantage	law of diminishing returns
capital	law of increasing cost
capital consumption allowance	market system
command system	pleasure-pain calculus
comparative advantage	production frontier
consumer sovereignty	production possibilities curve
convergence hypothesis	regeneration of wants
entrepreneurial ability	resource payments
factors of production	resources
"guns" and "butter"	scarcity
labor	specialization
land	unlimited wants

Questions for Review

1. What is the basic economic problem? Why is it that society has not been able to solve it?

2. What did Adam Smith mean when he wrote of the "invisible hand"?

3. How can an individual's efforts to promote his or her own well-being also further the well-being of society?

4. How does a market economy create incentives for specialization of labor? What is a negative aspect of specialization?

5. What does a movement along the production possibilities curve suggest? What does a point inside the curve suggest?

6. Banker Smith can open 15 new accounts or close 10 loans. Banker Jones can open 20 new accounts or close 5 loans. Draw their production possibilities curves. What is Banker Smith's cost of opening 1 new account? What is Banker Jones's cost of closing 1 loan? If they can specialize, who should open new accounts and who should close loans?

7. In a pure market system, distribution of income is based on individual ownership of resources and the value the market places on those inputs. What does this mean for people who are unable to contribute to the production process?

8. Command and market economies solve the five fundamental economic problems quite differently. Describe how the solutions to the following problems might be determined in a market economy and in a command economy.
    a) How many of each size of shoes a shoe manufacturer will produce.
    b) Whether or not to install ATMs in new locations.
    c) Whether mechanical paint sprayers or human workers will be used in an automobile assembly plant.
    d) How many automobiles to produce in one year.
    e) What price to charge for a movie.
    f) Whether a firm will sell its products only at one location or use mail order.

ENDNOTES

1. The interesting thing about savings is that they can lead to an improvement in the ability of an economy to grow and thus reduce problems of scarcity in the future. For a complete treatment of the impact of savings on long-term growth, refer to the discussion on production possibilities.

2. For an interesting overview of the Soviet economic system, see Seweryn Bialer, *The Soviet Paradox: External Expansion, Internal Decline* (New York: Alfred A. Knopf, 1986).

3. Adam Smith, *Inquiry into the Nature and Causes of the Wealth of Nations* (New York: Random House, Modern Library, 1937), p. 423.

4. See Sar A. Levitan and Martha R. Cooper, *Business Lobbies: The Public Good and the Bottom Line* (Baltimore, Md.: The Johns Hopkins University Press, 1983).

ECONOMICS IN THE NEWS

Concern about the decline of America's strength in world markets has led many people in the United States to conclude that the federal government must become involved in efforts to return the country to its economic dominance. As you have learned, however, the idea that government should intervene in the economy is contrary to free market capitalism. This article, discussing recent shifts in Soviet pricing policies, illustrates some of the complexities inherent in controlling and subsidizing consumer goods.

In Soviet Future: Strawberry Test

Buyer Reaction to Prices Will Reflect on Gorbachev Plan

By Felicity Barringer
Special to *The New York Times*

MOSCOW, June 27—At the Central Market today, a vendor sat behind an assortment of choice strawberries, telling the few inquiring shoppers that the berries cost the equivalent of $5.50 a pound. There were few buyers, and no line.

At the same time on a street out back, a Government truck pulled up and delivered 30 small crates of strawberries—some ripe, some overripe, some moldy—at $2.40 a pound. A scolding saleswoman shoveled them into the bags of customers who had formed a 15-minute line.

The strawberry scene spoke eloquently of the bizarre anomalies of the Soviet pricing system and its byproducts: unreasonably high or low prices and long lines for products whose quality is uneven at best.

Complex of Controls and Subsidies

The rigid pricing system is a complex fabric of Government controls and subsidies with isolated patches of quasi-free market economies, including farm markets that sell produce from private plots.

It is this system that Mikhail S. Gorbachev is proposing to alter with his program, newly endorsed by the Communist Party, to gradually introduce price flexibility in the Soviet economy.

Inherent in the issue of prices, according to Western and Soviet analysts, are the key difficulties that face most of Mr. Gorbachev's initiatives in his broad drive to remake Soviet society:

Reining in a powerful bureaucracy, in this case the State Committee for Prices, known by the acronym Goskomtsen. It sets more than 200,000 wholesale and retail prices annually, on everything from raw materials like ore and grain to bread, shoes, chinaware and cars.

Potentially tampering with a basic tenet of Communist ideology and the Soviet social contract, in this case overall price stability and dramatically low prices on basic foods, housing, education and mass transit.

Taking a cumbersome, inefficient but predictable system and introducing an element of the unknown, in this case, a limited role for competitive forces and the possibility of politically explosive inflation. Food price increases in Eastern Europe have sometimes touched off protest and political instability.

'Jumping Out Into the Unknown'

A Western diplomat predicted last week that conservatives would call the pricing innovations a threat to the basic order of Communism. The current system, he said, is a known quantity, but Mr. Gorbachev's proposals are "jumping out into the unknown."

How fast and how far Mr. Gorbachev will jump on the price issue is still under discussion, according to Abel G. Aganbegyan, the economist who was selected to explain Mr. Gorbachev's new proposals at a news conference.

Mr. Aganbegyan explained that the alternatives under discussion were either a stage-by-stage shift in the present pricing mechanisms, with the first stage affecting only wholesale prices, or an overall re-examination of wholesale, retail and agricultural prices, with no changes before 1990.

Instrument of Efficiency

The guidelines for Mr. Gorbachev's economic changes, approved Friday by the Communist Party's Central Committee, said prices should be made "an effective instrument for raising the efficiency of social production, for developing economic management methods and for deepening cost-accounting and self-financing."

The role of the price-fixing committee would be reduced in part by increased freedom of factories and large enterprises to contract directly with each other for industrial goods.

The Central Committee program said that wholesale prices should be amended to reflect production costs more accurately and that raw materials and fuel—such as heating oil—should be priced to reflect production cost and to discourage waste.

Until now, according to American specialists, wholesale prices were supposed to be roughly equivalent to production cost. But there was little incentive to keep costs down because of widely available subsidies.

In contrast, retail prices were supposed to be set at a level that would guarantee a balance between supply and demand. This was a goal that was largely unmet, judging by the periodic shortages of everything from fruit to furniture.

Meat and Bread Subsidized

Prices were also used to insure that some products were accessible to low-paid workers. Meat in state stores in Moscow and other cities sells at less than half the cost of production. Like other foods, particularly bread, it is heavily subsidized. But buyers often have to wait in line for meat that is of low quality, if available at all. In farmers' markets, it is likely available but higher priced.

According to Mr. Gorbachev's speech Thursday, the Soviet economy spends 72 billion rubles a year (more than $115 billion) in subsidies. More than 50 billion rubles of this goes to agriculture.

The farm subsidy has increased 150 percent in the last 10 years, and is now more than 12 times the 1966 level of four billion rubles, according to articles in the Soviet press.

"What is happening?" asked a professor of economics, R. Khasbulatov, writing in Komsomolskaya Pravda. "Agricultural productivity is virtually at a standstill" and the inefficiency is forcing up subsidies.

He said such subsidies were paid for in part by inflated prices on goods like imported jeans (marked up sevenfold) and similar products.

The average Soviet wage is slightly under 200 rubles a month, or $310. Even with subsidies, about 30 percent of the total is spent on food, according to a 1985 Soviet survey—compared with 19 percent by American families, Soviet economists said.

To increase the prices of bread and meat, for example, which have changed little in decades, without increasing salaries is to ask for social unrest. In Poland in 1976, an increase in food prices was canceled after widespread protests, strikes and, in one city, riots.

But to increase the salaries inevitably means an increased price for the goods that the worker produces—and the essential elements for inflation are then present.

In his remarks, Mr. Aganbegyan stressed that whatever price changes were made would come only after "wide discussion with the population."

The rise in food costs, he said, would "result in raises for the lower-paid population, for those who have large families, and so on."

And what about inflation? The word did not appear in the discussion of prices in the Central Committee blueprint. The most it would caution was: "It is necessary. . .to overcome the tendency toward the growth of prices on the basis of the development of the competitive power of enterprises."

This was a prescription for letting competition achieve the desired pricecutting effect.

Copyright © 1987 by the New York Times Company. Reprinted by permission.

CHAPTER FOUR

THE CONCEPTS OF DEMAND AND SUPPLY

Objectives

After reading this chapter, you should be able to

•

define the laws of supply and demand

•

list and describe the determinants of supply and demand

•

construct and interpret a demand schedule
and curve, and a supply schedule and curve

•

explain the difference between a change in demand and
a change in quantity demanded, and
the difference between a change in supply and
a change in quantity supplied

•

describe the effects of changes in supply
and/or demand on market equilibrium

THE CONCEPT OF DEMAND

In the previous chapter we discussed how the market economy determines how much to produce and what price to charge for the myriad of goods and services available to consumers. The price information generated by the market also performs the important function of rationing scarce resources among various users. Two major forces are at work in free and competitive markets: large numbers of buyers (demand creators) and sellers (suppliers). Buyers and sellers act independently and without collusion. These two economic agents behave in fairly predictable fashions. Through years of observation, economists have been able to translate this behavior into the two fundamental tenets of all competitive markets: the law of demand and the law of supply. These laws should not be interpreted in the same sense as physical laws. The laws of supply and demand are based on the assumption that humans are basically rational beings and thus behave in predictable ways. However, as these economic laws are based on human behavior, exceptions to them do arise.

The Law of Demand

The law of demand states that there is an inverse relationship between the price of a product or service and the quantity demanded for that product or service, provided that all other factors or variables that could influence demand are held constant. This proviso is called the *ceteris paribus* assumption. The law of demand describes the effect of a product price change on the quantity demanded of that particular product: as the price of a product rises, the quantity demanded falls, and vice versa. While the law of demand accounts only for the impact a product price change will have on quantity demanded, many other variables can also influence demand.

The Demand Equation and The Determinants of Demand

The relationship expressing how the quantity demanded of a given product or service is related to the factors or variables that might cause this amount to change is called the demand equation. The factors that can influence the level of demand are called the determinants of demand. The general form of demand equation for most goods is expressed as follows:

$$Q_d = f(P, Y, W, T, E, P_r, N, e)$$

Q_d is the dependent variable and represents the total quantity demanded.

The independent variables are:

- P = price of the product/services
- Y = income of consumers
- W = wealth of consumers
- T = taste or preferences of consumers
- E = inflation or inflation expectations
- P_r = *prices of related goods/services*
- N = number of consumers
- e = error term, or sum of all other influences on demand.

A change in any one of the independent variables in the demand equation will alter the amount demanded. Nonprice factors are constantly changing, and changes in these factors may be more important in scope and magnitude than a change in price. The impact of a change in the nonprice factors can be examined by observing the signs of the individual coefficients for each variable. The demand equation given below illustrates the normal relationships that exist between the nonprice factors and the quantity demanded. Some of the variables have a positive/negative sign ($\pm$), indicating that either a direct or an indirect relationship is possible.

$$Q_d = a - bP \pm cY + dW + eT + fE \pm gP_r + hN + e$$

Income (Y)

The sign of the income variable coefficient can be positive or negative. For most goods and services, the sign is positive because as consumer income rises, consumers are willing to purchase more of most products. On the other hand, as income falls, consumers reduce their demand. Goods and services for which demand varies directly with consumer income are called normal products. The vast majority of consumer purchases are classified as normal products. However, the demand for certain unique products varies inversely with consumer income. In other words, as income rises, consumers demand less of these goods. When income falls, consumers demand more of these goods. These goods and services are known as inferior products. This does not mean that these products are substandard in quality. These products may be substitutes for higher-priced items, unaffordable in times of shrinking income. For example, certain foods such as beans, ground beef, and dried milk may experience increased demand as incomes fall. Conversely, as incomes rise and steak once again becomes affordable, the demand for lower-priced substitutes may fall.

Wealth (W)

As consumers increase their level of wealth, they are likely to begin accumulating possessions, adding to their deposit account balances, and raising the value of their stock and land portfolios. They may also be more inclined to buy consumer goods. The increase in wealth provides a safety net or cushion and helps consumers overcome the anxiety that often accompanies large or frivolous purchases. In addition to the psychological boost to spending, increased wealth provides investment incentives. Consumers may elect to transform their wealth into funds that can be used for additional consumption. Therefore, as consumer wealth rises, demand can be expected to increase. As consumer wealth falls, demand will likely decrease.

Taste (T)

As the old saying goes, "There's no accounting for taste!" Consumers' preferences often change like the wind. Changes in taste are sometimes effected by advertising and promotional techniques, the influence of clever and creative fashion designers, and the media. However, in some cases, changes in consumer preference seem to have no identifiable cause. Regardless of the sources of such changes, the effects of demand are obvious. Demand for a good or service increases as consumers' collective taste for the product grows. Demand for a product declines, and may completely vanish, if consumer preferences turn away from the product. Recent examples of products that have experienced rapid growth in demand due to taste changes include Cabbage Patch dolls, foreign-make automobiles, and "running shoes" (as opposed to just plain sneakers). On the other hand, consumer demand for leisure suits, AM radios, and 8-track tape players has plummeted because of changes in society's taste.

Price Expectations (E)

Current demand for products can be influenced by consumer expectations of future changes in price. For example, consumers in the market for a new home may delay their purchase if they believe that interest rates on mortgages will fall in the near future. As a result of these decisions, current demand for housing will decline. If, however, they expect prices to rise, consumers may shift a planned future purchase to the present in order to take advantage of the current prices. In this case, current demand increases as a result of consumer expectations.

Price of Related Goods (P_r)

The sign of this coefficient may be positive or negative depending upon the functional relationship that exists between the primary commodity and the related good. If the two products are considered to be functional substitutes, the sign will be positive: that is, a rise in the price of good X will cause the demand for good Y to rise. For example, if consumers view a demand deposit account at a commercial bank to be no different from a demand deposit account at a thrift institution, then an increase in fees or minimum balance requirements at a commercial bank (thus, a real price increase) will boost the demand for checking accounts at a nearby thrift. If the two products are used together as a pair, they are said to be complements. The relationship between the demand for good X and the price change of a complementary good Y is inverse. In this case, the coefficient of the independent variable is negative. For example, if the price of videocassette recorders falls, the demand for videotapes is likely to rise. Complementary relationships exist for French-cuffed shirts and cuff links, tennis rackets and balls, skis and ski masks, and so on.

Most often, however, the coefficient of this factor is neither positive nor negative, but zero. A rise or fall in the price of good X will have no impact on the demand for good Y. Such products are called independent goods. Examples include the following set of commodities: rain coats and autos, eye glasses and butter, and orange juice and personal computers.

Number of Consumers (N)

Obviously, the more consumers in a market, the larger the demand. Thus, a bank can increase the demand for bank services by opening a branch in a new community. Similarly, the demand for a bank's products will decrease if it is located in a declining neighborhood.

Other Factors (e)

Factors such as time, advertising, and promotional efforts—even the weather—can affect demand. The effects of random factors on demand are captured in the error term. Their influence may cause increases or decreases in demand. A combination of these random forces may offset the effects of the individual factors.

The Demand Schedule

Within a dynamic economy, the various determinants of demand can change constantly. However, to simplify the discussion that follows, we will invoke the ceteris paribus assumption and allow only the product's price to vary. Nonprice variables will be marked by a rule—for example, $\overline{Y}$, to indicate that the ceteris paribus assumption is in effect and the value of the variable is being held constant. The ceteris paribus assumption will be lifted later so that you may observe what happens to demand in a dynamic economy. Our demand equation can now be restated as follows:

$$Q_d = a - bP \pm c\overline{Y} + d\overline{W} + e\overline{T} + f\overline{E} \pm g\overline{P}_r + h\overline{N} + \bar{e}$$

A demand schedule depicts ordered pairs of price and quantity demanded as dictated by the demand equation. The schedule reveals the quantity of a product consumers are willing and able to purchase at a particular price during a given period of time. Thus, it displays the quantity demanded at various prices. It also indicates the price that consumers will pay when quantities are at specific levels.

A demand schedule shows buyer intentions. Of course, the combination of price and quantity that will ultimately exist depends on the intentions not only of buyers, but also of producers.

The demand schedule is expressed as the intentions of buyers for a certain time period, t. Assigning a specific length of time enables us to set the limits of the buyers' intentions. Thus, in a demand schedule, the quantity of a given product's demand must be cited in terms of amount per hour, day, week, month, and so on.

Consider the following hypothetical demand equation for good X. For simplicity, the nonprice variables have been held constant and therefore eliminated from the equation.

$$Q_{d_x} = 100 - 25 P_x$$

We can create a demand schedule for good X per unit of time, t (table 4.1).

Table 4.1 Demand Schedule, Good X

Unit Price (dollars)	Quantity Demanded/t
4	0
3	25
2	50
1	75
0	100

t = Units of time.

The demand schedule is a reflection of the law of demand. At a price of $4 per unit, demand for good X during time t, is zero. At a price of $3, 25 units of good X would be demanded per unit of time t. If the price were lowered to $1, then quantity demanded would be 75 units. As the price decreases, the quantity demanded increases. Conversely, increases in prices lead to decreases in demand. For example, if the price is raised from $1 to $2, demand falls from 75 units to 50 units.

The rationale behind the law of demand is built upon the concept of diminishing marginal utility. As an individual consumes more and more of a certain good, marginal utility—or buyer satisfaction—decreases. For example, the first slice of a pizza brings great joy to a hungry shopper. The second slice may still be consumed with pleasure, but perhaps with less enthusiasm. As the shopper's hunger is satiated, the pizza's marginal utility diminishes along with it. And those shoppers who consume a third, fourth, and fifth slice of pizza are likely to discover that eventually, a product purchase can bring negative marginal utility! In other words, additional consumption of good X is generally accompanied by decreasing satisfaction. As purchase satisfaction decreases, consumers will no longer pay the price they were initially willing to pay.

ECONOMICS FOR BANKERS

The Demand Curve

The demand schedule we created for good X can be easily transformed into graphic form (figure 4.1). The set of ordered pairs of price and quantity is transposed onto the x and y coordinates. (See chapter 2 for a review of two-dimensional graphs.) The quantity demanded of good X per unit of time is placed on the horizontal x-axis. Price per unit is placed on the vertical y-axis.

Figure 4.1 Consumer Demand Curve, Good X
$Q_{d_x} = 100 - 25P_x$

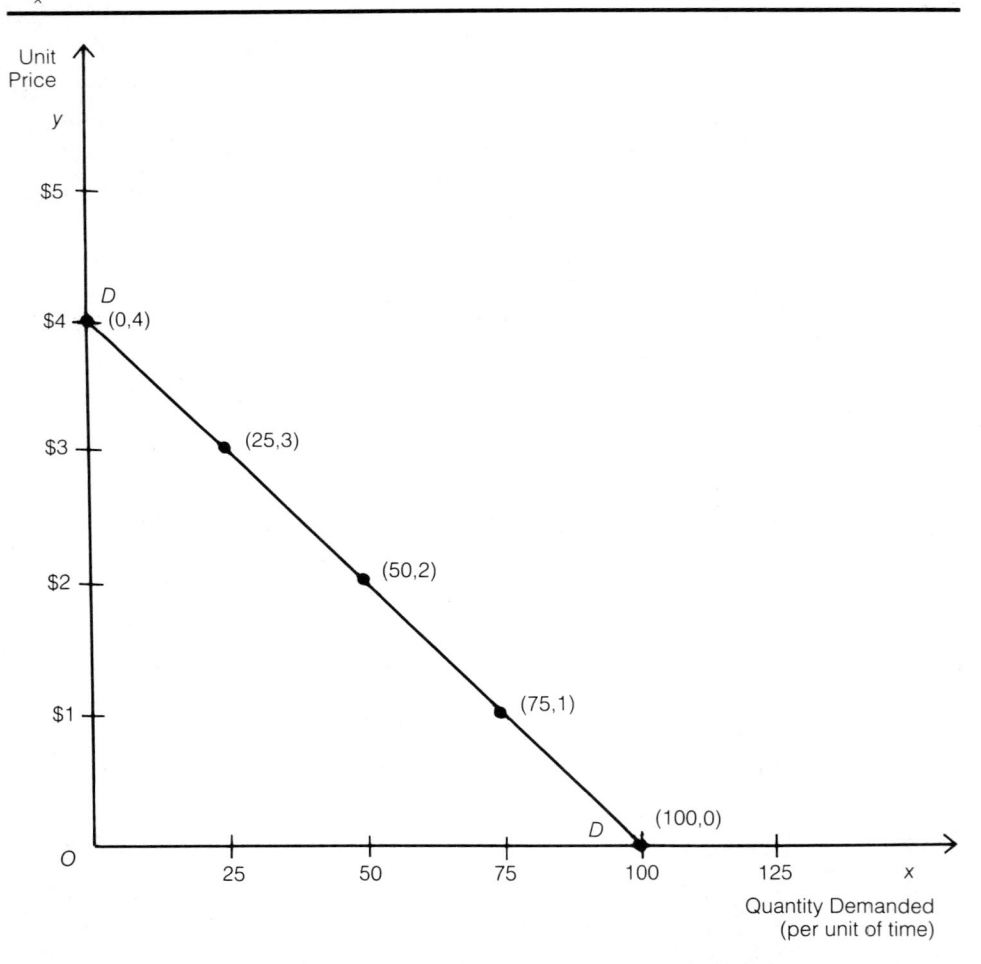

108

Normally, the independent variable (price in this instance) is placed on the horizontal axis, and the dependent variable (quantity) is placed on the vertical axis. Economists have elected not to follow mathematical convention here and reverse the standard placement of the dependent and independent variables.[1]

The demand for good X is represented by curve *DD*. The curve slopes downward to the right, reflecting the tenets of the law of demand. Note that the demand curve provides no more information than the demand schedule or the demand equation. It is merely a picture of the same data. Yet the graph offers a number of advantages over the demand schedule or equation. It is simpler in form and much easier to manipulate than schedules or equations. In the study of economics, graphs are considered the preeminent tool of economic analysis.

The Market Demand Curve

So far, we have examined the price-to-quantity calculus of a single consumer. However, most markets contain a large number of consumers. These consumers obviously have individual reactions to price and quantity. What looks like a bargain to one consumer may represent a classic "rip-off" to another. Does the demand analysis break down at this point because all consumers do not share a common demand equation? The answer is no, not at all. The demand equation can be broadened to encompass all consumers by using an aggregate term called "market demand." Market demand represents the total quantity demanded by all consumers at various prices. Determining the market demand is a simple matter of summing the individual quantities demanded at each price.

Consider a single economy with four consumers, A, B, C, D (table 4.2). The total market demand is the sum of the individual quantities demanded at each price. For example, when the price of good X is $3 per unit, consumer A demands 25 units; consumers B, C, and D, 35, 15, and 105 units, respectively. The market demand at this price is 180 units. (25 + 35 + 15 + 105). The market demand equation is also the sum of the individual demand curves (table 4.3).

Table 4.2 Market Demand Curve, Good X and Four Consumers

Price (dollars)	A/t	B/t	C/t	D/t	Total Market M/t
4	0	30	−10	90	110
3	25	35	15	105	180
2	50	40	40	120	250
1	75	45	65	135	320
0	100	50	90	150	390

t = Units of time.

Table 4.3 Market Demand Equation

Demand equations:

Consumer A	$Q_{d_A} = 100 - 25P_x$
Consumer B	$Q_{d_B} = 50 - 5P_x$
Consumer C	$Q_{d_C} = 90 - 25P_x$
Consumer D	$Q_{d_D} = 150 - 15P_x$
Market demand equation	$Q_{d_M} = \sum_{i=A}^{D} (Q_{d_i})$
Market demand	$Q_{d_M} = 390 - 70P_x$

Market demand can also be depicted graphically, as a market demand curve (figure 4.2). Notice that the market curve $D_m D_m$ is the horizontal sum of the individual quantities at any specific price on each demand curve.

Even if the market has thousands and thousands of consumers, the method of determining demand does not change. Total market demand is simply the sum of individual demand amounts.

Figure 4.2 Market Demand Curve
(The sum of individual demand curves)

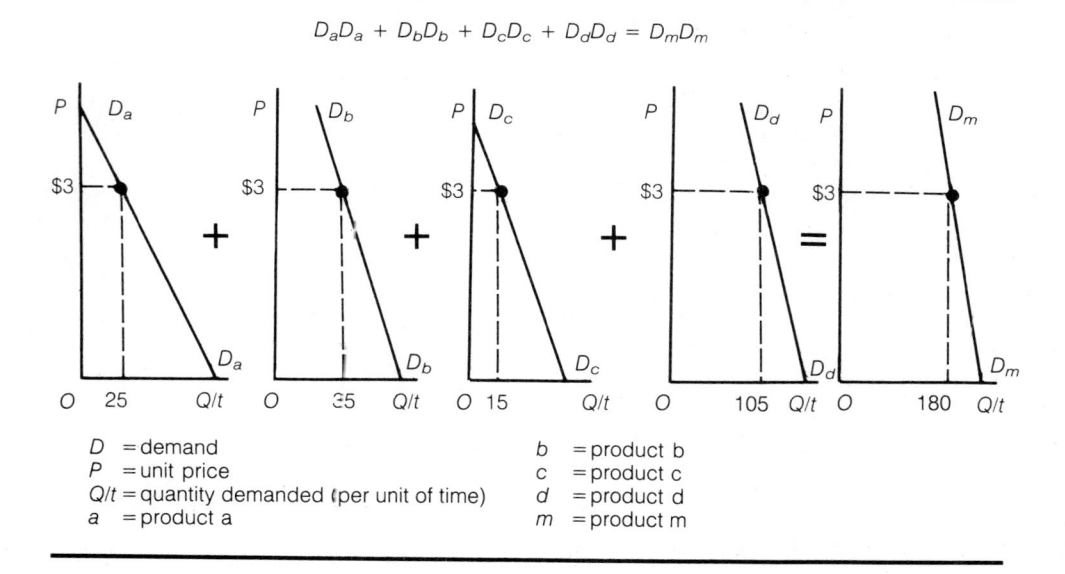

$$D_a D_a + D_b D_b + D_c D_c + D_d D_d = D_m D_m$$

At $P = \$3$: $Q_a = 25$, $Q_b = 35$, $Q_c = 15$, $Q_d = 105$, $Q_m = 180$

D = demand
P = unit price
Q/t = quantity demanded (per unit of time)
a = product a
b = product b
c = product c
d = product d
m = product m

Changes in Demand vs. Changes in Quantity Demanded

One of the most confusing situations in real-world demand analysis occurs when a price change is followed by a change in quantity demanded, and both changes are in the same direction. In other words, sometimes a price increase precedes an increase in quantity demanded. Similarly, a price decrease can be followed by a decrease in quantity demanded. This occurrence is contrary to the law of demand, which dictates that an increase in price leads to a decrease in quantity demanded, and vice versa. The explanation for this contradiction lies in the distinction between "change in demand" and "change in quantity demanded."

A change in demand occurs when any of the nonprice factors in the demand equation change. For example, if consumer income changes or prices of related goods change, consumers will demand more or less of good X at every given price, depending upon the direction and magnitude of the changes in the nonprice factors. A change in demand causes the demand equation, schedule, and curve to change. A change in demand can be equated with a shift in the demand curve.

When the demand curve shifts outward (toward the right), this indicates an increase in demand. Such a shift might occur because of a rise in income, a change in consumer taste that improves the product's desirability, or the launch of a major advertising campaign.

A decrease in demand is indicated by an inward shift of the demand curve (toward the left). A decrease in demand may occur because of a rise in income (if the product is inferior), unfavorable publicity surrounding the safety of the good, or, perhaps, a decrease in the price of a substitute product.

A change in demand will cause the whole demand curve to shift (figure 4.3). Curve D_0D_0 represents the original demand curve. If there is a change in any of the nonprice determinants of demand that would cause an increase in demand, the demand curve will shift to the right (to curve D_1D_1). A decrease in demand will result in a shift to the left (to curve D_2D_2).

A change in quantity demanded differs from a change in demand. A change in quantity demanded is caused by a change in one factor in the demand equation—the price of the product. If nonprice factors are also changing simultaneously, then the ceteris paribus assumption must be invoked. A change in quantity demanded results in a movement along, up, or down the existing demand curve (figure 4.4). There are no shifts in the curve's position. The demand equation and schedule are constant. The only change is a movement from one ordered pair of price and quantity demanded to another.

A change in quantity demanded can be shown as a movement from point A to point B along curve D_0D_0. At point A, price is P_0 and quantity demanded is OQ_0. However, if the price were lowered to P_1, there would be an increase in quantity demanded. This new level of quantity demanded is represented by amount OQ_1. The change in quantity demanded can

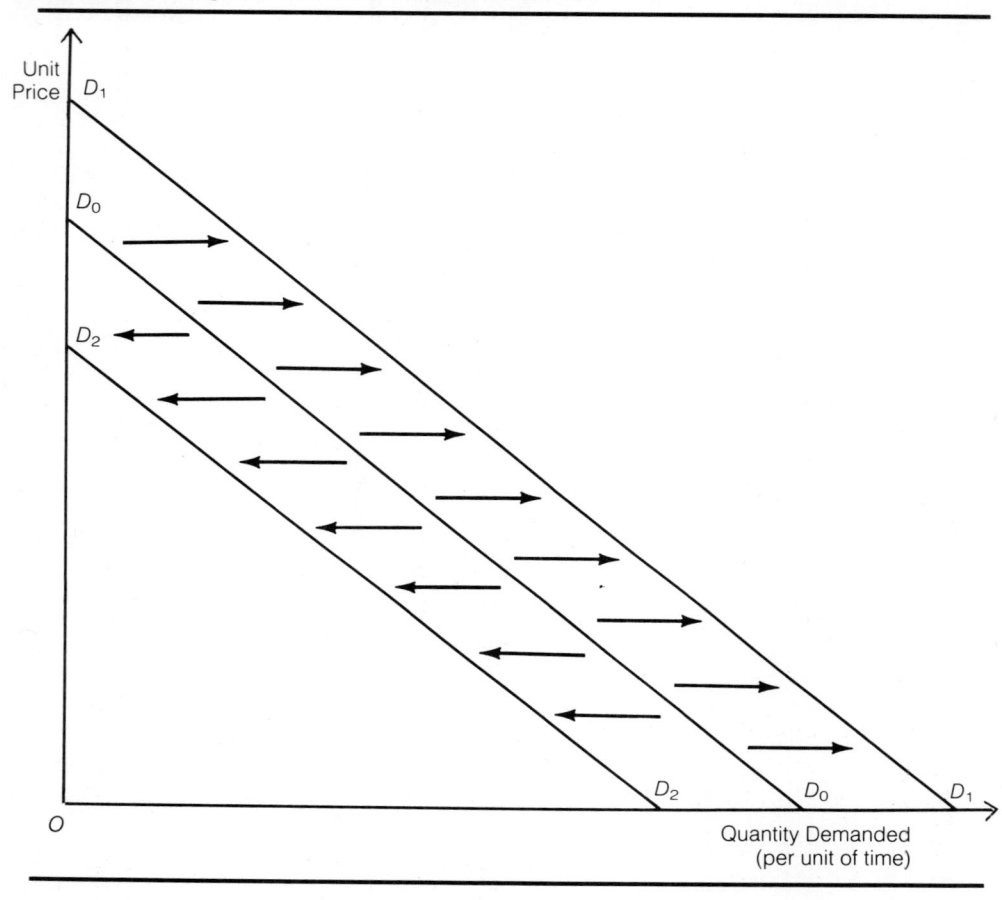

Figure 4.3 Change in Demand and Demand Curve Shifts

be expressed as distance Q_0Q_1. Notice that the other determinants of demand are held constant (ceteris paribus), and the only change in this instance is a movement down the curve.

To repeat: if a change in demand occurs, the whole demand curve shifts. This shift is caused by a change in one of the determinants of demand other than price. If a change in quantity demanded occurs, the curve remains in place, but a movement along the curve results from a change in the price of the product, with all other factors held constant.

When a real-world price increase leads to an increase in quantity demanded—or when an increase in quantity demanded leads to a real-world price increase—consumers have experienced a change in one or more of the nonprice variables in the demand equation. In other words, there has been a change in quantity demanded as well as a change in demand (see figure 4.5).

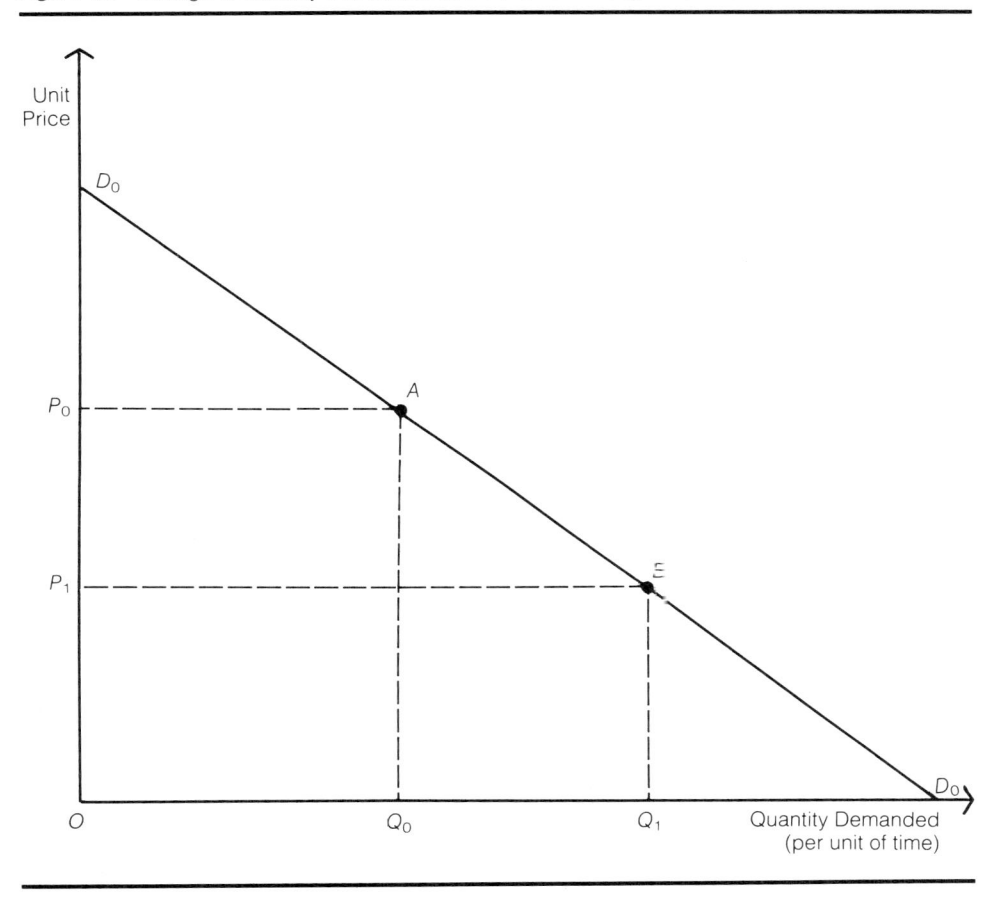

Figure 4.4 Change in Quantity Demanded and Movement Along the Curve

In figure 4.5, the original price-to-quantity relationship is shown as point A on demand curve D_0D_0. P_0 represents the price, and OQ_0 is the quantity demanded. If the price of good X were to increase to P_1, and all other factors held constant, the new ordered pair would be found at point B on curve D_0D_0. The price increase would cause a decrease in quantity demanded to OQ_0'. The law of demand predicts this outcome. However, if one or more of the other determinants of demand were to change at the same time, and those changes led to an increase in demand, the new demand curve might be one like D_1D_1. Now, consumers are willing to purchase more of good X at every price. Our new point of demand is point C on curve D_1D_1. At price P_1, consumers will demand quantity OQ_1 of good X.

The answer to this puzzle is simple. The rise in the quantity demanded following the price increase did *not* occur because of the original price change. The increase occurred

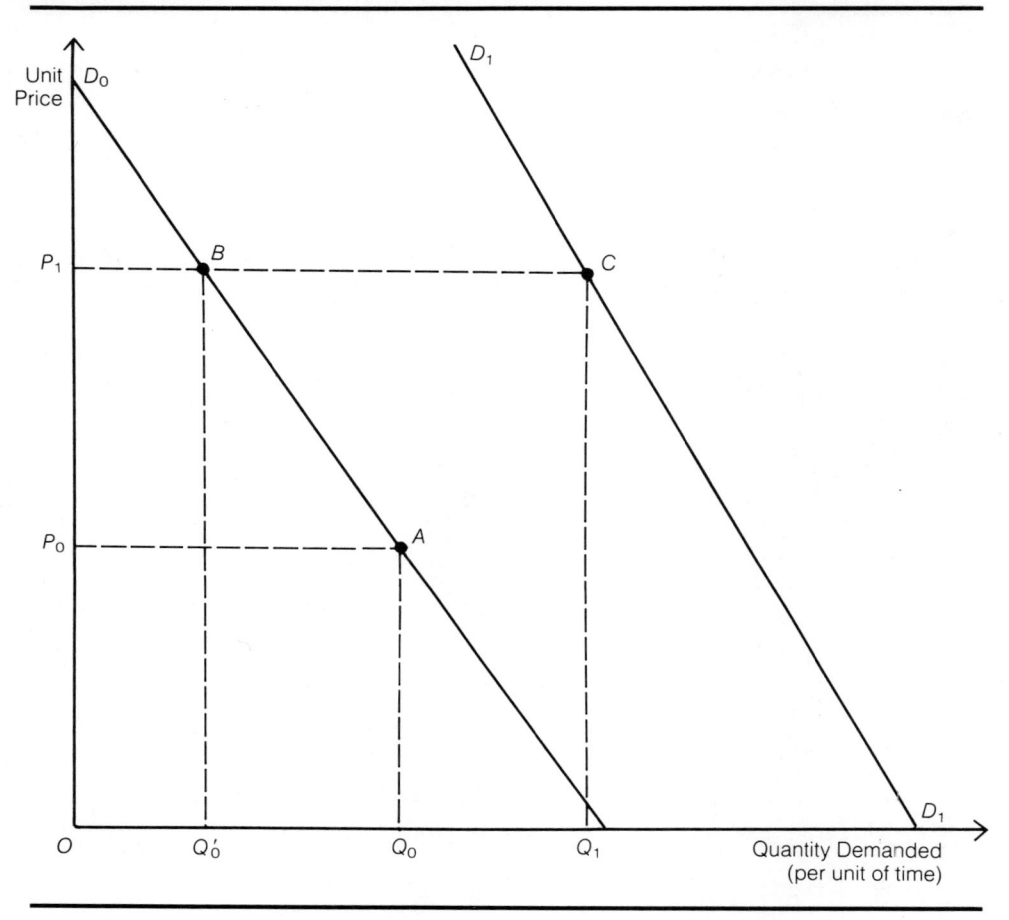

Figure 4.5 Change in Demand and Change in Quantity Demanded

because one of the nonprice determinants of demand changed. In other words, the change in demand overshadowed the change in quantity demanded.

An example of this phenomenon is the recent history of Japanese automobile sales in the United States. In the 1980s, the price of Japanese cars has risen dramatically. Yet sales of these imports have continued to rise, even in the face of voluntary import restraints. The increase in quantity demanded must be explained by factors other than price. American consumers perceive a high quality of workmanship in Japanese cars, and thus, preferences have shifted to reflect the increased desirability of Japanese makes. Of course, the high cost of gasoline in the early 1970s and the demand for fuel-efficient transportation served as the initial step in the escalating demand for the economical Japanese models.

An example of the opposite phenomenon, in which price and quantity demanded are both decreasing, is the recent sales pattern of black-and-white television sets. The price of these television sets has fallen steadily over the past few years. Yet, sales of black-and-white sets have virtually dried up. The law of demand would dictate that the price decreases lead to increases in quantity demanded and higher sales. However, consumer taste has changed. The rapid expansion of color programming and the availability of low-cost color sets have reduced the demand curve for black-and-white sets.

THE CONCEPT OF SUPPLY

While the concept of demand makes intuitive sense to most students of economics, the concept of supply is not as easily grasped. It can be viewed from the orientation of the individual or corporate seller of a product. The motivations of the producers and sellers of products are diametrically opposed to those of buyers. While consumers search for bargains, sellers try to obtain the highest possible prices for their goods. Price in this case acts as a control valve, inducing suppliers to offer products for sale or discouraging them from doing so. For any product, there is likely to be a minimum value or price, below which no supplier will offer it for sale. But, as the price is raised above this minimum value, suppliers are induced to offer increased quantities to buyers in the marketplace.

The Law of Supply

The law of supply states that there is a direct relationship between the price of a product or service and the quantity supplied of that product or service, under the condition of ceteris paribus. Thus, as the price of a product rises, the amount of the product that suppliers are willing and able to offer for sale will also increase. On the other hand, as the price decreases, the amount of the product that suppliers are willing and able to offer for sale will decrease, provided all other factors that influence supply are held constant.

The Supply Equation
And the Determinants of Supply

The supply equation is similar in design and construction to the demand equation. The quantity supplied is the dependent variable, and the price and the other determinants of supply are independent variables. The general form of the supply equation can be expressed as follows:

$$Q_s = f(P, E, C, N, T, G, e)$$

Q_s is the dependent variable and represents the total quantity supplied.
The independent variables are:
- P = price of product or service
- E = inflationary or deflationary expectations
- C = cost of production or resource cost
- N = number of suppliers
- T = technology
- G = government imposed taxes or subsidies
- e = error term, or sum of all other influences on supply.

As with the demand equation, a more specific supply equation can be created in which the signs for the coefficients for each variable are shown. These signs show the direction of movement in total supply when one of the determinants of supply changes. Such an equation is given below:

$$Q_s = a + bP - cE - dC + eN + fT - gG + e.$$

This equation shows that price varies directly with quantity supplied. The plus sign of coefficient b (the price term) is a reflection of the law of supply. However, as you can see, the signs of other coefficients are not all positive.

Inflation or Deflation Expectation (E)

In planning for the future, suppliers must formulate predictions about price movements. If they expect prices to rise sharply in the future, they will withhold some or all of their current production and thus, decrease supply. The negative sign of the expectation variable's coefficient (c) reflects this inverse relationship. An expectation of future price increases (inflation) leads to a decrease in current supply. An expectation of future price decreases (deflation) leads to an increase in supply.

Cost of Production (C)

As labor or material expenses rise, firms grow less willing to maintain current supply quantities at the old prices. Therefore, an increase in the cost of production leads to lower supply quantities at each price. The reverse holds for a decrease in resource costs. The negative sign of coefficient *d* reflects this inverse relationship. Cost of production is also called resource cost.

Number of Suppliers (*N*)

As the number of suppliers of a particular good grows, the amount of the product offered for sale at any given price increases. Similarly, as suppliers exit an industry, the quantity supplied decreases. This variable is directly related to quantity supplied; thus, the sign of the coefficient (*e*) is positive.

Technology (*T*)

This variable is closely related to cost of production. Presumably, improvements in production technology will lower production costs. Therefore, one might expect a similar relationship between quantity supplied and changes in technology. However, the sign of the coefficient (*f*) is positive because a technological advance is likely to lead to greater supply.

Government Taxes and Subsidies (*G*)

Certain taxes are viewed by suppliers as added costs of production. The impact of cost increases on supply has already been discussed. Subsidies are generally considered to be a "negative tax," so an increase in subsidies should lead to increases in supply. Using this perspective, the sign for the coefficient (*g*) must be negative.

Other Factors (*e*)

Variables other than those specifically described in the supply equation can affect supply. The price of related goods is one example. These additional factors can be lumped together in the error term, *e*.

As in the study of demand, it is helpful to isolate the effect of price changes on supply without the influence of the nonprice variables. This can be accomplished by applying the ceteris paribus assumption. The supply equation that results is given below:

$$Q_s = a + bP - c\overline{E} - d\overline{C} + e\overline{N} + f\overline{T} - g\overline{G} + \bar{e}.$$

The Supply Schedule

The supply schedule consists of the ordered pairs of quantity supplied and price (*Q,P*) as dictated by the supply equation. It shows the various quantities of products that suppliers are willing and able to bring to market at specific prices during a given period of time.

Table 4.4 Unit Price and Quantity Supplied, Good X

Unit Price (dollars)	Quantity Supplied t
4	90
3	65
2	40
1	15
0	−10 (0)

t = Units of time.

A supply schedule (table 4.4) can be constructed from the following hypothetical supply equation for good X. This equation includes only the price variable as an independent variable. The other independent variables have been held constant using the ceteris paribus assumption.

$$Q_s = -10 + 25P$$

The supply schedule shows that, as price rises, quantity supplied is increased. As price falls, quantity supplied decreases. This schedule indicates that at a price of zero dollars, −10 units of good X are supplied. While this may seem to make little sense, the message should be clear: there is some price between $1 and $0 at which no amount of supply of good X will be forthcoming. We can find that minimum price by setting the supply equation equal to zero and solving for P:

$$Q_s = -10 + 25P$$
$$0 = -10 + 25P$$
$$(0 + 10)/25 = \$0.40$$
$$P = \$0.40.$$

Thus, at a price of $0.40, the supply of good X is cut off completely.

The Supply Curve

Proceeding in the same manner as we did in the case of the demand curve, we can construct a supply curve (figure 4.6).

THE CONCEPTS OF DEMAND AND SUPPLY

Figure 4.6 Supply Curve
$Q_s = -10 + 25P$

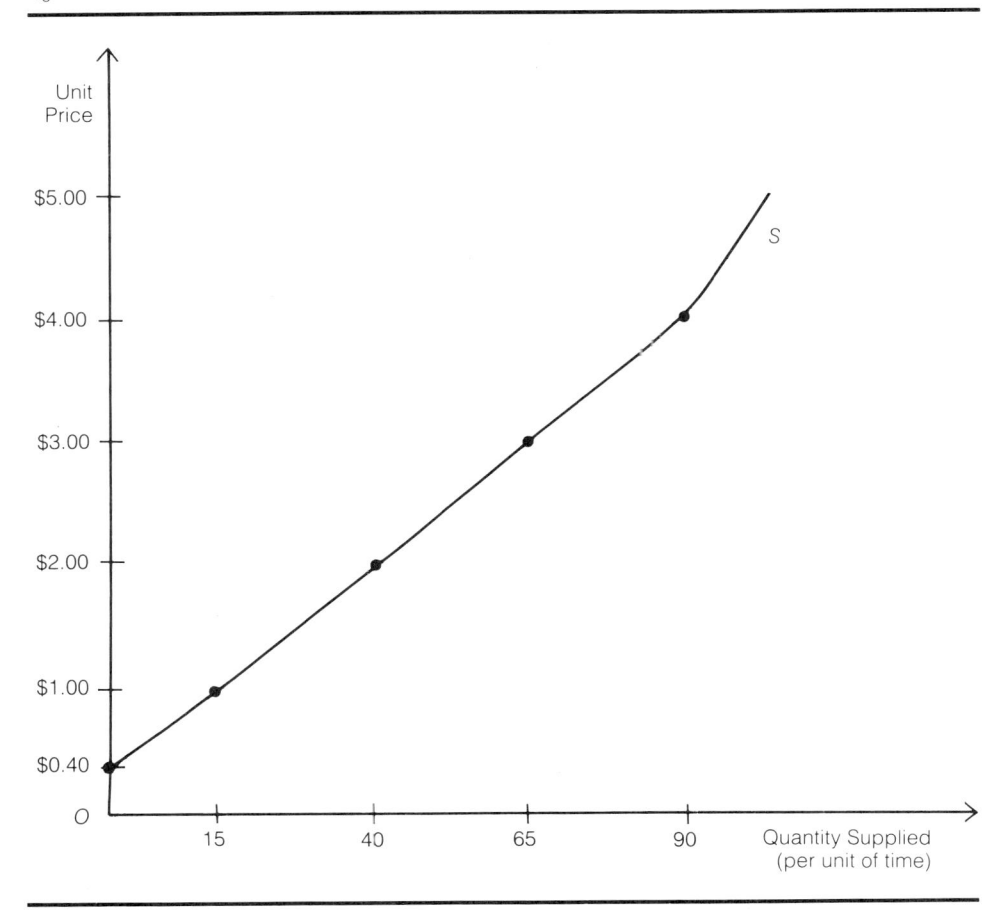

Here, quantity supplied replaces quantity demanded on the horizontal axis. The vertical axis still reflects the price per unit of good X. The supply curve slopes upward to the right, reflecting the direct relationship between price and quantity supplied. The supply curve intercepts the price axis at $0.40, indicating that at a price of $0.40 per unit, the quantity supplied is zero.

While a market supply curve has not been constructed for this example, it should be clear that the appropriate market supply curve is determined in the same manner as the market demand curve. It is constructed by summing the individual quantities demanded at each price.

ECONOMICS FOR BANKERS

Changes in Supply vs. Changes in Quantity Supplied

Figure 4.7 graphically illustrates the difference between a "change in supply" and a "change in quantity supplied." The logic is equivalent to that used in the case of changes in demand and changes in quantity demanded.

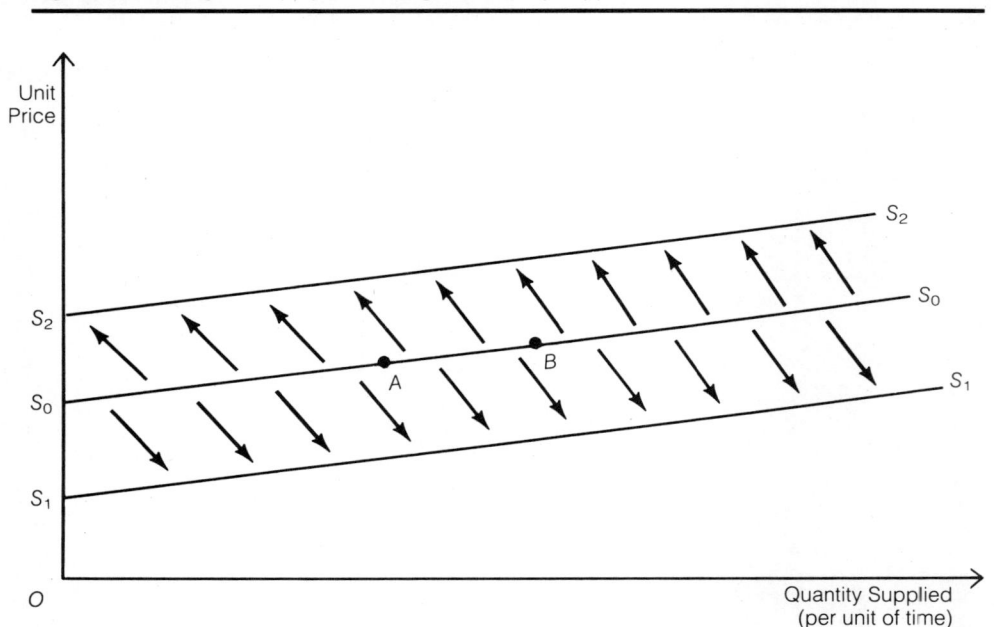

Figure 4.7 Change in Supply and Change in Quantity Supplied

In figure 4.7, point A on supply curve $S_0 S_0$ represents our original position. If the price of good X increases, there will be a change in quantity supplied, or a movement along the supply curve, to a new location such as point B. However, a change in one of the determinants of supply other than price will shift the curve itself—either to $S_1 S_1$, reflecting an increase in supply, or to $S_2 S_2$, reflecting a decrease in supply. To summarize, a change in quantity supplied is represented by a movement along the supply curve and is caused by a price change only. A change in supply, however, is represented by a shift in the whole curve and is caused by a change in one or more of the nonprice determinants of supply.

SUPPLY, DEMAND, AND THE MARKET SYSTEM

Demand encompasses the wishes of consumers while supply represents the hopes of suppliers. These dreams collide in the marketplace. As the forces of supply and demand come together, an invisible "collective bargaining" process ensues. This struggle both trims the consumer's wish list and deflates the hopes of suppliers. The end result is the establishment of a single price, called the equilibrium price, that balances quantity demanded with quantity supplied.

Market Equilibrium: The Marriage of Supply and Demand

The establishment of any price other than the equilibrium price leads to instability in the market. The conditions created as a result of market instability will force a revision in the price to the level at which the market is "cleared"—and quantity demanded is once again equal to quantity supplied. Consider a market supply and demand curve for good X (figure 4.8).

If a price of P_1 is established, the market will be unstable. At P_1, quantity supplied exceeds quantity demanded. A surplus of good X will develop, and market forces will lower prices.

If a price of P_2 is set, again the market will be unstable. At P_2, quantity demanded exceeds quantity supplied. A shortage of good X will arise, and market forces will raise the price of good X.

There is only one price at which neither a surplus nor a shortage will occur. That is the equilibrium price, P_e. At P_e, the quantity demanded and quantity supplied equal OQ_e. This is the price that clears the market of surpluses or shortages.

The amount of the surplus or shortage is easily derived from an analysis of the curves. At price P_1, amount OQ_1 is being offered for sale by firms, while amount OQ_2 is being Likewise, at price P_2, firms are willing to supply only amount OQ_2, while at that low price, consumers demand OQ_1. The amount of the shortage is ($OQ_1 - OQ_2$) or quantity Q_2Q_1. Notice that as long as the price is held above P_e, a surplus will develop. As long as the price is below P_e, a shortage of good X will exist. In either case, market forces will push the price toward the market clearing price, the equilibrium price of P_e. The quantity of good X supplied at the equilibrium price is called the equilibrium quantity.

Of course, not all consumers and firms are pleased with the equilibrium price and quantity level. Those consumers who are unwilling to pay a price of P_e or higher for good X

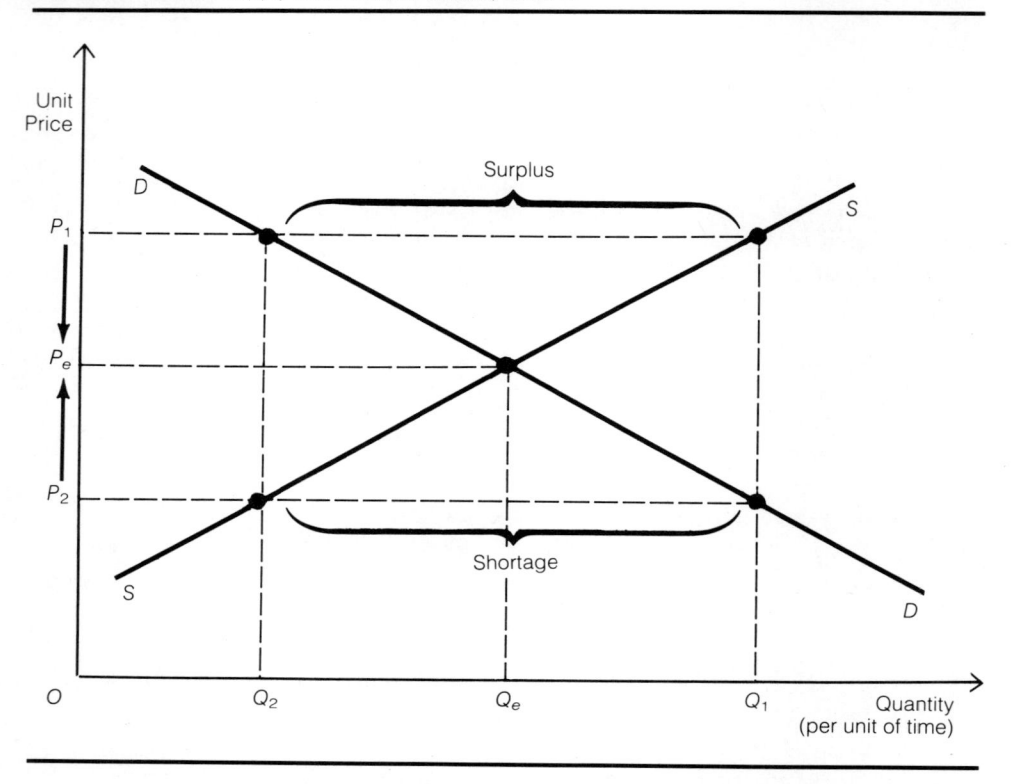

Figure 4.8 Market Supply and Demand Curves, Good X

are now unable to purchase any amount of good X. Any supplier who demands a price for good X above P_e is also disappointed.

How Changes in Demand and Supply Impact Market Equilibrium

A market in equilibrium remains stable until a change occurs in demand and/or supply. In reality, consumer tastes, expectations, income, and other demand variables change quite frequently. Conditions are also constantly changing on the supply side. Technological improvements, cost adjustments, and business openings and closings occur daily in modern economies. These changes precipitate changes in demand and supply that alter the conditions for market equilibrium. For any given market in any given time frame, eight different scenarios may develop. These separate changes in demand and supply have distinct effects on equilibrium price and quantity levels.

THE CONCEPTS OF DEMAND AND SUPPLY

Increase in Demand with Supply Constant

The equilibrium price and quantity will change in a particular way if demand increases while supply remains constant. This condition causes the demand curve to shift to the right (figure 4.9).

The original equilibrium price and quantity are represented by points P_e and Q_e respectively on curve D. If the demand for good X increases and the demand curve shifts to D', the new equilibrium condition will be P_e' and Q_e'. An increase in demand with supply constant normally leads to higher prices and greater quantity demanded.

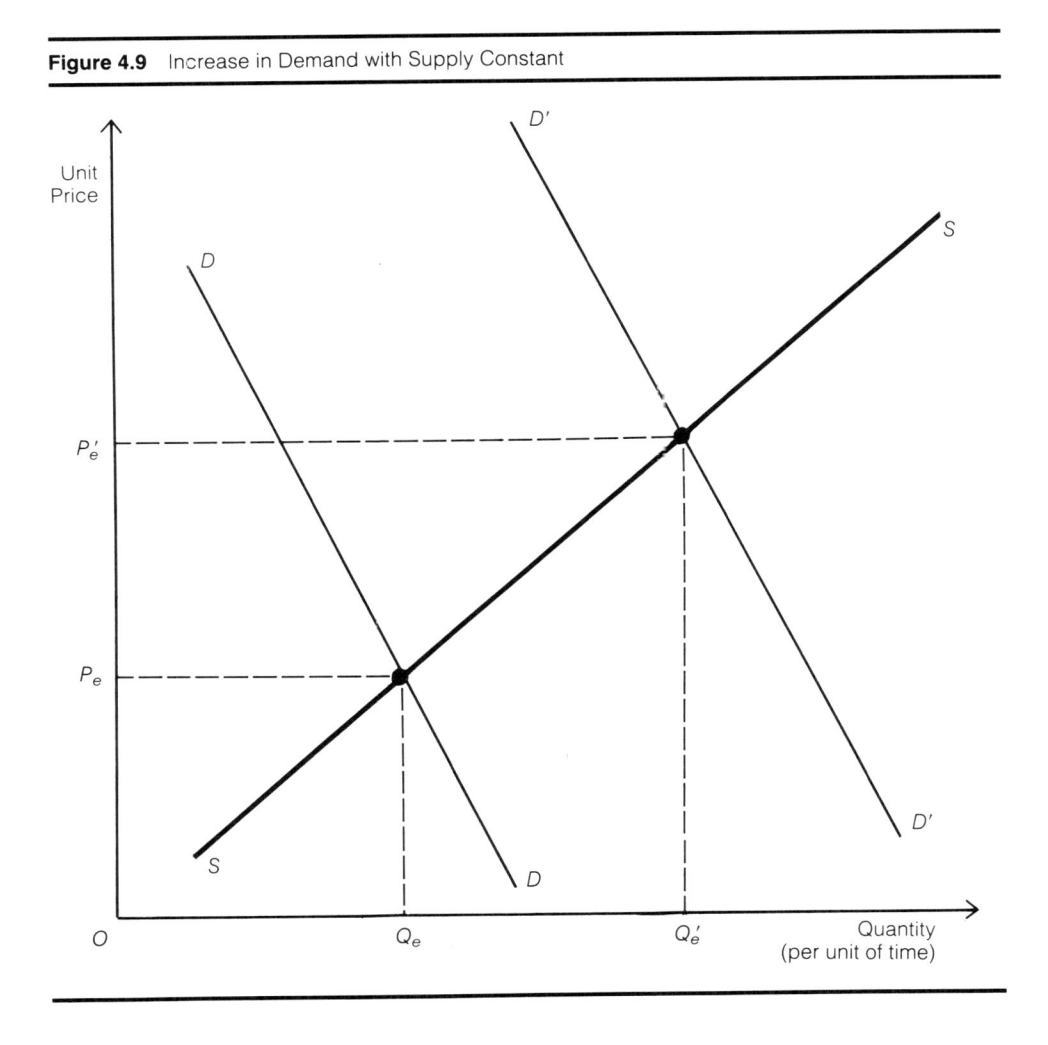

Figure 4.9 Increase in Demand with Supply Constant

123

Decrease in Demand with Supply Constant

A decrease in demand when supply remains constant will also change the equilibrium price and quantity (figure 4.10). Once again the original equilibrium price and quantity are P_e and Q_e respectively on curve D. A decrease in demand will shift the demand curve downward and to the left, to D'. The new equilibrium price and quantity will be lower than before.

Increase in Supply with Demand Constant

You should be able to predict what happens to equilibrium price and quantity in this instance. If supply is increased with demand constant (figure 4.11), consumers should be able to obtain more of the product at lower prices.

The shift in the supply curve to the right results in a lower price, P_e', and greater equilibrium quantity, Q_e'. This condition is a windfall for consumers!

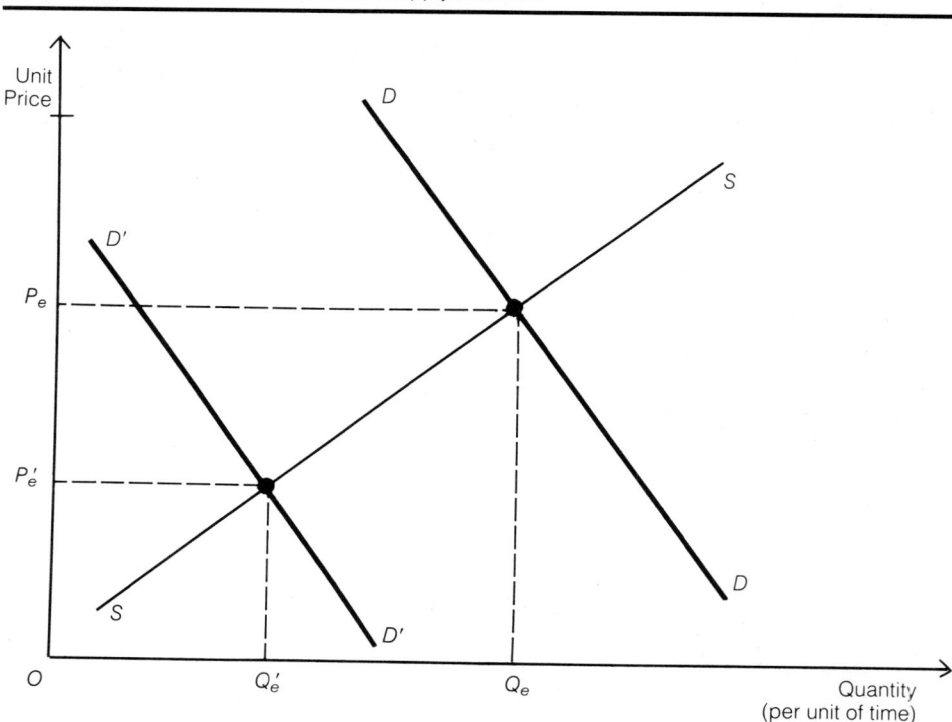

Figure 4.10 Decrease in Demand with Supply Constant

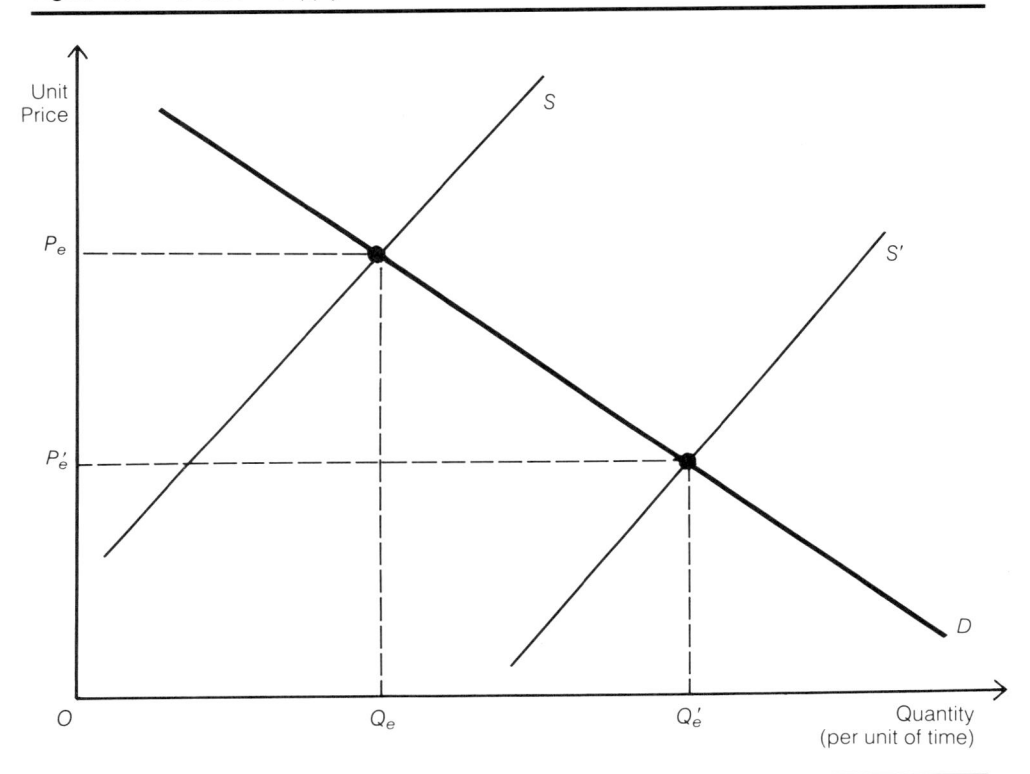

Figure 4.11 Increase in Supply with Demand Constant

Decrease in Supply with Demand Constant

A knowledgeable consumer winces at this predicament. A reduction in supply necessarily leads to higher prices and a cut in the quantity supplied in the new equilibrium. The shift of the supply curve (figure 4.12) causes the equilibrium price to rise to P_e' *and equilibrium quantity to fall to* Q_e'.

The first four scenarios have been relatively straightforward and easy to follow. When either supply or demand remains constant, you can predict with certainty the effect a change in the other factor will have on both equilibrium price and quantity. However, in the final four cases, the direction of the change in equilibrium price and quantity will be impossible to estimate without further analysis. The direction of a price or quantity change will be indeterminate unless information is provided as to the relative magnitude of the changes in supply and demand.

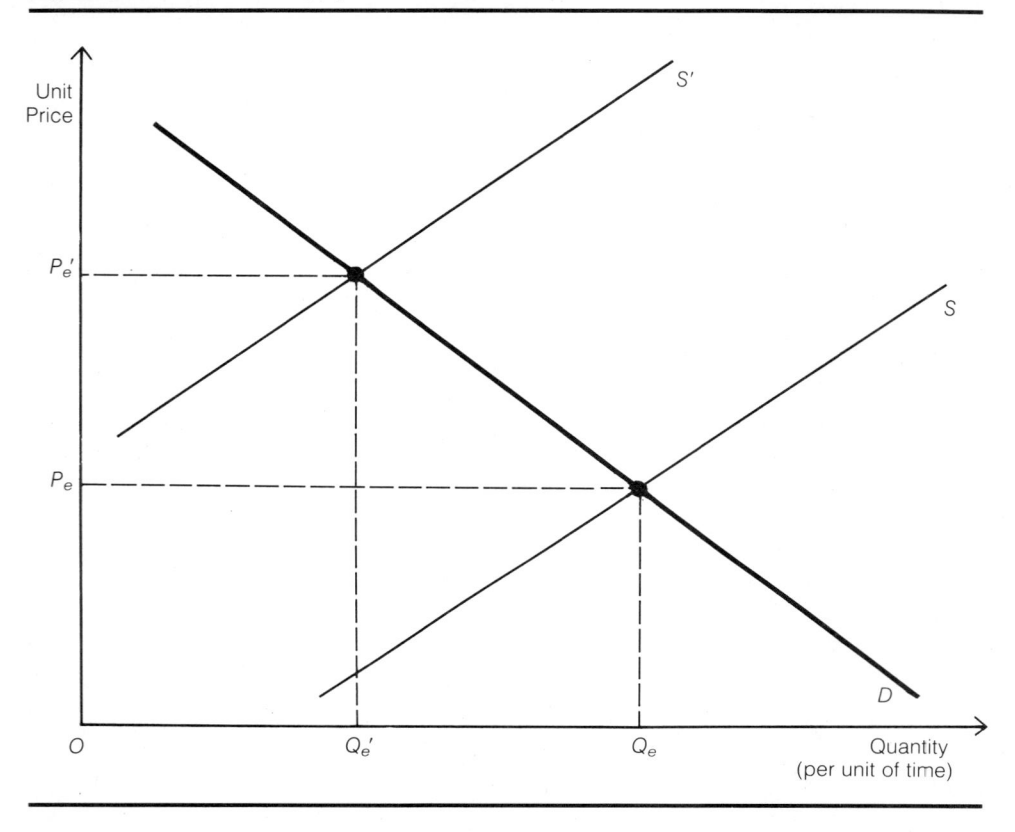

Figure 4.12 Decrease in Supply with Demand Constant

Increase in Demand with Decrease in Supply

Increased demand and decreased supply spell trouble for price-conscious consumers. Either change will lead to higher prices, and their combined effect will be similar. However, the effect of these changes on equilibrium quantity is uncertain. Taken separately, an increase in demand tends to raise quantity and a decrease in supply tends to lower it. Their combined effect thus depends upon the magnitude of the individual shifts. If the increase in demand is greater than the decrease in supply, the result will be a larger equilibrium quantity. However, if the increase in demand is smaller than the decrease in supply, the result will be a smaller equilibrium quantity. If the demand and supply change by identical proportions, their individual effects will cancel each other out and the equilibrium quantity will remain the same. These conditions can be illustrated graphically (figure 4.13). When the changes in demand and supply are of equal magnitude (panel a), the new equilibrium price is higher (P_e'), but the equilibrium quantity is unchanged.

THE CONCEPTS OF DEMAND AND SUPPLY

Figure 4.13 Increase in Demand with Decrease in Supply

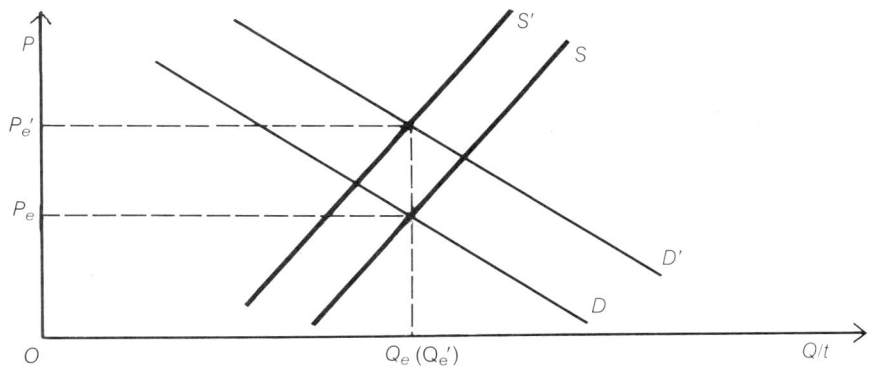

Panel a: Supply and demand changes are of equal proportion.

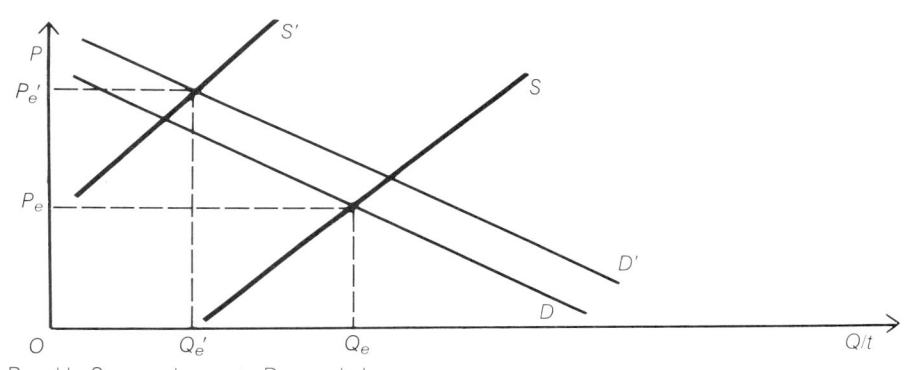

Panel b: Supply change > Demand change

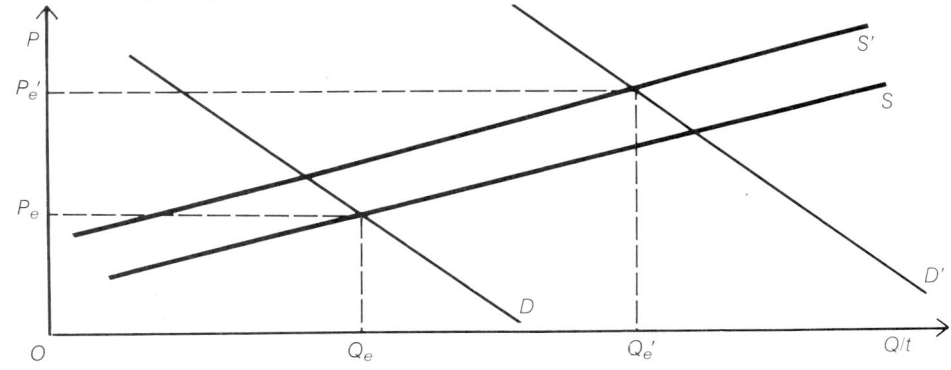

Panel c: Supply change < Demand change

P = Unit price
Q/t = Quantity (per unit of time).

When the decrease in supply is larger than the increase in demand (panel b), the equilibrium price rises as predicted to P_e' and the equilibrium quantity drops to Q_e'.

When the increase in demand is larger than the decrease in supply (panel c), the equilibrium price rises to P_e' and the equilibrium rises to Q_e'.

Increase in Supply with Increase in Demand

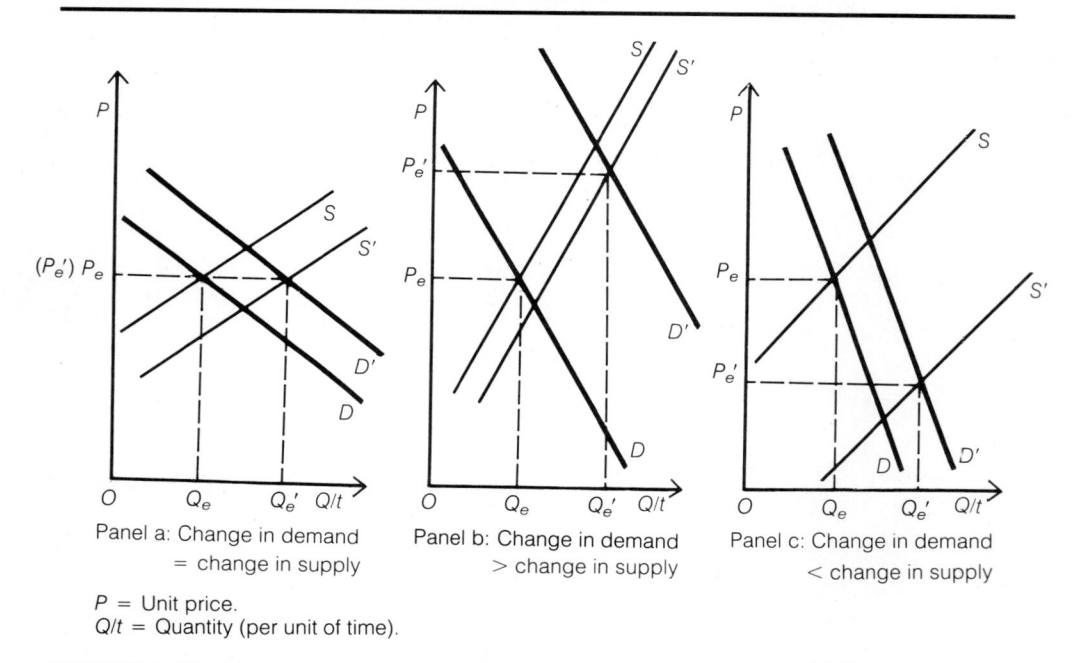

New firms are quick to enter growing markets if demand is increasing and the profit picture is appealing. Thus, the sixth combination of changes in supply and demand probably occurs more frequently than the other scenarios. To determine how an increase in supply with an increase in demand will affect price and quantity, it is helpful to examine the effects of the changes individually.

Increases in supply and increases in demand both tend to raise the equilibrium quantity. Taken together, they will clearly have the same effect. However, while increased demand tends to raise the equilibrium price, an increase in supply tends to lower it. The ultimate change in price is determined by the relative magnitudes of the individual shifts. As in the previous example, there are three possible outcomes, each of which may be depicted graphically (figure 4.14).

Figure 4.14 Increase in Supply with Increase in Demand

Panel a: Change in demand = change in supply

Panel b: Change in demand > change in supply

Panel c: Change in demand < change in supply

P = Unit price.
Q/t = Quantity (per unit of time).

First, the increases in demand and supply may be of equal magnitude (panel a). These changes offset each other and leave the equilibrium price unchanged (at P_e). The increase in demand may be greater than the increase in quantity supplied (panel b). The result is an increase in the equilibrium price (from P_e to P_e').

Finally, supply may change by a greater proportion than demand (panel c). This condition forces the price down (from P_e to P_e').

Notice that in all three cases, equilibrium quantity has increased.

Check Your Understanding

Changes in supply and changes in demand each affect market equilibrium in predictable ways. As shown by the material above, however, when changes occur in both supply and demand, the net effect depends on which change has occurred in greater proportion—in a sense, on which change is dominant. Check your understanding of the concepts discussed in this chapter by analyzing how the following two situations will affect the equilibrium price and equilibrium quantity at a given market:

A. Decrease in Demand with Increase in Supply
B. Decrease in Demand with Decrease in Supply

For each of these situations, ask yourself the following questions:

1. What is the effect of the change in demand?
2. What is the effect of the change in supply?
3. If the change in demand equals the change in supply, how does this affect the equilibrium price? The equilibrium quantity?
4. If the change in demand is greater than the change in supply, how does this affect the market equilibrium? If the change in demand is smaller?

Finally, using figures 4.9 through 4.14 as models, construct graphs that show the changes in the market supply and demand curves that can be predicted for situations A and B.

Answer: By itself, a decrease in demand will shift the demand curve downward and to the left, lowering the equilibrium price and quantity. An increase in supply will also tend to lower prices but will raise the equilibrium quantity. A decrease in supply, on the other hand, will ordinarily raise the equilibrium price and lower the equilibrium quantity.

Continued

> In situation A, the decrease in demand with an increase in supply will lower the equilibrium price. The equilibrium quantity may remain unchanged (if the amount of the decrease in demand equals the amount of the increase in supply); it may go down (if the decrease in demand is greater than the increase in supply); or, it may go up (if the decrease in demand is smaller than the increase in supply). This last possibility is similar to the digital watch industry example discussed above.
>
> In situation B, the decrease in demand with a decrease in supply will result in a lower equilibrium quantity, but the change in equilibrium price will depend on the relative magnitude of the changes in demand and supply. Again, if the changes are equal, they will cancel each other out—and the equilibrium price will remain the same. If the change in demand is greater than the change in supply, the price will go down. If the change in demand is smaller than the change in supply, the price will go up.

SUMMARY

Two independent forces that affect free and competitive markets are supply and demand. The impact of these forces on each other and on the market follows distinct patterns, which can be analyzed.

The law of demand states that the relation between a product's price and the quantity demanded is inverse—that is, as price rises, less is demanded. Factors that may affect demand include the income, wealth, and taste of consumers; price expectations; prices of related goods; market size; and various nonmonetary factors.

The law of supply states that the relation between price and quantity supplied is usually direct. In other words, as the price of a product rises, more is supplied. Factors that may affect supply include price expectations, production or resource costs, number of suppliers, technology, government taxes and subsidies, and other nonmonetary factors.

The equilibrium price is the price of a commodity at which neither a surplus nor a shortage will occur in the market. If any price other than the equilibrium price is established, market instability will force a revision in the price until equilibrium is reached. On a graph, the equilibrium price appears where the supply curve and the demand curve intersect.

In theory, a market in equilibrium remains stable unless a change occurs in demand, supply, or both. In the real world, demand and supply curves are constantly shifting. A change in demand or a change in supply may result in a new equilibrium price, a new equilibrium quantity, or both, depending on the relative shifts of the curves.

Movements along supply and demand curves result from changes in the price of the commodity while the other determinants of supply and demand remain constant. These movements are known as changes in the quantity supplied and changes in the quantity demanded.

KEY WORDS

ceteris paribus	error term
change in demand	independent goods
change in quantity demanded	inferior products
change in quantity supplied	law of demand
change in supply	law of supply
complementary goods	market demand
demand curve	market demand curve
demand equation	market equilibrium
demand schedule	market supply curve
determinants of demand	normal products
determinants of supply	price of related goods
diminishing marginal utility	supply curve
equilibrium price	supply equation
equilibrium quantity	supply schedule

Questions for Review

1. A retail clothing store recently lowered the price of double-breasted suits by 50 percent, yet sales declined. Does this mean the law of demand is invalid? Explain.

2. The demand for pocket calculators has risen dramatically in the past few years, yet their price has fallen. Show graphically what must have happened in the calculator market.

3. In the 1970s, U.S. motorists experienced gasoline shortages. Many states rationed gasoline using the numbers on license plates. Owners of vehicles with odd-numbered plates could purchase gasoline on odd-numbered days. Those with even-numbered plates could drive up to the pumps on even-numbered days. This worked well unless your car had even-numbered license plates and you had to take a long trip on an odd-numbered day. Explain the simple market solution to this problem of a shortage. What would be the repercussions of a market solution?

4. Draw a supply and demand diagram for the frozen orange juice market. Label the initial price and quantity.

   a) Show what would happen to the price and quantity if a freeze destroyed a large portion of the crop.

   b) Show what would happen if the price of apple juice fell drastically.

   c) Show what would happen if researchers discovered natural vitamin C was helpful in the prevention of certain health disorders.

5. A surplus of a particular good normally indicates a misallocation of resources to the production of that good. How does the price system restore efficiency?

6. What would happen to the demand for home equity loans in your bank in each of the following situations?

   a) The bank announces that the processing fee for the loans will increase by 5 percent, effective 2 weeks from today.

   b) The federal government grants a 20 percent reduction in federal personal income taxes.

   c) The price of houses increases.

   d) Apartment rents increase to the point where they are higher than a typical monthly mortgage payment.

7. Assuming that producers and consumers choose and act in their own respective self-interest, how can there ever be market equilibrium?

8. How can expectations of economic conditions affect supply?

9. Why is it so important to distinguish between changes in demand and changes in supply from changes in quantity demanded and changes in quantity supplied?

10. Some people buy more of some goods, such as gold jewelry and exotic foreign cars, as their prices go up. Does this negate the law of demand? Explain.

ENDNOTES

1. Economists respect mathematics and use it to a great extent in their work. The reason for their apparent disregard of mathematical convention here is that Alfred Marshall, the economist who first constructed and popularized the demand curve around 1890, either ignored or was unaware of this convention. He placed price on the vertical axis and quantity on the horizontal. Out of tribute to Marshall, economists have constructed the demand curve in this form ever since.

ECONOMICS IN THE NEWS

Price Stability Encourages Oil Industry

Rise From $18 Floor Expected; Drilling Lags

By James Tanner
and Youssef M. Ibrahim
Staff Reporters of *The Wall Street Journal*

Confidence is growing in the oil industry that some stability has returned to world petroleum markets.

Oil companies still are cautious about stepping up exploration spending—reduced by 40% since last year's oil-price collapse—but the consensus is that petroleum prices will hold around the current level of $18 a barrel and then rise before year's end.

"There are encouraging signs that the worst times for our industry may be ending," says Richard M. Morrow, chairman of Amoco Corp.

Among the signs cited by Mr. Morrow and other oil executives and analysts are anticipated further gains in world petroleum demand this year, coupled with indications of rapid declines in excess petroleum inventories despite a lingering gasoline glut in the U.S. Even more important is the mounting evidence of a new-found discipline within the Organization of Petroleum Exporting Countries, whose push for increased market share caused oil prices to collapse last year.

Price projections by both OPEC and the oil industry have often been wrong in the past, of course. Thus, most oil companies plan to hold spending down for several more months until there is further proof that prices won't fall back to last year's $10 low. But if prices hold at the current level or rise, "by later this year we'll see drilling beginning to recover and positive year-to-year comparisons in capital expenditures," says Paul Mlotok, international oil analyst at Salomon Brothers Inc. Many U.S. oil operators insist they won't resume much exploration in this country, however, until the price of oil again reaches $25 a barrel.

Senior OPEC officials aren't too eager to declare an end to their struggle to reverse the oil-market volatility of last year, which saw prices plunge to $10 a barrel from $28 at the beginning of 1986. So far, they say, OPEC has successfully passed the toughest test that was anticipated since its December decision to sell oil only at prices equivalent to $18 a barrel.

A widespread oil company boycott failed to sway the cartel from its resolve to stick with fixed prices, eliminate secret discounts and limit its 13 members' total production to less than 15.8 million barrels a day. Now, as demand for OPEC oil slowly returns, the danger is that some oil producers won't resist the temptation to sell more oil than their individual quotas permit.

"We are now passing the danger mark," says a senior OPEC official who asked not to be identified. "If everyone keeps output low we will be on much firmer ground for the rest of the year. It isn't unlikely that prices could go to the $20 level."

Industry sources say OPEC by and large stuck with the ceiling of 15.8 million barrels a day in the first quarter. But that may have been the result, at least in part, of a slackening in demand for OPEC oil since the new fixed-price schedule went into effect Jan. 1. Many petroleum refiners, particularly in the U.S., were hurt by shrinking profit margins because of higher crude costs and refused to commit to long-term contracts at OPEC's official prices.

But the refiners are beginning to run down their crude inventories to the point where they must buy oil again whatever the price. As a result, OPEC's production is rising above the first-quarter level. According to Oil Buyers Guide, a trade newsletter, OPEC output in the first three weeks of April averaged 16.4 million barrels a day.

Industry analysts say it is too early to suggest that OPEC is breaking discipline, because output figures tend to be higher at the beginning of the month, when producers are loading more tankers with exports. Another important barometer is what action OPEC will take at its June meeting.

Still, demand for OPEC oil is expected to be higher during much of the remainder of this year. Peter F. Holmes, chairman of Shell Transport & Trading Co., the British partner of the Royal Dutch/Shell Group, estimates the call on OPEC oil to average 16.9 million barrels a day for all this year and then increase further at a rate of around one million barrels a day each year after 1987.

"OPEC just went through the worst," agrees Mr. Mlotok of Salomon Brothers. He looks for a 1.3% increase in 1987 petroleum demand in the non-communist world. OPEC should benefit from the increased demand because non-OPEC production is expected to remain flat at 28 million barrels a day.

The senior planner of one major U.S.-based oil company foresees a smaller increase in the non-communist world's demand—only 1%—to 47.7 million barrels a day for 1987 from 47.2 million barrels a day in 1986. But he expects a continuing drop in non-OPEC production, largely in the U.S.—where output began falling sharply last year in the wake of the oil-price collapse—and in the North Sea.

The planning official thinks demand for gasoline will rise faster than for other fuels, easing the burdensome buildup of motor-fuel inventories in the U.S. Overall, he says, the world's above-ground supplies of oil were drawn down by about 200 million barrels in the first quarter. Inventories should decline an additional 100 million barrels to reach a "comfortable" level of about 4.2 billion barrels for the industry, he says. "If no one gets reckless," he says, that could happen over the next four to six weeks—holding prices firm at $18 a barrel or higher for the remainder of the year.

The spot, or non-contract, price of West Texas Intermediate, the barometer of U.S. oil prices, rose 15 cents, to $18.85 a barrel, yesterday.

Industry sources generally expect oil prices to rise next year by at least as much as the inflation rate. Eventually, they suggest, prices will rebound beyond the prior peak of $40 a barrel, although there's little agreement on the timing.

Though drilling costs plunged in the wake of the 1986 oil-price collapse, the heavily drilled U.S. remains one of the world's highest-cost producers. Oil operators in the U.S., as elsewhere, are more confident that OPEC's $18 price will stick, but they say that this isn't enough to spur much new drilling.

This mood is underscored by the continuing slump in U.S. drilling even though oil prices currently are $4 a barrel higher than the 1986 average of $14 a barrel. As of last week, according to the latest Hughes Tool Co. count, only 765 drilling rigs were operating in the U.S. That was 15 more rigs than were active the preceding week, but the latest count still is down from the 855 units that were active a year earlier and sharply lower than the 4,500 rigs operating at the late-1981 peak.

"At the absolute minimum level of prices, we are going to have to have somewhere between $22 and $25 a barrel and a fairly long period of stability to get any activity (in U.S. exploration)," says H.B. Scoggins, president of the Independent Petroleum Association of America, which represents more than half of the nation's estimated 10,000 independent oil operators.

Major oil companies are also unlikely to increase their exploration spending for some months, at least in the U.S., even if prices remain firm at $18 a barrel or rise.

Oil prices are back near a level, however, that could spur further development of existing oil fields in the U.S., as well as additional exploration for natural gas if prices for that fuel continue to move in lock step with those for oil.

Reprinted by permission of *The Wall Street Journal*, © Dow Jones & Company, Inc., 1987. All Rights Reserved.

CHAPTER FIVE

DEMAND AND SUPPLY IN THE MARKETPLACE

Objectives

After reading this chapter, you should be able to

- explain how a change in a product's price affects supply and demand curves
- describe how changes in quantity demanded or in quantity supplied can influence prices
- explain the difference between price supports and price ceilings
- describe how usury laws affect supply and demand for money
- describe the effects of minimum wage laws on supply and demand for labor
- discuss the concept of elasticity
- determine the elasticity coefficients of demand and supply
- list and describe the five categories of elasticity coefficients
- define and use the arc formula to measure demand elasticity and supply elasticity
- calculate elasticity of demand using a demand curve
- measure elasticity of demand using the revenue test
- describe the most important determinants of elasticity of supply and demand
- explain the concepts of cross elasticity of demand and income elasticity of demand
- discuss the concept of elasticity of demand for labor

The concepts of supply and demand and their interaction in the marketplace are powerful tools of economic analysis. Specific markets are studied to explain behavior in prices and output. Supply and demand theory is also used to study the resource market and to explain wage and salary movements, interest rates, and rents, etc. In this chapter, we will examine the role of the supply and demand market mechanism using numerical values for prices and quantity supplied and demanded, and several actual product and service markets. Finally, we will explore the very important concept of elasticity.

MARKET EQUILIBRIUM: A NUMERICAL EXAMPLE

We can create supply and demand curves for a hypothetical product, good X (figure 5.1). Given a price of $3 per unit of good X, the quantity supplied at this price is indicated by point c on the supply curve (S). At $3 per unit, 150 units of X will be supplied. However, at that relatively high price, quantity demanded—point b on the demand curve—is only 50 units. The quantity supplied exceeds the quantity demanded by distance bc. This represents a surplus of 100 units of good X.

If the unit price falls to $1 as firms scramble to sell off the excess supply, specific changes will occur in both quantity demanded and quantity supplied. Remember that these are changes in *quantity* demanded and supplied, not changes in demand and supply. The *price* of the product has changed but the other determinants of supply and demand have not. The lower price will cause quantity demanded to rise. Quantity demanded will move down curve D from point b to point e. At point e, quantity demanded is 175 units of good X. The lower price also forces quantity supplied to slide down curve S from point c to point d. At point d, quantity supplied is 35 units of good X. At the $1 price, quantity demanded exceeds quantity supplied by 140 units. This shortage is represented by distance de.

The shortage will stimulate the firms to raise the price of good X. The bidding stops slightly above $2, where, at point a, quantity demanded and supplied are equal to 100 units of good X.

APPLICATIONS OF SUPPLY AND DEMAND

To a banker, the most important economic "price" is the interest rate. It may seem strange to view the interest rate as a price, but that is exactly what it is: a price paid for funds. Deposits are the primary source of bank lending power. Financial institutions compete to attract the deposits of customers by offering services (such as check-writing privileges) or promising future interest payments. Economic agents needing financing for the purchase of goods or services usually come to a bank (or other financial institution) to obtain these

ECONOMICS FOR BANKERS

Figure 5.1 Supply and Demand Curves, Good X

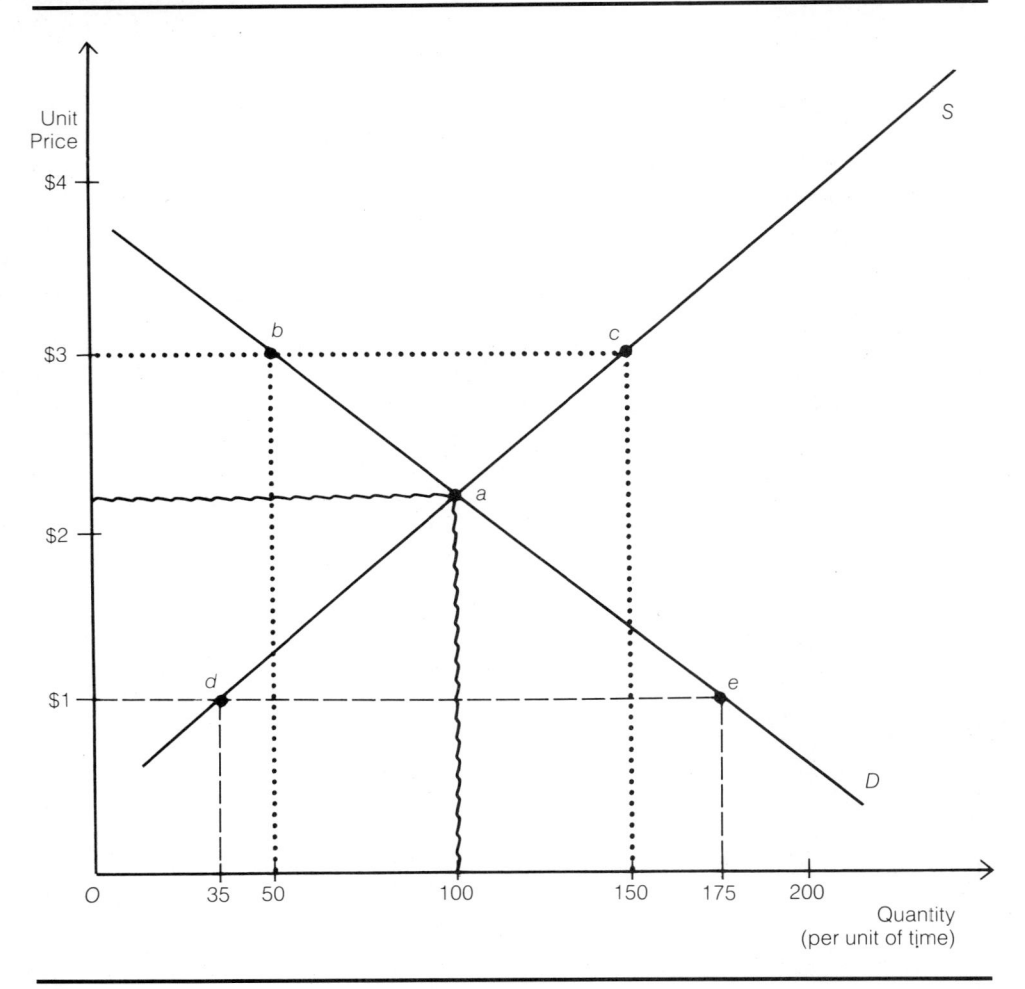

funds. The flow of loanable funds and their price—interest—is controlled by the market mechanism.

If we plot the supply and demand curves for loanable funds (figure 5.2), notice that the label of each axis is different from the label used when we plot the supply and demand curves of a product. Here, the horizontal axis represents the quantity of loanable funds, measured in dollars per time period. Do not confuse this with the vertical (price) axis of the product demand and supply curve. Here, the dollar term represents an amount of funds. On the price axis, the dollar term is a measure of a value or price, not an amount.

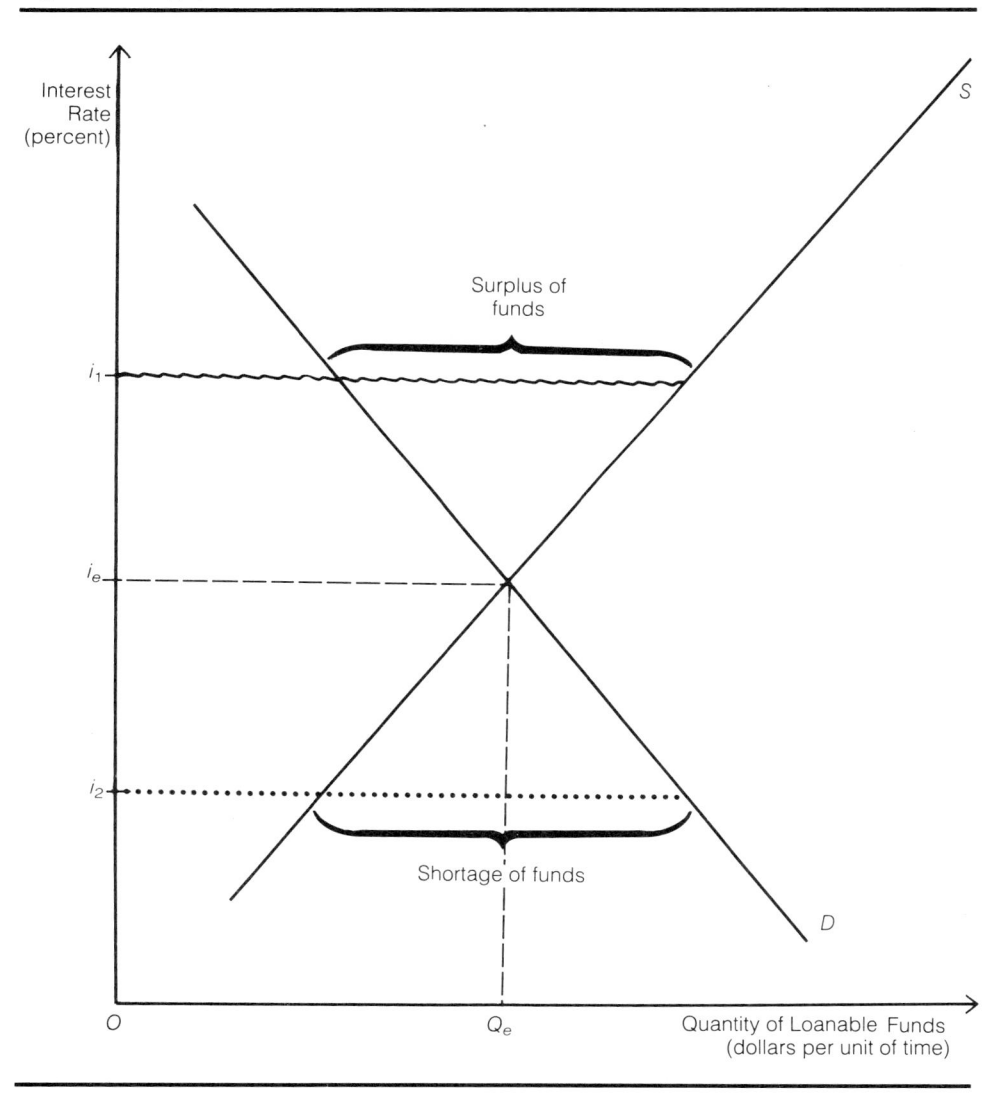

Figure 5.2 Supply and Demand Curves, Loanable Funds

The vertical axis shows the range of interest rates measured in percentages. If the interest rate is i_1, quantity supplied exceeds quantity demanded. At these "high" rates, a surplus of funds exists and interest rates will begin to fall. If the interest rate is i_2, quantity supplied is less than quantity demanded. A shortage of funds would tend to push rates up to an equilibrium position i_e, and the equilibrium quantity of such a price would be Q_e.

Change in Supply and Demand of Loanable Funds

The supply and demand of loanable funds can be influenced by a number of factors. A major influence on the supply of funds available to the commercial banking industry is the actions of the Federal Reserve.[1] A change in the demand or supply of loanable funds will cause a shift in the curves, which will alter interest rates and the equilibrium quantity.

When economists speak of interest rates, they realize there are many different rates attached to various financial instruments. Interest rates depend primarily on the maturity and riskiness of the loan. One of the best-known interest rate measures is the prime rate. The prime rate can be understood as a benchmark that a bank establishes from time to time and uses in computing an appropriate rate of interest for a particular loan contract. This benchmark is generally based on numerous considerations, including the bank's supply of funds, cost of funds, administrative costs, and competition from other suppliers of credit.

The prime rate changes with market supply and demand conditions. In recent years, this "price" of money has changed frequently in response to market forces (table 5.1). In 1980, the prime rate changed 39 times.

The equilibrium price can vary from relatively low to relatively high rates. The average annual price of money (table 5.2) between 1975–86 ranged from a low of 6.82 per-

Table 5.1 Changes to Prime Rate Charged by Banks on Short-Term Business Loans, 1929–86

Year	No. of Changes	Year	No. of Changes	Year	No. of Changes
1929	1	1949	0	1969	3
1930	1	1950	1	1970	5
1931	1	1951	3	1971	13
1932	1	1952	0	1972	7
1933	1	1953	1	1973	17
1934	0	1954	1	1974	23
1935	0	1955	2	1975	21
1936	0	1956	2	1976	8
1937	0	1957	1	1977	6
1938	0	1958	3	1978	15
1939	0	1959	2	1979	15
1940	0	1960	1	1980	39
1941	0	1961	0	1981	25
1942	0	1962	0	1982	12
1943	0	1963	0	1983	3
1944	0	1964	0	1984	10
1945	0	1965	1	1985	3
1946	0	1966	3	1986	4
1947	1	1967	3		
1948	1	1968	5		

Source: Federal Reserve Board.

Table 5.2 Average Prime Rate, 1947–86

Year	Percent	Year	Percent	Year	Percent
1947	1.52	1961	4.50	1975	7.86
1948	1.85	1962	4.50	1976	6.84
1949	2.00	1963	4.50	1977	6.82
1950	2.07	1964	4.50	1978	9.06
1951	2.56	1965	4.54	1979	12.67
1952	3.00	1966	5.62	1980	15.27
1953	3.17	1967	5.63	1981	18.87
1954	3.05	1968	6.28	1982	14.86
1955	3.16	1969	7.95	1983	10.79
1956	3.77	1970	7.91	1984	12.04
1957	4.20	1971	5.70	1985	9.93
1958	3.83	1972	5.25	1986	8.17
1959	4.48	1973	8.02		
1960	4.82	1974	10.80		

Source: Federal Reserve Board.

cent in 1977 to a high of 18.87 percent in 1981, an increase of approximately 200 percent in 4 years. The average annual prime rate for 1985 is roughly half the 1981 average.

The determinants of supply and demand for loanable funds are manifold and complex, and go beyond the scope of this text. But it might be an interesting task for you to speculate on the factors that affect changes in the prime rate.[2]

Gasoline Prices: Supply and Demand

The U.S. gasoline shortage of the 1970s was accompanied by sharply escalating prices at the pumps. The initial thrust behind the price hikes was the formation and ascent to power of the Organization of Petroleum Exporting Countries (OPEC). Formed in 1960 as an effort to combat low crude oil prices, this cartel was able, through production cuts and the effects of a U.S. embargo, to raise the price of crude oil from approximately $2.50 per barrel in the early 1960s to $12.00 per barrel in 1973.

Since crude oil is a raw material in the production of gasoline, this cost increase forced gasoline suppliers to shift their supply curves upward to the left—in other words, to decrease supply. Gasoline suppliers also ''demanded'' a higher price for every possible quantity of gasoline sold in order to recover their inflated operating costs. At the same time, American motorists were consuming gasoline at unprecedented rates. Domestic-built cars were large and luxurious, and generally had low gas mileage. New regulations required the attachment of antipollution devices that further lowered automobiles' gasoline efficiency ratings (miles per gallon). Other factors, such as the increased number of commuters and a growing interstate highway system, spurred demand for gasoline even higher.

ECONOMICS FOR BANKERS

The combination of decreasing supply and increasing demand resulted in skyrocketing prices. The price of gasoline soared from about $0.50 per gallon in 1977 to approximately $1.30 in 1981. The history of gasoline prices can be traced through demand and supply analysis. Figure 5.3 shows the shifts in demand and supply from 1977–81.

In figure 5.3, D_1 and S_1 represent the supply and demand curves for gasoline in 1977. The equilibrium price was approximately $0.50 per gallon. Increased demand and supply by 1981—curves D_2 and S_2 respectively—resulted in a rise in price to well above $1 per

Figure 5.3 Supply and Demand for Gasoline, 1977 and 1981

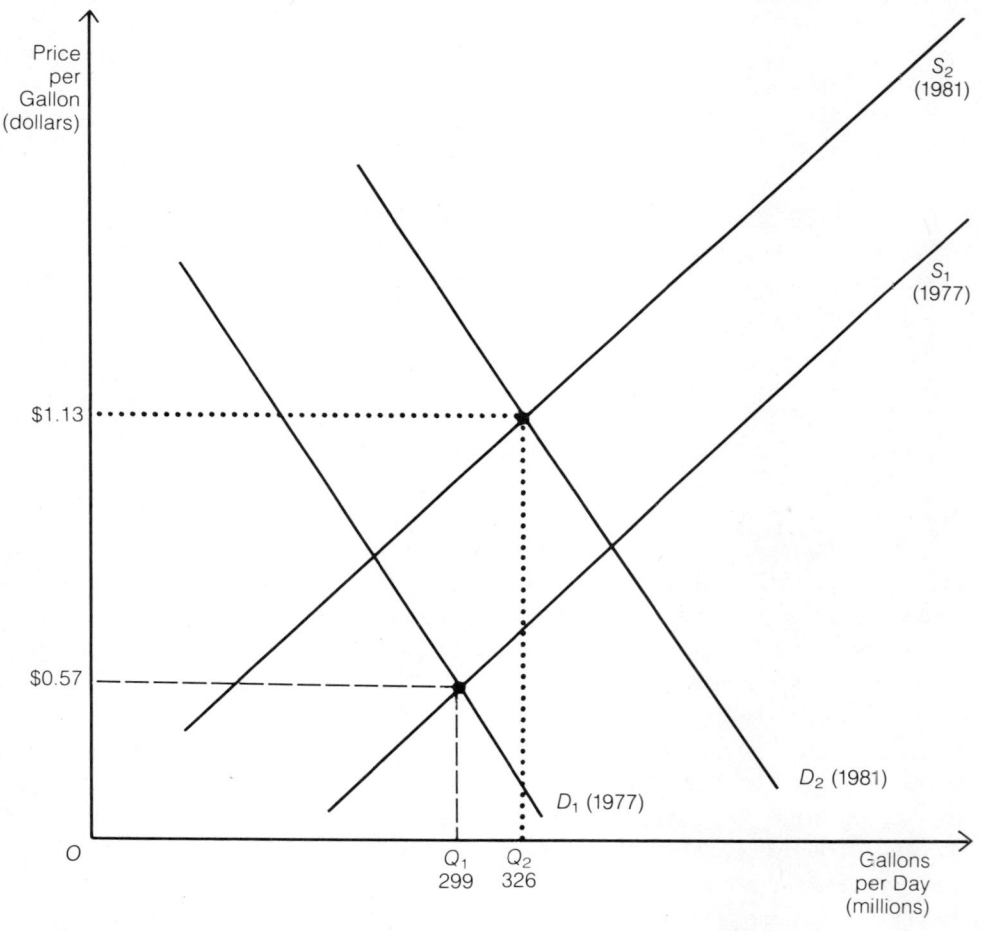

Source: Data from Statistical Abstract of the U.S., 1987 U.S. Department of Commerce. Bureau of the Census, pp. 470, 590.

146

Table 5.3 Price and Consumption of Gasoline

Year	Average Price per Gallon (dollars)	Gallons Consumed per Car
1973	0.39	736
1975	0.57	685
1980	1.19	579
1981	1.31	555
1982	1.22	563
1983	1.16	555

Source: Statistical Abstract of the U.S., 1987, U.S. Department of Commerce, Bureau of the Census, pp. 470, 590.

gallon. Table 5.3 shows gasoline price consumption figures for selected years around this tumultuous period.

At one point in the crisis, the U.S. government intervened by imposing price limits on retail sales of gasoline. While there were sporadic reports of "cheating" on the part of some gas station owners, the federal price limits "froze" prices as designed. However, the market—in this case, domestic oil companies—reacted by reducing quantity supplied. The artificially "low" price diminished consumers' desire to conserve fuel and simultaneously increased quantity demanded. When quantity demanded exceeds quantity supplied, the outcome is inevitable: shortages. The shortages shocked and angered American motorists, who blamed OPEC for the entire fiasco. Yet, a solution to the shortage problem was there all along. The free market solution would have been to let the price rise to its equilibrium level. Higher prices would have spurred stronger conservation efforts, reduced demand, and stimulated supply. Indeed, in recent years, OPEC's power has shown signs of weakening. Conservation efforts on the part of consumers have stabilized demand, while increased exploration led to the discovery and development of new sources of oil. Crude oil prices have fallen substantially, and the price of gasoline has followed suit. During the crisis, however, political solutions to the market problem were sought. These solutions will be explored in the next section of this chapter.[3]

MARKET INTERVENTION

The gasoline price freeze imposed during the 1970s to protect motorists from "exorbitant" prices is just one example of government attempts to control the market equilibrium price. Federal, state, and local governments have passed numerous pieces of legislation that attempt to regulate prices in certain markets. Government-established prices are called price supports and price controls.

Price Supports vs. Price Controls

A price support establishes the legal price for a product at a level above market equilibrium. These prices are sometimes called "price floors" because the market price may not fall below them. Price supports are established when the market price is considered to be too low for suppliers.

A price control fixes the legal price at a level below market equilibrium. These prices are also known as "price ceilings" because they establish a maximum price, or ceiling price, above which the market price may not rise. A price ceiling is sought when the market equilibrium price is considered to be too high for consumers. Establishing a price ceiling was the market intervention technique used during the gasoline shortage.

The arguments supporting market intervention are numerous and can be compelling. It is important to remember, however, that the market does not distinguish between normal and artificially set prices—it simply seeks out that price which equates quantity supplied with quantity demanded. We will examine some specific cases in which market intervention has been used. The issue of government intervention in markets is a normative issue, which generates strong opinions and heated debate among economists.[4]

Usury Laws

Many states have passed usury laws that stipulate a maximum interest rate lending institutions may charge for various types of loans. A usury law operates as a price control or ceiling.

The legal limit on the rate of interest that may be charged for the use of bank credit cards varies from state to state (see table 5.4). A lending institution may legally offer credit cards with an interest rate of 24 percent in the District of Columbia, but would be subject to heavy civil and criminal penalties for doing so in the state of Michigan. Normally, usury

Table 5.4 Bank Credit Card Finance Charges: Maximum Allowed by Law for Selected States, 1985

State	Amount (percent)
District of Columbia	24
Florida	18
Georgia	18
Hawaii	18
Kentucky	21
Louisiana	18
Michigan	18
North Dakota	18
Rhode Island	21
Tennessee	24
West Virginia	18

Source: Office of the General Counsel, American Bankers Association, 1985.

laws have no effect on the credit markets. When market interest rates are safely below the usury limits, the usury law is not triggered—and the market operates to allocate scarce resources to their most highly valued uses. However, when supply and demand conditions change, and lending institutions are forced to pay high interest rates on deposit instruments, the market interest charged on loans can rise above the usury limit. Because of the limits imposed by the law, portions of the bank's lending activity may become unprofitable. The bank may be forced to curtail such activity, and some bank customers may be unable to receive financing, even if they are willing to pay market rates. In other words, a shortage of credit develops.

Minimum Wage Laws

As part of the Fair Labor Standards Act of 1938, the U.S. Congress introduced a minimum wage law, which provided, for certain classes of workers, a minimum wage of $0.25 per hour. That minimum has been raised many times through the years and is currently $3.35 per hour. Future increases in the minimum wage have already been approved. The minimum wage acts as a price support, or floor price.

Most Americans support this minimum wage law. The arguments for this law are mostly humanitarian in nature: proponents hold that the minimum wage should raise the income of workers in the lower end of the wage scale and thus help eliminate poverty, or that the law can help offset employer exploitation of unskilled workers. Others argue that the minimum wage will permit individuals to maintain proper nutrition and health levels, which should improve productivity, or that the dignity provided by a decent basic wage will help inspire the unskilled worker to seek new skills and higher educational levels.

Arguments against the minimum wage center around the unemployment side effect caused by the imposition of a wage above market equilibrium. We can demonstrate the effects of the minimum wage by analyzing supply and demand curves in a hypothetical market for unskilled workers (figure 5.4).

Let us assume that the market-determined wage would be W_e with OL_e units of labor hours available to workers. If W_e is considered substandard, and government sets a minimum wage of W_m, the market forces cannot reach equilibrium. At wage rate W_m, the labor quantity supplied (the total number of individuals who enter the labor market) is at point B. At point B, the quantity of labor hours is OL_1. However, the labor quantity demanded by business at wage rate W_m is represented by point A of the demand curve. At point A, the quantity of labor hours is OL_2. This creates a surplus of labor represented by distance AB, or OL_1-OL_2. This surplus normally manifests itself as teenage unemployment.

Critics of the minimum wage argue that high teenage unemployment is a very serious problem. The teenage unemployment rate is consistently higher than the general unemployment rate (see table 5.5). Economists disagree as to the real effect of the minimum wage on teenage unemployment. However, a relationship between the wage support and disproportionately high teenage unemployment rates is difficult to dispute.

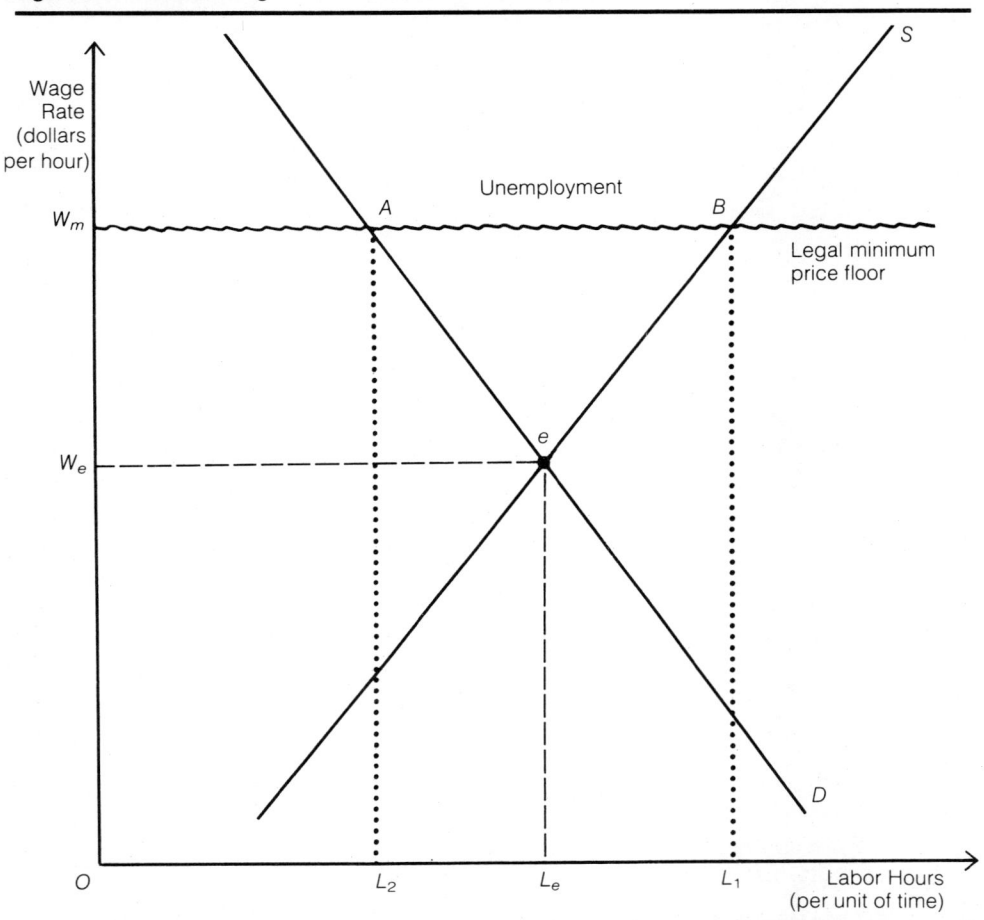

Figure 5.4 Minimum Wage and the Market for Unskilled Labor

Table 5.5 Teenage Unemployment, 1979–86

	Unemployment Rate	
Year	General	Teenagers
1979	5.8	16.1
1980	7.1	17.8
1981	7.6	19.6
1982	9.7	23.2
1983	9.6	22.4
1984	7.5	18.9
1985	7.2	18.4
1986	7.0	18.3

Sources: *Statistical Abstract of the U.S.*, 1987, no. 662, p. 390; and *Economic Indicators*, March 1987.

THE CONCEPT OF ELASTICITY

One of the most useful tools of economic analysis is the family of elasticity measures.[5] Basically, an elasticity value shows how one variable changes in response to the change of a related variable. The magnitude and direction of the change is encompassed in the elasticity coefficient.

The elasticity coefficient measures the degree of responsiveness, or elasticity, between variables. For the two variables x and y, where $y = f(x)$, the elasticity measure between x and y can be stated in a number of ways. In the three formulas below, e represents the elasticity coefficient:

$$1) \; e = \frac{\text{percentage change in } y}{\text{percentage change in } x}$$

OR

$$2) \; e = \frac{\Delta y / y}{\Delta x / x}$$

OR

$$3) \; e = \frac{\frac{\Delta y}{\Delta x}}{\frac{y}{x}} = \frac{\text{marginal value}}{\text{average value}}.$$

The numerical representation of elasticity is called the coefficient of elasticity. The coefficient of elasticity is the ratio of percentage changes of each variable. It can also be found by dividing the marginal value of a function by its average value.

Of all the members of the elasticity family, price elasticity of demand is the most used by economists. Price elasticity of demand is also called elasticity of demand, or demand elasticity.

Price Elasticity of Demand

Recall that, according to the law of demand, as the price of a good falls, ceteris paribus, consumers will demand more of the good. Conversely, as the price rises, quantity demanded will fall. By itself, this law is useful for general analysis; but the concept of elasticity reveals by "how much" demand varies with price changes.

Price elasticity describes by how much quantity demanded increases or decreases in response to a price change. The exact amount of the change in price and quantity can be found in the elasticity coefficient.

The formal designation of the price elasticity of demand coefficient for good X is:

$$e_d = \frac{\text{percentage change in quantity demanded of good X}}{\text{percentage change in the price of good X}}.$$

Following the logic of the law of demand, we discover that the elasticity coefficient of demand is normally a negative number. An increase in price—a change in price by a positive percentage—will lead to a negative percentage change in quantity demanded. Similarly, a decrease in price (a negative change) will lead to an increase in quantity demanded (a positive percentage change). The ratio of these changes will be negative. Because the coefficient is understood to be negative, the price elasticity of demand coefficient is often expressed as an absolute number, $|e_d|$ without the minus sign.

Elasticity Categories

Economists classify the elasticity coefficients into five distinct categories. The classifications relate to the value of the coefficient.

Relatively Elastic

When the elasticity coefficient of good X is greater than 1 (written $|e_d| > 1$), demand for good X is said to be *relatively elastic,* or simply, *elastic*. For example, if the price of good X rises by 10 percent and sales fall by 20 percent, the elasticity coefficient is calculated as follows:

$$|e_d| = \frac{-20\%}{+10\%} = 2.0.$$

The elasticity coefficient, 2.0, is greater than 1: demand is elastic. If, for good Y, a price increase causes a 50 percent fall in sales, the elasticity coefficient is calculated this way:

$$|e_d| = \frac{-50\%}{+10\%} = 5.0.$$

The coefficient is 5.0 and demand is again considered to be elastic. Note that demand for good Y is more elastic than demand for good X.

Inelastic

When the elasticity coefficient is less than 1 (written $|e_d|<1$) demand is said to be inelastic. For example, if a price increase of 10 percent of good X leads to a 9 percent drop in quantity demanded, the elasticity coefficient is equal to:

$$|e_d| = \frac{-9\%}{+10\%} = .90.$$

The elasticity coefficient is .90 and therefore demand for good X is considered inelastic. If, for good Y, a 10 percent price decrease leads to a 5 percent increase in quantity demanded, the elasticity coefficient is calculated as:

$$|e_d| = \frac{+5\%}{-10\%} = .50.$$

The coefficient is .50 and demand is inelastic. And the demand for good Y is more inelastic than the demand for good X. In general, the larger the elasticity coefficient, where $|e_d|>1$, the more elastic demand is said to be. The smaller the elasticity coefficient, where $|e_d|<1$, the more inelastic demand is considered to be. The remaining three elasticity categories can be considered special cases.

Unitary

When $|e_d|=1$, a given percentage change in price is matched by an identical change in quantity demanded, ignoring the differences in sign. When the elasticity coefficient is equal to 1, demand is said to be unitary, or said to have unit elasticity. In reality, few products or services have elasticity coefficients of exactly 1. It is most useful when thought of as a boundary separating the elastic and inelastic ranges.

Infinitely Elastic

The fourth category of elasticity is elasticity taken to the highest possible value of $|e_d|$, or infinity. Thus, the title, infinitely elastic, or perfectly elastic. When a product is infinitely elastic, a very small change in price causes a strong change in quantity demanded.

Perfectly Inelastic

The final category of elasticity is called perfectly inelastic. A product that is perfectly inelastic has an elasticity coefficient of zero. In other words, a change in price, up or down,

ECONOMICS FOR BANKERS

does not change the quantity demanded. Essentially, for such products, the quantity demanded is independent of the price.

It is normally very difficult to judge the elasticity of demand from observing the general shape of a demand curve. This is because, on a downward-sloping linear demand curve, the elasticity coefficient *changes* from point to point. However, these last three special cases of elasticity can be illustrated graphically (figure 5.5).

Demand curve D_i represents a product with zero elasticity, while D_e is a demand curve with infinite elasticity. Demand curve D_u is a demand curve with unit elasticity. Demand curve D_u is an example of a rectangular hyperbola discussed in chapter 2.

Measurements of Demand Elasticity

Three methods can be used to measure the elasticity range of a product: the arc formula, the demand curve, and the revenue test. The choice of which measurement to use depends on the degree and kind of information desired.

The Arc Formula

The primary method used to measure the elasticity coefficient is called the arc formula. The arc formula is a refinement of the general elasticity formula. You will recall that the formula used to determine elasticity is:

$$|e_d| = \frac{\text{percentage change in quantity demanded}}{\text{percentage change in price of good}}.$$

Using the formula, we can calculate the price elasticity of demand and coefficient for a hypothetical good X (see table 5.6) with a change in price from $10 to $9:

$$|e_d| = \frac{\frac{Q_2 - Q_1}{Q_1} \times 100\%}{\frac{P_2 - P_1}{P_1} \times 100\%},$$

where P_1 and Q_1 represent the old price and quantity and P_2 and Q_2 represent the new price.

$$|e_d| = \frac{\frac{125 - 100}{100}}{\frac{9 - 10}{10}} = \frac{\frac{25}{100} \times 100\%}{\frac{-1}{10} \times 100\%} = \frac{25}{10} = 2.5.$$

154

Figure 5.5 Elasticity of Demand: Special Cases

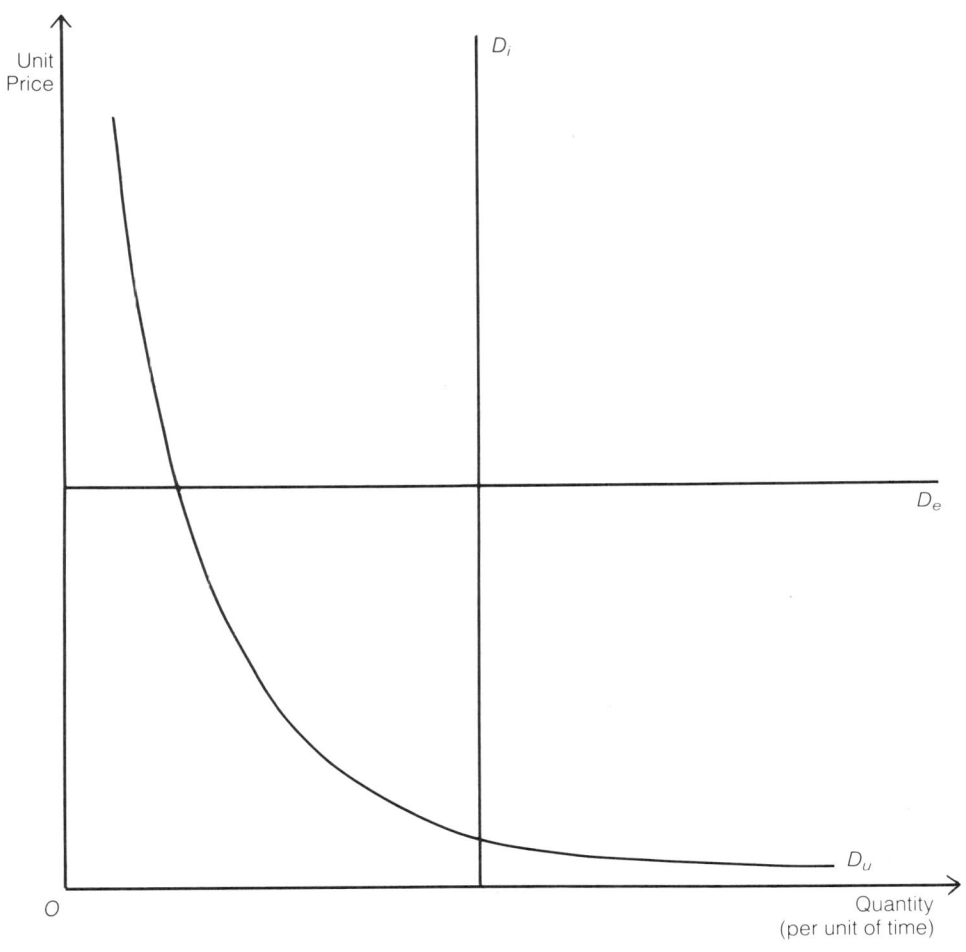

Table 5.6 Unit Price and Quantity Demanded, Good X

Unit Price (dollars)	Quantity Demanded
10	100
9	125
8	150
7	175

The elasticity coefficient is 2.5. If the price of good X is, at a later time, raised to $10 from $9, the new elasticity coefficient would be:

$$|e_d| = \frac{\frac{100-125}{125}}{\frac{10-9}{9}} = \frac{\frac{-25}{125}}{\frac{1}{9}} = 1.8.$$

It is disquieting to find a difference between the elasticity coefficient of a price decrease for product X (2.5) and that of a price increase (1.8). Why is there a difference in values when the changes have been of the same magnitude? The original values chosen for price and quantity determine the percentage change. The arc formula bypasses this problem by averaging the price and quantity points. The arc formula can be stated as follows:

$$|e_d| = \frac{\frac{Q_2 - Q_1}{(Q_2 + Q_1)/2}}{\frac{P_2 - P_1}{(P_2 + P_1)/2}} = \frac{\frac{Q_2 - Q_1}{Q_2 + Q_1}}{\frac{P_2 - P_1}{P_2 + P_1}}.$$

Using the arc formula, the elasticity coefficient of good X when price is increased or decreased is the same. A price decrease from $10 to $9 yields an elasticity of 2.11:

$$|e_d| = \frac{\frac{125-100}{125+100}}{\frac{9-10}{9+10}} = \frac{\frac{25}{225}}{\frac{-1}{19}} = 2.11.$$

A price increase from $9 to $10 yields the same coefficient:

$$|e_d| = \frac{\frac{100-125}{100+125}}{\frac{10-9}{10+9}} = \frac{\frac{-25}{225}}{\frac{1}{19}} = 2.11.$$

The Demand Curve

Demand elasticity can also be measured from a product's demand curve. For a linear demand curve, you can calculate elasticity at any point along the curve (see figure 5.6).

To find elasticity at point A on curve DD', first drop a vertical line to the horizontal axis (line segment AB in figure 5.6). The elasticity formula can be written as:

$$|e_d| = \frac{\frac{\Delta Q}{\Delta P}}{\frac{Q}{P}} = \frac{\Delta Q}{\Delta P} \times \frac{P}{Q}.$$

The slope of demand curve DD' at point A is $\Delta P/\Delta D$, or AB/BD'; therefore, $\Delta Q/\Delta P = BD'/AB$. Price is represented by distance AB and quantity demanded by OB. The elasticity at point A can now be expressed as:

$$|e_d| = \frac{BD'}{AB} \times \frac{AB}{OB} = \frac{BD'}{OB}.$$

Since distance BD' equals distance $0B$, the elasticity coefficient equals 1. Similarly, the elasticity at point C can be expressed as:

$$|e_d| = \frac{\Delta Q}{\Delta P} \times \frac{P}{Q} \text{ OR } \frac{ED'}{CE} \times \frac{CE}{OE} = \frac{ED'}{OE}.$$

Since distance ED' is greater than distance OE, the coefficient of elasticity is greater than 1. At point F, the elasticity measure is calculated as:

$$|e_d| = \frac{\Delta Q}{\Delta P} \times \frac{P}{Q} = \frac{GD'}{FG} \times \frac{FG}{OG} = \frac{GD'}{OG}.$$

Since distance GD' is less than distance OG, demand is relatively inelastic at point F. Therefore, along a straight-line demand curve starting from the price where $|e_d| = 1$ (the price corresponding to the midpoint of the relevant quantity demanded range), all prices above the midpoint price represent the elastic range of the demand curve, and all prices below this range represent the inelastic range. It is possible to determine the exact value of the elasticity coefficient at any given price when the price and quantity axes are appropriately labeled.

Figure 5.6 Elasticity and the Demand Curve

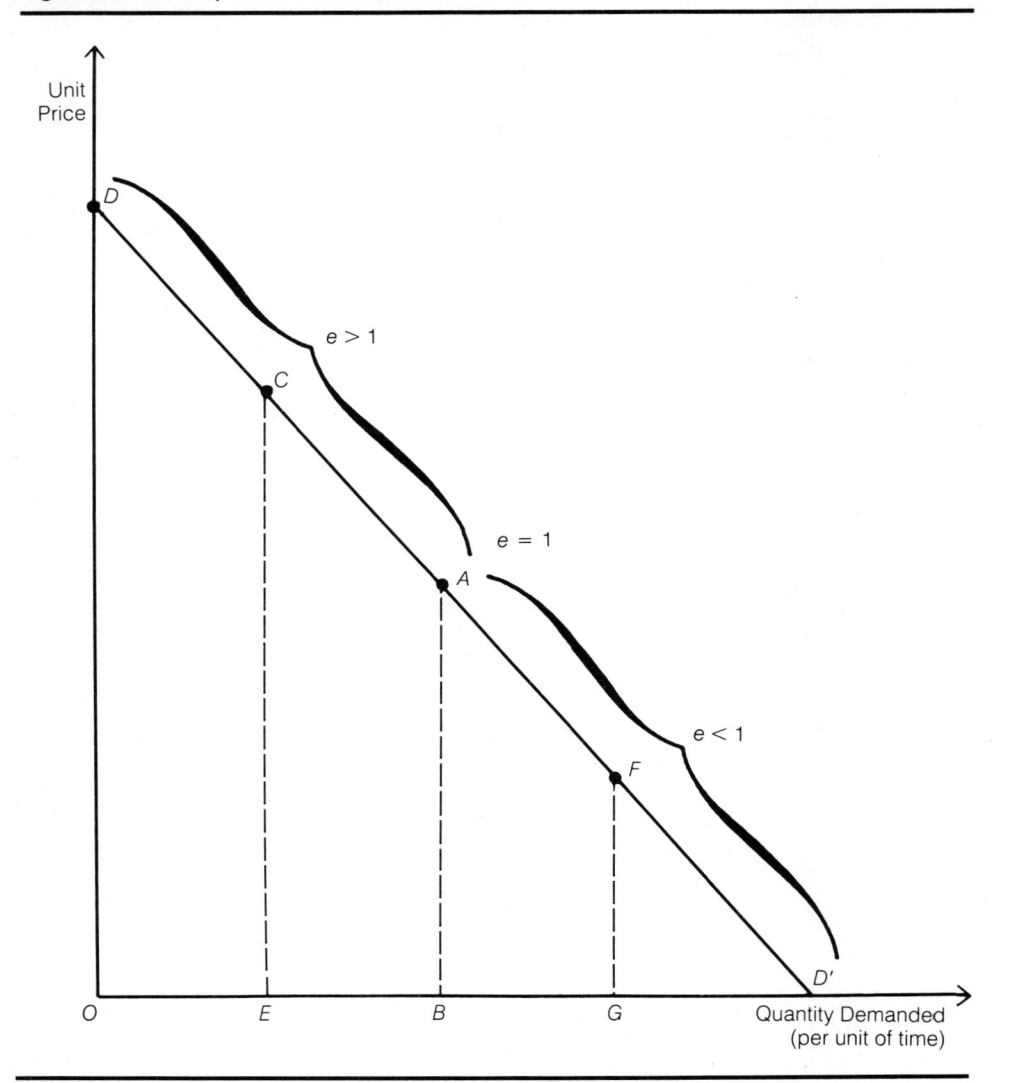

Check Your Understanding

Use the information in figure 5.7 and the formula for elasticity of demand to determine the elasticity coefficient of good X at a unit price of $5. Then, find the elasticity coefficient at a unit price of $8. Try it yourself before reading the correct answers below.

Did you remember to express the answers as absolute values?

Answer: In figure 5.7, the elasticity coefficient of good X at a price of $5 per unit is equal to $|.83|$. The calculation is written as follows:

$$|e_d| = \frac{11-6}{6-0} = \frac{5}{6} = |.83|.$$

The elasticity coefficient of good X at a unit price of $8 is $|2.67|$. The calculation is written as follows:

$$|e_d| = \frac{11-3}{3-0} = \frac{8}{3} = |2.67|.$$

With a slight alteration, this approach to the measurement of elasticity may also be used to measure elasticity at any price from a nonlinear demand curve (see figure 5.8). To find elasticity at point P on curve DD', we must first construct a tangent to point P, and use this tangent as a proxy for a straight-line curve. Elasticity is then calculated as discussed above. In figure 5.8, the line tangent to point P is labeled AB, and the line connecting P to the quantity axis is PC. Line AB, the tangent to point C on curve DD' becomes the proxy demand curve. Elasticity at point P is then calculated as follows:

$$|e_d| = \frac{\Delta Q}{\Delta P} \Big/ \frac{P}{Q} = \frac{\Delta Q}{\Delta P} \times \frac{P}{Q} = \frac{CB}{PC} \times \frac{PC}{OC} = \frac{CB}{OC}.$$

ECONOMICS FOR BANKERS

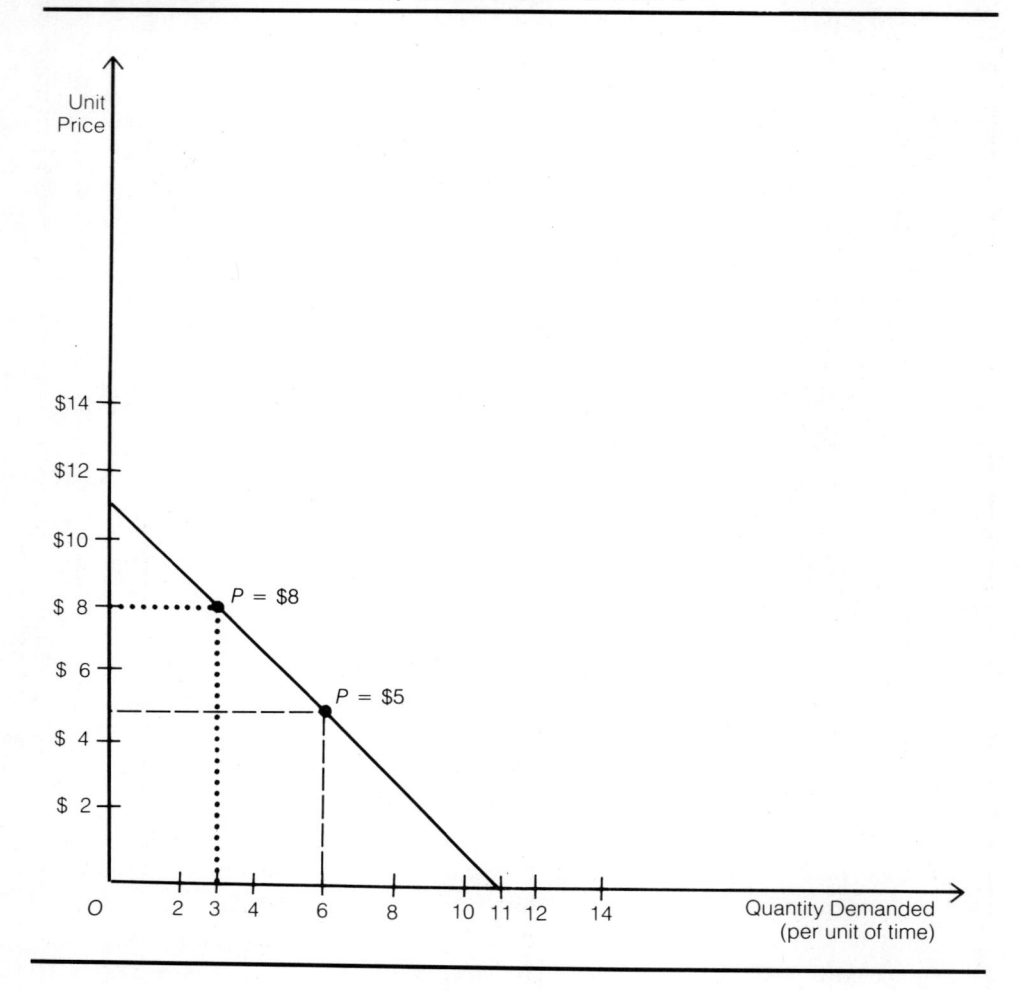

Figure 5.7 Measurement of Elasticity from a Linear Demand Curve

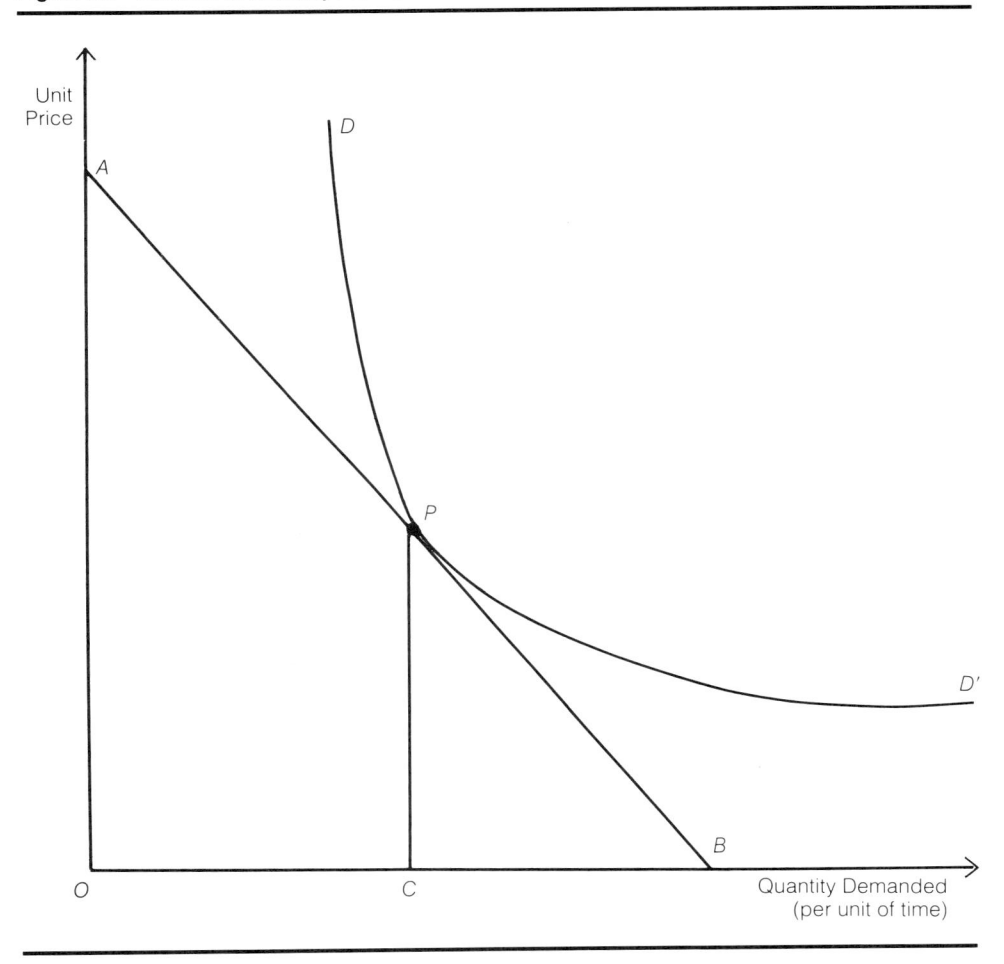

Figure 5.8 Estimate of Elasticity From a Nonlinear Demand Curve

The Revenue Test

The third method of measuring the elasticity range of a product is called the revenue test. Total revenue to a firm for selling good X is defined as price times quantity sold. If the price is changed and sales adjust, the resulting difference between the previous total revenue and the new total revenue is called marginal revenue. Marginal revenue can be defined as the change in total revenue caused by a one-unit change in quantity sold.

Consider an array of price, quantity demanded, total revenue, marginal revenue, and elasticity values for a firm selling good X (table 5.7).

Table 5.7 Price, Quantity, Revenues, and Elasticity

Price of Good X (P)	Quantity Demanded (Q)	Total Revenue (TR = P×Q)	Marginal Revenue $\left(MR = \frac{\Delta TR}{\Delta Q}\right)$	Elasticity $\left(e = \dfrac{\dfrac{Q_2 - Q_1}{Q_2 + Q_1}}{\dfrac{P_2 - P_1}{P_2 + P_1}}\right)$
$16	0	$ 0		0.0
14	5	70	70/5 = 14	15.0
12	10	120	50/5 = 10	4.3
10	15	150	30/5 = 6	2.2
8	20	160	10/5 = 2	1.3
6	25	150	−10/5 = −2	0.8
4	30	120	−30/5 = −6	0.4
2	35	70	−50/5 = −10	0.2

In table 5.7, when price equals $14, 5 units are demanded, and total revenue is $70. Marginal revenue is equal to the change in total revenue divided by the change in quantity demanded: $70/5 or $14. The arc elasticity between $16 and $14 is −15 or |15|. If the price is lowered to $12, demand rises to 10 units of good X. At this price, total revenue is $120, and marginal revenue is $10, calculated as follows:

$$\frac{\Delta TR}{\Delta Q} = \frac{\$120 - \$70}{10 - 5} = \frac{\$50}{5} = \$10.$$

The arc elasticity between a price of $14 and a price of $12 is equal to −4.3, or |4.3|.

If we move from a price of $8 to $6, however, notice that total revenue declines from $160 to $150. At this point, marginal revenue becomes negative:

$$MR = \frac{\Delta TR}{\Delta Q} = \frac{\$150 - \$160}{25 - 20} = \frac{\$-10}{5} = \$-2.00.$$

Here, the arc elasticity between prices $8 and $6 is inelastic, at −.80, or |.8|.

If prices were to drop still further, from $6 to $5, total revenue would decline further to $120, marginal revenue would be $−6 and arc elasticity would become −.4, or |.4|.

When demand is elastic ($e_d > 1$), a decrease in price causes total revenue to increase, while an increase in price causes total revenue to decrease. When demand is inelastic ($e_d < 1$), an increase in price causes total revenue to increase, and a decrease in price causes a decrease in total revenue. When demand is unitary ($e_d = 1$), a price change in either direction leaves total revenue unchanged. As you can see from table 5.7, as long as demand elasticity for good X is greater than 1, a cut in price leads to an increase in revenue (marginal revenue is positive). However, when elasticity of demand falls below 1, further price cuts lower total revenue and marginal revenue is negative.

This information can be very useful to the suppliers of good X. If they are faced with inelastic demand, they may raise revenue simply by increasing price. If demand is elastic, a drop in price can be used to raise total sales revenue. Remember, however, that sales revenues are not identical to profits. Costs must be factored in to determine profits. Nonetheless, many firms can profit from price cuts when demand is elastic.

Matinee movie prices, off-peak airline fares, and off-season hotel room rates are examples of attempts to manipulate price in order to benefit from the elasticity of demand. Conversely, the inelasticity of demand helps explain why there are no sales or discounts for other products, such as surgery, prescription drugs, and late-night towing service. The revenue test is summarized in table 5.8.

Table 5.8 Revenue Test for Elasticity

Combined Pattern of Change Price and Revenue	Price Elasticity of Demand
Increase — Decrease Decrease — Increase	$e_d > 1$
Increase — No change Decrease — No change	$e_d = 1$
Increase — Increase Decrease — Decrease	$e_d < 1$

DETERMINANTS OF ELASTICITY OF DEMAND

Various factors affect the elasticity of demand for goods and services. We will discuss only the most notable ones here. The importance of the product to the individual consumer is a major factor in the determination of elasticity of demand. Necessities and basics of life normally are more inelastic than luxury items. Consumers can live without many products. For some individuals, medical products or services may be essential to life. We can expect low, even zero elasticities for some vital necessities.

The number of substitute products or services available to consumers also influences elasticity. The greater the number of substitutes, the more elastic the demand tends to be, and the fewer the number, the more inelastic. For example, barring collusion between station owners, one is likely to find lower gasoline pump prices at a busy intersection with service stations on all four corners than at a single station located at an isolated exit on a deserted stretch of interstate highway. At the busy crossroads, there are a large number of substitutes for any given station, so demand will tend to be more elastic than when no substitutes are available.

The first two factors—importance and availability of substitutes—tend to blend together. The product of gasoline, taken by itself, tends to have an inelastic demand. It is certainly a necessity for anyone who uses a car for commuting to and from work, shopping, and so on. Yet the final elasticity of gasoline on the market is modified by other factors, like the number of substitute vendors available to the consumer.

Elasticity also depends on the degree of substitution available *between* various products. For example, while food is a basic necessity of life, the wide variety of foods available in most grocery stores makes the selection of a menu highly elastic.

Another major determinant of demand elasticity is the portion of disposable income required to purchase the particular product or service. Products that represent minor portions of our total expenditures tend to have inelastic demands. On the other hand, an item that takes up a larger percentage of total expenditures tends to have an elastic demand. For example, would you decrease your consumption of ketchup if the price increased by 50 percent? Probably not, because your total budgeting outlay on ketchup is miniscule. In contrast, if restaurant prices were to rise significantly, you may decide to limit consumption. The demand coefficient of ketchup is more inelastic than that of dining out.

The elasticity of demand of a general category of products is different from that of a specific brand of the product. As one progresses from a general product classification to a specific product, elasticity generally increases. This effect is related to the availability of substitutes. For example, the demand for auto loans in general may be inelastic, yet the demand for an auto loan from Bank A in a market with many substitute lenders may be much more elastic. Similarly, the demand for automobiles tends to be less elastic than the demand for Fords.

Finally, the length of time allowed for the adjustment of demand to price changes also influences elasticity. For example, when home heating fuel costs rose sharply in the 1970s, homeowners could do very little in the short term to decrease demand, other than lower thermostats and wear sweaters. So, consumption of fuel did not drop substantively when prices rose. Over time, however, homeowners made adjustments, such as installing insulation and storm windows, caulking sealants, and making fireplace improvements, in order to improve the fuel efficiency of their homes and curtail consumption. As time passed, demand elasticity increased to reflect such long-term adjustments.

Table 5.9 Demand Elasticity Estimates

Commodity or Service in Demand	Estimate Short Run	Long Run
Salt	—	0.1
Water	—	0.4
Beer	—	0.7–0.9
Housing	—	1.0
Physicians' services	0.6	—
Medical and hospitalization insurance	0.3	0.9
Gasoline	0.2	0.5
Automobiles	—	1.5
Electricity (household utility)	0.1	1.9
Gas (household utility)	0.1	10.7
Intercity bus	2.0	2.2
Air travel	0.1	2.4
Motion pictures	0.9	3.7

Sources: Hendrik S. Houthakker and Lester D. Taylor, *Consumer Demand in the United States, 1929–1970* (Cambridge, MA: Harvard University Press, 1966 and 1970 editions); U.S. Department of Agriculture; Kenneth G. Elzinga, "The Beer Industry," in Walter Adams, ed., *The Structure of American Industry* (New York: MacMillan, 1977); Llad Phillips and Harold L. Votey, Jr., *Economic Analysis of Pressing Social Problems* (Boston: Houghton Mifflin Co.). Reprinted with permission of the publishers.

Economists have attempted to estimate the elasticity of demand for various products (table 5.9). Generally, measures of short-run elasticity tend to be lower than long-run measures of elasticity. Also, products and services which are viewed as necessities tend to have lower elasticities than luxury items. With respect to bank products, it appears that elasticity of demand for loans varies with the maturity of the loan. Short-run debt appears to be inelastic while long-term debt is relatively inelastic. Bear in mind, however, that the demand elasticities for any individual bank will vary with the degree of bank and nonbank competition, customer demographics, and other factors.

ELASTICITY OF SUPPLY

Producers also respond to price changes by adjusting quantity supplied. The magnitude of this response is a measure of elasticity of supply. The definition of elasticity of supply for a product or service is the percentage change in quantity supplied for a good divided by the percentage change in price, ceteris paribus.

The general formula used to calculate elasticity of supply is similar to the one used for elasticity of demand. The formula appears as follows:

$$e_s = \frac{\text{percentage change in quantity supplied of good X}}{\text{percentage change in the price of good X}}.$$

Unlike the elasticity of demand coefficient, however, the sign of supply elasticity is always positive in accordance with the law of supply. A positive change in price will lead to a positive change in the quantity supplied, and a negative price change will lead to a negative change in the quantity supplied.

When e_s is greater than 1, supply is said to be relatively elastic. When e_s is less than 1, supply is relatively inelastic. And, like demand elasticity, supply elasticity can be equal to 1, 0, and infinity.

When e_s is equal to 1, supply elasticity is called unitary. When e_s is equal to 0, elasticity of supply is perfectly inelastic. As e_s approaches infinity, elasticity of supply is called infinitely elastic. On a graph, when a supply curve is vertical, e_s is equal to 0. When a supply curve is horizontal, supply is infinitely elastic.

The Arc Formula

Elasticity of supply can be calculated from a supply schedule with the use of the arc formula:

$$e_s = \frac{\dfrac{Q_{s_2} - Q_{s_1}}{Q_{s_2} + Q_{s_1}}}{\dfrac{P_2 - P_1}{P_2 + P_1}}.$$

Once again, let us consider an array of information for good X (table 5.10).

Table 5.10 Unit Price and Quantity Supplied, Good X

Unit Price (dollars)	Quantity Supplied
5	100
4	90
3	80
2	70
1	60

Using the arc formula, the elasticity of supply for a price change from $4 to $5 is calculated as follows:

$$e_s = \frac{\dfrac{Q_{s_2} - Q_{s_1}}{Q_{s_2} + Q_{s_1}}}{\dfrac{P_2 - P_1}{P_2 + P_1}} = \frac{\dfrac{100 - 90}{100 + 90}}{\dfrac{5 - 4}{5 + 4}} = \frac{\dfrac{10}{190}}{\dfrac{1}{9}} = .47.$$

At .47, supply is said to be relatively inelastic.

DETERMINANTS OF ELASTICITY OF SUPPLY

The most important determinant of elasticity of supply is time—the length of time between the initial price change and the adjustment of the quantity supplied. Within a short period of time, relatively little can be accomplished to increase output. For example, consider an automobile manufacturer who experiences a rapid increase in the price of automobiles (figure 5.9). When the price changes initially, the firm may be able to speed up production slightly, or offer overtime to employees to increase output. Yet the firm is constrained by the maximum attainable speed of the assembly line. In the intermediate term, the firm could perhaps purchase components from other suppliers to increase output, and in the long run, the manufacturer could opt to expand production facilities. Therefore, the long-run supply of autos is more elastic than the short-run supply. In the figure, supply curve S_{SR} represents the automobile firm's short-run supply curve. S_{LR} represents the long-run curve. If price changes from P_0 to P_1, the firm can adjust output very little in the short run. Supply is relatively inelastic. The firm is limited by plant size and assembly-line speed. Yet, some production changes can be accomplished to raise output slightly from Q_0 to Q_{SR}. However,

Figure 5.9 Time and Elasticity of Supply

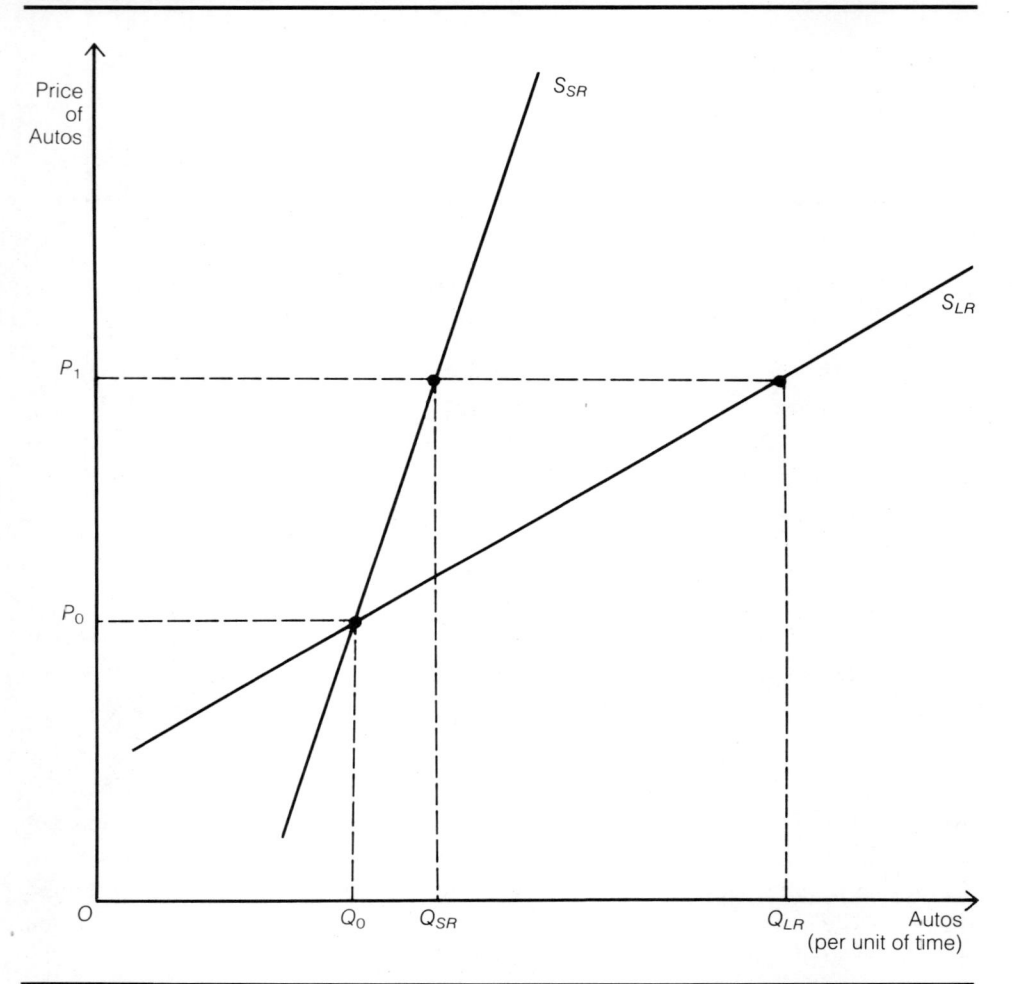

in the long run, the existing plant can be expanded, or a new plant constructed, and supply can be shifted to curve S_{LR}. After the passage of time, supply has become more elastic, and output can be increased much more, from Q_{SR} to Q_{LR}.

Time is not the only determinant of elasticity of supply. The more easily and efficiently factors of production can be substituted from one task to another, the higher elasticity of supply becomes. Also, certain products can be stored in inventory, without spoilage, or at relatively low storage costs. The larger the inventory level, the more responsive, or elastic, quantity tends to be.

OTHER MEASURES OF ELASTICITY

Cross Elasticity of Demand

You may recall from our discussion of the determinants of demand the impact that a change in the price of a related good has on quantity demanded. The measurement of the magnitude of this impact is called cross elasticity of demand. Cross elasticity of demand between good X and good Y can be defined as the percentage change in quantity demanded of good X divided by the percentage change in the price of good Y. The value of the coefficient of cross elasticity e_{xy} is computed by use of the following formula:

$$e_{xy} = \frac{\%\Delta Q_{d_x}}{\%\Delta P_y},$$

where e_{xy} = cross elasticity of demand coefficient
Q_{d_x} = quantity demanded of good X
P_y = price of good Y.

The cross elasticity coefficient reveals useful information regarding the relationship between the two products. If the value of e_{xy} is greater than zero, or positive, the two goods can be substituted for each other. The higher the value, the more the products can be used as substitutes for each other. If the sign of e_{xy} is less than zero, or negative, the goods are used in a complementary fashion. Finally, as e_{xy} approaches zero, the two products are independent, or unrelated in consumption.

Cross elasticity of demand can be calculated by use of the arc formula:

$$e_{xy} = \frac{\dfrac{Q_{x_2} - Q_{x_1}}{Q_{x_2} + Q_{x_1}}}{\dfrac{P_{y_2} - P_{y_1}}{P_{y_2} + P_{y_1}}}.$$

Income Elasticity of Demand

When consumer incomes increase, the quantity demanded of most products also increases, and vice versa. The measure of the responsiveness of demand to income changes is called the income elasticity of demand. The income elasticity of demand is defined as the percentage change in quantity demanded divided by the percentage change of income of the average consumer. The income elasticity coefficient (e_y) of good X can be written as:

$$e_y = \frac{\%\Delta Q_d}{\%\Delta Y},$$

where e_y = income elasticity of demand coefficient,
Q_d = quantity demanded of good X, and
Y = income of consumers *(Note: The letter Y is normally used to denote income.)*

If the value of e_y is greater than 0, then good X is a "normal" good. However, for certain products, an increase in income brings about a decrease in quantity demanded, and vice versa. In such cases, e_y will be less than 0, and the products are labeled "inferior" goods.

The calculation of e_y should be made using the arc formula, as follows:

$$e_y = \frac{\frac{Q_2 - Q_1}{Q_2 + Q_1}}{\frac{Y_2 - Y_1}{Y_2 + Y_1}}.$$

Elasticity of Demand for Labor

An extension of the demand elasticity measure to the labor resource market creates a hybrid elasticity. The elasticity of demand for labor measures the responsiveness of a firm's labor requirement to increases or decreases in wages. The elasticity of demand for labor can be defined as the percentage change in the quantity of labor demanded divided by the percentage change in wages. The elasticity coefficient of the demand for labor can be written as:

$$e_l = \frac{\%\Delta Q_l}{\%\Delta W},$$

where e_l = elasticity of demand for labor,
Q_l = quantity demanded of labor, and
W = wage rate.

If e_l is greater than zero, demand for labor is said to be elastic; if e_l is less than zero, demand is called inelastic. Obviously, the value of e_l determines just how much of an employment loss or gain will occur after a wage increase or decrease.

In the collective bargaining arena, labor unions prefer a very inelastic demand for labor. A low elasticity of demand for labor increases a union's bargaining leverage, because a large wage hike will have few job security repercussions. On the other hand, if the elasticity is high, then even small wage increases could lead to job losses.

The value of this critical elasticity measure is dependent upon three major factors. First, what is the percent of labor in the cost of production? If the production process is very labor-intensive, then a wage hike may lead to price increases, which can reduce quantity demanded of the firm's final product. The amount of sales lost depends upon a second factor: the elasticity of demand for the final product. If the workers produce a product with high elasticity of demand, then a price hike will cause a proportionally larger drop in sales. This would have a negative impact on job security. However, if the workers produce a necessity or a product with inelastic demand, the price hike caused by higher wages would be absorbed by the consumer with little loss of job security. The third factor that influences elasticity of demand for labor is the ability of management to substitute other factors of production for labor, or their ability to shift production to a lower-cost site (called "outsourcing").

Many experts trace the decline of the U.S. steel industry and the subsequent job loss experienced by steelworkers to the failure of union leadership to pay close attention to the elasticity of demand for steelworkers. It is argued that the United States Steelworkers officials believed erroneously that the demand for the labor of their members was very inelastic. They did not expect that significant job losses would occur as a result of their high wage settlements.[6]

SUMMARY

The intersection of a market demand curve with a market supply curve represents the price at which the market is in equilibrium. If prices rise above the equilibrium point, quantity demanded falls. If prices fall below the equilibrium point, quantity demanded rises.

A decrease in supply accompanied by increasing demand leads to higher prices. On the other hand, an increase in supply with a decrease in demand leads to lower prices.

Government intervention in the market system includes establishing of price controls and price supports, passing usury laws, and establishing minimum wage laws.

Elasticity measures the sensitivity or responsiveness of quantity demanded (or quantity supplied) to changes in price and other factors. Elasticity can show five different responses to changes in price. The arc formula, the demand curve, and the revenue test are three methods used to measure elasticity.

The determinants of elasticity of demand include the product's importance to the consumer, the number of substitutes available, the degree of substitution between various products, the portion of disposable income taken up by the purchase, the desire for a specific brand, and the length of time allowed in the measurement for the adjustment of demand to price changes.

Elasticity of supply is the change in quantity supplied over the change in price. The arc formula can be used to calculate elasticity of supply as well as elasticity of demand.

Determinants of supply elasticity include the length of time between the initial price change and the adjustment of quantity supplied, the ease with which other resources can be substituted, storage potential, and inventory size.

In addition to price elasticity, two other kinds of elasticity are cross elasticity of demand and income elasticity of demand. Cross elasticity of demand measures the change in the quantity purchased of a product in response to changes in the price of another product. Income elasticity of demand measures changes in the quantity purchased of a good in response to changes in income.

The elasticity of demand for labor measures the responsiveness of a firm's labor requirement to wage changes.

KEY WORDS

arc formula
cross elasticity of demand
elasticity
elasticity coefficient
elasticity of supply
Fair Labor Standards Act
income elasticity of demand
inelastic
infinitely elastic (inelastic)
marginal revenue
minimum wage

nonlinear demand curve
perfectly elastic (inelastic)
price controls (ceilings)
price elasticity of demand
price supports (floors)
prime rate
relatively elastic (inelastic)
revenue test
unitary
usury laws

Questions for Review

1. Rent controls are in effect, in one form or another, in many U.S. cities. It seems obvious the tenants living in rent-controlled housing benefit from such market intervention. Yet some economists argue that even the tenants lose in the long run. List some of the costs and benefits of rent control.

2. "The minimum wage law has done more to exacerbate America's long-run crime problem than either drugs or poverty." Comment on this statement.

3. The prime rate of interest changed only 25 times between 1929 and 1965. Yet the prime rate changed over 125 times between 1973 and 1980. How can you account for the instability of the prime rate in the late 1970s?

4. Given the following information, use the arc formula to find the income elasticity of demand for good X between the second and third year.

Year	Income	Quantity Demanded of Good X
1	$10,000	1,000
2	15,000	3,500
3	20,000	4,500

5. The First National Bank recently raised its fees for safety deposit boxes by 25 percent. From experience, the bank has calculated the price elasticity of demand for safety deposit boxes to be $-.50$. What will happen to bank revenues derived from deposit box rentals? If rentals totaled $50,000 before the price hike, calculate the rental revenue after the price hike.

6. The 100,000-strong iron workers union has just won a 15 percent wage hike after a lengthy strike. If the elasticity of demand for labor, e_l, is 2.0, are any ironworkers likely to lose their jobs after the wage increase goes into effect?

7. Price and sales information for good X and good Y are provided below. Are the goods substitutes or complements? Use the arc formula to find the cross elasticity of demand between good X and good Y, when the price of good Y changes from $12 to $13.

Year	Price of Good X (dollars)	Quantity Demanded of Good X	Price of Good Y (dollars)	Quantity Demanded of Good Y
1	10	20	15	60
2	9	30	14	75
3	8	40	13	90
4	7	50	12	105
5	6	60	11	120

8. The Pennsylvania turnpike commission needs to raise $100 million in additional tolls for badly-needed road repairs. The turnpike commissioner is urging that tolls be lowered by 20 percent to increase usage of the toll road in order to raise revenue. An economist, hired as a consultant to the commissioner, recommends a doubling of the current toll structure. Discuss the elasticity of demand estimates of the commissioner and the consultant. Which toll recommendation would probably lead to an increase in revenue? Why?

ENDNOTES

1. For a detailed explanation of the Federal Reserve System and its influence on the money supply, see David Friedman, *Money and Banking* (Washington, D.C.: American Bankers Association, 1985).

2. For more information on factors influencing the price of loanable funds, see Roy E. Moor, "Economics of Financial Markets," *Business Economics,* vol. 20, no. 2 (April 1985), pp. 37–42.

3. The U.S. market reaction to the changing of oil prices is explored by B. Trehan, "Oil Prices, Exchange Rates, and the U.S. Economy: An Empirical Investigation," in *Economic Review* no. 4, (Fall 1986), pp. 25–43.

4. For an interesting discussion of market intervention, see Robert Kuttner, "Where the Free Market Falls Short," *Business Week,* June 30, 1986, p. 20 and Walter W. Heller, "Activist Government: Key to Growth," *Challenge* (March/April 1986), pp. 4–10.

5. The first person to describe the concept of an equilibrium price and the output resulting from the interaction of supply and demand was British economist Alfred Marshall. He is also credited with systematizing the use of elasticity. His *Principles of Economics,* published in 1890, was a leading text in economics for over 40 years, and many of his ideas can be found in modern texts.

6. See L. Browne, "Steel—An Industry Beset on All Sides," *New England Economic Review* (May/June 1985), pp. 35–43.

ECONOMICS IN THE NEWS

Democrats Seek Higher Minimum Wage And White House Quickly Opposes It

By Cathy Trost
Staff Reporter of *The Wall Street Journal*

WASHINGTON—Congressional Democrats squared off against the Reagan administration as legislation was introduced to increase the minimum wage to $4.65 over three years.

The measure, introduced yesterday by Sen. Edward Kennedy (D., Mass.) and Rep. Augustus Hawkins (D., Calif.), would increase the wage from its current level of $3.35 an hour in a series of annual steps.

The wage would rise to $3.85 in 1988, $4.25 in 1989, and $4.65 in 1990. Automatic increases would follow in later years so that the minimum wage would equal half the average wage for non-supervisory private workers, which currently is $8.88 an hour.

The legislation is intended to "make the minimum wage a living wage," said Sen. Kennedy, chairman of the Senate Labor Committee. He called it the most "important poverty program that we in this Congress can pass—without adding one nickel to the deficit." He appeared at a news conference with Rep. Hawkins, who is chairman of the House Labor Committee.

The Reagan administration immediately announced it would oppose an increase. "The administration cannot stand by while some in Congress propose an action which will further deny opportunity to America's young men and women," said Labor Secretary William Brock.

Congressional supporters of an increase contend that the minimum wage has been sharply eroded by inflation since the last increase six years ago, and that a full-time worker earning the minimum wage generally doesn't make enough to keep his or her family above the poverty level.

But critics argue that an increase could cost jobs and fuel inflation. An increase would cause "a sharp reduction in employment opportunities for unskilled workers" and put "more people on welfare," as businesses cut hours or fail to create new jobs, warned the Minimum Wage Coalition to Save Jobs, which represents a variety of businesses and trade groups.

Any increase will result "in the loss of job opportunities for thousands of kids," said Mr. Brock, who added that it was important to "concentrate on how we get our kids into the work force, rather than on ways to keep them out." The administration has long supported a subminimum wage for youths, and Mr. Brock also has emphasized the need for job-training and education programs.

Sen. Kennedy lashed back at industry complaints, saying that each of the six times Congress has raised the minimum wage since it was established nearly 50 years ago, "we have heard dire prophecies of unemployment, inflation and bankruptcy. And six times these prophecies have been false."

He cited the findings of a commission established by Congress after it last voted to increase the wage. Those findings showed that a raise "has no significant impact on adult unemployment, youth unemployment, inflation, or the viability of business enterprises."

Sen. Kennedy and Rep. Hawkins both said they expected to gain bipartisan support for the legislation.

Sen. Kennedy predicted that hearings will be held in May, with mark-up in June and passage in July. Continued opposition from the administration would "hopefully be rejected" by Congress, he said, although the administration has "demonstrated the ability to flip-flop on issues" in the past. Rep. Hawkins predicted action by the House in early September.

Reprinted by permission of *The Wall Street Journal*, © Dow Jones & Company, 1987. All Rights Reserved.

CHAPTER SIX

GOVERNMENT AND THE MIXED ECONOMY

Objectives

After reading this chapter, you should be able to

•

describe some characteristics of a mixed economy

•

describe several ways in which government intervenes in the marketplace

•

define spillover costs and benefits
and describe the consequences of each

•

explain how taxes and subsidies are used to overcome externalities

•

explain the difference between the ability-to-pay theory
and the benefits-received theory of taxation

•

list and define three types of tax rates

•

categorize a number of taxes as progressive, regressive, or proportional

•

explain the relationship between tax shifting and elasticity of demand

•

compare U.S. tax rates with those of several other countries

THE PRIVATE SECTOR AND THE ROLE OF GOVERNMENT

As was discussed in chapter 3, the U.S. economic system is not a pure market economy. The U.S. economy is actually a *mixed* economy. That is, both private individuals and government wield influence in the marketplace. This mixed economy is capitalistic in nature. The factors of production are privately owned and they are put to profitable use under the generally competitive conditions of the free market.[1]

However, the role of government in the American economy has grown considerably over the years. Some sectors of the economy have received various forms of protection through regulation and legislation. Farmers, consumers, and workers have received government support. Banking, transportation, and communication are three major industries regulated by the government. In unregulated industries, government has pursued other means of fostering true competition. Government intervention represents another kind of effort to reach the four major economic goals of efficiency, stability, fairness, and growth.

Adam Smith would be disturbed to learn of the many functions and activities of government in the world's showcase of modern capitalism, the United States of America. In *The Wealth of Nations,* he suggested that for a capitalistic economy to thrive and grow, the size and scope of government would have to be limited to the barest essentials. Smith's prescription for the functions of government was to limit governmental activities to national defense, public utilities, a criminal justice system, and activities which improve the flow of commerce. This doctrine of limited intervention, or laissez-faire, was followed closely in the early development of the U.S. economy. Government's role has since grown to include many other activities. Today's government is involved in virtually every aspect of economic life. Table 6.1 shows the growth in government since 1970 in terms of federal and state and local outlays, expenditures, receipts, and employment figures. This growth is a controversial topic. However, we will discuss only the economic role of government, and not the sociological or political significance of its involvement. Within this framework, we will examine governmental attempts to promote, regulate, and most important, stabilize the private sector.

Promotion of Economic Activity

Government taxation policies, grants, subsidies, and regulations are intended to promote the development of new industries and to foster overall economic growth. Low-interest loans to small businesses, guaranteed student loans, and tax-financed university research are just a few examples of public attempts to foster economic growth.

Government involvement in business and industry ranges from regulations protecting the health and safety of American workers to pollution-control legislation. The logic behind

Table 6.1 Growth in Government Size

	Unit of Measure	1970	1975	1980	1982	1983	1984	Average Annual Percent Change 1970–80	80–83	83–84
Federal outlays	$Billions	195.7	324.2	576.7	728.4	796.0	852.0	11.4	11.0	5.4
Defense	Percent	41.8	26.7	23.2	25.4	26.4	26.7	(NS)	(NS)	(NS)
Nondefense	Percent	58.2	73.3	76.8	74.6	73.6	73.3	(NS)	(NS)	(NS)
Federal receipts	$Billions	192.8	279.1	517.1	617.8	600.6	667.0	10.4	5.1	11.0
Social Security taxes	Percent	23.0	30.3	30.5	32.6	34.8	36.3	(NS)	(NS)	(NS)
Corporation taxes	Percent	17.0	14.6	12.5	8.0	6.2	8.5	(NS)	(NS)	(NS)
Federal debt outstanding	$Billions	382.6	544.1	914.3	1,147.0	1,381.9	1,577.0	9.1	14.8	14.1
State and local government:										
Direct expenditures	$Billions	148.1	268.2	432.3	521.0	564.8	543.4	11.3	8.4	7.8
General revenue	$Billions	130.8	228.2	382.3	456.2	486.9	599.0	11.3	9.3	5.9
Percent federal	Percent	16.7	20.6	21.7	19.1	18.5	17.9	(NS)	(NS)	(NS)
Percent from property taxes	Percent	26.0	22.6	17.9	18.0	18.3	17.8	(NS)	(NS)	(NS)
Debt outstanding	$Billions	143.6	219.9	335.6	410.2	454.5	505.3	8.9	10.6	11.1
Federal civilian employment	1,000	2,881	2,890	2,898	2,848	2,875	2,942	0.1	−0.3	2.4
State and local employment	1,000	10,147	12,084	13,315	13,071	13,159	13,494	2.8	−0.4	2.5
Military personnel	1,000	3,066	2,128	2,051	2,109	2,123	2,138	−3.9	1.2	0.7

NS—Not significant.
Source: Statistical Abstract of the U.S., 1986, U.S. Depart. of Commerce, Bureau of the Census, p. xxiii.

regulation is that government must intervene if and only if the private sector has refused or failed to address large-scale problems or is unable to administer regulations effectively. Some argue that any attempt by the public sector to interfere in private matters constitutes overregulation. The attempts to deregulate various businesses in the 1980s bear witness to some of the problems that can result from overregulation. Yet, most people agree that a certain amount of regulation is essential to safeguard the competitive forces of the private sector.

One of the most traumatic periods in U.S. history signaled an end to its laissez-faire economic tradition. The Great Depression of the 1930s pushed people's faith in a free market economy to the limit. It became apparent that, while the market economy could propel a nation forward with explosive economic growth and prosperity, a free market economy was also susceptible to long periods of economic malaise. Bouts of recession, depression, panic, business failures, and high unemployment occurred with alarming regularity. The Great Depression was interrupted by World War II, but when the economy returned to peacetime status, Congress quickly addressed the issue of the market system's instability. In 1946, Congress passed the Full Employment and Economic Stabilization Act, which charged the executive branch of government with the responsibility of maintaining full employment and stabilizing the business cycle. The act also established the Council of Economic Advisors, a select group of economists who advise the president on matters of economics. The role of government as a stabilizer of economic activity will be addressed further in chapter 8.

Overcoming Marketplace Failures

Externalities

Economists place great faith in the free market system of supply and demand. However, economists also realize the system is not foolproof. One potential cause of free market failure is called economic spillovers, or externalities.

Spillovers or externalities occur because the effects of production of goods and services as well as the consumption of these products cannot be isolated. Often, there is a "fallout" effect between products: in some cases, the consumption of a product by consumer A affects consumer B. Consumer B may receive a positive or negative spillover, or externality. For example, you are at the movies and the person sitting next to you has purchased candy at the snack bar before the movie's start. At a critical point in the film, your neighbor decides to open the treat. The noise of the cellophane wrapper being removed causes you to miss a crucial passage of the dialogue. You have just received a negative externality. You had nothing to do with the economic transaction—the purchase of the candy—but you were victimized by it.

The production process can also generate negative or positive externalities. Air and water pollution are serious examples of the negative externalities that can result from production. A firm engages in private production, but spoils everyone's air and water. The market system sometimes fails to internalize the costs and benefits that are borne by individuals and groups unrelated to the primary activity.

Spillover, or externalities, can also bring benefits rather than costs. Benefits occur when individuals unrelated to the economic activity benefit from it. For example, an individual who attends college and becomes skilled in a certain area may create future spillover benefits for all: many advances in food production, disease prevention, and science have resulted from the efforts of researchers educated in our public school system. Similarly, the owner of an apple orchard benefits when the orchard is pollenized by the bees owned by the nearby beekeeper. Whether the spillover involves benefits or costs, the economic system has no way of internalizing its effects.

In the case of spillover costs, the individuals who precipitate the spillover do not pay the complete costs of their activities; in the case of external benefits, the primary economic agents do not receive all of the full benefits of their activities. In the first case, certain costs are forced onto others. If the costs were internalized completely, the primary economic agents would be required to absorb these additional costs and, as a result, the supply of the product or service would tend to shrink. In the latter instance, if the total benefits could somehow be "returned" to the primary economic agent, demand for these activities would be increased. These market failures lead to misallocation of resources and economic inefficiency. Resources will be overallocated unless spillover costs are internalized. Resources will be underallocated unless spillover benefits are internalized.

Taxes and Subsidies

One obvious solution to the problem of externalities is for government to make those responsible for spillover costs pay the total costs of production. In the case of air and water pollution, tax penalties and pollution-control regulations are meant to help internalize the spillover costs. For example, in an attempt to clean up auto exhaust pollution, Congress imposed strict air pollution standards on all auto makers. These regulations led to the adoption of catalytic converters, which require the use of more costly no-lead fuels. Motorists were forced to internalize the costs of reducing air pollution, paying higher automobile purchase prices and fuel costs. These penalties and regulations tend to decrease supply of the product in the marketplace, and correct the resource misallocation. Figure 6.1 depicts a competitive market showing substantial spillover costs.

In figure 6.1, DD and S_1S_1 represent the original demand and supply conditions. If the supplier were made to pay, or internalize, all costs of production, the supply curve would shift to S_2S_2. The vertical distance between the two supply curves represents the dollar value of the external costs. This internalization reduces quantity to Q_i. Therefore, if the situation were left alone, Q_iQ_e would represent the amount of overallocation of resources to the production of this good or service. The supply curve might be shifted by the imposition

GOVERNMENT AND THE MIXED ECONOMY

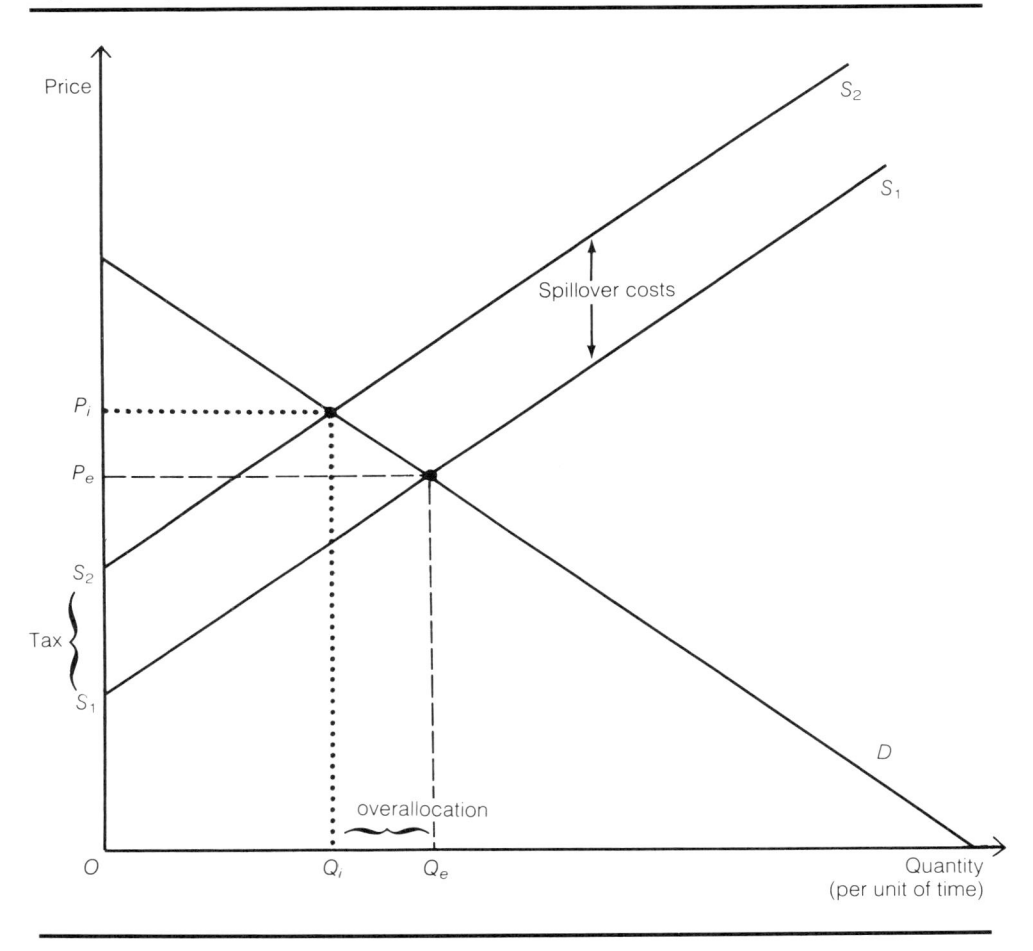

Figure 6.1 Spillover Costs in a Competitive Market

of a tax, by the cost of purchasing required pollution control equipment, or by fines levied for violation of the regulation.

The problem of underallocation of resources (figure 6.2) arises when external benefits are ignored by the market system. In figure 6.2, curves $D_e D_e$ and SS represent the original demand and supply conditions. If the consumers of these goods were able to receive all the benefits derived from their consumption, the demand curve would shift to $D_i D_i$. At $D_i D_i$, all benefits are internalized. The vertical distance between $D_e D_e$ and $D_i D_i$ represents the value of the extended benefits to society. Through internalization of benefits, consumers could be induced to expand consumption from Q_e to Q_i. Output $Q_e Q_i$ represents the underallocation of resources if these external benefits are left unattended. The overall welfare of society

183

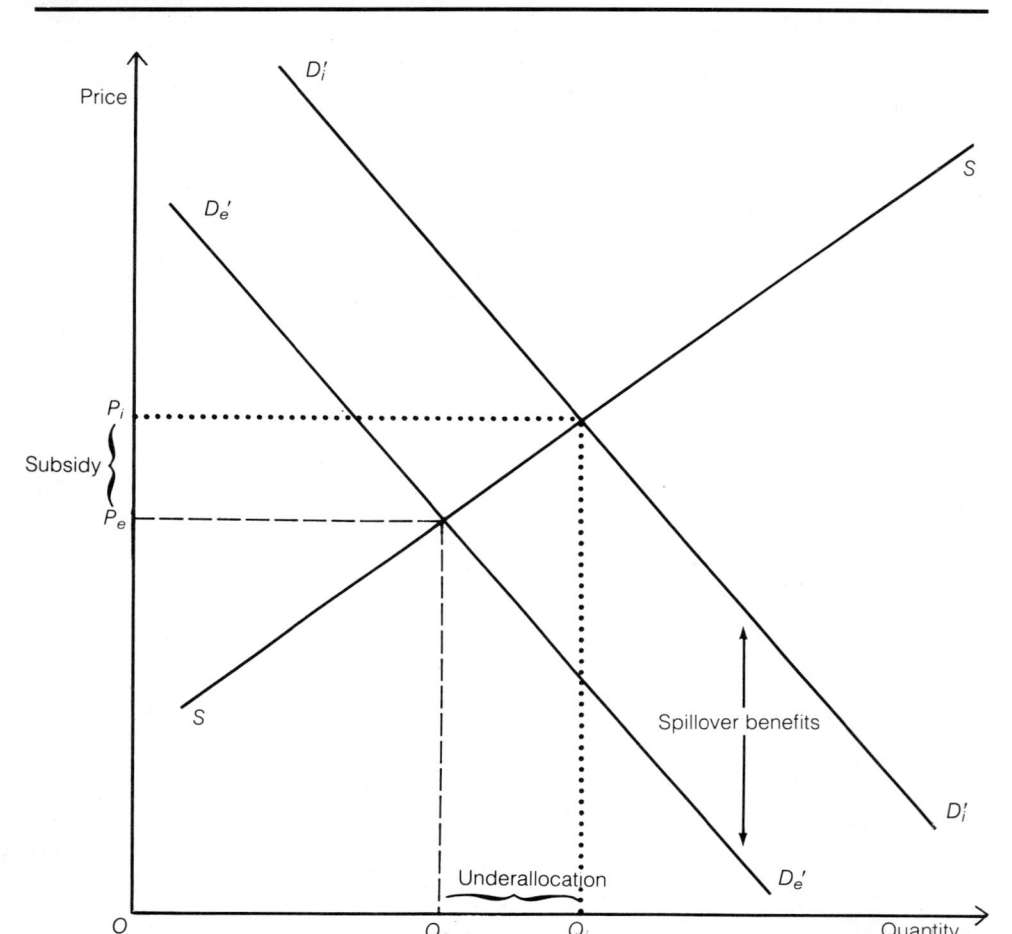

Figure 6.2 Spillover Benefits in a Competitive Market

could be improved if consumption of this good were increased from Q_e to Q_i. This increase in demand could be accomplished through government subsidies. A government subsidy is a payment to households or businesses, enabling them to produce or consume a product at a lower price (or in larger quantities) than would otherwise be possible.

Farmers have been the recipients of government subsidies under a system of direct payments since 1950. The government compensates farmers for the difference between the market price they receive and some higher target price established according to a selected base period in the past.[2]

Bankers participate in a kind of subsidy by providing the mechanism by which the government attempts to increase the external benefits of education. Student loan programs permit many students to attend college, some of whom might not have the opportunity to do so were subsidized assistance not available.[3]

Maintaining Competition

The efficiency and prosperity seen by Adam Smith as the result of the "invisible hand" of the market mechanism depend upon the assumption that all economic agents in the marketplace are going to "play fair." The "invisible hand" provides no solution to the problem of cheating or "overcompeting." In the rush for profits, firms may resort to collusion to control markets and prices. Predatory pricing procedures may drive rivals out of business, eliminating the constraints of competition. When competition breaks down, the government must intervene with antitrust enforcement. The problems created by "corporate bigness" and government's response will be discussed in chapter 8.

REVENUES AND EXPENDITURES IN THE PUBLIC SECTOR

The public sector of the economy comprises three major levels of government: federal, state, and local. Each level provides different services to the private sector. The various spending categories at each level of government are shown in table 6.2. Overall federal spending rose from $253.5 billion in 1975 to $664.0 billion in 1984. It almost tripled in 9 years. State and local expenditures show a similar trend. While the percentage of the total government expenditure that is devoted to defense remained the same (37 percent) and some expense categories decreased (for example, education), other expense categories increased dramatically. The amount of money devoted to interest payments on the federal debt increased from 9.8 percent of total expenditures in 1975 to 16.4 percent in 1984. The rise in interest debt is part of the overall concern about the burden of the federal deficit.[4]

The major source of funding for government (table 6.3) is taxation. Keeping pace with rising expenditures, the public sector's total tax revenue has more than doubled. About 60 percent of the revenue collected by the federal government is from various types of taxes assessed on private sector activities. Relatively minor sources of revenue include the U.S. postal service, national park fees, and insurance trust revenue.

Tax Theories

Regardless of the type of government, taxes are the lifeblood of government. Taxation can be defined as the legal and systematic method of transferring spending power from the

Table 6.2 Government Expenditures, 1975 and 1984 (billions of dollars)

	1975		1984	
Function	Federal	State and Local	Federal	State and Local
Total, all functions	**253.5**	[a]**230.7**	**664.0**	[a]**505.1**
Direct general	203.9	229.7	565.0	503.4
Intergovernmental	49.6	[b]1.0	99.0	[b]1.7
National defense and international relations	93.9	(x)	248.0	(x)
Postal service	12.7	(x)	26.6	(x)
Education	16.1	87.9	26.1	176.1
Highways	5.1	22.5	11.0	39.4
Public welfare	26.6	28.2	63.8	66.4
Health and hospitals	8.0	18.8	17.0	46.4
Natural resources[c]	14.7	7.7	62.2	15.8
Housing and urban renewal	5.1	3.5	17.1	9.3
Space research and technology	3.3	(x)	7.2	(x)
Air transportation	2.0	1.4	3.8	3.6
Social insurance administration	2.7	1.5	5.9	2.6
Interest on general debt	25.0	8.8	109.2	28.7
Other and combined	38.3	50.4	66.1	116.9

x. Not applicable.
Source: *Statistical Abstract of the U.S.*, 1987, no. 430, p. 251.
a. Excludes duplicative transactions between state and local governments.
b. State contributions to federal government.
c. Except for 1975, includes parks and recreation.

private sector to the public sector. For years, people have debated just how the costs of providing government services should be allocated among citizens.

Benefits Received

One of the earliest theories of taxation was founded on the concept of "benefits received." This method of taxation tried to mirror the private sector system of goods and service distribution. If you wanted to wear custom-made clothes, you had to pay the tailor. If you wanted to use the public highway, you had to pay the toll. Taxes should be levied on those who derived direct benefits from public services.

While this theory of taxation may appear to be fair and equitable on the surface, many problems surface upon its implementation. For example, does a resident of Washington, D.C., derive more benefits from the national defense system than a rancher in Montana? If the answer is yes, how can the benefits received and the tax burden be allocated? If a homeowner never has a fire in his or her home and, consequently, never needs to call upon the local fire department, should the homeowner be exempted from supporting the fire department? For many public goods, it is virtually impossible to assign specific amounts of

Table 6.3 Government Revenues, 1975 and 1984 (billions of dollars)

	1975		1984	
Source of Revenue	Federal	State and Local	Federal	State and Local
Total revenue	**303.5**	**[a]264.0**	**754.0**	**652.1**
General revenue	223.0	[a]228.2	531.1	542.8
Intergovernmental[b]	1.2	47.1	1.6	97.1
From federal government	(x)	47.1	(x)	97.1
From state governments	1.2	(a)	1.6	(a)
From own sources	221.7	181.1	529.5	445.8
Taxes[b]	190.0	141.5	414.8	320.2
Property	(x)	51.5	(x)	96.5
Individual income	122.4	21.5	296.0	64.6
Corporation income	40.6	6.6	56.9	17.0
Sales, gross receipts and customs[b]	21.1	49.8	49.5	114.1
General	(x)	29.1	(x)	75.2
Selective[b]	16.8	20.7	38.0	38.9
Motor fuel	4.5	8.3	10.7	12.6
Alcoholic beverages	5.3	2.1	5.4	3.1
Tobacco products	2.3	3.4	4.7	4.3
Public utilities	2.9	3.1	4.5	9.5
Death and gift tax	4.6	1.4	6.0	2.2
Charges and miscellaneous[b]	31.8	39.7	114.7	125.6
Postal service	9.6	(x)	24.4	(x)
Education	(z)	9.1	—	20.6
Hospitals	(z)	6.0	0.1	20.6
Natural resources[c]	3.0	0.8	22.6	2.9
Sewerage and sanitation	(x)	2.5	(x)	8.6
Utility and liquor stores	(x)	13.3	(x)	40.6
Insurance trust revenue	80.5	22.5	222.9	68.7

— Represents zero or rounds to zero.
x. Not applicable.
z. Less than $50 million.
Source: Statistical Abstract of the U.S., 1987, no. 429, p. 251.
a. Aggregates exclude duplicate transactions between state and local governments.
b. Includes other amounts not shown separately.
c. Includes parks and recreation.

"benefits received" because the benefits are not quantifiable. All citizens benefit from social goods such as national defense, public education, medical and sanitation services, and police and fire protection. It is impossible to decide how to equitably divide the burden of paying for these benefits among groups of people.

Perhaps the biggest problem with the benefits-received theory of taxation is that some citizens are unable to afford even the most essential services. It makes no sense to think that the recipients of welfare or public assistance should—or could—provide the revenue needed to fund these services!

Primarily because of these two problems, the benefits-received theory of taxation has been virtually abandoned. However, remnants of this system still remain. For example, federal excise taxes on gasoline sales are used to support the highway trust fund. Entry fees at government-owned parks are another example of the "user pay" concept. Turnpike, bridge, and tunnel tolls may be the best examples of taxes based on benefits received. However, the basic theory behind the vast majority of tax plans today is the ability-to-pay principle of taxation.

Ability to Pay

The ability-to-pay theory ignores the benefits-received concept. It borrows nothing from the older principle. Under the new theory, citizens are levied taxes based either on "natural" wealth or on income. Individuals with greater financial resources pay a larger share of taxes than those with less wealth or income. But what is "larger?" How much more should the wealthy pay? Politicians constantly struggle to answer this question. Issues of fairness and incentives must be addressed. For example, if the tax on wealth is perceived to be too large, incentives to consume more and save less receive a boost. On the other hand, an income tax structure that is perceived to be too harsh may reduce the incentive to work and increase the incentive for leisure.

The consequences of reduced incentives to work and save can be disastrous for an economy. The tax system must be structured in a fashion that minimizes the damage to both work and saving incentives. The primary method used to classify tax schemes measures the change in tax liability as relative to changes in income or wealth.

Progressive, Proportional, and Regressive Taxes

Under the ability-to-pay system, tax rates can be differentiated by the proportion of income taxed. Any tax liability is based on the following formula:

$$\text{tax base} \times \text{tax rate} = \text{tax liability}.$$

The tax base is the dollar value of property, wealth, or income. The tax rate is the percentage of income or wealth to be taxed, measured in the amount of tax paid per dollar of wealth or income. Tax liability represents the total dollar amount of the tax per person. Tax liability is also defined as the total tax yield to the government. The three major classifications of the tax scheme are progressive taxes, proportional taxes, and regressive taxes.

A progressive tax is any tax on income or wealth for which the tax rate increases as the dollar value of wealth or income rises, and decreases as income or wealth decreases.

A proportional tax is any tax on income or wealth for which the tax rate is constant, regardless of changes in the dollar value of income or wealth.

A regressive tax is any tax on income or wealth in which an inverse relationship exists between the tax rate and income or wealth. In other words, the tax rate rises as the dollar value of one's income or wealth decreases, and falls as the value increases.

Table 6.4 Hypothetical Income Tax Schedule

	Column 1 Income or Wealth (dollars)	Column 2 Tax Liability (dollars)	Column 3 Average Tax Rate (percent) (Col. 2/Col. 1)	Column 4 Marginal Tax Rate (percent) (Δ Col. 2/Δ Col. 1)
A.	5,000 10,000 15,000	1,500 1,600 750	30 16 5	2 5
B.	20,000 25,000 30,000	2,000 2,500 3,000	10 10 10	10 10
C.	35,000 40,000 45,000	3,500 6,000 9,000	10 15 20	50 60

To illustrate these classifications we can construct a hypothetical income tax schedule (table 6.4). Column 1 lists income or wealth categories. Column 2 shows the total taxes due or tax liability for every tax base category. Column 3 is a ratio of tax liability to tax base, or average tax rate, and column 4 shows the marginal tax rate, which is the change in tax liability divided by changes in income or wealth.

In panel A, as income rises from $5,000 to $15,000, the average tax rate falls from 30 percent to 5 percent. This panel represents a regressive tax. Even though an individual who earns $15,000 has a larger tax liability than the $5,000 income earner ($750 versus $500), the tax is regressive, because the average tax rate falls as income or wealth rises. It is the average tax rate that determines the tax classification, not the tax liability. Tax liability may increase as the tax base increases, yet the tax is still regressive. The classification depends solely on the relationship between the average tax rate and changes in the tax base. If the average tax rate rises as the tax base falls (or vice versa), the tax is classified as regressive.

In panel B of table 6.4, the tax rate remains constant throughout the tax base range. Regardless of whether income or wealth rises or falls, the average tax rate is constant. This is called a proportional tax. That is, tax liability is a fixed proportion of income. In this hypothetical example, the fixed proportion has been established at 10 percent of income or wealth.

Panel C of table 6.4 portrays a tax scheme that raises the average tax rate as income progresses from one level to the next. This is called a progressive tax. It is not progressive in the sense that it is necessarily modern or appropriate. The term "progressive" in this sense is used to explain a tax for which the average rate becomes "progressively" larger as income rises.

Table 6.5 Two Progressive Tax Schemes

Tax Scheme A			Tax Scheme B		
Income (dollars)	Tax Liability (dollars)	Average Tax Rate (percent)	Income (dollars)	Tax Liability (dollars)	Average Tax Rate (percent)
10,000	1,000	10.000	10,000	1,000	10.000
20,000	2,001	10.005	20,000	4,000	20.000
30,000	3,003	10.010	30,000	9,000	30.000
40,000	4,006	10.015	40,000	16,000	40.000

Figure 6.3 Proportional, Regressive, and Progressive Taxes

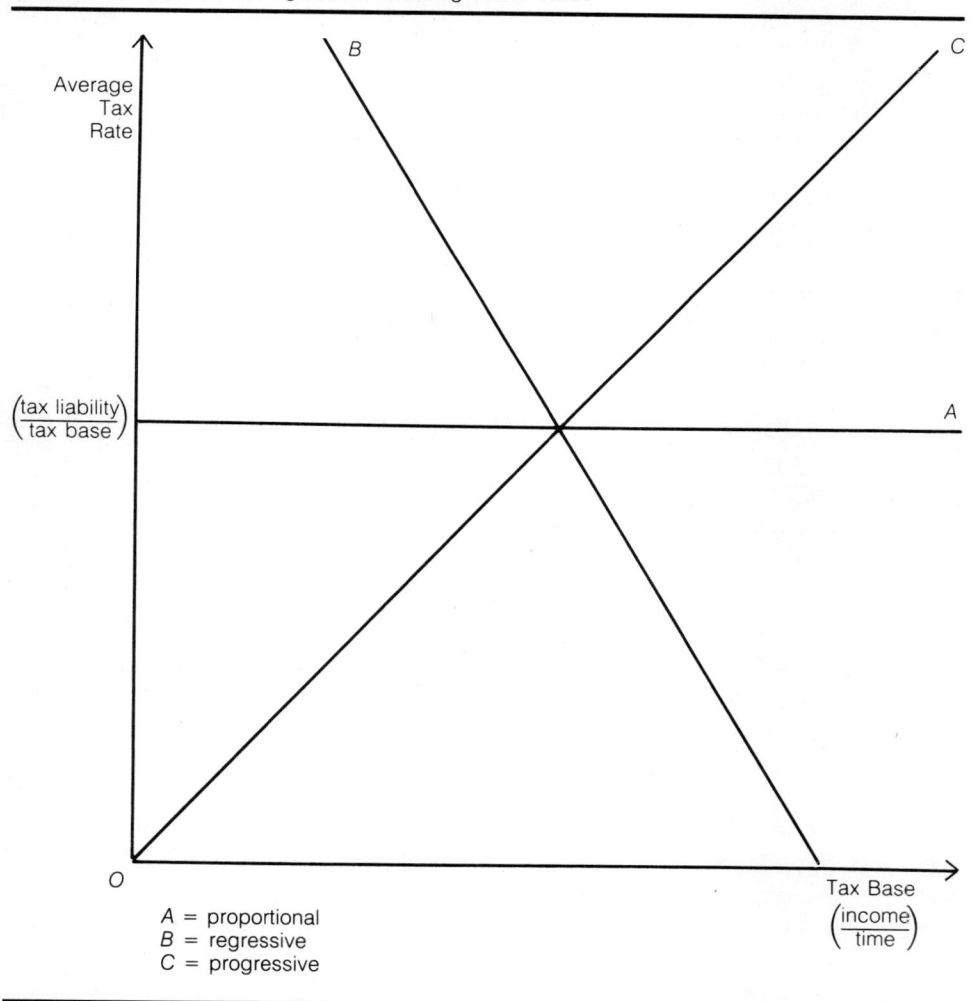

A = proportional
B = regressive
C = progressive

Taxes may vary in the degree to which they are regressive or progressive. Table 6.5 shows two tax schemes, both of which are labeled progressive. Yet tax scheme B is clearly "more progressive" than tax scheme A.

The three major types of taxes may be represented graphically (figure 6.3). Curve *A* represents proportional taxes. It is horizontal, reflecting its constant average tax rate. Curve *B* is a regressive tax. The curve is downward, sloping to the right, which shows the average tax rate falling as income rises. Curve *C* shows a progressive tax schedule. Here, as income rises, the average tax rate also rises.

Tax Classifications

Most common taxes can be placed in one of the three classifications described above.

Federal Income Tax

Income taxes are based on the amount of income that remains after certain, legally defined items are deducted from an individual's total income. The federal income tax is generally considered to be progressive. However, deductions and exemptions can influence the actual tax paid.[5] Table 6.6, which shows the amount of taxes paid by income class and the average tax rate by income group, demonstrates the progressive nature of the federal income tax.

Table 6.6 Federal Income Tax for a Single Person, 1986

Taxable Income (dollars)	Tax Liability (dollars)	Average Tax Rate (percent)[a]
15,000	1,927	12.8
20,000	3,054	15.3
25,000	4,354	17.4
30,000	5,841	19.5

Source: IRS Tax Tables, 1986.
a. Subject to rounding error.

Social Security Tax

The social security tax is a federal tax on wages. It is a fixed percentage proportion of income up to a set maximum. In 1985, an employee and his or her employer each paid Social Security taxes of 7.05 percent on the worker's first $39,600 wage income. The 1985 Social Security tax ceiling was $39,600. The tax rate and income maximum are established by Congress. The tax is proportional for income levels up to the set maximum, then regressive for income levels above the maximum. Once a worker's yearly income reaches the maximum level, he or she no longer has to pay the Social Security tax. Overall, the Social Security tax is regressive.[6]

Sales Taxes

Many state and local governments have sales taxes which are a fixed percentage of consumption expenditures. Some states exempt certain consumption categories—for example, food and prescription drugs. However, since families with low incomes normally spend a greater percentage of their income on consumption, or alternatively, save a smaller portion of their income than high-income families, the effective average tax rate drops as income rises. Sales taxes are classified as regressive taxes.

Occupational Privilege Taxes

Many localities charge a fixed-dollar tax for every individual employed within the limits of their jurisdiction. This class of taxes is clearly regressive. The tax is the same amount for the bank teller as it is for the bank president.

State Income Taxes

Many states have income taxes calculated on a fixed percentage of gross income. These taxes are normally considered proportional, because the tax rate is constant across all income classes.

Property Taxes

It is difficult to categorize property taxes. If property and real estate values are correlated with individual income levels, a fixed property tax rate per dollar value of property can be considered proportional. If, on the other hand, upper-income individuals hold wealth in nontaxable forms such as stocks and bonds, or if the tax code does not provide relief for elderly homeowners who, as a result, lose a relatively higher proportion of their income to property taxes, these taxes might be considered regressive.

Hidden Taxes

In many localities, citizens have forced passage of laws limiting future tax increases. These tax-limiting laws have squeezed budgets for many local governments, making it difficult to improve, or even maintain existing government services.[7] Even in areas that have no laws limiting taxes, political and economic realities have pressured taxing authorities into controlling taxes. Faced with stagnant revenues and escalating budgetary needs, many local governments have resorted to "hidden taxes." These hidden taxes may take the form of fees charged for government services that exceed the actual cost of service. Municipal water, electric, and sewer authorities may charge rates far greater than the average cost of the service. In other words, a "profit" is earned on utility revenues. These surpluses are normally transferred into a general fund where they are used to supplement local tax revenues. These taxes are called hidden because citizens are normally not aware that, for example, a portion of their utility bills is used to fund nonutility expenses. Some argue against hidden taxes on the grounds that they conceal the real cost of government. Also, to the extent that local taxes may serve as deductions in the calculation of an individual's federal tax liability, hidden taxes deny citizens a legal tax savings.

If we ignore hidden taxes, can we conclude what the net tax burden for U.S. citizens really is? When all taxes are lumped together, are taxes progressive, proportional, or regressive? When government transfer payments (welfare payments, food stamps, Social Security benefits, and so on) are included as "negative taxes," the total tax burden of federal, state, and local taxes appears to be about 25 percent of income. Joseph Pechman of the Brookings Institution reached this conclusion in his 1985 study of the overall distribution of the tax burden in the United States for the period 1966–85.[8] Pechman estimated the incidence of all three public sector government units for 1985. He concluded that the total tax burden is approximately proportional to income, at a rate of about 25 percent. The progressive income and property taxes are offset by regressive Social Security and sales taxes.

Tax Incidence and Tax Shifting

While taxes may be levied on and paid by one economic agent, it is very possible for the actual tax burden to be shifted to another. Tax incidence refers to the economic agent who must, in the final analysis, pay the tax. The tax incidence normally shifts through higher prices. Standard supply and demand analysis can be used to demonstrate the process of shifting tax burdens from producers to consumers.

The ability of a firm to shift the incidence of a tax forward to consumers depends to a great extent on the price elasticity of demand for the firm's product. The more elastic the demand for the product, the more responsive consumers are to a change in price. If the firm attempts to raise the product's price after a tax increase, resistance to the price increase could thwart the shift wholly or in part. This process can be analyzed with supply and demand curves (figure 6.4).

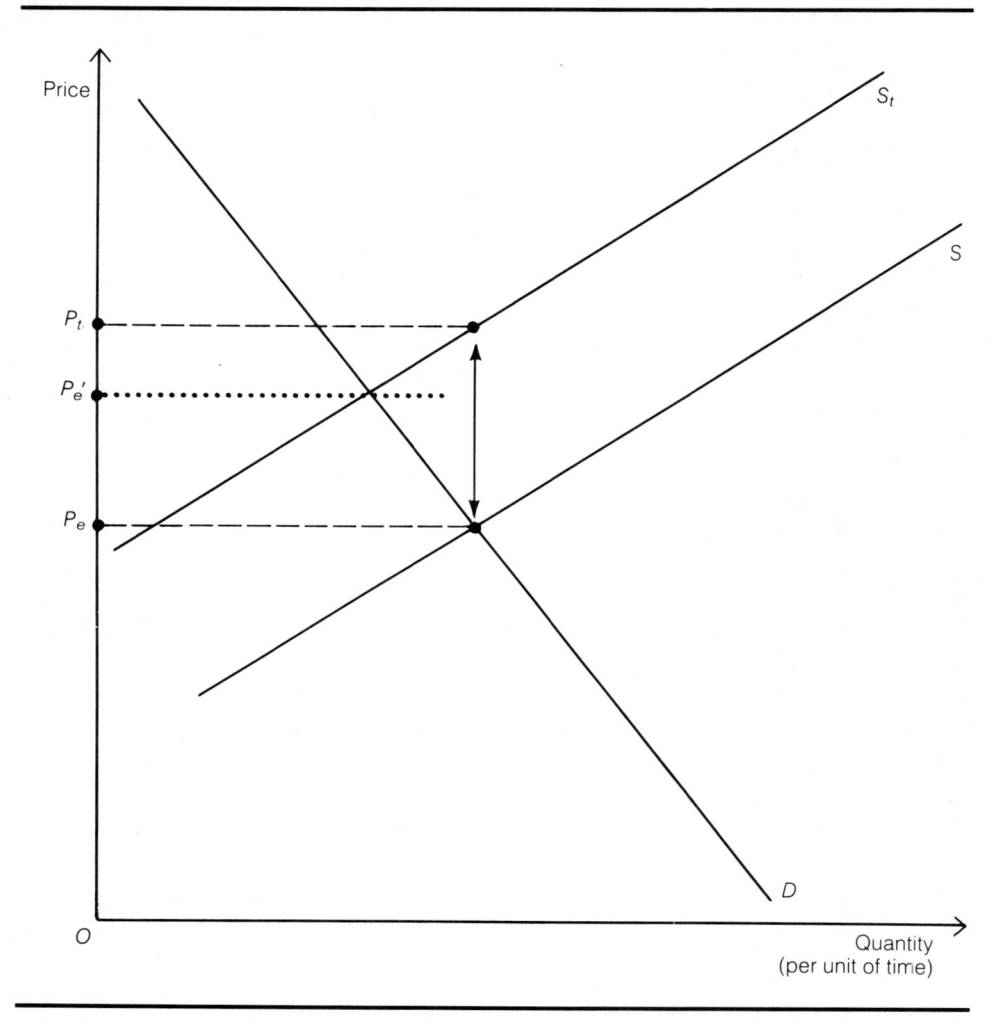

Figure 6.4 Sales Tax Incidence and Elasticity of Demand

In figure 6.4, the sales tax increase results in a shift of the supply curve backward to the left from S to S_t. The supply curve shifts vertically by the amount of the tax or distance $P_e P_t$. The equilibrium price before the tax hike is P_e', and after the tax hike is P_e'. Notice that the increase in price, $P_e P_e'$, is *less* than the tax increase $P_e P_t$. In this case, the firm was not completely successful in shifting the tax increase to consumers. Only a portion of the tax was borne by the consumer; the remainder was paid by the firm. A firm can only be successful in shifting the complete amount of the tax to consumers when demand is completely inelastic.

GOVERNMENT AND THE MIXED ECONOMY

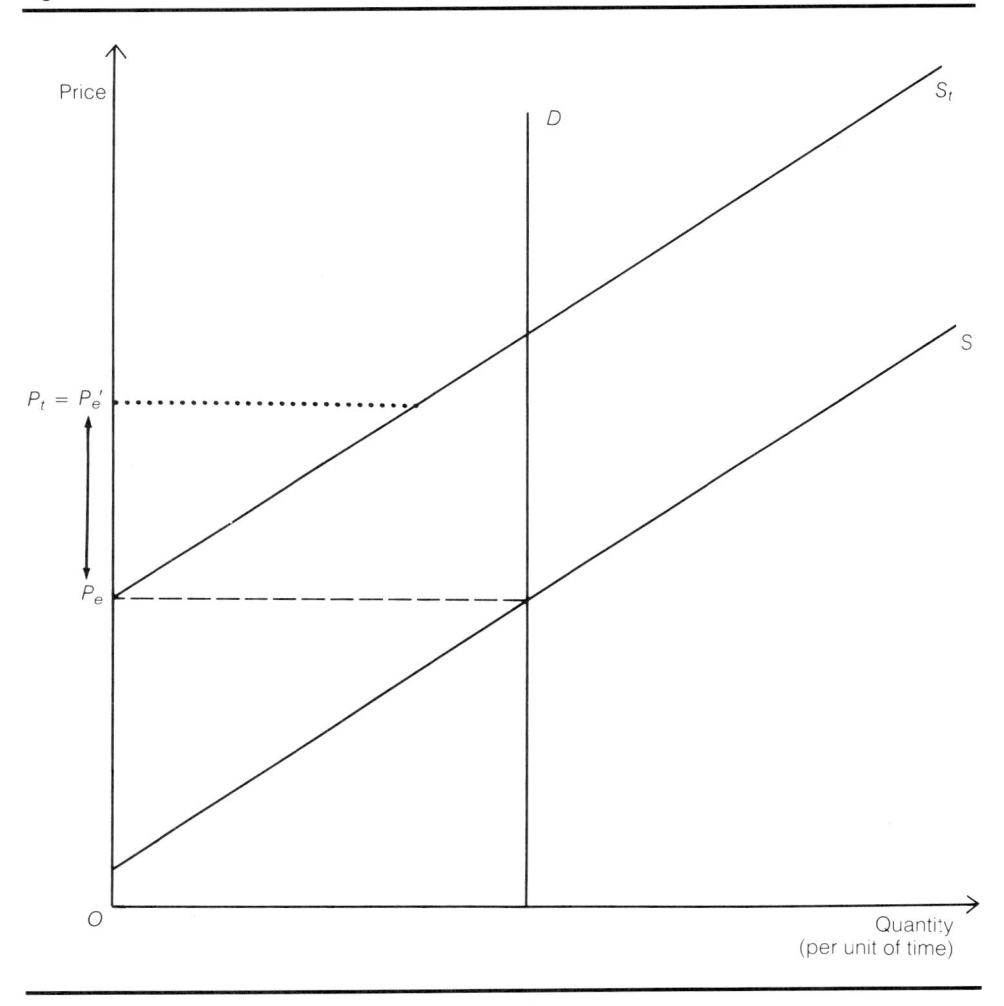

Figure 6.5 Sales Tax Incidence and Completely Inelastic Demand

Figure 6.5 shows a demand curve which is completely inelastic (vertical). Here, when the tax takes effect and the supply curve shifts from S to S_t, the new equilibrium price, P_e', is increased by the whole amount of the tax, or amount $P_e P_t$. In this situation, the consumers are forced to bear the entire tax burden. The tax is paid under the guise of higher prices.

At this point, you should see the relationship between tax incidence and elasticity of demand. The more inelastic the demand, the greater the proportion of tax that can be shifted. The more elastic the demand for the product, the smaller the proportion of tax that can be shifted. If demand is infinitely elastic (figure 6.6), any attempt to shift taxes will fail

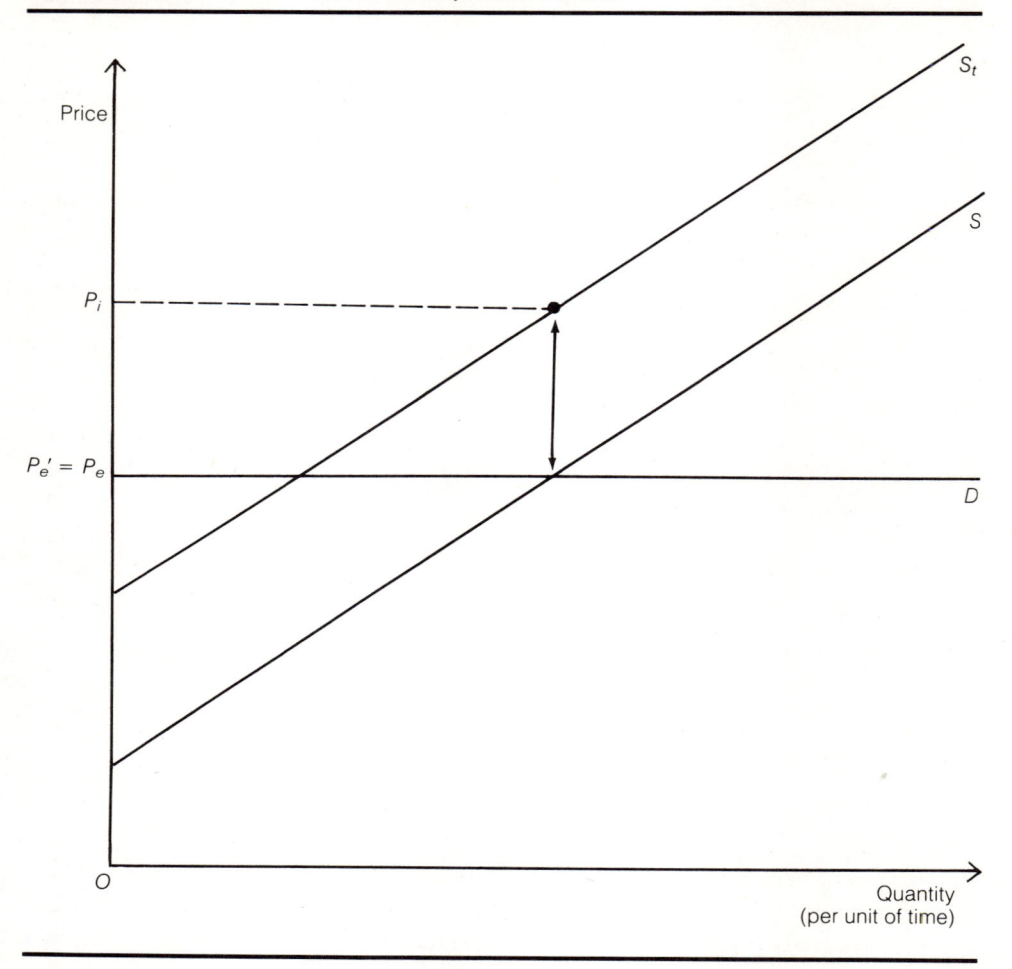

Figure 6.6 Sales Tax Incidence and Infinitely Elastic Demand

completely. Here, the curve is completely elastic (horizontal). The shift in the supply curve has no impact on the equilibrium price. Any attempt to pass the tax hike through to consumers is doomed to failure. The prices before and after the tax increase are unchanged ($P_e = P_e'$). The tax increase, equal to $P_e P_t$, must be absorbed completely by the producer.

Taxes Worldwide

How do taxes in the U.S. compare with those in the major non-Communist economic powers? Quite a range in tax revenue levels exists among the countries of the world

Table 6.7 Tax Revenues as a Percentage of Gross Domestic Product (GDP)

Country	1975	1980	1983	1984
United States	29.6	30.4	29.0	29.0
Austria	38.6	41.2	40.9	42.0
Belgium	41.1	43.7	45.6	46.7
Canada	33.0	32.0	33.4	33.7
Denmark	41.4	45.5	46.5	48.0
France	37.4	42.5	44.6	45.5
Japan	20.9	25.5	27.2	27.4
Sweden	43.9	49.4	50.6	50.5
United Kingdom	35.5	35.3	37.9	38.5

Source: *Statistical Abstract of the U.S.*, 1987, p. 828.

(table 6.7). In 1984, 50.5 percent of Sweden's gross domestic product consisted of national, local, and social security taxes. In other words, almost 51 cents out of every dollar's worth of production became revenue for Swedish tax authorities. In contrast, only 27.4 cents out of every dollar's worth of production went into Japan's tax coffers. The percentage in the United States also is relatively low. Generally, those countries with higher tax revenues as a percentage of total output tend to have very generous and complex social welfare systems. Those nations with relatively lower tax bills tend to rely more on private financing for social services.

SUMMARY

The mixed economy of the United States represents a system in between the pure market and pure command systems. Major economic questions are decided by the private sector (households and businesses) and the public sector (government).

Government involvement in the marketplace takes several forms. It promotes economic growth and stability, attends to the health and safety of its citizens, and fosters and, in some cases, controls competition through regulation.

The production or consumption of some goods creates spillovers or externalities in the form of benefits or costs incurred by parties other than the original producer or consumer. Two means of dealing with spillovers are adjusting the true costs and benefits so that all are internalized, or government regulation.

Federal, state, and local government expenditures have increased significantly in recent years. The U.S. national defense system and interest on the federal debt are relatively large expense items.

The chief source of revenue for the federal budget is taxation. Taxes may be regressive, proportional, or progressive. At first, taxes were primarily based on the benefits-received concept. Now, taxes are most often based on the principle of ability to pay. Governments may supplement tax revenues by instituting "hidden" taxes through inflated charges for municipal services.

Sometimes those who have been taxed can shift the burden to someone else. Producers may do this by raising prices. The ability of producers to pass the tax burden on to consumers depends largely upon the product's price elasticity of demand.

KEY WORDS

ability-to-pay theory	progressive tax
benefits-received theory	proportional tax
Council of Economic Advisors	regressive tax
externalities	spillovers
Full Employment and Economic Stabilization Act	tax base
	tax incidence
government subsidy	tax liability
hidden taxes	tax rate
laissez-faire	"user pay"
negative taxes	

Questions for Review

1. Give some current examples of taxes based on the "benefits-received" theory of taxation.

2. How might the costs of benefits provided by the public sector be reduced?

3. What justification can you use to defend a market system's government support of education?

4. In recent years, there has been a push toward cutting federal aid to states. State and local governments are being urged by some to shoulder the burden of maintaining services. What are the implications of this approach with regard to taxes, fairness, and tax incidence?

5. Another recent trend is "privatization" of public services. Governments are contracting with private firms to provide traditionally public services like medical care for the poor and elderly, and maintenance of prisons. What are some of the advantages and disadvantages of this trend?

6. How do subsidies increase output of a particular product? Do you think subsidies are a good idea for farmers? Why or why not?

7. Do government regulations focus on influencing the supply of goods or the demand for them?

8. How can a sales tax be both proportional and regressive?

9. In table 6.3, government expenditures for education increased from $16.1 billion in 1975 to $26.1 billion in 1984. However, critics charge that the federal government has abandoned our educational system. Comment.

10. Give an example of a spillover cost of producing some good. Give an example of a spillover benefit of producing some good.

ENDNOTES

1. See J. Greenwald, et al., "A New Age of Capitalism," *Time,* vol. 128, no. 4, July 28, 1986, pp. 28–34+.

2. See Milton H. Spencer, "Our Farm Problem: A Case Study," *Contemporary Economics,* 6th ed., (New York: Worth Publishers, Inc., 1986), pp. 432–41; and Ward Sinclair, "Administration Would Tighten Rules for Receiving Farm Subsidies," *The Washington Post,* March 15, 1987, p. A13.

3. See William F. Buckley, "The Feds and College Aid," *National Review,* vol. 38, no. 46, August 1, 1986; and William Bennett, "Time to End Student Loan Subsidies?" *U.S. News and World Report,* vol. 101, no. 8, December 1, 1986.

4. See Henry Kaufman, *Interest Rates, the Markets, and the New Financial World* (New York: Times Books, 1986); and Robert Eisner, *How Real is the Federal Deficit?* (New York: Free Press, 1986).

5. The 1986 tax law revision makes significant changes in tax rates, deductible items, and allowable exemptions. When the new rates are fully effective in 1988, individual taxes are projected to fall an average of 6.1 percent. See Leonard Wiener and Robert J. Morse, "Playing to Win by the New Tax Rules," *U.S. News and World Report,* September 1, 1986, pp. 49–51.

6. See James Dale Davidson, "The Poor Pay and the Rich Ride: Social Security Rip-off," *The New Republic,* November 11, 1985, pp. 12, 14.

7. See K. Bradbury, H. Ladd, "Changes in the Revenue-Raising Capacity of U.S. Cities, 1970–82," *New England Economic Review* (March/April 1985), pp. 20–37.

8. Joseph A. Pechman, *Who Paid the Taxes, 1966–85* (Washington, D.C.: Brookings Institution, 1985).

ECONOMICS IN THE NEWS

The growing trend of deregulation of American businesses has been especially controversial in the banking industry. This article discusses the effects of regulation on banks and the problems that must be resolved before deregulation may proceed.

Review & Outlook: Banking on Deregulation

A lot of high-priced banking talent hopped the shuttle from Wall Street to the Federal Reserve in Washington last week to argue over four words in a 1933 statute. The Glass-Steagall Act prohibits deposit-taking banks from being "principally engaged" in underwriting "ineligible securities," thus separating commercial banks and investment banks.

The idea behind this New Deal legislation was to protect depositors by restricting the kinds of investments banks could make with funds in demand accounts. Some bank regulation is necessary, but the notion that the Depression was caused by too little regulation is a myth. Brookings senior fellow Robert E. Litan wrote recently that "there was no evidence that the securities underwriting practices were a significant cause of the collapse of the banking system or that certain highly publicized abusive underwriting practices were widespread." In our view, the Depression was caused by protectionism, but showed up first in the financial markets because they correctly anticipated political actions and their economic effect.

Whatever the original value of the commercial/investment bank distinction, the markets have eroded it. For one thing, no industry is more international than banking. U.S. banks' foreign competitors are not hobbled by Glass-Steagall. Commercial banks discovered that the only way they could get into new financial services was to get passports for their employees. London and Tokyo have become beehives of American bank subsidiaries underwriting corporate debt and making other investments denied them in the U.S. On the other foot, when Goldman Sachs went looking for an infusion of capital, it found a commercial bank that wasn't bound by Glass-Steagall—Japan's Sumitomo.

The big irony is that restricting the investments that banks can make *increases* the risk to depositors. The very key to bank soundness is a diversified loan portfolio. Restricting thrift institutions to fixed-rate mortgages was a blunder only regulators could make. Ditto the farm credit system. Commercial banks haven't been able to diversify their portfolios into new instruments like mortgage-backed securities; instead, they're stuck with Third World debt. Commercial banks are especially troubled by being frozen out of the commercial-paper market. This short-term corporate debt is now a $300 billion market, up from $15 billion only 20 years ago. By issuing this paper, the big investment banks have eaten away at the commercial banks' best, least risky clients.

Only about one-third of all assets held by financial institutions are now held by commercial banks, down from more than half in 1946. Thrifts, insurance companies, pension funds and investment banks now hold the bulk of financial assets. Bankers have responded to this loss of business in a healthy way. They don't want protection, they want freedom to compete.

Congress has been the stumbling block. Despite the slogan of "American competitiveness," Democratic Reps. Fernand St Germain and Charles Schumer have sandbagged all efforts to reconsider Glass-Steagall. Fed Chairman Paul Volcker has also begged Congress for years to take up the issue, even urging that commercial banks be allowed into all kinds of underwriting, including corporate. Wearying of congressional inaction, the banks have come knocking at Mr. Volcker's door.

Citicorp, J.P. Morgan and Bankers Trust have applied to the Fed for permission to have their holding companies begin underwriting commercial-paper, mortgage-backed securities and municipal revenue bonds. Brokers at the big investment banks now perform the bulk of these activities. The three banks pledged in their applications that the new activities would not exceed 15% of the business of the holding companies. While Mr. Volcker doesn't think the Fed has the power to undo Glass-Steagall on its own, the 15% limitation puts the Fed on the spot since this seems within the "principally engaged" test.

The problem is that there are a handful of issues that have to be resolved before the barriers for commercial banks can be lowered. Chief among these is the role of explicit FDIC guarantees, and implicit Fed guarantees to prevent a string of bank failures. Commercial banks obviously get a benefit from federal insurance, which they shouldn't use for gambling with risky investments. Gerald Corrigan, president of the New York Federal Reserve Bank, has published a long paper trying to sort out what kind of regulation will have to remain.

While details have to be worked out, the markets have already made a big step toward deregulation almost inevitable. And as usual, the markets are right; more competition among financial institutions will cut costs and promote efficiency. The only question is how deregulation will come—through the Fed, by inducing banks to exchange federal charters for state ones, or by exporting the banks to London. By far the best solution would be for Congress to get to work moving the laws into the modern age.

Reprinted by permission of *The Wall Street Journal*, © Dow Jones & Company, 1987. All Rights Reserved.

CHAPTER SEVEN

BUSINESS ORGANIZATION

Objectives

After reading this chapter, you should be able to

•

describe the three major forms of business organization and
list some advantages and disadvantages of each

•

list some of the largest corporations in America and
explain some of the ways in which that list has changed over the years

•

list and describe several major antitrust laws

•

explain the difference between horizontal and vertical mergers,
and forward and backward mergers

•

describe the use of absolute concentration ratios, relative concentration ratios,
and the Herfindahl-Hirschman Index in measuring economic concentration

•

describe the relationship between industry profit levels and
industry concentration

•

list and describe several barriers to market entry

TYPES OF BUSINESS ORGANIZATION

The four factors of production (land, labor, capital, and entrepreneurial ability) are combined in a business enterprise to produce goods and services. Many business enterprises are small, with only a few employees; some have only one. Other enterprises are extremely large, with thousands of employees and sales larger than the GNP of certain small nations. The forms of business enterprise or organization have been categorized as sole proprietorships, partnerships, and corporations.

A look at the distribution and relative size of the three types of businesses is revealing. Sole proprietorships are overwhelmingly the most dominant form, comprising over 70 percent of all business enterprises. There are over 10 million such firms. These include farmers and professionals who are self-employed. Partnerships represent 10 percent of all businesses, and corporations, 20 percent. Table 7.1 shows the numerical breakdown of types of businesses in operation in the United States. While the sole proprietorship is the most popular form of business enterprise, the corporation is the most dominant in terms of sales. Table 7.2 shows how corporations dominate the American business scene in terms of output of goods and services. Why do some businesses organize as sole proprietors, some as partnerships, and others as corporations? Advantages and disadvantages accrue to each form of business organization.

Table 7.1 Types of Businesses in the United States (thousands)

Unit	1970	1975	1980	1983
Sole proprietorships	9,400	10,882	12,702	10,704
Partnerships	936	1,073	1,380	1,542
Corporations	1,665	2,024	2,711	2,999
Total	12,001	13,979	16,793	15,245

Source: Statistical Abstract of the United States, 1987. U.S. Department of Commerce, Bureau of the Census, p. 503.

Table 7.2 Receipts by Type of Business (billions of dollars)

Unit	1970	1975	1980	1983
Sole proprietorships	238	339	506	465
Partnerships	93	147	292	291
Corporations	1,751	3,199	6,361	7,135
Total	2,082	3,685	7,159	7,891

Source: Statistical Abstract of the U.S., 1987, p. 503.

Sole Proprietorships

The sole proprietorship is the simplest and most common form of business organization. The individual proprietor is the sole owner of the plant, equipment, and resources of the business undertaking, and while the firm may have other employees, the owner is completely responsible for the firm's performance. Sole proprietorships include the entire range of unincorporated, one-owner businesses, farms, and professional practices.

Advantages

A sole proprietorship is simple to organize, plan, and open for business. There are relatively few legal requirements. Often little expertise, business experience, or education is required. However, there is a strong incentive to work toward the objectives of the enterprise, because all profits accrue to the sole proprietor.

Sole proprietors enjoy a great deal of freedom in making decisions and taking action. The sole proprietor is literally his or her own boss.

Disadvantages

All losses of the proprietorship become the personal liability of the owner. Creditors can attach business assets and personal assets. Credit availability is limited to the credit rating of the sole proprietor, so business expansion can be difficult and relatively costly.

The business's resources are normally limited to the personal wealth of the sole proprietor, and efficient—but expensive—technology may be beyond the proprietor's grasp.

Because of their limited size, many sole proprietorships are unable to survive difficult economic times; they fail not because of the proprietor's shortcomings, but because of the swings of the business cycle.

It is difficult to liquidate or sell the business. A sole proprietor must find a buyer with virtually identical goals and interests.

Finally, although business expertise is not a requirement, the lack of it has proven fatal to many sole proprietorships. The sole proprietor generally bears responsibility for production, marketing, sales, advertising, public relations, and more. Balancing the demands of this tremendous workload requires considerable skill and flexibility. It is estimated that only 30 percent of new small businesses are still functioning 5 years after start-up.

Partnerships

The partnership form of business organization is the combination of two or more individuals who agree to own, operate, and share the expenses and proceeds of their enterprise in a predetermined fashion. The partnership requires a contract or agreement between or among the parties. This agreement is normally quite detailed and a written contract is used in most partnerships, but sometimes a verbal contract suffices. A number of systems of managements are possible, of which the most common form is the general partnership. Partnerships may include silent partners, secret partners, and dormant partners.

A silent partner has full financial, investment, and profit rights, and shares the debt obligations of the general partner. However, the silent partner does not normally participate in the day-to-day management of the firm. An example of a silent partner may be an older individual who brings status to the business but who has no interest in being an active participant.

The secret partner has full financial and legal ties to the firm but is not known to the public as a partner. The owner of a towing service may be a secret partner in an auto body repair business.

A dormant partner combines the characteristics of the silent and the secret partner. The dormant partner is not publicly known to be a partner and has no involvement in the managerial decision-making process. For example, a physician may be a dormant partner in a pharmacy.

Advantages

Additional individuals can bring added wealth and resources to the organization, and partnerships are only slightly more difficult to organize than sole proprietorships.

Some forms of partnership that allow for secret or dormant partners permit the business involvement of people who, for public image reasons, could not otherwise participate.

Individual partners may have special areas of interest or expertise permitting greater specialization and higher productivity than would be possible under a series of individual proprietorships.

Disadvantages

All partners are legally responsible for the business debts of the partnership; creditors may attach the partnership's assets as well as the private assets of each partner. Moreover, liability is not limited to individual decisions: each partner is responsible for the liabilities incurred by any and all of the associates.

The financial resources of a partnership still may be insufficient to obtain state-of-the-art technology.

The very essence of a partnership can lead to managerial roadblocks. Disagreements over policy and direction are common in partnerships. Critical decision making may be delayed, resulting in increased expenses and missed opportunities.

In some organizations where there are a large number of partners, more ambitious partners may break off and establish their own business, taking lucrative clients and valuable proprietary information with them.

Termination of the partnership following the withdrawal or death of one of the partners may be cumbersome. If the surviving partner or partners desire to continue, they must attempt to purchase the withdrawing or deceased partner's share of ownership. To account for the possibility of death of a partner, many partnerships purchase life insurance for all partners, the proceeds of which can be used to buy back the lost share from the deceased's estate. This practice permits the continued operation of the business without lengthy probate difficulties.

Corporations

Corporations are legal entities. Corporations can own property, secure debt, engage in legal battles, and produce and market goods and services.[1]

Advantages

The corporation is distinguished from other forms of business enterprise by its limited liability. The stockholders of a corporation are liable for the debts of the firm only to the extent of their investment in the ownership securities. In the event of bankruptcy, creditors normally may not attach the private assets of stockholders. Only the assets of the corporation (the legally responsible entity) are available for attachment by creditors.

Because of the advantages of limited liability to a stockholder, corporations can attract many investors whose combined wealth can be enormous. Expensive high-technology equipment and production processes are more readily obtainable by a successful corporation.

Transfer of ownership shares is relatively simple for the corporation. Rather than conduct the exhaustive search for a buyer that a sole proprietor may have to undertake, ownership shares in corporations can be sold by a simple phone call to a broker. Corporations can endure through generations of different stockholders.

Because corporations tend to be relatively large and wealthy, they are better able to withstand economic shocks that would destroy partnerships and sole proprietorships. Corporations have a long life expectancy.

Corporate funds of ownership permit intense specialization. Employing large numbers of people, corporations can obtain specialists who, through their combined effort, can be much more productive than an equal number of sole proprietors.

Corporations currently enjoy a small tax advantage over other types of business in the form of a lower maximum marginal tax rate.

Disadvantages

Corporations can only be established by obtaining a state charter. While corporate charter requirements vary from state to state, they are relatively expensive and difficult to obtain.

Normally, the owners of a corporation are not its managers. In the largest of corporations, many shareholders may not even know the names of top management. This is called separation of ownership and control. Corporate policy and direction may run counter to the beliefs of individual stockholders. Yet, when stocks are widely held, individual shareholders have little voice in the control of the organization. It appears that the same kind of voter lethargy that is common in democracies also takes place in large corporations. As in a democracy, this can prove expensive for the disenfranchised. Management decisions to purchase a corporate aircraft, award bonuses, and delegate other expensive perquisites may be made at the expense of dividends.

Although corporate profits are taxed at a special business rate, if these profits are not retained for future business development, but distributed as dividends to shareholders, double taxation occurs: the dividends are also taxed as personal income to shareholders. If the business were organized as a sole proprietorship, profits would only be taxed once, albeit at a slightly higher maximum marginal rate.

An interesting variation on the standard corporation is the "subchapter S corporation." This is a relatively small corporation that qualifies and elects to be taxed as a partnership under subchapter S of the Internal Revenue Code. Under this option, taxable income and certain liabilities of the corporation flow through to the individual proprietors as part of their tax reports.

THE EVOLUTION OF AMERICAN INDUSTRY

Valuable insights into the evolution of corporate America can be gained by observing the biggest American corporations over time (table 7.3).

Table 7.3 Top 10 American Businesses, Selected Years (by annual sales)

1909	1958	1985
U.S. Steel	Standard Oil of NJ	General Motors
Standard Oil of NJ	General Motors	Exxon
American Tobacco	U.S. Steel	AT&T
International Mercantile Marine	Gulf Oil	Mobil
International Harvester	Mobil Oil	Ford Motor
Anaconda Copper	Texaco	IBM
U.S. Leather, Inc.	Ford Motor	Texaco
Armour Meat Packing Company	Du Pont Chemical	Chevron
American Sugar Refinery	Standard Oil of Indiana	Sears Roebuck
Pullman Company	Standard Oil of California	Du Pont

Source: Data obtained from the U.S. Department of Commerce.

The combined impact of changing technology, shifts in consumer tastes and preferences, social and political forces, and managerial performance is visible in the history of corporations. In 1909, the U.S. economy relied heavily on agriculture and foodstuffs. By 1958, the auto and petro-chemical industries had matured to a point of dominance. Yet, by 1985, the importance of auto and oil had declined slightly, while the telecommunications and computer industries were emerging as significant forces in the economy.

BIGNESS VS. ECONOMIC EFFICIENCY: ANTITRUST ECONOMICS

The "invisible hand" which theoretically drives firms to high productivity and efficiency while encouraging low prices and increased consumer choices is contingent upon the competition of a large number of participants. Adam Smith warned against the possibility of dishonest entrepreneurs who might attempt to bypass the rigors of fair competition by joining forces with rival firms. Once combined, whether financially or spiritually, with competitors, such firms might find it easy to gouge a public faced with few, if any, alternate sources of supply. High prices, shoddy products, and poor service would result. Some kind of antitrust action would have to be used to restore competition. The basic deterrents employed to prevent firms from engaging in anticompetitive behavior in the U.S. are antitrust laws.

Antitrust Legislation

There are six major antitrust laws currently in force in the U.S. (table 7.4). The major purpose of these laws is to prevent the monopolization of industry and to restrict unfair methods of competition. The economic and legal definitions of "monopoly" differ slightly. The economic definition of a monopoly is a market in which only one firm exists. The legal definition of monopoly includes markets or industries that have more than one firm if the market or industry is dominated by a single firm. The legal monopoly is more closely allied to the economists' "oligopoly market." The term oligopoly refers to a market with a few relatively large firms.[2]

In a competitive market firms normally can increase their market share through acquisition or merger. There are three basic types of mergers.

A horizontal merger occurs between two firms in the same industry. If the First National Bank purchased the Second National Bank, this merger would be classified as a horizontal purchase.

A vertical merger occurs when two firms merge that are related somehow in the resource supply, production, or delivery markets.

Table 7.4 Major Antitrust Laws

Title and Date	Major Provision
Sherman Antitrust Act (1890)	Forbids restraints of trade, monopoly, and attempts to monopolize
Clayton Antitrust Act (1914)	Forbids practices whose effects may be to lessen substantially the degree of competition or to tend to create a monopoly
Fair Trade Commission Act (1914)	A supplement to the Clayton Act; forbids unfair methods of competition
Robinson-Patman Act (1936)	The "Chain Store Act"—a supplement to the Clayton Act, forbids payment of brokerage fees when no independent broker is employed; granting of discounts to manufacturers, retailers, and wholesalers unless such concessions are made to all buyers on proportionately equal terms; price discrimination; and charging lower prices in one locality than in another when the intent is to destroy competition or eliminate a competitor
Wheeler-Lea Act (1938)	An amendment to the FTC Act; forbids unfair or deceptive acts or practices in interstate commerce, defines "false advertising"
Celler-Kefauver Act (1950)	An amendment to the Clayton Act; forbids corporations from acquiring stock or assets of a competitor if such acquisitions lessen competition or tend to create a monopoly

There are two distinct types of vertical mergers: forward mergers and backward mergers. A forward vertical merger occurs when a firm acquires a firm "ahead" in the production chain. For example, if a clothing manufacturer purchases a chain of retail clothing stores, this acquisition is a forward vertical merger. A backward vertical merger occurs when a firm purchases a supplier. If the clothing manufacturer acquires a fabric mill, it has executed a backward vertical merger. In the financial area, an automobile manufacturer might expand vertically by acquiring a finance company.

Finally, a conglomerate merger involves two firms from separate industries. If our vertically integrated clothing manufacturer were to diversify and purchase an airline, this acquisition would be classified as a conglomerate merger.

The Justice Department treats each of these merger types differently. A horizontal merger between two large firms can weaken competition in certain markets, whereas a vertical merger may actually improve economic welfare if there is a gain in efficiency from the vertical integration of firms. Table 7.5 traces the merger movement by industry type for recent years.

Table 7.5 Merger and Acquisition Transactions

Industry Classification of Seller	Number of Mergers			
	1981	1982	1983	1984
Oil and gas	76	80	111	102
Banking and finance	335	426	331	251
Insurance	89	81	67	66
Mining and minerals	40	31	18	12
Food processing	69	52	74	58
Transportation	31	40	36	36
Retail	87	86	90	130
Brokerage and other investment firms	46	56	63	86

Source: W.T. Grimm & Co., *Mergerstat Review*, 1984. As published in *Statistical Abstract of the U.S.*, 1987, p. 524.

Measures of Bigness

How is "bigness" measured? Specific indicators of size are used to distinguish between high-concentration and low-concentration industries.

Absolute Concentration Ratio

The most popular measure of economic concentration is called the absolute concentration ratio. The ratio is normally stated in terms of a four-firm or eight-firm concentration ratio, depending on the total number of firms in a given industry. The four-firm concentration ratio is the most common, and it can be defined as the percentage of sales or assets held by the largest four firms. The ratio is determined by dividing the sum of the sales of the four largest firms in a market by total market sales. Total assets may also be used as a unit of measure, but the results are typically similar to those found using sales-based measures. Table 7.6 shows the four-firm concentration ratio of selected firms. The four-firm ratio is one of the popular measures of concentration because it is easy to calculate and because it is more easily understood by laymen than the more esoteric measures of concentration.

Despite its advantages, use of the absolute concentration ratio exclusively in determining the state of competition within an industry can be criticized on a number of areas. The ratio does not describe the degree of competition among the four largest firms. It may be possible to have a very competitive market with only a few large firms. The four-firm ratio also does not account for the competitive effects of imports, nor is the impact of interindustry competition included in the basic four-firm measures. For example, many highly concentrated industries face stiff competition from related industries.

The fourth criticism of the four-firm ratio is related to the point noted above: the ratio depends to a great extent on how the "market" is defined. If the market is defined in a very narrow sense, the four-firm ratio may be very high. If, on the other hand, the "market" is

Table 7.6 Four-firm Concentration Ratios for Selected U.S. Manufacturing Industries

Industry	Number of Firms	Four-Firm Concentration Ratio[a] (percent)
Internal combustion engines	202	48
Wood household furniture	2,430	16
Envelopes	196	28
Paint and allied products	1,170	24
Glass containers	41	50
Household refrigerators and freezers	39	94
Electric lamps	113	91
Hard surface floor coverings	12	99
Sporting and athletic goods	1,453	17
Surgical and medical instruments	766	32
Transformers	240	52
Small arms	138	51
Aluminum sheet, plate, and foil	39	74
Ready-mixed concrete	4,161	6
Petroleum refining	282	28

Source: Adapted from *1982 Census of Manufacturers*, U.S. Department of Commerce.
a. Concentration ratios based on dollar value of shipments.

defined in a very broad sense, the four-firm ratio may be reduced to insignificance. For example, the "major television broadcasting market" is very highly concentrated, yet the "television market" is only one small part of the entire "entertainment market."

The final criticism of the four-firm ratio is that the measurement may misrepresent the degree of competition in regional or local markets. For example, the national four-firm concentration ratio for commercial banks is quite low, but a study of regional or local markets may reveal extensive concentration.

At least one of the above drawbacks can be eliminated when the four-firm concentration ratio is combined with the four-firm relative concentration ratio.

Relative Concentration Ratio

The four-firm relative concentration ratio measures the corporate size of the largest four firms. The largest firm is given an index value of 100, and the second, third, and fourth largest firms are assigned values based on their size compared to the leader. The general formula for a relative concentration ratio is as follows:

$$\left[100 - \left(\frac{\text{sales of \#2 firm}}{\text{sales of \#1 firm}}\right)^* - \left(\frac{\text{sales of \#3 firm}}{\text{sales of \#1 firm}}\right)^* - \left(\frac{\text{sales of \#4 firm}}{\text{sales of \#1 firm}}\right)^* \right].$$

*expressed as a percentage

Table 7.7 Annual Sales: Major Petroleum Firms, 1985
(millions of dollars)

Company	Sales
Exxon	86,673
Mobil	55,960
Texaco	47,500
Chevron	41,742
Amoco	26,921
Atlantic Richfield	21,723
Phillips Petroleum	15,636
Tenneco	15,270
Occidental Petroleum	14,534
Sun	14,435
Others combined	107,278

Source: Reprinted from April 18, 1987 issue of *Business Week* by special permission, copyright © 1987 by McGraw-Hill, Inc.

For example, a four-firm relative concentration ratio of (100 – 100 – 100 – 100) would mean the four largest firms in an industry are of equal size, while a ratio of (100 – 50 – 50 – 25) reveals that the second and third largest firms in the industry are of equal size at half the size of the leader. The fourth largest firm is only 25 percent as big as the leader, and half the size of the second and third largest firms. The technique of calculating the four-firm relative and absolute concentration ratios can be shown with the use of actual data (table 7.7). The four-firm absolute ratio can be calculated by dividing the industry sales total by the combined sales of the top four firms—EXXON, Mobil, Texaco, and Chevron. Total industry output is listed as $447,672 million. The top four firms' sales equal $231,875 million. Therefore, the four-firm concentration ratio is equal to .52. The four-firm relative ratio is calculated as follows:

$$100 - \frac{X_2}{X_1} - \frac{X_3}{X_1} - \frac{X_4}{X_1},$$

where $X_1, X_2, X_3,$ and X_4 are the sales of the largest, second, third, and fourth largest firms respectively.

The individual ratios are expressed as percentages. The four-firm relative concentration ratio for the oil and gas market is (100 – 65 – 55 – 48). In other words, there were three firms of relatively equal size (Mobil, Texaco, and Chevron) engaged in the production of fuel in 1985, and their industry leader, EXXON, was approximately 1.5 times larger than its nearest rival.

The Herfindahl-Hirschman Index

The Herfindahl-Hirschman Index (H-HI) combines the benefits of the absolute and relative concentration indices. The index increases as absolute concentration increases and with increasing dominance by a few firms. The index measures the sum of individual market shares, each squared, of all the firms in a given industry. The formula for the Herfindahl-Hirschman Index is as follows:

$$\text{H-HI} = \sum_{i=1}^{n} \left(S_i\right)^2,$$

where H-HI = Herfindahl-Hirschman Index, and
S = Market share of firm 1 to n expressed as a percentage.

The higher the H-HI value, the more concentrated the market in both the absolute and relative sense. Table 7.8 constructs various hypothetical market concentrations and the calculation of the Herfindahl Index for each.

Table 7.8 Herfindahl Index for Four Hypothetical Markets

Market	Firm	Market Share (percent)	Herfindahl Index (HHI)
A. Two firms	A	50	
	B	50	$(50)^2 + (50)^2 = 5{,}000$
B. Two firms	A	80	
	B	20	$(80)^2 + (20)^2 = 6{,}800$
C. Three firms	A	33.3	
	B	33.3	
	C	33.3	$(33.3)^2 + (33.3)^2 + (33.3)^2 = 3{,}327$
D. Ten firms of equal size	A	10	
	B	10	
	C	10	
	D	10	
	E	10	
	F	10	
	G	10	
	H	10	
	I	10	
	J	10	$(10)^2 + (10)^2 + \ldots + (10)^2 = 1{,}000$

Table 7.9 Herfindahl Calculations of Oil and Gas Industry, 1985

Company	Market Share (percent)[a]	Market Share Squared
Exxon	19.4	376.36
Mobil	12.5	156.25
Texaco	10.6	112.36
Chevron	9.3	86.49
Amoco	6.0	36.00
Atlantic Richfield	4.9	24.01
Phillips Petroleum	3.5	12.25
Tenneco	3.4	11.56
Occidental Petroleum	3.2	10.24
Sun	3.2	10.24
Other	23.9	n/a[b]
	Herfindahl Index (H-HI)	835.76

Source: Information on market share is available from company reports, industry trade publications, and other business publications.
a. Subject to rounding error.
b. The Herfindahl squared value for the category "other" is not the square of the summed market shares (23.9) but instead the sum of the squared market shares of all remaining small firms.

In market A, where there are only two firms of equal size, the H-HI is 5,000. In market B, which has two firms of unequal size, the H-HI is equal to 6,800. In other words, as the distribution of output between and among firms becomes uneven, the Herfindahl-Hirschman Index indicates the relative concentration by growing in size. As a comparison of markets C and D illustrates, as markets become more competitive, with larger numbers of rivals, the index becomes smaller.

The H-HI for the oil and gas industry (table 7.9) is calculated by summing the squares of the industrial market shares.

By itself, the number in the index is relatively meaningless. It has no way of showing if the structure of a given industry is highly concentrated vis-à-vis other industries. Industry structure and concentration depends, to a great extent, on the combination of technology, efficiency, firm size, total market sales potential, foreign competition, local market conditions, and other factors not assessed by the index. Normally, however, an H-HI under 1,000 is considered to be unconcentrated and competitive. An H-HI between 1,000 and 1,800 is considered moderately concentrated, and an index over 2,000 is considered to be highly concentrated. Table 7.10 shows the Herfindahl Index for selected industries.

In 1982, the Antitrust Division of the Justice Department issued new merger guidelines (table 7.11) based on the Herfindahl-Hirschman Index. The new merger guidelines denote H-HI ranges which might trigger a Justice Department challenge.

The Justice Department is not required to challenge every merger which fails the Herfindahl test. The joint venture of Toyota and General Motors, which created the Saturn Auto subsidiary, was attacked by Chrysler as being a violation of the merger guidelines. Chrysler officials warned that the merger would raise the Herfindahl-Hirschman Index to a

Table 7.10 Herfindahl Index for Selected U.S. Manufacturing Industries

	Herfindahl Index (H-HI)[a]
Highly concentrated: (H-HI $\geq$ 1,800)	
Chocolate and cocoa	2,214
Malt beverages	2,089
Chewing and smoking tobacco	2,564
Carpets and rugs	1,892
Tire cord and fabric	2,584
Greeting card publishing	2,840
Organic fibers, noncellulosic	2,349
Flat glass	2,032
Gypsum products	1,993
Mineral wood	2,081
Moderately concentrated: (H-HI = 1,000 to 1,800)	
Dog, cat, other pet food	1,167
Cookies and crackers	1,401
Canned and cured seafoods	1,683
Wood TV and radio cabinets	1,049
Sanitary paper products	1,328
Building paper and board mills	1,409
Industrial glasses	1,530
Soap and other detergents	1,306
Tires and inner tubes	1,591
House slippers	1,262
Unconcentrated: (H-HI $<$ 1,000)	
Rice milling	871
Confectionary products	584
Animal and marine fats	414
Bottled and canned soft drinks	109
Manufactured ice	125
Men's and boys' neckwear	311
Distilled liquor	741
Women's and misses' outerwear	86
Brick and structural clay tile	263
Mining machinery	575

Source: Adapted from *1982 Census of Manufacturers*, U.S. Department of Commerce.
a. Concentration index based upon dollar value of shipments.

level six times greater than that permitted by the guidelines, and demanded a merger challenge. The Justice Department chose not to challenge the merger. The guidelines are, after all, only guidelines. Other factors must be considered. In this case, the U.S. auto industry struggle to compete with the Japanese may have weighed heavily in the Justice Department's decision not to intervene. Perhaps the Justice Department concluded the merger would permit General Motors to learn a great deal about Japanese management techniques and production methods. These lessons would lead to a more viable and competitive industry in the long run.

Table 7.11 Justice Department Merger Guidelines (based on the Herfindahl Index)

Herfindahl Index (H-HI)	Market Classification	Merger Action
Less than 1,000	Unconcentrated	No challenge
Between 1,000 and 1,800	Moderately concentrated	Challenge new merger if index increases by more than 100 points as a result of merger
Greater than 1,800	Highly concentrated	Challenge any merger if index increases more than 50 points as a result of merger

Source: Antitrust Division, U.S. Justice Department.

Bigness and Profits

Is there a strong correlation between concentration in any given industry and profitability? Economic theory would predict that, where competition is strong and rigorous, and where entry into the industry by new firms is not blocked or impeded, profits should be pushed to the barest minimum. This level of profit is called normal or business profit. Normal profits include only the opportunity costs of the owner's total capital and entrepreneurship investment in the enterprise. If, for example, capital can earn a 10 percent rate of return in the capital markets, then firm owners who are earning a 10 percent profit will not desire to liquidate their investment. They are earning a normal rate of return. Normal profit is the return necessary to maintain capital levels in a given industry. If the same firm earns 18 percent profit, economists would say the firm is earning an 8 percent economic profit. Economic profits represent returns to capital above and beyond those levels needed to keep capital in an industry. In other words, economic profits are those returns above normal profits. If the firm's returns go back to 10 percent, we can say the economic profits are zero, but normal profits are maintained.

When firms in any given industry are able to earn economic profits, a signal is released to other economic agents. These economic agents will try to enter the industry to reap the benefits of economic profit. The new competition inspired by the lure of economic profit will tend to reduce profits for all competitors. New firms will continue to enter the industry until the economic profits have returned to zero, and firms again earn only normal profits. If average profits fall below the normal profit level, some competitors will leave or exit that industry. Competition and supply will be reduced until profits return to a normal level.

Firms may try to block this mechanism. If mergers and acquisitions in an industry constantly erode the structure of an industry, reducing the number of viable competitors and thereby raising the concentration level, can economic profits be earned and sustained? The economic evidence is not clear in this matter. While many highly concentrated, low-competitive industries tend to have profits much higher than lower-concentrated, competitive industries, this is not a universal phenomenon. Research economists continually study various industries to determine the relationship between industry structure and profit concentration.[3]

BARRIERS TO MARKET ENTRY

Economic theory tells us that industries earning economic profits will soon experience the entry of new competition. Yet the evidence indicates this does not always occur. Some firms seem to be able to earn economic profits but not have to face fresh competition. One theory holds that the existing profitable firms sometimes erect barriers that prevent potential firms from entering the market.

Barriers to market entry can be both legal and economic in nature. A firm can obtain patents for key production methods or processes. U.S. patent prohibition extends for 17 years. During this period, the firm holding the patent can obtain a strong market position. Firms facing foreign competition can seek import quota protection from Congress. The domestic steel and auto industries benefit from "voluntary" quotas that act as an effective barrier to entry. Other legal barriers include licensing or charter requirements imposed by government regulatory bodies.

One of the most effective barriers to entry is consumer brand loyalty. Firms with strong market positions can create strong brand loyalty through effective marketing and advertising campaigns. The long-term import of this conditioning is often an effective barrier to entry. For example, in the 1960s, Heinz Foods entered the canned soup market which had been dominated by industry leader Campbell. The new firm's sales record was disappointing. Heinz undertook consumer taste studies to find out why the Heinz products couldn't gain a foothold in the market. When consumers were asked to rate the two soups in a blind taste test, approximately 50 percent of the subjects preferred Heinz products to Campbell's. When the subjects were asked their preference between soups served in labeled containers, however, 95 percent preferred Campbell's—even when the labels on the containers were switched! In other words, subjects preferred soup labeled Campbell's even when the soup actually was Heinz. Faced with this brand loyalty, Heinz dropped out of this market.

An important economic barrier to entry occurs when the new entrant would not be able to produce at the same cost level as the existing firm. The existing firm's technology or skilled work force generates a cost advantage which cannot be overcome by a competitor new to the industry. In this case, the established firm could sell its product at a price that a potential entrant could not match, because of the entrant's higher average costs, yet maintain its own economic profits. The existing firm's technique of pricing carefully to limit entry yet still generate economic profits is called limit pricing.

Certain industries rely on frequent model changes or product performance adjustments to bar entry. For example, a potential entrant may be able to raise enough capital to introduce a new competitive product. But if the established firms, with substantial economic resources at their disposal, can respond by introducing a "new generation" product, the new entrant may not be able to stay in the market. This can be an effective barrier in industries where new models require expensive retooling or promotional expenses.

THE HEALTH OF AMERICAN BUSINESS

New businesses are being started every day. Other businesses are closing their doors, for a variety of reasons. Table 7.12 contains birth and death statistics for U.S. firms for selected years. Table 7.13 lists business failures by industry sector.[4]

Table 7.12 Industrial and Commercial Failures: Number and Liabilities

Year	Total Concerns in Business[a]	New Incorporations	Failures[b]
1960	2,708,000	183,000	15,445
1965	2,527,000	204,000	13,514
1970	2,442,000	264,000	10,748
1975	2,679,000	326,000	11,432
1980	2,780,000	534,000	11,742
1984	4,885,000	635,000	52,078

Source: Statistical Abstract of the U.S., 1987, p. 509; also U.S. Bureau of Economic Analysis, Business Conditions Digest, June issues.
a. Data through 1980 represent the number of names listed in July issue of Dun & Bradstreet Reference Book. Data for 1984 represent the number of establishments listed in the Dun's Census of American Business. The base was changed due to expanded business failure coverage.
b. Includes concerns discontinued following assignment, voluntary or involuntary petition in bankruptcy, attachment, execution, foreclosure, etc.; voluntary withdrawals from business with known loss to creditors; also, enterprises involved in court action . . . which may or may not lead to discontinuance; and businesses making voluntary compromise with creditors out of court.

As table 7.12 indicates, there has been rapid growth in the total number of new enterprises established between 1960 and 1984. The total number of concerns increased by approximately 80 percent during this period. However, the number of business failures per year also increased, by more than 200 percent during the same period.

Table 7.13 portrays the recent struggles of the farming and service sectors. Relatively large increases in the number of failures of agricultural, forestry, and fishing enterprises, as well as in the number of failures in the general service sector, occurred between 1984–85.

Table 7.13 Business Failures by Industry Sector, 1985 and 1986

Industry	1985	1986	Percentage Change 1985–86
Agriculture, forestry, and fishing	2,699	2,622	−2.9
Mining	796	911	14.4
Construction	7,005	7,037	0.5
Manufacturing	4,869	4,740	−2.6
Transportation and public utilities	2,536	2,552	0.6
Wholesale trade	4,836	4,815	−0.4
Retail trade	13,494	13,524	0.2
Finance, insurance, and real estate	2,676	2,771	3.6
Services	16,649	20,912	25.6

Source: Economic Analysis Department, The Dun & Bradstreet Corporation, 1985–86 *Business Failure Record*.

SUMMARY

A business may be organized as a sole proprietorship, a partnership, or a corporation. Sole proprietorships are most prevalent but corporations are biggest in terms of sales. Each form of business has its advantages and disadvantages for its owners.

The list of American corporate powerhouses has changed over the years, reflecting changes in technology, consumer taste, and managerial performance.

Various antitrust laws have been passed by Congress as a means of preventing monopolies and promoting healthy competition. Antitrust laws are used to prevent some kinds of business mergers.

Mergers can be horizontal, between businesses of the same type, or vertical, between a company and another company that either precedes or follows it in the production chain. Vertical mergers can be forward or backward.

The absolute concentration ratio, the relative concentration ratio, and the Herfindahl-Hirschman Index are three methods used to measure the economic concentration of firms in an industry.

Industries that are in highly concentrated and not very competitive markets may have profits that are significantly greater than those of industries in less concentrated and more competitive markets.

In those industries where economic profits exist, economic forces will be set in motion that encourage new entries. Existing firms, in an effort to protect their profit positions, may attempt to erect barriers to entry.

Barriers to market entry include patents, import quotas, licensing fees, limit pricing by existing firms, brand loyalty of consumers, start-up costs to new firms, and the introduction of "new and improved" products by established producers.

KEY WORDS

antitrust laws
conglomerate merger
corporation
dormant partner
economic profit
four-firm concentration ratio
Herfindahl-Hirschmann Index
horizontal merger
limit pricing

normal (business) profit
oligopoly market
partnership
relative concentration ratio
secret partner
silent partner
sole proprietorship
subchapter S corporation
vertical merger (forward, backward)

Questions for Review

1. Under the Reagan administration's Justice Department appointees, antitrust action against vertical mergers decreased sharply, yet administration concern over vertical mergers is still quite high. Explain this apparent contradiction.

2. Define the market for financial services in both a narrow and broad sense. What new firms enter the financial services industry when the market is broadly defined?

3. Given the market data shown below, find (a) the four-firm absolute concentration ratio, (b) the four-firm relative concentration ratio, and (c) the Herfindahl Index.

Firm	Sales
A	$1000
B	935
C	850
D	300
E	200
F	150
G	25

4. Given the market data shown in question 3, how would the Justice Department view a merger between firms A and B?

5. Banking is a very competitive, low-concentration industry. No single bank or group of banks can control the national markets. Competition is fierce, even at the regional level. However, at the community level, some banks can possess considerable market power and generate relatively high economic profits. Theoretically, these high economic profits should lead to the entry of new banking organizations. Yet, in certain areas, new entry rates are low. What barriers to entry exist in banking markets?

ENDNOTES

1. For an interesting perspective on corporations and their role in the American economy, see John Kenneth Galbraith, "The Corporation," *The New Industrial State* (Boston: Houghton Mifflin, 1976).

2. Robert A. Katzmann describes the original intentions of U.S. antitrust legislation and argues for broader interpretation in "The Attenuation of Antitrust," *The Brookings Review* (Summer 1984), pp. 23–27.

3. Walter Adams and James Brock describe how the concentration of corporate power in America has had unhealthy results in their book, *The Bigness Complex: Industry, Labor, and Government in the American Economy* (New York: Pantheon, 1986).

4. Bank failure rates have been the topic of many articles on banking and business. One such article is Anthony W. Cyrnak's "Recent Bank Failures," *Weekly Letter*, the Federal Reserve Bulletin of San Francisco, April 11, 1986, pp. 1–3.

ECONOMICS IN THE NEWS

Mergers & Acquisitions
Savings Banks Figure in Several Fed Decisions

Recent decisions of the Federal Reserve Board include an approval of an Alabama acquisition over the dissent of Chairman Paul Volcker.

This transaction barely passed competitive muster, arousing a dissent from Chairman Paul Volcker and Governor Wayne Angell. They would have conditioned approval on a divestiture of offices to alleviate the perceived anticompetitive effects.

In the Tuscaloosa banking market, the transaction would result in the largest organization, First Tuscaloosa Corp., getting just a tad larger. The majority of the Board found several mitigating circumstances. AmSouth's absolute and relative sizes in the market were small. Indeed, AmSouth was the smallest depository institution in the market. In the context of the market's overall competitive structure, the increase in market concentration would be modest. Since AmSouth's entry into the market in 1976, its market share had remained unchanged despite a substantial increase in the market's deposits. Four other commercial banking organizations, including the largest organizations in the state, would remain as competitors in the market. Thrift institutions have a significant market presence, controlling approximately 37 percent of the market's total deposits. Two of the thrifts are the largest and second largest thrift institutions in the state. And finally, a broad range of competitive services are offered by credit unions, consumer and commercial finance companies, and other providers of financial services.

The dissent of Chairman Volcker and Governor Angell was as follows:

We would also approve the proposed acquisition by AmSouth of First Tuscaloosa, but unlike the majority of the Board, we would require AmSouth, as a condition of approval, to divest an office or offices equivalent to its current position in the market. We would do so because, in our view, given the already highly concentrated nature of the Tuscaloosa banking market, the proposal without a divestiture would unduly reduce the competitive forces at work in the area.

We agree with the majority that the increase in concentration in the market consequent upon the merger is small. The question posed, however, is whether, in a market already so highly concentrated, a merger involving the dominant bank in the market with another viable competitor should be approved without a divestiture designed to maintain existing competitive options. In this case of a highly concentrated market, we believe that an acquisition that will eliminate an effective and forceful competitor from the market and further concentrate the market share of the dominant institution in that market should not go forward.

Reprinted by permission of the *Banking Expansion Reporter*, April 20, 1987, Vol. 6, No. 8.

CHAPTER EIGHT

INDIVIDUALS IN THE U.S. ECONOMY

Objectives

After reading this chapter, you should be able to

•

describe some ways growth, aging, relocation, and education
have affected the population of the United States

•

define the civilian noninstitutional population

•

distinguish between functional and personal distributions of income

•

ascertain labor's share of total national income
in any given year

•

discuss where and, in general, why wage differentials occur

•

give a brief history of unions in the American workplace

•

describe some of the major U.S. labor laws

•

explain why unions have been losing power in several American industries

POPULATION TRENDS

Growth

The 1985 U.S. resident population was 238.7 million. The population of the U.S. has increased steadily since World War II, but at two distinct rates in two distinct time periods. Between 1944 and 1964, the population rose from 138.9 to 191.9 million—an average annual increase of approximately 2.0 percent. Using the simple 70 rule as a guide, this rate would lead to a doubling of the population every 35 years. However, in the next 20 years, from the end of 1964 to 1984, the population increased by only 44.7 million—an average annual rate of roughly 1.1 percent. In other words, the rate of increase in our population has declined by nearly 50 percent in the last 2 decades. If the current trend continues, the U.S. population will double in some 64 years. This slowdown in population growth has occurred because of a reduction in the birth rate, accompanied by a stable death rate. In addition to the natural changes brought about through births and deaths, the population changes because of migration (see figure 8.1). The U.S. birth rate has fallen from a post-World War II high of 24.9 births per 1,000 population in 1955 to a 1985 rate of 16.0 births per 1,000. At the same time, the death rate has dropped from a post-World War II high of

Figure 8.1 Components of Population Change, 1960–85

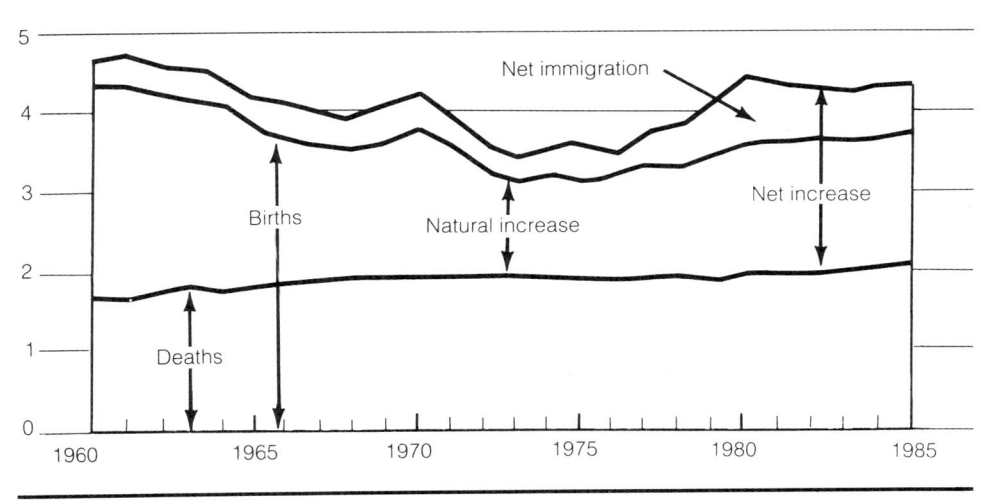

Source: Statistical Abstract of the U.S., 1987, U.S. Department of Commerce, Bureau of the Census, p. 6.

9.6 deaths per 1,000 population in 1950 to 8.6 per 1,000 in 1985. The post-World War II legal immigration rate ranged from a high of 3.5 immigrants per 1,000 population in 1980 to 1.9 immigrants per 1,000 population in 1985.

Age

Perhaps the most interesting characteristic of America's current population is the increase in the average age (table 8.1). The economic implications of an aging population are significant and largely beyond the scope of this text.[1] However, the significance of this population change to the banking industry is critical.

Table 8.1 United States Resident Population, Median Age for Selected Years

Year	Median Age (years)
1850	18.9
1860	19.4
1870	20.2
1880	20.9
1890	22.0
1900	22.9
1910	24.1
1920	25.3
1930	26.4
1940	29.0
1950	30.2
1960	29.5
1970	28.0
1980	30.0
1985	31.5

Source: *Statistical Abstract of the United States*, 1987, U.S. Department of Commerce, Bureau of the Census, p. 18.

Bank products and services tend to attract customers who are between 39–50 years of age. Many individuals reach their peak earnings potential in those years. Customers in this age bracket are normally relatively large retail depositors. In addition, they tend to make excellent loan customers because of their specific credit needs and excellent credit ratings. The population in this age group will increase dramatically in the near future (table 8.2), as will the population between 40 and 44 years of age. Those banks positioned to meet the needs of these burgeoning age groups will grow accordingly.

After 1990, growth in the age groups between 25 and 44 years old are projected to decrease through the year 2,000, by which time the largest age cohort will be moving into the 45–64 age group. The under-25 age group, in decline since the mid-1960s, is projected to continue declining at an accelerating rate.

Table 8.2 Bank Customer Growth Pattern: Population Projection by Age Bracket, 1980–90

Age Bracket	Percentage Change
20–24	−14.17
25–29	+6.55
30–34	+21.31
35–39	+37.26
40–44	+48.28
45–49	+25.92

Source: Current Population Reports, 1980, U.S. Department of Commerce, Bureau of the Census, series P-25, nos. 917, 952, and 985.

Mobility

The U.S. population is highly mobile. However, research shows that mobility of individuals tends to decrease with age (table 8.3). The most mobile Americans are between 25 and 29 years old. In 1981, 70.4 percent of this group changed residence. At the same time, only 16.2 percent of individuals 65 years or older chose to move. A great deal of this youth mobility can be attributed to the process of "emptying the nest." However, even in the older age groups, mobility seems to be fairly strong. In addition, it appears that residents of the western states seem to be far more mobile than the rest of the nation. Westerners appear to be significantly more mobile than Northeasterners.

Table 8.3 Mobility of Americans

	Percentage Distribution, 1985		
Age and Region	Nonmovers (same house in 1980)	Movers	Movers from Abroad
5–9 years old	47.9	50.0	2.1
10–14 years old	57.8	40.5	1.7
15–19 years old	64.4	33.4	2.2
20–24 years old	39.1	58.0	2.9
25–29 years old	26.5	70.4	3.2
30–34 years old	40.9	56.5	2.6
35–44 years old	58.8	39.4	1.8
45–54 years old	72.9	26.2	0.9
55–64 years old	79.0	20.2	0.9
65 years old and over	83.5	16.2	0.3
Northeast	66.9	31.3	1.8
Midwest	60.9	38.3	0.8
South	56.0	42.4	1.6
West	49.6	47.4	3.3

Source: Current Population Reports, 1987, series P-20.

Educational Attainment

The U.S. population tends to be highly educated. In 1985, roughly 7 out of 10 Americans aged 25 years and older had earned high school diplomas. Approximately 19 percent of this age group had completed at least 4 years of college (figure 8.2). The educational status of the population increased dramatically during the 40-year period between 1940 and 1980. In 1940, approximately 2 out of 10 Americans 25 years of age or older had completed high school and only 4.6 percent had completed at least 4 years of college.

The increase in educational levels has led to great advances in productivity and quality of life, yet related problems have surfaced. This elevation in educational levels has raised worker expectations and increased demand for a limited number of supervisory and management jobs. Worker discontent escalates when these rising expectations are not fulfilled.

Figure 8.2 Educational Attainment of Americans 25 Years and Over

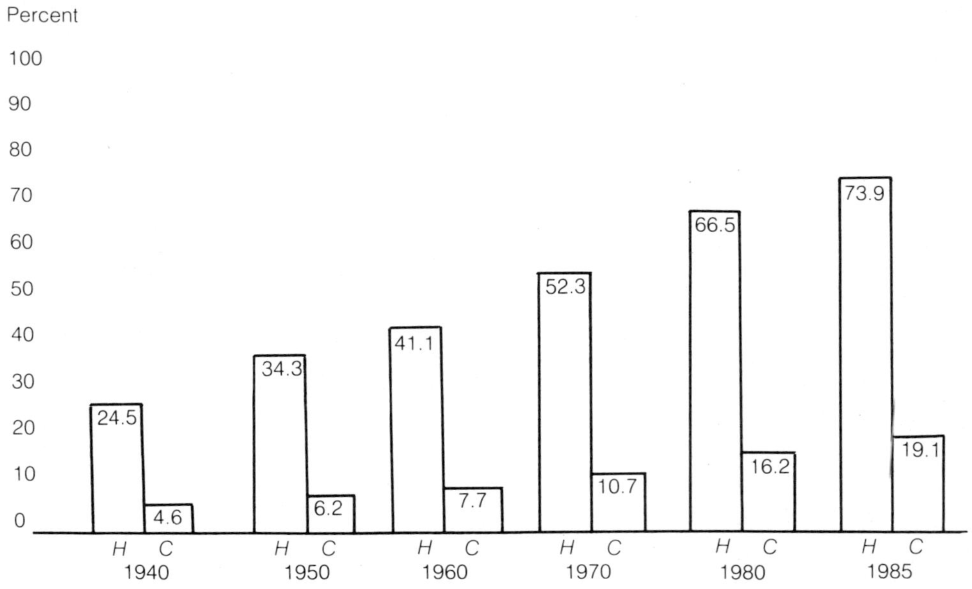

Year	H (4+ years high school)	C (4+ years college)
1940	24.5	4.6
1950	34.3	6.2
1960	41.1	7.7
1970	52.3	10.7
1980	66.5	16.2
1985	73.9	19.1

H = 4 years or more of high school.
C = 4 years or more of college.

Source: Data from Statistical Abstract of the U.S., 1987, U.S. Department of Commerce, Bureau of the Census, p. 121.

Advances in education have not been shared equally among American racial and ethnic groups. In 1980, about one-half of black Americans over 25 years old had not earned high school degrees, and the percentage of blacks with college degrees was only half as large as that of white college graduates. Yet the rate of increase in educational level for minorities has been high (figure 8.3). In 1940, only 7 out of 100 blacks 25 years or older were high school graduates. But by 1985, over half of this group held secondary school diplomas. The proportion of blacks who have obtained college degrees has also risen dramatically since 1940. This influx of college-educated minorities into the labor force will increase the competition for highly sought positions.

Figure 8.3 Educational Attainment of Black Americans 25 Years and Over

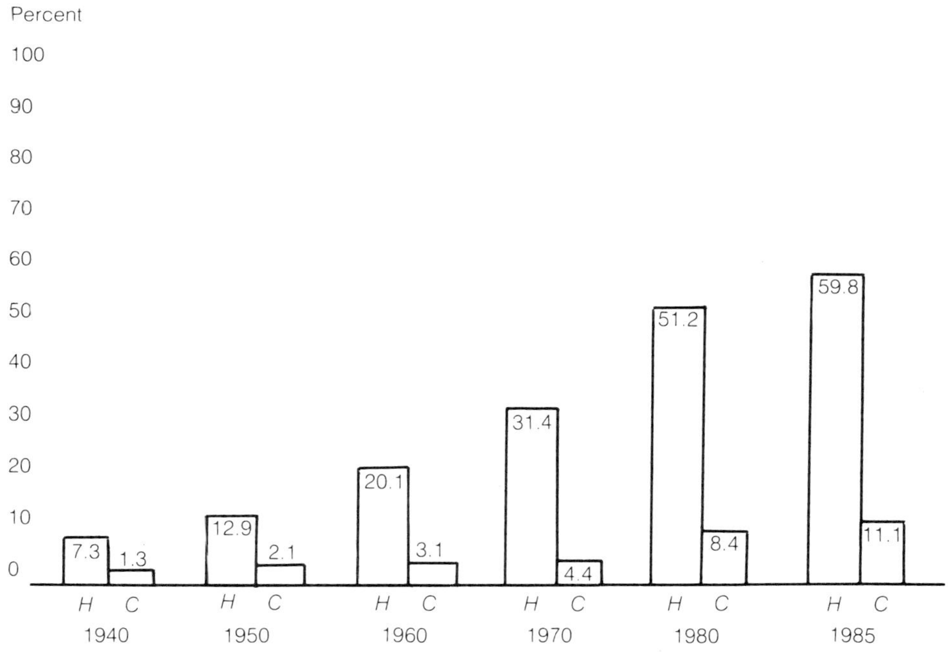

Year	H (4+ years high school)	C (4+ years college)
1940	7.3	1.3
1950	12.9	2.1
1960	20.1	3.1
1970	31.4	4.4
1980	51.2	8.4
1985	59.8	11.1

H = 4 years or more of high school.
C = 4 years or more of college.

Source: Data from Statistical Abstract of the U.S., 1987, U.S. Department of Commerce, Bureau of the Census, p. 121.

THE LABOR FORCE

The portion of the U.S. population that is over 16 years of age, not institutionalized, and not in the armed services is called the civilian noninstitutional population (CNP). The CNP represents the potential, or maximum, number of employees who could be employed in the economy. Groups of people in the population who are not included in the CNP are either too young for employment, unable to enter the work force, institutionalized, or in the armed services. The CNP comprises all those individuals in the civilian labor force (persons working or actively seeking work) plus those eligible to work but not in the labor force (persons not working and not seeking work). This latter group consists mostly of students, homemakers, and retired employees.

The civilian labor force includes all individuals who are either gainfully employed or unemployed but seeking work. The percentage of the CNP that is made up of the civilian labor force is called the civilian labor force participation rate. It is a rough measure of the propensity of the economic agents in the population to be used as an economic resource. Labor force participation rates for males over 20 years of age approached 90 percent in the years immediately following World War II, but have fallen recently.

One of the most amazing economic events of the last 40 years is the remarkable rise in the female labor force participation rate. The adult female rate has risen dramatically, from 31.8 percent in 1948 to approximately 55 percent by 1985. Table 8.4 shows the labor force participation rate by sex, race, and age for 1985 and a projection for 1995.

While women have increased their participation in the work force, roughly 1 out of 3 female employees are considered part-time employees compared with 1 out of 10 males. Nevertheless, changing economic conditions, demographics, and social norms have led to an increased role for women in the workplace.

U.S. INCOME STATISTICS: FUNCTIONAL VS. PERSONAL DISTRIBUTIONS

Individuals act as economic agents in two distinct capacities. On the one hand, like the other factors of production, people are represented in the supply side of production—labor and entrepreneurial ability. As such, workers, managers, and executives receive income for their contributions to the production process. On the other hand, once income is received and goods and services are placed in the market, individuals affect the economy as consumers. Individual people and household units are both considered economic agents as income earners and consumers.

Two methods are used to determine the distribution of income. The functional distribution of income shows, in a very rough fashion, the total amount of income earned by

Table 8.4 Civilian Labor Force Participation

	Participation Rate (percent)	
Race, Sex, and Age	1985	1995 (projected)
Total	64.8	66.6
Whites	65.0	66.8
Male	77.0	75.8
Female	54.1	58.4
Blacks	62.9	65.3
Male	70.8	70.8
Female	56.5	60.8
Males	76.3	75.3
16–19 years	56.8	57.9
20–24 years	85.0	87.3
25–34 years	94.7	93.7
35–44 years	95.0	94.3
45–54 years	91.0	90.4
55–64 years	67.9	62.6
65+ years	15.8	11.0
Females	54.5	58.9
16–19 years	52.1	51.2
20–24 years	71.8	76.3
25–34 years	70.9	81.1
35–44 years	71.8	80.5
45–54 years	64.4	71.3
55–64 years	42.0	42.7
65+ years	7.3	5.5

Sources: U.S. Bureau of Labor Statistics, *Employment and Earnings*, monthly; *Monthly Labor Review*, November, 1985; and unpublished data as given in *Statistical Abstract of the U.S.*, 1987, no. 639, p. 376.

the four factors of production. Remember that the owners of the factors of production must be paid in order to induce them to permit use of these scarce resources in the production process. The resource payments made to these owners take the forms of wages, interest, rent, and profits. The annual sum of these resource payments represents the functional distribution of income (table 8.5). It is also the measure known as national income.

Table 8.5 Functional Distribution of Income, 1985

	Billions of Dollars	Percentage of Total Income
Compensation of employees	2,372.7	72.8
Proprietor's income	242.4	7.4
Rental income	57.4	1.8
Corporate profits	299.0	9.2
Interest	287.7	8.8
Total income	3,259.2	

Source: *Economic Report of the President*, 1986.

ECONOMICS FOR BANKERS

The vast majority of income earned by the factors of production is in the form of payments to labor. Compensation to employees includes all wages and salaries as well as the value of employer contributions for social insurance, private pensions, health and welfare funds, and worker's compensation insurance costs. Proprietor's income is income earned by small business owners, farmers, professionals, and others. A very small portion of proprietor's income belongs in the rent, interest, and profit categories, but the simpler definition is sufficient for the purposes of this book.

The wage and salary portion of total income was about 80 percent in 1985. The owners of the other factors of production received about 20 percent of the total income in the form of interest, profits, and rents. This split of total income between workers and the owners of production has been fairly constant since 1940 (table 8.6).

The personal distribution of income indicates the amount of income earned by individual households. The income of households for 1985, distributed across the entire household population, covers a broad range (table 8.7). An individual household earning over $50,000 in 1985 is in the 86th percentile of households—that is, 85.3 percent of all households made less than $50,000 in 1985. A household earning under $5,000, by contrast, was in the eighth percentile: only 7.7 percent of all households earned less than $5,000 in 1985.

Table 8.6 Labor's Share vs. Owner's Share, National Income

Year	National Income	Labor's Share[a]	Owner's Share[b]	Labor's Share	Owner's Share
	(billions of dollars)			(percentage of total)	
1940	79.6	64.8	14.8	81.4	18.6
1950	239.8	194.2	45.6	81.0	19.0
1960	424.9	348.8	76.1	82.1	17.9
1970	832.6	698.5	134.1	83.9	16.1
1980	2203.5	1818.9	384.6	82.5	17.5

Source: Economic Report of the President, 1986.
a. Labor share is sum of wage, salaries, and proprietor's income.
b. Owner's share is sum of rents, interest, and profits.

Table 8.7 Income Distribution by Households, 1985

Income Range (dollars)	Percentage of Households in Range	Percentage of Households in Range or Below
Under 5,000	7.7	7.7
5,000–9,999	12.4	20.1
10,000–14,999	11.5	31.6
15,000–19,999	10.9	42.5
20,000–24,999	10.0	52.5
25,000–34,999	17.0	69.5
35,000–49,999	15.8	85.3
50,000 and more	14.8	100.0

Source: Statistical Abstract of the U.S., 1987, p. 432.

Table 8.8 Current- and Constant-Dollar Median Family Income for Selected Years

Year	Median Family Income in Current Dollars	Median Family Income in Constant Dollars (1985)
1950	3,319	13,736
1960	5,620	18,907
1970	8,734	24,197
1980	17,710	23,121
1985	23,618	23,618

Source: Statistical Abstract of the U.S., 1987, p. 431.

Table 8.9 Family Income Distribution by Quintile, 1985

Quintile Ranking	Percentage Distribution of Aggregate Family Income
Lowest Fifth	4.6
Second Fifth	10.9
Third Fifth	16.9
Fourth Fifth	24.2
Highest Fifth	43.5
Top 5 percent	16.7

Source: Statistical Abstract of the U.S., 1987, p. 437.

If all household incomes were ranked from the highest to the lowest, median family income would measure the income status of the middle family (table 8.8). The median family income is the income level at which 50 percent of all families earn more and 50 percent of all families earn less. The median family income can be measured in both current and constant (inflation-adjusted) dollars. According to table 8.8, the current-dollar median family income has increased over time; but when the income is adjusted for inflation, median family income can decrease, as it did between 1970 and 1980.

Data about the median family income can be misleading because it does not show the relative distribution of family income. Table 8.9 portrays how aggregate income was distributed in 1985. The population has been divided into fifths, or quintiles, and ranked from the poorest quintile to the richest. If the income were evenly distributed, each quintile would earn 20 percent of total income. As table 8.9 shows, the distribution is far from even. In 1985, the three poorest quintiles each earned less than 20 percent of the total income, and the richest group earned over 40 percent. In fact, the richest 5 percent of all families received over 16 percent of total income.

The distribution of income portrayed in table 8.9 includes only money income, and does not include any nonmonetary income. For example, the value of food stamps, Medicare, Medicaid, and government-sponsored goods and services is not calculated. If the value of these goods and services were included, the distribution of "income" would be less skewed toward the upper income groups.[2]

Poverty in America

In 1964, the Social Security Administration created an index used to quantitatively define poverty in America. (Since then, the index has been revised twice: once in 1969 and again in 1980.) Like the income distribution measure, the poverty index is based on money income and does not reflect noncash benefits such as food stamps, Medicaid, and public housing. The Department of Agriculture's 1961 economy food plan was used as a guide in determining consumption requirements. The poverty thresholds are updated yearly to reflect changes in the consumer price index, and average poverty levels are established for families of various sizes (table 8.10).

Table 8.10 Weighted Average Poverty Levels
(based on money income for families and unrelated individuals)

Size of Unit	1970 (dollars)	1985 (dollars)
1 person	1,954	5,469
Under 65 years	2,010	5,593
65 years and over	1,861	5,156
2 persons	2,525	6,998
Householder under 65	2,604	7,231
Householder 65 and over	2,348	6,503
3 persons	3,099	8,573
4 persons	3,968	10,989
5 persons	4,680	13,007
6 persons	5,260	14,696
7 persons or more	6,468	n.a.
7 persons	n.a.	16,656
8 persons	n.a.	18,512
9 persons	n.a.	22,083

n.a. = Not available.
Source: Statistical Abstract of the U.S., 1987, p. 416.

The incidence of poverty does not fall equally on all segments of the population (table 8.11). In 1969, 12.1 percent of the population was below the poverty level. While 1985's rate of 14.0 percent reflects an increase of less than 2 percent, it represents an increase of 9 million people. Nearly one-third of all black American families were below the established poverty level. It has also been estimated that 39 percent of all women fall below the poverty line, compared with 32 percent of all men. Thirty-two million women fall below the poverty line and another 8 million are classified as "near poor" (income levels up to 25 percent higher than the poverty level).[3]

Between 1978 and 1984, the share of families with incomes of $35,000 or more (in 1984 dollars) grew from 29 percent to 34 percent. However, the average real income of the poor has also fallen further below the poverty thresholds.[4]

Table 8.11 Persons Below the Poverty Level, by Race and Family Status, 1985

Unit	Number (millions)	Percentage of Population
All persons	33.1	14.0
White	22.9	11.4
Black	8.9	31.3
In families with female householder, no husband present	16.4	33.5

Source: Statistical Abstract of the U.S., 1987, p. 443.

Occupational Earnings

Not only do earnings differ from household to household, but there are also significant differences in wages and salary across occupations (table 8.12). Much of the variation in occupational earnings can be explained by supply and demand theory. However, a discussion of the reasons for interindustry and intraindustry occupation wage differentials goes beyond the scope of this book. Obviously, differences in natural abilities and aptitudes between and among workers, educational attainment, labor union activity and strength are just a few of the possible factors. In addition, discrimination on the basis of race, sex, and age may account for a significant portion of the occupational wage differentials.[5]

In virtually every job category, women make considerably less than men. Hourly wages range from a low of $4.47 to a high of $10.25 within the male category, and a lower, but similarly wide range is found in the female category.

The wage differential between the sexes is more striking in white-collar positions (table 8.13). The differential between the sexes here results from two separate forces. First, the top white-collar positions are still dominated by men, and most firms pay higher salaries

Table 8.12 Median Hourly Earnings, by Job Category

Job Category	Median Hourly Earnings (dollars)		
	Total	Male	Female
Managerial and professional specialty	9.13	10.25	8.57
Technical, sales, and administrative support	5.73	7.03	5.44
Service occupations	4.19	4.62	3.98
Precision production, craft, and repair	9.20	9.60	6.06
Operators, fabricators, and laborers	6.53	7.30	5.30
Farming, forestry, and fishing	4.43	4.47	4.18

Source: U.S. Bureau of Labor Statistics, unpublished data, as reported in Statistical Abstract of the U.S., 1987, no. 683, p. 404.

Table 8.13 Median Weekly Earnings, White-Collar Jobs
(by occupational group and sex, 1985)

Occupation	Men (dollars)	Women (dollars)
Managerial and professional	580	404
Executive, administrative, and managerial	586	389
Technical support	467	331
Sales occupations	440	223
Administrative support	397	272
Service occupations	276	188

Source: Bureau of Labor Statistics, "Weekly Earnings of Wage and Salary Workers: Second Quarter 1985," table 3.

for more complex and responsible positions. Second, discrimination based on sex still affects the American labor market.

The wage differential between male and female blue collar jobs is relatively small, vis-à-vis white-collar positions. This smaller differential can be traced to the "democratic effect" collective bargaining has had on wage structures. In mixed-member labor organizations, hourly earnings are listed in the labor agreement by job, or job classification, not by sex.

HISTORY OF COLLECTIVE BARGAINING

The employees of virtually every sector of American industry are organized to some extent: school teachers, police, firefighters, professional engineers, industrial workers, nurses, airline pilots, even bank employees. However, the extent of unionization has been declining. In the late 1950s, total union membership was over 25 percent of the civilian labor force. By 1985, the percentage had fallen to only 16 percent.

With the passage of the National Labor Relations Act (NLRA) in 1935, which guaranteed certain workers the right to organize and bargain collectively, union membership skyrocketed. By the end of World War II, union membership had quadrupled to roughly 15 million members. Thereafter, the pace of membership growth slowed. By 1980, about 20 million workers were organized. This slowdown in growth has meant that union membership has failed to keep pace with the growth in the labor force. By 1980, union representation as a percentage of the labor force was at the lowest level since 1950: roughly 18 percent.

Union membership roll counts are no longer an accurate measure of the number of workers represented by a formal labor organization. Beginning in 1960, there has been rapid growth of government employee associations and professional groups. Many of these organizations engage in collective bargaining activities. If these employee associations are combined with the more traditional labor organization, total union membership was equal to 22.4 million workers in 1984, or about 20 percent of the labor force (figure 8.4).

Figure 8.4 Union Membership in the U.S., 1900–85

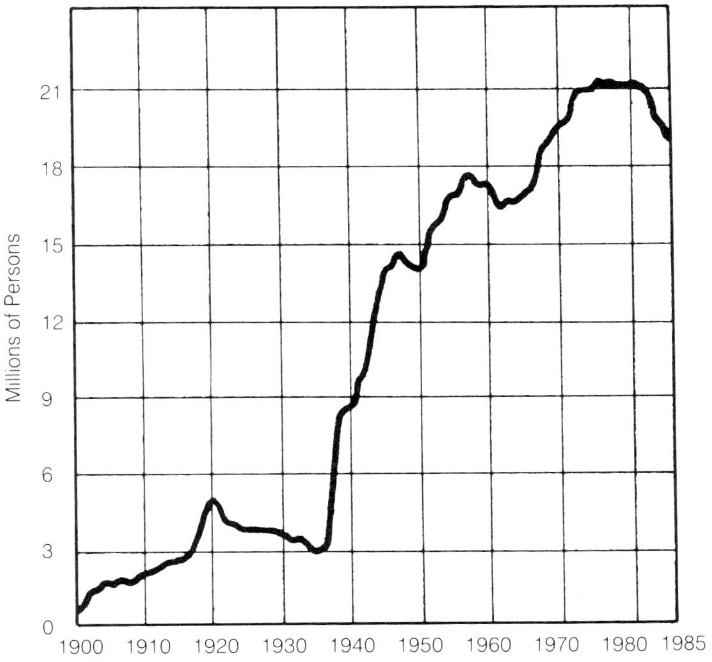

Source: Handbook of Labor Statistics. 1986. U.S. Department of Labor Bureau of Labor Statistics.

Unions have a long history in the United States. Even before the Declaration of Independence, skilled artisans in handicraft and domestic industries joined together in benevolent societies, primarily to provide members and their families with financial assistance in the event of serious illness, debt, or death of the wage earner. Although these early associations had few of the characteristics of present-day labor unions, they did bring workers together to consider problems of mutual concern and to devise ways and means for their solution.

Craftsmen such as carpenters, shoemakers, and printers formed separate organizations in Philadelphia, New York, and Boston as early as 1791, largely to resist wage reductions. These unions were confined to local areas and were usually weak because they seldom included all the workers available to practice the craft. Generally, they continued in existence for only a short time.

Strikes, during which workmen quit working as a group, paralleled the development of organization and collective bargaining. The New York bakers were said to have stopped work to enforce their demands as early as 1741. The first authenticated strike was called in 1768 by the New York tailors to protest a reduction in wages.

As unions became stronger, the wage question increased in importance and employers organized to resist wage demands. Where circumstances appeared favorable, employers attempted to destroy the effectiveness of a union by hiring nonunion workers and by appealing to the courts to declare the labor organization illegal. Unions were prosecuted as "conspiracies in restraint of trade" under an old English common law doctrine that combinations of workmen to raise wages could be regarded as a conspiracy against the public.

The attempt of courts to apply this conspiracy doctrine aroused a controversy that lasted throughout most of the nineteenth century. Slowly, judicial attention was shifted from the question of whether a mere combination of workmen constituted a conspiracy to the legality of the means they used to gain their ends. While unions, as such, became regarded as "lawful," strikes, boycotts, and other attempts of workers to secure their demands were the subject of legal action in the courts for many decades.

During the union-employer struggles of the 1880s, the labor movement itself became the scene of a decisive contest over its future structure. The Knights of Labor championed a nationwide organization of labor based upon the direct affiliation of local unions and city centrals cutting across trade lines. This approach had been tried unsuccessfully several times.

By 1881, the nucleus of a new coalition of organizations had taken shape. Devoted to "pure and simple unionism," its main goals were higher wages and improved working conditions. In 1886, this coalition of unions met in Columbus, Ohio and formed the American Federation of Labor (AFL). Samuel Gompers was elected president of this new national union. The newly founded American Federation of Labor favored a national federation based primarily on existing national trade or craft unions.

In the 3 decades following 1890, the AFL consolidated its position as the principal federation of American unions. The first decade of growth was slow, but from 1900 to 1904 membership rose rapidly, from half a million to a million and a half, and then increased irregularly to 2 million by the outbreak of World War I. During and immediately following the war years, membership again rose rapidly and reached more than 4 million in 1920.

The emergence of labor as an influential national economic group did not occur without opposition or setbacks. However, despite vigorous and sometimes violent employer opposition to unions, an increasing number of "trade" or collective bargaining agreements resulted from direct negotiations between unions and employers. The stabilization of industrial relations and the attainment of job security are considered by many authorities to be important factors in the success of AFL trade unionism in that period.

The economic depression and widespread unemployment that followed the 1929 stock market crash further reduced union membership to 3.25 million by 1932.

Although the decline in union membership was a serious blow to the labor movement, about 3 million workers retained their membership during the worst years of the depression. These workers provided vital centers of growth ready to respond to improved economic conditions, especially when many of the obstacles to union growth were removed by changes in public policies.

New Labor Laws

The Railway Labor Act of 1926, although limited to railroad transportation, marked the beginning of a new era in labor law. This act was based on the premise that peaceful labor-management relations should be maintained by free collective bargaining between employers and unions. Railroad workers were assured the right to organize and join unions without employer interference.

Next came the Norris-LaGuardia Act of 1932. It brought to an end what has been called, in the history of labor-management relations, the era of "government by injunction." The act drastically limited judicial restrictions on strikes, picketing, and boycotts, and forbade the use of the "yellow dog" contract whereby workers, as a condition of employment, agreed not to join a union.

In the spring of 1933, the incoming administration of President Franklin D. Roosevelt obtained the passage of the National Industrial Recovery Act (NIRA). Section 7(a) of this law guaranteed the right of employees to organize or join unions of their own choosing and to bargain collectively with their employers. The NIRA was invalidated by the Supreme Court in May of 1935, but in July of the same year the principles stated in the labor section were incorporated in the National Labor Relations (Wagner) Act.

The Wagner Act was the most significant labor law thus far enacted in the United States. It guaranteed employees "the right to self-organization, to form, join, or assist labor organizations, to bargain collectively through representatives of their own choosing, and to engage in concerted activities for the purpose of collective bargaining or other mutual aid or protection." The act went beyond a statement of principles; it created the administrative machinery of the National Labor Relations Board. As a government agency, the board was given, among other duties, the following functions: (1) to prevent and remedy employers' "unfair labor practices" which discouraged or interfered with the self-organization of employees or with the practice of collective bargaining; and (2) to determine the bargaining unit in cases of controversy and hold secret "representation" elections to decide which union, if any, the employees wanted to represent them for bargaining purposes, and with which the company, by law, had to bargain collectively.

This trend toward a more favorable government policy was one of the main causes of the success unions enjoyed in the organizing work which followed in the mid-1930s. This new government attitude was also reflected in the enactment of the Fair Labor Standards (Wage-Hour) Act in 1938, the Social Security Act in 1935, and the Walsh-Healy (Public Contracts) Act in 1936.

Increases in union membership in the mid-1930s were most conspicuous in the mass-production industries. The Wagner Act, however, established a basic code to encourage free collective bargaining and virtually ended company-dominated unions and employer-controlled employee representation plans.

The 2-year expansion of total union membership brought about a rise from less than 3 million in 1933 to 3.75 million in 1935. By 1937, membership had almost doubled, advancing to 7.25 million. This growth in union membership was accompanied by internal political bickering. A struggle developed between the supporters of traditional craft unions and those who wanted to open membership to the newly emerging industrial unions with their semiskilled and unskilled workers. After a bitter struggle, in 1938 a new national union emerged from the parent AFL to promote the organization of mass production workers. The union was called the Congress of Industrial Organizations (CIO). The CIO elected John L. Lewis, then president of the United Mine Workers, as the new president. Lewis was a bitter rival of the old established AFL.

The difficulties that continued to exist between the AFL and the CIO did not prevent the growth of unionism. On the contrary, the rivalry generated by the two large federations stimulated the organizing efforts of the unions in each group. By the end of 1941, union membership had climbed to over 10 million members.

The end of World War II in 1945 led to new problems for organized labor. More than 10 million servicemen and -women were demobilized in the 12 months following V-J Day, August 14, 1945. Thousands of factories retooled to meet the demands of a civilian, peacetime economy.

Beginning in the autumn of 1945, a number of strikes occurred in the oil, automobile, steel, and coal industries. Altogether, 42 large strikes, each involving 10,000 or more workers, occurred between August 1945 and July 1946.

The unsettled labor-management situation after the war revived and greatly strengthened opposition to the Wagner Act. Senator Robert A. Taft, a leader in the demand for change, argued that although the act had been passed to aid unions in maintaining an appropriate "balance" of rights and responsibilities between workers and employers, it had gone "far beyond" such a balance in its actual administration. He and Congressman Fred A. Hartley sponsored a rewriting of the act. The resulting measure, the Labor-Management Relations (Taft-Hartley) Act, gained such widespread support that, despite strong objections by organized labor and a presidential veto, it became law on June 23, 1947.

The concept of striking a "balance" between unions and employers led to the development of a list of "unfair labor practices" applying to unions, along with a list applying to employers. Refusal to bargain in good faith, engaging in secondary boycotts, stopping work over a jurisdictional or interunion dispute, and charging excessive initiation fees to keep new members out of a union were considered by the law to be unfair. Employers, as well as workers, were permitted to appeal to the National Labor Relations Board against unions in connection with such practices. Certain practices could be opposed by suing in court for damages. Restrictions on the use of injunctions were eased. Section 14(b) of the Taft-Hartley Act allowed the states to adopt more restrictive legislation against union security clauses than was provided in the federal law. This is called the right-to-work law.

Special rules were written into the Taft-Hartley Act for handling controversies or strikes which, in the judgment of the President, could create or threaten emergencies by imperiling the national health or safety.

The Taft-Hartley Act also established the Federal Mediation and Conciliation Service as a separate agency of the government. This service offers assistance to labor and management in arriving at peaceful settlement of labor disputes, particularly if they threaten substantial interruption of interstate commerce.

For about 10 years after the passage of the Taft-Hartley Act in 1947, trade union membership expanded at about the same rate as nonagricultural employment was increasing. At the same time, an aggressive collective bargaining approach opened up new vistas for American workers. The AFL and CIO merged in December 1955 after 20 years of bitter and costly rivalry.

Soon after the merger, however, the largest union in the federation—the Teamsters—was expelled. In 1959, the Labor-Management Reporting and Disclosure (Landrum-Griffin) Act brought the government directly into the regulation of union affairs on a broad scale; union membership began to decline, in both absolute and relative numbers, for the first time since the depression; a host of writers began to discuss what they felt was a growing crisis in American labor. In July 1968 the United Auto Workers (UAW), another of the larger AFL-CIO unions, left the AFL-CIO and, with the Teamsters, formed the short-lived Alliance for Labor Action.

By the mid-sixties, however, union membership had begun to rise again, particularly as public employees turned to unions in increasing numbers. Equally prominent was the influence of the AFL-CIO in securing significant legislation on private pension and welfare plans and the workplace environment. New developments in organizing workers and significant new legislation had resulted in progress toward many of labor's goals. The AFL-CIO coordinated a number of unionization campaigns in specific areas, and gave financial assistance and moral support to organizing drives among farm workers and public employees.

Between 1956 and 1974, membership in government employee unions had increased by almost 2 million members to 2.9 million. In recognition of the growing importance of organizations of public workers, the AFL-CIO in 1974 established a separate public employee department, one of the largest departments in the federation.

Other public employees, such as teachers, and some professional employees such as athletes and nurses, joined professional associations. These associations performed many of the functions of unions, including collective bargaining. Among the most important of these associations are the National Education Association, the Major League Baseball Players Association, and the American Nurses Association. In 1974, these professional associations had more than 2.6 million members.

The 1980s has been one of the darkest periods in union history. Back-to-back recessions in the early 1980s and deregulation of major industries have led to what has been labeled a period of concessionary bargaining. Under concessionary bargaining, unions attempt to maintain their hard-fought gains. Employers insist on long lists of "give-backs" including substantial wage reductions. For example, in 1982, the Teamsters agreed to (1) negotiate a new labor contract well in advance of the contract expiration date; (2) accept wage increases that are below inflation increases; and (3) accept work rule changes that will increase productivity. These give-backs were a direct result of the increase in competition from nonunion truckers allowed by the deregulation of the trucking industry. Similarly, facing increased competition from independent, nonunion air carriers in the early 1980s, PAN AM was able to wrestle these concessions from their flight attendants: (1) a 10 percent wage cut and wage freeze; (2) a 16 percent increase in flight-service hours without increases in labor costs; and (3) a reduction in restrictive work rules, which will lead to additional productivity gains.

The managements of steel, auto, rubber, and chemical industries have also won concessions of various sorts from their unionized employees. Some of these industries have been under attack from low cost foreign competitors; others have seen the overall demand for their products drop. Finally, some firms have relocated in order to move away from areas of strong union power. For example, when attempts to obtain significant cost reductions were unsuccessful, Mack Truck of Allentown, Pennsylvania, decided to close the local truck assembly plant and construct a new plant in South Carolina—a right-to-work law state, where union opposition could be expected to be of little consequence.[6]

It appears that the traditional strongholds of union power (steel, coal, autos, rubber, and other basic industries) face increasing pressure for a slowdown in wage, salary, and benefit package growth. The management of these firms will use plant relocation and foreign outsourcing as collective bargaining "trump cards."

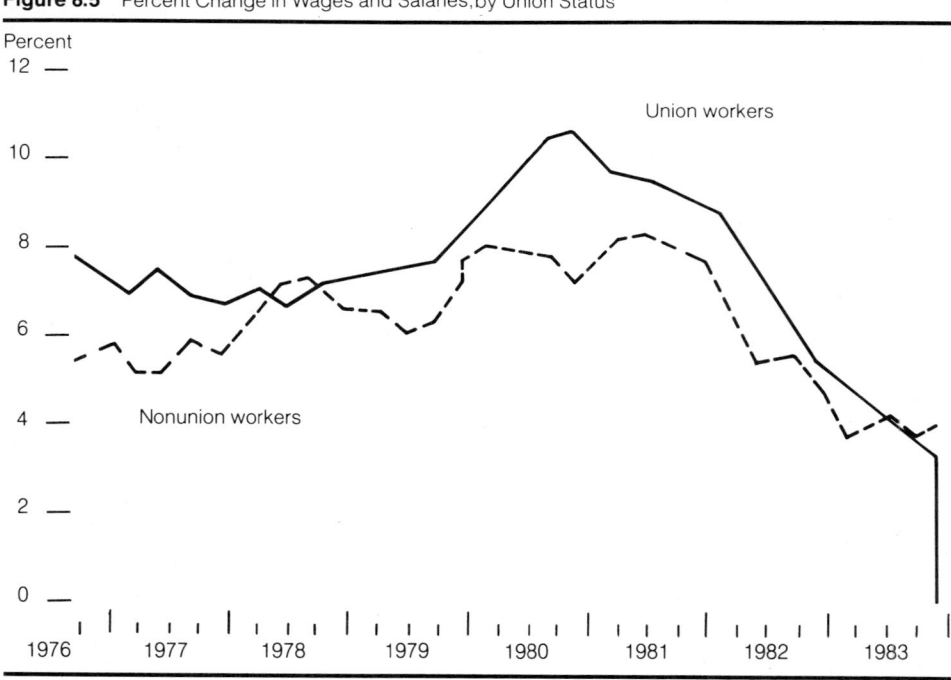

Figure 8.5 Percent Change in Wages and Salaries, by Union Status

Wages and Collective Bargaining

Since the early 1900s, membership in a union (or coverage under a collective bargaining agreement) generally has resulted in pay levels that are higher than those received by nonunion workers (figure 8.5). Differences in the rates of increase in pay of union workers, as measured by the Bureau of Labor Statistics' Employment Cost Index, were especially large in 1980, a year of double-digit inflation. The high inflation rate triggered large cost-of-living increases for workers covered by union contracts. More recently, increases in prices and rates of pay have slowed for all workers.

Labor unions have been successful in narrowing the wage gap between skilled and unskilled union members. Historically, wage differences between skilled and unskilled craftsworkers have been substantial, but over the past several decades they have narrowed considerably (figure 8.6). For example, in the building construction trades, journeymen's wages were about double those of unskilled workers at the turn of the century; by the early 1960s, journeymen earned about a third more than unskilled workers. The relative positions of skilled and unskilled wages has remained fairly stable in the last 2 decades.

Perhaps the most important advantage unionized workers have over nonunionized employees is the inclusion of the cost-of-living adjustment clause (COLA) in many labor agreements. The advantage is much more apparent during periods of rapidly rising prices.

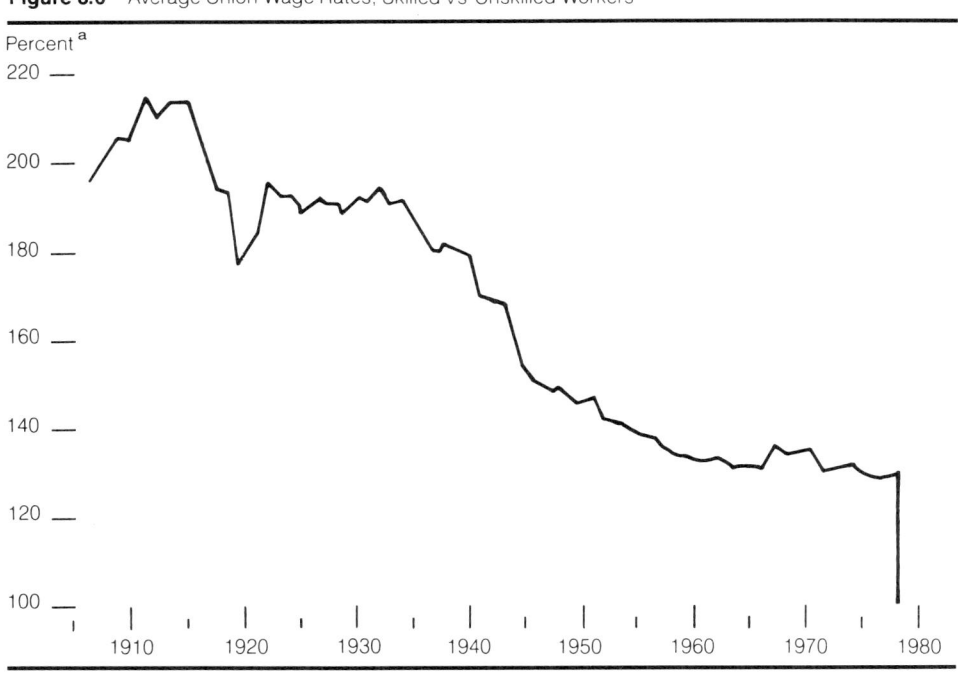

Figure 8.6 Average Union Wage Rates, Skilled vs Unskilled Workers

[a]Average union wage rates for journeymen as a percentage of rates for helpers and laborers, building construction.

As 1984 began, the wages of almost three-fifths of the nearly 8 million workers covered under major collective bargaining agreements were subject to automatic cost-of-living adjustments. A decade earlier, less than a third were covered by COLA clauses.

Historically, COLAs have helped workers to recover some of the purchasing power that is lost as a result of price increases. Typically, half to two-thirds of the cost of a rise in prices is recovered when a COLA is triggered. (Some COLA clauses also decrease wages when prices fall.) The size of the adjustment depends on several factors, including the formula used to calculate the COLA. This may include a "cap" on the size of the COLA and the timing of the COLA review process. COLAs generally go into effect after the Consumer Price Index has changed by an amount specified in the collective bargaining agreement.

The percentage of union workers covered by some type of COLA clause for the years 1978–82 went down (figure 8.7). This may have been caused by cost pressures placed on management during a period of high inflation. Companies may be willing to substitute other benefits if the union agrees to remove or modify the COLA clause. In a period of moderate inflation, management has less fear of COLAs.

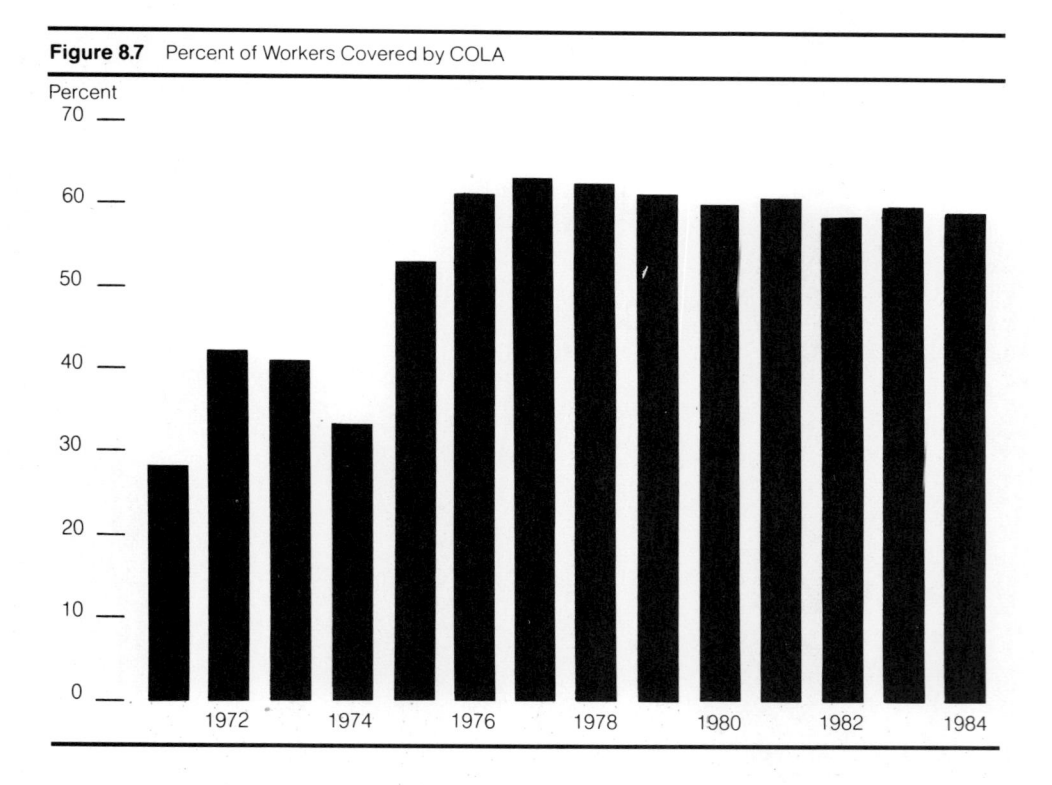

Figure 8.7 Percent of Workers Covered by COLA

SUMMARY

While the U.S. population continues to grow, it grows at a slower rate than in the past. The birth rate has declined and the death rate has stabilized. The net effect is that the U.S. population is aging. This trend will have an effect on the types of products and services offered by banks. In the near future, the mushrooming wealth of a middle-aged group of customers will greatly influence the marketing mix of commercial banks.

Statistically, U.S. citizens are very mobile, and often move several times during their lives. The U.S. population is also becoming increasingly educated.

The civilian noninstitutional population (CNP) includes all persons at least 16 years of age, who are not institutionalized and not in the armed forces. The civilian labor force participation rate is the percentage of the CNP in the labor force.

A significant change in U.S. civilian labor force participation has been the tremendous increase in the number of women working outside the home.

Functional income distribution is the annual sum of all rents, wages, interest, and profits paid to the owners of the factors of production. About 80 percent of the total national income is distributed in the form of wages and salaries.

Personal income distribution represents the amount of income earned by individual households. While the U.S. median family income has increased, the number of poor people has also increased. Blacks and women bear a disproportionately large share of the burden of poverty.

Wages and salaries differ across occupations. This is due, in part, to the factors of supply and demand, individual differences, and labor union activity. However, age, race, and sex discrimination still appear to influence wage differentials, even though such discrimination is illegal.

Collective bargaining is negotiation between a firm's management and a union for the purpose of agreeing on mutually acceptable wages and working conditions for employees. While union membership and influence have declined recently, unions have had a powerful effect on working America.

The Railway Labor Act, the Norris-LaGuardia Act, the Wagner Act, the Fair Labor Standards Act, and the Labor Management Relations Act (Taft-Hartley Act) influenced the size, power, and direction of the American labor movement.

KEY WORDS

American Federation of Labor
civilian labor force participation rate
closed shop
concessionary bargaining
Congress of Industrial Organizations
consumer price index
functional distribution of income
Landrum-Griffin Act

National Industrial Recovery Act (NIRA)
National Labor Relations Act (NLRA)
National Labor Relations Board
Norris-LaGuardia Act
poverty index
Railway Labor Act
right-to-work law
Taft-Hartley Act

Questions for Review

1. Why was the Taft-Hartley Act a unique law with regard to labor unions?

2. What is the Fair Labor Standards Act and what is its significance?

3. Why is the Norris-LaGuardia Act important?

4. How effective have labor unions been in increasing labor's share of the national income?

5. With respect to demand and supply in the labor market, what are the objectives of unions? How does a union attempt to accomplish these objectives?

6. In 1986, the number and magnitude of major work stoppages (strikes or lockouts) rose sharply after declining for the previous 2 years. What do you think are some of the causes of this trend?

7. What is the trade-off between income equality and economic efficiency and growth?

8. Discrimination on the basis of age, sex, and race is prohibited in the American workplace. In what ways does it still appear? Why is discrimination such a difficult practice to eliminate?

9. Median money income grew rapidly during the 1970s and early 1980s, yet median real income remained about the same over this time period. Discuss.

ENDNOTES

1. One serious implication of an aging population is the strain on our Social Security system. For an interesting article on this problem, see "The World Crisis in Social Security," *The Futurist* (February 1983), pp. 11–13.

2. For readers interested in estimates of income distributions that attempt to account for these in-kind transfers, see G. William Hoagland, "The Effectiveness of Current Transfer Programs in Reducing Poverty" (Washington D.C.: Congressional Budget Office); and Edgar K. Browning, "The Trend Toward Equality in the Distribution of Net Income," *Southern Economic Journal* (July 1976).

3. See the article by William O'Hare, in *American Demographics* (May 1986), pp. 22–25. See also Martin Brofenbrenner, "Income Distribution and 'Economic Justice'," *Journal of Economic Education*, (Winger, 1986), pp. 35–51.

4. See Beth B. Hess, "The New Faces of Poverty," *American Demographics* (May 1983), pp. 26–31.

5. See Albert Rees, *The Economics of Work and Pay* (New York: Harper & Row, 1973).

6. See Robert Kuttner, "Can Labor Lead," *The New Republic*, March 12, 1984, pp. 19–25; and Aaron Bernstein, "Productivity—Not Pay Cuts—Will Keep Union Members Working," *Business Week*, August 25, 1986, p. 32.

ECONOMICS IN THE NEWS

AFL-CIO Forms Unit to Monitor, Coordinate Activity at Banks

By Jeffrey Marshall

NEW YORK—The American Federation of Labor and Congress of Industrial Organizations is creating a new unit to monitor and coordinate labor efforts to exert pressure on banks and other corporations.

Ten or 11 people will be hired to staff a Washington office that is being remodeled to handle the new unit, according to Murray Seeger, director of information for the Washington-based AFL-CIO. The department will be known as the Office of Comprehensive Organizing Strategies and Tactics, he said.

Formation of the organizing office by the nation's foremost labor body may signal a new phase in labor's largely unfruitful campaign to pressure banks to adopt labor goals and permit unionization. Only 28 banks in the country are unionized, according to one recent count, and local union efforts to steer deposits and customers away from certain banks have had limited success.

"We're always cautious about expanding authority unless [AFL] affiliates want us to do so; clearly, they do want it," said Mr. Seeger of the new office. He added that the AFL-CIO would not do any actual organizing, but would work to coordinate such activities by affiliates.

A major role of the new office, he said, would be to gather information on "financial interlocks" between companies and union pension fund investments. Pension fund investments—some in the billions of dollars—represent a potent weapon in the unions' arsenal, for threats of withdrawal can get a bank's attention very quickly.

However, a spokesman for Corporate Campaign Inc.—a New York-based group that works with unions to fight corporate policies it sees as antiunion—called the AFL's decision to restrict the unit's role largely to information-gathering "the least controversial and the least political" approach to the situation.

"Their perspective is not as defined as ours," he added.

Corporate Campaign is headed by Ray Rogers, who has been in Minnesota for months spearheading the fight by union meat-packers against Geo. A. Hormel & Co. One part of that effort was a picketing and leafleting campaign against First Bank System, a leading lender to Hormel.

Mr. Rogers has led unions in a number of successful organizing efforts, some of which also involved banks. Manufacturers Hanover Trust Co., for instance, was threatened with the withdrawal of hundreds of millions of dollars in pension fund accounts in a bitterly fought effort to unionize textile workers at J.P. Stevens & Co. Stevens eventually signed contracts with the textile workers union late in 1980.

Unions in Europe have been aggressively pushing to organize white-collar workers in multinational banks there, so far with little effect. One union, the International Federation of Commercial, Clerical, Professional, and Technical Workers, said recently it would consider boycotting international financial transactions as part of a campaign to win concessions.

Reprinted by permission of *American Banker*, © 1986. All Rights Reserved.

CHAPTER NINE

NATIONAL INCOME ACCOUNTING

Objectives

After reading this chapter, you should be able to

- describe the three major components of national income accounting

- list some uses of national income accounting

- define the two methods of measuring national output

- list the four major economic sectors whose combined output is called the gross national product

- define the gross national product (GNP)

- name the components of the expenditure approach to calculating gross national product

- state some of the reasons why the gross national product is not a perfect measure of the nation's health

- describe other national income accounts including net national product, national income, personal income, and disposable personal income

- explain how price indexes are used to adjust the GNP for price changes

NATIONAL INCOME ACCOUNTING

The U.S. Department of Commerce has developed a framework for monitoring the magnitude, health, and performance of the U.S. economy. This structure consists of three major branches: National Income and Product Accounting (NIPA), capital finance and balance sheet accounting, and input-output accounting. The concepts and principles used in national income accounting are very similar to those used by businesses at the microeconomic level.

Components of the National Income Accounting System

The NIPA is the most widely used system of accounts, and shows the composition of the nation's total output as well as the distribution of total income generated during the production process.[1] The capital finance and balance sheet accounts, also called flow of funds accounts, illustrate how financial intermediaries and financial instruments transform income saved into investments, and portray the asset and liability shifts that result from these savings-to-investments activities. The flow of funds accounts also show the current U.S. balance sheet of total assets and liabilities at a certain point in time. Finally, the input-output accounts trace the flow of resources (input) through the production process among industries, and list the value added (output) by industry. These accounts also include data on the commodities included in national output.

International accounts are also incorporated into the national income accounting framework. These accounts include balance of payments and balance of trade accounts that reflect the level of economic activity occurring between U.S. economic agents and the rest of the world. Regional accounts disaggregate national output by geographic subdivision and thus permit analysis of local economic health.[2]

Purpose and Uses

The primary purpose of national income accounting is to produce an understandable, complete record of the economy's performance. National income accountants answer questions concerning the size, composition, and use of the country's output. The accounts also provide vital information about the process or mechanism used to produce and distribute total output. The accounts must be coherent, manageable, and above all, an accurate reflection of the forces in the economy.

National income accounting plays a crucial role in economic policymaking at the highest levels of government. National income accounts are used by individuals and corporations in planning and marketing, as part of academic and governmental research efforts, and to compare U.S. economic performance with that of foreign nations.

Methods

National income accounting measures the nation's output of goods and services. With few exceptions, this measurement concentrates on the sales and purchases of the market economy. Department of Commerce accountants recognize the existence of a large amount of nonmarket economic activity, but find it very difficult to account for such "off-the-books" transactions and activities in any orderly fashion.[3] Moreover, by far most of the economic activity in the U.S. is market driven and occurs in organized markets where recordkeeping is relatively easy. National income accountants rely heavily on these records to calculate the nation's output.

National income accountants sum the "final user" accounts of individual economic agents, even though some of the economic agents may not produce formal, structured, and accepted accounting statements. In the absence of proper documentation, the accountants make and use estimates in their calculations. All individual transactions are segregated into one of four distinct economic groups or sectors. Each sector contains economic agents who engage in similar transactions and react to economic events and policy in like fashion. Uniform accounts are then developed for each major group and are used to illustrate the broad categories of economic activities in which each sector is engaged. The four major economic sectors are (1) consumers or households; (2) business; (3) federal, state, and local governments; and (4) foreign.

The combined economic output of these four sectors is called the gross national product (GNP). The GNP is the single most important measure of economic activity.

GROSS NATIONAL PRODUCT

The GNP is defined as the total dollar value of all new final goods and services produced in the economy in one year. While this definition is straightforward and virtually self-explanatory, some additional comments are required.

The GNP is measured in dollars because the monetary unit is the most useful common denominator for all goods and services. Consider the problem of adding tons of steel, cubic feet of natural gas, gallons of milk, square yards of fabric, and hours of a professional's services. All products and services sell for a price in the marketplace and thus have monetary value. The market price, or final sales value, is used as the basis for GNP calculation.

Unfortunately, price changes affect the value of output from year to year. The purchasing power of a dollar is lower during periods of inflation and higher during periods of deflation. National income accountants adjust the GNP by offering a current-dollar GNP estimate and a constant-dollar (real, or adjusted) GNP. The methods used to adjust national output figures are discussed later in this chapter. Current-year GNP figures are adjusted to accommodate price changes so that output from different periods may be compared and real changes determined and measured.

The GNP is a measure of final goods and services. A great deal of economic activity occurs between and among individual enterprises as raw materials progress through the production process in the sometimes long journey to the end user. However, to include the value of the transactions at each step of the production process in the GNP would be a gross miscalculation of final output. The final price paid by the end user incorporates the expenses incurred at the previous stages: gathering the raw materials, producing, marketing, distributing, and selling the product. The value added at each of these stages comprises the product's final dollar value. Thus, the GNP does not include intermediate sales—only final or end-user sales.

The GNP is based on the value of new production. While a substantial volume of business in certain used products (for example, cars and housing) exists, the value of any used item—an item produced, sold, and thus included in a previous GNP calculation—represents a duplication. To include its resale value in the current GNP calculation would result in double counting. Of course, the dollar value of current services connected with the sale of used goods should be included in the GNP calculation. The sales commissions and brokerage fees earned by the marketing agents of used products represent values of current services and are properly included in the GNP.

The vast array of production that takes place outside the marketplace presents another problem for national income accountants. How can the value of nonmarket activity be captured in GNP calculations? The accountants have had mixed success in incorporating nonmarket activity into GNP calculations. For example, when an individual rents living space, the value of that transaction is a market activity and is simply added to the GNP. However, many Americans own their homes. The value of owner-occupied housing might escape calculation if it were not for a rental equivalent estimate. The GNP includes an estimate of the rents homeowners would receive if they rented their properties to others. Similarly, many farmers grow much of their own food and this nonmarket consumption should be included in the GNP. If farmers were to purchase foodstuffs in the market, the value of their food consumption could be easily calculated. Estimates of the market value of nonmarket food consumption are included in the GNP.

Certain nonmarket production activity is either too difficult to estimate or virtually impossible to predict, and thus is not included in the GNP calculation. Plumbers, house painters, and others sell services to customers on the open market and may also perform these valuable services on their own properties. The value of do-it-yourself work is not included in the GNP. Similarly, the value of homemaking services such as cooking, cleaning, and childcare is not included in the GNP. However, as more women have entered the labor force, working couples have increasingly hired others to perform routine household duties. As contracted services, these once-nonmarket activities become market activities and are included in the GNP.

Finally, some market activities are actually nonproductive in nature, and thus are excluded from GNP calculations. For example, government transfer payments to individuals (Social Security benefits, welfare payments, unemployment compensation, and so on) are income to the individual recipients but are not considered as income for national income accounting purposes. These payments constitute shifts or transfers of existing funds from one group to another, rather than the results of current production. Thus, the value of these transfer payments is excluded from the GNP. However, when the recipients of these payments purchase new, final goods and services in the marketplace, these purchases are, of course, included. Similarly, the values of all stock and bond sales are not included in the GNP calculation: these sales do not represent current production. They are merely a swapping of money assets for securities, and vice versa. Only that portion of a security exchange that represents the value of the broker's commission and fees is included in current production.

Methods of GNP Calculation

Two methods are used to calculate the GNP. The first method is called the expenditure approach, or flow of funds approach. Using this method, the GNP equals the sum of personal consumption expenditures, gross private domestic investment, government purchases of goods and services, and net exports (exports less imports). The alternate method is called the income approach, or flow of income approach. In this approach, the income of the four factors of production are summed, along with employee compensation, interest, rents, proprietors' income, dividends, undistributed corporate profits, corporate income taxes, and two nonincome amounts: depreciation and indirect business taxes. These two methods result in essentially identical GNP calculations. The numbers differ only by a small statistical discrepancy, reflecting measurement error. Although both GNP calculation methods are used, the expenditure approach is the more popular of the two.

Personal Consumption Expenditure (PCE)

The PCE represents the total value of goods and services of individuals and the operating expenses of nonprofit institutions (such as churches, charities, or colleges). Also included in the PCE is the estimated market value of all food, fuel, clothing, rentals on dwellings, and financial services received through bartering by consumers. The estimated rental value of owner-occupied dwellings is also included, but private purchases of residential units are classified separately as gross private domestic investment.

Personal consumption expenditures are broken down into three separate categories: durables (products with more than a 3-year economic life), nondurables, and services. The total of these items under PCE represented approximately 65 percent of total GNP in 1985 (table 9.1).

Table 9.1 United States Gross National Product and Components, 1985 (billions of dollars)

Categories	Subtotals	Total	Percentage of GNP
Personal consumption expenditure			
Durable goods	360.8		9.0
Nondurable goods	912.5		22.9
Services	1,308.6		32.8
		2,581.9	64.7
Gross private domestic investment			
Nonresidential fixed investment	475.7		11.9
Residential fixed investment	185.6		4.6
Change in business inventories	9.1		0.2
		670.4	16.8
Government purchases of goods and services			
Federal	353.9		8.9
State and local	460.7		11.5
		814.6	20.4
Net exports			
Exports	370.4		9.3
Imports	(444.8)		(11.1)
		(74.4)	(1.9)
Gross National Product		3,992.5	100%[a]

Source: Adapted from *Economic Report of the President*, 1986, table B-1, p. 252–53.
a. Subject to rounding error.

Expenditures for services now dominate the U.S. economy. We spend approximately the same amount of money on goods (durables and nondurables) as we do on services. This is a relatively recent development. The percentage of the GNP accounted for by each of the four major expenditure sectors has changed over time (table 9.2). In 1950, the goods segment of personal consumption expenditures (durables plus nondurables) exceeded service spending by more than a two-to-one margin. By 1985, however, more money was spent on services than on goods.

Motor vehicles and household furniture normally account for 75 to 90 percent of all durable-good spending. About 50 percent of the nondurable category is made up of food and drink sales. The major components of the services category are rents and rental equivalents, medical services, and recreational services. In 1983, rentals and rental equivalents amounted to 34 percent of all service expenditures. National income accountants estimate the rental-equivalent value of all owner-occupied dwellings and include those estimates in the service component of the PCE.

Table 9.2 United States Gross National Product and Components, Selected Years, 1940–85

Categories	1940	1950	1960	1970	1980	1985
			Percentage of GNP			
Personal consumption expenditures						
Durables	7.8	10.7	8.4	8.4	8.0	9.0
Nondurables	37.0	34.1	29.7	26.6	24.9	22.9
Services	26.2	21.9	26.0	27.9	30.4	32.8
Total	71.0	66.7	64.1	62.9	63.3	64.7
Gross private domestic investment						
Nonresidential fixed investment	7.7	9.6	9.5	10.3	11.8	11.9
Residential fixed investment	3.5	7.1	5.1	4.0	4.5	4.6
Change in business inventories	2.2	2.3	0.6	0.3	(0.3)	0.2
Total	13.4	19.0	15.2	14.6	16.0	16.7
Government purchases of goods and services						
Federal	6.1	6.6	10.5	9.7	7.6	8.9
State and local	8.1	6.7	8.9	11.7	11.8	11.5
Total	14.2	13.3	19.4	21.4	19.4	20.4
Net Exports						
Exports	5.4	5.0	5.8	6.8	12.8	9.3
Imports	(3.7)	(4.2)	(4.6)	(6.0)	(11.7)	(11.1)
Total	1.7	0.8	1.2	0.8	1.1	(1.8)

Note: Subject to rounding errors.
Source: Adapted from *Economic Report of the President*, 1985.

Gross Private Domestic Investment (GPDI)

The investment component of the GNP is the sum of fixed capital goods purchased by private business and nonprofit institutions, and the value of the change in the physical volume of inventories held by private businesses. The GPDI includes all private purchases of dwellings, regardless of the motive for purchase.

The three major components of the GPDI are nonresidential fixed investments, residential fixed investments, and changes in business inventories.

Nonresidential fixed investments include producer-durable equipment and structures. Producer-durable equipment is all new equipment and net purchases of used equipment that are chargeable to fixed asset accounts for which depreciated, or capital consumption allowance, accounts are maintained. This equipment must have an expected economic life of one year. Structures include buildings, barns, public utilities, hotels, motels, as well as certain long-life equipment such as blast furnaces, nuclear reactors, oil and gas wells, and mining installations.

The fixed residential structure component of the GPDI includes all purchases of residential structures and all additions to such structures. Even newly constructed college dormitories are included in this estimate.

Changes in business inventories represent fluctuations in the physical volume of farm and nonfarm inventories valued at the average selling price for the period.

The GPDI component of the GNP also includes capital consumption allowance total (gross) investment before the application of depreciation charges. It does not include any public investment projects (bridges, roads, and so on), as this type of spending is already accounted for under the government component of the GNP. In 1985, GPDI accounted for roughly 17 percent of the total GNP (see table 9.2). The largest share of the GPDI was nonresidential fixed investments of $475.5 billion, or 11.9 percent of the GNP. Investment spending normally accounts for around 15 percent of the GNP while individual components of investment experience a greater degree of fluctuation. The amount of nonresidential fixed investment is influenced by many factors including cost of capital, profit expectation, and current tax consequences of investment spending.

Government Spending

The two major categories of government spending are (1) federal and (2) state and local. This component of the GNP represents the total amount of government spending on newly produced goods and services, and total compensation for government employees at all levels. It also includes gross investment in capital projects such as highways, schools, and dams. Transfer payments, interest paid on government debt, and subsidies are excluded from this component.

Total government spending in 1985 amounted to some $814.6 billion (see table 9.1), with federal expenditures accounting for $353.9 billion. State and local government spending amounted to about $460.7 billion. In 1985, approximately 20 percent of the nation's GNP could be attributed to government spending, with the combined state and local spending effort exceeding that of the federal government. This has not always been the case. For example, in 1950, only 13 percent of the GNP was accounted for by total government spending (see table 9.2). However, since the 1960s, government spending has held steady at about 20 percent of the GNP.

Net Exports

This component of the GNP represents total U.S. exports minus imports. Exports are domestically produced goods and services and are considered part of total national production. Imports represent the production of other countries. They are included in the national income accounts and subtracted from total domestic output. In 1985, the United States exported $370.4 billion worth of goods and services (see table 9.1). However, we purchased $444.8 billion in goods and services from our trading partners. Therefore, in 1985, net exports was a negative $74.4 billion. In 1940, 1950, and 1960, exports accounted for roughly 5 percent of the GNP, and imports around 4 percent (see table 9.2). Net exports have remained roughly 1 percent. This may belie the recent dramatic growth in foreign trade. In 1980, however, exports and imports each accounted for over 10 percent of the GNP, double the 1950 to 1970 averages.

The sum of these component expenditures equals the gross national product. In mathematical form,

$$GNP = C + I + G + X_n,$$

where C = personal consumption expenditures,
I = gross private domestic investment,
G = total government spending, and
X_n = net exports (exports less imports).

Imperfections of the GNP

While the GNP is the most widely used measure of our economy's production, and generates newspaper headlines every quarter when it is announced, it is not the perfect measuring device. Many greet an increase in the GNP as a symbol of America's incredible economic achievement; but many others criticize the same growth as symbolic of industrial excesses. Growth in the GNP is cherished by some who seek a higher standard of living, and bemoaned by others who are concerned with the impact production may have on the quality of life and our fragile environment.[4]

No Qualitative Measure

The GNP is a gross measure. It places a total dollar value on all of the goods and services produced in one year. Whatever is produced is somehow measured. The GNP measures productive activity but does not distinguish whether any particular production activity is good or bad for society. The GNP is not a measure of social welfare. If the GNP rises 10 percent in one year but street crime increases by 20 percent during the same period, we may be worse off as a society. Cigarette sales, liquor sales, and legal sales of pornography are included in the GNP. Some people argue that these activities are damaging not only to the end users of the products, but also to society in general.

In a similar vein, the GNP does not account for negative or positive externalities that result from the production of certain products. If a firm pollutes the environment in the production process, GNP accounts do not deduct the cost of the damage to society; this has led some environmentalists to call the GNP "gross national pollution." Ironically, the cost of attempts to recover pollution from the environment is measured in the GNP.

Limited Measure of Leisure Time

Compared with past generations, and with workers in many other countries today, many Americans benefit from enormous amounts of leisure time (table 9.3). The average length

Table 9.3 Average Weekly Hours of Production Workers (on private nonagricultural payrolls for selected years)

Year	Average, All Industries
1950	39.8
1955	39.6
1960	38.6
1965	38.8
1970	37.1
1975	36.1
1980	35.3
1985	35.1

Source: Bureau of Labor Statistics.

of the workweek has fallen dramatically. In addition to shorter work hours, employees have received increasingly large fringe benefit packages that include pay for time away from work. Vacation, holiday, and personal leave benefits have been extended for many workers. The GNP has not been able to measure these activities directly. However, individual purchases of vacation homes, recreational vehicles, sporting goods, and other recreational goods and services are counted as part of GNP. Therefore, to a limited extent, the GNP accounts capture a portion of the value of increased leisure time.

No Measure of Improvements in Goods and Services

The GNP tends to ignore important quality changes in goods and services that reflect technological advances, increased knowledge, and so on. If the quality improvement is reflected in increased prices, the improvement may be measured to some extent. Still, many improved products and services replace their predecessors without price increases and, sometimes, with price decreases. For example, the latest generation of computers is faster and more powerful than earlier models, yet prices for computer goods have generally declined. Similarly, decreases in quality may escape measurement.

National income accountants do attempt to measure quality changes in those goods that make up a large portion of our budget. For example, annual quality estimates are made on American automobiles. However, for the most part, quality changes are not incorporated into the GNP.

No Measure of Individual Welfare

The GNP is a measure of total output. It does not reflect the individual's share in this output. The average individual can be less well-off even if the GNP is rising over time. This situation can occur if the population rises faster than the GNP, and/or the distribution of GNP becomes more unequal.

Many argue that the GNP per capita (the GNP divided by total population) is a stronger measure of national welfare than GNP. If population growth outpaces output or GNP growth, the average standard of living of the population declines. This situation exists in many third world countries.

Similarly, the GNP does not measure the distribution of output among individuals. It is only an aggregate measure of production. Therefore, if GNP growth is accompanied by a more unequal distribution of output, the standard of living of the average individual may decline.

The Underground Economy

The "underground economy" consists of both legal and illegal activities, which the economic agents attempt to conceal in order to reduce or eliminate their tax liabilities or to avoid legal prosecution. Considerable amounts of money change hands in illegal business transactions involving narcotics, gambling, prostitution, and loan sharking. The revenues from these activities are not reported, and the initial spending on these products and services goes unmeasured. However, when the recipients of the income from these illegal activities purchase goods and services in the legitimate marketplace, these secondary expenditures are, of course, measured. Therefore, the underground economy may serve as only a temporary refuge as eventually this income is respent and captured in the GNP calculation.[5] In addition, recent changes in GNP accounting methods have been able to capture, in part, the impact of the underground economy.

Legal but unreported income includes undeclared tips and gratuities, certain cash-only transactions, and "off the record" services. Individuals attempt to conceal this type of economic activity to reduce tax burdens or retain transfer payment benefits linked to maximum income levels.

Estimates of the extent of legal and illegal activities range from 5 percent to 30 percent of the GNP. The government tries to estimate the size of the underground economy in order to gauge the tax revenue loss from such activities. Estimates are made using one of two different methods. The first method is a direct investigation of the income history of both tax return filers and nonfilers. The second approach is more subtle. Trends in the probable amounts of unreported income are deduced from a historical time series of the currency held by the public. This approach is based on the fact that the participants in this hidden economy generally eschew any written record of their activity. Transactions tend to be conducted using cash or payment in kind (barter). Therefore, canceled checks, credit card receipts, bank statements, and other records are not used.

An Internal Revenue Service study indicated that, in April 1976, approximately $80 billion of currency was held by the public (table 9.4).

Table 9.4 The Underground Economy
(legal and illegal activities, 1976 estimates)

Illegal Activities	Income (billions of dollars)
Illegal drugs	23.6
Bookmaking	5.0
Numbers	3.0
Other gambling	2.0
Prostitution	1.6
Total	35.2
Legal, unreported activities	
Self-employed	39.5
Wages and salaries	26.8
Total	66.3
Total Income	101.5

Source: U.S. Department of the Treasury, Internal Revenue Service.

With nearly 80 million households in the U.S. at that time, the statistics would imply that the average holding of currency was roughly $1,000 per household. Since undeposited or uninvested currency earns no interest, however, the cost of holding this amount of cash would seem prohibitively high, even for a wealthy household. It appears that a few, perhaps members of the underground economy, hold a disproportionate amount of cash.

Drug trafficking appears to be the major revenue producer among illegal activities, with gambling (bookmaking and numbers) running a close second. The tax revenue loss related to the total amount of unreported income from illegal activities is approximately $9 billion. The bulk of the unreported legal activity income is attributed to self-employed individuals, although a surprisingly large amount of wage and salary income is paid to workers but not reported.

OTHER NATIONAL INCOME ACCOUNTS

The national income accounts (table 9.5) are not limited to estimates of the gross national product. A number of other accounts reveal a great deal about the economic health and stature of our nation. These supplemental accounts are created by making specific deductions and additions to the gross national product. These supplemental accounts are net national product (NNP), national income (NI), personal income (PI), and disposable personal income (DPI).

Table 9.5 National Income Accounts, 1985
(billions of dollars)

Gross national product	3,992.5
Less: Capital consumption allowance	(438.2)
Equals: Net national product	3,554.3
Less: Indirect business taxes[a]	(338.7)
Equals: National income	3,215.6
Less: Corporate profits	(299.0)
Net interest	(287.7)
Contributions for social measures	(354.9)
Plus: Government transfer payments to individuals	465.2
Personal interest income	456.5
Dividends	78.9
Business transfer payments	19.3
Equals: Personal income	3,293.9
Less: Personal taxes	(493.1)
Equals: Disposable personal income	2,800.8
Less: Personal consumption expenditures	(2,581.9)
Interest paid by consumers to business	(87.4)
Net personal transfer to foreigners	(2.1)
Equals: Personal saving	129.4

Source: Adapted from *Survey of Current Business*, U.S. Department of Commerce, Bureau of Economic Analysis.
a. Includes indirect business taxes and nontax liabilities, business transfer payments, and subsidies.

Net National Product (NNP)

Gross private domestic investment is part of the GNP calculation. The GPDI includes the amount of funds spent on replacing capital equipment and plants worn out in the production process. This wearing out, or consumption, of the plant and equipment necessary for production is called the capital consumption allowance, or depreciation. To a certain extent, the inclusion of capital consumption allowances in the GNP calculation overstates true output. For example, a business owner may cite bottom-line improvements in efficiency and increased profit resulting from a new computer system without accounting for the cost of the improvement: the added expense of the new technology.

Net national product is the gross national product minus the capital consumption allowance. It is an improved measure of national output because it accounts for the lost production capacity caused by the production process itself. In terms of the production possibility theory, capital consumption expenditure represents the amount of capital goods expenditures necessary to maintain any current production possibility curve in its present position. Failure to pay for the current period's depreciation charges reduces the economy's potential output, and the production possibility frontier shifts backward, toward the origin.

The gross national product adjusted by the capital consumption allowance is equal to net national product. NNP is the sum of personal consumption expenditures, government spending, net exports, and net private domestic investment. Net private domestic investment (NPDI) is equal to GPDI minus capital consumption.

National Income (NI)

National income is the aggregate income that originates in the production of goods and services to the labor and property resources supplied by all economic agents. It is therefore a measure of the factors of production costs of all goods and services produced. The factor costs are recorded as income in the form in which they accrue to economic agents. The incomes are measured in pretax dollars, and consist of compensation of employees, proprietors' income, rental income of persons, corporate profits, and net interest. National income differs dramatically from the GNP. National income excludes depreciation, indirect business taxes (such as sales, excise, and business property taxes), business transfer payments, and current surplus of government enterprises. National income does include business subsidies, however. Therefore, national income is identical to net national product except for the removal of indirect business taxes from the latter.

Personal Income (PI)

The third supplemental national income account is called personal income. This account includes income received from all sources—that is, from participation as an economic agent in the production process, from government and business transfer payments, and from government interest payments on government debt (which is treated for accounting purposes as a transfer payment). However, personal income is not a measure of national output because it excludes certain incomes, such as contributions for Social Security, undistributed corporate profits, and corporate income taxes, that accrue in production, but are not distributed to individuals. These incomes earned, but not received, must be subtracted from national income to arrive at personal income. In summary, personal income is equal to national income minus all corporate income taxes, retained (undistributed) corporate profits, and Social Security contributions, plus all transfer payments.

Disposable Personal Income (DPI)

The final supplemental national income account measures the amount of income households have to either spend or save, after deducting all personal taxes. This measure of income is called disposable personal income. Personal taxes include all tax payments (net of refunds) for income, estates and gifts, and personal property. Disposable personal income is equal to personal income minus personal taxes.

Disposable personal income can be either consumed or saved. The amount we save as a nation influences the growth rate of our economy. Recall our discussion of the ''guns vs. butter'' decision required under production possibilities theory. For a nation's economy to achieve long-term growth, it is essential to forgo current consumption and invest in capital goods—human capital as well as physical plant and equipment. The flow of savings provides the major source of funds required for this investment spending.

Table 9.6 Comparison of Savings Rates (percentage of income)

	United States	Japan	United Kingdom	West Germany
1970–74	8.5	20.6	10.1	14.9
1975–79	7.5	22.7	12.4	14.2
1980–84	6.6	21.0	12.9	13.6
1985	5.1	22.5	11.9	13.0

Source: Robert M. Giordano, "Myth and Reality of Japanese Influence on the U.S. Treasury Securities Market," *Financial Market Perspectives*, Goldman Sachs Economic Research, September–October 1986, as cited in C. Alan Garner, "Tax Reform and Personal Saving," *Economic Review*, February 1987, (Federal Reserve Bank of Kansas City), p. 13.

The amount of one's income that is consumed compared with the amount saved depends upon a number of factors. The more important factors include the return on savings, interest rewards, and the tax implications of interest income derived from savings. A great proportion of interest income earned from savings is treated as taxable income. Conversely, interest paid on some loans is tax deductible. Some economists believe that U.S. tax laws thus create an incentive for consumption and a disincentive for saving. This may be a major cause of the relatively low U.S. savings rate as compared with that of a number of other industrialized countries (table 9.6).

ADJUSTING GNP FOR PRICE CHANGES

Since the GNP calculation is basically derived by multiplying price by quantity, changes in price can distort the final GNP measure. We are concerned primarily with estimating the total national output in real terms, or total quantity. Yet since dollar values are the only common denominator between and among goods and services, we are saddled with the problem of making annual GNP comparisons when prices of goods and services are either rising or falling. For example, if 10 million units of good X are sold in year 1 at $3 per unit, the contribution to the GNP for that year would be $30 million (10 million × $3). However, if in year 2 another 10 million units of good X are sold, now at $4 per unit, the GNP will increase by an additional $10 million to a total of $40 million (10 million × $4), even though real production remained unchanged at 10 million units. Similarly, if the price of good X falls to $2 in year 3, and 10 million units are sold, the real GNP will be significantly understated. Inflationary pressures tend to result in an overestimated real GNP, while deflationary pressures tend to result in an underestimated real GNP.

National income accountants have developed a method to adjust the current-dollar GNP for price changes. The accountants deflate the unadjusted, current dollar GNP during periods of price increases and inflate it during periods of falling prices. The resulting GNP, after adjustment, is called the constant-dollar, real, or adjusted GNP (table 9.7). Table 9.7 shows price and quantity data for a simplified economy with only one product, good X. Column 2 represents the real output of good X. Column 3 represents the average price per unit of good X. Column 4 shows the annual current-dollar or unadjusted GNP. The figures in column 4 are obtained by multiplying the output of good X (column 2) by the average price of good X (column 3).

Table 9.7 Computation of Adjusted Hypothetical GNP

(1) Time Period (years)	(2) Output of Good X	(3) Price per Unit of X	(4) Unadjusted or Current-Dollar GNP (2) × (3)	(5) Price Index (year 1 = 100)	(6) Adjusted or Constant-Dollar GNP (4)/[(5)/100]
1	10	$10	$ 100	100	100
2	20	10	200	100	200
3	20	15	300	150	200
4	30	20	600	200	300
5	20	50	1,000	500	200
6	40	20	800	200	400

A study of current-dollar GNP (column 4) reveals that this unadjusted measure shows the values of the nation's output rising rapidly through year 5, then falling in year 6. However, a more careful inspection reveals the bias in current-dollar GNP caused by price fluctuations. The jump in the GNP between years 2 and 3, when GNP increased from $200 to $300, was caused by inflation; the real output of good X did not change. Similarly, the unadjusted GNP jumped from $600 to $1,000 between years 4 and 5, even though real production of good X actually declined by 10 units! The drop in output was lost because of the severe price inflation during this period. It appears that output dropped even more between years 5 and 6, as the unadjusted GNP fell from $1,000 to $800. In reality, however, the decrease in price from $50 to $20 per unit between years 5 and 6 was significant enough to mask an actual increase in real output. Obviously, reliance on the current-dollar GNP is foolish. National income specialists deal with this problem by adjusting the current-dollar GNP with a device called a price index.

The price index allows money-valued output changes to be measured with a common measuring device. A particular year is chosen as the base year, and the prices that exist in that year are compared with those of all other years. In this fashion, it is possible to determine the extent of price changes relative to the base-year reference point. The general formula for a price index is given as:

$$\text{Price index} = \frac{\text{Current-year price}}{\text{Base-year price}} \times 100.$$

The index allows price changes to be expressed in percentage terms. In Table 9.6, column 5 represents the price index for years 1 through 6.

To illustrate the calculation, we can compute the price index for year 3. In our example, we have chosen year 1 as the base year.

$$\text{Price index} = \frac{\$15}{10} \times 100 = 150.$$

A price-index value of 150 for year 3 means that, in year 3, prices were 150 percent of the base-year price. To obtain the adjusted GNP shown in table 9.7, one more step is required. To adjust a current-dollar GNP, apply the formula shown below:

$$\text{Adjusted GNP} = \frac{\text{Unadjusted GNP}}{\text{Price index}/100}.$$

The denominator simply transforms the price index from a percentage to a decimal. Thus, for year 3, the formula yields the following:

$$\text{Adjusted GNP} = 300/1.5 = 200.$$

Comparing the annual adjusted, or constant-dollar, GNPs shown in column 6 presents a clear picture of the real output fluctuations in the economy.

Check Your Understanding

In using a price index to make adjustments to the GNP, the choice of a base year is arbitrary. The choice of one year over another will not affect the adjustment process. Check your understanding of this process by calculating the price index and adjusted GNP for year 3 in table 9.7, using year 4 as the base year. Then, find the price indices and adjusted GNPs for all other years, using year 4 as the base year.

Answer: Using the formula for a price index, calculate as follows:

$$\text{Price index} = \frac{15}{20} \times 100 = 75.$$

A price index of 75 for year 3 means that, in year 3, prices were 75 percent of the base-year price. The adjusted GNP equals $300 divided by .75, or $400. The change in the base year has changed the numbers that result from the calculations, but not the relationships that hold among the numbers. Using year 4 as the base year, the price indices and adjusted GNPs for years 1 through 6 would appear as follows:

(1) Time Period (years)	(2) Output of Good X	(3) Price per Unit of X	(4) Unadjusted (current-dollar) GNP	(5) Price Index (year 4 = 100)	(6) Adjusted (constant-dollar) GNP
1	10	$10	$100	50	200
2	20	10	200	50	400
3	20	15	300	75	400
4	30	20	600	100	600
5	20	50	1,000	250	400
6	40	20	800	100	800

The pattern of the numbers in the price index and adjusted GNP columns matches the pattern in table 9.7.

INFLATING AND DEFLATING THE GNP

Table 9.8 shows actual historical GNP data for the U.S. economy for recent years. Column 2 shows the actual, published, or unadjusted GNP that occurred in each year. Column 3 lists the average price levels that existed in each year as measured by the U.S. Department of Commerce implicit price deflator (1982 = 100). The implicit price deflator for the GNP is a current-weighted price index (1982 = 100) and is obtained by dividing the current-dollar GNP by the constant-dollar GNP for each period. It is a weighted average of the detailed price indices used in the deflation of GNP. It is weighted by the composition of the constant-dollar output for each quarter. That is, the price indices for each quarter are weighted by the ratio of the quantity of the item valued in 1982 prices to the total output in 1982 prices. Therefore, changes in the implicit price deflator reflect changes in prices as well as changes in the composition of the GNP. Column 4 lists adjusted or constant 1982-dollar GNP, derived by dividing the current-dollar GNP of column 2 by its corresponding price index (expressed as a decimal).

Table 9.8 Current-Dollar vs. Constant-Dollar GNP, Selected Years (billions of dollars)

(1) Year	(2) Current or Unadjusted GNP	(3) Price Index[a] (percent) 1982 = 100	(4) Constant-Dollar GNP (1982 dollars)
1978	2,249.7	72.2	3,115.2
1979	2,508.2	78.6	3,192.4
1980	2,732.0	85.7	3,187.1
1981	3,052.6	94.0	3,248.8
1982	3,166.0	100.0	3,166.0
1983	3,401.6	103.8	3,277.7
1984	3,774.7	108.1	3,492.0
1985	3,992.5	111.7	3,573.5
1986	4,206.1	114.5	3,673.4

Source: U.S. Department of Commerce, Bureau of Economic Analysis.
a. Price index used is the U.S. Department of Commerce Implicit Price Deflator.

Because of steady price increases from 1978 through 1985, the unadjusted GNP must be inflated for all years prior to 1982. Lower current-year prices must be translated into relatively higher (1982) prices. The unadjusted GNP for all years after 1982 must be deflated. Higher current-year prices must be translated into relatively lower (1982) prices. To find the value of the 1980 GNP in constant 1982 dollars, inflate the 1980 current-year GNP as follows:

$$\frac{\text{Unadjusted 1980 GNP}}{\text{1980 Price index}/100} = \text{Adjusted 1980 GNP}$$

$$\frac{2{,}732.0}{0.857} = \$3{,}187.8$$

In other words, prices in 1980 were, on average, considerably lower than those of 1982. Therefore to express the 1980 GNP in 1982 prices, we inflate the 1980 GNP. The adjusted 1980 GNP reported in table 9.8 is $3,187.1—not $3,187.8. This minor difference reflects whether the numbers are rounded before or after performing the calculation.

Similarly, to find the value of the 1984 GNP in constant 1982 dollars, we deflate the 1984 current-year GNP.

$$\frac{\text{Unadjusted 1984 GNP}}{\text{1984 Price index}/100} = \text{Adjusted 1984 GNP}$$

$$\frac{3{,}774.7}{1.081} = \$3{,}491.85$$

Prices in 1984 were relatively higher on average than in 1982. Again, the number obtained above differs slightly from that shown in the table because of rounding. Therefore, it is necessary to deflate the 1984 GNP in terms of the 1982 GNP. The adjustment of each GNP to constant 1982 dollars permits us to investigate changes in real output by, in effect, holding all prices constant from one year to the next.

The adjustment process described above is of considerable importance to banks. Imagine a bank posting an annual profit of x dollars, year after year. Obviously, an adjustment for the effect of higher prices would pare down the real, or constant-dollar, profits, and quite possibly show a declining constant-dollar profit performance over time. In addition to profits, virtually every economic variable subject to the distortion caused by price changes should be adjusted to some base-year reference point.

SUMMARY

The U.S. Department of Commerce has three systems for monitoring the country's economy. These include National Income and Product Accounting (NIPA), capital finance and balance sheet accounting, and input-output accounting.

National income accounting is an important component of policymaking, planning, marketing, and research efforts in the public as well as the private sector.

The gross national product (GNP) is the single most important measure of economic activity. It is defined as the total dollar value of all new final goods and services produced in the economy in one year. The GNP is the sum of personal consumption expenditures, gross private domestic investment, total government spending, and net exports. The expenditure method and the income method are two means of measuring national output.

The GNP has several flaws as a measuring tool. It does not discriminate "healthy" from "unhealthy" production, fails to capture the value of increased leisure time, ignores quality improvements, does not measure the average individual's well-being, and, because of the existence of unreported legal and illegal economic activity, underestimates the true level of U.S. productivity.

Other national income accounts measure net national product, national income, personal income, and disposable personal income.

The GNP must be adjusted to accommodate price changes. A price index is created using the current-year price and a base-year price. The resulting value is called the adjusted, or constant-dollar, GNP. Unadjusted GNP is also known as current-dollar GNP.

Americans generally do not save as much as citizens in other countries. Some say this is because U.S. tax laws create an incentive for spending and a disincentive for saving.

KEY WORDS

constant-dollar (real, adjusted) GNP
current-dollar GNP
disposable personal income (DPI)
durables
expenditure approach
government transfer payments
gross national product (GNP)
gross private domestic investment (GPDI)
implicit price deflator
income approach
input-output accounting

national income (NI)
national income and product accounting (NIPA)
net national product (NNP)
net private domestic investment (NPDI)
nondurables
personal income (PI)
rental equivalents
services
value added

Questions for Review

1. Discuss what problems would occur in trying to compare the U.S. GNP with the GNP of the U.S.S.R.

2. If a Third World country used the same methodology to calculate its GNP as the U.S. does, explain how the Third World nation's GNP might be seriously underestimated.

NATIONAL INCOME ACCOUNTING

3. The service component of the personal consumption expenditure has grown rapidly in recent years and has inflated the U.S. GNP growth rate. Observers note that many of the new services are not essential in nature and do little to enhance the U.S. standard of living. List some nonessential services and comment about them.

4. In 1975, the current-dollar GNP was $1,549.2 billion and the constant-dollar GNP (adjusted to 1972 dollars) was $1,231.6. If (1972 = 100), find the implicit price deflator (price index) for 1975.

5. The U.S. GNP in 1947 was $233.1 billion. If the implicit price deflator (1972 = 100) in 1947 was 49.6, find the value of the 1947 GNP in constant 1972 dollars.

6. Given the following data, assess the profitability performance of the Third National Bank for the 1980–82 period.

Year	Net Income (millions of dollars)	Price Index (1972 = 100)
1980	125.0	178.4
1981	129.5	195.1
1982	135.6	206.9

7. Explain the difference between the following national income accounts:
   a) Gross national product (GNP) and net national product (NNP).
   b) Gross private domestic investment (GPDI) and net private domestic investment (NPDI).
   c) Personal income (PI) and disposable personal income (DPI).

8. Gambling and prostitution are legal activities in Great Britain. This tends to inflate its GNP relative to that of the U.S., where these activities are outlawed. Comment.

9. Given the following data, find the GNP, NNP, NI, PI, and DPI.

Interest income	=	$ 100	Indirect business taxes	=	$280
Personal consumption			Personal taxes	=	420
expenditure	=	2,000	Transfer payments	=	500
GPDI	=	500	Social Security contributions	=	270
Exports	=	500	Retained corporate earnings	=	45
Imports	=	400	Corporate taxes	=	60
Government spending	=	600	Depreciation	=	400

277

ENDNOTES

1. Simon Kuznets, Nobel Prize-winner in economics, is largely responsible for developing the major concepts of national income and products accounts. See Simon Kuznets, *National Income and Its Composition: 1919 to 1928* (New York: National Bureau of Economic Research, 1941). He pointed out in a later work that a high national income is no guarantee of the nation's citizens' happiness. For example, increasing specialization may foster worker boredom, tension, and stress. See Simon Kuznets, *National Income: A Summary of Findings* (New York: National Bureau of Economic Research, 1946).

2. See Robert P. Parker, "National Income and Product Accounts: The Comprehensive Revision," *Business Economics*, vol. 21, no. 3 (July 1986), v. XXI, n.3, pp. 5–9.

3. See "IRS Sheds Light on Underground Economy," *U.S. News and World Report,* September 26, 1985.

4. See Kenneth Boulding, "Fun and Games with the Gross National Product—The Role of Misleading Indicators in Social Policy," in *The Environmental Crisis* ed. Harold W. Helfrich, Jr. (New Haven: Yale University Press, 1970).

5. See Carol S. Carson, "The Underground Economy: An Introduction," *Survey of Current Business* (May 1984), pp. 21–37. See also L. Saunders "What the Mattress Knows (The Underground Economy)," *Forbes*, vol. 136, no. 1 (July 1, 1985), p. 96.

ECONOMICS IN THE NEWS

Economy Grew At 4.3% Rate In First Quarter

By Rose Gutfeld
Staff Reporter of *The Wall Street Journal*

WASHINGTON—A drop in imports and a rise in inventory investment pushed economic growth to a much faster 4.3% annual rate in the first quarter, the Commerce Department said.

The rise in the real gross national product, the inflation-adjusted value of the economy's output of goods and services, followed a meager 1.1% growth pace in the fourth quarter and was the largest since a 5% rate in the second quarter of 1984. Many analysts, however, contended the report exaggerated the economy's underlying strength and masked sluggishness.

"The number was big, but the economy was weak in the first quarter," said Allen Sinai, chief economist at Shearson Lehman Brothers Inc. in New York. Robert Wescott, vice president at Alphametrics Corp. in Bala Cynwyd, Pa., agreed, saying, "It's a basically weak report."

Both economists contended that the inventory buildup was excessive in light of weak demand and said that a slowdown in inventory investment is likely restraining growth in the current quarter. Much of the inventory accumulation occurred in the auto industry, which has cut production recently. The report showed that consumer spending fell for the second consecutive quarter. Capital spending also declined.

Accompanying the acceleration in growth was a resurgence in inflation. Prices, as measured by a GNP-based measure known as the deflator, rose at a 3.5% annual rate in the quarter after increasing at a subdued 0.7% pace in the fourth period.

On the other hand, a narrowing of the trade deficit again contributed to growth for the second quarter in a row. While recent monthly figures have shown the deficit expanding, those reports aren't adjusted for inflation or for seasonal change, as the GNP figures are.

In a briefing for reporters, Commerce Undersecretary Robert Ortner said the rise in inflation "may be some cause for concern." He said, however, that much of the rise reflected higher energy prices and said he still expects inflation to be moderate this year.

Growth Estimate

The department also said that the after-tax profits of U.S. corporations rose 6.3% in the fourth quarter, rather than the 6.1% it initially estimated. This gain was the sharpest since an 11.4% rise in the third quarter of 1983.

The GNP figure does bolster the chances that the economy will reach the Reagan administration's prediction of 3.2% growth for 1987. A White House spokesman told reporters that "the administration regards these first-quarter figures with enthusiasm, noting that they exceed our forecast for 1987 growth by more than a full percentage point."

Mr. Ortner said the drop in imports in the first quarter largely reflected a reduction in oil shipments. Exports also fell, however, reflecting declines in exports of farm goods and aircraft. Mr. Wescott called the export decline "evidence that weak growth abroad is starting to take its toll."

Some economists were more bullish on the outlook. Robert Dederick, chief economist at Northern Trust Co. in Chicago, said that demand is strengthening in the current quarter and the trade balance is continuing to improve. Some of the softness in capital spending was expected, he said, following the strong fourth-quarter purchases in advance of tax-law changes that imposed less generous depreciation schedules for some items.

"The economy is still in a slow-growth channel," he said. "This doesn't tell me we're breaking out on the high side, but it doesn't tell me to be pessimistic, either," Mr. Dederick added.

On profits, the department said the fourth-quarter rise brought them to a $144.5 billion annual rate from a $135.9 billion pace in the third quarter. For all of 1986, profits rose a revised 2% to $134 billion from $131.4 billion. Previously, the department reported this 1986 increase at 1.9%.

Before-Tax Profits

Before taxes, profits rose a revised 8% to a rate of $259.6 billion, after increasing 5.6% in the fourth quarter to a $240.4 billion pace. Previously the department said before-tax profits rose 7.7% in the fourth quarter.

The department's measure of profits from current production rose a revised 3% in the fourth period to a $311.2 billion pace after rising 3% in the third quarter to a $302 billion pace. This figure, which many analysts consider a better gauge of corporate financial health, is adjusted to eliminate the effects of inflation on inventories and to reflect capital depreciation more accurately.

The department originally put this rise at 2.8%.

The department's measure of corporate cash flow grew 0.4% in the fourth quarter to a $391.9 billion pace after rising 1.3% to a $390.4 billion rate. Originally this figure was put at 0.3%.

The first-quarter increase brought GNP to an annual rate of $3.735 trillion from $3.696 trillion in the fourth quarter. Before inflation adjustment, fourth-quarter GNP ran at a $4.339 trillion annual rate compared with a $4.259 trillion pace in the third quarter.

Reprinted by permission of *The Wall Street Journal*, © Dow Jones & Company, 1987. All Rights Reserved.

CHAPTER TEN

THE BUSINESS CYCLE

Objectives

After reading this chapter, you should be able to

- describe the role of the National Bureau of Economic Research (NBER)

- define business cycles in macroeconomic terms

- characterize business cycle peaks, troughs, expansions, contractions, recessions, and depressions

- describe several theories that explain business cycle movements

- explain the concepts of leading, lagging, and coincidental indicators, and give an example of each one

- explain why composite indexes are more reliable than individual indexes

THE BUSINESS CYCLE

We now turn our attention to the most critical aspect of our economic existence—the business cycle. The real GNP does not grow at a steady, moderate pace. In fact, the level of real output is subject to relatively wild swings in behavior. At times, real GNP growth is slow and steady. Very abruptly, the level of activity may begin to decline (this is called negative growth). Or the economy may enter into a period of stagnation, where months go by without major improvement in output. Then, almost without warning, production might burst forward, straining the economy's production capacity. These swings in economic activity, tracked over time, make up the business cycle.

Phases

The major arbiter of business cycle phenomena in the U.S. is the National Bureau of Economic Research (NBER), located in Cambridge, Massachusetts. The NBER defines a business cycle as a period of "expansions of economic activity, followed by similarly general recessions, contractions, and revivals, which merge into the expansion phase of the next cycle." A theoretical business cycle is portrayed graphically in figure 10.1.

The major indicator of economic activity is real, or inflation-adjusted, GNP. Real GNP is measured on the vertical axis. Time is measured on the horizontal axis. The units used to measure time are normally 3-month periods or quarters. These units of measurement are used because they coincide nicely with the statistical release dates for the quarterly GNP estimates made by the U.S. Department of Commerce.

Business cycle turning points are defined as moments in time when economic activity changes directions. In other words, turning points represent occasions when real GNP

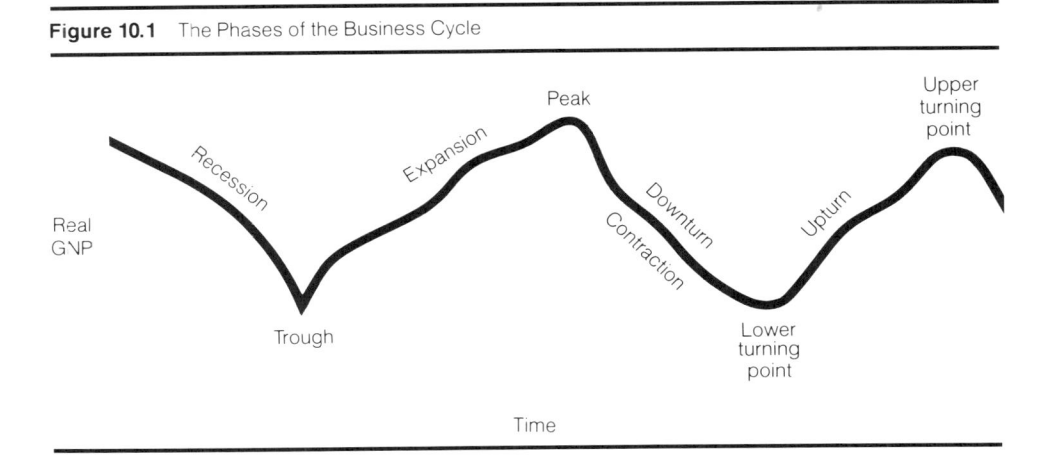

Figure 10.1 The Phases of the Business Cycle

growth is at a relative peak or relative trough. A peak is the point at which real output shows the largest relative deviation above the long-term trend line of economic activity. At this point, capacity is at or near full utilization, and full or near-full employment is normally achieved. A trough is the point at which real output shows the largest relative deviation below the long-term trend. At this point, consumption spending is normally quite low and investment is normally minimal. These turning points, also called upper and lower turning points, have been identified by date since 1854. These dates, called "business cycle reference dates," signal the completion of a cycle. A business cycle can be characterized by the number of months or quarters that pass as the economy moves from one trough to the next trough. Since 1854, the NBER has established the existence of 29 distinct U.S. business cycles. The cycles range in duration from a low of 14 months (from the trough of July 1980 to the next lower turning point of November 1982) to a high of 117 months (from the trough of February 1961 to that of November 1970). The last trough to be dated, as of this writing, was November 1982.

Expansion and Contraction

The expansion phase of the business cycle is defined as the rise in business activity and real output from the lower turning point, or trough, to the peak, or upper turning point. For the 29 business cycles completed since 1854, the average length of the expansion phase has been approximately 35 months.

The contraction phase of the business cycle is defined as the fall in business activity and real output from the peak, or upper turning point, to the trough, or lower turning point. The contraction phase is usually much shorter than the expansion phase. For the 29 cycles completed since 1854, the average contraction has lasted approximately 18 months.

The post-World War II history of the average lengths of expansions and contractions differs significantly from the period 1854 to 1982. In 1946, the government passed the Employment Act. Among other provisions, the act created the Council of Economic Advisors to advise the government on policy matters relating to cyclical fluctuations in economic activity. The evidence shows that the economy has benefited greatly from this policy advice (table 10.1). From 1946 to 1982, through eight complete cycles, the average length of the expansion phase of the cycle has been 44 months while the contraction phase has averaged only 12 months. The 105-month expansion phase from March 1961 to November 1969 was the longest ever recorded.

Recessions and Depressions

While there are no strict definitions of the terms "recession" and "depression," there is a generally accepted rule of thumb that the NBER will designate a contraction phase a

Table 10.1 Dates of Peaks and Troughs of Business Cycles in the United States, 1854–1982

Monthly				Quarterly			
Trough		Peak		Trough		Peak	
December	1854	June	1857	IV	1854	II	1857
December	1858	October	1860	IV	1858	III	1860
June	1861	April	1865	III	1861	I	1865
December	1867	June	1869	I	1868	II	1869
December	1870	October	1873	IV	1870	III	1873
March	1879	March	1882	I	1879	I	1882
May	1885	March	1887	II	1885	II	1887
April	1888	July	1890	I	1888	III	1890
May	1891	January	1893	II	1891	I	1893
June	1894	December	1895	II	1894	IV	1895
June	1897	June	1899	II	1897	III	1899
December	1900	September	1902	IV	1900	IV	1902
August	1904	May	1907	III	1904	II	1907
June	1908	January	1910	II	1908	I	1910
January	1912	January	1913	IV	1911	I	1913
December	1914	August	1918	IV	1914	III	1918
March	1919	January	1920	I	1919	I	1920
July	1921	May	1923	III	1921	II	1923
July	1924	October	1926	III	1924	III	1926
November	1927	August	1929	IV	1927	III	1929
March	1933	May	1937	I	1933	II	1937
June	1938	February	1945	II	1938	I	1945
October	1945	November	1948	IV	1945	IV	1948
October	1949	July	1953	IV	1949	II	1953
May	1954	August	1957	II	1954	III	1957
April	1958	April	1960	II	1958	II	1960
February	1961	December	1969	I	1961	IV	1969
November	1970	November	1973	IV	1970	IV	1973
March	1975	January	1980	I	1975	I	1980
July	1980	July	1981	III	1980	III	1981
November	1982			IV	1982		

Source: U.S. Department of Commerce, Bureau of Economic Analysis.

recession only when the downturn has lasted for at least 6 consecutive months. A depression is essentially a severe and prolonged recession. President Harry S. Truman, however, distinguished between the two terms: he said a recession is when your neighbor loses his job; a depression is when you lose your job.

The Great Depression was a terrible disaster for America. In the summer of 1929, industrial production in America began a long, precipitous decline that continued until 1933. In the fall of 1929, the U.S. Stock Market took a disastrous plunge, petrifying every sector of the economy. Many banks failed: the number of commercial banks decreased by almost 35 percent between 1929 and 1933.[1] Unemployment rates soared to almost 25 percent of the labor force. A new president, Franklin D. Roosevelt, was inaugurated in March 1933 and led the nation in its struggle to recover with innovative government-sponsored employment programs.[2]

Recessions are characterized by reductions in consumer spending, drops in sales, factory closings, and heavy unemployment. However, recessions normally lead to a decrease in the inflation rate and, in certain cases, to falling prices or deflation. By contrast, the expansion phase of the business cycle leads to increased consumer spending, new or expanded factories, and increased employment opportunities.

An unfortunate side effect of the rapid buildup in economic activity is rapidly rising prices. Rapid, unanticipated price increases can drastically reduce the buying power of certain groups. Because of the powerful effects of unchecked, sharp shifts in economic activity on employment rates and prices, these phenomena have been the bane of modern economic systems. The mission of macroeconomic policymakers is to subdue these wild swings in economic activity. One of the major economic goals is to place the economy on a growth path that approximates the ideal long-run trend line of stable activity and gradual expansion. If we cannot reach this lofty goal, a second-best solution is to moderate the amplitude of the cycle (see figure 10.2).

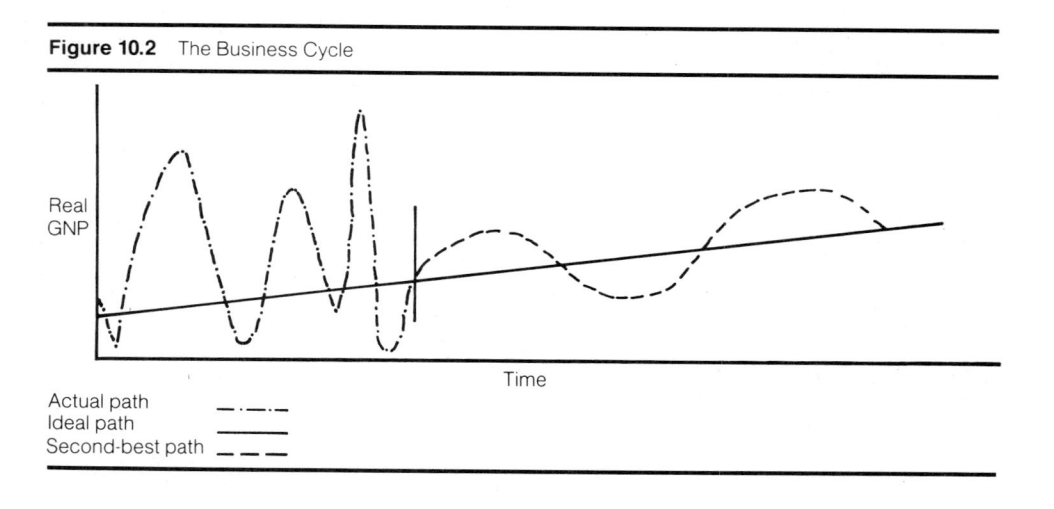

Figure 10.2 The Business Cycle

Actual path —·—·—
Ideal path ———
Second-best path ————

Business Cycle Theories

Numerous attempts have been made to explain the causes of fluctuations in economic activity. There is little agreement as to why these phenomena occur. Some theories are strictly economic, political, or sociological in nature. At least one theory is based upon physical science. Certain theories are based on internal economic forces, others on external economic or political ones. Some are all-inclusive, seeking to explain the very nature of the business cycle, while others address limited and specific causes of economic fluctuations. Several of the more popular theories on business cycle fluctuations are described below.

Underconsumption Theory

Early economists concentrated on underconsumption as the major threat to economic peace. Thomas Malthus, best known for his population essays, was a distinguished and learned economist. While Malthus did not articulate a complete theory, he hinted in the *Principles of Political Economy* (1820) that recessions, depressions, and panics can be started by lack of spending. As spending slows, sales fall, business orders decrease, and factories reduce output. This reduction in hours of work cuts employee earnings, and workers' ability to purchase goods and services is reduced. This cycle feeds on itself, and plant closings and unemployment result.

John Hobson, an early twentieth-century economist, argued that because income is distributed unequally, over-saving on the part of the wealthy and upper-income groups could precipitate slowdowns in spending, which could also lead to plant closings and unemployment.

Monetary and Credit Theories

Monetary and credit theories argue that the expansion of output requires an elastic money supply. Any rigidity in the source of credit or money supply can stunt economic growth, creating conditions that can lead to economic collapse. Similarly, an overly elastic supply of credit can lead to excessive borrowing by merchants, which at first leads to increased production. But, as the process continues, manufacturing capacities are soon reached, prices rise, and price inflation leads to the next contraction.

Marxist Theory

Other theories of the business cycle have been proposed by opponents of capitalism who despised the capitalistic system for its unequal distribution of wealth between workers and the owners of the means of production. The most famous of these theories was proposed by Karl Marx.

In 1867, the first volume of Marx's famous work, *Das Kapital* (translated *Capital*), was published. In it, Marx portrayed the recurring and intensifying struggle between the capitalists and workers. He called this trend in business cycles the "laws of motion" of all capitalistic systems. Marx based his argument on the concept of "surplus value." Marx held that the wage a worker will receive under competitive conditions will only be sufficient to maintain the worker and his family physically. This wage is called the "subsistence" wage. Marx further argued that the value of the product the laborer produces is generally much higher than this subsistence wage. The difference between the total value of a worker's output and the subsistence wage the worker receives is called "surplus value." Because the capitalists own the means of production, this surplus value accrues to the capitalists.

Marx argued that the drive to create "surplus value" leads to exploitation of workers. Competition in the marketplace leads to introduction of labor-saving devices, and as all firms add to their capital stocks, unemployment from technological advances leads to an army of unemployed. The workers no longer have income to purchase the products of the capitalists. Consumption dwindles as additional labor-saving devices are installed to lower costs even further. Yet the number of income-earning employees fails to keep pace with the output of goods and services. As firms try to sell their bloated inventories, prices and profits tumble, business failures escalate, and the great crisis of capitalism ensues. Firms that are able to emerge from the ruins consolidate, and the economy moves forward again. As the cycle continues, however, the failure of these giant firms creates even more hardship.

Marx argued that capitalist economies would continue for a time from cycle to cycle, but that each cycle would intensify until, ultimately, there would be a final business cycle. Marx claimed that the centralization of the means of production and socialization of labor would at last reach a point where they become completely incompatible.[3]

Structural Theory

Many economists argue that the rise of large monopolistic firms and large, inflexible labor unions causes structural rigidities in the economic system that can precipitate changes in the business. For example, if a low-cost foreign competitor enters the U.S. market, competition will force American firms to match the lower prices of the new market entrants. The current cost structure of the American firms may be too high to generate profits at the new price level, and it may be difficult to lower costs. Labor costs, for example, may be fixed by long-term labor contracts.

If the U.S. firms do not meet the price competition, sales begin to drop and worker layoffs begin. Because the number of employees in these industries may be quite large, the total drop in income and thus consumption spending can be large enough to affect other industries. Because of the economic interdependence of communities, this localized recession can soon spread across the country. In a period of "hard times," it is particularly difficult for a firm to extract wage and benefit concessions from the union. Ultimately, the firm may opt to relocate to a nonunion location, or outsource production to a foreign land, leaving a large pool of unemployed workers with limited spending power and limited opportunities for future employment.

Investment Theory

Unlike underconsumption or oversaving theories, investment theories hold that business-cycle instability is caused by too little saving. These theorists argue that the normal, slow expansion of an economy is easily disrupted if the required level of investment in plant and equipment is not sustained.

Economist I.M. Clark of Columbia University refined this theory with his concept of the acceleration principle. This principle relates the level of net investment spending, the rate of growth of aggregate demand, the stock of capital goods, and the level of income. According to the acceleration principle, for net investment to occur, the level of aggregate demand must be increasing and the utilization of the current capital stock must be at maximum capacity. If the growth rate of investment spending is to be maintained, the rate of growth of the GNP must accelerate. If it does not, investment spending can decrease or even fall to zero. The acceleration and deceleration of investment spending causes swings in overall economic activity. The acceleration principle will be discussed in more detail in chapter 12.

Cyclical Innovation Theory

Joseph Schumpeter, a famous Austrian-born economist, argued that business cycles are partially the result of technical innovations and inventions and the new products that are thus introduced to the economy. New products and technology are born through the creative efforts of innovators. These innovations create new business opportunities, which quicken the pace of economic activity and stimulate economic growth. Eventually, the economic possibilities of the innovations are exhausted and expansion of output ceases. Economic contraction ensues, and continues unless—or until—new and better innovations are introduced. Schumpeter observed that the expansions and contractions could be further driven by the credit practices, speculation, overexpansion, and uncertainty generated by the frenzy of economic activity surrounding the innovation.

Schumpeter held that innovations themselves occur in regular cycles of 50 to 60 years in length, which he called the Kondratieff cycles.[4] According to Schumpeter, the first such cycle began in the 1780s and ended with the development of steam power and British textile manufacturing. The second 60-year cycle, lasting to the end of the nineteenth century, was caused by the development of massive railroad lines and improvements in iron and steel technology. Thomas Edison is credited with starting the third cycle with the innovations associated with the development of electricity. Schumpeter acknowledged shorter subcycles intertwined among the Kondratieff, most notably a medium-length 10-year cycle called the Juglar, and a short, 3- to 4-year cycle called the Kitchin. These cycles were named in honor of their discoverers, Clement Juglar and Claude Kitchin. Schumpeter believed that the cycles were linked together in continuous operation. He held that the troughs of all three cycles had occurred simultaneously only once—in 1929![5]

Military Buildup Theory

Many economists have observed that, in the U.S., major war periods and heavy defense spending in nonwar years have all led to economic expansions. Some contend that the long period of expansion from 1961 to 1969 was likely fueled by spending for the war effort in Southeast Asia. Proponents of the military buildup theory hold that the end of hostilities generally causes a cutback in defense outlays, resulting in a business contraction.

Politics and the Business Cycle

Edward Tufte, a political scientist, believes that economists should focus on the American national political scene in order to explain business cycle theory. Tufte claims that incumbent politicians influence economic activity through policymaking in an effort to improve their chances for re-election. Tufte uses election and economic business cycle data to show a high correlation between elections and economics. He proclaims the following pattern describes most periods between 1948 and 1978: "a 2-year cycle in the growth of real disposable income per capita, with accelerations in even-numbered years and decelerations in odd-numbered years. A 4-year presidential cycle in the unemployment rate, with downturns in unemployment in the months before the presidential election and upturns in the unemployment rate usually beginning from 12 to 18 months after the election."[6]

Sunspot Theory

In the late nineteenth century, British economist William Stanley Jevons attempted to reduce all of economics to mathematics and science. Jevons held that the discovery of sunspots in 1801 by Sir William Herschel was a significant economic as well as scientific finding. These usually severe bursts of radioactive storms on the surface of the sun cause the earth to be bombarded with large doses of solar radiation. Jevons reasoned that the extra doses of radiation must affect weather patterns. Changes in rainfall amount can influence crop yields in agriculture, which in turn influence the general level of business in all economic sectors. Jevons offered the following proof for his theory: the average duration of the business cycle for the approximately 150-year period between 1721 and 1878 was 10.46 years. Sir William Herschel estimated the sunspot cycle to be 10.45 years! Jevons held this statistical correlation to be causal and not a random occurrence. He died convinced that sunspots caused fluctuations in economic activity.[7]

Self-Fulfilling Prophecy Theory

Some experts consider business cycles to be the results of mass hysteria—an economic version of the lemming effect. Periodic swings in consumer spending behavior are thought to be the results of undue optimism or pessimism. For example, the fear of a recession on the part of consumers can precipitate the recession because, as consumers begin to worry about job security, house payments, and other debt problems, they make conscious decisions to postpone spending—keeping the car one more year, or putting off a planned vacation until "good times" return. If enough consumers cancel their spending plans, this lack of consumption can trigger an economic downturn. Similarly, once in the depths of a recession, expectations of recovery can actually hasten a business upturn.

Modern economic thought places far less emphasis on ascertaining the causes of the business cycle. Instead, massive efforts are under way in an attempt to reduce the number and severity of economic fluctuations. Today's economists focus on predicting the dates of the business cycle's turning points or, once a severe contraction or overheated expansion begins, on determining the appropriate fiscal and monetary policy actions required to end the disturbance. Most of these predictions and calculations are based on information from economic indicators or econometric models.

ECONOMIC INDICATORS AND ECONOMETRIC MODELS

All economic agents can benefit from advance warning of key turning points in the business cycle. However, economists' current forecasting ability is not much different from that of the weather forecasters. Weather forecasting is often quite accurate in the short run, fairly accurate over an intermediate period, and rather poor in the long run. Economic forecasts have a similar record. Later in the chapter we will evaluate the performance of the major econometric forecasts, but first we will consider a simple, yet effective method of forecasting business cycle changes.

Economic Indicators

As noted earlier, the period from 1929 to 1941 was one of the most devastating eras in the economic history of the United States. After the worst years, between 1929 and 1933, when real GNP fell by almost 30 percent, the economy recovered slightly from 1934 to 1936. A sharp contraction reappeared in 1937–38. Battered and bruised from recent economic events, Secretary of the Treasury Henry Morgenthau, Jr., asked the private, nonprofit National Bureau of Economic Research for assistance.

Secretary Morgenthau requested a series of economic indicators that could be used to forecast the end of the 1937–38 recession in particular, and all turning points in general. Morgenthau had realized that certain economic indicators reach their peak or trough before the economy as a whole reaches its peak or trough. In order to predict when changes in the overall economy would occur, economists had only to observe the changes in these "leading" economic indicators.

The NBER had as a member of its staff a brilliant young economist named Arthur F. Burns, who would later serve as Federal Reserve Board chairman. Burns selected a list of economic indicators that seemed to predict turning points in the economy with surprising accuracy. The first list of leading economic indicators was released by the Department of the Treasury in 1938.

Over the years, there have been many changes to the original list. A subdivision of the Department of Commerce, the Bureau of Economic Analysis (BEA), has taken over the original duties of the private-sector NBER, and publishes a wide variety of economic and business indicators. Their primary publication is the monthly *Business Conditions Digest*. Economic and business indicators are organized by time series. A time series is an array of economic data recorded sequentially at equal time intervals. For example, weekly money supply, monthly unemployment rates, and quarterly GNP estimates are all economic time series.

Although business cycles vary in duration and intensity, they normally are of sufficient duration to permit cumulative movements in other time series, which also display cyclical movement. Some series relate more closely to the general business cycle than others. The BEA has classified the various time series according to how well they perform as indicators.

Certain indicators stand out because of the consistency with which their movements have paralleled business cycles, the regularity of their timing at turning points in aggregate economic activity, and the prominence of their cyclical fluctuations relative to shorter activities within the economic system.

The list of time series is quite long, but three groups of indicators particularly deserve attention. These three series are the leading, coincidental, and lagging economic series.

Leading Indicators

Turning points of some economic time series typically occur before the dates marking the peaks and troughs of the general business cycle. These time series are called leading indicators. This group of indicators relates primarily to future production and employment needs of business. The BEA examined and rated over 300 individual series for their ability to "lead" the general cycle. The following six criteria were applied in the assessment and selection process:

- Economic significance: how well understood and how important is the role in business cycles of the variable represented by the time series data?
- Statistical adequacy: how well does the given series measure the economic variable or process in question? Is it a true reflection of reality?
- Timing at revivals and recessions: how consistently, in terms of a month lead time, has the series led the successive business cycle turns over time?
- Conformity to historical business cycles: how regularly have the movements in the specific indicator reflected the expansions and contractions in the economy at large?

- Smoothness: how promptly can a cyclical turn in the series be distinguished from directional change associated with shorter (mainly irregular) movements?
- Currency or timeliness: how promptly are the statistics available and how frequently are they reported?

Of all the time series tested and scored by the BEA, 12 separate indicators emerged as clear-cut winners in their ability to predict turning points. One has since been dropped. The 11 remaining leading indicators, along with a weighted average of all 11 called the composite leading index, are released monthly by the Department of Commerce.

The composite leading index is considered a much more reliable indicator than any of the individual series that make up the composite.

Each business cycle possesses its unique characteristics as well as aspects which it shares with other cycles. As we have learned, there is no single, proven, and accepted cause of cyclical fluctuations. Moreover, how the individual indicators would perform in a particular episode is likely to depend on which of many causes of a cyclical reversal are then in operation. Some leading indicators, then, would prove most useful in one set of conditions, others in a different set. To increase the chances of getting true signals, and reduce the likelihood of getting false ones, it is advisable to rely on all such potentially useful leading indicators as a group.

Another important reason for combining the leading series into a composite index is that the measurement errors in individual indicators are often large. To the extent that the data errors in the different indicators are independent, the risk of being misled can be reduced by evaluating the signals, not from any one series viewed in isolation, but from a combination of series.

The leading indicators tend to be sensitive not only to sustained cyclical fluctuations in the economy but also to frequent disturbances of all kinds. Hence, the month-to-month changes in these series tend to reflect the short, erratic fluctuations much more than the longer cyclical movements. By combining the series into an index, some of that "noise" is eliminated. Thus, the composite leading index can be much smoother than any of its individual components. The rationale behind each of the 11 leading economic indicators is discussed below.

Average Workweek

Current production is intended for future consumption. Products produced today are stored in inventory for future sale and delivery. If future sales are expected to increase above present levels, a perceived need for increased inventories will be reflected in a longer workweek. Likewise, expectations that future sales will decrease below present levels are revealed by a shortened work week.

Initial Unemployment Claims

These are the average weekly initial claims for state unemployment insurance. The individual states supply the statistics to the Department of Commerce, which compiles them into a national total and announces the claim every month. An increase in these claims indicates a slowing of consumer spending is near, as consumers adjust to reduced income levels.

New Orders of Consumer Goods

This indicator is defined by the Department of Commerce as a measure of new orders for durable goods (excluding capital goods and defense products), and of unfilled orders in selected nondurable goods industries. A rise in new orders indicates that future production levels will be increased. Similarly, a decrease in new orders portends reduced production in the future.

Standard & Poor's 500 Stock Index

This indicator is similar to the Dow Jones Average in that it reflects price changes of common stocks. It shadows the stock price movements on the New York Stock Exchange and includes prices of 500 actively traded stocks. The stock index is reported each weekday in the *Wall Street Journal* and in many other newspapers. This index is said to reflect the consensus of investors regarding the economy's future performance: a rise in the index indicates that investors believe future performance will be strong, and a fall in the index indicates the opposite.

New Contracts and Orders for Plant and Equipment

This is a measure of all new contracts and orders for commercial and industrial construction, privately owned nonbuilding construction (such as bridges and utility construction), and manufacturers' new orders of nondefense capital goods. Much of the construction information used is compiled by the F.W. Dodge Division of McGraw-Hill. An increase in this indicator implies additional future employment and output as firms attempt to fill new orders, and vice versa.

Building Permits

Permits for new private housing units are issued by local governments. The issuance of a permit normally occurs several months before construction actively begins. Although the *Federal Reserve Bulletin* and the *Survey of Current Business* report the actual number of units authorized, the composite leading index uses an index showing monthly changes. A rise in the number of building permits means that, in the near future, the construction industry and its suppliers will experience an escalation in volume.

Vendor Performance

Although all of the indicators cited purport to show national economic conditions, vendor performance actually measures an aspect of a specific local economy. Each month the Purchasing Management Association of Chicago surveys Chicago-area businesses to determine whether they are experiencing delays in delivery. A decrease in vendor performance indicates slower deliveries, which implies a "busy" business sector. Increased vendor performance may reflect slower sales.

Inventory Changes

This indicator measures month-to-month changes in manufacturing and trade inventories, as well as unfilled manufacturer's orders. However, unfilled orders for capital goods and defense products are not included in the series. This series is a weighted 4-month moving average. Increases in inventory levels signal changes in the overall business cycle.

Changes in Sensitive Prices

This indicator measures the change in the crude materials component of the producer price index (previously called the wholesale price index). It is of particular importance because included in the list of crude materials are crude petroleum, natural gas, and coal. Other crude materials included are iron ore, scrap metal, crude natural rubber, and waste paper. An increase in sensitive prices signals a potential increase in demand for these products and perhaps a quickening of the economy's pace.

Money Supply (M2)

M2 includes M1 (coin, currency, demand deposits, traveler's checks, and other checkable deposits) plus money market mutual fund balances, savings and small time deposits, and other balances. Increases in M2 indicate a rise in potential spending power in the economy.

Change in Business and Consumer Credit Outstanding

This series measures the change during a month in the seasonally adjusted amount of consumer and business debt outstanding. The basic data include all short- and intermediate-term credit used to finance the purchases of commodities and services for personal consumption or to refinance debts originally incurred for such purposes. The indicators also include credit extended to businesses. Increases in credit demand can foreshadow a rise in consumer and business spending.

Critics of the composite leading index argue that while some of the individual indicators have the support of economic theory behind them, other individual components seem to have been included without any accompanying economic logic. Economic forecasting with leading indicators thus seems to be more of an art than a science.[8] Regardless of the lack of economic purity of the leading indicators, the true test of its value is how well the composite index works. Ideally, the composite leading index should consistently turn down prior to general business cycle troughs and turn up before business cycle peaks.

Gary Gorton, an economist in the Department of Research at the Philadelphia Federal Reserve Bank, tested the performance of the composite leading index in all business cycles from 1948 to 1970, and found the performance mixed.[9] Gorton concluded, however, that the composite leading index, if used properly and in conjunction with other economic evidence, was a fair indicator of business cycle turning points.

Leading Index Performance

The most important estimate of a leading indicator's performance measures its ability to predict business cycle turning points. A less important measure of its performance is the ability to predict movements of economic activity all along the cycle.

Using turning points to measure the accuracy of the composite leading index involves matching changes in the index with later changes in the business cycle. The main problem here is determining the appropriate number of months that the indicator must display the required behavior before declaring that the index is predicting a turning point.

Because short-term changes in the composite leading index often result from random movements, any change in the index may be reversed simply by the passage of time. For example, if the index declines for 2 consecutive months, using a 2-month rule of thumb, you could conclude that it predicts a downward turning point in economic activity. Using a 3-month rule of thumb, however, if the index falls for 2 months but then, in the third month, rises above the level announced 3 months earlier, you would not predict a turning point. The number of months chosen is quite arbitrary.

Analyzed using a 1-month rule of thumb, the composite leading index successfully predicted every turning point from 1948–70, but it also predicted roughly 33 turning points in economic activity that did not occur.[10] Use of a short-term measurement can lead to many false signals. Accuracy improves as longer-term measurements are adopted, but the length of time of advance notice is reduced.

The leading indicators apparently predict troughs more accurately than peaks. Consequently, the length of time available for accurate advance notice declines more quickly for peaks than for troughs as the number of months chosen for the measurement goes up. The convention is to use periods of 3 months.

Even though the leading indicators give occasional false signals, much of the time the composite leading index is very successful. It does not normally miss turns in the direction of economic activity, but the number of months by which the index precedes or follows the turning points in general business varies from one period to the next. Also, the average length of the lead time is different for peaks than it is for troughs. The performance of 12 leading indicators as well as of the composite leading index, in terms of lead time (advance notice) provided for business cycle turning points, is shown for the period from July 1953 to November 1982 (table 10.2). (Note: In 1987, net business formation was dropped from the list.) The number of months of advance notice is shown in parentheses.

In table 10.2, panel A shows the peak and trough dates of 12 leading indicators and the composite leading index, which correspond to contractions in economic activity as defined for reference-point contractions. For example, the January 1980 contraction of the general business cycle was preceded by a contraction of the composite leading index 10 months earlier. (The composite index began to decline in March 1979.) In other words, using the 3-month rule of thumb, the index would have provided 7 months' advance notice of a recession. Similarly, the August 1957 contraction in general economic activity occurred some 23 months after the index began to contract in September 1955. Application of the 3-month rule here would have given some 20 months of warning. Yet the composite leading index only gave 3 months' advance notice of the July 1981 contraction, and application of a 3-month rule of thumb would have canceled out the lead time. Forecasting with leading indicators is problematic precisely because the lead time is variable.

Panel B illustrates the lead time for forecasting the beginning of economic expansion. In general, these lead times are either very short or nonexistent. For example, the July 1980 expansion was preceded by a May 1980 peak of the composite leading index—a 2-month warning. Fortunately, advance notice for this turning point is not nearly as critical as the reference date for contractions.

Clearly, forecasting with leading indicators has its drawbacks. However, these indicators still possess many advantages: they offer a low acquisition cost, simplicity, and basic dependability. While all prognosticators accept that no two cycles are alike in duration, intensity, and causation, the leading economic indicators seem to provide an economical way to estimate the "average" disturbance.

Coincidental Indicators

Individual economic time series data that closely parallel the general business cycle are termed "coincidental indicators." These individual indicators hit their peaks and troughs at about the same times as the business cycle. They neither lead nor follow the overall cycle,

Table 10.2 Specific Peak and Trough Dates, Leading Indicators

Panel A: Specific Peak Dates Corresponding to Contractions Beginning in:

	July 1981	Jan. 1980	Nov. 1973	Dec. 1969	Apr. 1960	Aug. 1957	July 1953
Average workweek, production workers, mfg.	5/81 (−2)	3/79 (−10)	4/73 (−7)	10/68 (−14)	5/59 (−11)	11/55 (−21)	4/53 (−3)
Initial claims, state unemployment insurance (inverted)	7/81 (0)	9/78 (−16)	2/73 (−9)	1/69 (−11)	4/59 (−12)	9/55 (−23)	9/52 (−10)
New orders, consumer goods, in 1972 dollars	5/81 (−2)	12/78 (−13)	3/73 (−8)	11/68 (−13)	2/59 (−14)	7/55 (−25)	4/53 (−3)
Vendor performance, slower deliveries	4/81 (−3)	3/79 (−10)	5/73 (−6)	6/69 (−6)	10/59 (−6)	10/55 (−22)	7/52 (−12)
Index of net business formation[b]	12/80 (−7)	10/78 (−15)	10/72 (−13)	4/69 (−8)	3/59 (−13)	6/55 (−26)	1/53 (−6)
Contracts and orders in 1972 dollars	4/81 (−3)	3/79 (−10)	11/73 (0)	4/69 (−8)	3/59 (−13)	11/56 (−9)	2/53 (−5)
New building permits, private housing	9/80 (−10)	6/78 (−19)	12/72 (−11)	2/69 (−10)	11/58 (−17)	2/55 (−30)	11/52 (−8)
Change in inventories on hand and on order, in 1972 dollars (smoothed[a])	7/81 (0)	5/78 (−20)	3/73 (−8)	12/68 (−12)	4/59 (−12)	9/56 (−11)	2/53 (−5)
Change in sensitive prices (smoothed[a])	10/80 (−9)	4/79 (−9)	4/73 (−7)	2/69 (−10)	10/58 (−18)	9/56 (−23)	NSC
Index of stock prices, 500 common stocks	11/80 (−8)	NSC	1/73 (−10)	12/68 (−12)	7/59 (−9)	7/56 (−13)	1/53 (−6)
Money supply M2 in 1972 dollars	NSC	1/78 (−24)	1/73 (−10)	1/69 (−11)	NSC	4/56 (−16)	NSC
Change in credit outstanding	5/81 (−2)	1/79 (−12)	2/73 (−9)	1/69 (−11)	6/59 (−10)	6/55 (−26)	10/52 (−9)
Composite index of 12 leading indicators	4/81 (−3)	3/79 (−10)	3/73 (−8)	4/69 (−8)	5/59 (−11)	9/55 (−23)	3/53 (−4)

298

Panel B: Specific Trough Dates Corresponding to Expansions Beginning in:

	Nov. 1982	July 1980	Mar. 1975	Nov. 1970	Feb. 1961	Apr. 1958	May 1954
Average workweek, production workers, mfg.	9/82 (−2)	7/80 (0)	3/75 (0)	9/70 (−2)	12/60 (−2)	4/58 (0)	4/54 (−1)
Initial claims, state unemployment insurance (inverted)	9/82 (−2)	5/80 (−2)	3/75 (0)	10/70 (−1)	2/61 (0)	4/58 (0)	9/54 (+4)
New orders, consumer goods, in 1972 dollars	10/82 (−1)	6/80 (−1)	3/75 (0)	10/70 (−1)	1/61 (−1)	4/58 (0)	10/53 (−7)
Vendor performance, slower deliveries	9/82 (−6)	6/80 (−1)	2/75 (−1)	12/70 (+1)	3/60 (−11)	12/57 (−4)	12/53 (−5)
Index of net business formation[b]	9/82 (−2)	6/80 (−1)	2/75 (−1)	8/70 (−3)	1/61 (−1)	4/58 (0)	3/54 (−2)
Contracts and orders in 1972 dollars	8/82 (−3)	5/80 (−2)	12/75 (+9)	10/70 (−1)	3/61 (+1)	3/58 (−1)	3/54 (−2)
New building permits, private housing	10/81 (−13)	4/80 (−3)	3/75 (0)	1/70 (−10)	12/60 (−2)	2/58 (−2)	9/53 (−8)
Change in inventories on hand and on order, in 1972 dollars (smoothed[a])	1/83 (+2)	8/80 (+1)	4/75 (+1)	3/70 (−8)	2/61 (0)	3/58 (−1)	11/53 (−6)
Change in sensitive prices (smoothed[a])	12/81 (−11)	6/80 (−1)	1/75 (−2)	1/71 (+2)	8/60 (−6)	11/57 (−5)	NSC
Index of stock prices, 500 common stocks	7/82 (−4)	NSC	12/74 (−3)	6/70 (−5)	10/60 (−4)	12/57 (−4)	9/53 (−8)
Money supply M2 in 1972 dollars	NSC	5/80 (−2)	1/75 (−2)	4/70 (−7)	NSC	1/58 (−3)	NSC
Change in credit outstanding	11/82 (0)	5/80 (−2)	3/75 (0)	10/70 (−1)	4/61 (+2)	2/58 (−2)	12/53 (−5)
Composite index of 12 leading indicators	3/82 (−8)	5/80 (−2)	2/75 (−1)	10/70 (−1)	12/60 (−2)	2/58 (−2)	11/53 (−6)

NSC. No specific cycle. This means no specific turning point in the indicator can be found to correspond with the reference date turning point.
Source: Adapted from *Business Conditions Digest*, February 1985, U.S. Department of Commerce. Bureau of Economic Analysis.
a. A "smoothed" data series is one in which the data has been adjusted for "random shocks" or aberrations during any one period. The most commonly used method of smoothing data is to use moving average data.
b. Net business formation was dropped from the composite index of leading indicators in 1987.

but closely align with general economic behavior. The major coincidental indicators are personal income, industrial production, nonagricultural employment, and manufacturing and trade sales.

Employees on Nonagricultural Payrolls

This indicator measures the total number of persons employed in nonagricultural establishments. It is seasonally adjusted. Data are obtained from the "establishment survey" conducted each month by the BLS. An establishment is defined as an economic unit that produces goods and services, such as a factory, mine, or store. It is usually at a single physical location and is engaged predominantly in one type of economic activity. Industries include mining, construction, manufacturing, wholesale and retail trade, government, finance insurance and real estate, electric and gas utilities, transportation, and other services.

Industrial Production Index

This index measures changes in industrial production in the economy. It includes all manufacturing, mining, and utility industry output (including government enterprises). Farm production, construction activity, transportation, and trade and service industries are excluded.

Personal Income Less Transfer Payments

This is a measure of total personal income received by individuals, including unincorporated businesses and nonprofit institutions. Excluded are transfer payments. These are defined as income received by individuals and businesses for which no current services have been rendered. Examples of transfer payments are Social Security benefits, Medicare payments, unemployment compensation, and food stamps.

Manufacturing and Trade Sales

This series measures the monthly volume of sales of manufacturing, merchant wholesalers, and retail establishments in constant dollars. It is a gross indication of business sales activity.

Like the 11 leading indicators, the 4 major coincidental indicators are combined into a composite index (table 10.3).

Table 10.3 Specific Peak and Trough Dates for Selected Coincidental Indicators

Panel A: Specific Peak Dates Corresponding to Contractions Beginning in:

	July 1981	Jan. 1980	Nov. 1973	Dec. 1969	Apr. 1960	Aug. 1957	July 1953
Employees on nonagricultural payrolls	7/81 (0)	3/80 (+2)	10/74 (+11)	3/70 (+3)	4/60 (0)	3/57 (−5)	6/53 (−1)
Personal income less transfers in 1972 dollars	8/81 (+1)	1/80 (0)	11/73 (0)	NSC	5/60 (+1)	8/57 (0)	6/53 (−1)
Index of industrial production, total	7/81 (0)	1/80 (0)	6/74 (+7)	10/69 (−2)	1/60 (−3)	3/57 (−5)	7/53 (0)
Mfg. and trade sales in 1972 dollars	4/81 (−3)	5/79 (−8)	11/73 (0)	10/69 (−2)	1/60 (−3)	2/57 (−6)	3/53 (−4)
Composite index of 4 coincident indicators	7/81 (0)	1/80 (0)	11/73 (0)	10/69 (−2)	1/60 (−3)	2/57 (−6)	5/53 (−2)

Panel B: Specific Trough Dates Corresponding to Expansions Beginning in:

	Nov. 1982	July 1980	Mar. 1975	Nov. 1970	Feb. 1961	Apr. 1958	May 1954
Employees on nonagricultural payrolls	12/82 (+1)	7/80 (0)	4/75 (+1)	11/70 (0)	2/61 (0)	5/58 (+1)	8/54 (+3)
Personal income less transfers in 1972 dollars	10/82 (−1)	7/80 (0)	3/75 (0)	NSC	12/60 (−2)	4/58 (0)	4/54 (−1)
Index of industrial production, total	11/82 (0)	7/80 (0)	3/75 (0)	11/70 (0)	2/61 (0)	4/58 (0)	4/54 (−1)
Mfg. and trade sales in 1972 dollars	10/82 (−1)	5/80 (−2)	3/75 (0)	11/70 (0)	1/61 (−1)	4/58 (0)	12/53 (−5)
Composite index of 4 coincident indicators	12/82 (+1)	7/80 (0)	3/75 (0)	11/70 (0)	2/61 (0)	4/58 (0)	8/54 (+3)

NSC. No specific cycle. No specific turning point in the indicator can be found to correspond with the reference date turning point.
Source: Adapted from *Business Conditions Digest*, February 1985, U.S. Department of Commerce, Bureau of Economic Analysis.

ECONOMICS FOR BANKERS

In table 10.3, panel A shows the coincidental series peaks relative to reference-dated turning points for business cycle contractions. Panel B displays the coincidental series troughs dates corresponding to reference-dated expansions. In panel A, notice that the peak dates of the composite index of coincidental indicators exactly duplicates the peak dates of the economy for the 1973, 1980, and 1981 contractions. The trough dates of the composite index matched the economy's reference-dated expansions in 1958, 1961, 1970, 1975, and 1980, and lagged by only 3 months in 1954 and 1 month in 1982.

Lagging Indicators

The peaks and troughs of six important economic time series typically follow the turning points in general business activity. These series are referred to as lagging indicators.

Labor Cost per Unit of Output, Manufacturing

This indicator measures, in physical terms (hours), the change in labor costs per unit of output. It is the percentage change over 4-quarter intervals in the number of employee hours required to produce a unit of output, which is the reciprocal of output per personhour.

Ratio of Manufacturing and Trade Inventories to Sales

This indicator measures the value of manufacturing and trade inventories as a percentage of total sales.

Average Duration of Unemployment in Weeks

Figures for this indicator are based on data collected in a household survey of the labor force. Measurements are taken on the average length of time, in weeks, during which persons classified as unemployed had been continuously looking for work, or (in the case of persons on layoff) since the termination of the most recent employment.

Ratio of Consumer Installment Credit Outstanding to Personal Income

This indicator measures the amount of consumer installment debt as a percentage of personal income. Consumer purchases of items such as automobiles and home appliances tend to increase this ratio. It is a general measure of consumer indebtedness and of consumer ability to make additional purchases.

Commercial and Industrial Loans Outstanding

This indicator measures the average dollar amount of business loans outstanding each month. Included are data on all loans for commercial and industrial purposes except those secured by real estate. Loans to financial institutions and loans for the purpose of purchasing or carrying securities are also excluded. However, commercial paper issued by nonfinancial companies is included.

Average Prime Rate Charged by Banks

The prime rate measures the interest rate banks charge their most creditworthy business customers for short-term loans. This rate is the base used to scale upward the rates charged on most loans to other business customers. It is not as sensitive as money market instrument rates, which fluctuate daily in response to short-term changes in supply and demand. Rather, its movements tend to be infrequent, changing only by increments of at least .25 of a percentage point. Major banks tend to change their prime rate in response to increasing differentials with selected open market money rates.

The vast majority of lagging indicators reflect investment costs or consumer borrowing levels (table 10.4). A composite index of the six major lagging indicators is also released.

In table 10.4, panel A relates peaks of the lagging indicators to the dates beginning contractions in the overall economy. For example, while an overall business cycle contraction began in November 1973, the composite lagging index continued to move forward for 13 months afterwards, and did not begin to turn down until December 1974. Panel B shows the trough dates that correspond to the dates beginning periods of expansion in general economic activity. The most recent period of expansion began in November 1982; however, the composite lagging index continued its fall through October 1983, during a period in which the U.S. economy was well on its way toward business recovery.

If the leading, coincidental, and lagging indicators are working ideally, the relationship between and among the turning points of the indicators and the general business cycle approaches the hypothetical turning points shown in figure 10.3. In the figure, the shaded area represents the reference dates for a recession in the general business cycle. The leading indicators peak (P) before the recession begins and reach a trough (T) before the recession is concluded. The coincidental indicators' peak (P) and trough (T) mirror those of the general business cycle and occur at the same time. The lagging indicators' peak (P) occurs after the recession begins, while the trough (T) begins after the economy has escaped the recession.

Table 10.4 Specific Peak and Trough Dates for Selected Lagging Indicators

Panel A: Specific Peak Dates Corresponding to Contractions Beginning in:

	July 1981	Jan. 1980	Nov. 1973	Dec. 1969	Apr. 1960	Aug. 1957	July 1953
Average duration of unemployment (inverted)	12/81 (+5)	7/79 (−6)	9/73 (−2)	10/69 (−2)	6/60 (+2)	9/57 (+1)	9/53 (+2)
Ratio, constant-dollar inventories to sales, mfg. and trade	1/82 (+6)	5/80 (+4)	3/75 (+16)	11/70 (+11)	1/61 (+9)	4/58 (+8)	12/53 (+5)
Labor cost per unit of output, mfg.— actual data as a percentage of trend	1/82 (+6)	6/80 (+5)	3/75 (+16)	3/70 (+3)	2/61 (+10)	4/58 (+8)	12/53 (+5)
Average prime rate charged by banks	8/81 (+1)	4/80 (+3)	9/74 (+10)	2/70 (+2)	7/60 (+3)	12/57 (+4)	2/54 (+7)
Commercial and industrial loans in 1972 dollars	10/82 (+15)	3/80 (+2)	9/74 (+10)	8/70 (+8)	NSC	9/57 (+1)	5/53 (−2)
Ratio, consumer installment credit to personal income	NSC	NSC	2/74 (+3)	11/69 (−1)	12/60 (+8)	1/58 (+5)	4/54 (+9)
Composite index of 6 lagging indicators	1/82 (+6)	4/80 (+3)	12/74 (+13)	3/70 (+3)	6/60 (+2)	12/57 (+4)	12/53 (+5)

Panel B: Specific Trough Dates Corresponding to Expansions Beginning in:

	Nov. 1982	July 1980	Mar. 1975	Nov. 1970	Feb. 1961	Apr. 1958	May 1954
Average duration of unemployment (inverted)	7/83 (+8)	1/81 (+6)	1/76 (+10)	6/72 (+19)	7/61 (+5)	10/58 (+6)	5/55 (+12)
Ratio, constant-dollar inventories to sales, mfg. and trade	1/84 (+14)	1/81 (+6)	11/78 (+44)	2/73 (+27)	4/62 (+14)	5/59 (+13)	5/55 (+12)
Labor cost per unit of output, mfg.— actual data as a percentage of trend	NA	7/81 (+12)	7/76 (+16)	12/72 (+25)	12/61 (+10)	5/59 (+13)	6/55 (+13)
Average prime rate charged by banks	7/83 (+8)	8/80 (+1)	4/77 (+25)	3/72 (+16)	11/65 (+57)	8/58 (+4)	7/55 (+14)
Commercial and industrial loans in 1972 dollars	10/83 (+11)	3/81 (+8)	4/77 (+25)	1/72 (+14)	NSC	8/58 (+4)	8/54 (+3)
Ratio, consumer installment credit to personal income	NSC	NSC	2/76 (+11)	4/70 (−7)	11/61 (+9)	11/58 (+7)	11/54 (+6)
Composite index of 6 lagging indicators	10/83 (+11)	4/81 (+9)	4/76 (+13)	2/72 (+15)	11/61 (+9)	8/58 (+4)	4/55 (+11)

NA. No available data to determine the turning point of the indicator.
NSC. No specific cycle. No specific turning point in the indicator can be found to correspond to the reference date turning point.
Source: Adapted from *Business Conditions Digest*, February 1985, U.S. Department of Commerce, Bureau of Economic Analysis.

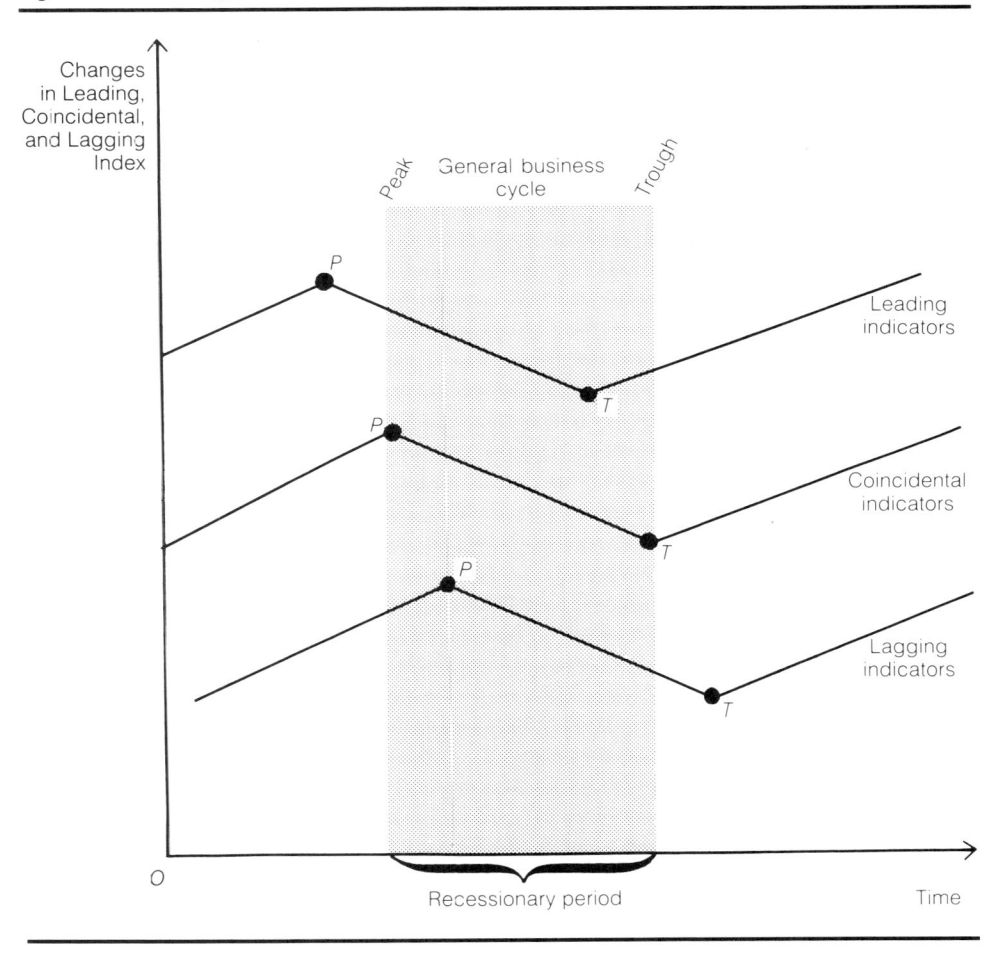

Figure 10.3 Leading, Coincidental, and Lagging Indicators and the Business Cycle

No index of economic indicators can perform well if used mechanically and in isolation from other information tools. Good results can be expected only if the current behavior of the index is interpreted with experienced judgment and in light of other evidence. Even then, of course, various external factors can occasionally distort the relationships among the leading, coincident, and lagging indicators of business expansion and contraction. Structural changes in the economy will also affect these relationships.

TRACKING THE COMPOSITE LEADING INDEX

Leonard H. Lempert, director of Statistical Indicator Associates (SIA), North Egremont, Massachusetts, and publisher of the weekly *Statistical Indicator Reports*, has prepared the following checklist for bankers to use in assessing cyclical indicators.

A Checklist for Assessing Cyclical Indicators

Bankers in the U.S. are inundated with economic statistics. Many of these figures are accompanied by "analyses" by media, political, and professional individuals, who possess varying amounts of expertise and bias. To make sense of the diverse and sometimes conflicting views surrounding economic information, bankers need guide rules. The 14 suggestions that follow should help bankers make their own assessments of economic indicators.

- Identify every economic statistic with respect to its cyclical timing. Is the indicator one that conforms to the major movements of the economy and consistently moves ahead of, with, or after major economic turning points? Is it a leading, coincident, or lagging indicator? The Commerce Department's *Business Conditions Digest* will help you identify the indicators.
- Statistics covering different periods are released at different times during the month. Early in a month, employment statistics are released that cover the previous month. Later in the month, manufacturing and trade statistics are released for 2 months earlier. A few days later, another figure may be released that covers the previous quarter. Do not confuse figures covering like periods with figures covering different periods.
- Judge an indicator's underlying direction by assessing its data for the latest month, over the last 3 months, from the date it reached an earlier high or low, or over any period of time during which it appears to have established a trend.
- There is no simple rule for accepting a trend in the composite leading index as predictive of an oncoming turning point in the economy. A 2-month decline—or even a 3-month decline—need not indicate that a recession lies ahead. Assess the magnitude of the decline relative to the magnitude of declines in the index prior to previous recessions. Assess the behavior of the composite leading index in the light of movements in the composite index of coincidental indicators and the composite lagging index. Is the coincidental composite showing signs of slowing up? Is the lagging composite showing signs of an inordinate speeding up? If so, be alert to trouble ahead!
- Find the last established reference date in the Commerce Department's *Business Conditions Digest*, SIA's weekly reports, or some other reliable source. In 1987, the last date identified was the trough in November 1982. Thus, in early 1987, the economy was in the fifth year of an upswing.

You will also want to distinguish among the current movements of leading, coincident, and lagging indicators. When assessing current activity, use the coincident indicators: industrial production, nonagricultural employment, personal income, manufacturing, and trade sales. Are they moving upward more slowly or faster than previously? Are they moving upward together or is one or more hesitating, perhaps even weakening?

If you wish to include the quarterly GNP figure, be careful. Quarterly data shows how one quarter compares with the previous quarter, but not how the economy fared from month to month during the quarter. In assessing what the economy currently is doing, it is best to stick with the four basic monthly coincident indicators. Do not be tempted to consider common stock prices or the money supply or the inventory-to-sales ratio or other economic measures whose timing of ups and downs tend to lead or to lag the economy as a whole.

- Anticipate recession. If the economy is in an upswing, you will want to look for signs that this expansion is coming to an end. Look for weaknesses in the leading indicators and excessive increases in the lagging indicators.

    For example, in mid-1984, the composite leading index dropped fairly substantially for 2 months, then more or less leveled off for the remainder of the year. This drop and leveling-off could be interpreted as a recessionary alert. But the failure of the composite leading index to resume a downtrend signaled that the recession was not to be. The economy flattened out from March 1985 through July 1985 and failed to live up to its growth potential for the remainder of 1985, but no real recession occurred.

    Excessive increases in the lagging indicators may not follow short-lived weaknesses in the leading indicators. The composite lagging index rose after mid-1984, but not very strongly. Moreover, one very important lagging indicator, the prime interest rate, actually declined. This, too, was evidence that the economic upswing was not running away with itself and courting major trouble.

- Anticipate recovery from recessions. If the economy is in a recession, you will want to look for telltale signs of its coming to an end, such as renewed strength in the leading indicators together with significant corrections of the excesses that had developed in the lagging indicators.

    The emphasis here is on the leading and lagging indicators, not on the coincident indicators. Coincidental indicators tell us where the economy is, not where it is going. The coincident indicators establish the parameters of the recession: they move downward until the recession is over. For example, in 1982, the composite index of coincidental indicators reached a trough in December 1982—virtually simultaneously with the November 1982 end of the recession. The composite leading index, on the other hand, reached a low in March 1982; and by November 1982, it had been moving upward for 8 months. Usually, leading indicators turn upward only a couple of months before the economy changes from recession to recovery.

In 1982, soon after the leading indicators started to improve, the composite lagging index began to decline fairly sharply. This decline meant that the excesses created in the preceding recovery and in the recession up to that time were being corrected. The ratio of inventories to sales was steadying rather than climbing; labor costs per unit of output were falling and becoming less oppressive to manufacturers; and the prime interest rate had plummeted.

- Recognize that the first release of the composite indexes does not include complete data for the latest month shown. One or 2 indicators are usually missing from the 11 leading indicators; 1 out of 4 will be missing from the coincidental composite; and 2 out of 6 generally are missing from the lagging composite. These missing indicators can, when they become available, significantly change the individual composites and especially the ratio between the coincidental and lagging composites.
- The ratio of the coincidental-to-lagging composites is a long-lead leading indicator. It gives you some early statistical evidence for assessing movements in the lagging indicators as excessive (hence, a threat to expansion) or as corrective (hence, a sign of recovery).
- Strength or weakness in any of the composite indexes may be attributed to one or only a few indicators. To evaluate this relative strength or weakness, find a "diffusion" index—an index that shows the percentage of expanding indicators among any particular group of indicators. Based on the direction of its centered, 3-month moving average, give a rising indicator a value of 1; a leveling-off indicator a value of ½; and a declining indicator a value of 0. Add up the points and divide by the number of indicators in the group to express it as a percent.
- Do not rely on quarterly economic measures as indicators of what is currently going on. Quarterly data tell you how one quarter as a whole compares with the previous quarter as a whole. Quarterly data do not tell you what has happened from month to month in the most recent quarter. A second quarter may exceed a first quarter, thus hiding May and June decreases.
- Similarly, comparisons of current data with data for the same month a year ago provide no evidence whatsoever of whether an indicator is currently moving upward or downward. You have to know what has happened in the intervening months.
- Never draw a conclusion from the limited data shown for a particular indicator in a news release. Compare it yourself with earlier data for the same indicator going back several months. Media designations of "up" or "down" are often oversimplified. You need to know how earlier data have been revised and whether the "up" or "down" describes a comparison with last month, with a previous low or high, or with the same period a year ago. If you can, chart the new data against data you have already charted for the last couple of years.
- Do not confuse absolute changes in some economic measures with percentage changes in other economic measures. Do not confuse monthly or quarterly percentage changes in an

economic measure with annual rates of change in other economic measures. Annual rate changes are more than 12 times the corresponding monthly percentage change and more than 4 times the corresponding quarterly change.

This checklist will help you not only to assess the economy yourself, but also to assess what others say about the economy.

HIGH-TECH ECONOMIC FORECASTS

A whole new service industry has developed involving the marketing of econometric forecasts. Firms like Data Resources, Inc., and the Kent Economic and Development Institute center their major business thrust around their econometric forecasts. Other forecasters are associated in some way with institutions of higher education (UCLA Business Forecasting Projects and Georgia State University). Financial and nonfinancial corporations may also prepare and market their own estimates of future economic developments. The Bureau of Economic Analysis of the U.S. Department of Commerce also prepares a very sophisticated economic forecast. There are literally hundreds of organizations that try to estimate future economic activity.

The first major econometric forecast was made by the Wharton School of the University of Pennsylvania in 1963. Under the direction of Lawrence R. Klein, the Wharton model became known worldwide for its large scope and uncanny accuracy. Lawrence Klein was recognized as a pioneer in econometric forecasting work when he was awarded the Nobel Prize in 1980. In 1980, Klein formed a private consulting firm called Wharton Econometric Forecasting Associates, Inc. In 1986, Wharton and Chase Econometrics merged to form a new Wharton Econometrics.

Basically, econometric models use systems of mathematical equations to simulate real-world behavior. These equations are fitted with historical data and manipulated by statistical techniques to estimate the "best fit" values of future economic variables. The original Wharton model was comprised of only 20 equations, which represented the largest sectors of our economy. Today's models include macroeconomic estimates of the GNP, interest rates, unemployment, and inflation, and also industry-specific data (for example, automobile sales). The modern model may contain over 1,000 equations and provide estimates of up to 10,000 separate variables. Most models generate quarterly forecasts for the next 4 to 12 quarters (1 to 3 years). Some forecasters update their forecasts quarterly while others provide monthly forecasts.

Econometric forecasters do not simply plug historical data into their equation systems, push the button, and let the computer calculate the forecast. The forecasters use a raw, computer-generated forecast as a base reference point into which they incorporate their judgments of recent economic and political events, past errors, recent data announcements, and even the predictions of others to arrive at the final published forecast.

Accuracy of Econometric Forecasts

The accuracy of econometric models has been criticized by forecast users since the first forecasts began to appear in the 1960s. The greatest criticism occurs during periods of economic or political shock, when the forecasts may differ radically from historical experience.

For example, the imposition of wage and price controls under the Nixon Administration (1971–74), the OPEC oil embargo of 1973–75, the Iranian revolution-caused oil crisis of 1978–79, and the foreign debt problem of 1982 were shocks to the economic system that were difficult to anticipate. Forecasters try to develop enough skill and savvy to anticipate such events and adjust the model as required.

Stephen K. McNees, economist and vice president of the Federal Reserve Bank of Boston, is considered by many to be the "master scorekeeper" of the forecasters. McNees regularly evaluates the performance of the top forecasters and publishes these results as a service for the forecast-user community. McNees underscored the importance of judgment in forecasting when he commented:

> while the model-builder may assume that the future will resemble his model's description of the past, the essence of forecasting is to try to anticipate ways in which the future is likely to differ from the particular historical period on which the model is based. . . . The lesson of the past 15 years seems to be that 'special' extra-model events occur with sufficient frequency that forecast users should be cautious in accepting any mechanically generated, 'pure model' forecast unthinkingly. Economic models can more properly be regarded as a tool for enhancing a forecaster's understanding of the economy and its history than as a substitute for careful analysis.[11]

The accuracy of macroeconomic forecasts varies from period to period. Some time periods are tumultuous and uncertain; others are calm and relatively predictable. McNees charted the average forecast errors in GNP, real GNP, implicit price deflator, and the unemployment rate made by the major forecasting organizations from 1971 to 1985. Some of his findings are shown in table 10.5. The annual average forecasting errors (in terms of percent deviation from actual statistics) differed from year to year. Apparently, certain events in 1975, 1981, and 1982 were not anticipated, and large forecasting errors occurred.

Table 10.5 also shows the average error and the average absolute error for the entire period. The average error can be misleading. For example, a 5-percent overestimation (+5 percent) of real GNP can be offset during the next period by a 5-percent underestimation (−5 percent). Under a simple average-error calculation, this combination would result in zero error for the period. The average absolute error provides a better performance evaluation because this average disregards the direction of the error and calculates the average error without regard to sign.

Table 10.5 Historical Variability of Forecast Errors
(Median of One-Year-Ahead Forecasts)

Forecasting Period Ending in	GNP	Real GNP	Implicit Price Deflator (1972=100)	Unemployment Rate
		(percentage points)		
1975:1	3.5	6.0	−4.0	−2.4
:2	2.7	4.4	−1.9	−2.8
:3	.8	−.4	.5	−1.4
:4	−.3	−1.4	.6	−.1
1976:1	−1.7	−2.4	−.1	.7
:2	1.6	1.1	.4	.5
:3	2.8	1.2	1.3	−.2
:4	2.1	.8	1.2	−.6
1977:1	2.0	1.1	.9	−.6
:2	−.3	−.2	.1	−.3
:3	−2.1	−1.3	−.5	0
:4	−.7	−.2	−.4	0
1978:1	1.7	1.5	.1	.5
:2	−1.8	−.7	−1.1	.5
:3	−2.1	−.1	−1.9	.6
:4	−3.9	−1.4	−2.2	.6
1979:1	−3.2	−.4	−2.5	.4
:2	−1.3	.7	−1.8	.7
:3	−2.1	−.6	−1.6	.7
:4	−1.3	−1.0	−.9	.8
1980:1	−1.8	−1.5	−.1	.5
:2	−.5	−.1	−.6	0
:3	−1.1	−.4	−.7	−.1
:4	−1.5	−.1	−1.1	.1
1981:1	−4.5	−3.8	−.9	.7
:2	−4.8	−3.8	−.5	.9
:3	−2.0	−1.5	−.4	.3
:4	1.4	.3	1.3	−.7
1982:1	7.1	4.6	1.7	−1.5
:2	6.4	4.6	1.3	−2.1
:3	6.7	3.9	2.5	−1.6
:4	6.8	3.7	2.9	−2.0
1983:1	5.3	3.0	1.7	−1.6
:2	2.9	.6	2.4	−1.1
:3	.4	−1.7	1.9	.4
:4	−1.4	−2.6	1.2	1.7
1984:1	−2.4	−3.3	.8	1.6
:2	−2.1	−2.5	.6	1.6
:3	−.8	−1.5	1.1	.9
:4	−.1	−1.4	1.3	.4
1985:1	1.2	0	1.1	0
Average Error	−.1	.3	−.5	−.1
Average Absolute Error	2.1	1.6	1.4	.7

Source: McNees, Stephen K. "Which Forecast Should You Use?" *New England Economic Review*, Federal Reserve Bank of Boston, July/Aug. 1985, p. 4.

SUMMARY

The nation's real output (GNP) does not grow at a smooth, steady pace. Instead, it goes through periods of acceleration and retardation. The path of this movement is called the business cycle. The National Bureau of Economic Research (NBER), in Cambridge, Massachusetts, takes responsibility for tracking business cycle phenomena.

Expansions are increases or upward movements in business activity. Contractions are declines in business activity. A peak (or upper turning point) is a point in the business cycle at which real output reaches the highest level above the existing, long-term trend line. A trough (lower turning point) is the point at which real output reaches the lowest level below the existing long-term trend line.

Generally speaking, an economy must experience 2 consecutive quarters of contractions before it is said to be in a recession. A severe, prolonged recession is called a depression.

Many theories have been propounded regarding the causes of business cycles, involving the following factors: underconsumption (or oversaving); an inelastic (or overly elastic) money supply; the flaws of capitalism; the rise of large, monopolistic firms and inflexible labor unions; undersaving; innovation; war; politics; sunspots; and self-fulfilling expectations.

Leading economic indicators are time series whose movements tend to foreshadow that of aggregate economic activity. The composite leading index is a collection of 11 of the best-performing individual leading indicators.

Coincidental economic indicators are time series whose movements tend to coincide with that of aggregate economic activity. The index of composite coincidental indicators is a collection of four of the most important individual coincidental indicators.

Lagging economic indicators are time series whose movements tend to follow that of aggregate economic activity. The composite lagging index is a collection of the six dominant individual lagging indicators.

Many organizations attempt to forecast the economy, some using changes in the economic indicators as guides, others using sophisticated econometric models.

KEY WORDS

acceleration principle
Arthur F. Burns
average workweek
Bureau of Economic Analysis
coincidental indicators
composite index of coincidental indicators
composite lagging index
composite leading index
Council of Economic Advisors
diffusion index
Edward Tufte
Employment Act of 1946
John Hobson
Joseph Schumpeter
Karl Marx
Kondratieff Cycle
Lawrence R. Klein
National Bureau of Economic Research
Standard & Poor's 500 Stock Index
Stephen K. McNees
time series
William Stanley Jevons

Questions for Review

1. A country is experiencing low unemployment, rising income, and increasing output. In what phase of the business cycle is the economy operating? Describe the inverse phase.

2. List three major difficulties in economic forecasting.

3. Net business formations was recently dropped as an indicator used in calculating the composite leading index. One component of net business formations was the number of new telephone hookups and disconnects as reported by AT&T. Can you suggest a reason why this indicator was dropped? Can you suggest a replacement?

4. Business cycle theories are often separated into two groups: those external to the economic system of a country and those internal to it. Characterize the theories described in this chapter as external or internal.

5. What caveats would you offer to a banker who wants to purchase the services of an economic forecaster?

6. Describe the optimal path of the business cycle. Describe the next-best path. Why are gradual shifts preferred to sharp, unexpected movements?

ENDNOTES

1. See Milton Friedman and Anna Schwartz, *A Monetary History of the U.S., 1867–1960* (Princeton, N.J.: Princeton University Press, 1963), chapter 7; also see Milton Friedman and Anna Schwartz, *The Great Contraction, 1929–1933* (New York: National Bureau of Economic Research, 1964).

2. See John Kenneth Galbraith, *The Great Crash, 1929* (Boston: Houghton Mifflin, 1955) and Studs Terkel, *Hard Times: An Oral History of the Great Depression in America* (New York: Pantheon Books, 1970).

3. Karl Marx, *Capital*, reprinted in *Classics of Economics*, ed. Charles W. Needy (Oak Park, IL: Moore Publishing Company, Inc., 1980).

4. Schumpeter credits Nicolai D. Kondratieff with the discovery of these very long cycles of economic activity. Kondratieff defined his cycles in a paper, "The Long Waves in Economic Life," *Review of Economic Statistics* (November 1935), pp. 105–15.

5. See Joseph A. Schumpeter, "The Analysis of Economic Change," *Review of Economic Statistics* (May 1935), pp. 1–10.

6. Edward R. Tufte, *Political Control of the Economy* (Princeton, N.J.: Princeton University Press, 1978), p. 27.

7. While Jevon's sunspot theory is only of historical interest today, there is evidence that suggests sunspots do influence weather and climatic conditions. And certainly, during intense solar storms, worldwide satellite communication capabilities are interrupted and diminished.

8. For a discussion of the issues regarding behavioral explanations of time series indicators, see Thomas J. Sargent and Christopher A. Sims, "Business Cycle Modeling Without Pretending to Have Too Much 'A Priori' Economic Theory," *New Methods of Business Cycle Research*, Federal Reserve Bank of Minneapolis, October 1977.

9. See Gary Gorton, "Forecasting With the Index of Leading Indicators," *Business Review*, Federal Reserve Bank of Philadelphia (November/December 1982), pp. 15–27.

10. See H.O. Stekler and Martin Schepsman, "Forecasting With an Index of Leading Series," *Journal of the American Statistical Association*, vol. 68, no. 342 (June 1973), pp. 291–296.

11. Stephen K. McNees, "Which Forecast Should You Use?" *New England Economic Review*, Federal Reserve Bank of Boston (July/August 1985), p. 40.

ECONOMICS IN THE NEWS

Is There Really A Business Cycle?

No, say some academic economists. They argue that unpredictable shocks— not monetary or fiscal policy— cause ups and downs in the economy.

By Marc Levinson

After four years of economic expansion, the pessimists are on the prowl. With the recovery aging, those who insist that business cycles run in patterns contend it is too late to expect the lackluster economy to turn around. "The current expansion is relatively long by postwar standards," cautions Jerry Jasinowski, executive vice president of the National Association of Manufacturers. "It's highly unlikely that we will see a strong rebound this late in the cycle." Adds Robert Dederick, chief economist of Chicago's Northern Trust Co., "There is a cyclical inevitability."

While this past-is-prologue approach to economic forecasting is still dominant among business economists, a new view is taking root in the nation's universities. Academic economists are developing radical new definitions of the business cycle and how it works—definitions that challenge the conventional understanding of the economy's movements.

The most popular of the new approaches is called the "real business cycle" theory. Developed by Finn Kydland of Carnegie-Mellon University and Edward Prescott of the University of Minnesota, it asserts that recoveries and recessions do not occur in a pattern; nor are they caused by either changes in the money supply, as monetarists have long asserted, or changes in consumer demand, as Keynesians have contended.

Using complex and controversial statistical methods, real business cycle proponents insist that what is commonly labelled a "cycle" is just a series of random movements. "It's easy to read patterns into data when they're not there," says Edward Prescott.

Economic swings, according to the new theory, are precipitated by unforeseen, unpredictable shocks that affect the cost of production, such as the oil price surges of 1973 and 1979 or the U.S. drought of 1972. According to the new theory, the deep recession of 1981–82 could have been caused by the 1979 oil price hike, the rapid increase of women in the labor force and the unexpected oversupply of personal computers. But unlike the overwhelming majority of economists, real business cycle theorists contend the Federal Reserve's tight money policies were irrelevant.

Shocks can be positive as well as negative. The invention of a new technology, for example, could cause the economy to expand.

The new theory poses a major challenge

Reprinted with permission, BUSINESS MONTH magazine, December, 1986. Copyright © 1986 by Business Magazine Corporation, 38 Commercial Wharf, Boston, MA 02110.

to traditional business cycle thinking. While Keynesians and monetarists have their differences, they both believe that high interest rates choke off booms and that low rates kindle recovery. They also agree that the different sectors of the economy (housing, retailing, capital equipment) move in a predictable pattern within each cycle.

That concept of the business cycle stems from the work of scholars such as Geoffrey Moore, director of the Center for International Business Cycle Research at Columbia University. Moore concedes that each cycle is different, but believes that historic patterns offer clues to the economy's future course. "You can say something about the characteristics of different parts of the economy by knowing what the characteristics were in the past," he contends.

If real business cycle theory is correct, companies might as well fire their forecasters. Unlike changes in the money supply or consumer demand, real shocks are unobservable until they actually happen. As Carnegie-Mellon theorist Martin Eichenbaum points out, "It's hard to know when the next shock will be." Without knowing, it is impossible to predict whether the next downturn will occur in a month—or in a decade.

Real business cycle theory also lightens the workload of government policymakers. If shocks occur randomly, government intervention to smooth out fluctuations in the business cycle is obviously a waste of time. "Less attention is going to be directed at fluctuations," says Minnesota's Edward Prescott.

Even academics, who disagree with the real business cycle approach, are distancing themselves from the popular view of an economy moving inexorably from peak to trough. Most academic economists now agree that the length of the current economic expansion is unimportant in forecasting the next one. "Expansions do not seem to age in the sense that there's a higher and higher probability of a recession starting," says Brown University's William Poole.

Moreover, most economists now accept the idea that shocks do play a role in the business cycle. "I don't think that this explains a great deal, but it does explain some," concedes Victor Zarnowitz of the University of Chicago, one of the leading academic experts on cycles.

Economists are also moving away from the long-accepted view that the business cycle fluctuates around a long-term growth trend, usually estimated at about 3% per year. N. Gregory Mankiw of Harvard University and John Campbell of Princeton University maintain that a recession this year means the economy's output will remain lower than it otherwise would have been—forever. "There really isn't any tendency to revert to trend," Mankiw asserts. "Reverting to trend means that a period of slower growth should be followed by a period of faster growth, and that doesn't happen."

Traumas that make the entire economy shudder, such as the OPEC oil boycott, are obviously uncommon events. Their rarity makes it tricky for advocates of the real business cycle theory to pinpoint the shocks responsible for each swing in the economy.

To compensate for the paucity of big shocks, they postulate a constant series of small shocks, such as the invention of a new technology or a change in demographics, that combine to buffet the economy in unpredictable ways. Still, skeptical academics argue that small shocks are not enough to change the course of the entire economy. "You've got to have something that's aggregate," insists Harvard's Lawrence Katz.

And Kydland and Prescott's assertion that shocks are the *only* cause of fluctuations has unleashed a storm of controversy. Says Princeton economist Ben Bernanke, who believes that bank failures and financial panics frequently trigger recessions: "Where they fall short is making the extreme claim that *all* business cycles are caused by these things."

Real business cycle theory is still a long way from being accepted in academia. The Keynesian school argues that by focusing only on shocks it ignores the possibility that fluctuations in consumer demand can cause booms and recessions. In addition, both Keynesians and monetarists reject the contention that major changes in the growth of the money supply have nothing to do with the state of the economy. And in the business world, most forecasters also give short shrift to the notion that only a bolt from the blue can send the economy into a tailspin.

Nonetheless, the current economic upswing has yet to conform to the traditional pattern. In the fourth year of expansion, interest rates are still declining rather than rising and the nation's factories are producing far below their capacity.

What does this mean for 1987? The new theory, of course, insists that that question is unanswerable. A depression could be in the offing or we could get the upswing President Reagan insists is on the way. After all, real cycle proponents such as the University of Rochester's Charles Plosser always offer the same forecast: "A boom is just as likely as a bust."

CHAPTER ELEVEN

UNEMPLOYMENT

Objectives

After reading this chapter, you should be able to

- explain what the unemployment rate measures

- identify and explain the uses of the current population survey

- define the three categories into which the adult noninstitutional population is divided: employed, unemployed, and "not in the labor force"

- explain the differences that categorize short-term, long-term, and very long term unemployment

- define the "discouraged worker" and discuss issues surrounding the effect discouraged workers have on the unemployment rate

- list and define the three major types of unemployment: cyclical, structural, and frictional

The term "unemployment" evokes visions of the Great Depression, Dust Bowl farmers, and long queues of people waiting for government relief. However, the concept of unemployment is one of the most confusing and least understood in all of economics. For example, some people interpret the announcement that "the U.S. unemployment rate rose to 8.4 percent last month" to mean that 8.4 percent of the population is out of work. Others believe it means that 8.4 percent of all workers lost their jobs last month. Both of these interpretations are false. This chapter focuses on the concept of unemployment, its statistical measurement, and some of the problems associated with the structure of the official unemployment rate.

DEFINITION OF UNEMPLOYMENT

The most commonly held misconception about the unemployment rate is that it represents the percentage of the total population not working. Another frequently held, but erroneous, belief is that an individual must have experienced a layoff or been the victim of a discharge to qualify as unemployed. In reality, the unemployment rate measures the percentage of the civilian labor force that is currently unemployed, but still actively seeking work.

The official unemployment rate is based upon data collected by the Bureau of the Census. The Bureau of the Census conducts a monthly survey of households called the current population survey (CPS). The results of the monthly survey are processed by the Bureau of Labor Statistics (BLS). The BLS announces the official unemployment rate early in the month for the preceding month. However, the accuracy of the official rate depends to a great extent upon the design, structure, and implementation of the CPS.

The Current Population Survey

The CPS covers 60,000 households from over 1,000 localities in every state and the District of Columbia.[1] The survey is conducted in the same week every month—the week of the 19th day of the month. The survey questions always pertain to the preceding week, that of the 12th day of the month. The households chosen as the sample group represent approximately 1 out of 1,300 households, or 1 out of every 120,000 individuals. A given household remains in the sample group for 4 months, is then removed for 8 months, then readmitted to the sample for 4 months. Therefore, each household is sampled for 8 months over a 16-month period. The interviewers who actually conduct the survey make personal visits to the households in 3 out of 8 months and conduct phone interviews for the remaining 5 months. The interviewer asks questions about the labor force activities of all household members who are over 16 years of age and not in mental, penal, or other institutions. The sum of all individuals in this group is called the noninstitutional population.[2] In 1985, the adult noninstitutional population numbered roughly 179.9 million, while the adult civilian noninstitutional population was 178.2 million.[3]

The results of the survey place all of the members of this population in one of three categories. The first category is called "employed."

The category of employed persons includes five groups. First, it includes all individuals who, during the survey week, did any work at all in their own business, profession, or farm. The individual need work only 1 hour to be considered employed. If an individual worked Monday of the survey week but was laid off Tuesday, that person would still be considered employed. Second, all individuals who received no income but worked at least 15 hours for a family enterprise are included. The survey also includes all individuals who were not at work during the survey week, but who had jobs or businesses from which they were temporarily absent. Workers on sick leave, vacation, strikes, and so on are considered employed. Workers need not receive pay for such absences in order to be included in this group. All members of the armed forces stationed in the U.S., and all foreigners working temporarily in the United States but not living in an embassy make up the final two groups.

Persons excluded from this category include those who work in their homes (housewives and househusbands) and volunteers in hospitals, churches, and social or charitable organizations.

The second category of the adult noninstitutional population is called "unemployed." Unemployed persons are all individuals who have had no employment during the survey week, but who were ready and available for work and made specific efforts or attempts to secure employment sometime during the preceding 4 weeks, or were waiting to be recalled to a job from which they had been laid off, or were waiting to report to a new job within at least 30 days.

The crucial criterion here is that one must be actually seeking work to be counted among the unemployed. Yet the test for "actively seeking work" is not very stringent. Contacting a friend concerning a job vacancy is considered an acceptable job-search technique.

The third category is made up of persons "not in the labor force." Those not in the labor force include all individuals at least 16 years old who are not employed and not actively seeking employment. These persons are classified as "keeping house," "in school," "retired," "unable to work" because of long-term disability, and "other." The "other" category includes the voluntarily idle, seasonal workers who did not work during the survey week, and those who did not look for work because they believed there were no jobs available. This last group includes a very important component of the population called the discouraged worker. We will discuss the discouraged worker below.

In 1982, of the civilian noninstitutional population of 172.3 million, 62.1 million (roughly 35 percent) were categorized as "not in the labor force." Of the remaining 110.2 million individuals considered to be in the labor force, 99.5 million were considered employed and 10.7 million unemployed. The official unemployment rate is calculated as the percent of the labor force that is unemployed, using the following formula:

$$\text{Official unemployment rate} = \frac{\text{Number of unemployed}}{\text{Number of unemployed} + \text{number of employed (labor force)}} \times 100\%.$$

For 1985, the figures are:

$$9.7\% = \frac{10.7 \text{ million}}{110.2 \text{ million}} \times 100\%.$$

Seasonal Adjustment of Unemployment

Throughout the year, the size of the labor force and the levels of employment and unemployment change with regular seasonal events such as changes in weather, holidays, reduced or expanded production, and school openings and closings. Seasonal adjustment attempts to balance these seasonal variations in order to present the underlying economic conditions. For example, the actual unemployment rate skyrockets in June and plummets in September as students enter and exit the labor force for the summer months. The published, seasonally adjusted rate removes this special variation to show the more fundamental time series movements.

Much attention is paid to the unemployed group in the survey. Questions are designed to categorize each unemployed person according to his or her status at the time the person began to seek employment. All unemployed persons are placed in one of four groups that correspond to the four major reasons for unemployment. The four major groups are job losers, job leavers, reentrants, and new entrants.

Job losers are all individuals whose employment ended involuntarily and who began searching for a new position immediately, and all persons on either temporary or indefinite layoff. Job leavers are all persons who quit or otherwise left their employment voluntarily and immediately began looking for work. Reentrants are all individuals who had previously held a job lasting at least 2 weeks, but who were out of the labor force prior to their latest job search. New entrants are all persons who have never worked at a full-time job lasting at least 2 weeks.

For the decade 1973–83, in most years the largest single category for reason for unemployment has been job losers, and the recession years of 1975 and 1982 showed sharp increases in job losses (table 11.1). The category of job leavers seems to be relatively unaffected by the business cycle. From 1967–83, this group ranged from .5 to .9 points of the overall unemployment rate. The new worker category displays the same sort of stability.

Table 11.1 Unemployed Persons and Unemployment Rates by Reason for Unemployment, 1973–83

(Numbers in thousands)

Year, sex, age, and race	Number unemployed							Unemployment rate						
					Entrants							Entrants	
	Total	Job Losers	Job Leavers	Total	Reen-trants	New Workers	Total	Job Losers	Job Leavers	Total	Reen-trants	New Workers

TOTAL

1973	4,365	1,694	683	1,989	1,340	649	4.9	1.9	0.8	2.2	1.5	0.7
1974	5,156	2,242	768	2,144	1,463	681	5.6	2.4	0.8	2.3	1.6	0.7
1975	7,929	4,386	827	2,715	1,892	823	8.5	4.7	0.9	2.9	2.0	0.9
1976	7,406	3,679	903	2,823	1,928	895	7.7	3.8	0.9	2.9	2.0	0.9
1977	6,991	3,166	909	2,916	1,963	953	7.1	3.2	0.9	3.0	2.0	1.0
1978	6,202	2,585	874	2,742	1,857	885	6.1	2.5	0.8	2.7	1.8	0.9
1979	6,137	2,635	880	2,623	1,806	817	5.8	2.5	0.8	2.5	1.7	0.8
1980	7,637	3,947	891	2,799	1,927	872	7.1	3.7	0.8	2.6	1.8	0.8
1981	8,273	4,267	923	3,083	2,102	981	7.6	3.9	0.8	2.8	1.9	0.9
1982	10,678	6,268	840	3,569	2,384	1,185	9.7	5.7	0.8	3.3	2.2	1.1
1983	10,717	6,258	830	3,628	2,412	1,216	9.6	5.6	0.7	3.3	2.2	1.1

Source: *Handbook of Labor Statistics*, U.S. Department of Labor, Bulletin 2217, June 1985, p. 80.

The largest single trend in recent U.S. unemployment rates has been the slow but steady growth in the reentrant category. This change has been a direct result of increased labor force participation by women.

A second important measure of unemployment is the length of time labor force participants are out of work. Obviously, a short period of unemployment may result in only a temporary setback to the individual and minimal economic damage. A long period of joblessness, however, can cause severe psychological damage as well as economic devastation to an individual. The length of time a person is unemployed but continuously seeking work is called duration of unemployment. For example, for persons on layoff, duration represents the number of weeks since job termination. If the person is subsequently employed for a period of 2 or more weeks, or if he or she drops out of the labor force, the duration count stops.

The duration of unemployment is divided into three categories: short-term, long-term, and very long term unemployment. Short-term unemployment lasts less than 5 weeks; long-term unemployment duration is between 5 and 14 weeks; and very long term unemployment duration is over 15 weeks.

The percentage of unemployed people experiencing various lengths of unemployment varies with the business cycle. The percentage of jobless workers who experience very long term unemployment climbs during economic downturns with longer layoff periods and lessened employment opportunities. Accordingly, the proportion of short-term joblessness declines.

The third quarter of 1979 was a recent peak in U.S. business activity, and the first quarter of 1983 was a period when the economy was just coming out of the 1981–82 recession (see figure 11.1). Prior to the short-lived 1980 recession, roughly 20 percent of all unemployed persons were jobless for 15 weeks or more. This proportion rose during the 1980 recession and then declined slightly during the brief 1981 recovery. As the 1981–82 recession deepened, the proportion of very long term unemployed workers rose to over 40 percent by the first quarter of 1983.

Duration of unemployment is one of the six lagging economic indicators. The reason the cyclical pattern of the duration of unemployment lags behind the overall business cycle and overall jobless rate is that, at the onset of a downturn, the jump in the number of job losers temporarily lowers the average duration of a continuing spell of unemployment. As the recession progresses, however, the average duration of unemployment rises as workers find it increasingly difficult to find new jobs. When the economy enters a period of recovery, the number of job losers declines sharply; but the average duration of unemployment continues to rise, and the duration only begins to decline after many of the longer-term unemployed find jobs. A comparison of unemployment, average duration of employment, and changes in the business cycle over time illustrates this relationship (see figures 11.2 and 11.3).

Duration of unemployment is normally expressed as "mean duration" in weeks. As we learned in chapter 2, the mean or arithmetic average can be quite misleading as a

ECONOMICS FOR BANKERS

Figure 11.1 Unemployment by Duration, Selected Quarters, 1979 and 1983

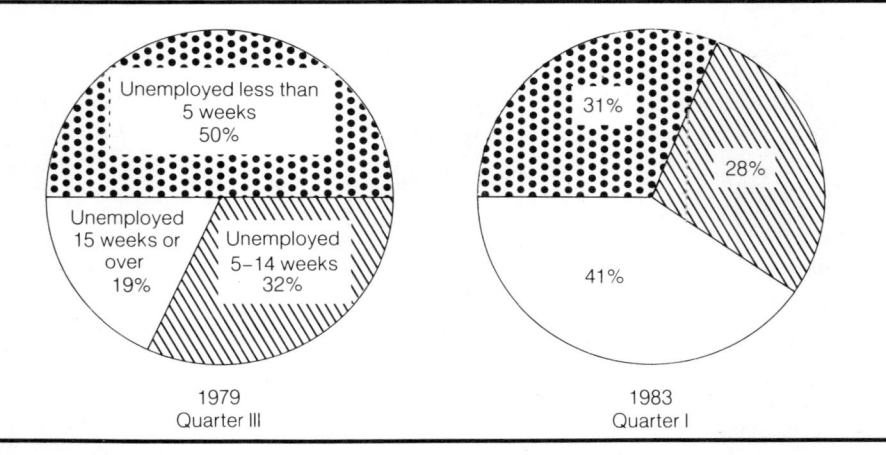

1979 Quarter III
- Unemployed less than 5 weeks: 50%
- Unemployed 5–14 weeks: 32%
- Unemployed 15 weeks or over: 19%

1983 Quarter I
- 31%
- 28%
- 41%

Source: Data adapted from *Handbook of Labor Statistics.*
U.S. Department of Labor, Bureau of Labor Statistics, June 1984.

Figure 11.2 Unemployment Rate and Average Duration of Unemployment, 1953–83

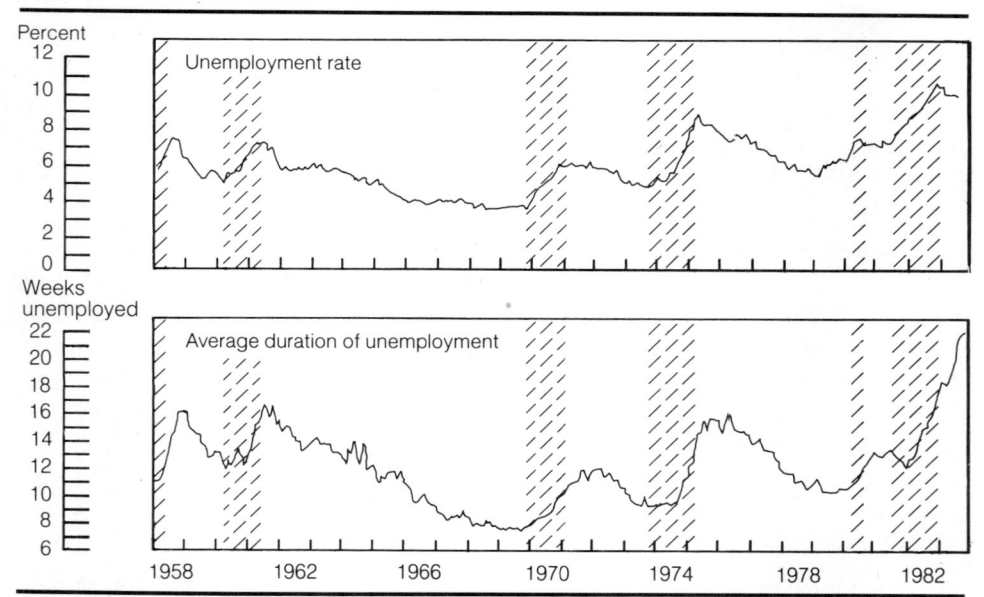

Note: Shaded areas denote recession periods.
Source: Data adapted from *Handbook of Labor Statistics.*
U.S. Department of Labor, Bureau of Labor Statistics, June 1984.

Table 11.2 Duration of Unemployment, 1984–86

Duration of Unemployment (weeks)	Annual Average (thousands of people)		
	1984	1985	1986[a]
Fewer than 5	3,350	3,498	3,311
5 to 14	2,451	2,509	2,441
15 and over	2,738	2,305	2,056
15 to 26	1,104	1,025	969
27 and over	1,634	1,280	1,087
Mean duration (weeks)	18.2	15.6	14.9
Median duration (weeks)	7.9	6.8	6.8

Source: *Monthly Labor Review*, Bureau of Labor Statistics, March 1986, p. 66.
a. Jan. 1986—annual rate.

measure of central tendency. For example, in 1984, the average mean duration of unemployment was 18.2 weeks; however, for the same period, the median duration of unemployment was only 7.9 weeks. Similarly, by January 1986, the mean duration had dropped by 3.3 weeks to 14.9 weeks, while the median duration fell by only slightly more than 1 week to 6.8 percent. This indicates the existence of a relatively large group of very long term jobless individuals. Table 11.2 shows the duration of unemployment for 1984–86.

DISCOURAGED WORKERS

Critics of the official unemployment rate claim that the rate seriously underestimates the actual number of unemployed because it fails to account for the discouraged worker. The discouraged worker is defined as an individual who either fails to enter or drops out of the labor force. The individual may feel that no job exists for someone of his or her qualifications and skills, or may have searched unsuccessfully for a suitable position for some time, only to give up in frustration. Discouraged workers are not counted as unemployed persons in the official statistics. If they were, the official unemployment rate would be much higher. However, the government does acknowledge the existence of discouraged workers and attempts to estimate the size of this group. For example, in 1982, the BLS estimated that over 1.5 million workers became discouraged and left the labor force. The official unemployment rate in 1982 was 9.7 percent; however, if the discouraged workers were included as unemployed, the revised rate would have been substantially higher (table 11.3). The adjusted rate would increase from 9.7 percent to almost 11.0 percent of the labor force.

The discouraged worker may resurface in the official statistics as an unemployed reentrant in the labor force. This movement in and out of the labor force is only part of the constant turnover that takes place among the unemployed. Roughly only half of the unemployed in a given month will still be jobless in the next month. The other half either

Table 11.3 Estimate of Unemployment, Including the Discouraged Worker, 1982

Official rate	
Civilian noninstitutional population	172,271,000
Civilian labor force[a]	110,204,000
Civilian labor force as a percentage of population:	*64 percent*
Employed members of the civilian labor force	99,526,000
Unemployed members of the civilian labor force	10,678,000
Unemployment rate:[b]	*9.7 percent*[c]
Adjusted rate	
Discouraged workers[d]	1,576,000
Unemployed plus discouraged workers	12,254,000
Adjusted civilian labor force	111,780,000
Adjusted unemployment rate:[e]	*11.0 percent*

Source: Employment and Earnings, Monthly, U.S. Bureau of Labor Statistics.
a. The civilian labor force includes those who are currently employed or are seeking employment.
b. Unemployed persons as a percentage of the civilian labor force.
c. This table excludes resident members of the armed services. In 1982, the civilian unemployment rate was 9.7 percent. The all-worker rate was 9.5 percent. This latter rate includes resident members of the armed forces.
d. Members of the civilian noninstitutional population who are not seeking employment.
e. Unemployed persons (including discouraged workers) as a percentage of the civilian labor force (ncluding discouraged workers).

finds jobs or withdraws from the labor force. Because of this turnover, the total number of individuals who actually experience a spell of unemployment during a year is considerably greater than the published average level. For example, the published average monthly level of unemployment in 1981 was 7.5 percent. Yet 23.4 million persons experienced unemployment at some time during 1981—2.8 times the annual average unemployment rate. In other words, over 21 percent of the labor force experienced a period of unemployment in 1981, but the average at any given month was only 7.5 percent. A good rule of thumb in estimating "real unemployment" is that the percentage of the labor force that will suffer at least one period of unemployment during a given year is approximately three times the official average rate.[4]

UNDEREMPLOYMENT

The problem of underemployment is one of the most pressing issues facing the American business community. An underemployed worker is working at a job below his or her skill or educational level. The economy is unable to generate a sufficient volume of professional positions to accommodate an increasing supply of well-trained and highly educated people. These individuals accept positions for which they are overqualified, and can easily become bored and disenchanted.

The official unemployment rate does not and, in fact, cannot measure the magnitude of underemployment. A close proxy for an underemployment measure may be the number of employees who quit or resign from their jobs; however, even this measure is imperfect. Some job leavers may resign for reasons unrelated to the skill level of the job. It is also impossible to measure the number of individuals who stay at lesser jobs because they are afraid or unable to switch to a more appropriate position. To combat the adverse side effects of underemployment, many firms have instituted job enrichment programs in order to satisfy the job demands of the underemployed workers. Other firms have preferred to avoid the problem by making it a practice not to hire overqualified applicants.

TYPES OF UNEMPLOYMENT

Economists classify unemployed individuals by types or causes of unemployment. There are three major types of unemployment.

Cyclical Unemployment

Individuals who suffer from cyclical unemployment are victims of downturns in economic activity. A decrease in spending, which leads to a decrease in sales and orders, can cause firms to lay off employees in an effort to cut costs and reduce losses. Cyclical unemployment tends to move with the business cycle.

The trend in overall cyclical unemployment in the post-World War II era has been marked by eight business cycles (figure 11.3). The overall unemployment rate rose sharply during each of these recessionary periods and declined during the subsequent recovery or expansion phase. The majority of the changes in unemployment during these periods are cyclical in nature.

Since the 1960s, the reductions in unemployment achieved during each expansion phase have nonetheless left the jobless rate at higher levels than prior to each recession. For example, during the shortest recovery following a brief 1980 recession, the jobless rate fell from 7.8 percent in July 1980 to 7.2 percent one year later, just before the 1981–82 downturn. With the return of cyclical unemployment, however, the rate reached 8.8 percent by the end of 1981 and reached a post-World War II record high of 10.8 percent by the end of 1982. With the economic expansion in 1983, 1984, and 1985, the rate ended 1985 at 7.2 percent.[5] The rate continued to fall, and by mid-1987 stood at 6.1 percent.

Past business cycle patterns provide insight about both current and future events. For example, early in an economic downturn, before unemployment begins to rise, employers tend to cut back the number of hours worked per week. As a result, the proportion of persons working part time for economic reasons tends to increase early in a recession. As the recession deepens, the unemployment rate rises because employers are decreasing their

Figure 11.3 Unemployment Rate and the Business Cycle, 1948–83

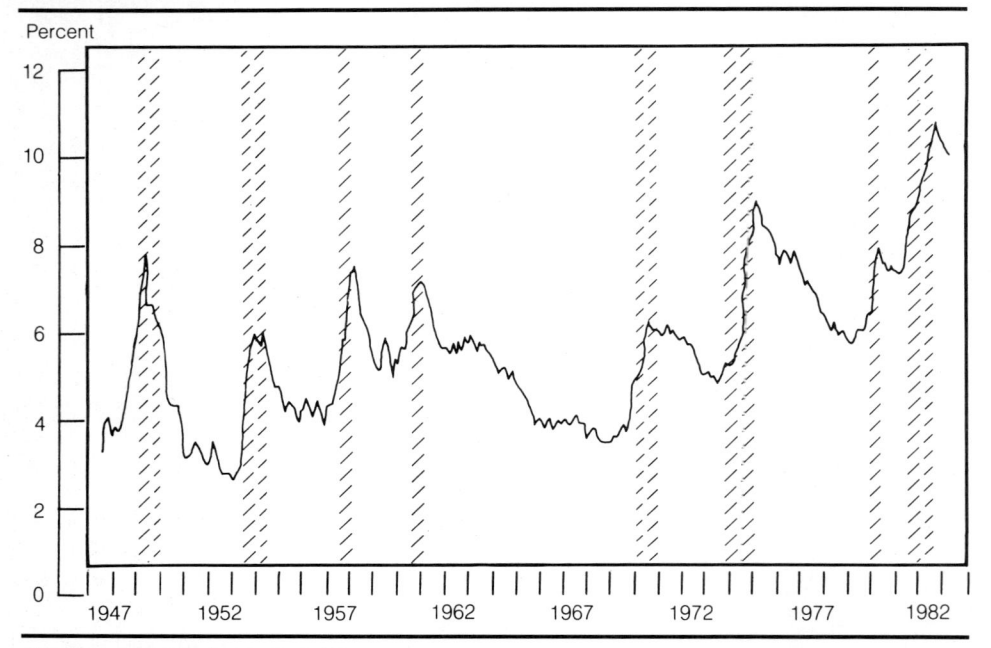

Note: Shaded areas denote recession periods.
Source: Data adapted from *Handbook of Labor Statistics.*
U.S. Department of Labor, Bureau of Labor Statistics, June 1984.

work forces, first laying off workers and then perhaps terminating some jobs. This phase becomes evident when the proportion of job losers to total unemployed goes up and the overall jobless rate accelerates upward. Initially, the average duration of joblessness may remain unchanged or even decline as newly unemployed workers lower the average. Over time, the average duration of unemployment will begin to rise. As the duration of unemployment lengthens, some workers may become discouraged and drop out of the labor force. When the business cycle passes its trough and begins recovery, the order reverses itself as employers begin to lengthen hours, rehire workers, and expand payrolls with new positions.

Structural Unemployment

Not all unemployed workers are without work because of layoffs. Many unemployed people in the 1980s have never held a job; others lack the education and skills to fill available jobs, or have been displaced from a job by new technology or foreign competition.

Structurally unemployed workers are those whose jobs have been permanently eliminated. For example, the Northeast region of the United States has experienced a large number of plant closings. The closing of a large plant may leave many employees emotionally depressed and confused about their options for the future. These structurally unemployed workers may have to relocate to new regions in order to find suitable employment. Workers who choose to stay behind may encounter bleak employment opportunities unless they are able to use other skills or retrain for different kinds of work.

A great deal of the recent structural unemployment in the U.S. has been concentrated in the primary metal and automobile industries. These industries have unemployment rates far higher than other sectors of the economy (figure 11.4). The Northeast and Midwest, hard-hit by structural unemployment in these industries, have come to be called the "rust belt" as a result.

Structural unemployment may also occur in industries that are vulnerable to cyclical swings in sales. Workers in the goods-producing sector are affected severely by the

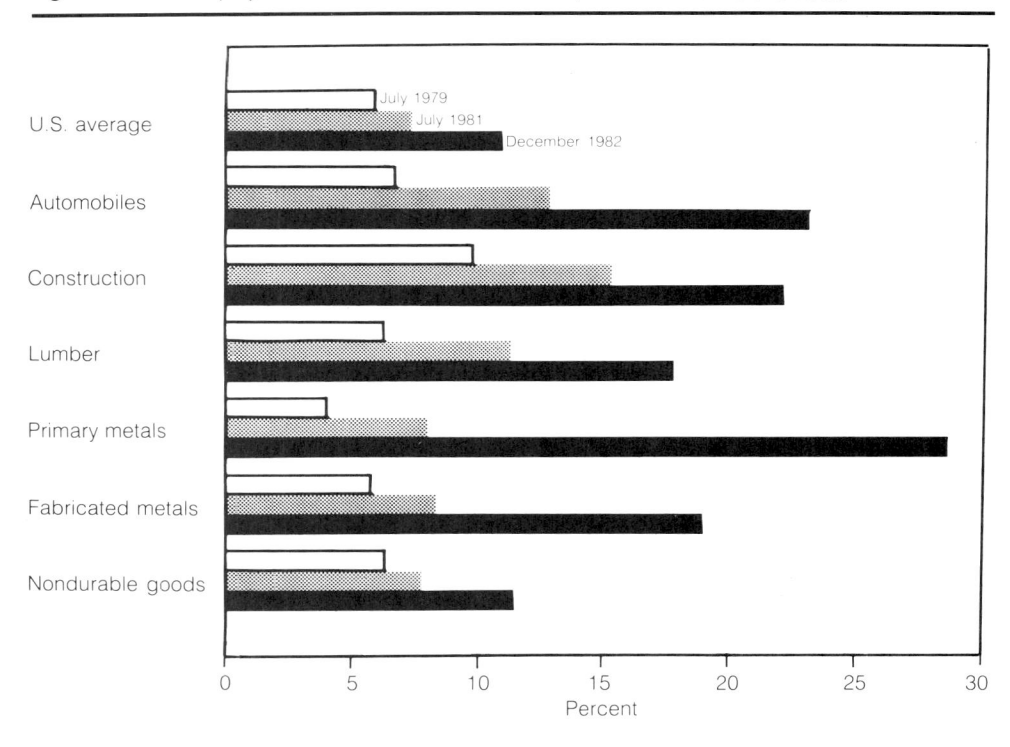

Figure 11.4 Unemployment Rates in Selected Industries, Selected Months and Years

Source: Data adapted from *Handbook of Labor Statistics*, 1983, U.S. Department of Labor, Bureau of Labor Statistics.

Figure 11.5 Unemployment Rates for Major Industry Divisions, Selected Quarters and Years

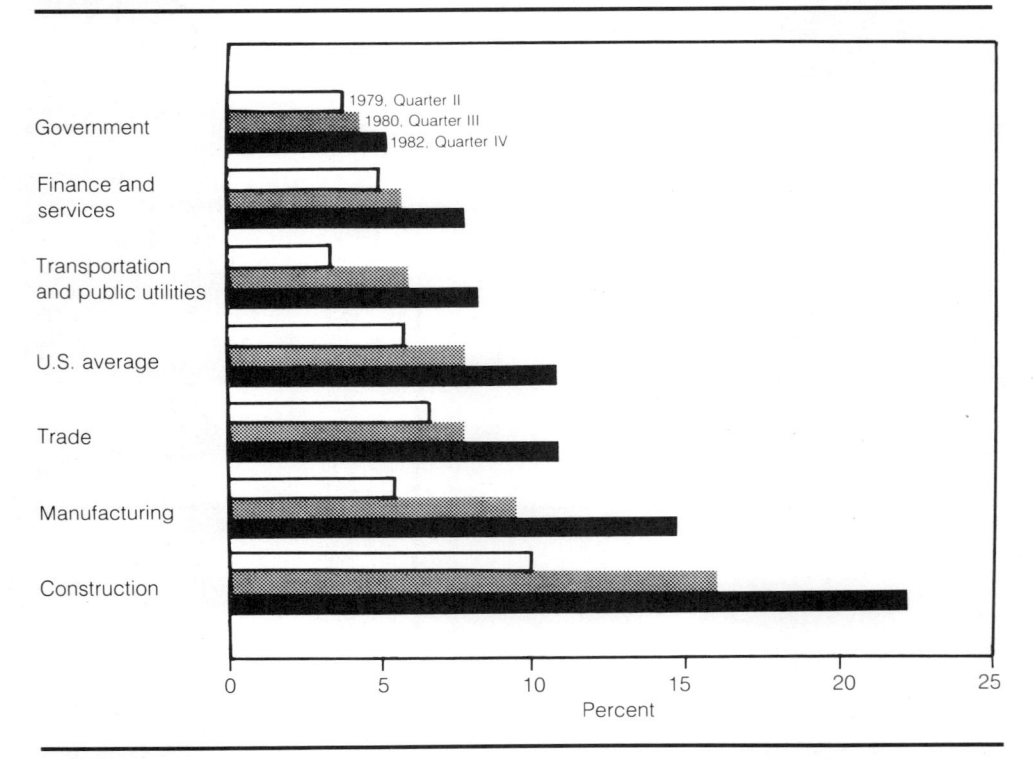

Source: Data adapted from *Handbook of Labor Statistics.* 1983. U.S. Department of Labor. Bureau of Labor Statistics.

recessions. Also, high interest rates can choke off spending for interest-sensitive products of the housing and automobile industries. Although all industries suffer during cyclical downturns, employees in transportation, public utilities, finance and service industries, and government are less affected by structural and cyclical unemployment than workers in the goods-producing sector (figure 11.5). Workers in the service sector enjoy relatively greater job security.

Frictional Unemployment

Frictionally unemployed individuals are jobless because of some sort of barrier or friction in the labor force. For example, if an unemployed factory worker leaves the rust belt and decides to begin a new career working with computers in California, this person may remain unemployed until he or she obtains the necessary skills to gain a position in the new field. Frictional unemployment can also be caused by labor-management disputes, by the uncertainty and hesitancy of first-time job seekers, or by discrimination.

Frictional unemployment is more likely to affect people who are young, who are members of a minority group, or who are blue-collar workers. Some demographic groups carry a disproportionate share of unemployment (figure 11.6). For example, while people 16–24 years old represented only about 1 in 5 workers in the civilian labor force in 1982, 2 in 5 of the unemployed fell into this age group. Black workers were only 1 in 10 in the labor force compared to 2 in 10 of the jobless.[6] Hispanic workers were also overrepresented among the unemployed, and blue-collar workers comprised about 30 percent of the nation's work force, but 45 percent of the unemployed.

Minority groups generally experience unemployment at a much higher level than white workers. Jobless rates for black workers in 1982 were more than twice those of white workers, a pattern that has generally persisted over the past 3 decades. Unemployment rates

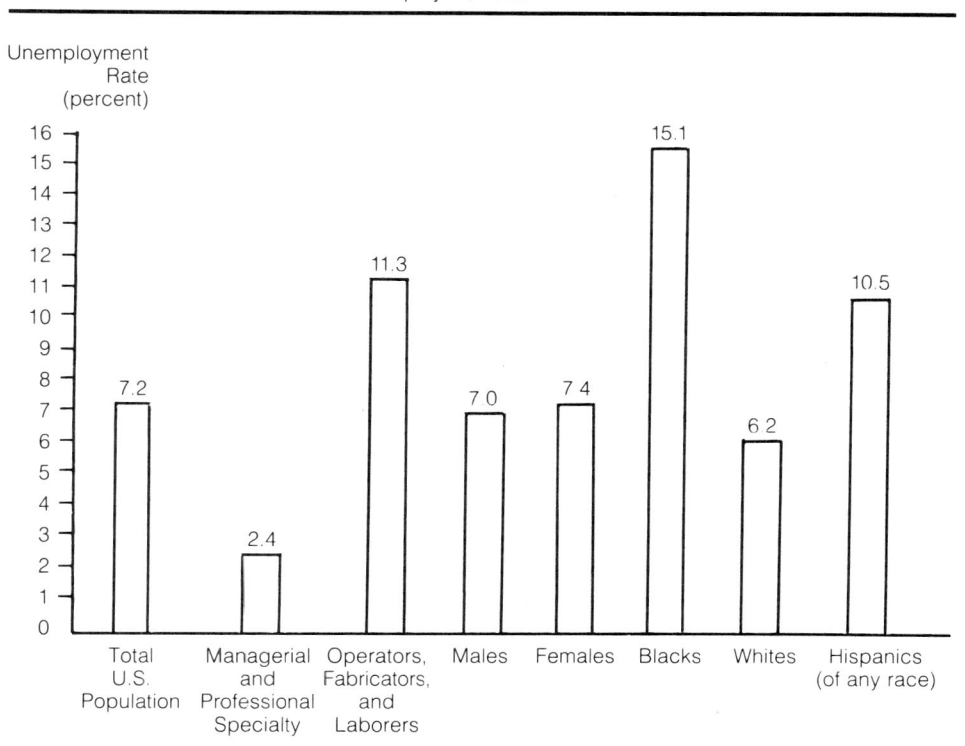

Figure 11.6 Characteristics of the Unemployed, 1985

Category	Unemployment Rate (percent)
Total U.S. Population	7.2
Managerial and Professional Specialty	2.4
Operators, Fabricators, and Laborers	11.3
Males	7.0
Females	7.4
Blacks	15.1
Whites	6.2
Hispanics (of any race)	10.5

Source: Data adapted from Statistical Abstract of the U.S., 1987, U.S. Department of Commerce. Bureau of the Census.

for persons of Hispanic origin tend to be about 1.5 times higher than those for non-Hispanics. Rates of joblessness among Hispanics vary among Mexican, Puerto Rican, and Cuban subgroups, reflecting diverse cultural backgrounds, age composition, educational levels, residential patterns, and other factors. Interpretations of unemployment data concerning minority groups should reflect an awareness of such variations.

Blue-collar workers typically bear a higher incidence of unemployment than white-collar employees. Blue-collar workers are concentrated in the cyclically sensitive goods-producing industries, and hence are more likely to lose their jobs during economic downturns. Nonfarm laborers, the least-skilled blue-collar group, normally have the highest jobless rate; white-collar workers, particularly those in professional or managerial fields, typically have the lowest jobless rates.

Joblessness among adult workers declines as educational attainment rises. This is one of the strongest incentives for additional schooling. Among persons 25 years of age and over, the more years of school completed, the less the likelihood of unemployment (figure 11.7). Workers with less than 4 years of high school are three times more likely to be unemployed than those with 4 years of college.

Unemployment data, in conjunction with other major indicators, help us to assess the economic health of a nation. Unemployment statistics are also useful for viewing the human implications of business cycle trends. Examining the characteristics of unemployed workers and the nature of their joblessness may contribute to a better understanding of one of society's most important problems.

Figure 11.7 Unemployment Rates by Education, 1982
(persons 25 years and older)

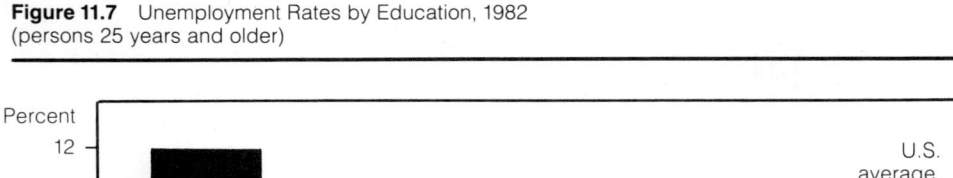

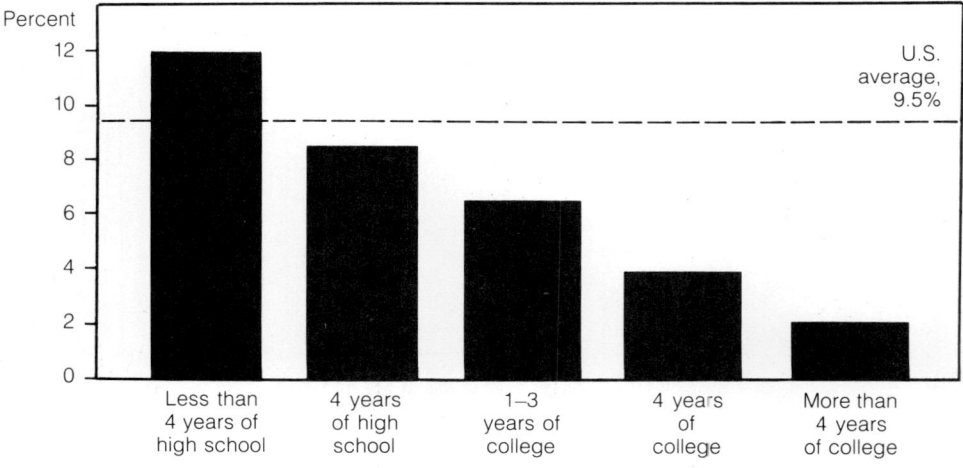

Source: Data adapted from *Handbook of Labor Statistics*, 1982. U.S. Department of Labor. Bureau of Labor Statistics.

The official jobless rate is primarily an indication of the amount of labor available but not used in the economy at a given time. Unemployment statistics, per se, are not designed to measure economic hardship although public attention is often focused on the hardships experienced by jobless workers and their families. It is possible to disaggregate unemployment into various components that shed some light on the relative welfare of workers. For example, variations in unemployment by marital status, age, race, gender, and type of employment can be identified.

Monthly statistics on the labor force and unemployment are a "snapshot" of a particular point in time; they do not reveal the constant flux that occurs in the pool of unemployed persons.

SUMMARY

The unemployment rate is a measure of the percentage of the civilian labor force that is unemployed but actively seeking work. The official unemployment rate is announced by the U.S. Bureau of Labor Statistics, using data gathered by the U.S. Bureau of the Census.

The noninstitutional population consists of all American citizens over 16 years of age who are not institutionalized. The members of this group may be employed, unemployed, or "not in the labor force" (not employed and not looking for work).

Unemployed noninstitutionalized people may be categorized as job losers, job leavers, reentrants, or new entrants. Unemployment is also categorized by its duration: short-term, long-term, or very long term.

During economic downturns, the percentage of jobless workers who are unemployed for more than 15 weeks (very long term) increases.

Discouraged workers are persons who either fail to enter or drop out of the work force. The official unemployment rate would be much higher if discouraged workers were incorporated in the calculation.

There is constant turnover in the ranks of the unemployed. The actual number of people who will be unemployed at least once during a given year is considerably higher than the official U.S. unemployment rate.

Underemployment is another condition that cannot be measured easily. In some cases, the educational level of a worker is higher than is required in his or her current position.

Cyclical unemployment results from business recessions or depressions because decreases in consumer demand lead to layoffs in certain industries. A certain kind of cyclical unemployment follows the patterns of the seasons. Workers in goods-producing industries are particularly vulnerable to cyclical unemployment.

Structural unemployment can be very prolonged. It arises when the location and/or skill requirements of job openings do not match the location and skills of available workers. Changes in technology, markets, or political priorities can feed structural unemployment.

A third type of unemployment is frictional unemployment. It arises primarily because our economic system is incapable of matching people with jobs instantly and smoothly. Often, the frictionally unemployed are people out of work because they are between jobs. Discrimination against minorities, the young, the elderly, and women is another source of frictional unemployment.

Unemployment does not affect all people in our nation equally. Youth, minorities, and blue-collar workers are among those persons most likely to experience unemployment. Lower levels of education or employment in a cyclically sensitive industry (one that is affected by economic fluctuations) also make the worker more vulnerable to joblessness. Workers with more than one of these characteristics have a greater likelihood of unemployment; black teenagers, for example, historically have had high jobless rates even in the best of economic times.

KEY WORDS

adult noninstitutional population
Bureau of Labor Statistics
current population survey
cyclical unemployment
discouraged worker

duration of unemployment
frictional unemployment
structural unemployment
unemployment rate

Questions for Review

1. The evening news reports that the number of workers with jobs has increased in the most recent month. The morning news also reports that the unemployment rate has increased. Can both of these reports be accurate? Explain why or why not.

2. Explain how an auto worker might be affected by cyclical unemployment. By structural unemployment.

3. How might the underground economy, described in chapter 10, affect the unemployment rate? Name some of these legal or illegal underground occupations.

4. Not all of the unemployed are without jobs involuntarily. Why would someone choose to be out of work?

5. A genetic engineer, unable to find work in her field, takes a job as a bicycle messenger. Should she (and her unused scientific skills) be counted as unemployed? How should she be classified?

ENDNOTES

1. For a detailed description of the current population survey, see U.S. Bureau of Labor Statistics, *Concepts and Methods Used in Labor Force Statistics Derived from the Current Population Survey*, Bureau of Labor Statistics, Report No. 463, series P-23, no. 62, October 1976.

2. If military personnel are excluded from the noninstitutional population, this group is called the civilian noninstitutional population. The Bureau of Labor Statistics publishes unemployment rates for both the "civilian labor force" (excluding the military) and the "labor force," which includes military personnel.

3. Bureau of Labor Statistics, *Employment and Earnings*, monthly.

4. See Del Marth, "Does the Jobless Rate Do the Job?" *Nation's Business*, November 1982.

5. An interesting perspective on the lower unemployment rate is presented by Lance Compa, a labor attorney with the United Electrical, Radio, and Machine Workers of America. In an editorial in the *Washington Post*, Compa notes that while the unemployment rate has dropped considerably in recent years, the new jobs are often "low-paying jobs with short hours, small benefits and bleak futures." Forty-four percent of the new jobs, according to Compa, pay at or below the minimum wage. See Lance Compa, "So We Have More Jobs—Low-Paid, Part-Time Ones," *Washington Post*, March 15, 1987, p. C1-2. See also Alan Blinder, "A 7-Percent Jobless Rate is Just Not Good Enough," *Business Week*, February 3, 1986.

6. See Katharine L. Bradbury and Lynn E. Browne, "Black Men in the Labor Market," *New England Economic Review*, Federal Reserve Bank of Boston (March/April 1986), pp. 32–42, for a description of the deteriorating employment situation of black men.

ECONOMICS IN THE NEWS

Forced to Make a Fresh Beginning

Layoffs pose the challenge of a lifetime

By Barbara Rudolph. Reported by Lisa Kartus/Chicago and Thomas McCarroll/New York

Bobbie Cooper, a communications manager for MCI, the long-distance phone company, had just returned from her Thanksgiving holiday when she was called into her boss's office. "We are eliminating your position," Cooper was told. At first the message did not quite register. "So where am I going?" she asked. The explanation that followed was painfully clear: she was being fired. Recalls Cooper: "It hit me like a ton of bricks. I was in a state of shock." Cooper, 44, had worked for IBM and one of its subsidiaries for 24 years. She was transferred to MCI when IBM bought a minority stake in the smaller firm last March. Even though Cooper got a severance package of nearly $38,000 from MCI, she remains stunned as she looks for a new job: "They told me to clear my desk and pack my things. And I was gone, just like that. Poof."

Whatever length of service, in small companies or sprawling conglomerates, everyone from floor sweepers to senior executives is facing the possibility of job loss. Despite the merits of restructuring, corporations seem well aware that their new austerity moves pose unprecedented challenges for their employees. By and large, affected firms are trying to ease the pain. More companies than ever before are relying on early-retirement schemes and generous severance packages to entice voluntary resignations as a means of meeting slimming goals. For some employees, no amount of compensation can adequately make up for the loss of the job. But for others, the golden handshake can provide a liberating opportunity to get out of a dead-end job and start afresh somewhere else.

Getting fired, though, is always a jolt. Once the shock has worn off, many people are left with a fragile sense of self-esteem. Even those who remain at work are affected by layoffs, suffering both from what is often called survivor's guilt and from apprehension about their own jobs. Says Elizabeth Uporsky, 30, an accounts-receivable specialist at AT&T, which is undergoing major staff reductions: "Everybody is walking around on pins and needles wondering if they're going to be next. We're reminded of what's happening every day. We have rows and rows of empty cubicles and desks."

For the former occupants of those empty desks, finding a new job can prove difficult. Though the unemployment rate has declined from 10.8% to 6.7% since the 1981–82 recession, the jobless level is still high by historical standards. Since so many companies are resorting to layoffs simultaneously, job seekers may encounter more competitors seeking fewer opportunities. Those who have worked in specialized jobs often find that their particular skills are not readily transferable to new jobs.

More and more companies try to help departing employees find work. Seven years ago, 16% of the 1,000 largest industrial companies offered job-placement or counseling services for out-going employees. Today, 51% do. In addition, private agencies set up to help laid-off workers find jobs are proliferating. Some 300 of these outplacement firms now operate, compared with twelve companies a decade ago. Says Robert Hecht, chairman of Lee Hecht Harrison, a New York City-based outplacement firm: "Years ago people thought only deadbeats and the lame ended up in outplacement. But that has changed."

Many refugees from large corporations land jobs in fast-growing small companies or start their own businesses. John Cain, 47, left General Electric two years ago when his job as a manager in computer operations was phased out. A 23-year veteran at GE, Cain decided to "chase a life-long dream," which was to be his own boss. He founded Connecticut-based Scientific Systems, which markets an electronic filing and word-processing program designed for job seekers. Says Cain: "Had I not left GE, I probably would have never been able to pursue this. I wanted to prove to myself that I wasn't ready to be set out to pasture."

After 15 years as an accountant for Denver-based Haley-Roth, a health-care firm, Virginia Hughes, 66, is trying to parlay her part-time work as a wedding planner into a full-time career. John Nostrand, 51, had worked for Union Carbide for 15 years when, in December 1985, he took early retirement from his $45,000-a-year job as a manager of factory automation. Nostrand now works as a consultant for the Coopers & Lybrand accounting firm, making about 15% more than he did at Carbide.

Other laid-off workers find they are happier even without their old paychecks. Two years ago, Harry Marsh lost his $30,000-a-year job as a structural engineer for Chicago-based CBI Industries after working there for 18 years. After he had unsuccessfully looked for work for eight months, Marsh decided to stay home with his daughter, 14, and son, 11. His wife earns enough at Bell Laboratories to support the family, and Marsh has launched a small upholstery business that brings in about $5,000 a year. Now that they are saving on taxes, commuting, child care and other expenses, the family's financial position is not much below what it was when Marsh worked at CBI.

The upheavals in corporate America are likely to make large companies lose some of the allure they once held for job seekers. Certainly people will no longer count on a corporation to provide lifetime job security. Says Paul Hirsch, professor of business policy at the University of Chicago Graduate School of Business: "The new culture is to keep your nose clean and your bags packed. The moral that people see around them is, if you fall in love with your company, you're going to get burned."

That is at once too harsh and oversimplified. But at least one lesson is clear: just as companies must adjust to changing times and tougher competitive conditions, so must their employees learn to do the same.

Copyright 1987 Time Inc. All rights reserved. Reprinted by permission from TIME.

CHAPTER TWELVE

INFLATION

Objectives

After reading this chapter, you should be able to

- define inflation
- define the consumer price index (CPI)
- explain how items in the CPI are weighted and classified
- explain why it is incorrect to think of the CPI as a cost-of-living index
- explain why the CPI cannot be used to make interarea comparisons of living costs
- state the relationship between inflation and purchasing power
- explain the effects of inflation on savers and spenders, debtors and creditors, earners of fixed and flexible incomes, and the public and private sectors
- list and describe eight major sources of inflation
- describe the real output effects of inflation
- define hyperinflation
- discuss the trade-off between unemployment and inflation, using the Phillips Curve concept

This chapter will focus on the concept of inflation, its effects, the process used to measure price changes, the proper application of the measurement device, causes of inflation, and the deadly combination of high inflation and unemployment.

DEFINITION OF INFLATION

Inflation is a condition in which the economy experiences a general increase in the average price level of all goods and services. Note that inflation refers to the average price level of goods and services. In practice, the prices of certain individual items may decrease. But, on average, the price level rises. The term "average," moreover, does not mean simply the average increase of *all* goods and services. If we only purchased cars and toothpicks, a 100 percent increase in the price of toothpicks and a 0 percent increase in the price of cars would average out to be a 50 percent price hike. Clearly, to be meaningful, the weight given a particular price increase must somehow be linked to the importance of that item in consumer budgets. The actual measurement of inflation is a very controversial topic in economics. We now turn our attention to the methodology used in measuring the inflation rate.[1]

The Consumer Price Index (CPI)

The primary statistic used to describe price changes in the U.S. is the consumer price index (CPI). The consumer price index is a measure of the average change in the prices paid by urban consumers for a fixed market basket of goods and services. It is calculated monthly for two population groups, one consisting only of wage earners and clerical workers and the other consisting of all urban families. The wage-earner index (CPI-W) is a continuation of the historic index that was introduced well over a half-century ago for use in wage negotiations. The wage-earner index represents about 40 percent of the noninstitutional population of the U.S. As new uses developed for the CPI in recent years, the need for a broader and more representative index became apparent. The all-urban index (CPI-U), introduced in 1978, is representative of the buying habits of about 80 percent of the noninstitutional population. The methodology for producing the index is the same for both populations. The CPI-U and its major components are shown for selected periods in tables 12.1 and 12.2. The first table shows the CPI in index-number form and the second table shows the equivalent percentage changes in the index numbers.

Table 12.1 Consumer Price Indexes, Selected Years

(1967 = 100, except as noted; monthly data seasonally adjusted, except as noted by NSA)

Period	All items[a] NSA	Food	\multicolumn{8}{c}{Housing}	Appar-el and upkeep	\multicolumn{3}{c}{Transportation}	Medical care	Ener-gy[b]	All items less food, energy, and shelter
			Total[a]	\multicolumn{4}{c}{Shelter}	Fuel and other utilities		Total[a]	New cars	Motor fuel			
				Total	Renters' costs (Dec. 1982=100)	Home-owners' costs (Dec. 1982=100)	Mainte-nance and repairs NSA								
Rel. imp.[c]	100.0	16.2	42.9	27.8	8.0	19.6	0.2	7.9	6.3	17.2	4.6	2.9	5.4	7.4	48.6
1982	289.1	285.7	314.7	337.0	......	......	334.1	350.8	191.8	291.5	197.6	389.4	328.7	416.1	245.6
1983	298.4	291.7	323.1	344.8	103.0	102.5	346.3	370.3	196.5	298.4	202.6	376.4	357.3	419.3	258.4
1984	311.1	302.9	336.5	361.7	108.6	107.3	359.2	387.3	200.2	311.7	208.5	370.7	379.5	423.6	271.2
1985	322.2	309.8	349.9	382.0	115.4	113.1	368.9	393.6	206.0	319.9	215.2	373.8	403.1	426.5	281.6
1986	328.4	319.7	360.2	402.9	121.9	119.4	373.8	384.7	207.8	307.5	224.4	292.1	433.5	370.3	291.2

Source: *Economic Indicators*, U.S. Department of Labor, Bureau of Labor Statistics, February 1987.
a. Includes items not shown separately.
b. Fuel oil, coal, and bottled gas; gas (piped) and electricity; and motor fuel.
c. Relative importance, December 1985.

Table 12.2 Changes in Consumer Prices, All Urban Consumers

(Percent change from preceding period; monthly data seasonally adjusted, except as noted by NSA)

Period	All items[a]	Food	Housing Total[a]	Shelter Total[a]	Renters' costs	Home-owners' costs	Fuel and other utilities	Apparel and upkeep	Transportation Total[a]	New cars	Motor fuel	Medical care	Energy[b]	All items less food, energy, and shelter
							Change, December to December, NSA							
1982	3.9	3.1	3.6	2.4	.....	.....	9.7	1.6	1.7	1.6	−6.5	11.0	1.3	6.1
1983	3.8	2.6	3.5	4.7	5.1	4.5	1.8	2.9	3.9	3.4	−1.7	6.4	−.5	5.0
1984	4.0	3.8	4.2	5.2	5.9	5.1	4.2	2.0	3.1	2.4	−2.4	6.1	.2	4.4
1985	3.8	2.7	4.3	6.0	6.3	5.9	1.9	2.9	2.6	3.5	3.0	6.7	1.8	3.7
1986	1.1	3.8	1.8	4.6	5.0	4.6	−5.7	.9	−5.9	5.8	−30.6	7.7	−19.7	3.4

Source: *Economic Indicators*, February 1987.
a. Includes items not shown separately.
b. Fuel oil, coal, and bottled gas; gas (piped) and electricity; and motor fuel.

History of the CPI

The CPI was initiated during World War I when rapid increases in prices, particularly in shipbuilding centers, made such an index essential for calculating cost-of-living adjustments in wages. Studies of family expenditures were conducted in almost 100 industrial centers over a 2-year period (1917–19) in order to establish weights for the index that actually reflected the relative importance of goods and services purchased by consumers. In 1919, the Bureau of Labor Statistics began publication of separate indexes for 32 cities. Regular publication of a national index, the U.S. city average, began in 1921. A new study was made in the mid-1930s, and a revised index was introduced in 1940.

The first comprehensive post-World War II revision of the index was completed in January 1953, using weights from the 1950 expenditure survey. At that time, not only were the weighting factors, list of items, and sources of price data updated, but improvements in pricing and calculation methods were introduced. Medium-size and small cities were added to the city sample to make the index representative of prices paid by all urban wage-earner and clerical-worker families.

A 1964 revision introduced new expenditure weights based on the spending patterns in 1960–61 of single persons as well as families, and using updated samples of cities, goods and services, and retail stores and service establishments. A similar revision was completed in 1978, incorporating new expenditure weights from a 1972–73 consumer expenditure survey, new retail outlet samples from a 1974 point-of-purchase survey, and population data from the 1970 census. It also introduced the second index, the more broadly based CPI for all urban consumers (CPI-U), which took into account the buying patterns of professional and salaried workers, part-time workers, the self-employed, the unemployed, and retired people, in addition to wage earners and clerical workers.

In January 1983, the BLS changed the way in which homeownership costs are measured. A rental equivalence method replaced the asset-price approach to homeownership costs for the CPI-U. This change separated shelter costs from the investment component of homeownership so that the index would reflect only the cost of shelter services provided by owner-occupied homes.

The most recent revision of the CPI occurred in 1986. A new market basket, based on the expenditures reported by all urban residents (80 percent of the total U.S. population) between the years 1982 to 1984, was introduced. In addition, the BLS has announced its intentions to change the reference base year, 1967, to a more recent period. This change will occur sometime after January 1988.

The monthly CPI is first published in a news release between the 20th and 25th of the month following the month in which the data are collected. Thus, the index for January is published in late February.

The CPI is not an exact measure of price change. It is subject to sampling or estimating errors, which reflect statistical limitations rather than mistakes in the index calculation.

Calculating the CPI

The CPI is based on a sample of prices of food, clothing, shelter and fuels, transportation, medical services, and the other goods and services that people buy for day-to-day living. Price changes are captured by regularly repricing essentially the same market basket of goods and services. The current aggregate cost is compared with the cost of the same market basket in a selected base year. The base year is chosen arbitrarily and has no impact on the actual annual inflation rates. As noted above, the base year currently used for the CPI is 1967. In other words, the level of consumer prices in 1967 is considered equal to 100 index points. Monthly changes in actual prices of goods and services are converted into their index point equivalents.

A change to a later base year merely produces a measuring device of a different calibration. To interpret the index, simply compare a given index value with the base year. For example, the CPI-U in December 1985 was 327.4. The base-year index is (1967 = 100). The same market basket that cost $100 in 1967 would cost approximately $327.40 in December 1985.

As noted, the base period is expected to change sometime after January 1988. Many anticipate that the change will be to (1982–84 = 100). Nevertheless, whatever year(s) the BLS selects to be the new base period, the change involves little more than an arithmetic change to make the index numbers easier to comprehend. For example, the conversion of the annual index numbers for the CPI from a 1967 base to a 1977 base involves dividing the index numbers by the 1977 CPI (181.5) and multiplying by 100. This amounts to a change as follows:

Consumer Price Index, by Year

Base	1967	1969	1973	1977
1967 = 100	100.0	109.8	133.1	181.5
1977 = 100	55.1	60.5	73.3	100.0

To measure the changes in consumer prices, representatives of the BLS actually go into approximately 24,000 stores and business establishments in 85 different cities to record the prices of specific items: hamburger, for example, and other cuts of meat. They will price a specific shirt, a specific dress, a specific suit, a specific electric appliance, a specific can of vegetables, and so forth. On each successive visit, they will price the same items or, if the item is no longer being sold, the closest thing to it. The businesses visited include grocery and department stores, hospitals, filling stations, and other types of stores and service establishments. Prices of food, fuels, and a few other items are obtained every month in all 85 locations. Prices of most other goods and services are collected in alternating months in either the five largest urban areas or other selected areas. Prices of most goods and services are obtained through visits by trained representatives. Mail questionnaires are used to obtain public utility rates, some fuel prices, and certain other items. Rent and property taxes are collected from about 18,000 tenants and 18,000 housing units, respectively.

People who give information do not always report accurately. Precautions are taken to guard against errors in pricing that would affect the index most seriously. The field representatives who collect the price data and the commodity specialists and the clerks who process them are well trained to watch for unusual deviations in prices that might be due to errors in reporting.

Weights and Relative Importance in the CPI

In calculating the consumer price index, price changes for the various items in each urban area are averaged together with weights that represent their importance in the spending of the appropriate population group (table 12.3).

The weight of an item in the CPI is derived from records on public expenditures for that item as determined by the consumer expenditure survey. This survey provides data on the average amount of goods and services consumed by the index population during the survey period.

The relative importance of an item is also taken into consideration. The relative importance shows the share of total expenditure an item is expected to command if quantities consumed remain constant while prices follow their historical path. Although the quantity weights of items in the market basket remain fixed, the relative importance of items changes over time, reflecting the effect of price changes. Items whose prices rise faster than the average become relatively more important. Thus, the relative importance of transportation in the index of all urban consumers, which was 18 percent in December 1977, rose to nearly 22 percent in December 1982. During the same period, the relative importance of apparel fell from 5.8 percent to 5.2 percent, even though the same amount and quality of clothing figured in the calculation. The published data on relative importance are used to answer such questions as what was the effect on the overall CPI of a particular price change (for example, gasoline prices) for a particular period?

It is important to realize that the CPI is not a cost-of-living index. The CPI merely compares the cost of a market basket of goods and services in any given period with the same market basket of goods and services of a base period. This does not mean consumers will purchase the same kinds and quantity of goods and services today as they purchased in 1967. Consumers often adjust their purchases, substituting lower-priced products for relatively high-priced products. For example, if beef prices escalate more quickly than chicken prices, consumers tend to purchase more chicken and less beef. The CPI does not take this sort of consumer behavior into account. The price index assumes consumption of the same market basket period after period. Because of this limitation, it is essential to

Table 12.3 Consumer Price Index: Relative Importance of Major Groups, 1982–84

Item	Relative Importance (percent)
All items	100.000
Food and beverages	17.840
Housing	42.637
Apparel and upkeep	6.524
Transportation	18.696
Medical care	4.796
Entertainment	4.380
Other goods and services	5.128

Source: U.S. Department of Labor, Bureau of Labor Statistics.

remember that the CPI is only a price index—not a cost-of-living index. Many erroneously equate the CPI with a measure of living costs.

There are other drawbacks to the use of the CPI as a cost-of-living measure. A true cost-of-living measure accounts for increases in income taxes or Social Security taxes; the CPI does not. The CPI can only account for those tax changes that are incorporated into the final prices of goods and services included in the market basket.

It takes some time for the CPI to reflect changes in spending patterns for new products and services. For example, the rise of fast-food and convenience-store shopping came after the construction of the current market basket. Because of this, the CPI does not currently account for changes in the pattern of consumer expenditures resulting from the incorporation of these new products and services.

The CPI cannot report changes in lifestyle. It measures the price changes for a sample of products used by a certain population group in the base year, without regard to the demographics of that population group.

The CPI is based on money expenditure, so it does not reflect noncash consumption. For example, changes in fringe benefits or nontaxed government-supplied services can influence living expenses but are not measured in the CPI.

Special Problems: Quality Changes and Seasonal Adjustments

One of the most difficult conceptual problems in compiling a price index is finding a way to accurately measure changes in quality. Products and consumption patterns are constantly changing. For example, with each model change of an automobile, the BLS must try to distinguish between the increase in price due to inflation and the increase in price due to quality change. A quality change in a new model of an item should not be expressed as a price change, since the index measures the cost to consumers of purchasing a constant market basket of goods and services of constant quality through time.

Ideally, estimates would be obtained for each dollar-value quality change resulting from a change in the model or item priced. Such an estimate would reflect how much consumers value the quality change. However, direct measurement of the value consumers place on quality change is rarely possible. Therefore, the BLS uses an indirect method to measure the quality change by evaluating the additional cost associated with producing the change in quality. For new automobile features, this estimate is based on all costs incurred in manufacturing plus the established company markup to the selling price of passenger cars. This estimate of costs applies to all new features that are installed as standard equipment—that is, all new features on cars in the same or comparable series. For items that replace or modify some previously existing feature, the estimate is based on the difference in cost between the old and the new feature. In other words, the estimate of cost for new items is computed for both the new and the old feature. The difference between these values is used as the estimate of quality change.

Quality adjustments exclude changes in style or appearance, such as the use of chrome trim, unless these features have been offered as options and purchased by a large proportion of customers. Also, new technology sometimes results in better quality at the same or reduced cost. When the resulting change in cost is minimal or difficult to ascertain, it is ignored and prices are compared directly.

Seasonally adjusted data are presented in the CPI alongside unadjusted data. Seasonal adjustment removes the estimated effect of changes that normally occur at the same time and in about the same magnitude every year, such as price movements resulting from changing climatic conditions, production cycles, model changeovers, holidays, and sales.

Uses of the CPI

The CPI is often used as a measure of inflation and serves as an indicator of the effectiveness of government economic policy. It is also used for economic analysis. Components of the CPI, such as the CPI series for food consumed at home, are also important as measures of price change for segments of the consumer's budget, and are used to analyze changing patterns of consumer behavior.

The CPI is used also as a deflator of other economic series; that is, it is used to adjust other series for price changes and to translate these series into inflation-adjusted values. Retail sales and hourly and weekly earnings are series for which the CPI is often used as a deflator. CPI components are used as deflators for most personal consumption expenditures in the calculation of the gross national product. For a review of how the price index is used to adjust the GNP, turn to chapter 9. A third major use of the CPI is to adjust income payments. More than 8.5 million workers are covered by collective bargaining contracts, which provide for increases in wage rates based on increases in the CPI. In addition to private sector workers whose wages or pensions are adjusted according to changes in the CPI, the index now affects public sector payments to more than 50 million persons, including Social Security beneficiaries, food stamp recipients, and retired military and federal civil service employees and their survivors. Under the National School Lunch Act and the Child Nutrition Act, national average subsidies for school lunches and breakfasts are adjusted annually by the secretary of agriculture on the basis of the change in the CPI series, "Food Away From Home."

The Economic Recovery Tax Act of 1981 provided for adjustments to the income tax structure based on the changes in the CPI-U in order to prevent inflation-induced tax rate increases. These adjustments are designed to offset the phenomenon called "bracket creep." Bracket creep occurs when inflation-driven wage hikes push taxpayers into higher tax rate categories (brackets).

Just as the CPI should not be used as a cost-of-living index, it should not be used to measure the differences in price levels between and among cities. The local city and regional CPI information released by the BLS cannot be used to determine "high cost" or "low cost" cities or regions. Why? Because these area indexes measure only the average change in price for each area since the base period. The indexes say nothing about the level of prices at the beginning of the base period.

Local area CPIs can be used to determine whether prices in one area are rising faster or slower than prices in other areas (or in the nation as a whole). However, it is impossible to tell from those separate indexes whether prices are higher in one area than another. This is because the CPI measures only the change in prices. It does not measure the price levels. In the February 1986 consumer price index for selected U.S. cities (table 12.4), the all-item CPI-U (1967 = 100) for Pittsburgh was 330.1 and for Philadelphia was 320.1. This does not

Table 12.4 Consumer Price Index, All Urban Consumers, Selected Areas (1967 = 100)

	CPI-U Index Feb. 1986
U.S. city average	327.5
Philadelphia, PA-NJ	320.1
Chicago, IL-Northwestern IN	326.4
Detroit, MI	322.9
L.A.-Long Beach-Anaheim, CA	326.6
New York, NY-Northeastern NJ	322.3
Pittsburgh, PA	330.1
Atlanta, GA	336.9
Buffalo, NY	310.1
Cleveland, OH	350.2
Dallas-Forth Worth, TX	347.0
Honolulu, HI	301.2
Houston, TX	337.2
Kansas City, MO-KS	321.1
Minneapolis-St. Paul, MN-WI	339.9
San Francisco-Oakland, CA	341.1

Source: U.S. Department of Labor, Bureau of Labor Statistics.

necessarily mean that prices or living costs were higher at that time in Pittsburgh than in Philadelphia.

What the index numbers do indicate is that since the base year, the prices of a fixed market basket of goods and services in Pittsburgh have been rising at a greater rate than those in Philadelphia. While both the Pittsburgh and Philadelphia indexes have 1967 as the base period, that does not mean the price levels were the same in both cities in 1967. The base-period index ignores the actual prices: the prices in both cities, which may have been different, were arbitrarily set at 100. Furthermore, the Pittsburgh index measures only the change in prices for Pittsburgh, and the Philadelphia index measures only the change in prices in Philadelphia.

Suppose that in 1967, the actual dollar cost of the CPI market basket was $125 in Chicago and $100 in Atlanta. For purposes of the CPI, both would be arbitrarily labeled "100," as has been done in the following hypothetical example:

	Chicago	Atlanta
Cost of market basket in 1967	$125	$100
1967 Index	100	100
Price increase 1967–76	20% ($25)	25% ($25)
1976 Index	120	125
Cost of market basket in 1976	$150 ($125 + $25)	$125 ($100 + $25)

Note that the index for 1976 is 120 for Chicago and 125 for Atlanta—an increase since 1967 of 20 percent for Chicago and 25 percent for Atlanta. The higher 1976 index for Atlanta indicates that the cost of the market basket rose faster (by a greater percentage) in Atlanta. This will not, however, support the conclusion that the actual cost of the market basket is higher in Atlanta than in Chicago. In our example, the 1976 cost of the market basket would still be higher in Chicago than in Atlanta ($150 versus $125).

In terms of dollars and cents, each city started from a different point in 1967. There is nothing in the CPI figures to tell us which city had higher prices then, or which had higher prices in 1976. To make interarea comparisons, then, you must supplement CPI information with data about the actual price levels in the areas being compared.

A Banker's Guide to Using the CPI

Bankers should be able to translate the announced changes in the CPI index number system into meaningful inflation percentage rates. Table 12.5 shows index increases and percent-

Table 12.5 Consumer Price Index, 1965–86
(1967 = 100)

Year	Index	Change from Previous Year Points	Change from Previous Year Percentage
1965	94.5	—	—
1966	97.2	2.7	2.9
1967	100.0	2.8	2.9
1968	104.2	4.2	4.2
1969	109.8	5.6	5.4
1970	116.3	6.5	5.9
1971	121.3	5.0	4.3
1972	125.3	4.0	3.3
1973	133.1	7.8	6.2
1974	147.7	14.6	11.0
1975	161.2	13.5	9.1
1976	170.5	9.3	5.8
1977	181.5	11.0	6.5
1978	195.4	13.9	7.7
1979	217.4	22.0	11.3
1980	246.8	29.4	13.5
1981	272.4	25.6	10.4
1982	289.1	16.7	6.1
1983	298.4	9.3	3.2
1984	311.1	12.7	4.3
1985	322.2	11.1	3.6
1986	328.4	6.2	1.9

Source: Economic Report of the President, 1987.

age changes for selected years. The 1977 index was 181.5—up 81.5 index points from the base year (100.0) in 1967. This means that the cost of the market basket in 1977 was 81.5 percent greater than the cost of the same basket of goods and services in 1967.

In this example, measured against the base period of 1967, each index point is equal to one percentage point. But as we shall see below, the only time an index point is the equivalent of a percentage point is when it is being measured against the base year.

Computing Percent Changes in CPI Index Numbers

It is important not to confuse index points with percentage points. Except as indicated above, a one-point change in CPI does not equal a 1-percent change. When the measurement is made from the base period to some subsequent point in time, the index series readily shows not only the increase in index points, but also the increase in percentage (the inflation rate). Measurements between other points in time, however, require some additional computations to derive the change in terms of percentage.

For example, in 1968, the CPI advanced to 104.2, an increase over 1967 of 4.2 points and 4.2 percent. This increase, measured against the base year (1967), produces a situation in which the change in points and the change in percentage are identical. This is not the case in any other year. The index in 1969 moved up to 109.8, an increase of 5.6 points above 1968. That increase, however, was equal to 5.4 percent over the 1968 index. And in 1970, the index advanced an additional 6.5 points over 1969, which amounted to 5.9 percent over the 1969 index.

The formula used to compute a percentage increase or decrease in the CPI (or in any set of data) is as follows: (1) divide the amount of the change by the figure from which the change occurred, then (2) multiply by 100. An 81.5 percent change in the CPI from 1967 to 1977 is actually 81.5 index points (the amount of change) divided by 100 (the figure from which the change occurred). Multiplying the dividend (0.815) by 100 yields 81.5 percent. Similarly, the change from 1966 through 1972 would be 125.3 minus 97.2, or 28.1 index points for the amount of change, divided by 97.2, which comes to 0.289. The decimal is multiplied by 100, in order to obtain the percentage—in this case, 28.9 percent. In the same way, between 1965 and 1967, the CPI increased 5.8 percent. The amount of change, 5.5 (100 − 94.5) is divided by 94.5, and then multiplied by 100.

Using the conversion formulas from chapter 2, you can convert month-to-month changes in the CPI to a percentage change at an annual rate. The CPI can also be used to calculate the rate of inflation between 2 years. To do so, you simply divide the most recent CPI by the earlier one, subtract one from the total and multiply the resulting number by 100. The formula is expressed as follows:

$$\text{Inflation rate} = \left[\frac{\text{CPI in most recent year}}{\text{CPI in earlier year}} - 1 \right] \times 100.$$

For example, the CPI in 1969 was 109.8, and in 1974, 147.7. To find the rate of inflation between 1969 and 1974, divide 147.7 by 109.8, subtract one, and multiply by 100.

$$\left[\frac{147.7}{109.8} - 1 \right] \times 100 = 35\%$$

THE EFFECTS OF INFLATION

Inflation is a major economic problem. Certainly the fact that prices rise over time can be viewed as potentially harmful to consumers. But what is it that makes inflation dangerous to an economy? Do not rising prices, ceteris paribus, mean increasing revenues for businesses and, perhaps, higher profits? Would not these higher profits mean greater dividends, salaries and wages, and so on? Is inflation a simple matter of taking money out of the economy's left pocket and placing it into its right? One fact is clear: the effects of inflation are not distributed evenly across all economic agents. To understand why this is so, you must remember the definition of inflation given at the beginning of the chapter. It is the average price level that rises. To further complicate matters, the average price level does not increase at a steady, smooth pace. Thus, inflation is very difficult to predict.

Some people are very good at predicting inflation. These people may be able to adjust their economic behavior to compensate for and perhaps even take advantage of rising prices. Others may be employed in situations in which long-term wage contracts include clauses that link future payments to inflation levels. Many labor agreements contain cost-of-living adjustment (COLA) clauses that increase future wage rates in the event of inflation. Congress has provided for the effects of inflation on the income of retired citizens by indexing Social Security benefits. Commercial banks have attempted to protect the real value of loan payments from inflation by the adoption of variable rate loans.

Other people, however, fail to anticipate inflation or perhaps are unable to modify their earning, spending, and lending activities to adjust for inflation. These people may suffer economic losses as a result.

In any case, the end result of inflation is a redistribution of wealth in an unsystematic, inequitable fashion. Before looking at winners and losers in times of inflation, it is important to understand how inflation affects the purchasing power of one's money.

There are two types of income. Money, or nominal income, is simply the amount earned for work performed. This amount is unadjusted for inflation. Real, or adjusted, income has been "deflated" to remove the distortions of inflation. Recall that any nominal income value can be adjusted by the following formula:

$$\text{Real income} = \frac{\text{Nominal income}}{\text{Price index (expressed as a decimal)}}.$$

In percentage terms, the formula is approximated by the following:

$$\Delta \text{ Real income} = \Delta \text{ Nominal income} - \Delta \text{ Price level}.$$

For example, if an employee's nominal or money income increases by 12 percent in a year, and prices rise by 10 percent in the same period, real income is said to have increased by only 2 percent. Similarly, a 12 percent increase in nominal income, accompanied by a 15 percent rise in the price level, will lead to a 3 percent decrease in real income.

Thus, inflation is inversely related to the purchasing power of the dollar. As the rate of inflation increases, the value of your money decreases. The change in the value of a dollar from a base-year period is expressed as the reciprocal of the CPI written as a decimal (1/CPI). Table 12.6 illustrates the value of a dollar for various periods compared with a base year of 1967. Notice, a 1967 dollar lost $.20 by 1972, was worth $.55 in 1977, and by 1985 was worth only $.31 in terms of a 1967 dollar's purchasing power.

Table 12.6 Consumer Price Index and the Value of a Dollar

Year	CPI	Value of Dollar [1/(CPI/100)]
1967	100.0	1.00
1972	125.3	0.80
1977	181.5	0.55
1982	289.1	0.35
1985	322.2	0.31

Source: U.S. Bureau of Labor Statistics.

Savers and Spenders

As a whole, savers suffer most from unanticipated inflation. As the inflation rate rises, the real value of the amount saved in terms of purchasing power decreases. The worst erosion occurs in cash holdings where no interest is earned to offset the inflation. For example, from 1967 to 1985, the CPI-U increased from 100 index points to approximately 327.0. In other words, every $1 put away as savings in 1967 had a purchasing power value of only $ .31 in 1985 [$1/(3.27/100)]. Of course, the vast majority of financial instruments available to savers, from savings accounts to bonds, earn interest. However, if the rate of interest earned on savings is less than the rate of inflation, a net loss of purchasing power can still result. For example, a bondholder earning 10 percent interest per annum but faced with 13 percent inflation suffers approximately a 3 percent erosion in the value of the interest payment per year.

This adverse effect on the value of savings is one reason why runaway inflation can be sustained. Consumers may be tempted to "buy" now and beat future price increases rather than save current income. Inflation-induced spending fuels the inflation by creating excess demand in the marketplace.

Debtors and Creditors

Price level increases can drastically alter the calculus that exists between creditors and debtors. Inflation tends to punish creditors and benefit debtors. Remember, inflation reduces the purchasing power of a dollar. Debtors therefore repay creditors with dollars that are worth less than those originally loaned. Of course, interest charges may more than offset the damage to the real value of the loan. However, if interest rates do not keep pace with inflation, the creditor essentially winds up paying the debtor to put the lender's money to use. This situation underscores the significant difference between nominal and real interest rates. The nominal rate of interest is the stated or posted rate of interest. The real rate of interest is the inflation-adjusted nominal interest rate. For example, if the stated rate of interest for a loan is 9.5 percent per year and inflation is measured at 5.0 percent for the period, the real rate of interest is 4.0 percent. Certain fixed-rate loans of long duration can actually yield a negative real interest rate for the lender. The negative real interest rates suffered by many creditors in the high-inflation years of 1978–81 may have prompted the adoption of variable rate loans.

Fixed-Income and Flexible-Income Earners

Those individuals who, for some reason or another, have sources of income that are fixed, or relatively fixed, will face purchasing power reductions of their income as the average price level rises. For example, retired individuals on fixed monthly pensions or annuities can suffer drastic losses in real income. As noted above, in practice, at least a part of this problem has been addressed for Social Security recipients by the indexation of benefits. Also, certain workers whose incomes are held constant for long periods without the benefits of periodic review or cost-of-living adjustments can be damaged. Basically, any income group whose income increases at a slower rate than the rate of inflation suffers a real income decline. Conversely, those individuals whose incomes increase faster than the inflation rate, gain.

Employees who have extraordinary market power, or who benefit from a strong union representation, may be able to demand and receive income increases that exceed inflation. Workers in expanding industries may also gain while those in older, declining sectors, or those without strong organized power may lose. However, in a fully employed economy, rising prices must mean greater incomes for someone. Therefore, higher prices could mean higher profits or increased compensation for all employees involved in profit sharing.

Not all union employees receive total real wage protection from COLA clauses. Very few COLA clauses have 100 percent pass-through language. That is, most COLA clauses increase wages by only a certain fraction of the inflation rate. Other COLA clauses require a threshold amount of inflation to occur before the COLA benefits begin. In other words, if a COLA clause promises an increase in wages if and only if inflation exceeds 5 percent, workers will receive no benefit from COLA if inflation is less than 5 percent. If inflation is 4.5 percent, the COLA clause is inoperative. Real wages are therefore cut by 4.5 percent and the employee must rely on other negotiated compensation benefits for relief.

Public and Private Sectors

One of the greatest sources of income redistribution occurs between the public and private sectors. The public sector is, of necessity, a major debtor. From local municipal bond projects to massive federal borrowings, the public sector receives large amounts of funds from the private sector. In inflationary periods, the real value of that debt decreases. Thus, a real-wealth redistribution from the creditors in the private sector to the debtors in the public sectors occurs. Also, to the extent that inflation leads to higher nominal or money wages, the tax revenues of certain states and the federal government rise dramatically. The progressive structure of the federal income tax leads to extremely large inflation windfalls that accrue to the federal government. The Reagan administration took steps to eliminate bracket creep by incrementally indexing tax rates beginning with the 1985 tax year.

THE SOURCES OF INFLATION

One of the greatest controversies among economists is the source or cause of inflation. Many economists hold that inflation is a money phenomenon and is the result of excessive growth in the money supply. Other economists blame inflation on massive federal deficits, or on large union-sponsored wage increases that are unrelated to productivity, or on monopolistic pricing practices of large firms in noncompetitive industries, or on the predatory pricing practices of cartels such as OPEC. Other economists hold a more eclectic view, blaming inflation on all of the above causes plus a few others. It may be useful to think of inflation as a collection of types, caused by different things. Seven major types of inflation are discussed below.

Demand-Pull Inflation

This traditional form of inflation links rising prices to excess demand. When the total demand (spending) of consumers, businesses, and governments exceeds the supply of goods and services available, prices are pulled up by the competitive pressures generated by that spending. Typically, total demand increases faster than the supply of goods available when there is rapid growth in the nation's money supply. Some economists characterize demand-pull inflation as a condition in which "too much money chases too few goods."

Cost-Push Inflation

In this form of inflation, prices are "pushed" up by producers who offset increases in their production costs by marking up prices and passing costs on to consumers. Powerful labor unions are sometimes blamed for cost-push inflation. Through threat of strikes, union employees may receive very large wage increases. Companies may attempt to "push" these new costs onto the end users of the product.

This is not to say that every labor cost increase is inflationary. Labor cost increases can be offset by productivity increases. For example, if worker productivity rises by 3 percent, a 5 percent wage hike will increase unit labor costs by only 2 percent. On the other hand, if a firm experiences declining productivity, unit labor costs may increase at a greater rate than wages. A 5 percent wage hike coupled with a 5 percent reduction in productivity can mean a 10 percent increase in unit labor costs, and depending upon both the percentage of labor costs in total costs and competitive conditions, prices may be increased accordingly.

The link between demand-pull and cost-push inflation is called the wage-price spiral. As demand-pull pressure drives up prices, workers seek higher wages to compensate for their loss of purchasing power. To the extent that they succeed in obtaining higher wages, they drive up production costs. Producers raise prices in an effort to offset these cost increases and to protect their profit margins. With prices higher, workers again see a loss in the purchasing power of their incomes and press for still higher wages. If obtained, these higher wages drive up production costs and the cycle continues. COLA clauses only strengthen the spiral.

Scarcity-Induced Inflation

This term refers to a condition of rising prices caused by a natural or cartel-induced shortage of a key commodity or good. In the 1970s, America's inflation was aggravated by a worldwide drought that created a scarcity of wheat and grain (and drove up food prices) and by OPEC's control of world oil supplies and fivefold increase in the price of oil.

Administered Inflation

This type of inflation is triggered by profit-hungry firms that, because of a noncompetitive market advantage, are able to raise prices with relative ease. The most highly publicized cases of administered inflation in recent years were the pricing policies of the oil companies during the oil crisis, and the automobile companies' raising of prices in the face of declining sales.

Expectation-Induced Inflation

If economic agents anticipate inflation, or if a round of inflation has begun, they may take action that actually increases inflationary pressures. For example, consumers may attempt to cushion the impact of future price hikes by increasing current purchases. Large corporations may also participate in these forward-buying schemes in anticipation of higher prices. The resulting increase in demand for goods and services leads to higher prices.

Inflation Resulting From Government Deficits

That massive government deficits can be inflationary should come as no surprise. When individuals buy government securities, their savings are channeled to the government. These savings are transformed into government spending on goods and services or into transfer payments to individuals (which eventually are placed in the spending cycle). This type of inflation can be viewed as a subset of demand-pull inflation. If these deficits are financed by simple money creation, the effect on prices can be dramatic.

Foreign Exchange Rates and Inflation

If the exchange-rate value of the dollar declines, a portion of that change in value may show up in higher prices for imports and the domestic goods that compete against those imports.[2] When the value of the dollar depreciates, the prices of imports and exports change. The magnitude of the price change depends upon the amount of dollar depreciation, and the amount of the depreciation "passed through" to export and import prices. The degree of the pass-through depends upon the products involved, producer profit margins, capacity utilization, expectations regarding future foreign exchange values, and competitive conditions. Dollar depreciation can cause import prices to rise, which will lead to increases in the consumer price index. One popular rule of thumb is that a 10 percent depreciation in the dollar leads to a 1.5 percent increase in consumer prices over a 3-year period.[3] Inflation caused by dollar depreciation can precipitate additional wage and price inflationary pressure.

Eclectic View

Economic researcher D.W. Cho recently polled economists as to how they formed their own inflationary expectations.[4] Cho surveyed members of the National Association of Business Economists and asked economists to identify what information they use to develop expectations concerning the future inflation rate. The economists were provided a selection of possible inputs including economic variables, popular economic indicators, and certain noneconomic factors. The three most frequently cited variables were past inflation rates, changes in money supply, and wage rates. Other important sources were oil prices, government deficits, prices of certain key raw materials, and wage rates and settlements.

INFLATION AND REAL OUTPUT

So far, our examination of the effects of inflation has been made under the assumptions that the economy is at full employment and real output (GNP) is constant. Under such conditions, inflation simply transfers wealth from one group or sector to another. However, this ideal situation does not match reality: the GNP is not fixed, and the economy is rarely at full employment. Recent events indicate that, more than simply redistributing the total income of our economy, inflation also leads to changes in real output and employment.

Mild demand-pull inflation may act as a stimulus to economic activity. If prices rise because of excess demand, and revenues rise before wages and material costs catch up, business profits will increase. This profit increase may lead to production increases, new investments in plant and equipment, and subsequent increases in employment and earnings. Of course, this increase in economic output can only occur if there are idle resources available in the economy.

Inflation may also lead to a reduction of real output. If inflation is severe enough, the drop in output can become a full-blown economic recession. Let us start with a full-employment, constant real output condition. As a number of firms attempt to increase prices, perhaps in response to a significant increase in labor costs, employees in those sectors of the economy who have been unable to extract similar wage gains may turn away from those products. If these products are in major industries such as auto and steel, the loss of sales and subsequent drop in production and employment could reverberate through the entire economy. In an attempt to reduce losses, these firms may raise prices still further, creating a condition of rising prices with below full-capacity levels of output and employment. The end result is an inflationary recession, a condition that has been dubbed stagflation. The U.S. economy experienced stagflation from 1979 to 1981, when the inflation rates of 13.3 percent, 12.4 percent, and 9.4 percent for those 3 years were accompanied by unemployment rates of 5.8 percent, 7.0 percent, and 7.5 percent. The combined effects of simultaneous inflation and unemployment can be devastating to an economy, and extremely frustrating for policymakers.

Inflation and Unemployment

The combined effects of inflation and unemployment can be quite unpleasant to many economic agents. A method to measure the combined effect of both inflation and unemployment has been developed, which is called the discomfort index. The discomfort index is the sum of the unemployment rate and the rate of increase in the consumer price index. For example, in 1980 the inflation and unemployment rates were 12.4 and 7.0, respectively, which describes a discomfort index of 19.4. By 1986, the discomfort index fell to 8.0.

It is the belief of most economists that the stagflation experienced by the U.S. economy in the 1978–81 period was anomalous. Normally, an economy experiences either relatively high inflation or relatively high unemployment, but not both problems at once. The consensus on inflation normally locates the primary source of inflation in either excessive growth in the money supply or demand-pull inflation. However, the inflation component of the 1978–81 stagflation has been traced to cost-push, or administered, inflation. It appears incorrect to blame excess aggregate demand for the inflation when unemployment and unused capacity are at high levels. Noted economist Abba Lerner has explained past stagflation this way: "Prices may rise because of pressures by sellers who insist on raising prices even though they may find it not especially easy to sell. We would then have not a buyer-induced inflation but a seller-induced inflation."[5]

ECONOMICS FOR BANKERS

Stagflation aside, the vast majority of our post-World War II economic history has been characterized by either inflation or unemployment. It is apparent that, for most periods, reductions in inflation can only be accomplished by increases in unemployment, and reductions in unemployment will normally only occur if inflation rises. The first economist to popularize this economic policy dilemma was A.W. Phillips. In a famous 1950 article, Phillips, a British economist, showed evidence of the trade-off between wage-rate growth and unemployment.[6] Phillips had found that, in Great Britain, a rather stable negative relationship existed between unemployment and wage-rate growth (figure 12.1). Line PP' shows the best-fit relationship between changes in money wage rates (a proxy for inflation) and unemployment. This line is known as the Phillips Curve. In the British experience, attempts to push unemployment below 4 percent lead to increasingly large doses of inflation, and on the other hand, attempts to reduce inflation (in other words, to approach very low increases in money wages) can only come about through large additional increments in unemployment.

Figure 12.1 Phillips Curve for Great Britain, 1861–1913

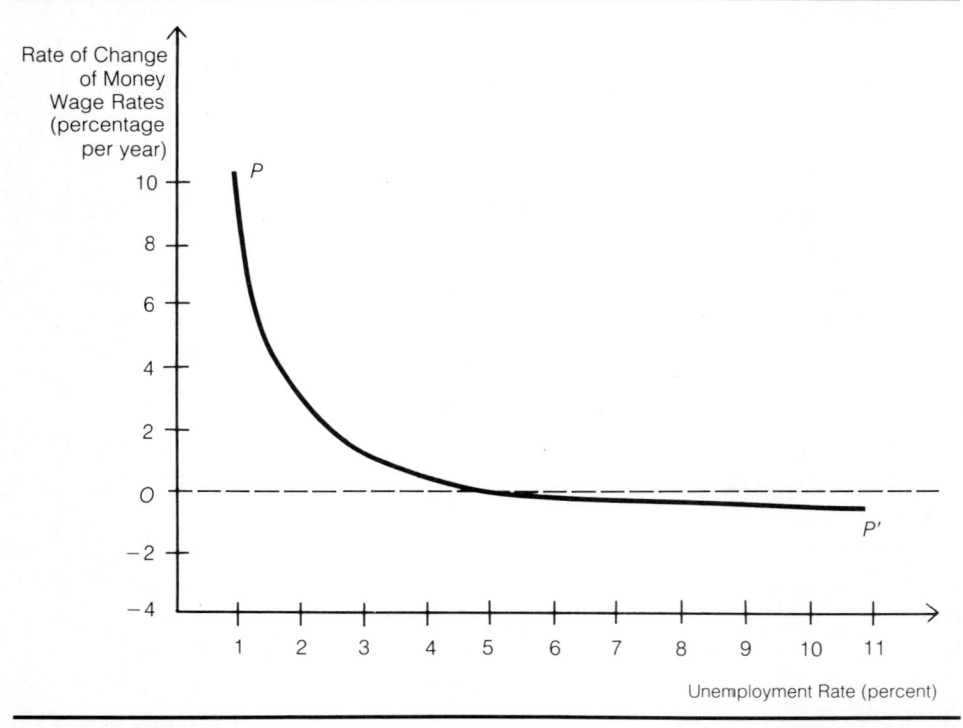

Source: A.W. Phillips, "The Relation between Unemployment and the Rate of Change of Money Wage Rates in the United Kingdom, 1861–1957." *Economica* New Series 25 (November 1958) pp. 283–299.

INFLATION

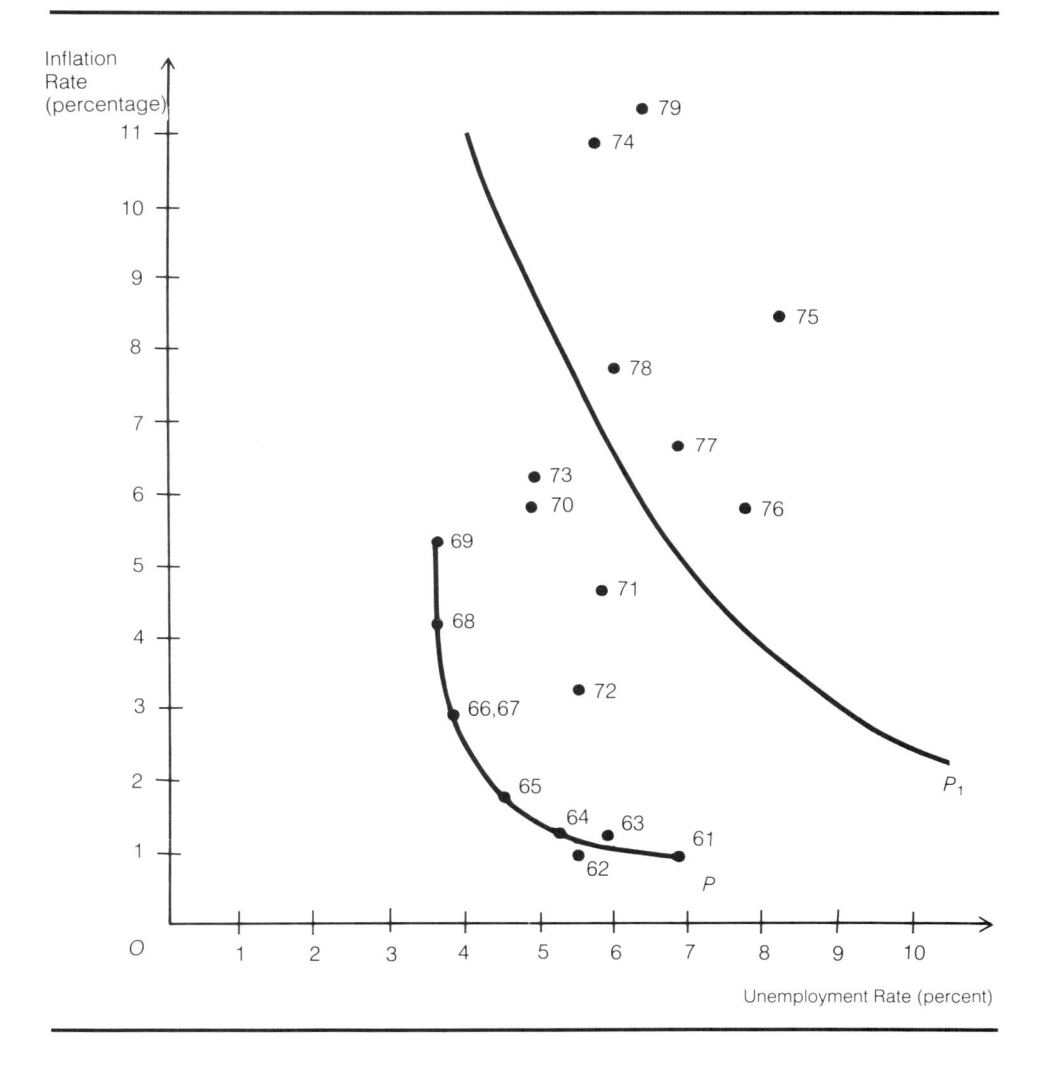

Figure 12.2 Phillips Curves for the United States, 1960s and 1970s

Use of the Phillips Curve has become so widespread that the trade-off between inflation and unemployment has become known simply as the "Phillips Curve dilemma." In more recent analyses, the rather awkward "change in money wage rates" label for the vertical axis on the original curve has been replaced by the more tractable "inflation rate."[7]

Figure 12.2 shows two Phillips Curve diagrams for the U.S. economy, one (P) for the decade of the 1960s and the other (P^1) for the 1970s. Notice how the 1960s Phillips Curve of inflation and unemployment upholds the standard trade-off. However, the 1970s curve portrays a much different relationship. While the relationship between the variables is still inverse, the entire curve has shifted outward to the right, away from the origin. In other words, the inflation rates of the 1960s can only be maintained in the 1970s by a much higher level of unemployment. Conversely, in order to reduce unemployment to the levels of the 1960s, the 1970s inflation penalty was much higher. This analysis suggests that while the inflationary pressures of the 1960s were of the typical demand-pull variety, the inflation of the 1970s was of a different kind, perhaps cost-push or administered inflation.

The first half of the 1980s shows mixed results (table 12.7). In the years 1980–82, the economy experienced both relatively high levels of inflation and unemployment. These data suggest a pattern similar to that in the 1970s. The data for 1983–85, however, reveal an inflation-employment pattern reminiscent of the 1960s. If this pattern continues, economic policy options in the late 1980s, while still difficult, will be much brighter than those of the 1970–82 period.[8]

Table 12.7 Phillips Curve Data for the 1980s

Year	Inflation Rate (percent)	Unemployment Rate (percent)
1980	12.4	7.0
1981	8.9	7.5
1982	3.9	9.5
1983	3.8	9.5
1984	4.0	7.4
1985	3.8	7.0
1986	1.1	6.9

Source: U.S. Department of Commerce.

If we plot Phillips Curve data for the 1960s through the 1980s, the information may at first appear chaotic (figure 12.3). However, if the general shape of the curve is superimposed on the data for each decade, the graph reveals an interesting series of progressions away from and back toward the origin (figure 12.4).

Curve P again represents the 1960s. Curves P_1 and P_2 represent early and later periods in the 1970s, and curve P_3 is the pattern for the early 1980s. Curves P_1 through P_3 progress away from the origin, indicating an overall pattern of rising inflation and rising unemployment. Each major shift in the curve is signaled by a dramatic jump in the unemployment rate (in 1971, 1974–75, and 1980–82), after which unemployment drops back slightly while inflation rises.

Since 1982, however, both unemployment and inflation have dropped substantially, pushing the curve back toward the origin. The unemployment and inflation rates for 1986 are remarkably close to the rates experienced in 1961. In a sense, the years 1982–86 describe a break in the acceleration of inflation and unemployment. A Phillips Curve constructed for the late 1980s may, as a result, resemble the curve for the 1960s very closely.

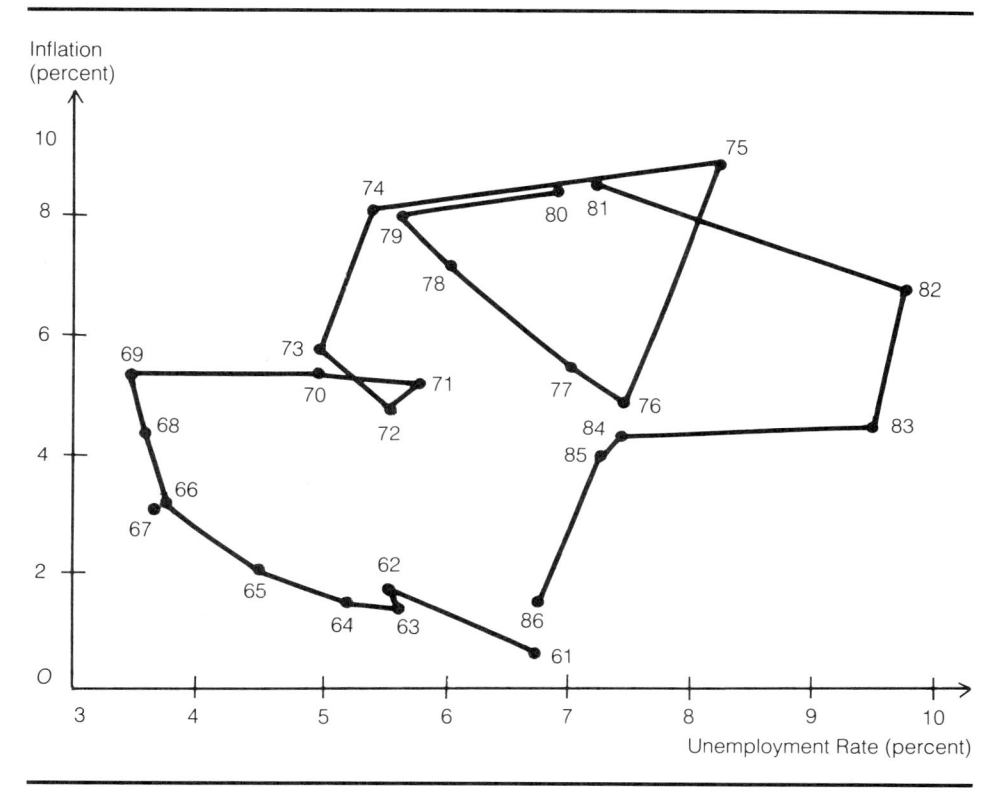

Figure 12.3 Phillips Curve Data, 1961–86

Hyperinflation

In some countries, inflation rates regularly exceed 100 percent per year. While there is no official definition of the term, it is safe to call inflation rates exceeding 100 percent hyperinflation. Normally, hyperinflation is a monetary phenomenon. When governments require funds to purchase goods and services, it is always a temptation for them to simply print money rather than tax their citizens. This politically expedient measure is extremely dangerous and invariably leads to hyperinflation. The most famous instance of hyperinflation occurred in post-World War I Germany. In an effort to pay staggering war reparations and reconstruct a devasted infrastructure, the German government resorted to simply printing currency to "create" government spending power. Inflation leaped from a base of 100 in 1919 to almost 1,200,500,000,000 by 1923. In 1923 alone, inflation of consumer prices amounted to almost 4 trillion percent. This type of inflation crippled the currency and

ECONOMICS FOR BANKERS

Figure 12.4 Phillips Curves, 1961–86

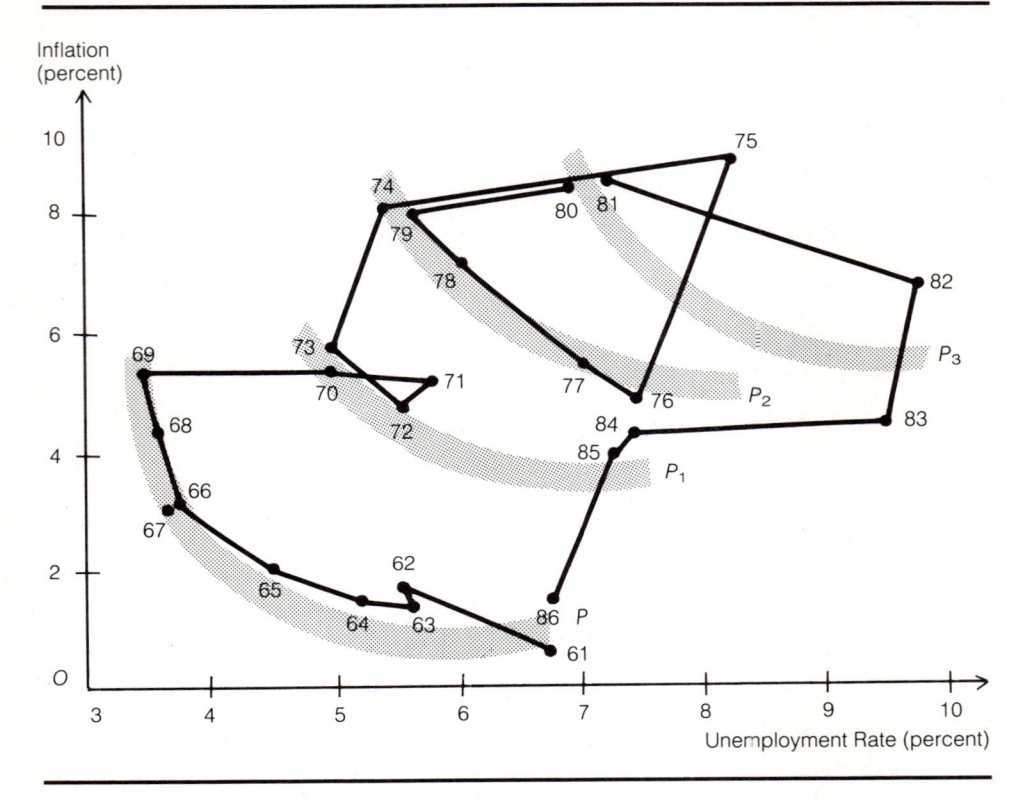

reduced Germany to a barter economy. Workers refused to accept payment in money. Many workers demanded and received food as salary. Those workers who did accept currency actually had to carry their weekly earnings home in horse-drawn wagons! The real value of the savings of millions of middle-class Germans was reduced to virtually nothing. Many experts believe the losses and bitterness experienced by the Germans during this period laid the groundwork for the frustration and hatred that would erupt some 15 years later.

The German hyperinflation following World War I is not, however, the worst case of hyperinflation. Following World War II, the Hungarian government began printing pengo notes in earnest. In 1940, one U.S. dollar could be exchanged for 6 Hungarian pengos. By 1946, the exchange rate had risen to one U.S. dollar for 6.3 quintillion pengos. A quintillion is a 100 followed by 18 zeros. To get from 6 to 6,300,000,000,000,000,000 took a 5-quadrillion percent inflation rate!

SUMMARY

Inflation is a substantial, sustained increase in the average level of prices. The inflation rate measures the rate of increase of prices.

The consumer price index is a commonly used measure of inflation based on changes in the price of a specific market basket of goods and services that an average urban family would purchase. The CPI is released monthly by the Bureau of Labor Statistics. It is not, however, a perfect measure of inflation: the CPI does not reflect any one person's purchases, nor can the market basket be changed quickly enough to keep pace with changing consumption patterns.

Inflation decreases the purchasing power of the dollar. The quantity of real goods and services that can be purchased for a given sum of money decreases during periods of inflation. Inflation results in a redistribution of income in an unsystematic, inequitable manner primarily because some people are unable to anticipate and/or compensate for its effects. Inflation is particularly hard on savers, fixed-income earners, and, generally, creditors.

The major types of inflation include demand-pull inflation, which reflects excess aggregate demand, and cost-push inflation, which occurs in the absence of demand pressures, perhaps fueled by unions and big business. Other sources of inflation include scarcity, a lack of competition, expectations of consumers and producers, government deficits, and foreign exchange rates.

The Phillips Curve represents a statistical relationship between unemployment and inflation. Every point on the curve represents a unique combination of inflation and unemployment. The relationship normally is inverse. It appears that small reductions in the unemployment rate require a trade-off in the form of large increases in the inflation rate, and vice-versa.

Hyperinflation is a situation in which prices rise dramatically with little or no increase in output. Unchecked growth in a nation's money supply can trigger hyperinflation.

ECONOMICS FOR BANKERS

KEY WORDS

administered inflation
all-urban index
base year (period)
consumer expenditure survey
consumer price index (CPI)
cost of living
cost-push inflation
demand-pull inflation
expectation-induced inflation
forward buying

hyperinflation
inflation
market basket
negative real interest rate
nominal interest rate
Phillips Curve
real interest rate
scarcity-induced inflation
stagflation

Questions for Review

1. Why must the BLS continually revise the contents of the CPI market basket?

2. The CPI-U in 1980 was 246.8. If the base-year index is (1967 = 100), how much did a market basket of goods cost in 1980?

3. What economic conclusions can you draw from the following statements, singly and in combination?
   a) The 1983 CPI-U for Houston, TX was 320.6.
   b) The 1983 CPI-U for Buffalo, NY was 284.5.

4. If your nominal income increased by 10 percent last year and the inflation rate was 15 percent, by how much did your real income increase (or decrease)?

5. If Mr. Smith stashed $150 in a safe deposit box in 1967, what was the purchasing power of that money in 1985?

6. When are variable rate loans most appealing to bankers? Why? When are they most appealing to borrowers? Why?

7. Describe the connection between demand-push and cost-pull inflation.

8. Suppose Mrs. Jones purchased a home for $70,000 in 1980 and sold it for $75,000 in 1984. Calculate her real profit (or loss).

ENDNOTES

1. The material in this chapter regarding the price index has been condensed from material prepared by the Bureau of Labor Statistics. A detailed discussion on the methods used to construct the price index can be found in the 1987 revision of *The Consumer Price Index*, U.S. Department of Labor, Bureau of Labor Statistics, report 736, January 1987.

2. This discussion is based upon the research of Gerald H. Anderson. See Gerald H. Anderson, "How Desirable is Dollar Depreciation?" *Economic Commentary*, Federal Reserve Bank of Cleveland, December 15, 1985.

3. See Peter Hooper and Barbara Lowry, "Impact of the Dollar Depreciation on the U.S. Price Level: An Analytical Survey of Empirical Estimates," *International Finance Discussion Papers No. 128* (Washington, D.C.: Board of Governors of the Federal Reserve System, January 1979).

4. Dong W. Cho, "Formation of Inflationary Expectations by Business Economists," *Business Economics*, vol. 21, no.2 (April 1986), p. 35.

5. Abba P. Lerner, "Inflationary Depression and the Regulation of Administered Prices," *The Relationship of Prices to Economic Stability and Growth* (Compendium of Papers submitted by Panelists Appearing before the Joint Economic Committee) 85 Cong. 2 Sess. (Washington, D.C.: U.S. Government Printing Office, 1958), pp. 257–68; reprinted in *Readings in Macroeconomics*, ed. M.G. Mueller, (New York: Holt, Rinehart and Winston, 1966), p. 362.

6. A.W. Phillips, "The Relation Between Unemployment and the Rate of Change of Money Wage Rates in the United Kingdom, 1861–1957," *Economica*, New Series 25 (November 1958), pp. 283–99.

7. The relationship between changes in money wage rates and inflation is as follows: if wages grow at a rate faster than labor productivity, inflation is likely to result. If labor productivity growth exceeds the growth in money wages, deflation likely will occur. If money wage growth equals labor productivity growth, prices will probably remain stable. Phillips estimated that at a 2 percent annual increase in productivity, price stability would occur if unemployment were 2.5 percent per annum. At unemployment rates below 2.5 percent, Britain would normally experience inflation, and unemployment would have to be pushed to 5.5 percent to stop wage increases.

8. See Robert J. Gordon, "Understanding Inflation in the 1980s" *Brookings Papers on Economic Activity*, no. 1 (1985), pp. 263–99. See also, Beryl W. Sprinkel and Thomas Gale Moore, "Inflation, Disinflation, and the State of the Macroeconomy," *Economic Report of the President, 1986*, pp. 23–40.

ECONOMICS IN THE NEWS

Major labor contracts in 1986 provided record low wage adjustments

Negotiations again focused on efforts to curb labor costs and save jobs by providing small wage increases, wage decreases, and wage freezes; many settlements provided lump sums instead of wage increases or to offset decreases

John LaCombe and Joan Borum

In 1986, major collective bargaining settlements in private industry provided record low wage and compensation adjustments, reflecting both employers' and unions' efforts to curb labor costs. Their task was made easier by continued moderate upward pressures on wages from comparatively small increases in consumer prices. According to the Bureau of Labor Statistics' 19-year-old series on private industry agreements covering 1,000 workers or more,[1] wage adjustments—the net effect of decisions to increase, decrease, or not change wages—under settlements reached during 1986 averaged 1.2 percent in the first contract year and 1.8 percent annually over the contract term. . . . The settlements covered 2.5 million workers.

This was the fifth consecutive year in which settlements produced average wage adjustments that were substantially below those registered prior to 1982. . . . Wage adjustments which were actually put into effect during 1986, stemming from settlements negotiated that year and those reached in prior years, also averaged a record low—2.3 percent.

The last time parties to 1986 settlements negotiated (usually in 1983 or 1984), they agreed to contracts that specified average wage adjustments of 3.5 percent the first year and 3.2 percent annually over the term.

Total wage adjustments—those specified at the time of settlements plus any subsequent cost-of-living adjustments (COLA's)—averaged 4.0 percent a year over the contract term. This was the smallest on record, and occurred while the Consumer Price Index for Urban Wage Earners (CPI-W) was rising 3.5 percent a year (between December 1982 and December 1985).

The average size of total wage adjustments under expiring agreements has dropped steadily since 1983 because the size of specified wage changes declined and because smaller price increases produced lower wage increases triggered by COLA's. As shown in the following tabulation, the contracts preceding 1986 settlements yielded larger total wage adjustments when they included a COLA clause.

	Average wage adjustment (in percent) per year in contracts	
	With COLA	Without COLA
Total adjustment .	4.2	3.7
Specified	2.7	3.7
COLA	1.6	—

This marks a return to the pre-1983 pattern in which expiring contracts with COLA clauses provided smaller specified wage adjustments than those without, but COLA's more than made up the differences.

The bargaining climate

Bargaining during 1986 took place in a mixed national economic climate. The Consumer Price Index for Urban Wage Earners rose 0.7 percent during the year (the smallest rise since 1961) and unemployment continued to hover around 7 percent. Negotiators focused on both old and new problems, including: depressed markets and competition from abroad in the steel, aluminum, and copper industries; competition from nonunion firms in retail trade and construction; competition from both union and nonunion carriers in the airline industry; and the breakup of long-standing bargaining relationships in the steel and telephone communications industries. The most common issue was how to curb labor costs and retain jobs.

A number of contracts addressed this issue by such indirect methods as restructuring jobs or changing work rules. Other more direct approaches included historically low wage increases, freezes, or cuts; lump-sum payments (which are not included as wages in this series) instead of wage increases or to offset wage cuts; lower wage adjustments in the first than in subsequent years of multi-year contracts; and the suspension or elimination of COLA clauses.

Wage increases, decreases, and freezes

Average wage increases under 1986 settlements were the smallest on record for this series—2.9 percent the first contract year and 2.7 percent a year over the contract life. First-year increases were received by 1,730,000 workers, while 526,000 workers had no wage change and 230,000 sustained wage cuts averaging −9.2 percent. Subsequently, wage increases will go to 218,000 workers with no wage change and 15,000 with a wage decrease in the first contract year. Thus, over their term, contracts reached during 1986 will provide wage increases to 1,963,000 workers, about four-fifths of the total covered. Workers with increases were mostly in construction, railroads, telephone communication, public utilities, food stores, and health services.

The wages of about an eighth of the workers were frozen and those of about one-tenth were cut over the term of 1986 settlements, marking the fifth consecutive year in which substantial proportions of workers did not receive wage increases under settlements. . . . Workers with wage freezes were concentrated in construction, nonelectrical machinery manufacturing, and food stores. Workers sustaining pay cuts were mostly in steel manufacturing; some of them also took reductions in their previous agreement. . . .

---FOOTNOTE---
[1]The major collective bargaining agreement series for private industry covers 6.5 million workers in bargaining units with at least 1,000 workers. For definition of terms, see Current Labor Statistics, "Wage and Compensation Data," pp. 53–55. Additional tabulations from this series appear in the March 1987 issue of the Bureau's *Current Wage Developments*.

Excerpted from the *Monthly Labor Review*, May 1987, pp. 10-16.

CHAPTER THIRTEEN

CLASSICAL VERSUS KEYNESIAN ECONOMICS

Objectives

After reading this chapter, you should be able to

•

describe the economic relationships that exist between and among businesses, households, and governments, using the circular flow model

•

describe the economic roles each sector plays in the circular flow model of the economy

•

describe the basic tenets of Say's Law

•

explain how the classical economists used Say's Law and the concept of flexible wages and prices to conclude that the economy is basically self-correcting

•

explain how the Great Depression was a catalyst for the decline of the classical doctrine and the birth of Keynesian economics

•

list Keynes's major criticisms of the classical doctrine

What happens to an economy in a severe recession or depression? Do unemployment, factory closings, and despair continue unabated and, if so, for how long? What mechanisms or processes can offset the recessionary decline? Are these solutions internal to the economy, or must they be applied by an outside agent?

Historically, there have been two schools of thought regarding this question. The original theory, first proposed around 1800 and still embraced in a modernized form by many economists, is called the classical school of economic thought. Modern-day spokespersons of this theory are called neoclassical economists. This theory is based on the belief that any fluctuation in economic activity can be arrested and eventually corrected by market forces already in place in a free and open economy. The classical doctrine holds the economy to be, in effect, self-correcting.

Around 1930, a new body of thought developed that questioned the ability of an economic system to recover from economic disturbances. This revolution in economic thought was led by John Maynard Keynes, a prominent and wealthy British economist who criticized the classical dogma and suggested that an economy in trouble may not be able to recover unless outside forces were applied to correct internal deficiencies. Keynes developed a complete theory to accompany his policy recommendations. He has since become known as the father of modern economics.

This chapter investigates the foundations of classical economic thought and Keynesian critique of that doctrine, and introduces the basic tenets of Keynesian economics. To begin, however, it is helpful to study the basic flows of a typical economy in order to become familiar with the relationships that exist among the major economic agents. These flows are generally depicted in a diagram called the circular flow model (figure 13.1).

THE CIRCULAR FLOW OF THE U.S. ECONOMY

The circular flow model highlights the economic relationships between and among the major economic agents: businesses, households, and governments. It describes the major functions of each sector or agent, and also presents the three major markets of the economy: the input, product, and capital markets.

The households sector of the economy is the home of the owners of the four factors of production (land, labor, capital, and entrepreneurial ability). The households sector offers these resources to the business sector to use in the production of goods and services. The venue of these resource transactions is called the input market. The business sector then attempts to sell its goods and services in the product market to the household sector and the government sector. This flow of resources and products constitutes the real economy, as opposed to the monetary economy.

The money flows in our simplified model occur when the households sector receives resource payments (wages, rents, interest, and profits) from the business sector in return for

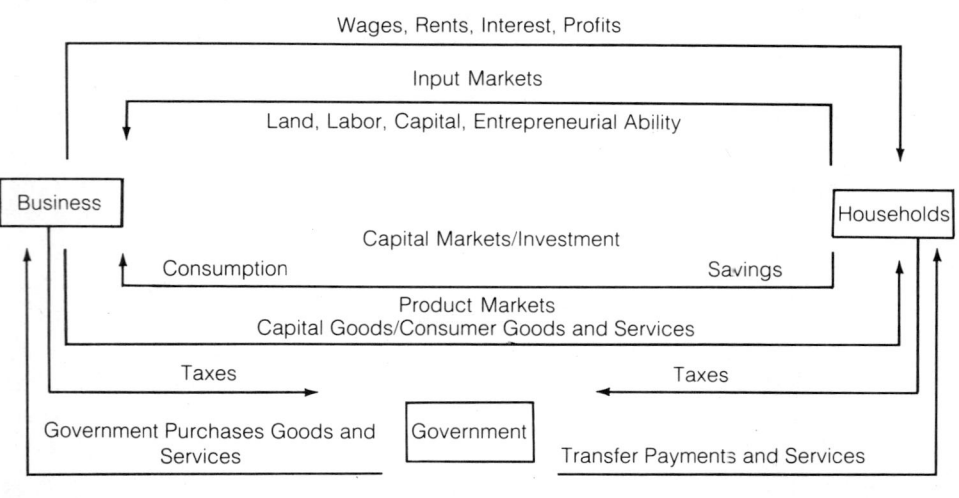

ECONOMICS FOR BANKERS

Figure 13.1 Circular Flow Model

```
                    Wages, Rents, Interest, Profits
          ┌─────────────────────────────────────────────────┐
          │              Input Markets                       │
          │   Land, Labor, Capital, Entrepreneurial Ability │
          │                    ↓                             │
   ┌──────────┐                                        ┌──────────┐
   │ Business │        Capital Markets/Investment      │Households│
   └──────────┘   Consumption              Savings     └──────────┘
          │          Product Markets                         │
          │   Capital Goods/Consumer Goods and Services      │
          │                                                  │
          │      Taxes →            ← Taxes                  │
          │                   ┌──────────┐                   │
          │ Government Purchases Goods and │Government│ Transfer Payments and Services
          │       Services    └──────────┘                   │
```

Source: American Bankers Association.

the use of the factors of production. This income is subsequently either (1) used to purchase goods and services in the product market, or (2) saved and/or placed in the capital markets where the funds act as a source of investment and consumption for others.

The government also plays an integral role in the economy. The government provides the legal framework, the domestic infrastructure, national defense, and social goods through legislation, taxation, and spending. Tax revenues flow to the government from both the households and the business sectors. The government uses these receipts to purchase goods and services and to provide transfer payments and services to both sectors. The government sector also enters the capital markets to obtain debt funding when government spending exceeds tax receipts. In the U.S., the federal government's role in the economy was expanded beyond that described in this model by the passage of the Employment Act of 1946. This law requires the executive branch of government to pursue policies that help to stabilize the business cycle, promote full employment and price stability, and ensure a minimum standard of living for all. Economists view the act of saving with caution. Savings can be considered a "leakage" in the circular flow. It might be helpful to think of the circular flow as the economy's body and the income and spending flows as its blood. If all of the income earned by the households sector is not spent on goods and services, the amount saved (not consumed) can be seen as a leakage from the system. For the system to remain healthy and vigorous, this "blood" (leakage) must be somehow "injected" back into the system. The primary purpose of the capital or investment market is to ensure that these "leakages" are returned to the economy as "injections" of additional consumption or investment spending. If these leakages are not returned to the economy, overproduction, unemployment, and loss of income may easily result.

THE CLASSICAL DOCTRINE

The classical statement of economic doctrine can be traced to a number of economists. Each of these individuals added points to the theory, and today, the sum of these arguments can be described as the classical theory. At the heart of the classical doctrine are the teachings of an 18th century French economist named Jean Baptiste Say. Say contended that a general economic glut is impossible. He held that the main source of the aggregate demand for goods and services is the flow of income to the owners of the factors of production. In other words, the mere act of producing products generates a stream of resource payments, which are then used to consume the products just produced. New resources are combined, adding to supply, but the new production also generates demand. The demand is backed by purchasing power received from the sale of resources in the input markets. The most simple distillation of Say's teachings has been formulated into what is now called the law of markets, or Say's Law: supply creates its own demand.[1]

Say's Law

David Ricardo, an English economist and contemporary of Say, was a leading spokesman of the classical doctrine of free markets. He added to Say's doctrine by asserting that not only was there an ability to purchase all that was produced, but there was also the desire to do so. If there has been one economic tenet that has withstood the test of time, it surely must be the classical argument that the desire for goods and services is infinitely large. Thus, Ricardo echoed Say's words and added that economic disturbances would as a result have very short life spans. He wrote:

> Say has, however, most satisfactorily shown, that there is no amount of capital which may not be employed in a country, because demand is only limited by production. No man produces, but with a view to consume or sell, and he never sells, but with an intention to purchase some other commodity, which may be immediately useful to him, or which may contribute to future production. By producing, then, he necessarily becomes either the consumer of his own goods, or the purchaser and consumer of the goods of some other person. . . . There cannot, then, be accumulated in a country any amount of capital which cannot be employed productively, until wages rise so high in consequence of the rise of necessaries, and so little consequently remains for the profits of stock, that the motive for accumulation ceases.[2]

Say's Law thus became the foundation for the classical doctrine of economic stability and growth. In 1776, Adam Smith told the world that capitalism could and would work. Free markets, self-interest, and the absence of government intervention were the essential ingredients of a successful society. Economic depressions and downturns were insignificant because the capitalistic economy was essentially self-correcting. Even population growth, a problem Thomas Malthus had thought might spell disaster for all societies, could be managed using this model.

In a growing nation, new workers and the new enterprises could be easily accommodated into the system, not by deploying existing firms and workers, but by producing their own products and offering these products in exchange. The market system, like the skin surrounding the human body, could stretch to fit an increasing volume of products. The marketplace was capable of expansion; it was not considered fixed or limited in size.

The classical economist did allow that overproduction or gluts of specific goods could occur. Yet these setbacks were seen as temporary, serving only as a sign for business to move to more profitable endeavors. The classical economists held that there are very powerful underlying forces at work which will tend to force the economy to full employment equilibrium.

The "Problem" of Savings

For the classical theory to hold, the flow of income generated in the production process must be spent in its entirety by the recipients. Proponents of classical theory believe that savings, or leakages from the circular flow, are injected back into the system as investment spending. The "problem" of savings is thus solved by investment.

Classical theory requires that the amount saved (leaked) be equal to the amount invested for the economy to maintain a full-employment equilibrium. Theoretically, the interest rate mechanism assures this result. Banks and other financial service businesses play a crucial role in this system. They collect the savings of households in what is called the loanable funds market and serve as conduits for these funds. The business sector borrows the funds and turns them into investment spending, which generates new employment opportunities. The injection of investment spending is theoretically sufficient to offset the leakage of savings. The market for loanable funds is shown in figure 13.2.

If the supply of loanable funds (savings) exceeds the demand for loanable funds (investment) the economy becomes depressed as leakages from the system exceed injections. In figure 13.2, at interest rate i_o, the quantity of loanable funds supplied is greater than the quantity demanded. In other words, the amount that people are willing to save exceeds the amount that business is willing to invest. At interest rate i_o, the economy experiences poor sales performance, layoffs, and reduced output.

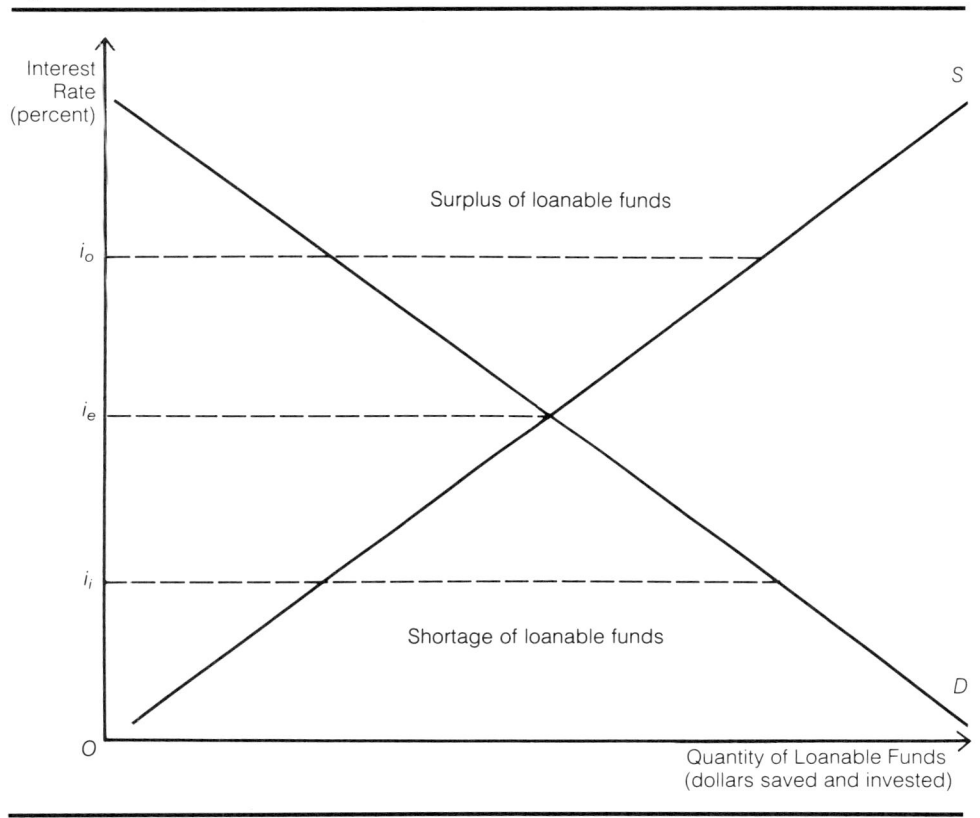

Figure 13.2 Savings and Investment in the Classical Model

[Graph showing Interest Rate (percent) on vertical axis and Quantity of Loanable Funds (dollars saved and invested) on horizontal axis. An upward-sloping supply curve S intersects a downward-sloping demand curve D at equilibrium interest rate i_e. Above equilibrium at i_0 is labeled "Surplus of loanable funds"; below equilibrium at i_1 is labeled "Shortage of loanable funds".]

The classical doctrine provides a simple answer for this dilemma. In free and open capital markets, the price of loanable funds (the interest rate) will begin to drop and continue dropping until the savings-investment conditions are stabilized at interest rate i_e. This equilibrium rate of interest equates the quantity supplied and quantity demanded for loanable funds. The amount saved equals the amount invested, and the economy returns to full employment, without inflation.

Similarly, at interest rate i_1, the amount businesses want to invest exceeds the amount consumers desire to save, resulting in a shortage of loanable funds. In response, capital market forces drive the interest rates up to i_e, where the shortage is eliminated. Again, a balance is struck between savings and investment—the total amount of the leakage is now equal to the total amount of the injection. In this way, the interest rate mechanism automatically provides for a level of total spending sufficient to maintain full employment.

Price-Wage Flexibility

One more loophole remains to be addressed by classical doctrine. Suppose the combined effects of Say's Law and the interest rate mechanism are not sufficient to generate a level of spending consistent with full employment. What if pockets of unemployment remain, and this unemployment begins to reduce total income and purchasing power? The classical theory has one more mechanism to protect against a prolonged bout of unemployment or product glut. In an open labor market, supply and demand forces operate to restore employment. Classical economists hold to the belief in free and open markets for labor and products as well as for loanable funds. If unemployment occurs, it does not last long, according to the classicists. Wage rates will drop, and businesses will then hire the unemployed in response to lower wage rates. One of the staunchest defenders of the classical doctrine, A.C. Pigou, was a prominent British economist who felt the only reason unemployment might linger is because wages were not sufficiently flexible.

> With perfectly free competition . . . there will always be at work a strong tendency for wage rates to be so related to demand that everybody is employed. . . . The implication is that such unemployment as exists at any time is due wholly to the fact that changes in demand conditions are continually taking place and that frictional resistances prevent the appropriate wage adjustments from being made instantaneously.[3]

Classical economists believe that unsold goods will lead to price declines, which rapidly increase the quantity demanded for these products. Increased sales spur greater and greater production, leading to worker recalls. Thus, within a short time, the economy automatically returns to its full employment level. This noninflationary level of full employment is referred to as natural employment. The companion natural unemployment rate is the amount of unemployment that would exist when the economy is at full employment, with noninflationary output. Natural unemployment consists of frictionally and structurally unemployed individuals.

The classical theory can be summarized as follows: all markets are assumed to be free, open, and competitive. Supply creates its own demand (Say's Law) and works to ensure that aggregate spending will match aggregate income. If spending falls short of income, the resultant savings will be transformed into investment spending through the free and open capital markets.

The interest rate mechanism will operate to eliminate any shortages or surpluses of loanable funds. The amount saved will equal the amount invested. If goods remain unsold, prices will drop to improve sales, and if unemployment persists, wage rates will adjust to increase employment to its natural level.

All of the above is done automatically. The economy is essentially self-correcting. The capitalist system does not require government intervention in the marketplace.

The classical policy prescription for economic fluctuations is thus one of laissez-faire. The government should not intervene; instead, Adam Smith's "invisible hand" will guide the economy back to prosperity.

MODERN CLASSICAL ECONOMICS

The classical doctrine described above has not passed out of favor. Many neoclassical economists still cherish the basic theory and advocate its strong laissez-faire policy recommendations. The neoclassical model can be demonstrated using aggregate demand and supply curve analysis.

An aggregate demand curve (figure 13.3) shows the total expenditures that economic agents are willing and able to undertake at various average prices. Total quantity demanded

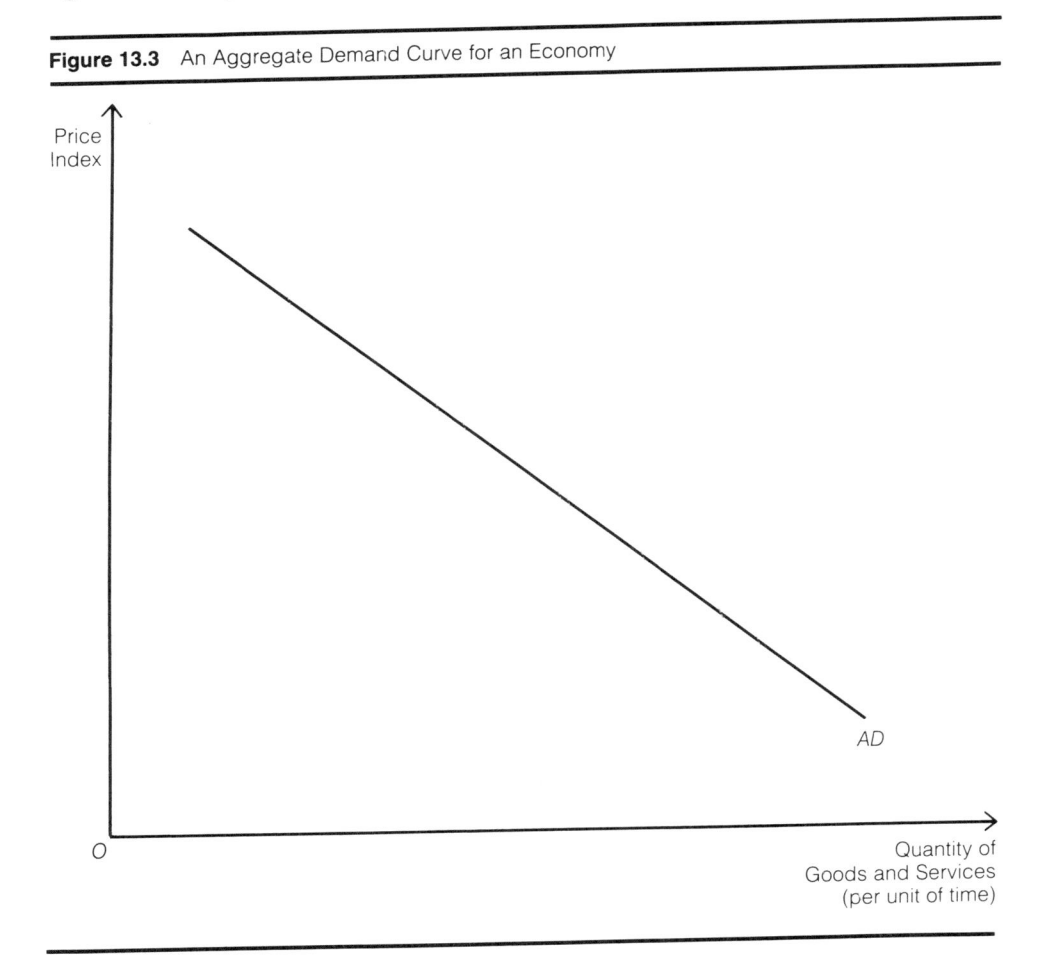

Figure 13.3 An Aggregate Demand Curve for an Economy

Figure 13.4 Two Aggregate Supply Curves

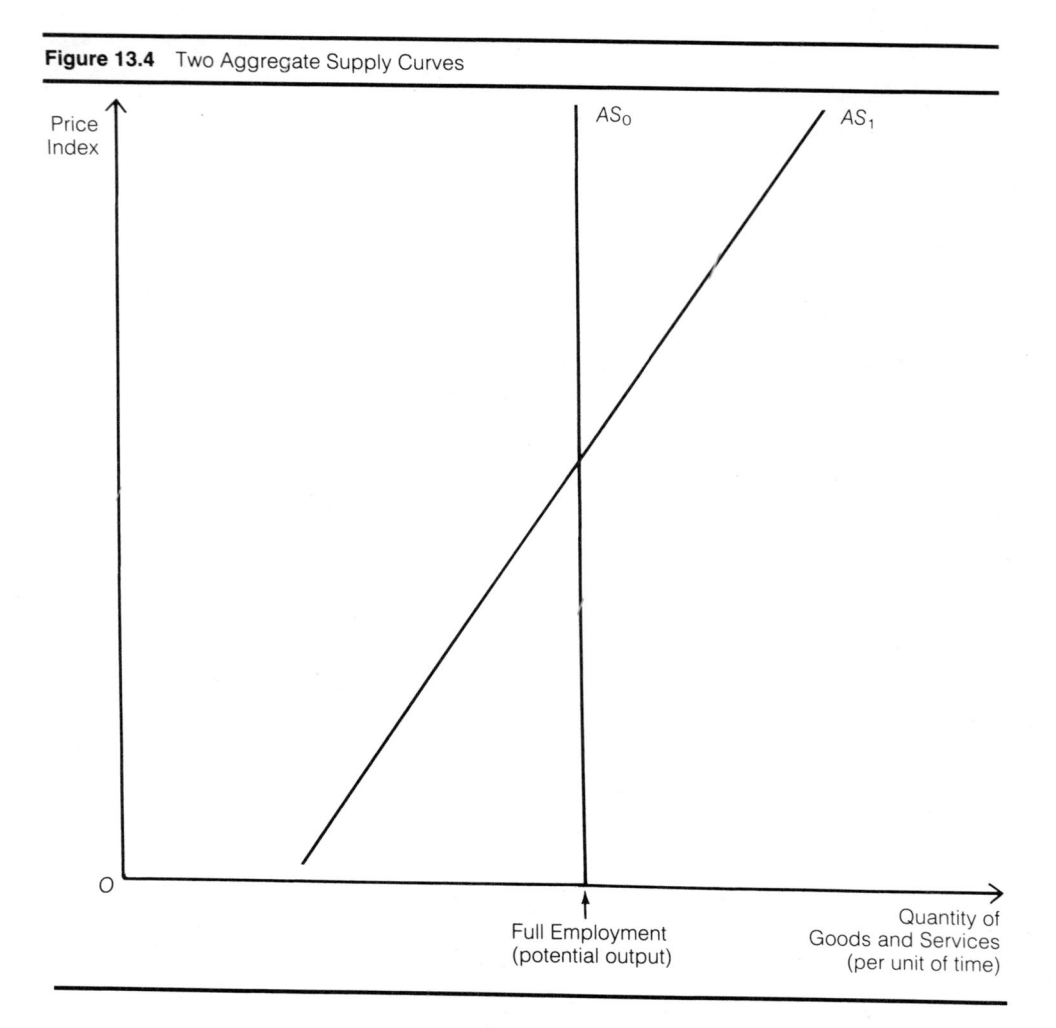

[Figure: Two aggregate supply curves plotted with Price Index on the vertical axis and Quantity of Goods and Services (per unit of time) on the horizontal axis. AS_0 is a vertical line at Full Employment (potential output); AS_1 is an upward-sloping line.]

(real GNP) is measured horizontally and is a function of the weighted average price of all goods and services. This average price level, expressed as an index, is shown on the vertical axis. The downward sloping curve implies that consumers, governments, businesses, and foreigners prefer larger and larger quantities of goods and services as the average price level falls.

The total supply, or aggregate supply curve (figure 13.4), reveals the total output suppliers are willing and able to supply at various prices.

Aggregate supply curve AS_0 represents the classical depiction of aggregate supply. Here the quantity of goods and services is fixed in the short run. Thus, aggregate supply is drawn as a vertical line. The output level associated with curve AS_0 is that amount that would be produced at the natural employment level. The unemployment amount at that

CLASSICAL VS. KEYNESIAN ECONOMICS

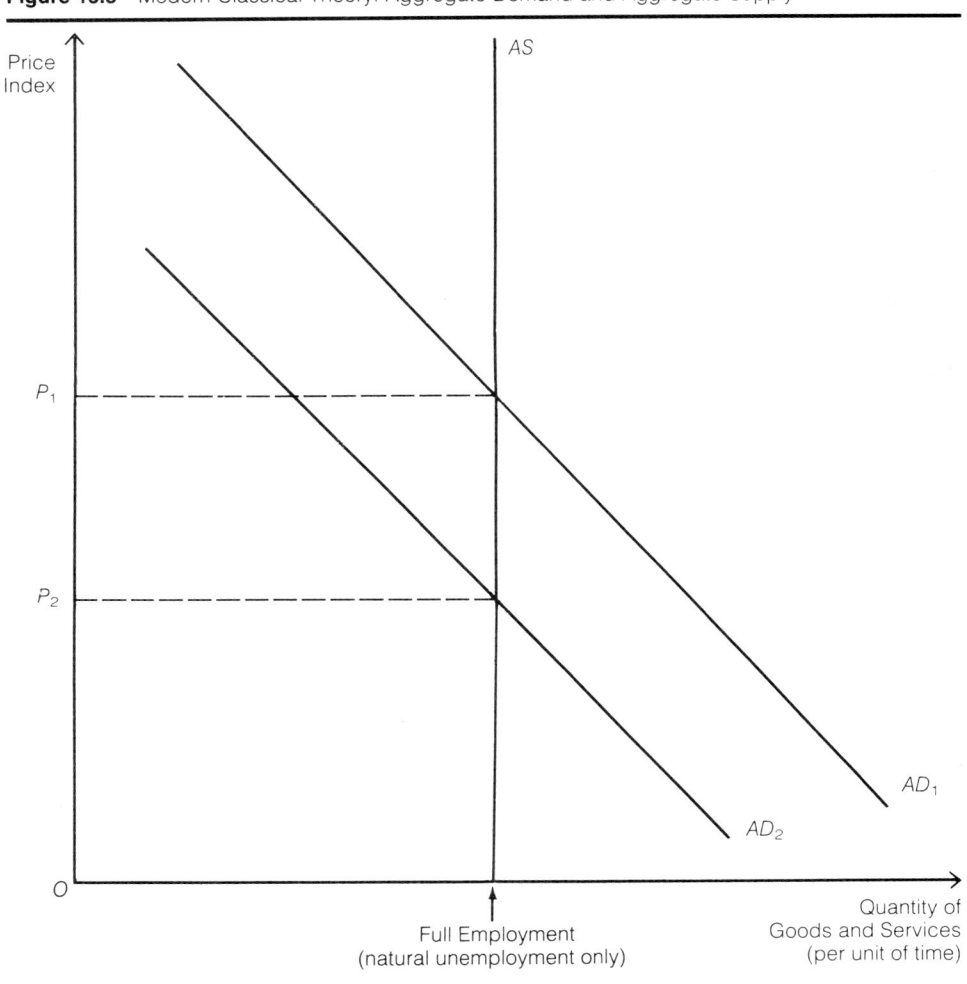

Figure 13.5 Modern Classical Theory: Aggregate Demand and Aggregate Supply

output would only consist of workers who are experiencing frictional and structural unemployment. Curve AS_1 shows aggregate supply that varies positively with the average price level. The classical theory would denounce the existence of a curve such as AS_1. The market-adjustment process described by the classical economists is depicted in figure 13.5.

The classical theory holds that any change in aggregate demand will only affect average prices, and that output and employment will not be altered. For example, a drop in aggregate demand from level AD_1 to AD_2 will lead to a price decrease from P_1 to P_2. Real output and employment will remain stable; or, if they are temporarily disturbed, output and employment will return to their natural levels as prices adjust to market forces.

Decline of the Classical Doctrine

If it were not for the Great Depression of the 1930s, there is a good chance the classical school of economic thought would still be the prevailing theory in use to explain economic disturbances. However, the economic magnitude and cruel length of the Great Depression created significant misgivings in the economic community. The economy was said to be self-correcting. Was it really? Where were all of those economic mechanisms that were guaranteed to bring full employment and stability? The Great Depression made everyone question old theories.

The 1920s was one of the most incredibly explosive decades in our economic history. The stock market set records year after year. A dollar invested in 1921 turned into $3 by 1929 through the rise of the Great Bull Market. However, in October 1929, the market collapsed. The effect of the crash is perhaps best encapsulated by a sad joke from that period: when a guest booked a room at a New York hotel, the desk clerk asked "For sleeping or for jumping?" The misery dealt to the average citizen was awful. Robert L. Heilbroner, an economic historian, reported these individual tragedies:

> In Muncie, Indiana—the city made famous by its selection as 'Middletown'—every fourth factory worker lost his job by the end of 1930. In Chicago, the majority of working girls were earning less than twenty-five cents an hour and a quarter of them made less than ten cents. In New York's Bowery alone, 2,000 jobless crowded into bread lines every day. In the nation as a whole, residential construction fell by 95 percent. Nine million savings accounts were lost. Eighty-five thousand businesses failed. The national volume of salaries dwindled 40 percent, dividends 56 percent, wages 60 percent.[4]

Against this backdrop, the classical doctrine came under attack. Classical theory appeared inconsistent with actual economic events. Was the theory based on faulty assumptions? Were the conclusions of the theory incorrect? Could a new and better theory be developed which could explain the lengthy depression? If so, what economic policy recommendations would be forthcoming? As the Depression lengthened, the classical doctrine began to lose supporters. Yet, it was 7 years before a new theory was offered as an alternative to the classical doctrine.

KEYNESIAN ECONOMICS

In 1936, John Maynard Keynes published *The General Theory of Employment, Interest, and Money,* and began what is now known as the Keynesian revolution of macroeconomic thought. Keynesian economics refuted the foundation of the classical doctrine and replaced it with a tighter, more concise, logically superior model. In addition, Keynes went beyond mere abstract model building by providing economic policy solutions to the major macroeconomic problems. Before we turn our attention to the Keynesian critique of the classical doctrine and Keynesian economics, let us look at Keynes, the man.

John Maynard Keynes

1883 was a significant year for economists. Karl Marx, the founder of communism and avowed enemy of capitalism, died. John Maynard Keynes, the founder—and perhaps the savior—of modern capitalism, was born. Keynes's economic fortunes and career achievements would turn out to be as successful as Marx's were unsuccessful. Yet both men have left important and significant legacies.

Keynes was the son of British economist John Neville Keynes, who was a successful academic and college administrator. His mother, a brilliant individual in her own right, was the mayor of Cambridge. Keynes was raised in an atmosphere of high intellectualism. His family expressed tremendous curiosity and concern for the various government policy issues and questions of the day. It should be no surprise that Keynes developed a taste for power and influence.

As a Cambridge-trained classical economist, Keynes became a professor at Cambridge as well as a consultant to business and government. He joined the Bloomsbury group, a loosely affiliated group of writers, scholars, and intellectuals who had profound influence on British culture and society.

Keynes's personal and professional life can only be characterized as exciting. He courted and married the beautiful Lydia Lopokova, a star Russian ballerina. He served as chairman of a large life insurance company; was a member of the British delegation to the Versailles Peace Conference; was appointed president of a prestigious theater; became a director of the mighty Bank of England; and was endowment fund manager for Cambridge University. His friends included Winston Churchill, Franklin Roosevelt, Bernard Shaw, Pablo Picasso, and Leonard and Virginia Woolf. Shortly before he died in 1946, he complained that he had only one regret in his life. He said, "I wish I had drunk more champagne." His research and academic interests were also significant. He wrote a number of books on a variety of topics. In 1919, he resigned from the Versailles Peace delegation and wrote a virulent attack on the "excessive" war reparations the Allies placed on Germany. In his *Economic Consequences of Peace,* Keynes warned that the economic recovery of all of Europe was more important than revenge:

> The danger confronting us, therefore, is the rapid depression of the standard of life of the European populations to a point which will mean actual starvation. . . . Men will not always die quietly. For starvation, which brings to some lethargy and despair, drives other temperaments to the nervous instability of hysteria and to a mad despair. And these in distress may overturn . . . and submerge civilization. . . .[5]

Keynes's major work, however, concerned the world of macroeconomics. Before the publication of his *General Theory* in 1936, he had given hints that he was about to rebel against the popular tide of classicalism. In 1930, he recommended that the British government develop public works projects to stimulate a sluggish economy. In 1933, in a minor pamphlet, *The Means to Prosperity,* he suggested the answer to the Great Depression could be found in expanded public works projects and massive government intervention in the economy. By 1936, he was so sure he had found the key to the economic puzzle that he wrote to George Bernard Shaw, "I believe myself to be writing a book on economic theory which will largely revolutionize . . . the way the world thinks about economic problems."[6] Indeed, the *General Theory* would prove to be as important as Smith's *Wealth of Nations* and Marx's *Das Kapital.*

Keynesian Critique of the Classical Doctrine

Keynes systematically attacked the alleged self-correcting features of the classical model. Keynes disputed the notion that an economy, once depressed, would automatically return to full employment, equilibrium or stability. Keynes's analysis showed that the economy would certainly move to a stable condition, but that the level of employment and economic activity at the new equilibrium point could be well below the natural, or full employment, level.

Keynes also disputed Say's Law. He saw merit in the concepts that production generates income and that income becomes the source of future demand. However, Keynes flatly denied the existence of a mechanism that would automatically equate planned savings with planned investment. Keynes argued that the interest-rate mechanism is far too fragile to take on such an important task. Besides, he pointed out, the acts of saving and investing are performed by two separate and unrelated sectors, households and businesses. These groups have different motivations and goals. While interest rates affect decision making regarding how much to save or invest, they are not the only determinant of savings and investment levels.

Keynes argued that people save for reasons unrelated to the interest rate. Noninterest rate determinants of savings include the need to save for retirement, unforeseen contingencies or emergencies, the desire for a higher standard of living or to build a fund of money to leave to one's heirs, and simple greed. Keynes argued that any one or combination of these factors may operate to counter the interest-rate mechanism. Therefore, even if interest rates change, there may be little if any change in the flow of savings if these determinants conspire to affect savings in an opposing manner.

Similarly, business investment decisions depend on determinants other than the rate of interest. Keynes argued that the overriding determinant of investment spending was the expected rate of profit from any particular project. If the value of an additional unit of capital goods exceeds the added cost of obtaining that good, the investment will be undertaken. The financing cost, or interest rate, is only one of the cost components. Thus, while interest rates are important, they are not the only consideration. As a result, the classical model will not be valid under certain circumstances.

For example, when interest rates fall, the classical assumption is that investment will rise. Keynes argued that if profit expectations are poor, low interest rates will not be sufficient inducement to cause businesses to invest. In other words, Say's Law could break down. The leakage of savings may not be replaced by injections of investments.

As the evidence from the 1930s indicates, the classical doctrine's relationship between interest rates and investment spending does not hold up to empirical testing (table 13.1). Keynes felt that the interest rate mechanism could not be counted on to influence savings and investment decisions. In fact, by Keynes's theory, savers may reject the lending option altogether and prefer to simply hold cash. This preference for cash holdings is called the liquidity preference function.

Table 13.1 Interest Rates and Investment Expenditures, 1929–41

Year	Interest Rate[a] (percent)	Investment Expenditure (billions of dollars)
1929	4.7	16.2
1930	4.5	10.3
1931	4.6	5.5
1932	5.0	.9
1933	4.5	1.4
1934	4.0	2.9
1935	3.6	6.3
1936	3.2	8.4
1937	3.3	11.7
1938	3.2	6.7
1939	3.0	9.3
1940	2.8	13.2
1941	2.8	18.1

Source: Adapted from Economic Report of the President, 1986.
a. Interest rate is Moody High Grade Aaa bond yield.

Keynes dealt the classical doctrine a major blow with the development of liquidity preference theory. Classical theory contends that the danger of a general glut can be averted if the leakages of savings can be injected back into the spending stream as investments. The liquidity preference concept upsets this process. The liquidity preference recognizes that people may desire to hold cash for speculative, precautionary, and transaction motives. However, the desire to hold cash is inversely related to the rate of interest. The opportunity cost of holding cash is forgone interest. Therefore, at high interest rates, liquidity preference is low, and as rates fall, the desire to hold cash increases (figure 13.6).

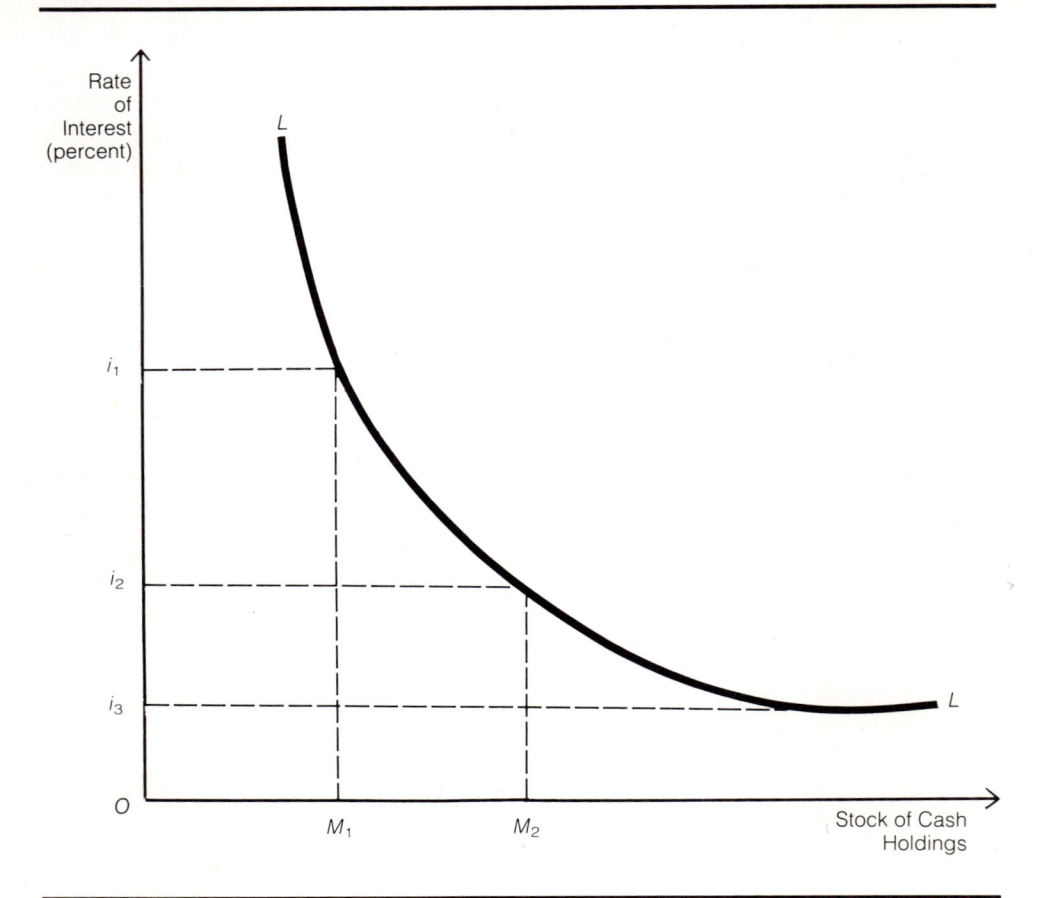

Figure 13.6 Keynesian Liquidity-Preference Curve

Following curve *LL*, as interest rates fall, the stock of cash holdings rises. At interest rate i_1, OM_1 stock of money is held by the public. If rates fall to i_3, the public will desire to increase cash holdings to OM_2. Of vital importance to the Keynesian analysis is the special shape of the liquidity preference curve. Notice that at interest rate i_3 and below, the public is not willing to decrease cash holdings. Conversely, increases in the money stock are not likely to push interest rates below i_3. Keynes called this condition the liquidity trap. In other words, even if lower interest rates could spur new investment—which may be unlikely for various reasons—at some point, interest rates will become inflexible. The point at which interest rates become inflexible defines the liquidity trap.

Keynes's final criticism of the classical savings-investment model is neatly expressed in this often-quoted passage from the General Theory:

> Ancient Egypt was doubly fortunate, and doubtless owed to this its fabled wealth, in that it possessed two activities, namely, pyramid-building, as well as the search for the precious metals, the fruits of which, since they could not serve the needs of man by being consumed, did not stale with abundance. The Middle Ages built cathedrals and sang dirges. Two pyramids, two masses for the dead, are twice as good as one; but not so two railways from London to York.[7]

Keynes's comment dramatically illustrates his awareness of the folly of reliance on the salvation of investment spending in a recession.

Why would a business want to invest in more production capacity when there already exists substantial unused capacity. If consumer spending is already depressed, it is unlikely that businesses will have rosy profits expectations. In fact, it is reasonable to assume that in a severe recession, a reduction in spending or an increase in the savings rate will lead to a reduction in the rate of investment instead of an increase. Therefore, the leakages of savings are likely to remain as idle funds in the hands of consumers or financial intermediaries. As long as these funds remain out of the circular flow of economic activity, unemployment and economic malaise could persist.

Keynes also criticized the classical proposition that, faced with unsold inventories of goods, businesses would cut prices in an effort to increase sales, and that the competition between and among unemployed workers would drive down wages and thus create an incentive for businesses to increase their hiring levels. Keynes did not believe that the labor and product markets were free and open. He felt that large monopolistic firms and giant labor unions wielded sufficient economic power to disrupt competitive markets. Keynes argued that monopolistic firms would rather lay off workers to cut costs than lower prices, and that large unions would be more concerned with obtaining larger and larger wage and benefit packages for the majority of their workers than worry about the unemployment consequences to only a few. In other words, the classical theory that wage and price flexibility offered a line of defense against a prolonged recession or depression was nothing more than window dressing. In reality, wages and prices tended to be flexible in only one direction: upward.

Keynesian Recommendations

The classical school advocates a laissez-faire doctrine of no government intervention to stabilize the business cycle. Keynesian economics takes the opposite approach. Keynes concluded, albeit reluctantly, that massive government intervention was the only way to save the free market economies from the Great Depression. In a letter to the *New York Times* in 1934, Keynes wrote, "I see the problem of recovery in the following light: How soon will normal business enterprise come to the rescue? On what scale, by which expedients, and for how long is abnormal government expenditure adjustable in the meantime?"[8] Keynes did not see government spending programs as permanent measures, but as abnormal and temporary assistance to a system in need of support. Also, even as early as the 1930s, many public works projects were looked upon as wasteful but essentially harmless projects. Keynes blasted the basic sensibility and quality of most public works projects in the following passage from *General Theory*:

> If the Treasury were to fill old bottles with banknotes, bury them at suitable depths in disused coal mines which are then filled up to the surface with town rubbish, and leave it to private enterprise on well-tried principles of laissez-faire to dig up the notes again . . . there need be no more unemployment, and, with the help of the repercussions, the real income of the community, and its capital wealth also, would probably become a good deal greater than it actually is. It would, indeed, be more sensible to build houses and the like; but if there are political and practical difficulties in the way of this, the above would be better than nothing.[9]

While the Keynesian policy directives of government investment were never undertaken on a large scale, many of President Roosevelt's New Deal programs of the 1930s embodied the essence of Keynesian economics. But the massive government spending programs required to bring about full recovery were never carried out: World War II unwittingly concluded the initial Keynesian experiment. Unemployment was quickly eliminated by the mobilization for war; but inflation from overspending began to rear its ugly head, and dramatic price increases occurred after the war. After World War II, Keynesian economics became the standard guide for governing modern market economies.

SUMMARY

The circular flow is a model that depicts the relationship between spending and income for the entire economy. Businesses, households, and governments are interrelated in the model. Households sell resources to and purchase goods and services from businesses. Household spending yields business income, which is, in turn, used to pay households for their resources. Government taxes households and businesses in order to finance government expenditures. The financial services industry takes deposits from households and businesses and uses them to finance investment spending.

Classical economics is a body of economic theory that emphasizes self-interest and the existence of universal economic laws. Say's Law (supply creates its own demand) epitomizes classical economic philosophy. Classical economists believe that markets work to balance supply and demand and that intervention is unnecessary.

John Maynard Keynes attacked classical economic philosophy on several fronts. He questioned the stability of the demand for money and the validity of Say's Law. He believed that prolonged periods of overproduction and unemployment were possible and that the market mechanism would not necessarily automatically correct this situation. The Great Depression, Keynes concluded, occurred because the economy became trapped in an equilibrium position with rampant unemployment. Government intervention was the only solution.

KEY WORDS

circular flow model
classical school
David Ricardo
John Maynard Keynes
liquidity preference function
liquidity trap
natural unemployment rate
Say's Law

Questions for Review

1. What fundamental belief separates classicists from Keynesians?

2. Describe the role played by the factors of production in input markets. What is meant by the circular flow of money in our economy?

3. How did passage of the Employment Act of 1946 affect government's role in the economy?

4. What are injections and why are they necessary?

5. What is Say's Law? How did Ricardo modify it?

6. According to classical doctrine, how will the economy react to a surplus of loanable funds? How will it react to persistent unemployment?

7. List and explain four Keynesian criticisms of the classical doctrine.

8. What is liquidity preference? How does it conflict with classical theory?

9. What did Keynes say about wage-price flexibility?

ENDNOTES

1. See Jean Baptiste Say, *Treatise on Political Economy* (Philadelphia: John Grigg, 1803).

2. David Ricardo, *The Works and Correspondence,* ed. Piero Scaffa, vol. 1 (Cambridge, England 1951–55), p. 290. Copyright © 1951, Cambridge University Press.

3. Arthur C. Pigou, *Theory of Unemployment* (London, England: Macmillan and Co., Ltd., 1927), p. 176.

4. Robert L. Heilbroner, *The Worldly Philosophers,* (New York: Simon and Schuster, 1972), p. 243.

5. John Maynard Keynes, *The Economic Consequences of Peace*, as quoted in Heilbroner, p. 251.

6. John Maynard Keynes, letter to George Bernard Shaw, as quoted in Heilbroner, p. 261.

7. John Maynard Keynes, *The General Theory of Employment, Interest, and Money* (New York: Harcourt, Brace, and World, Inc., 1936), p. 131. Reprinted by permission of Harcourt Brace Jovanovich, Inc.

8. Heilbroner, p. 268.

9. Keynes, *General Theory*. Reprinted by permission of Harcourt Brace Jovanovich, Inc.

ECONOMICS IN THE NEWS

What's Neo in Economics

An inquiry into three schools of modern economics, wherein the author asks whether his profession has a mainstream, or is completely at sea.

Edgar R. Fiedler, CB Economic Research

For a long time public debates about political economics have been dominated by the Keynesians and the monetarists. But while these arguments have droned on (or, occasionally, raged), another school of thought called the "neoclassical economics" was developing. Outside the halls of academe, this new approach to the economy and economic policy is little known, but by now it seems to have matured enough to be worth exploring a bit further.

The simplest way to do this perhaps is by reading the recently published *Conversations With Economists* (Rowman & Allanheld) by Arjo Klamer, a young economics professor at Wellesley College. Klamer traipsed around with a tape recorder under his arm interviewing 11 assorted academic economists, most of whom (but not all) speak only to other professors. The subject matter is highly theoretical; much of it is an example of what former Presidential adviser Herbert Stein had in mind when he said that, to the public, policy discussions among economists are "either incomprehensible or incredible." But with that limitation, the book is well done and especially useful for the professional who has not kept up to date on theory (*mea culpa*). The appeal of *Conversations* is enhanced by the fact that each of the participants is highly articulate—either that or Klamer's editing was superior, quite possibly both. . . .

The first point to make about *Conversations* is how nicely it reveals that the three schools are not so diametrically opposed to one another on every facet of economic theory as might be assumed from accounts of their differences in the media. Each theory accepts a large part of the earlier teachings, and builds from it and on it.

A second basic insight that *Conversations* brings out is that each theoretical school is far from monolithic. The differences between the monetarists and the Keynesians are greater than the differences among the individual members within each camp, but that does not mean that every Keynesian theorist sees eye to eye with every other Keynesian, or every monetarist with his compatriots. Like political parties, each theoretical camp fits a broad range of views under its tent.

The reality is, of course, that the views of all economic theorists lie along a continuum and, although it is convenient for some purposes to bunch them into groups, one should not be misled into thinking the bunching is neat and the views within each group are highly consistent.

Keynesianism (or, better, Neo-Keynesianism to reflect latter-day advancements). The central issue that separates Keynesian economics from its challengers (including the classical economists who were dominant before Keynes) is the instability of the economy and how government should respond. The economy does not operate continuously at high levels of prosperity, Keynesians argue, and when the business cycle takes a downward turn it is wrong to assume that, left to its own devices, the economy will promptly return to high employment. Our market system contains too many rigidities, such as sticky wages and prices, to permit the quick adjustments that would prevent serious recessions. Consequently, there is a crucial role for government: To minimize the serious costs of a weak economy, and especially to minimize unemployment, government should actively pursue spending, tax, and monetary policies that will reverse a recession or (symmetrically) restrain an inflationary boom. Properly handled, these policies will avoid prolonged recessions and inflation.

Monetarism. The most important tenet of monetarism (you will not be surprised to learn) is that money matters—and it matters a lot. It is *the* crucial determinant of how the overall economy performs. And what monetarists are talking about here is the supply of money, that is, the total *quantity* of money in the system and how fast it is rising or falling. Monetarists are normally not very interested in interest rates. Keynesians, on the other hand, put considerably less emphasis on monetary variables and, when they do, it's usually on interest rates rather than the money supply.

New Classical. Interpretation of the new-classical theory seems to come at three levels of sophistication. The simplest level, what might also be called the partisan political level, says that since the policy prescriptions of new-classical economists are always for a minimum of government intervention in the economy, this means that the new-classical economics is identical to monetarism. While it is true that the new-classicists are closer to the monetarists than to the Keynesians, the two schools are clearly not identical.

At the second level, the interpretation brings in the idea of *rational expectations,* which is the most salient idea of the new-classical economics. Rational expectations says that people understand how the economy works and use all information available to them in making their economic decisions. Thus, when the government changes its economic policy, people anticipate the consequences of the change and alter their behavior accordingly, which nullifies the intent of the policy change. Suppose, for example, the Federal Reserve decided to speed up the growth of money in order to increase employment. Rational expectations argues that business executives, workers, and consumers, in anticipation of the effects of a larger money supply, would all raise prices and wages proportionately. As a result, the intended effect of higher employment would be vitiated, and the only effect would be the unintended effect, a higher price level.

From *Across the Board,* May 1984, pp. 49–54. Reprinted by permission of Across the Board, The Conference Board Magazine.

CHAPTER FOURTEEN

FUNDAMENTALS OF KEYNESIAN ECONOMICS

Objectives

After reading this chapter, you should be able to

- list and describe the four components of aggregate demand

- define aggregate demand

- describe the consumption function and list several determinants of consumption

- graph a consumption curve and a savings curve, given the level of autonomous consumption, the amount of disposable income per period, and the portion of disposable income households will spend on consumption

- define and distinguish between marginal and average propensities to consume and to save

- define and distinguish between autonomous and induced changes in consumption

- define aggregate supply

- determine the equilibrium level of national income, given an aggregate supply schedule and the aggregate demand schedule

- explain the multiplier effect

- explain the paradox of thrift

- describe a recessionary gap

- describe an inflationary gap

FUNDAMENTALS OF KEYNESIAN ECONOMICS

In this chapter, we will develop what has become known as the Keynesian model of national income and employment determination. While much of this discussion will center on Keynes's original analysis, his work has been modified by others throughout the years. Economists now refer to the following analysis as simply "Keynesian Economics."[1]

You will recall from our discussion in chapter 13 that the Keynesian model differs radically from the classical doctrine. Keynes rejected the notion that the free enterprise system automatically reverts to full employment when its equilibrium has been disturbed. Furthermore, Keynes rejected the classical belief that the desired total spending in the economy (aggregate demand) will always equal the full-employment aggregate income. Instead, Keynesian theory argues that equilibrium may be reached at a level of income far below that required to generate full employment. This low equilibrium level need not be temporary.

The Keynesian model of income determination rests upon changes in aggregate demand or expenditures. If the economy experiences a reduction in the overall level of spending, the level of real output and employment may fall. If the drop in spending occurs while the economy is at full employment, a less-than-full employment level will result. If aggregate spending later increases, the economy may move back to full employment as real output and employment rise. Similarly, increases in aggregate spending when the economy is already at full employment levels can create inflationary pressures. These may lead to price increases with little or no change in real output. Keynesian theory is a demand theory of national income determination. In other words, changes in the economic condition, according to Keynes, are driven by changes in demand.

AGGREGATE DEMAND

In the previous chapter, the term "aggregate demand" was defined as the sum of all planned spending for the nation's output of goods and services. Total demand comprises the total spending plans of four sectors: consumers, business, government, and the foreign sector. These four components of demand can be summed algebraically as:

$$\Sigma D = C + I + G + (X - M),$$

where ΣD = Aggregate demand,
C = Consumption expenditures,
I = Business investment expenditures,
G = Government expenditures, and
$(X - M)$ = Net exports (Exports − Imports).

Consumption Expenditures

The largest and most important component of aggregate demand is consumption (C). Keynes studied why people consume and what makes consumers change their spending habits. He concluded that disposable income was the major determinant of consumption.

A convenient way to express the relationship between income and consumption is called the consumption function. The consumption function is an equation that can be transformed into a schedule or a graph. It relates the dollar value of the expenditures consumers plan to make to their disposable income.

It is unlikely that any two families spend their incomes in exactly the same way. The consumption function, however, is concerned not with particular families but with all consumers. The consumption function is designed to represent the spending habits of all. We can express this relationship for a hypothetical economy as:

$$C = C_o + bY_d,$$

where C = Consumption expenditures,
C_o = The amount households would consume if their disposable incomes were zero (autonomous consumption),
Y_d = Disposable income per period, and
b = The portion of disposable income households will spend on consumption.

C_o is called autonomous consumption and represents the level of consumption if consumers have no current income. The value of the b term is very important in the Keynesian model. Keynes argued that there exists a law of consumption under which "men are disposed, as a rule and on average, to increase their consumption as their income increases, but not by as much as the increase in their income."[2] Keynes believed that consumers would not spend every penny of an additional dollar of disposable income, but that they would save a portion of it.

The consumption function can be used to depict a set of alternative income and consumption patterns. For example, consider a consumption function with the following specifications:

$$C = \$1,000 + .8Y_d,$$

where C_o (autonomous consumption) = $1,000 (billions) and the portion of an additional dollar of disposable income consumed is 80 percent or .8.

From this consumption function we can select various hypothetical income levels and observe the effect on consumption (table 14.1).

FUNDAMENTALS OF KEYNESIAN ECONOMICS

Table 14.1 Planned Consumption and Savings at Various Disposable Income Levels (billions of dollars)

(Y_d) Disposable Income	(C) Consumption Expenditure	(S) Savings
3,000	3,400	−400
3,500	3,800	−300
4,000	4,200	−200
4,500	4,600	−100
5,000	5,000	0
5,500	5,400	100
6,000	5,800	200

If disposable income is $4,000 billion, then planned consumption will be $4,200 billion ($1,000 billion autonomous consumption plus .8 × $4,000 billion, or $3,200 billion). Savings will be a negative $200 billion. If income rises to $5,000 billion, then consumption will be $5,000 billion, and savings will be $0. If income is at $6,000 billion, consumers would elect to spend $5,800 billion and save $200 billion.

Several factors besides the level of disposable income influence consumption expenditure. The stock of consumer durables, attitudes toward thrift, and the balance of consumer debt outstanding can all influence the level of total consumption. So far, we have assumed these determinants to be held constant or unchanged. We will account for the possibility of change in these variables below.

The Consumption Curve

Figure 14.1 graphically depicts the consumption-income and consumption-savings relationship developed in table 14.1.

In figure 14.1, the consumption curve (C) crosses the vertical axis at $1,000 billion. This is the point at which disposable income is $0 and consumers are spending an amount equal to $1,000 billion on autonomous consumption. Autonomous consumption is the portion of total consumption that does not depend on the level of income. The savings curve (S) intercepts the vertical axis at − $1,000 billion. This negative savings is the amount by which personal spending outweighs personal income. Negative savings is also called dissavings. The $1,000 billion in autonomous consumption must be financed by either a reduction in savings or borrowing. The savings equation can be written as:

$$S = -\$1{,}000 \text{ billion} + .2Y_d.$$

That is, when disposable income is equal to zero, savings is equal to − $1,000 billion. For every $1.00 increase in disposable income, savings rises by $0.20. This representation of the saving-income relationship is called the savings function. The savings function can be derived from the general consumption function. Since $C = C_o + bY_d$, and since all income

Figure 14.1 Planned Consumption and Planned Savings Schedules

$C = 1,000 + .8Y_d$

$\Delta C = \$800$

$\Delta Y_d = \$1,000$

$S = -1000 + .2Y_d$

C, S = Consumed or saved.
Y_d = Disposable income.

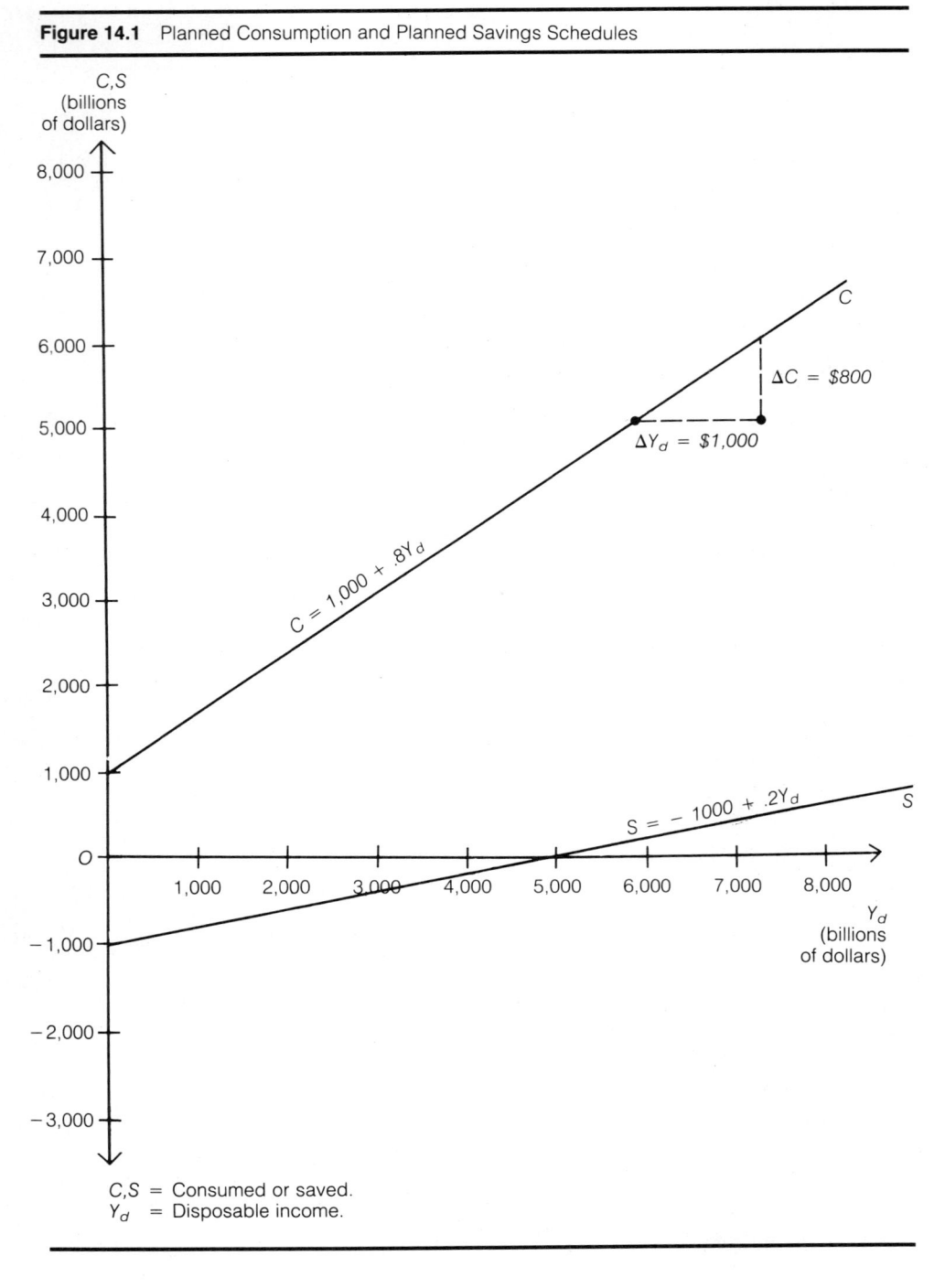

400

FUNDAMENTALS OF KEYNESIAN ECONOMICS

must by definition either be consumed or saved, $Y_d = C + S$. Solving for savings yields the following:

$$S = Y_d - C \text{ and}$$
$$S = Y_d - (C_o + bY_d) \text{ substituting } C = C_o + bY_d,$$
$$S = -C_o + (Y_d - bY_d), \text{ gathering terms}$$
$$S = -C_o + (1 - b)(Y_d).$$

In our hypothetical economy, since the consumption function is equal to $C = C_o + bY_d$ or $C = \$1{,}000$ billion $+ .8Y_d$, then $S = -\$1{,}000$ billion $+ (1 - .8)Y_d$ or $S = -\$1{,}000$ billion $+ .2Y_d$.

Marginal and Average Propensities to Consume

John Maynard Keynes labeled the relationship between the change in income and the change in consumption the marginal propensity to consume. It is defined as the fraction of any change in disposable income that is consumed. The formula used to calculate the marginal propensity to consume is written as follows:

$$\text{MPC} = \frac{\Delta C}{\Delta Y_d}.$$

The marginal propensity to consume is the "b" term in our consumption function, $C = C_o + bY_d$.

The MPC can be obtained from table 14.1 or figure 14.1. In table 14.1, at disposable income level $5,000, consumption is also $5,000. As income rises to $5,500, consumption increases to $5,400. Thus,

$$\text{MPC} = \frac{(\$5{,}400 - 5{,}000)}{(\$5{,}500 - 5{,}000)} = \frac{400}{500} = .80.$$

In other words, the $500 change in disposable income led consumers to increase their spending by 80 percent, or $400. In figure 14.1, the marginal propensity to consume is equal to the slope of the consumption function (b).

Another measure related to the marginal propensity to consume is the average propensity to consume (APC). The APC measures the percentage of total disposable income that is consumed. The formula for the APC is written as follows:

$$\text{APC} = \frac{C}{Y_d}.$$

From table 14.1, at income level $6,000, the APC = $5,800/6,000 = .97, while at income level $5,000, the APC = $5,000/$5,000 = 1.0. The APC explains what fraction of a dollar of disposable income, on average, is spent on consumption.

401

Marginal and Average Propensities to Save

Income can be either consumed or saved. Keynes also described the relationship between changes in income and changes in savings. The marginal propensity to save (MPS) is equal to the percentage of an additional dollar of disposable income that is saved. The formula for the MPS is written as follows:

$$MPS = \frac{\Delta S}{\Delta Y_d}.$$

The marginal propensity to save can be calculated in three ways. First, the MPS can be obtained using the general formula described above. When income rises from $5,000 to $5,500, savings jumps from $0 to $100. Therefore,

$$MPS = \frac{\Delta S}{\Delta Y_d} = \frac{\$100}{500} = .2.$$

The MPS is also equal to (1 − MPC). Using the data presented in table 14.1, if the MPC = .8, the MPS = (1 − .8) = .2. Finally, the MPS is the slope of the savings function (as shown in figure 14.1).

The average propensity to save (APS) is similar in concept to the APC and shows the fraction of total income that is saved. The general formula used to calculate the APS is written as follows:

$$APS = \frac{S}{Y_d}.$$

In table 14.1, at income level $6,000, savings is equal to $200, therefore:

$$APS = \frac{\$200}{\$6,000} = .03.$$

At income level $5,000, however, the APS becomes APS = S/Y = $0/$5,000 = 0. Added together, the APS and APC equal 1. Thus, the APS = 1 − APC, and the APC = 1 − APS. Table 14.2 presents the data from table 14.1 with columns added for the MPC, MPS, APC, and APS.

Table 14.2 Consumption, Savings, and Disposable Income: Marginal and Average Propensities (in dollars)

(Y_d) Disposable Income per Period	(C) Consumption Expenditures	(S) Savings	(APC) Consumption Disposable Income	(APS) Savings Disposable Income	(MPC) ΔConsumption ΔDisposable Income	(MPS) ΔSavings ΔDisposable Income
3,000	3,400	−400	1.13	−0.13		
3,500	3,800	−300	1.09	−0.09	0.80	0.20
4,000	4,200	−200	1.05	−0.05	0.80	0.20
4,500	4,600	−100	1.02	−0.02	0.80	0.20
5,000	5,000	0	1.00	0.00	0.80	0.20
5,500	5,400	100	0.98	0.02	0.80	0.20
6,000	5,800	200	0.97	0.03	0.80	0.20

Check Your Understanding

In table 14.2, the APC varies from 0.97 to 1.13 and the APS from 0.03 to − 0.13. The marginal propensity to consume is constant throughout at 0.80, and similarly, the marginal propensity to save remains at 0.20. Check your understanding of these concepts by recalculating the figures in table 14.2, using a different figure for autonomous consumption. For example, if autonomous consumption changes from $1,000 to $2,000, the new consumption function would be $C = \$2,000 + .8Y_d$. How does this affect the APC and the APS? The MPC and MPS?

Answer: Consumption expenditures for each level would be $1,000 higher. Concurrently, the figures in the savings column would decrease by $1,000. APC would rise, but APS would shrink. The MPC remains the same, at 0.80, and the MPS also remains the same, at 0.20. The first two rows of figures recalculated from table 14.2 are presented below to help you check your work:

Y_d	C	S	APC	APS	MPC	MPS
3,000	4,400	−1,400	1.46	−0.46	0.80	0.20
3,500	4,800	−1,300	1.37	−0.37		

Table 14.3 shows the APC and APS figures for the U.S. economy for selected years from 1930 to 1985.[3] The APC approached 1.0 in 1935. The national income level was so low, households consumed virtually their entire disposable incomes. In 1935, savings accounted for only 3.7 percent of disposable income. In 1945, however, the savings rate (APS) had leaped to 19.2 percent. This radical departure from trend was due to rationing programs instituted during World War II, which severely limited purchases of products in an effort to divert raw materials to the war effort. The long-run trend is for Americans' APS to average around 6.5 percent.

Autonomous Changes in Consumption

The Keynesian model is demand dependent. Changes in aggregate demand cause changes in the equilibrium level of national income. Since consumption is a major component of aggregate demand, it is important to distinguish between the two possible changes in the level of consumption, and to understand the causes of these changes.

Table 14.3 History of APC and APS: Selected Years, 1930–85

Year	(1) Disposable Personal Income	(2) Personal Consumption Expenditures	(3) Personal Savings	(4) Average Propensity to Consume	(5) Average Propensity to Save
1930	74.5	69.9	3.4	93.8	4.6
1935	58.5	55.7	2.1	95.2	3.7
1940	75.3	71.0	3.4	94.2	4.5
1945	149.1	119.5	28.7	80.1	19.2
1950	206.6	192.0	11.9	92.9	5.8
1955	275.0	253.7	16.4	92.3	6.0
1960	352.0	324.9	19.7	92.3	5.6
1965	475.8	430.4	33.7	90.5	7.1
1970	695.3	621.7	55.8	89.4	8.0
1975	1,096.1	976.4	94.3	89.1	8.6
1980	1,828.9	1,668.1	110.2	91.2	6.0
1985	2,800.8	2,634.8	115.2	94.1	4.1

Source: *Economic Report of the President,* 1986 (Washington, DC: U.S. Government Printing Office).

The first reason total consumption may change is that certain nonincome determinants of consumption may influence the individual consumption decisions of buyers. Any change caused by nonincome factors is called an autonomous change in consumption. Nonincome factors include, among others, consumer expectations, wealth, level of debt, new products introductions, and changes in marketing practices.

Consumer expectations of future events can lead them to change current expenditures. In chapter 4, we discussed the idea that consumers may change their demand for a product based upon their expectations of future price movements. Households will normally increase their purchases of products whenever a substantial future price increase is expected.

Similarly, if consumers expect large changes in future income levels, they may drastically change current consumption. As individuals approach retirement age, they often begin to reduce their consumption expenditures years in advance of their actual retirement. The fear of a future income drop increases their desire to save now. On the other hand, workers who expect large bonuses or substantial pay raises may celebrate the anticipated income with a shopping spree today.

Anticipated shortages of products can cause panic buying. During the 1979 gasoline crisis, motorists parked in long lines to keep topping off their fuel tanks. Others, more desperate, hoarded fuel in large underground tanks installed in their backyards.

The propensity to consume is also influenced by the stock of wealth consumers currently possess. Wealthy consumers with large stocks of durable goods may begin to save at higher rates. On the other hand, a large stock of wealth permits an individual to continue to consume at high levels in the event of a temporary decrease in income. The wealthy can begin to liquidate their stock of wealth by selling off various assets.

Changes in the age distribution of the population can also have an impact on wealth and consumption. As the "baby boomers" in the U.S. mature, the growth in the 35 to 50-year-old age bracket will mushroom. This age group traditionally attempts to add to their stock of durable goods at every opportunity. Some economists are predicting a significant economic boom as the result of increased spending by the baby boom generation.

The debt levels of consumers also have an impact on consumption. When the ratio of consumer debt-to-disposable income rises, consumers tend to restrict spending. Changes in the laws relating to credit practices can also influence consumption.

The introduction of new products can precipitate a major spending cycle on the part of consumers. For example, the introduction of home video products such as video recorders and video cameras has spurred sizable expenditures by many consumers.

The marketing tactics and financing innovations of the business sector can also influence consumption. For example, the auto industry introduced low-interest financing terms in the summer of 1985 as a way to boost lagging sales. As a result, the auto industry posted an all-time record sales year.[4]

Autonomous changes in consumption can cause the entire consumption function to shift (figure 14.2). If consumption increases because of a change in one or more of the nonincome determinants, the consumption curve (C) will shift to a curve like C'. This means that at any income level, consumers are planning to consume more than before and consequently save less.[5]

In figure 14.2, as the consumption curve shifts upward from C to C', the amount of consumption at OY_d income rises from OC to OC' ($\Delta C'$). The autonomous change in consumption can lead to a parallel or nonparallel shift in the consumption curve. In other words, for the general consumption function $C = C_o + bY_d$, C_o, and/or b, the MPS can change. A movement from C to C'' involves a decrease in the amount consumed at every income level. For example, at income level OY_d, consumption is lowered from OC to OC'' ($\Delta C''$).

Induced Changes in Consumption

An induced change in consumption occurs along the consumption function as the direct result of a change in income. It is assumed under an induced change in consumption that the nonincome determinants of consumption are held constant. The additional amount of consumption spending that is "induced" from a change in income depends upon the marginal propensity to consume. The higher or lower the MPC, the larger or smaller the change in consumption that results from a change in income. For example, in figure 14.3, consumption function C_1 is associated with a larger marginal propensity to consume than consumption function C_2.[6] When income changes from OY_1 to OY_2, the change in consumption for those consumers whose spending habits are portrayed by consumption function C_1 exceeds the change for consumers represented by C_2.

Figure 14.2 An Autonomous Change in Consumption

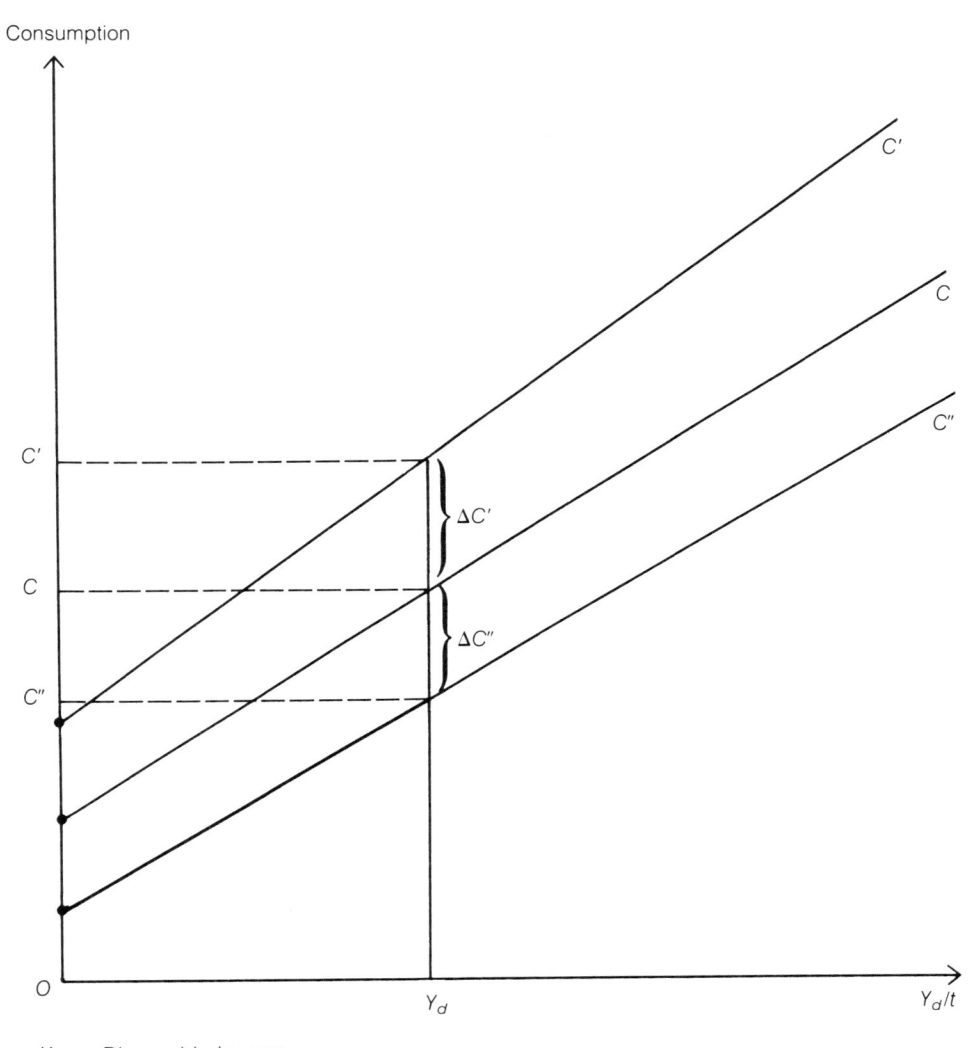

Y_d = Disposable income.
t = Units of time.

Figure 14.3 Induced Change in Consumption and the Marginal Propensity to Consume

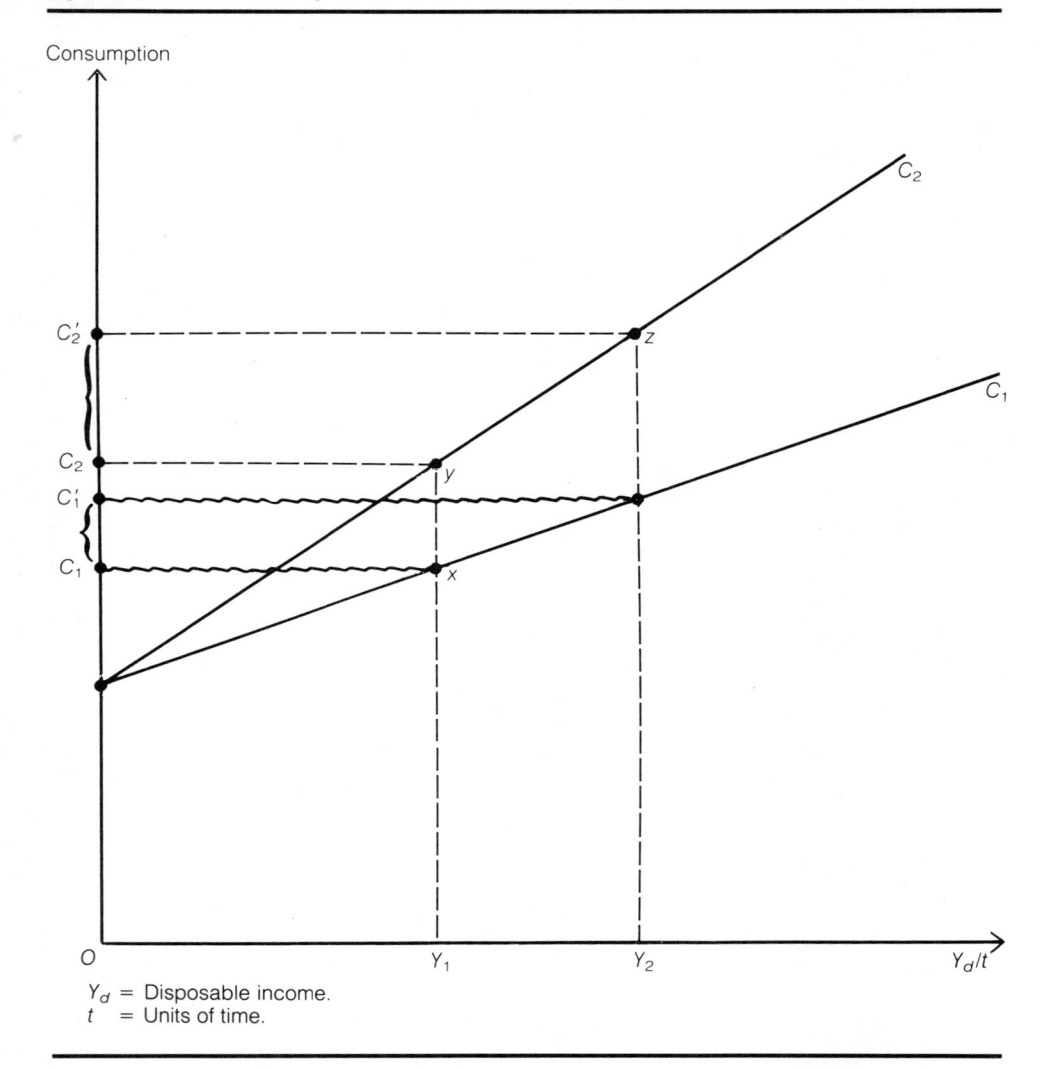

Y_d = Disposable income.
t = Units of time.

Figure 14.3 can also be used to illustrate the combination of an autonomous and induced change in consumption. We can begin at an initial income level of OY_1 on consumption function C_1, or point X. At point X, OC_1 represents total consumption. If a nonincome determinant of consumption causes consumers to increase their spending habits, the consumption function could change to curve C_2. Now at income level OY_1, consumption has risen to point Y, or consumption level OC_2. The movement from X to Y is an autonomous change in consumption. If income were to change from OY_1 to OY_2, consumption would increase to point Z, or consumption level C_2'. The movement from point Y to Z is an induced change in consumption.[7]

Investment Spending

The second component of aggregate demand is investment spending (I). The level of investment depends upon a number of variables. For simplicity, we will assume the level of investment is independent of the level of national income. Now the investment function can be written as $I = I_o$ and the investment function can be graphed as a horizontal line (figure 14.4). If investment spending were related to the level of income, then the investment function would follow the form $I = I_o + cY_d$ where I_o represents autonomous investment, and c can be viewed as a marginal propensity to invest. Notice the slope of this second curve is positive, reflecting the tendency for investment demand to rise as national income rises.

Investment spending can be added to the consumption demand to illustrate total private domestic demand, $C + I$ (figure 14.5). Here, the consumption function is added to the investment function, generating a new private domestic aggregate demand schedule. The aggregate demand curve ($C + I$) is parallel to the consumption function (C) because we have assumed investment to be exogenous, or external, to our model. Therefore, investment demand is equal to I_o, regardless of income.

Government Spending

The third component of aggregate demand is government spending (G). Let us assume, initially, that government spending is at a constant level, and exogenously determined. Later, we will vary the level of government expenditures and observe the changes in income. For now, we can simplify our analysis by establishing the level of government spending at a fixed, unchanging level. When G is added to the domestic private demand ($C+I$), the new aggregate demand can be called total domestic demand ($C+I+G$). The $C+I+G$ demand curve is illustrated in figure 14.6.

ECONOMICS FOR BANKERS

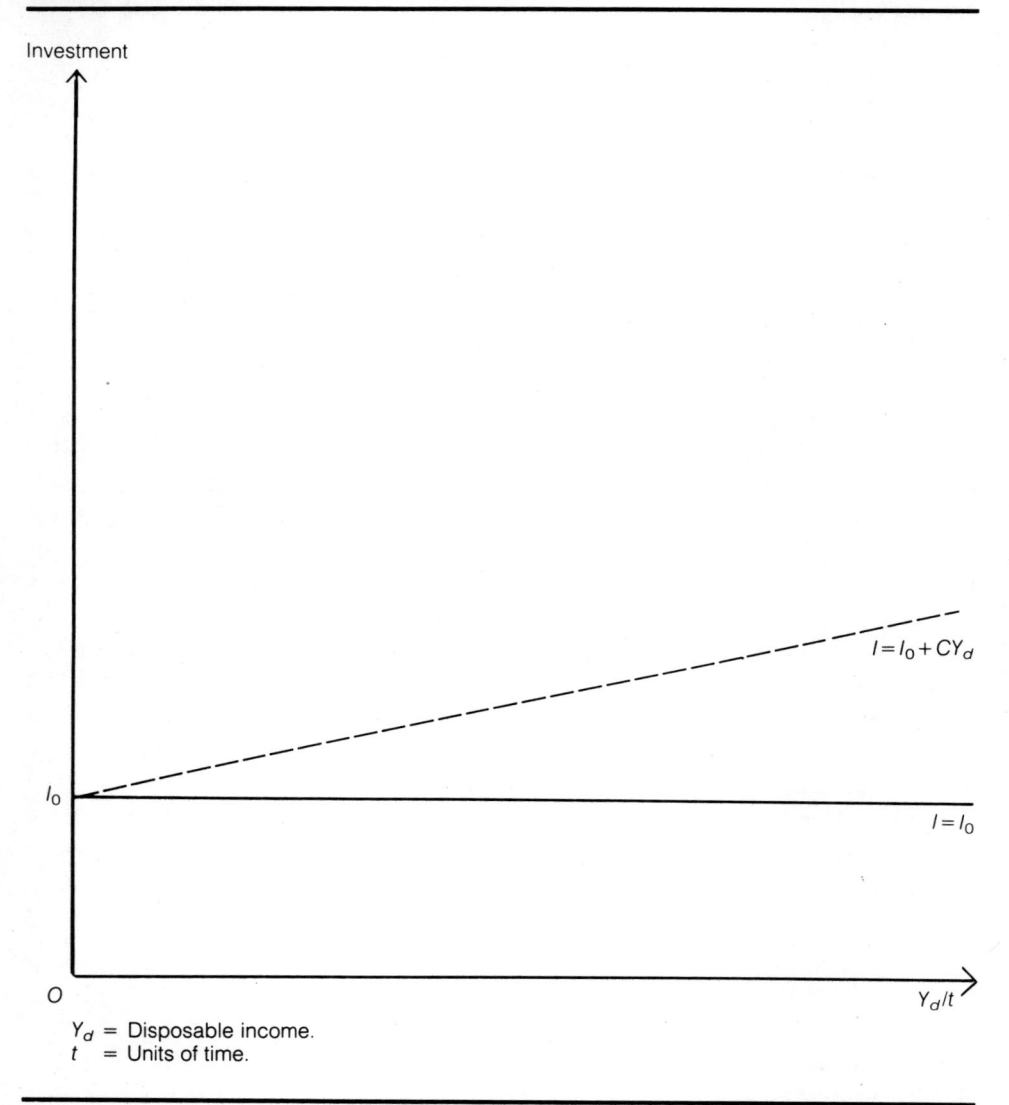

Figure 14.4 Investment Demand, Autonomous $I = I_0$

$I = I_0 + CY_d$

I_0

$I = I_0$

Y_d/t

Y_d = Disposable income.
t = Units of time.

FUNDAMENTALS OF KEYNESIAN ECONOMICS

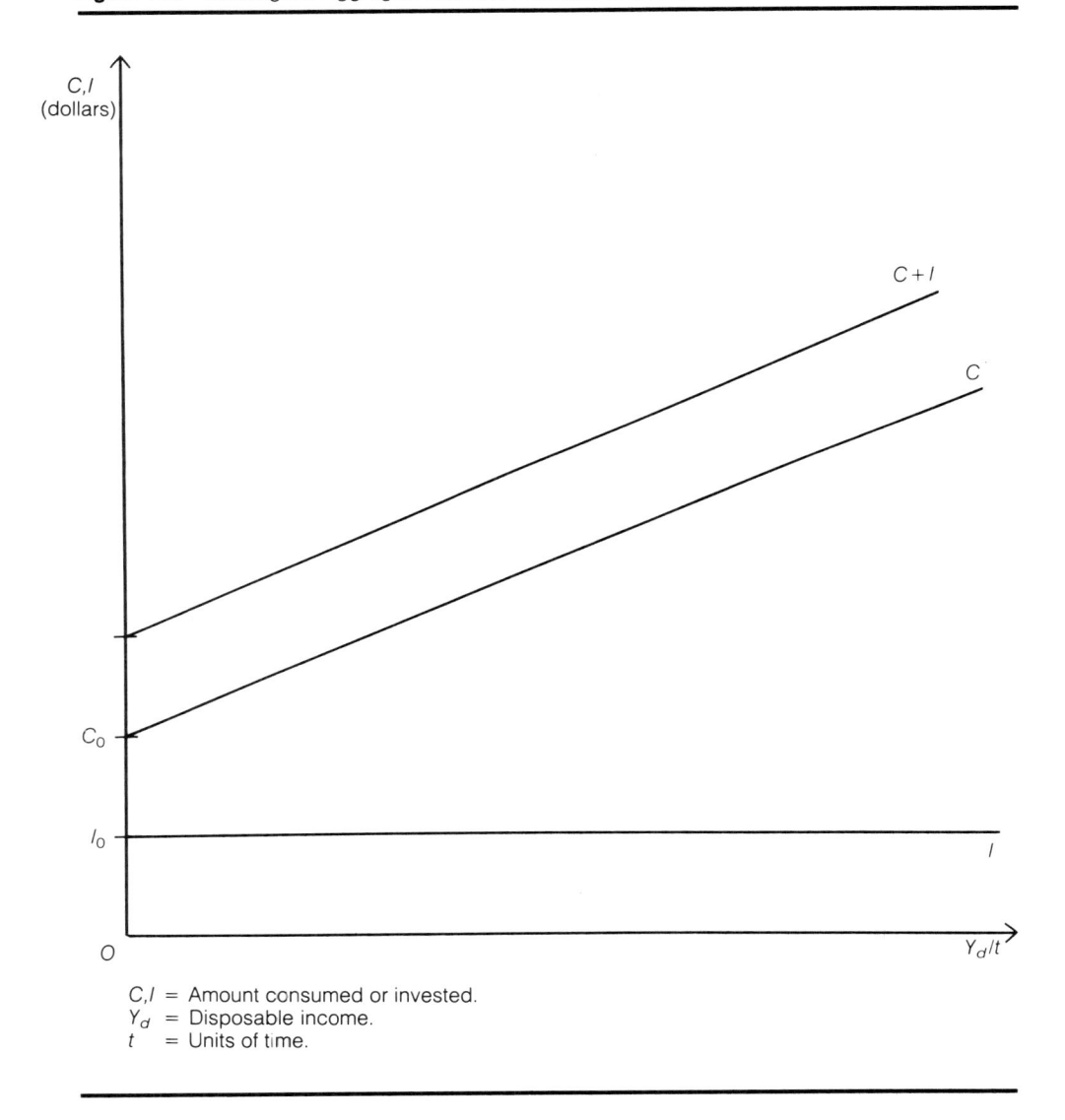

Figure 14.5 Building the Aggregate Demand Function: Investment Demand

C,I = Amount consumed or invested.
Y_d = Disposable income.
t = Units of time.

411

Figure 14.6 Aggregate Demand (Consumption, Investment, Government Expenditures, and Net Exports)

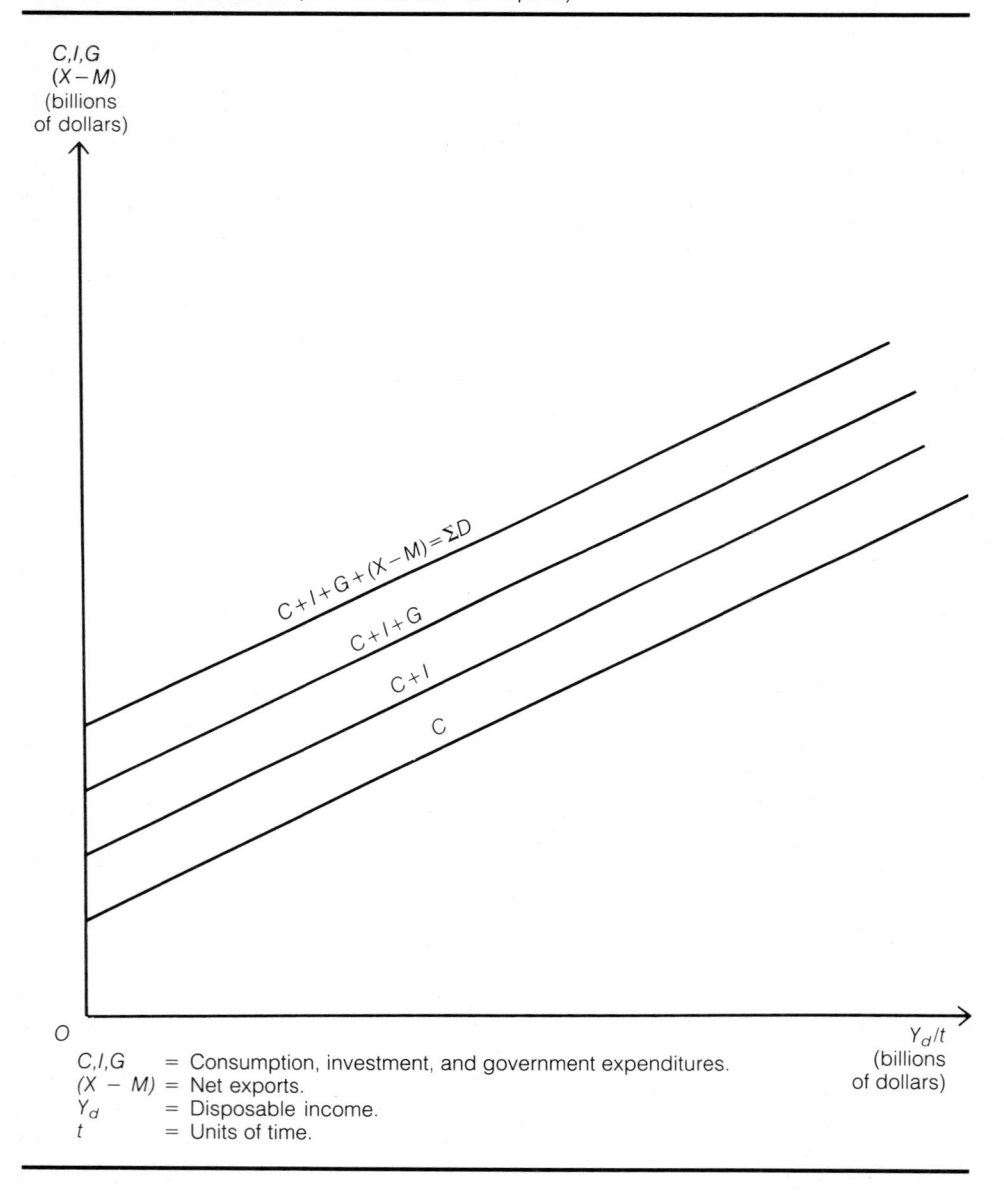

C, I, G
$(X - M)$
(billions of dollars)

$C + I + G + (X - M) = \Sigma D$
$C + I + G$
$C + I$
C

Y_d/t
(billions of dollars)

C, I, G = Consumption, investment, and government expenditures.
$(X - M)$ = Net exports.
Y_d = Disposable income.
t = Units of time.

FUNDAMENTALS OF KEYNESIAN ECONOMICS

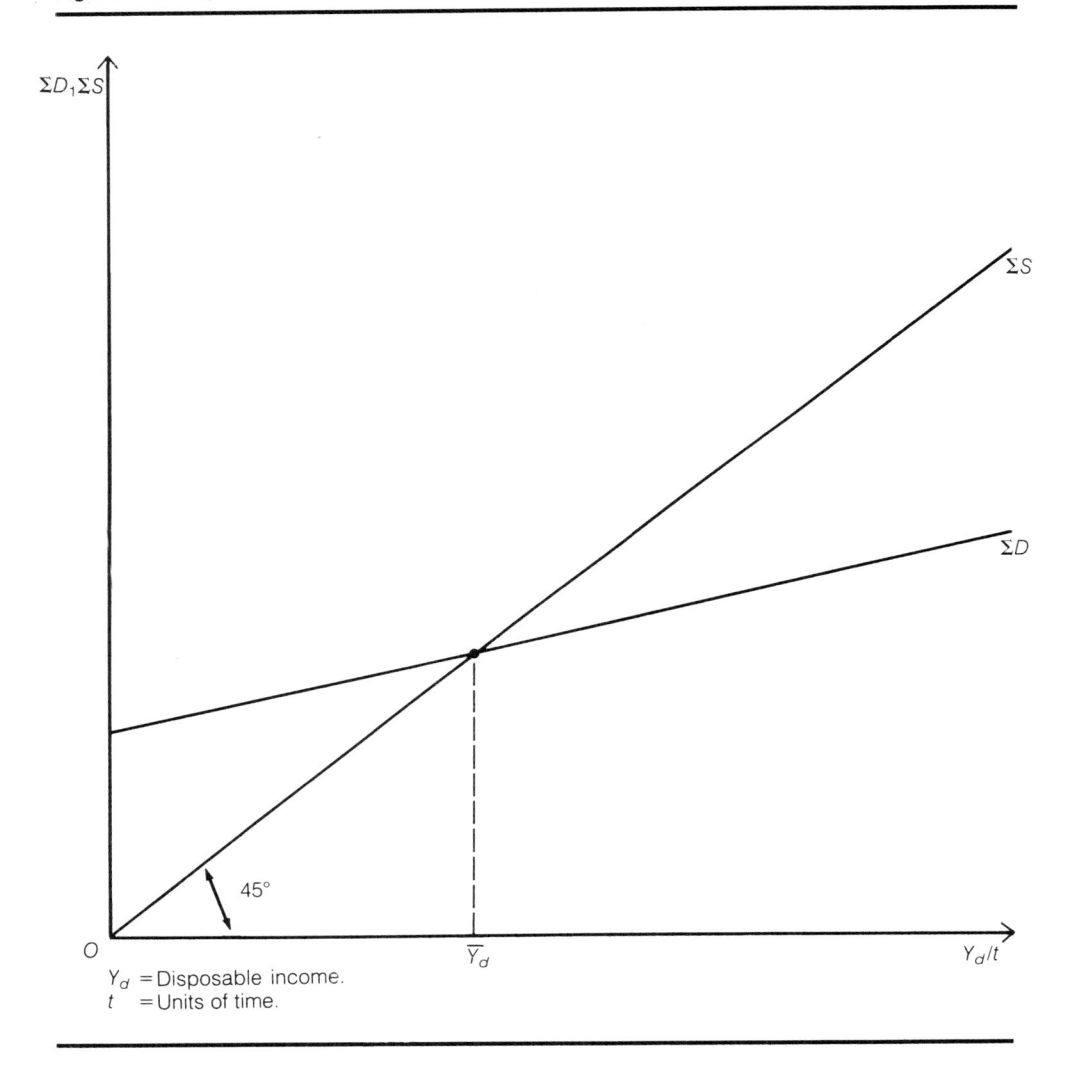

Figure 14.8 Equilibrium National Income

Y_d = Disposable income.
t = Units of time.

415

Changes in Investment Spending

Let us construct an array of aggregate supply, demand, and income data for a hypothetical economy (table 14.4). We will assume the absence of the government and foreign sectors to simplify our analysis. At an income level of $2,500 billion, the aggregate demand and aggregate supply are equal. At that equilibrium level of GNP, the aggregate demand generated by consumption (C) and planned investment (I) is such that all of the goods and services produced are purchased.

If national income is equal to $2,100 billion, however, total aggregate demand at that income level is $2,180 billion. How will the economy provide for the excess demand of $80 billion? Notice that businesses had planned to invest $40 billion. However, through a buy-down process, their inventories have been reduced by $80 billion. This is called unintended investments in inventories, and in this instance the investment value is negative. Consumers are demanding more products than are currently being produced, and consequently, firms are being forced to use the stocks of goods in inventory to accommodate the additional demand. However, this action will cause inventories to dwindle, and firms will attempt to replenish their inventories. This added production will stimulate production and increase national income and the amount of aggregate supply in the next period. This adjustment process continues until equilibrium is restored.

Alternatively, if income is at $2,800 billion, aggregate supply will exceed aggregate demand by $60 billion. In this case, production levels anticipated by business have exceeded actual demand. This excess production will be placed in inventory and accounted for as an unintended increase in investment of $60 billion. However, firms will react to this excessive buildup in inventories by slicing production targets. The net effect of this attempt to adjust production is a reduction in national income. Again, this process will continue until that level of national income where $\Sigma S = \Sigma I$.

Table 14.4 National Income Determination, Hypothetical Economy
(billions of constant dollars)

Income = Aggregate Supply = GNP	Consumption (C)	Savings (S)	Planned Investment (I)	Aggregate Demand (C + I)	Unintended Investment in Inventories	Effect on Income
2,100	2,140	−40	40	2,180	−80	increase
2,200	2,220	−20	40	2,260	−60	increase
2,300	2,300	0	40	2,340	−40	increase
2,400	2,380	20	40	2,420	−20	increase
2,500	2,460	40	40	2,500	0	no change (equilibrium)
2,600	2,540	60	40	2,580	+20	decrease
2,700	2,620	80	40	2,660	+40	decrease
2,800	2,700	100	40	2,740	+60	decrease
2,900	2,780	120	40	2,820	+80	decrease

Planned Savings Equals Planned Investment

A second method to determine national income equilibrium in a simple economy is to find that income level where planned savings equals planned investment. In table 14.4, at all income levels other than the equilibrium level of $2,500, planned savings (S) is either greater than or less than planned investment (I).

For example, at income level $2,400, $S = \$20$ and $I = \$40$, and at income level $2,900, $S = \$120$ and $I = \$40$. The object here is to equate planned saving and planned investment. Planned savings is always equal to total investment (planned investment combined with unintended inventory investment). For example, while planned investment exceeds savings by $20 billion at income level $2,400, unintended inventory investment is equal to $-\$20$. And at income level $2,900, S exceeds I by $80, but unplanned inventory investment is also $80.

Leakages Equal Injections

Another method exists for determining the equilibrium level of national income. You may recall from our study of the circular flow diagram that the economy tends toward equilibrium as long as the leakages (savings) from the spending cycle are somehow injected back into the system. If, however, total leakages exceed total injections, the level of economic activity eventually declines. If injections exceed leakages, economic activity increases. The leakages-equal-injections approach works here in a similar manner.

We can define leakages as income that, for one reason or another, is not spent in the domestic marketplace. A major leakage is savings (S), but other leakages include taxes (T) and imports (M). Injections can include any aggregate spending in the domestic economy that is not linked directly to national output or income. The major injection we have studied so far is investment spending (I), but government spending (G) and export expenditures also qualify as injections. National income equilibrium is reached when total leakages equal total injections, or $T + S + M = I + G + X$.

THE MULTIPLIER EFFECT IN KEYNESIAN ECONOMICS

One of the most significant components of Keynesian economic theory involves how a small change in aggregate demand can be magnified into a much larger change in national income. The process by which a given change in aggregate demand leads to a much larger change in income is called the multiplier effect.

An original change in the level of aggregate demand clearly can lead to a change in income. The multiplier effect tells us that the resulting change in income will be larger than the original change in demand—sort of an income bonus. How do we calculate the size of the multiplier and how does this multiplication in income occur?

If an increase in investment spending at $10 billion were to occur and, as a result, income were to increase by $30 billion, we would say the value of the multiplier is 3.0. If instead, the income were to increase to $40 billion, we would conclude the multiplier had a value of 4.0. The value of the multiplier is defined as the change in income divided by the actual change in aggregate demand.

The magnitude of the simple multiplier is directly related to the size of the marginal propensity to consume. The algebraic formula for finding the multiplier is written as follows:

$$\text{The multiplier } (m) = \frac{1}{\text{MPS}} = \frac{1}{(1-\text{MPC})}.$$

For example, if the MPC = .5, the multiplier is calculated $m = 1/(1-\text{MPC}) = 1/.5 = 2$. However, if the MPC increases to .75, the value of the multiplier is now $m = 1/\text{MPS} = 1/(1-\text{MPC}) = 1/.25 = 4$.

If the MPC equals .9, the multiplier is $m = 1/(1-.9) = 1/.1 = 10$. Therefore, the larger or smaller the MPC, the larger or smaller the size of the multiplier.

The multiplier effect can be shown from a simple numerical example. The multiplier derives its power from the spending-income-responding cycle. If consumer A increases his or her consumption, consumer B receives this spending as income. Consumer B saves part of this income and spends the remainder. Consumer C receives, as income, the expenditure of consumer B, saves part, and spends the rest. This process continues throughout the economy from round to round until the increase in consumption reaches zero. This round-by-round process is shown in table 14.5.

Table 14.5 The Multiplier Process
(original change in aggregate demand = $10)

Round	Change in Income	Change in Savings (MPS = 0.20)	Change in Savings (MPS = 0.20)
1	$10.00	$ 8.00	$ 2.00
2	8.00	6.40	1.60
3	6.40	5.12	1.28
4	5.12	4.10	1.02
5	4.10	3.28	0.82
All following rounds	16.38	13.10	3.28
Total	$50.00	$40.00	$10.00

Multiplier $= \dfrac{1}{\text{MPS}} = 5$.

In the first round of expenditures, the $10 in new aggregate demand becomes income for someone. Since the MPC is 0.80, this individual spends 80 percent—or $8.00—and because the MPS = 0.20, saves $2.00. In the second round, the $8.00 of consumption from round 1 becomes income for somebody else. This second individual also spends 80 percent and saves 20 percent. Therefore, additional consumption in round 2 amounts to $6.40 (0.80 × $8.00) and savings equals $1.60 (0.20 × $8.00).

In the third round, the $6.40 of additional consumption in round 2 creates income for somebody else. This individual also spends 80 percent and saves 20 percent of the newly found income. This cycle continues until the cycle is exhausted. The total income generated from the original $10 increase in spending is $50. The multiplier is confirmed to be equal to 5.0. Note that the total increase in new savings is equal to the original change in aggregate demand. This will always be the case. Moreover, the largest increases in income occur in the first few rounds. The increases in the later rounds become smaller and smaller. For this change in income to be permanent, the original change in aggregate demand must be sustained. If the change in aggregate demand is withdrawn, the process will be halted.

Check Your Understanding

The multiplier effect works for drops in total demand as well as for increases. If there is a $10 reduction in aggregate demand, the net effect will be a $50 decrease in total income. Check your understanding of the multiplier effect by duplicating the information from table 14.5, using an MPC of 0.50 or a multiplier of 2.0.

Answer: If your calculations are correct, you will have found that the magnitude of the total change in income is much less than that presented by the original table 14.5. The adjusted table is represented below:

Original change in aggregate demand = $10

Round	Change in Income	Consumption (MPC = 0.50)	Savings (MPS = 0.50)
1	$10.00	$ 5.00	$ 5.00
2	5.00	2.50	2.50
3	2.50	1.25	1.25
4	1.25	0.62	0.62
5	0.62	0.31	0.31
6	0.31	0.16	0.16
All following rounds	0.31	0.16	0.16
Total	$20.00*	$10.00	$10.00

*rounded

The Keynesian multiplier can also be shown graphically (figure 14.9). Panel A shows the aggregate demand and supply curves for a simple economy. This economy only has two components of demand: consumption and investment. We have further assumed the MPC to be equal to 0.8. The multiplier is, therefore, 5.0. Notice that when investment is increased, aggregate demand changes from $C+I$ to $C+I'$. As a result of the multiplier effect, the change in equilibrium national income is much larger than the original change in investment spending. The original change of $100 billion in investment spending leads to an increase of $500 billion in national income. In panel B, the effect of a decrease in investment spending is also shown. In this case, as investment spending declines by $100 billion, the equilibrium national income is reduced by $500 billion.

The multiplier effect applies to any change in the components of aggregate demand: consumption, investment, government, or net export expenditures. The final impact on the level of national income and employment is independent of the source of the change in spending.

THE PARADOX OF THRIFT

"A penny saved is a penny earned" and "save for a rainy day" are maxims many of us learn in childhood. There are certainly good reasons for individuals to increase their saving levels, but the issue of savings becomes clouded when we focus our attention on the whole economy.

Another element of Keynesian theory is the paradox of thrift. This apparent contradiction states that an individual can easily increase his or her level of savings, but if the economy or all individuals attempt to save more, it may lead under certain conditions to a decrease in national income, and as a result, total savings may not increase at all. The paradox of thrift is tied to the multiplier effect. If the savings attitudes of individuals change and lead to an attempt to save more, ceteris paribus, this will lead to a decrease in aggregate demand as consumption expenditures fall. Permanent decreases in aggregate demand will lead to amplified decreases in income, and the relatively larger decreases in income will reduce the ability to save.

RECESSIONARY AND INFLATIONARY GAPS: FORESHADOWING FISCAL POLICY

The major difference between the classical doctrine and Keynesian economics is the dispute over whether or not the economy can move toward a full-employment, noninflationary, equilibrium income level. Keynesian economics purports that the economy will reach an equilibrium position but that there is no guarantee the equilibrium position will be at a full-

FUNDAMENTALS OF KEYNESIAN ECONOMICS

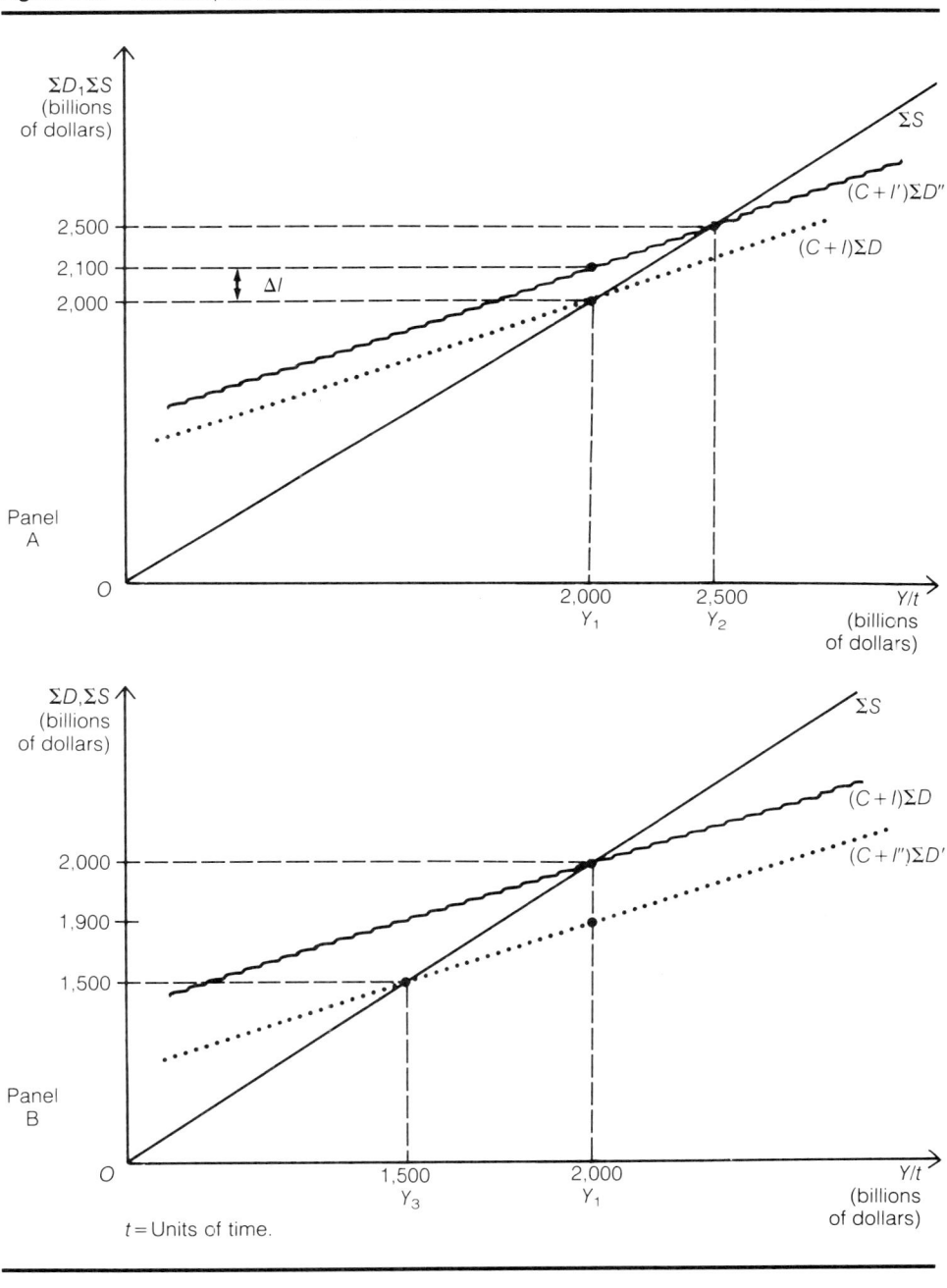

Figure 14.9 The Multiplier Effect for an Increase and Decrease in Investment Spending

Panel A

Panel B

t = Units of time.

Figure 14.10 Recessionary and Inflationary Gaps

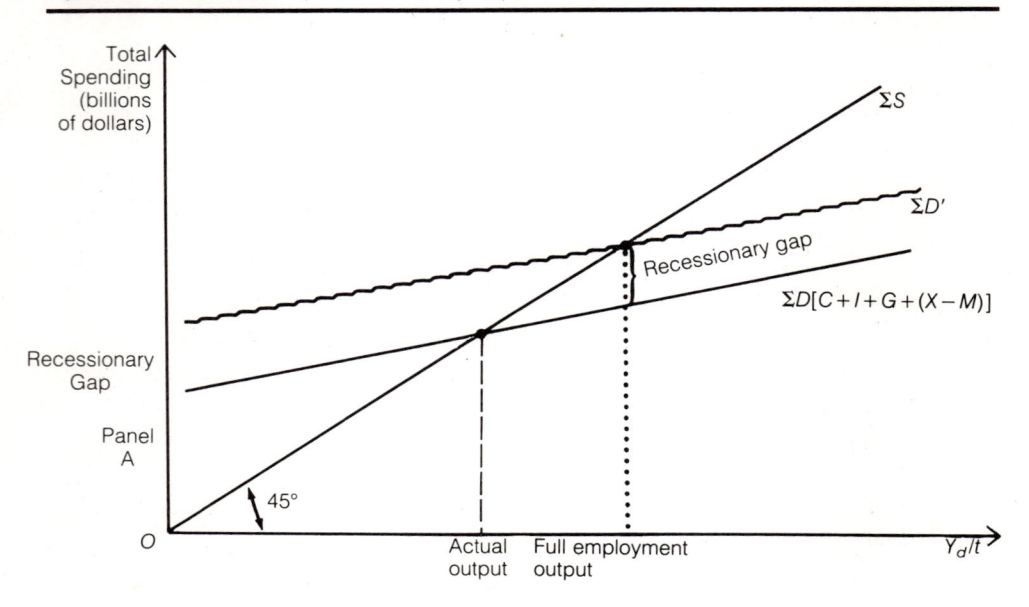

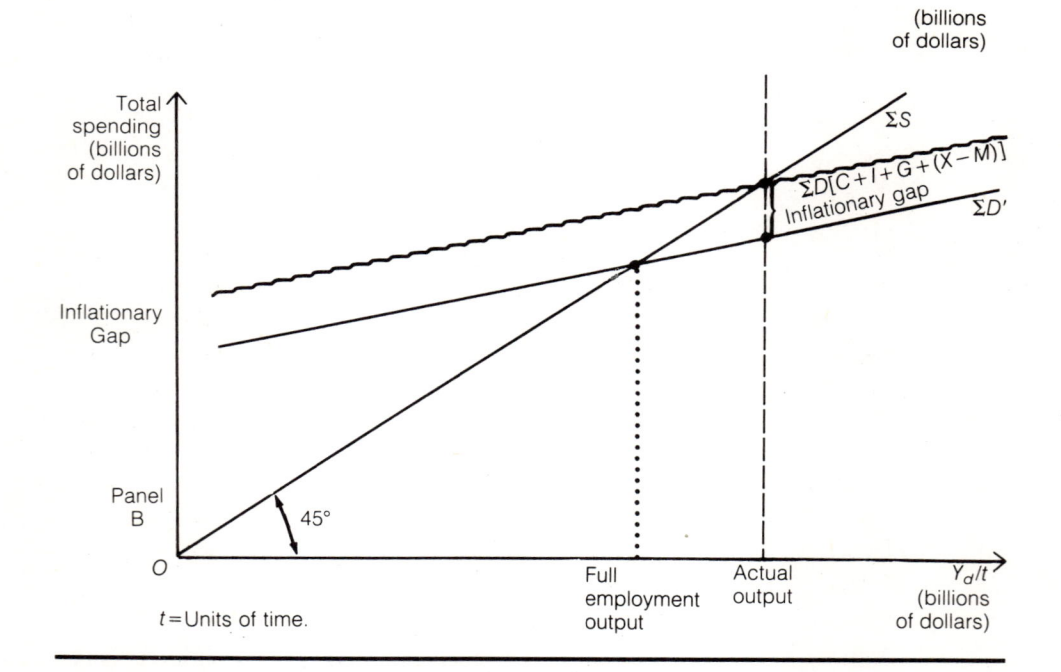

Total Spending (billions of dollars)
ΣS
ΣD'
Recessionary gap
ΣD[C+I+G+(X−M)]
Recessionary Gap
Panel A
45°
O
Actual output
Full employment output
Yd/t
(billions of dollars)
Total spending (billions of dollars)
ΣS
ΣD[C+I+G+(X−M)]
Inflationary gap
ΣD'
Inflationary Gap
Panel B
45°
O
Full employment output
Actual output
Yd/t (billions of dollars)

t = Units of time.

employment (noninflationary) level. The difference between the equilibrium levels reached by the economy and the ideal equilibrium level (at full employment, with no inflation) is called a recessionary inflationary gap. Figure 14.10 illustrates these two possibilities. In panel A, the full employment output is situated at a higher income level than actual output. This recessionary gap reflects unused capacity, idle factories, and high unemployment. Nevertheless, until aggregate demand increases, the gap will remain. The recessionary gap is measured as the change in aggregate demand necessary to move the economy to a full employment national income level. Because of the multiplier effect, the income gap is much larger than the aggregate demand or recessionary gap.

To Keynesians, the recessionary gap is the focus of fiscal policy. The major goal of fiscal policy is to find methods to reduce or eliminate the recessionary gap. In other words, the government should implement policies aimed at moving the aggregate demand curve ΣD upward toward the preferred position of $\Sigma D'$. The methods and analysis necessary to accomplish this objective are the subjects of the next chapter.

In panel B of figure 14.10, an inflationary gap is shown. The aggregate demand curve (ΣD) and aggregate supply curve (ΣS) intersect at a national income equilibrium level far above the full-employment equilibrium level. The vertical distance between ΣD and the preferred aggregate demand curve $\Sigma D'$ represents the amount of excess spending in the economy—the inflationary gap. This excess spending leads to classic demand-pull inflation. Since factories are already working at full-employment capacity, business is not able to respond with additional production, and the excess demand results in higher prices. The fiscal policy implications should be clear: the policy objective should be to somehow reduce aggregate demand downward from ΣD toward $\Sigma D'$. Because of the multiplier effect, the size of the income gap measured horizontally on the income axis is much more than the size of the inflationary gap measured vertically on the spending axis.

SUMMARY

Aggregate demand is the sum of all planned spending in an economy. The components of demand are consumption, investment, government, and the foreign sector spending. Consumption spending is the largest of the four components.

Aggregate supply is the total value of final goods and services produced at each possible income level.

Other factors that influence consumption spending levels include disposable income, wealth, consumer expectations, credit availability, attitudes toward thrift, and the supply of consumer durables.

The average propensity to consume and average propensity to save are measurements that reflect long-term relationships between consumption spending, savings, and disposable income. The marginal propensity to consume and marginal propensity to save show how total consumption and saving react to changes in total income.

When total spending equals total income, the economy is at equilibrium. At this point, total leakages (savings, taxes, and imports) equal total injections (investment, government, and export spending).

The multiplier effect explains how a particular change in total spending induces a significantly larger change in the equilibrium income level. The paradox of thrift follows this principle and holds that the desire to increase savings leads to a reduction in consumption spending. This, in turn, may cause a much larger decrease in the equilibrium income level and, as a result, affect the actual amount saved.

KEY WORDS

aggregate supply
autonomous change in consumption
average propensity to consume (APC)
average propensity to save (APS)
consumption function
dissavings
induced change in consumption
inflationary gap
law of consumption

marginal propensity to consume (MPC)
marginal propensity to save (MPS)
multiplier effect
paradox of thrift
recessionary gap
savings function
stock of wealth
total aggregate demand

Questions for Review

1. Recalculate the consumption function presented in table 14.2 using $200 as the level of autonomous consumption. How does this affect the APC and the APS? The MPC and the MPS?

2. Why does the APC differ from the MPC?

3. In addition to income, what other factors influence consumption levels?

FUNDAMENTALS OF KEYNESIAN ECONOMICS

4. Complete the following table using the assumption that 40 percent of any increase in income is spent on consumption. Graph the consumption and savings curves. Y_d = disposable income, C = consumption, and S = savings.

Y_d	C	S	APC	APS	MPC	MPS
$ 40	$56					
80						
120						
160						
200						
240						

5. When planned savings rises (the savings function shifts upward), income falls and the actual savings level is higher than before. What do Keynesians call this phenomenon?

6. Suppose the Y-intercept of the consumption function is $100 million and the MPC is 0.5. Create a table relating C and S to Y_d for all values of Y_d between $0 and $300 million (by $50 million intervals).

7. If C = $200 million, I = $100 million, G = $400 million, X = $50 million, and M = $150 million, what is aggregate demand?

8. Given the equation C = $100 + (.9)50, how much will households consume if Y_d = 0?

9. Why is Keynes's model said to be demand dependent?

10. What is the multiplier? How is its value determined?

425

ENDNOTES

1. For more information on Keynes, see Robert Lekachman, *The Age of Keynes* (New York: Random House, Inc., 1966). See also Dudley Dillard, *The Economics of John Maynard Keynes* (Englewood Cliffs, N.J.: Prentice-Hall, 1948).

2. John Maynard Keynes, *The General Theory of Employment, Interest, and Money* (New York: Harcourt, Brace, and World, Inc., 1936), p. 96.

3. The sum of APC and APS does not equal one because of the inclusion in disposable income of the interest paid by consumers to business and net personal transfer to foreigners. These items are excluded from consumption and saving, however.

4. Unfortunately for many banks, this low-interest financing by the financial arms of the giant auto firms has seriously eroded the automobile financing business for banks.

5. You should relate a change in autonomous consumption to the "change in quantity demanded" concept described in chapter 4. In fact, some authors have opted to call the change in consumption resulting from a change in a nonincome determinant as a "change in the amount consumed."

6. Recall that the marginal propensity to consume is the slope of the consumption function, and that the slope of C_1 is greater than the slope of C_2.

7. If a large number of consumers experienced an autonomous change in consumption, the added spending in the economy would lead to greater incomes, which would then cause an added induced change in consumption. This link between consumption, spending, and added consumption is discussed below under the multiplier concept.

8. The Greek letter Σ, sigma, is used here in the statistical sense, meaning "the sum of."

ECONOMICS IN THE NEWS

The Newest Name in Economics: John Maynard Keynes

Commentary by Norman Jonas and Joan Berger

The star of the American Economic Assn. convention in New Orleans Dec. 28-30 was a long-departed economist named John Maynard Keynes. The conferees were marking the 50th anniversary of Keynes's *General Theory of Employment, Interest and Money*, the book that transformed economic policymaking in the industrial world. But Keynes was much more than the birthday boy at this party.

His name was being bandied about because his ideas are returning to center stage, after enduring a decade of scorn, as economists grope for solutions to deepening worldwide problems of slow growth, excess capacity, unemployment, and severe trade imbalances.

The new appreciation of Keynes is not so much for his prescriptions of fiscal stimulus as for his revolutionary central thesis: Weak demand for workers and goods will not naturally revive if wages and prices soften. So Keynes advised government to step in to stimulate consumer demand and investment. His ideas were never abandoned by mainstream economists, but they became virtually useless in the 1970s, when the world's major economic problem became supply shortages rather than inadequate demand.

The Keynesians' loss was the monetarists' gain. As the 1970s wound down, the Keynesians were forced to accept the use of monetary restraint to subdue inflation. Grudgingly, the Keynesians also adopted the monetarist principle that stimulating demand to drive unemployment below some "natural" rate would be self-defeating because it would lead to higher inflation and ultimately even greater unemployment. In addition, the Keynesians gave ground to an elegant new school of classical economists known as rational expectationists, who hold that activist economic policies are inevitably frustrated by the public's perception that they will lead to higher inflation.

TOO MUCH OF EVERYTHING. But having made these concessions, the Keynesians are coming back into their own. Demand is once again the issue. Both industrial and developing nations are producing more than the world's peoples can afford to buy. The U.S. has artificially sustained its own demand since 1982 through supply-side tax cuts and has become the consumer of last resort for foreign goods.

The supply siders have no answer to the problem of gluts and underemployment. Nor do the monetarists, since their insistence on stable money growth precludes an activist response. Indeed, their thesis that monetary growth can be calibrated precisely to economic activity has been devastated in the past five years by chaotic shifts in velocity, the rate at which the money supply turns over. If no one can predict turnover, then the link between money, output, and prices collapses.

COMING TOGETHER. Neither side would concede defeat at the New Orleans meeting. Said monetarist Allan H. Meltzer of Carnegie-Mellon University: "We've really won. They've adopted a lot of our thinking." Keynesian Robert J. Gordon of Northwestern

University took a slightly different view: "Modern Keynesians have stolen many of the best ideas of the monetarists and the rational expectationists." But to disinterested observers, it looked more like convergence than a victory for either side, as leading Keynesians and rational expectationists alike urged the Federal Reserve to start targeting nominal gross national product instead of monetary growth—and monetarists seemed to go along. That, of course, means easier money to lower interest rates.

Beyond this, the Keynesians are still short on solutions for the economy's ills. Given the size of the budget and trade deficits, no one is talking about increased government spending or more tax cuts. But the Keynesians meeting in New Orleans had no hesitation about calling for the export of such old-fashioned remedies to other industrialized countries, particularly to West Germany and Japan, which seem bent on running huge trade surpluses by restraining domestic demand.

After the disappointments the public has experienced in recent years in the nostrums of just about every school of economics, it may be just as well that the Keynesians are not going overboard with proposals for saving the U.S. economy. What matters is that Keynesianism is still a useful framework for analyzing economic problems, if not a kit of solutions. In the long run, Keynes lives.

Reprinted from the January 12, 1987 issue of *Business Week*, by special permission. © 1987 by McGraw-Hill, Inc.

CHAPTER FIFTEEN

KEYNESIAN FISCAL POLICY IN ACTION

Objectives

After reading this chapter, you should be able to

•

identify the cause of an inflationary or deflationary gap

•

list and describe fiscal policy options for solving
inflationary and deflationary gap problems

•

describe the effects of government spending and taxation on the economy

•

explain the concept of the balanced budget multiplier

•

describe some of the automatic stabilizers
used to limit the severity and length of business-cycle fluctuations

•

describe expansionary and contractionary fiscal policies

•

define the four components of the fiscal policy timing lag

•

name four potential solutions to minimize timing lags

•

describe fiscal drag and differentiate between
the solutions of the Keynesians and the supply-side economists

•

identify four approaches to the federal budgeting process

•

define the crowding-out effect

•

list some criticisms of fiscal policy and four alternatives offered by its critics

The previous chapter set the stage for a discussion of the Keynesian prescription for economic disturbances. This chapter will focus on the preferred Keynesian reaction to aggregate demand—aggregate supply imbalances. The body of policy implications of Keynesian economics has become known as Keynesian fiscal policy. We will first examine the theoretical foundations of Keynesian fiscal policy, and then describe how these theoretical concepts are translated into real-life fiscal policy actions.

THE THEORY BEHIND FISCAL POLICY

In figure 15.1 both the inflationary gap and the recessionary (or deflationary) gap are shown. The aggregate supply curve appears as ΣS, and ΣD_1, ΣD_2, and ΣD_3 represent various levels of aggregate spending or demand. Income level Y_d^* is assumed to be the level of income that would generate full employment with price stability.

The only level of aggregate demand that ensures a level of national income capable of providing for full employment with price stability is the combination of consumption, investment, government and foreign sector spending shown as ΣD_1. Point A depicts the intersection of aggregate demand and aggregate supply at the full employment level of national income, Y_d^*. If the equilibrium level of national income was at level Y_d^*, no corrective fiscal policy would be required. However, if the equilibrium level of national income was either above or below this desired level, an inflationary or deflationary gap would result, and corrective fiscal policy measures could be instituted.

In the figure, an inflationary gap is shown as distance AB. This inflationary gap exists because the equilibrium level of income associated with aggregate demand, ΣD_3 exceeds the desired level of Y_d^*. The appropriate fiscal policy decision would be to reduce aggregate demand back to ΣD_1.

Similarly, a deflationary gap is shown as distance AC. The deflationary gap occurs because the equilibrium level of income associated with aggregate demand level ΣD_2 is less than the desired level of Y_d^*. The appropriate fiscal policy option would be to stimulate aggregate demand toward level ΣD_1.

An inflationary gap occurs when the equilibrium level of national income is greater than the level of national income consistent with full employment and price stability. The fiscal policy required to eliminate an inflationary gap is to reduce aggregate demand (figure 15.2). Current aggregate demand is shown in the figure as ΣD_o. This level of total planned spending leads to an equilibrium level of income of Y_d', which is greater than the full employment output Y_d^*. Total demand exceeds the productive capacity of the economy. Shortages of goods and services caused by this excess demand condition cause increases in the average price levels.

Figure 15.1 Inflationary and Deflationary Gaps

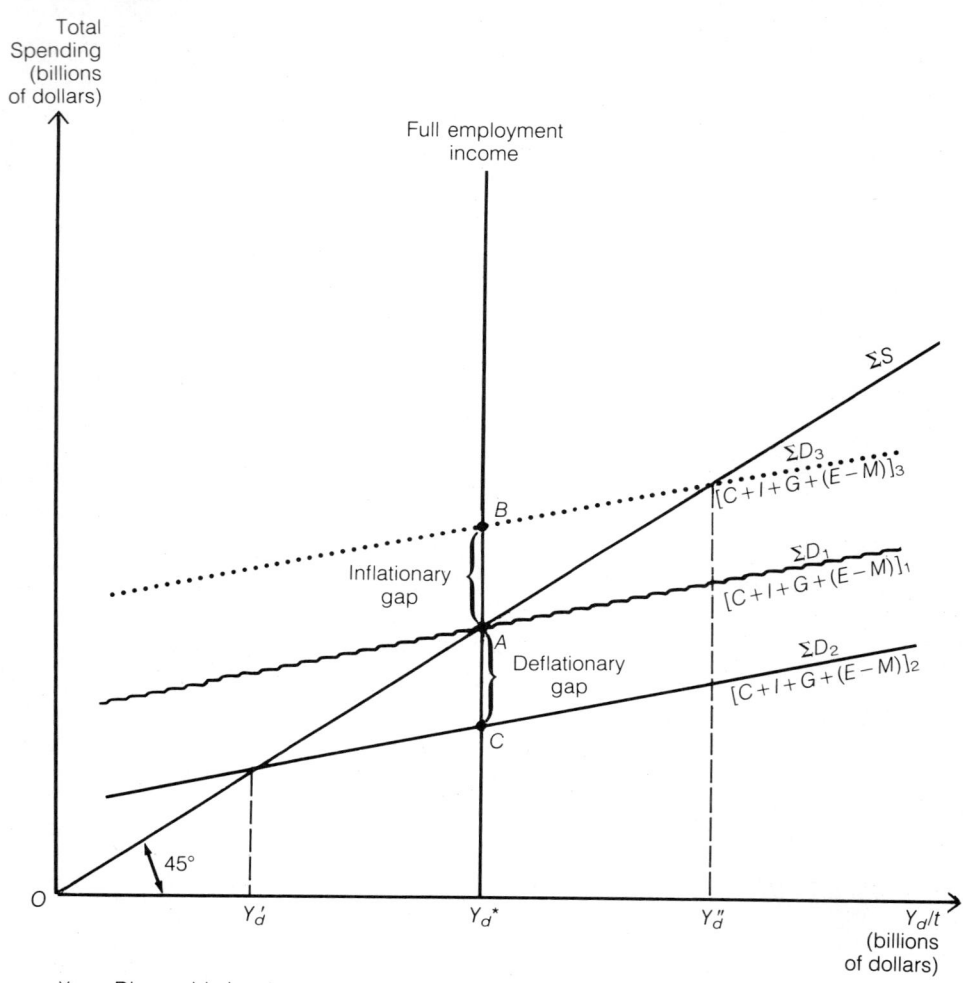

Y_d = Disposable income.
t = Units of time.

KEYNESIAN FISCAL POLICY

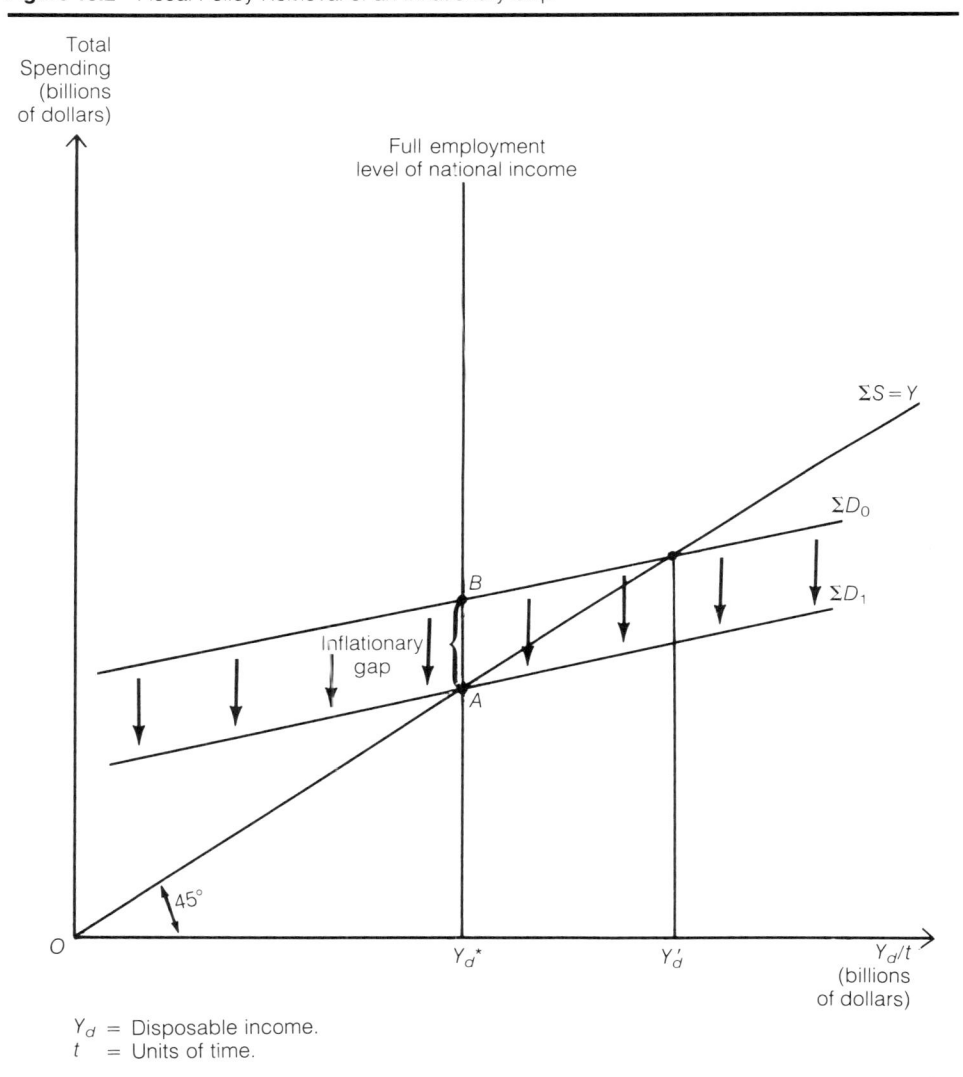

Figure 15.2 Fiscal Policy Removal of an Inflationary Gap

Y_d = Disposable income.
t = Units of time.

433

Figure 15.3 Fiscal Policy Removal of a Recessionary Gap

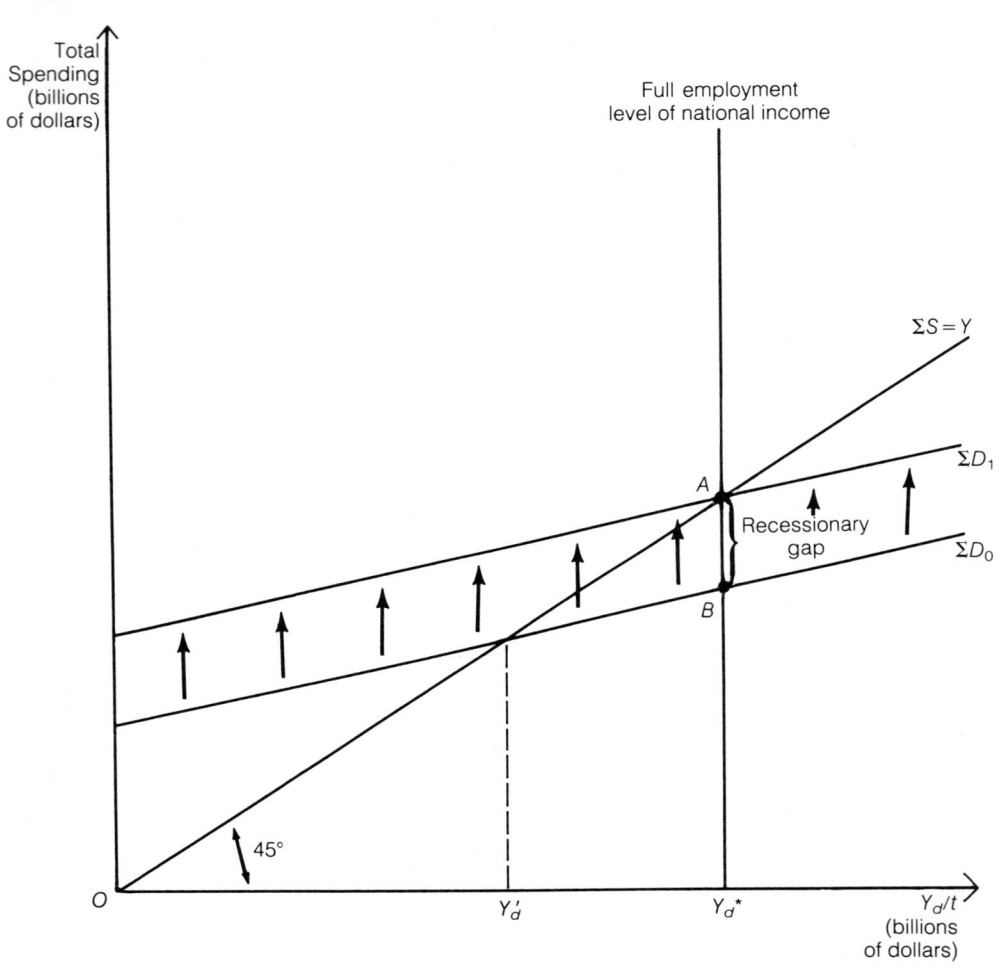

Y_d = Disposable income.
t = Units of time.

The policy implications of this economic dilemma are clear: the government should attempt to reduce aggregate demand by an amount equal to the value of inflationary gap of AB. In other words, reduce aggregate demand to level ΣD_1. Fiscal policy options can be of two basic types (figure 15.3). To reduce an inflationary gap, the government may (1) raise taxes to reduce the combined demands of the consumer, business, and foreign sector; or (2) reduce government spending.

It is one thing to suggest a reduction in aggregate demand to eliminate an inflationary gap. It is another matter to estimate the dollar value of the tax increase or cut in government spending that would lead to a full-employment noninflationary national income. This more exact process will be discussed below.

THE NUTS AND BOLTS OF FISCAL POLICY

To illustrate the mechanics of fiscal policy, we will construct a hypothetical economy with aggregate output and aggregate demand components (table 15.1).

In this example, the marginal propensity to consume is .75 and the marginal propensity to save is .25. Therefore, the simple multiplier has a value of 4.0. That is, any change in aggregate demand will lead to a fourfold change in equilibrium output. Also in this example, investment expenditure and net exports are assumed to be fixed, regardless of the level of output, at $150 and $50, respectively, and government expenditures are assumed to be initially $0. Given these conditions, the economy would attain equilibrium at an output level of $4,700. Here, aggregate demand is equal to aggregate supply. Alternatively, total leakage (savings) is equal to total injections (investment plus net exports) only at total output level $4,700. Now, let us see how our hypothetical economy is affected by adding government spending.

Effects of Government Spending

The equilibrium income level of this economy will change when government spending is initiated (table 15.2). If we assume that government spending is set at a level of $200, what effect does this have on the economy? We can trace two major changes in the economy. First, as was discussed in chapter 14, government expenditures are a component of aggregate demand, so the addition of government purchases in our economy raises the level of aggregate demand at all levels of output by the amount of the government expenditures. In this case, the aggregate demand figures are $200 greater at each income level than those in table 15.1.

Second, a major change in the equilibrium level of national output can be observed. The equilibrium level of output has increased from $4,700 to $5,500. This increase

Table 15.1 Hypothetical Economy Without Government Spending
(billions of dollars)

NNP=DI Total Output or Income	Consumption Spending (C)	Saving (S)	Investment Spending (I)	Government Spending (G)	Net Export Spending (X−M)	Aggregate Demand [C+I+G+(X−M)]
3,700	3,750	−50	150	0	50	3,950
3,900	3,900	0	150	0	50	4,100
4,100	4,050	50	150	0	50	4,250
4,300	4,200	100	150	0	50	4,440
4,500	4,350	150	150	0	50	4,550
4,700	4,500	200	150	0	50	4,700
4,900	4,650	250	150	0	50	4,850
5,100	4,800	300	150	0	50	5,000
5,300	4,950	350	150	0	50	5,150
5,500	5,100	400	150	0	50	5,300
5,700	5,250	450	150	0	50	5,450

Table 15.2 Hypothetical Economy with Government Spending
(billions of dollars)

Total Output or Income	Consumption Spending (C)	Saving (S)	Investment Spending (I)	Government Spending (G)	Net Export Spending (X−M)	Aggregate Demand [C+I+G+(X−M)]
3,700	3,750	−50	150	200	50	4,150
3,900	3,900	0	150	200	50	4,300
4,100	4,050	100	150	200	50	4,450
4,300	4,200	150	150	200	50	4,600
4,500	4,350	200	150	200	50	4,750
4,700	4,500	250	150	200	50	4,900
4,900	4,650	300	150	200	50	5,050
5,100	4,800	350	150	200	50	5,200
5,300	4,950	400	150	200	50	5,350
5,500	5,100	450	150	200	50	5,500
5,700	5,250	500	150	200	50	5,650

demonstrates the powerful effect of the multiplier. With a multiplier of 4.0, the $200 increase in aggregate demand caused by the addition of government spending raises the equilibrium level of income by $800. If we were now to reduce government expenditures from $200 to $0, the equilibrium level of output would fall by $800. Therefore, the multiplier can have a powerful expansionary and contractionary impact.

The government spending we have introduced requires financing. The traditional method of financing government spending is through taxation. But what would happen to our economy if we raised taxes in order to pay for this spending? Table 15.3 shows the effect of taxation on the equilibrium income levels. We have levied a lump-sum tax, or a tax where the total tax revenue is constant, regardless of the level of income, in the amount required to offset the government spending, or $200.

Table 15.3 Hypothetical Economy: Impact of Taxes and Government Spending (billions of dollars)

Total Output or Income	Taxes (T)	Disposable Income (DI)	Consumption Spending (C)	Saving (S)	Investment Spending (I)	Government Spending (G)	Net Export Spending (X − M)	Aggregate Demand [C + I + G + (X − M)]
3,700	200	3,500	3,600	−100	150	200	50	4,000
3,900	200	3,700	3,750	−50	150	200	50	4,150
4,100	200	3,900	3,900	0	150	200	50	4,300
4,300	200	4,100	4,050	50	150	200	50	4,450
4,500	200	4,300	4,200	100	150	200	50	4,600
4,700	200	4,500	4,350	150	150	200	50	4,750
4,900	200	4,700	4,500	200	150	200	50	4,900
5,100	200	4,900	4,650	250	150	200	50	5,050
5,300	200	5,100	4,800	300	150	200	50	5,200
5,500	200	5,300	4,950	350	150	200	50	5,350
5,700	200	5,500	5,100	400	150	200	50	5,500

The first impact of the tax is to create a divergence between national income and disposable income. Now consumers have $200 less income to spend on consumption at all levels of income. Notice, at every level of income, not only has the tax reduced disposable income but it has also lowered both consumption and saving. In other words, consumers have "paid" their tax bill by cutting back on both spending and saving. Since the MPC = .75 and the MPS = .25, consumers naturally reduced consumption by $150 (.75 × $200) and saving by $50 (.25 × $200). Therefore, the effect of the tax was to reduce both consumption and savings at all income levels by the amount of the tax.

Taxation has also affected the equilibrium level of output. The new equilibrium level of output can be determined in two ways.

Under the aggregate demand-aggregate supply approach, we find the equilibrium level of output stands at $4,900, down from the $5,500 level of table 15.2. The injection-leakages approach to income determination yields the same equilibrium level of income. Total injection includes government spending, investment spending, and net exports. Total leakages include savings and taxes. Only at the equilibrium level of income of $4,900 do total injection and leakages equal each other ($400).

The imposition of the lump-sum tax of $200 lowered equilibrium income from $5,500 to $4,900, or by $600. The addition of $200 of government spending caused, through the multiplier effect, an increase of $800 in equilibrium income. We also warned that if we were to remove the government spending, equilibrium income would fall by $800. In other words, if we increase taxes and government spending by equal amounts, equilibrium income rises by an identical amount. This phenomenon is known as the balanced budget multiplier.

The Balanced Budget Multiplier

The balanced budget multiplier holds that if there are equal and offsetting increases in both taxes and government spending, the equilibrium level of income will not remain the same, but will increase by the exact amount of the increase. In our example, before we introduced either government spending or taxation, the economy was in equilibrium at income level $4,700. Yet after we added $200 in taxes and $200 in government spending, the economy achieved its new equilibrium income at $4,900—precisely $200 higher than before.

This apparent paradox can be solved easily. Any change in government spending is immediately and fully transferred to a change in aggregate demand. A change in taxes, however, depending upon the value of the marginal propensity to consume, has a less-powerful effect on aggregate demand through the resultant change in consumption spending. In our example, the $200 tax bite reduced consumption demand by only $150 because the MPC was .75 (.75 × $200). The net effect of the tax increase ($150 reduction in aggregate demand) and the government spending increase ($200 increase in aggregate demand) is a $50 gain in aggregate demand. When the simple multiplier is applied, our $50 increase in aggregate spending is transformed into a $200 increase in equilibrium income. To calculate the impact on equilibrium income of a change in aggregate demand, use the following formula:

$$\Delta NI = (\Delta \Sigma D)(m),$$

where ΔNI = the change in equilibrium income,
$\Delta \Sigma D$ = the change in aggregate demand, and
m = the multiplier.

THE MATHEMATICS OF FISCAL POLICY

A slightly more complex hypothetical economy is presented in table 15.4 to illustrate the use of fiscal policy to drive the economy to full-employment equilibrium. We will use a number of familiar simplifying assumptions to keep the example clear: we assume that taxes are at a constant level, regardless of the level of national income; investment expenditures and net exports are also constant and unaffected by changes in income; government expenditures initially are fixed and unrelated to changes in the level of income and are considered part of our original aggregate demand schedule; prices are stable and any change in aggregate demand will affect real output, not prices.

In column 3, the unemployment rate associated with various levels of national income is shown. For example, at a relatively low level of output or income, say $3,900, unemployment is 8.0 percent, but as output rises to $4,700, the unemployment rate drops to 6.0 percent. Table 15.4, then, is a reconstruction of table 15.3 except for the addition of the unemployment data. The equilibrium level of income for the economy is $4,900. The unemployment rate associated with this equilibrium level of income is 5.5 percent. Suppose the government declares that the only acceptable level of unemployment (or the desired level of full employment) is 4.5 percent. Obviously, the equilibrium national output must be raised to the $5,300 level in order to force unemployment down to the desired 4.5 percent. The government may either lower taxes, raise spending, or do both in order to increase aggregate demand to drive up the equilibrium level of income from $4,900 to $5,300.

AUTOMATIC VS. DISCRETIONARY FISCAL POLICY

Automatic Stabilizers

In an effort to continually stabilize the business cycle, several automatic fiscal measures have been put in place. These stabilizers may be implemented without legislative approval.

Table 15.4 Fiscal Policy in Action
(billions of dollars)

National Income (Aggregate Supply)	Taxes	Unemployment Rate (percent)	Disposable Personal Income	Consumption Expenditure	Savings	Investment Expenditures	Government Expenditures	Net Export Expenditures	Total Expenditures $[C+I+G+(X-M)]$ (Aggregate Demand)
3,900	200	8.0	3,700	3,750	−50	200	150	50	4,150
4,100	200	7.5	3,900	3,900	0	200	150	50	4,300
4,300	200	7.0	4,100	4,050	50	200	150	50	4,450
4,500	200	6.5	4,300	4,200	100	200	150	50	4,600
4,700	200	6.0	4,500	4,350	150	200	150	50	4,750
4,900	200	5.5	4,700	4,500	200	200	150	50	4,900
5,100	200	5.0	4,900	4,650	250	200	150	50	5,050
5,300	200	4.5	5,100	4,800	300	200	150	50	5,200
5,500	200	4.0	5,300	4,950	350	200	150	50	5,350
5,700	200	3.5	5,500	5,100	400	200	150	50	5,500

Current rate ☐
Desired rate ⌐⌐

While the automatic stabilizers may not be strong enough to ward off a major recession or inflation, their combined actions certainly help to reduce the severity and length of an inflationary or recessionary period. These automatic devices include both tax and government-payment mechanisms.

Proportional and Progressive Income Taxes

Recall from chapter 6 that the vast majority of federal taxes levied on businesses and individuals are, at least in part, proportional or progressive in nature. These taxes help stabilize the economy.

For example, as income begins to fall at the outset of an economic downturn, the taxes actually collected by government units also decline. For a progressive tax, this decline in tax receipts can be acute; for a proportional tax, it is generally less acute. Given current tax laws, a reduction of $100 billion in the GNP would lead to a drop in tax receipts estimated at between $30 and $40 billion. (The exact amount of loss would depend upon the group of taxpayers most injured by the drop in economic activity.) The economy thus receives assistance automatically. The relatively lower tax liability is a boost to business and consumers. Proportionately more after-tax income is available for investment and consumption spending! While a drop in national income is serious, the impact of the drop is attenuated or softened by tax effects.

Similarly, the U.S. tax structure stabilizes the business cycle in an expansion phase. When national income and spending are rising and inflationary pressures are building, increased tax burdens remove spending power from the private sector. This reduction in spending tends to reduce inflationary pressures. All of these actions take place without deliberate intervention in the economy.

Unemployment Compensation and Other Transfer Payments

A large number of employees have partial income protection from job loss through the unemployment insurance system. The coverage and conditions vary by state; however, the basic automatic stabilizer function of unemployment compensation works this way: when a covered employee is laid off, that employee receives unemployment compensation. This compensation is not equal to the employee's normal income, but the compensation prevents the disaster of a total loss of income. Because this program also injects income into our economy exactly when income levels are falling because of rising unemployment, unemployment compensation payments help soften the potential drop in aggregate spending. Unemployed workers can continue spending, albeit at reduced levels.

Unemployment compensation also helps moderate expansions. The various state unemployment compensation programs are funded through the "premiums" paid by business. The premiums act as a slight drag on business cash flow during periods of robust economic activity, and this added business expense tends to reduce the absolute limits of business expansion, and perhaps reduce inflationary forces.

To summarize, during economic downturns, spending-power "injections" from unemployment compensation benefits are greater than the "leakages" of unemployment compensation premiums (taxes) paid by employers, and the net effect is a stimulation of the economy. During the inflationary, or expansionary, phase of the business cycle, leakages in the form of unemployment compensation taxes outweigh the injections of unemployment compensation benefits paid to employees and, on balance, the economy and inflationary forces are restrained.

Minor Automatic Stabilizers

There are a host of other government programs and private employee-employer contracts and relationships that tend to automatically stabilize the business cycle. For example, certain labor agreements contain supplemental unemployment benefit (SUB) clauses designed to supplement the income of laid-off workers. The labor contracts stipulate that the companies will fund the plans with the monies to be paid to laid-off employees during slack business periods. Private SUB plans affect the economy in the same fashion as the public sector's unemployment compensation programs.

Other public plans include welfare payments, farm subsidies, and other government subsidies that assist both consumers and corporations in times of economic distress. These programs help to deflect the economy's maximum potential decline.

FISCAL POLICY ISSUES AND PROBLEMS

Timing Lags

Because of the nature of discretionary fiscal policy decision making, it is likely that long time delays will occur between the time the need for action is perceived and the time the actual policy implementation causes changes in aggregate demand. If the economic problems that precipitated the need for policy action persist, the fiscal policy time lag damages the economy by simply prolonging economic suffering. Under certain conditions, the time lag can actually cause more serious economic problems to develop.

For example, assume the economy is currently suffering from high inflation caused by excess demand conditions, and the fiscal authorities attempt to implement policy that is designed to drain excess aggregate demand from the system. Implementation is delayed by the timing lags inherent in the fiscal policy decision-making process. During this delay, the economic conditions change and inflationary gaps are eliminated by internal market forces. If the change in the economy is not observed in time, the anti-inflationary policy might be set in motion. Now, "excess" aggregate demand is removed from a system already in equilibrium. This action could result in the creation of a recessionary gap. In other words, a fiscal policy designed to be countercyclical could, inadvertently, become procyclical, and drive the economy away from equilibrium. Obviously, timing lags represent a major practical problem for fiscal policy. Is it possible to shorten or eliminate the lag? To answer this question, we must investigate the nature and structure of the fiscal policy lag.

Fiscal policy time lags are broken into four categories: the recognition lag, the study lag, the implementation lag, and the effect lag. Together, these separate lags can add up to many months, even years.

The Recognition Lag

While economic activity takes place on a daily basis, the data collection required to record this activity takes time. Government economists and statisticians do a commendable job in preparing the various statistical economic time series that are used to evaluate and study the health of the economy, but the process itself is time-consuming, and reporting delays and data revisions are commonplace.[1] Months may pass before economists even recognize that a particular economic problem exists.

For example, you will recall from our earlier discussion of the business cycle that traditionally the economy must experience a decline in real income of at least 2 consecutive quarters (6 months) before a recession is declared. When you add to this the lag associated with final data collection, many months may elapse before the economy is officially diagnosed to be in a recession. Yet consumers and businesses are already suffering the effects of the economic downturn.

The Study Lag

The study lag is defined as the length of time required for the fiscal authorities (the Council of Economic Advisors, the executive branch, and Congress) to investigate the causes and possible array of solutions available to cure the aggregate-demand imbalance. Once the issue has been studied, concrete plans for action can be proposed. Meanwhile, certain groups in the economy continue to feel the discomfort of the existing imbalance. Once specific fiscal policy prescriptions have been proposed, the administrative, and/or political approval process begins.

The Implementation Lag

Because of the democratic structure of the U.S. government, the executive branch of government must secure congressional or legislative approval on spending and taxation matters. Those familiar with the legislative process of American politics understand the potential delays that can occur in obtaining congressional approval in matters affecting the federal budget. Congressional debate, committee investigation, lobbyist intervention, partisan logrolling, and media attention can create a long "traffic jam" for any well-intentioned proposal. The time required to formally promulgate the fiscal policy is called the implementation or administrative lag.

In practice, the executive branch frequently will try to shorten this delay by presenting the economic problem as a national emergency. The president may address the nation on prime-time television to alert the nation to the problem and urge swift congressional adoption of the fiscal policy programs.[2] Such actions sometimes help; unfortunately, however, this process can itself often seriously delay or even "kill" a fiscal policy proposal.

The Effect Lag

The final lag component, the effect lag, is simply the length of time it takes for the fiscal policy to actually cause the desired change in aggregate demand. For example, if the economy is suffering from a recession and a tax cut is recommended and adopted by Congress, the effect lag would consist of the time required to actually change the take-home pay of workers, plus the additional time required for wary consumers to spend their increased income. Eventually, this spending would lead to increased orders, sales expansion and recall of laid-off workers, and ultimately reduced unemployment.

Fiscal Policy Speedup

Can the problems of fiscal policy lag be reduced? A number of proposed solutions to the fiscal policy lag problem exist. One suggested improvement is to increase reliance on economic forecasts in fiscal policy formulations. While economic forecasting is still in its relative infancy, the reliability and usefulness of economic forecasts have improved dramatically in recent years. Incorporating forecasts into the policy-making process could shorten or eliminate many of the delays described above.

Second, if fiscal policy could in some way be removed or isolated from the political process, the implementation or administrative lag could be reduced. The Federal Reserve provides an excellent example of how an independent, nonpartisan agency can react quickly and decisively to bring about changes in monetary policy.

Third, projects instituted by fiscal policy design can be selected to speed or slow the desired change in aggregate demand. For example, major government construction projects such as dams, highways, and so forth, which are part of fiscal policy decisions, tend to be extremely slow in completion, and hence in bringing about changes in spending or output. Because of the nature and timing problems of government spending projects, recent fiscal policy has focused on the relatively speedy tax adjustment as the mainstay of fiscal policy.

Finally, an overall solution to the problem of fiscal policy lag may be to reduce the reliance on discretionary fiscal policy by either increasing the number and/or improving the impact of automatic stabilizers. Automatic stabilizers go into effect without the need for study or approval: they are, in a sense, pre-approved fiscal measures. One of the greatest challenges facing economists and fiscal policymakers is to develop and implement automatic stabilizers, which can be ready to "save" the economy when it encounters trouble without stifling the free-market mechanism. Policymakers must balance the need for built-in stability against the dangers of excessive regulation and awkward government bureaucracy.

Fiscal Drag

Another problem created by fiscal policy is fiscal drag. Fiscal drag occurs when the automatic stabilization impact of a tax structure drains off aggregate demand from the economy. For example, given a tax system that encourages automatic stabilization of income levels around a full-employment equilibrium level, any discretionary antirecessionary fiscal policy used will not be fully effective because the tax system drains new tax revenues from the newly generated income. In this situation, the automatic stabilizer reduces the effect of the discretionary fiscal policy decision.

The new supply-side school of economic thought urges reductions in government regulation, more limited government intervention in the economy, and massive tax cuts in order to improve private sector incentives and initiatives. Supply-siders find at least one aspect of Keynesian economics appealing, albeit for a completely different reason than the Keynesians themselves. The Keynesians and the supply-siders both support general tax cuts as an attempt to cure the problem of fiscal drag. Yet they differ as to the mechanism by which this fiscal policy action would operate.

Supply-side economists hold that fiscal drag can be defeated by general tax cuts through the increased work efforts and production that would be generated by the new incentives. They argue that high marginal tax rates stifle the desire to work. As individuals choose between work and leisure time, heavy tax penalties cause many to select greater amounts of leisure rather than work. This tends to lower production and output levels. Supply-siders claim that a general tax cut would alter this critical work-leisure calculus.

Keynesians, on the other hand, envision a more direct route between general tax cuts and the reduction of fiscal drag. They hold that tax cuts result in more disposable income for consumers and higher after-tax profits for business. This added income will be spent on greater amounts of goods and services by consumers, and on investment projects by business. The multiplier process will magnify these gains in spending to raise the economy to a higher, possibly even full-employment, level of aggregate output.

FEDERAL BUDGET POLICY

The interaction of government expenditures on goods and services and the tax policies used to pay for this spending makes up the world of the federal budget. Congressional policymakers must answer a number of important questions concerning fiscal policy and the federal budget. For example, is it the absolute goal of the government to balance the budget at all times? Should a balanced budget goal be subordinate to the need for fiscal policy? How should deficits and surpluses be managed? Should we print or borrow money to finance deficits? The answers to these and other questions have created a great deal of confusion and debate. We will investigate the basic budgeting philosophy in the remainder of this chapter and study the issue of deficit financing and the public debt in the next.

Several approaches to the budget process exist, four of which are discussed below.

The Annually Balanced Budget

One approach to the federal budget holds that the government must, under all circumstances, balance its budget on a yearly basis. The government should only spend an amount of money equal to its tax receipts. This view equates the federal budget to that of an individual or household. Debt is considered dangerous and should be avoided at all costs. Proponents of this approach argue that an annually balanced budget would have a neutral effect on the economy, and that an annually balanced budget is the only way to prevent a politically motivated Congress from spending the nation into debt. However, there are some problems with this position.

Assume that the budget is initially balanced and the economy is entering into an expansion phase. As the nation's output and income rise, so do the tax revenues of the federal treasury. In order for the government to balance the budget, tax cuts, new spending programs, or both would have to be instituted. However, these balanced budget maneuvers would hardly have a neutral impact on the economy: tax cuts and increases in government spending lead to increases in both national income and expenditures. These pressures in turn provoke an even more robust expansion.

Similarly, if the economy is in the contraction phase of the cycle, tax receipts will begin to fall as both output and income decline. With an annually balanced budget rule, the government would be forced to raise taxes, cut spending, or both in order to make up for the loss in tax revenues. These policies also are not neutral. Either policy, implemented at this time, would push the economy deeper into recession.

The Cyclically Balanced Budget

The cyclically balanced budget approach rejects the rule of annually accounting for tax receipts and spending. Instead, it requires an accounting over the length of the entire business cycle. In other words, the government would be free to run a deficit in those years when the economy is in a recession and suffering from a decline in spending, and to run a surplus in those years when the economy is experiencing excess aggregate demand and inflation. The theory here is that the total deficits will be offset by the total surpluses. Unfortunately, this is unlikely to occur in practice. Historical data indicate that recessions and expansions differ in both length and magnitude. There can be no guarantee that balancing surpluses and deficits would occur.

Functional Finance

A third approach to fiscal budgetmaking holds that whether the budget is balanced with regard to surpluses or deficits is of little importance. Instead, the major purpose of the budget is business cycle management. This view, which completely subordinates the issue of deficits and surpluses to fiscal policy considerations, is called the functional finance approach.

Functional finance proponents argue that the cost of constant deficits or an occasional surplus is a small price to pay for economic stability. They argue that a fully employed economy without inflation is far more desirable than a fiscally balanced federal budget in an unstable economy.

Opponents of this approach charge that functional finance leads to massive federal deficits and debt, and that this debt burden causes real long-term harm to the economy in the form of persistent inflation and distortions in private investment.

The Full-Employment Cyclically Adjusted Budget

The final approach to fiscal policy and the budget is called the full-employment cyclically adjusted budget. This approach assumes the existence of an ideal level of national output at which the unemployment rate (or, conversely, the employment level) is at an optimal level. In other words, a full-employment or high-employment income goal is set, and the budget that would exist under those conditions is determined. The actual budget in any given year is

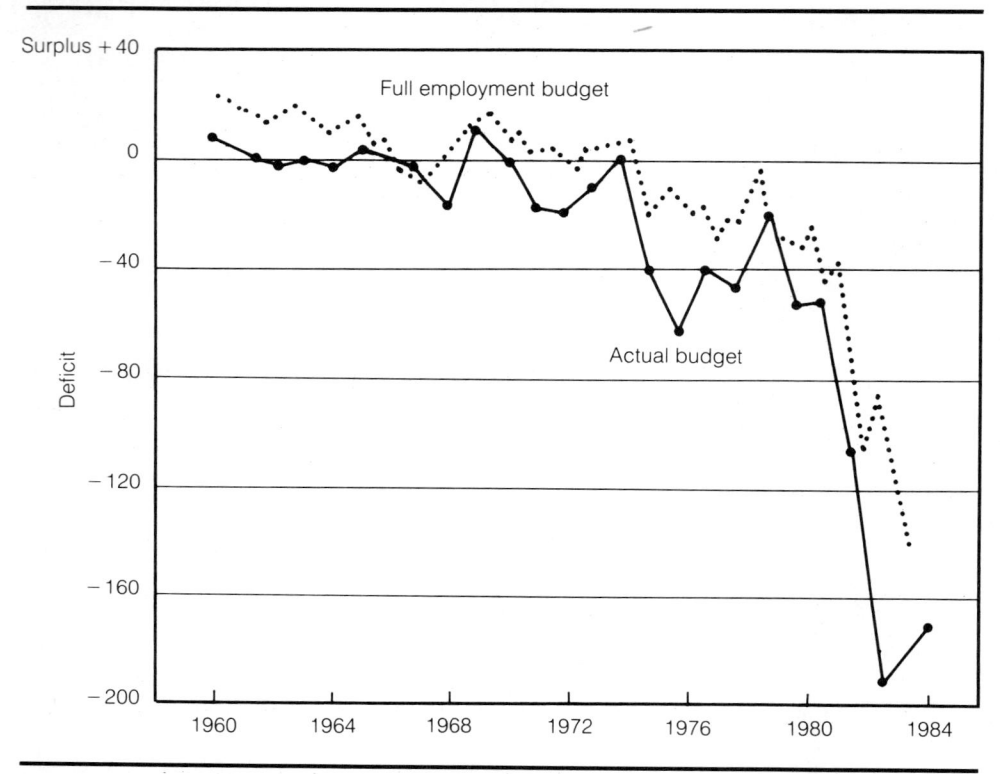

Figure 15.4 Actual and Full Employment Budgets 1960–84

Source: Office of Management and Budget, Federal Reserve Bank of St. Louis.

then compared with the ideal full-employment or high-employment budget. By comparing the actual budget expenditures in any year with the revenues of the ideal budget, policymakers can judge the influence of their current policy.

For example, it is possible for the actual budget to be in a deficit position, but when compared with full-employment budget revenues, the actual budget may be in balance or even show a surplus.

Figure 15.4 shows the relationship of the actual budget to the full-employment budget for selected years. Notice that both the cyclically adjusted budget and the actual budget have shown deficits for most of the years. Generally, the actual budget deficit has been larger than the full-employment or high-employment budget deficit for the majority of years. This indicates that the actual output level has been less than the full-employment output level for most of the period.

Printing Money

One way to finance a deficit is simply to print money. Most forms of deficit financing involve the issuance of government securities, but it is also possible to "finance" deficits through the printing press. As we have learned, however, this practice is extremely dangerous. The stimulus to the economy generated by printing money is much stronger than the stimulus generated when government debt is issued. Uncontrollable inflationary pressures may be generated when the choice to finance deficits by printing money is made.

The Crowding-Out Effect

A major criticism of fiscal policy in general is that when the government must run a budget deficit to support expansionary fiscal policy, the policy itself is ineffective and destabilizing because of the crowding-out effect. Crowding out occurs when the government finances the deficit through borrowing in the capital markets. This often-massive intrusion into the private capital market causes a dramatic increase in the demand for funds, and of course, an increase in the price of these funds (the interest rate). Higher interest rates tend to cut investment spending and certain forms of consumer demand tied to credit-market conditions. Therefore, what started out as an expansionary fiscal policy may actually lead to a reduction in aggregate demand in the investment and consumption sectors. If the crowding-out effect is large enough, the fiscal policy may be rendered completely ineffective.

There is much debate as to the real magnitude of the crowding-out effect. Everyone seems to agree that the impact of the crowding-out effect is far more severe during a period of business expansion than during a recessionary period. Some argue that during a recession, when tremendous "slack" already exists in the economy, the crowding-out effect could be virtually insignificant. Finally, others argue that if the monetary authorities increase the money supply to offset the added demand for money caused by the crowding-out effect, its impact could be minimized. However, such an increase in the money supply could be inflationary.

CRITIQUES OF KEYNESIAN FISCAL POLICY

Fiscal policy can be a powerful economic stabilization tool. However, timing problems, budget deficits, public debt issues, and the crowding-out effect all tend to dampen its effectiveness. One of the major issues surrounding fiscal policy concerns the size and implications of the public debt that results from deficit-finance policy. We will devote the next chapter to the study of this issue.

A number of economists have criticized the Keynesian-based model of fiscal policy, attacking both its structure and its practicality. One criticism even centers around the specific industries that normally bear the brunt of fiscal policy action. In the next section, we will examine the ideas of the major opponents of current fiscal policy.

Rational Expectation Theory

The rational expectation theory holds that all economic agents (investors, employers, employees, and so on) have a complete and thorough knowledge of our market system. Furthermore, the theory claims that these economic agents are able to ascertain any change in the government's economic policy and use this information in a "rational" manner. Economic agents use past government policy outcomes to predict future conditions, and they "expect" certain policies to have a precise impact on their economic condition. Rational expectation theorists argue that since economic agents are rational, any government policy aimed at altering the economy may be offset by the actions of these rational economic agents, who are acting in their own self-interest.

For example, assume strong recessionary pressures are gripping the nation. We would expect the government to undertake expansionary fiscal policy. However, in the past, workers have suffered real-wage losses from the inflationary pressures these budget-deficit-producing policies have generated. In order to protect themselves from anticipated inflation, workers will demand higher money wages. These higher wages can have a softening effect on profits and, subsequently, on future output and employment. Therefore, the hoped-for reduction in unemployment may be forestalled by the anticipatory actions of economic agents. In effect, fiscal policy effectiveness can be reduced by the actions of employees, consumers, or businesses who anticipate future economic change.

Wage-Price Guidelines and Controls

Many experts feel that fiscal policy is ineffective in fighting inflation because of the severe deflationary impact on output and employment. As an alternative, they offer a program of immediate relief in the form of wage-price guidelines or controls. These laws or recommendations attempt to limit the percentage of wage and/or price increases allowed. Such guidelines (usually voluntary) and controls (mandated by law) have been instituted in the past to control runaway inflation. They were used in one form or another during the 1960s by the Kennedy and Johnson administrations, in the Nixon administration's wage-price freeze of the early 1970s, and in President Carter's wage-price guideposts in the late 1970s.

Like the rational expectation theorists, those who support the use of rules to fight inflation argue that inflation is driven and sustained by inflationary expectations. They believe that wage-price guidelines and controls can stop continuously rising expectations. If these expectations are stopped, then workers and firms will not demand anticipatory wage and price increases. Proponents of this view also argue the policies have had a good track record in controlling at least short-run wage and price increases. The record does show moderate short-run success for these controls. However, in the long run, compliance and market forces can render the guidelines ineffective.

The major critics of wage-price guidelines and controls argue that a whole bureaucracy must be created to enforce compliance also. As certain economic resources become scarce, strong economic incentives arise to permit the free market to determine the wage or price paid to use those resources. As the free-market price accelerates beyond the legal price, illegal black markets may flourish.

Others contend that legally mandated wages and prices disrupt the efficiency of the free-market system. For example, rising demand for products normally brings higher prices, which signal the intricate web of economic forces to offer more resources for the production of this item. However, effective price controls limit this price rise, thus limiting the economy's ability to efficiently allocate resources.

Finally, with price controls, shortages of products generally develop. How are these products to be allocated among competing users? Fairness may demand a government-imposed rationing program. This only adds to the government bureaucracy. Motorists in certain states may recall the problems that arose with the various gasoline rationing plans of the late 1970s.

TIPS

TIPS stands for "Tax-Based Income Policies." Developed by Henry C. Wallace, Sidney Weintraub, and Arthur Okun, TIPS criticizes the industrial damage that frequently accompanies government economic policy. For example, fiscal and monetary policy aimed at curing inflation can be disastrous to those industries that produce interest-sensitive products. The authors of TIPS charge that government inflation fighting is often concentrated in a few sectors, which are forced to bear the brunt of the deflationary repercussions (plant closings and layoffs) of the policy. High interest rates can crush the construction industry and, to a lesser extent, the automobile and appliance industries.

As interest rates increase, sales and profits fall, resulting in worker layoffs and plant closings. In certain cases, the ripple effect can be dramatic. For example, steel, rubber, and other auto-related businesses decline as auto sales dip. The recent automobile cut-rate financing schemes are seen by many as an attempt by the auto makers to shield themselves from the damage caused by fiscal and monetary policy.

TIPS is designed to fight inflation without producing these adverse side effects. TIPS can be implemented in two different ways. In the TIPS "stick" version, firms are encouraged to control their wage increase. As we saw earlier, wage increases that exceed productivity can lead to cost-push inflation. Under a TIPS stick plan, firms whose average, annual wage increase exceeds some predetermined guideline level face tax penalties. In the TIPS "carrot" version, attempts are made to control inflationary wage increases by offering firms tax relief in the form of tax credits if their wage increases are in compliance with the established guidelines. Proponents argue that economic incentives of higher after-tax profits should be enough to keep wages under control. Opponents of TIPS (sticks) counter by stating that corporate taxes can easily be shifted forward to consumers, and any tax surcharge placed on corporations would probably be passed on to customers in the form of higher prices.

Supply-Side Economics

The newest critics of Keynesian-based fiscal policy are the supply-side economists. Supply-side theory holds that the preference for aggregate-demand-based fiscal policy has led to the deterioration of the production and aggregate-supply side of our economy. This neglect, caused by improper tax incentives for savings and investment as well as by excessive government regulation, has led to slow economic growth in terms of both output and productivity. According to the supply-siders, these conditions have created the relatively recent problem of stagflation (relatively high inflation and high unemployment occurring simultaneously).

Supply-side economists have urged sweeping changes in our tax code aimed at increasing the level of savings, investment, and work. Also, they have argued that many of our income-transfer programs, such as welfare and unemployment compensation, actually hurt the economy by fostering an attitude among certain workers that hard work and productivity are not necessary. They argue that these programs have created a perverse work ethic, encouraging the belief that layoffs do not matter because the income safety net is there to protect workers.

Finally, supply-side theorists urge deregulation for many industries. They argue that regulation has harmed certain industries by overprotecting inefficient firms from the rigors of competition. In a free, unregulated market environment, new competition would insure efficiency and lower prices.

The Reagan administration has embraced supply-side doctrine. Tax cuts, the abolishment of many social programs, and the deregulation of much of the transportation system are examples of supply-side economics in action. In the 1982 *Economic Report of the President,* Reagan announced the key elements in his supply-side program:

- decrease the growth in federal spending by sharp cuts in incentive-robbing welfare and social programs;
- reduce the burden of excess regulation of private enterprise by providing regulation relief;
- restore saving, investment, and work incentives by aggressive tax cutting;
- in cooperation with the Federal Reserve System, make a new commitment to monetary growth that would restore price stability, a stable currency, and healthy financial markets.

This program was specifically aimed at eliminating the stagflation that burdened the U.S. economy in the early 1980s.

SUMMARY

An inflationary gap is created when the equilibrium level of income associated with aggregate demand exceeds the desired level of national income. A fiscal policy decision to reduce aggregate demand is required. Choices include tax hikes and/or decreases in government spending. A deflationary gap occurs when the equilibrium level of income associated with a particular aggregate demand level is less than the desired level of national income. The fiscal policy option in this case is to stimulate aggregate demand.

The balanced budget multiplier is based on the concept that equal increases in taxes and government spending will raise equilibrium income by a comparable amount.

Automatic and discretionary stabilization methods may be applied in fiscal policy decisions. Automatic stabilizers include taxes, unemployment compensation, and other government and private programs. Planned (discretionary) methods include expansionary and contractionary measures.

Time lags between fiscal policy implementation and actual changes in aggregate demand are difficult to eliminate. The entire fiscal policy time lag comprises recognition lag, study lag, implementation lag, and effect lag. Approaches to reducing lag include increased reliance on econometric forecasting in the policymaking process, removing fiscal policymaking from the political arena, focusing efforts on the more easily changed components of aggregate demand, and increased use of automatic stabilizers.

Fiscal drag occurs when the automatic stabilization impact of an economy's tax structure cancels out the effect of newly generated income by draining off new tax revenues. Supply-side economists and Keynesians differ as to the best approach to defeating fiscal drag.

Different philosophies exist with regard to balancing the federal budget. Some believe that government must balance its budget on a yearly basis. Others believe that the budget should be balanced over the length of a complete business cycle. Still others believe that balancing the budget is irrelevant, and that business cycle management is the goal of fiscal budget making. Finally, some believe that a full employment goal should be set and the appropriate budget developed in recognition of that goal.

Crowding out occurs when a government finances a budget deficit by increased borrowing in the private capital markets, choking off the supply of funds for business investment and consumer spending.

Not everyone believes in the value and effectiveness of fiscal policy. Rational expectation theorists argue that the actions of knowledgeable and rational economic agents offset government fiscal policy decisions. Others feel that wage-price controls are more effective inflation fighters because they depress the continuous increase in expectations. Another approach is the tax-based income policy. Supply-side economists stress the need for modifying tax codes in order to increase savings, investment, and employment levels. They support deregulation of industry and decreased funding of many social programs.

KEY WORDS

annually balanced budget	expansionary fiscal policy
automatic stabilizer	fiscal drag
balanced budget multiplier	supplemental unemployment benefits
contractionary fiscal policy	(SUBs)
crowding-out effect	supply-side economics
cyclically balanced budget	TIPS
discretionary fiscal policy	unemployment compensation

Questions for Review

1. What phenomenon occurs when aggregate demand is so high that the equilibrium level of the gross national product exceeds the full employment level?

2. According to Keynesian thought, how does a decrease in government spending affect aggregate demand and the equilibrium level of output? Would such a move be considered contractionary or expansionary?

3. What is the effect that an equal increase (or decrease) in government spending and taxes will have on the equilibrium level of income?

4. What is the change in equilibrium income if the change in aggregate demand is $150 and the multiplier is 5.0?

5. What are deliberate actions taken by the government to control economic fluctuations called? Give an example of this kind of government action.

6. a) How can tax rates be used as economic stabilizers?
   b) "Reducing marginal tax rates provides incentives to work, save, and invest." Who would be more likely to say that—a Keynesian or a supply-sider?

7. List four causes of timing lags.

8. Budgetary surpluses may be generated by a high-employment economy, preventing it from reaching its maximum growth potential. What is this problem called? How do progressive tax systems contribute to the creation of such surpluses?

9. What is the conceptual difference between an annually balanced budget and a cyclically balanced budget? Which approach has as its underlying philosophy the belief that the federal government should be more concerned with promoting a full-employment but noninflationary level of national income than with balancing the budget?

10. When resources are used by the public sector that might otherwise be used by the private sector, business investment-spending levels are likely to fall. What is this phenomenon called? What is its effect on interest rates?

11. "The only fiscal policy moves that truly cause changes in people's behavior are the ones that are completely unexpected." What theory does this statement represent?

ENDNOTES

1. It is not uncommon for government statistics to be revised months or even quarters after they were first announced. These revisions are often so large that the direction of change (positive or negative) of a particular time series may actually be reversed.

2. These events can even take on the flavor of a political campaign. President Ford wore the famous "WIN" button on his suit lapel. The button represented his effort to defeat inflation. The "WIN" button was an acronym for "Whip Inflation Now."

ECONOMICS IN THE NEWS

Economic Policy: The Old Tools Won't Work

In an increasingly global economy, U.S. fiscal and monetary policies don't perform the way they used to.

by Marc Levinson

Since the advent of the New Deal more than half a century ago, the federal government has actively helped shape the course of the economy. Its ability, at least in the short run, to pump up the economy in hard times and slow it down when inflation began to boil up has been unquestioned. As recently as 1981, when a sharp cutback in money supply growth pushed the country into recession, or 1983, when the stimulative effects of a tax cut brought the economy back to health, the old elixirs worked as they had in the past.

But in 1986, things were different. Heady growth in the money supply, repeated cuts in the Federal Reserve Board's discount rate and record federal budget deficits all failed to juice the lackluster economy. The old linkages between the government's actions and the economy's responses have changed in ways economists do not fully understand. As a result, the government's economic tools have been partially blunted. Contends Lawrence Chimerine, chairman of Chase Econometrics, "The ability of policy changes to improve the economy is much smaller than ever."

The reason: the growing internationalization of the U.S. economy. Flexible exchange rates and the resulting mushrooming of international capital markets have made traditional economic policies act in unexpected ways. "No one has a reliable theory of exchange rates," says Paul Krugman, a professor of international economics at the Massachusetts Institute of Technology. "That makes it very difficult to be sure of the effects of macroeconomic policy."

These international connections make it increasingly difficult to aim economic weapons at purely domestic targets. Even thinking of "domestic" in terms of economic problems is misleading. "The problem is global overcapacity and global underconsumption," contends Steve Quick, an economist with the Joint Economic Committee of Congress. "But we have no tools. We have no global fiscal policy. We have no global monetary policy." Adds Harold Rose, chief economist of Britain's Barclays Bank: "It's very hard to see how we can get out of these problems by macroeconomic policy alone."

Certainly, the assumption that the government can "fine tune" the economy has been in disrepute since the early 1970s, when policymakers were helpless as they faced high unemployment and high inflation at the same time. But faith in the government's ability to deal with one of these problems at a time has remained strong. Now, however, the government's very ability to

---

Reprinted with permission, BUSINESS MONTH magazine, January, 1987. Copyright © 1987 by Business Magazine Corporation, 38 Commercial Wharf, Boston, MA 02110.

achieve some domestic goal—3% growth in output, 4% unemployment—appears increasingly limited. The jury is still out on whether these limitations are a temporary phenomenon or a permanent fact of life. . . .

There is no doubt that a $108 billion budget slash will cut domestic demand. It will also lower deficits and reduce the government's borrowing from abroad, driving down the dollar. But whether a more favorable exchange rate for exports will boost the economy more than lower government spending retards it is an open question. "We don't know the responsiveness of the economy to a changed deficit," contends economist Mickey D. Levy of Philadelphia's Fidelity Bank. "We don't know the lags." Concurs Rudolph Penner, director of the Congressional Budget Office, "If we had been analyzing that big a change twenty years ago, there wouldn't have been much debate that it would cause a recession."

In fact, economists now shy away from talking about "fiscal policy," because they believe a given amount of government spending can have vastly different effects on the economy, depending upon its purpose and method of financing . . . .

CHAPTER SIXTEEN

CURRENT MACROECONOMIC ISSUES: THE NATIONAL DEBT

Objectives

After reading this chapter, you should be able to

•

describe the size of public debt in relation to gross national product

•

explain how the debt burden (as defined by interest expense) has increased dramatically since 1960

•

list the owners of the public debt

•

list and describe four methods by which the government could repay the public debt

•

describe the effect of the public debt on investment spending

•

describe the intent, major provisions, and potential impact of the Gramm-Rudman-Hollings Balanced Budget Act of 1985

DEFINITION OF THE PUBLIC DEBT

As we have seen in chapter 15, modern economic fiscal policy can lead to recurring fiscal deficits. In years when actual income is below the full-employment level of income, the government may spend more than it receives in taxes in order to stimulate spending and employment. Similarly, a budget surplus may be appropriate when inflationary pressures are present, and in those years government tax revenues may exceed government expenditures (table 16.1). The combined effect of all years is equal to the current public debt, net of all debt that has matured and been retired by the fiscal authorities. This federal debt grew from approximately $17 billion in 1929 to an estimated $2,320.6 billion by 1987.[1]

The federal debt has grown dramatically since 1929. However, the full story is not simply one of massive growth in the federal debt. Observing patterns growth in the debt over time helps put the debt into context.

Table 16.1 Government Tax Receipts, Spending, Deficits, and Total Public Debt, 1929–87 (billions of dollars)

Fiscal Year or Period	Total Receipts	Total Outlays	Surplus or Deficit	Fiscal Year or Period	Total Receipts	Total Outlays	Surplus or Deficit
1929[a]	3.9	3.1	0.7	1965	116.8	118.2	−1.4
1933[a]	2.0	4.6	−2.6	1966	130.8	134.5	−3.7
1939	6.3	9.1	−2.8	1967	148.8	157.5	−8.6
1940	6.5	9.5	−2.9	1968	153.0	178.1	−25.2
1941	8.7	13.7	−4.9	1969	186.9	183.6	3.2
1942	14.6	35.1	−20.5	1970	192.8	195.6	−2.8
1943	24.0	78.6	−54.6	1971	187.1	210.2	−23.0
1944	43.7	91.3	−47.6	1972	207.3	230.7	−23.4
1945	45.2	92.7	−47.6	1973	230.8	245.7	−14.9
1946	39.3	55.2	−15.9	1974	263.2	269.4	−6.1
1947	38.5	34.5	4.0	1975	279.1	332.3	−53.2
1948	41.6	29.8	11.8	1976	298.1	371.8	−73.7
1949	39.4	38.8	.6	1977	355.6	409.2	−53.6
1950	39.4	42.6	−3.1	1978	399.6	458.7	−59.2
1951	51.6	45.5	6.1	1979	463.3	503.5	−40.2
1952	66.2	67.7	−1.5	1980	517.1	590.9	−73.8
1953	69.6	76.1	−6.5	1981	599.3	678.2	−78.9
1954	69.7	70.9	−1.2	1982	617.8	745.7	−127.9
1955	65.5	68.4	−3.0	1983	600.6	808.3	−207.8
1956	74.6	70.6	3.9	1984	666.5	851.8	−185.3
1957	80.0	76.6	3.4	1985	734.1	946.3	−212.3
1958	79.6	82.4	−2.8	1986[b]	777.1	979.9	−202.8
1959	79.2	92.1	−12.8	1987[b]	850.4	994.0	−143.6
1960	92.5	92.2	.3				
1961	94.4	97.7	−3.3				
1962	99.7	106.8	−7.1				
1963	106.6	111.3	−4.8				
1964	112.6	118.5	−5.9				

Sources: Department of the Treasury, Office of Management and Budget, and Department of Commerce, Bureau of Economic Analysis.
a. Not strictly comparable with later data.
b. Estimates.

Public debt has increased most dramatically during war years. The public debt rose from $50.7 billion at the onset of World War II to a staggering $271.0 billion by 1946 (see table 16.2). Public debt has also increased sharply in recessionary periods. In an attempt to stimulate the economy during periods of economic distress, the government must stimulate aggregate demand by spending an amount greater than tax revenues. For example, during the 1974–75 recession, federal deficits rose from $6.1 billion in 1974 to $53.2 billion in 1975. In the most recent recessionary period of 1980–82, deficits jumped from $73.8 billion in 1980 to $127.9 billion in 1982.

Recently, the supply-side argument that taxes should be cut to stimulate incentives led to the Economic Recovery Tax Act of 1981, which legislated phased-in tax-rate cuts for both individuals and corporations. The Tax Reform Act of 1986 calls for even lower rates. These tax reductions were not offset by equivalent reductions in government spending; therefore, federal deficits have grown dramatically since 1981. The total federal debt has grown from $914.3 billion in 1980 to a whopping $2,112.0 billion by 1986 for an increase in total debt of 130 percent.

Table 16.2 Public Debt Relative to GNP, 1940–87 (billions of dollars)

Year	Gross Federal Deficit	GNP	Debt as a Percentage of GNP	Year	Gross Federal Deficit	GNP	Debt as a Percentage of GNP
1940	50.7	95.8	53	1965	323.2	673.6	48
1941	57.5	113.0	51	1966	329.5	740.5	44
1942	79.2	142.2	56	1967	341.3	793.5	43
1943	142.6	175.8	81	1968	369.8	852.4	43
1944	204.1	202.0	101	1969	367.1	929.5	39
1945	260.1	212.4	122	1970	382.6	990.5	39
1946	271.0	212.9	127	1971	409.5	1,057.1	39
1947	257.1	225.0	114	1972	437.3	1,151.2	38
1948	252.0	248.5	101	1973	468.4	1,285.5	36
1949	252.6	264.1	96	1974	486.2	1,417.0	34
1950	256.9	266.9	96	1975	544.1	1,523.5	36
1951	255.3	314.7	81	1976	631.9	1,699.6	37
1952	259.1	342.7	76	1977	709.1	1,935.8	37
1953	266.0	365.1	73	1978	780.4	2,173.4	36
1954	270.8	369.4	73	1979	833.8	2,452.2	34
1955	274.4	387.6	71	1980	914.3	2,667.6	34
1956	272.8	418.0	65	1981	1,033.9	2,986.2	34
1957	272.4	441.2	62	1982	1,147.0	3,141.5	37
1958	279.7	449.8	62	1983	1,381.9	3,320.9	42
1959	287.8	479.5	60	1984	1,576.7	3,695.3	43
1960	290.9	507.7	57	1985	1,827.5	3,936.8	46
1961	292.9	519.0	56	1986[a]	2,112.0	4,192.2	50
1962	303.3	556.6	54	1987[a]	2,320.6	4,538.1	51
1963	310.8	588.6	53				
1964	316.8	629.4	50				

Source: Adapted from *Economic Report of the President*, 1986.
a. Estimates.

Public Debt and the GNP

While it is clear that public debt is growing absolutely, the overall U.S. GNP has also been growing. Table 16.2 indicates total debt, gross national product, and the national debt as a percentage of GNP for the years 1940–87. The national debt as a percentage of GNP fell from a post-World War II high of 127 percent to a low of 34 percent in the 1978–81 period. In other words, the debt has been gradually falling relative to the total size of the economy. Unfortunately, beginning in 1982, the debt as a percentage of national output has begun to rise. It is estimated to have jumped from 37 percent in 1982 to over 51 percent by 1987. The 34–50 percent range of the 1980s still compares favorably with the 34–100 percent range of 1948–79 period. However, the national debt has recently become a major political economy issue because of its sharp increase during 1980–85 and because of the reversal of the long-term, post-World War II downward trend of the debt as a percentage of the GNP.

Debt Burden

Another interesting aspect of the national debt involves the annual interest charges associated with the debt (table 16.3). The total interest charges in any given year are a function of the total amount of the debt and of the average interest rate of the various debt instruments issued to finance the debt. During high-interest periods, the debt burden can become quite large. In fact, by 1984 only income security and national defense cost the federal government more than the interest on the national debt. The $110 billion in interest payments represented the third largest item in the federal budget and 13.6 percent of all federal expenditures.

Table 16.3 Interest on National Debt and its Relation to GNP and Federal Expenditures

Year	Net Interest Payment Bill (billions of dollars)	GNP Bill (billions of dollars)	Federal Spending Bill (billions of dollars)	Interest as Percentage of GNP	Interest as Percentage of all Federal Spending
1964	8.0	629.4	118.5	1.3	6.8
1966	9.2	740.5	134.5	1.2	6.8
1968	11.3	852.4	178.1	1.1	6.3
1970	14.1	990.5	195.6	1.4	7.2
1972	14.4	1,151.2	230.7	1.3	6.2
1974	20.7	1,417.0	269.4	1.5	7.7
1976	26.8	1,699.6	371.8	1.6	7.2
1978	35.2	2,173.4	458.7	1.6	7.7
1980	53.3	2,667.6	590.9	2.0	9.0
1982	84.6	3,141.5	745.7	2.7	11.3
1984	115.5	3,695.3	851.8	3.1	13.6
1986[a]	135.3	4,192.2	979.9	3.2	13.8

Source: *Economic Report of the President*, 1986.
a. Estimates.

The debt burden or interest expense of the national debt has increased dramatically since the 1960s. Since 1964, the debt burden has risen from 1.3 percent of GNP and 6.8 percent of federal spending to 3.2 percent and 13.8 percent, respectively in 1986. In other words, in 1986 the federal government used roughly 3.2 percent of the GNP simply to pay the interest on the national debt.

Table 16.4 Ownership Share of Public Debt, 1984

Debt Holder	Estimated Percentage of Debt
U.S. government	16.4
Federal Reserve bank	10.3
Commercial banks	13.0
Individuals	9.3
Insurance companies	3.9
Money market funds	1.3
Corporations	2.9
State and local governments	11.1
Foreign accounts	11.4
Other owner[a]	20.4

Source: Department of the Treasury.
a. Includes savings and loan associations, credit unions, nonprofit organizations, etc.

Debt Ownership

To whom is the national debt owed? Many Americans erroneously believe that the public debt is held by foreigners and/or foreign governments. In reality, foreign ownership of the U.S. public debt is a relatively minor part of the total (table 16.4). Who, then, owns the debt? The answer is that the public owns the majority of the public debt. Commercial banks, money market funds, insurance companies, and private individuals own public debt securities. State and local governments own a share of the debt, and the federal government itself holds much of its own debt: approximately 25 percent of the national debt is held by government agencies and the Federal Reserve System.

PUBLIC DEBT ISSUES

Over the years, many concerns and issues have arisen with respect to the national debt and its impact on our economy. Many of these concerns and issues have been based on spurious logic; however, others merit serious consideration by economists and policymakers.

Government Bankruptcy

Perhaps the greatest misconception about the debt is the belief that ever-expanding government debt will, one day, render the federal government of the United States incapable of paying the interest and principal on its debt, and the U.S. will be forced into bankruptcy. This misconception is based upon an improper comparison between public and private debt.

Private individuals and corporations who borrow in the financial markets are under legal obligation to repay their debts. When these debts come due it may be possible, albeit difficult, to obtain additional financing for the purpose of refinancing the original debt; yet, sooner or later, the original debt must be paid. The lender is entitled to take legal action to enforce payment. Frequently, bankruptcy results from this legal attempt to enforce repayment. Repayment of debt in the public sector is governed under other conditions.

The government has available at least four methods by which it could repay its obligation. Fortunately the government chooses the most appropriate of these options, debt refinancing. When the government securities that represent the bulk of the federal debt mature, the government simply issues new debt to finance the repayment of the maturing debt.

A second method of retiring debt could be to raise taxes by an amount equal to the value of the maturing securities. This method, however, would tend to have a negative impact on aggregate demand; thus, if the economy were in a less than full-employment equilibrium state, such a fiscal policy would be damaging. On the other hand, if inflationary pressures caused by excess demand were present, this policy would be acceptable.

The government could, as a third option, simply reduce government spending in order to repay its debt that is due. The dangers of this policy are similar to those cited for raising taxes.

Finally, because the government issues currency, it is entirely possible for the federal government to retire its debt by simply printing money. We have previously discussed the potentially dire inflationary consequences that could result from such a policy. Nevertheless, if the government were somehow forced to repay the debt, it could respond by turning on the printing presses.

The National Debt Is Owed to Foreign Powers

Another popular misconception is that the people of the United States, through the national debt, are in debt to the rest of the world. Only a small portion of the debt is held by foreigners or foreign governments. By the mid-1980s, approximately 11.4 percent of the debt was held outside the U.S. However, two real concerns relate to foreign ownership of the debt. First, the percentage of the debt held outside the U.S. is rising and has more than doubled since 1960. There is a definite trend of increasing reliance on funding from outside sources. Second, when interest and principal payments are made to foreign debtholders, a transfer of real income occurs. This transfer arises when the funds paid to foreigners depart from the U.S. spending flow. This impact is lessened to the extent that foreigners reinvest in U.S. securities or purchase U.S. exports.

Huge Debts Mortgage The Future

Many economists say that today's citizens are mortgaging the future of their children by amassing such a large public debt. For example, by 1986, the U.S. per capita debt stood at approximately $8,000. However, as we have seen, the public itself owns much of this debt. While future generations will pay the interest on much of the debt generated today, those same generations will receive that same interest as income. To pay off the entire U.S. debt today, we would simply raise taxes and then use those tax revenues to repay domestic debtholders. The only major system drain would be the payments to foreign debtholders. However, one real concern is related to this popular misconception. While the national debt does not mortgage our children's future, it is possible that today's debt might reduce the size of our economy's future capital and asset base. This possibility arises from the adverse impact of federal debt on private investment levels.

The Crowding-Out Effect

Perhaps the most persuasive argument regarding the dangers of the national debt centers around the crowding-out effect. The crowding-out effect occurs as the government attempts to finance larger and larger deficits in the capital markets. This government borrowing increases the demand for loanable funds, which leads to an increase in the price of these funds. The increase in interest rates is linked to a reduction in private sector consumption and investment. For example, consumption expenditures are affected as higher interest rates lead to a reduction in new housing starts, auto sales, or any other interest-sensitive credit purchase. But the higher interest rates have a more important effect on the capital goods markets. To the extent that higher interest rates reduce private investment, the capacity of the economy to produce in the future may be diminished (figure 16.1). In other words, our long-term productivity may suffer if current investment spending is reduced by deficit-induced boosts in the cost of capital.

Figure 16.1 demonstrates the effect on investment spending of changes in the rate of interest through the investment demand curve. First, assume that the economy is at full employment. For some reason, the government incurs a budget deficit. The investment projects are represented according to expected profitability by curve I_D. The private investor who undertakes the most profitable project is willing to pay relatively higher rates

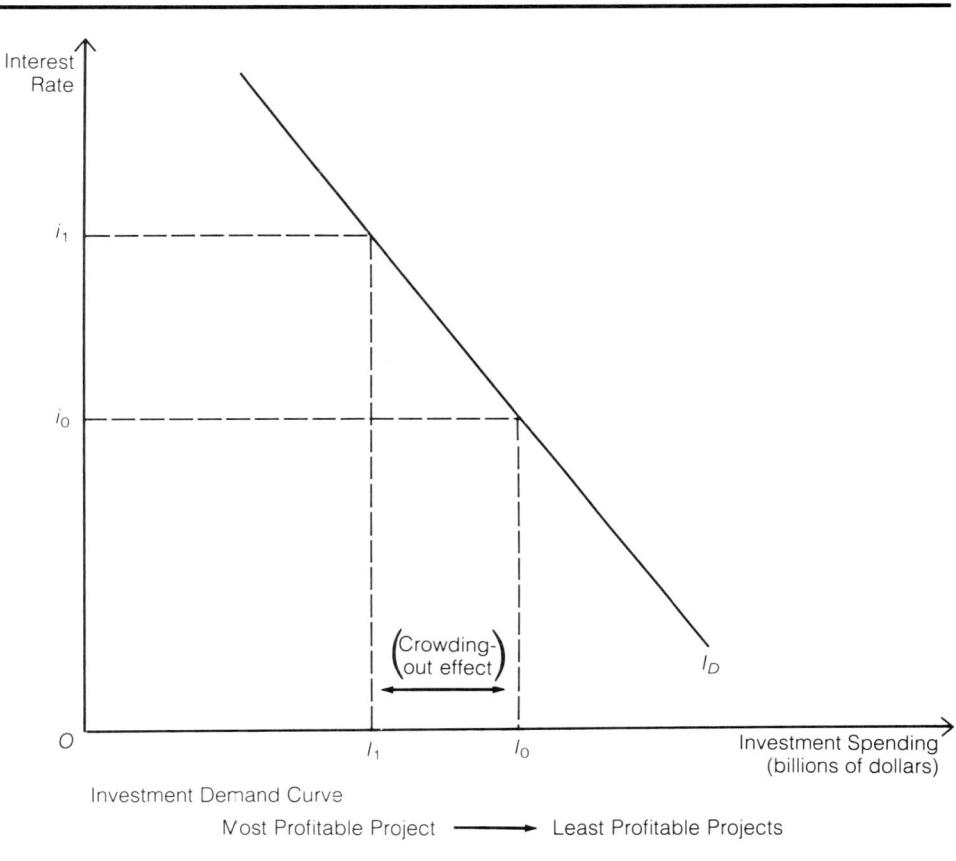

Figure 16.1 The Crowding-Out Effect

[Graph: Investment Demand Curve showing interest rate on vertical axis with i_1 above i_0, and investment spending on horizontal axis with I_1 to the left of I_0. Downward sloping I_D curve. Crowding-out effect shown as distance between I_1 and I_0. Most Profitable Project → Least Profitable Projects.]

than those investors who are projecting more modest rates of return on their projects. For example, if the current rate of interest is i_0, then the economy will invest an amount equal to I_0. However, if because of deficit financing, interest rates are forced upward to i_1, then the amount of investment spending will fall to I_1. The amount of investment spending presented by distance I_0–I_1 represents the crowding-out effect.

Critics of the crowding-out effect argue that it is unfair to investigate only the economy's loss of investment spending that results from crowding out. They hold that this loss in investment spending may be partially or completely offset by two separate factors: the gain in aggregate demand, which would result from the deficit stimulus, and, if the deficit is used to fund public sector projects, the advantages of public investment (figure 16.2).

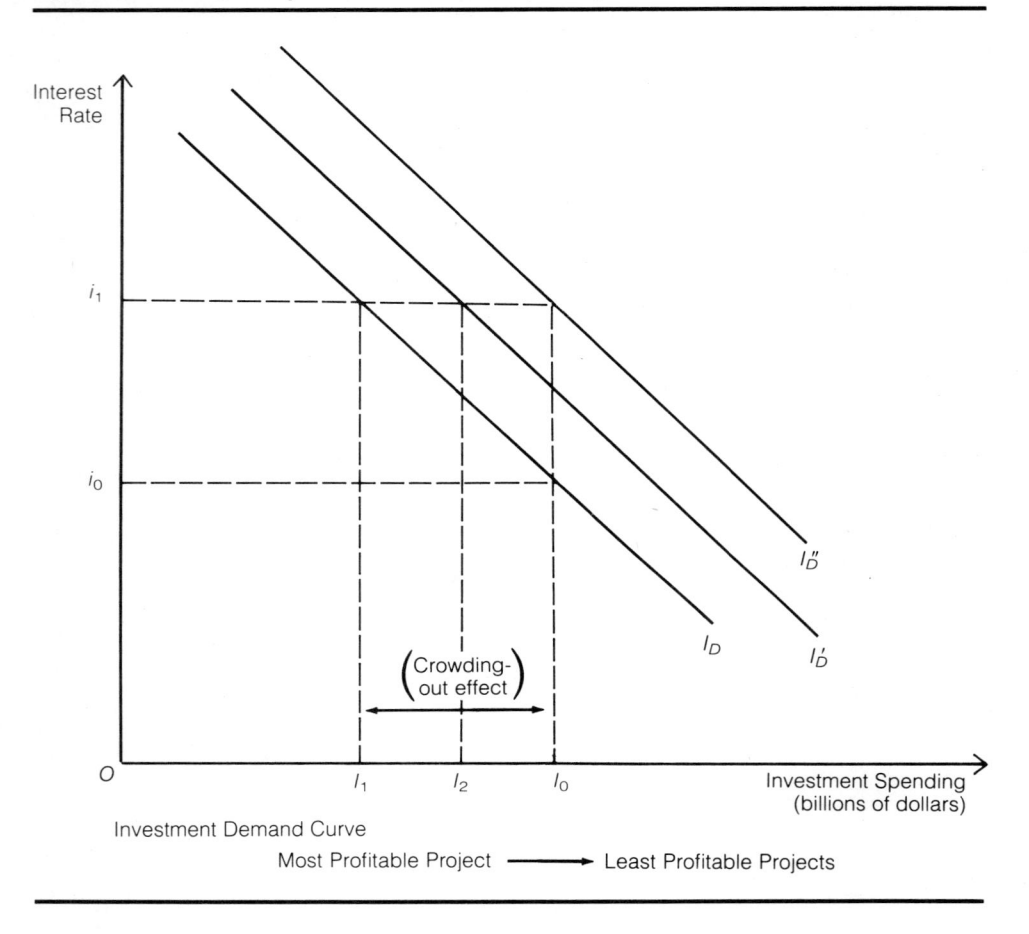

Figure 16.2 The Crowding-Out Effect and Deficit Spending

Investment Demand Curve
Most Profitable Project ⟶ Least Profitable Projects

Figure 16.2 shows the impact that deficit spending can have on the investment function. Here, we assume that the economy is in a recession with large amounts of underutilized resources available. The appropriate fiscal policy would be for the government to increase spending or decrease the tax burden. Either of these actions, or a combination thereof, would create a budget deficit, with resulting higher interest rates as the government issues new debt in the capital markets. As we have seen, the adverse impact of rising interest rates inhibits capital expansion, and worthwhile investment may be crowded out. However, given the underutilization of resources, other forces are also at work here, which may counterbalance the crowding-out effect.

The additional fiscal spending, enhanced by the multiplier, will lead to an increase in national income. This increase in national income could change the profit expectations of business if the demand increase is large enough, thus stimulating the purchase of additional plant equipment to meet the anticipated additional demand. The occurrence of either or both of these possibilities would lead to an increase in investment demand. This increase in investment demand is shown by a shift in the original investment demand curve I_D to position I_D'. At I_D' the crowding-out effect caused by the increase in the interest rate from i_0 to i_1 is softened. At I_1 on I_D', the new level of investment is I_2. Therefore, the crowding-out effect of deficit spending has been reduced from $I_0 I_1$ to $I_0 I_2$. If the shift in the investment demand curve is sufficiently great to move the curve to level I_D'', even at the increased rate of interest i_1 investment spending will return to I_0. The crowding-out effect has been offset entirely.

The second argument against the crowding-out effect centers around the impact of the spending associated with the budget deficit.

Many economists believe that federal spending on infrastructure projects like airports, interstate highways, or energy research can lead to future gains in productivity in the same fashion as private investment. The case has been made that many public investment projects are essential to future private investment. For example, it is unlikely that the airline and travel industry would be as large and employ as many people as it does were it not for the massive federal aid that supports airport construction and renovation. Only the federal government is large enough to undertake such massive projects as the construction of thousands of miles of interstate highways. These projects set the stage for a multitude of ancillary private ventures. Finally, many government-sponsored educational and research efforts would not survive without the public support. The benefits from such projects are difficult to measure; nevertheless, the value of the nation's human capital is undoubtedly enhanced by such expenditures.

The Explosion of Deficits in the 1980s

One final issue associated with the national debt has galvanized public pressure to do something about the debt. This problem is the virtual flood of red ink since the last (1980–82) recessionary period (table 16.5).

The average growth of the U.S. debt in the 1980s has been approximately 13.0 percent per annum. At this average rate, the federal debt would double roughly every 5½ years. This recent explosion of the debt can be traced to the Economic Recovery Tax Act (ERTA) of 1981, which basically cut taxes by 25 percent over a 3-year period and offered significantly lower capital-gains taxes and more attractive depreciation schedules. (The ERTA and other supply-side measures will be discussed later in this chapter.) However, these reductions in federal revenues were not offset by similar reductions in federal

Table 16.5 Recent Increases in Public Debt

Year	Deficit (billions of dollars)	Total Debt (billions of dollars)	Percentage Increase in Total Debt
1980	73.8	914.3	—
1981	78.9	1,003.9	9.8
1982	127.9	1,147.0	14.3
1983	207.8	1,381.9	20.5
1984	185.3	1,576.7	14.1
1985	212.3	1,827.5	15.9
1986[a]	202.8	2,112.0	15.6
1987[a]	143.6	2,320.6	9.9

Source: *Economic Report of the President*, 1987.
a. Estimated.

spending. As a result, the total debt more than doubled between 1980 and 1986. These huge deficits have forced experts to begin to find ways to lower the deficits. Several balanced budget amendments have been introduced in Congress. While most of these measures have been defeated and ridiculed for their effect on fiscal policy options, a relatively moderate balanced budget amendment was adopted by Congress in December 1985 in the form of the Gramm-Rudman-Hollings Act.

The Gramm-Rudman-Hollings Act

The Gramm-Rudman-Hollings Act is officially called the Balanced Budget and Emergency Deficit Control Act of 1985. This act established a schedule of steadily declining deficit target amounts beginning in 1986 and culminating in a required balanced budget by 1991. This bill is designed not to eliminate the national debt, but to slow the deficit growth. If all goes as planned, the annual deficit will reach zero by 1991, whereupon one or two events might occur. Should Congress decide to generate an annual surplus budget after 1991, as government securities mature, the government may pay off the principal of these securities with the accumulated surplus. A second approach may be to run an annually balanced budget each year after 1991 and simply refinance maturing debt with new debt. This approach would maintain the national debt level at the 1991 level. Does this portend an end to fiscal policy as we know it? On the surface, it appears that the act will seriously limit discretionary fiscal policy. However, the law has provided that, if the economy encounters a recession, the law's sequestration (budget-cutting) procedures can be suspended.

Major Provisions of the Act

The Balanced Budget Act stipulates that budget deficits must be decreased annually and specifies measures that must be taken to achieve this result.[2] The maximum deficit amounts set by the act for fiscal years 1986–91 are shown below:

Fiscal Year	Maximum Deficit (billions of dollars)
1986	$171.9
1987	144.0
1988	108.0
1989	72.0
1990	36.0
1991	0.0

If the deficit is estimated to exceed the maximum level by any amount in 1986 and 1991, or by more than $10 billion in the years 1987 through 1990, an automatic spending-reduction procedure is triggered. Except for trust and special funds, this involves the permanent cancellation of new budget authority and other authority to obligate and expend funds. For 1986, the outlay reduction is limited by the act to a maximum of $11.7 billion, regardless of the amount of the excess deficit. In later years, the amount of possible outlay reductions is not limited.

The first step in the sequestration process is a joint report by the director of the Office of Management and Budget (OMB) and the director of the Congressional Budget Office (CBO) to the comptroller general that estimates budget base levels, including the amount by which the projected deficit exceeds the maximum deficit amount for the fiscal year covered by the report. This report also provides OMB and CBO economic assumptions, including the estimated rate of real economic growth, and calculates the amounts and percentages by which various budgetary resources must be sequestered in order to eliminate any deficit excess.

If either the CBO or the OMB projects real economic growth to be less than zero for any 2 consecutive quarters, or if the Department of Commerce reports that real (inflation-adjusted) growth in the GNP is less than 1 percent for any 2 consecutive quarters, many of the provisions of the Balanced Budget Act can be suspended by the Congress, including sequestration orders that have not already gone into effect.

For fiscal year 1986, the joint OMB/CBO report to the comptroller general was made on January 15, 1986. For subsequent years, the directors will make an initial report on August 20 and a revised report on October 5 to reflect final congressional action on the budget during the month of September.

The comptroller general reviews the directors' reports and issues his own reports to the president and the Congress that confirm or modify the information reported by the OMB and the CBO. The comptroller general's reports are the basis for reductions in budgetary resources to be ordered by the president.

The comptroller general's role in the sequestration process has been challenged in the courts. On February 8, 1986, the District Court for the District of Columbia ruled that sequestration procedures were unconstitutional because the Gramm-Rudman-Hollings Act vests executive branch power in an officer who can be removed from office by the legislative branch of government. Later that same year the Supreme Court upheld the lower court's ruling. The original act, however, provided for such a contingency. Now the House and Senate budget committees will merge into a new ad hoc committee called the Joint Committee on Deficit Reduction. This new committee will establish a joint resolution of Congress detailing the required sequestration of funds. The spending cuts will take effect if this resolution is passed by Congress and signed by the president.

Gramm-Rudman-Hollings Budget Cuts

Several federally funded programs receive immunity from all budget cuts resulting from sequestration. These are interest payments on federal securities, Social Security benefits, Medicaid, food stamps, and most of the basic welfare programs. One-half of the budget cuts would come from defense spending and one-half from the nondefense side of the budget.

The Impact of the Gramm-Rudman-Hollings Act

Some analysts fear that an abrupt sizable reduction in budget deficits might at least temporarily weaken the economy. Their fears are linked to the reduction in aggregate demand that would result directly from budget cuts. This would lead to short-run reductions in output and employment. The greatest risk of a legislative-induced recession would be in the late 1980s, when the deficit is reduced drastically.

Others argue that any short-run economic weakening of the economy caused by federal spending cuts will be offset by the long-term salutary effect of a weakened crowding-out effect. If long-term interest rates decline as a result of sequestration, after a short initial time lag, business investment spending and other interest-sensitive private consumption spending should increase. Moreover, as relative interest rates decline, foreign demand for U.S. securities should also decline. The reduction in foreign demand for U.S. securities should reduce international demand for the U.S. dollar, which, ceteris paribus, would reduce the value of the dollar. A lower value for the dollar would increase U.S. exports and lower imports, eventually bringing an improvement in the deficit trade balance. Finally, an improved trade balance will tend to strengthen domestic output and employment.

In the long run, the act may have the following consequences. First, as the deficit shrinks, the total federal debt will grow more slowly, until it eventually reaches a zero-growth point. Eventually, the debt will decline relative to the GNP. A lower federal debt-to-GNP ratio will allow more private debt to finance capital formation, leading to higher long-term productivity and resulting in higher living standards for future generations.

Second, smaller federal deficits will make the U.S. less dependent on capital inflows from abroad. The foreign capital that has financed government spending on consumption goods rather than on productive investment will decrease. This will improve future domestic living standards by reducing our service debt obligations to foreigners.

Third, a shrinking federal debt will reduce the federal interest-payment problem. This reduces the possibility that the government may, at some point, be forced to amortize a large portion of the debt. The inflationary danger of printing money to handle large deficits will have been reduced.

Fourth, reduced deficits will provide insurance should the government have to resort to future heavy deficit financing in the event of a severe business cycle shock, war, or other national emergency.

Finally, the fixed-deficit targets of this act will certainly undermine the automatic-stabilizer effects of cyclical deficits. Recall from chapter 15 that our tax system generates deficits in periods of economic contraction and that these deficits cushion the economic slowdown by providing a stimulus to aggregate demand. Fixed-deficit targets will reduce the effectiveness of automatic stabilizers. However, the act does provide for suspension of the deficit-reduction process in the event of a serious economic disturbance.

Many economic analysts doubt that the deficit targets will ever be met. Their reservations stem from the many political and legal challenges that are bound to arise in decisions on how to reduce spending. Special interest groups will almost certainly delay the process through intense lobbying efforts. Some analysts believe that lobbying efforts may be strong enough to halt the sequestration process. Whether this will happen remains to be seen. The article that follows this chapter highlights the problems that may limit the effectiveness of this new law. Some observers are so skeptical they have developed still another solution to deficit reductions.

This solution uses a planned liquidation of federal assets to provide the government with funds to save the deficit reduction targets. The sale of federal assets such as Conrail or the Bonneville Power Administration is called privatization. Proponents of privatization believe that the process creates dual benefits. First, revenue from the sale of assets can be used to reduce deficits. Second, many feel that the private-sector acquisition of these concerns will lead to improved productivity. For example, Great Britain completed the sale of billions of dollars of state-owned companies in the early 1980s. This privatization has led to the resurgence of the British auto industry. However, privatization transactions only result in the change in ownership of existing assets. These transactions do not increase aggregate demand in the same fashion as do spending cuts and tax increases. Therefore, privatization should not be considered a substitute for discretionary fiscal policy. It is merely a debt-reduction measure, with a secondary benefit of more efficient resource use.

SUMMARY

A government may spend more than it receives, creating a budget deficit. Or its revenues may be greater than total outlays, creating a budget surplus. The U.S. government has been running a deficit for many years; consequently, the size of the public debt has grown dramatically.

The public debt as a percentage of the GNP has been rising in the 1980s. This represents a reversal of a long-term downward trend. Moreover, the percentage of the GNP used to pay the interest on the public debt has been rising rapidly. These two trends have prompted renewed concern with reducing the public debt.

While a portion of the federal debt is owned by foreign parties, much of it is held by government agencies, the Federal Reserve, banks, other financial businesses, and private citizens.

The government has four basic options for handling its debt. It can issue new debt to finance repayment of maturing government securities. It can also raise taxes, reduce government spending, or print money.

One reason for concern about the size of the public debt is that a growing debt may force interest rates to increase, thus crowding out private sector investment spending. Some economists believe that the increase in aggregate demand that results from deficit spending and the advantages of public spending projects may offset the decrease in investment spending caused by crowding out.

The Gramm-Rudman-Hollings Act, passed in 1985, provides for automatic budget cuts if Congress and the public are unable to agree on a plan to reduce the budget deficit. The goal of the act is a balanced federal budget by 1991. If successful, the act will not eliminate the debt but will slow its growth.

A shrinking federal debt may lead to increased productivity, lessen American dependence on other nations, reduce the federal interest-payment load, and provide a safety net in the event of national economic emergencies.

Privatization, or the sale of federal assets to the private sector, is seen by some as a potentially helpful tool in lessening the federal debt. While privatization may generate revenue to lower the deficit and increase productivity, it will not directly affect aggregate demand.

KEY WORDS

Economic Recovery Tax Act of 1981
Gramm-Rudman-Hollings Act of 1985
privatization

sequestration
Tax Reform Act of 1986

Questions for Review

1. Why did public debt increase sharply in the mid-1970s?

2. Identify the four approaches to retiring federal debt. Which approach do demand-side economists support? Which approach do supply-side economists support?

3. Under the Gramm-Rudman-Hollings deficit reduction plan, how can Congress and the president avoid automatic spending cuts?

4. Why is the amount of public debt owed to the foreign sector of growing concern?

5. What will be the effect of a lower public debt-to-GNP ratio?

6. "While the large, persistent budget deficits of the 1980s were undesirable, it is not clear that all deficits are bad." Do you agree or disagree with this statement? Why?

ENDNOTES

1. By "public debt," we refer only to the federal government's obligation. Actually, state and local governments can also have "unbalanced" budgets. However, between 1968 and 1986, the total of all state and local budgets have shown surpluses. For example, in 1985 all state and local tax revenues exceeded spending by $58.3 billion.

2. *The Economical Budget Outlook: Fiscal Year 1987–1991,* Congressional Budget Office, February 1986, pp. 86–87.

ECONOMICS IN THE NEWS

Gramm-Rudman Looks More Than Ever Like a Pipe Dream

By Douglas A. Harbrecht, edited by Stephen H. Wildstrom

Senator Pete V. Domenici (R-N.M.) once described the Gramm-Rudman balanced budget law as a "planned train wreck." The government got through the first year under Gramm-Rudman because nobody looked at the numbers too closely, but this year the deficit-reduction express is about to jump the tracks for good.

The law requires a deficit of no more than $108 billion in fiscal 1988. With the current-year deficit estimate at more than $170 billion, that target is beyond reach. To come close to the goal on paper, both Congress and the White House have resorted to an assortment of gimmicks remarkable even by federal budget standards. Says Joseph R. Wright Jr., deputy director of the Office of Management & Budget: "It's very obvious that the budget process is broken."

UNCOMPROMISING. The prospects for fixing it are poor. The Supreme Court decision striking down Gramm-Rudman's automatic spending cuts took the heat off policymakers. The once hoped-for "grand compromise" between President Reagan and Hill leaders won't happen. Instead, Reagan has taken to the hustings to blast the "tax-and-spend crew on Capitol Hill."

Left to their own devices, Democrats have produced a 1988 budget resolution that ties modest increases in military spending to Reagan's acceptance of a $19.3 billion tax increase and that cuts the federal deficit by $37 billion. But the resolution is likely to be flat-out ignored this year. Reagan's vow to veto "any tax hike that reaches the Oval Office" has sent Democrats and Republicans scurrying for the trenches. "There really is reason now to dig in and resist a tax hike at all costs," says Senator Malcolm Wallop (R-Wyo.). Adds Senate Budget Committee member Nancy L. Kassebaum (R-Kan.): "I don't see how you can have an agreement in an atmosphere so partisan."

Democrats are just as demoralized. House Democratic Caucus Chairman Richard A. Gephardt (D-Mo.) says there is no point in the Democrats' coming up with $19.3 billion in new taxes if President Reagan will veto them.

Tax increases would produce real money. That's more than can be said for many of the spending reductions called for. For example, the resolution proposes the sale of Rural Electrification Administration loans—for a gain of $7.2 billion in 1988. But budget-writers point out that the government will forgo future interest receipts. Furthermore, existing guarantees require the government to remain liable for any future defaults by borrowers. Another gimmick: The budget assumes $139 billion in interest costs. But that estimate is based on January rates. Since then, rates have risen sharply, and debt service will probably cost much more, bloating the deficit.

Some in Congress see a window of opportunity for making spending cuts and budget reforms. On July 17 the current national debt limit of $2.3 trillion expires. Senator Phil Gramm (R-Tex.) threatens to block an increase in the debt limit until lawmakers agree to put teeth back into Gramm-Rudman. But few take heart. "The changes being discussed are too monumental, and time is too short, for anything meaningful to happen," says Stanley Collender, budget analyst for Touche Ross & Co.

History provides an even more sobering assessment. Congress hasn't met a budget deadline since 1976 and has spent more than it estimated it would in budget resolutions in every year of the Reagan Administration. Deficits in every year have been higher than predicted. And despite perennial threats of a "veto strategy," Reagan has only vetoed one regular appropriations bill.

In the end, Congress will likely punt. The President is strong enough to block a tax hike but lacks the clout to force the big spending cuts he wants. The probable result: A fiscal 1988 deficit that won't fall much below $170 billion.

Reprinted from the July 6, 1987 issue of *Business Week*, by special permission. © 1987, by McGraw-Hill, Inc.

APPENDIX I

MONEY

Money is the high-octane "fuel" that propels the modern industrial economy. However, to merely say that the U.S. economy, or any industrial economy, needs money to fuel and sustain its standard of living and economic growth is to understate money's true role. For the individual, money not only provides a central economic frame of reference and a standard of comparison, it also provides freedom of choice; for society, it provides the most efficient means yet discovered to allocate scarce resources. Money also binds people to each other, integrating them into an economic system. It is a common economic language, whose use shapes and defines one's role in the economy, as a consumer exercising market "demand" for goods and services; as a saver, investor, and borrower; and as a taxpayer and recipient of government payments.

A FUNCTIONAL DEFINITION OF MONEY

Medium of Exchange

A nation's money consists of those items generally accepted in exchange for goods and services or in settlement of debt. In the simplest sense, money is nothing more than a nation's generally accepted medium of exchange.

Because any item can serve as a medium of exchange—from gold cubes to electronic entries in a computer—money cannot be defined meaningfully, or understood, in terms of its physical characteristics. For this reason, economists commonly define money in terms of its functions—what it does—rather than what it is made of or what it looks like. Although the most basic function of money is to serve as a medium of exchange, money has two other important functions: to serve as a unit of account and as a store of value.

Unit of Account

Any item that serves as a nation's medium of exchange—that has been generally accepted as its functioning money—will also serve as a nation's unit of account. In this capacity,

---

All material in Appendixes I, II, and III is excerpted from David H. Friedman, *Money & Banking* (Washington, DC: American Bankers Association, 1985).

money serves as a standard or yardstick for measuring the relative value, or worth, of goods and services. By using money as a standard of value, one knows, for example, that a $500 television set is twice as expensive as a $250 suit of clothes, and that if one's after-tax income is $2,000 per month, the television will cost the equivalent of 1 week of labor. Money is also used in this capacity to denominate the value of all the items on a company's balance sheet, such as inventories, fixed assets, and raw materials.

Store of Value

Money's third, and most critical, function is to serve as a store of value, a means to hold and accumulate purchasing power for future, general use. By serving as a store of value, money allows one to buy goods and services independently, without having to sell other goods and services in exchange.

This key characteristic distinguishes a money economy from a barter economy. In a barter economy, goods and services are exchanged for other goods and services. The lack of assurance that any given good in one's immediate possession will be accepted for a good one might want from someone else is a major drawback of a barter economy. The inability to preserve the quality and physical condition of all goods held in storage for future exchange is another. In essence, future generalized purchasing power cannot be accumulated efficiently or effectively in a barter economy.

General Acceptability

Any item can serve as a medium of exchange, and historically most items have—from the long-horned cattle "money" used by the pharaohs of ancient Egypt to the sharks' teeth "money" used by the people of Micronesia before World War II. As long as people are willing to accept an item in exchange for goods, services, or settlement of debt, that item is money.

GOLD STANDARDS AND BIMETALLIC STANDARDS

Many industrial nations, including the United States, attempted to regulate the value of their national money by operating under a gold standard or bimetallic (gold and silver) standard in the nineteenth century.

Under a gold standard, a nation would define the value of its money not in terms of purchasing power but in terms of a fixed weight of gold, and would allow for full convertibility of its paper money into gold at this predetermined rate of exchange. Gold standards worked well for brief periods of time, as long as the gold supply kept growing in pace with national production and income. However, when gold production slowed in the last third of the nineteenth century with the end of the California and Australia gold rushes, prices fell throughout the world.

Declining prices and wages caused by the gold shortage led to economic unrest in many countries in the 1870s to 1890s in the form of strikes, rising unemployment, and political instability. In the United States, falling prices moved farmers and unions to press aggressively for the government to use silver as well as gold as its monetary standard, an action that moved the government to adopt a bimetallic standard.

Under bimetallism, the U.S. Treasury agreed that it would exchange U.S. currency for either gold or silver at a predetermined weight ratio, for example, exchanging 16 ounces of silver for each ounce of gold. Bimetallism, however, worked even more poorly than the gold standard in maintaining the value of U.S. money. The problem with America's bimetallic standard was that other countries did not agree to maintain the same weight ratio of exchange. As a result, different value systems existed throughout the world for the same commodity monies.

Changes in the relative demand and supply for either gold or silver in any part of the world led to a rapid disappearance of the more expensive metal money from circulation. For example, as supply and demand changes drove up the price of gold, the cheaper metal silver would be used as the circulating money while the more expensive metal gold would be hoarded, melted down, or sold abroad, disappearing from circulation. This principle that "cheap money" will tend to drive "dear money" from circulation is known as Gresham's Law, so named for Sir Thomas Gresham who, as Britain's sixteenth-century Master of the Mint, first identified this economic phenomenon.

U.S. MONEY IN THE 1980s

In the United States, coin, paper currency, bank deposits on which checks can be drawn (checkbook money), and electronic funds transfers (EFTs) constitute the accepted media of exchange. Credit cards are commonly used payment devices, but they do not qualify as a medium of exchange.

Coin

Coin comprised only about 3 percent of U.S. money, or about $14 billion, in 1984. It is used mainly for day-to-day convenience transactions. Modern American coin, like most of the world's contemporary "small change," is made of various base metals whose intrinsic value is worth less than the amount stamped on the face of the coin.

U.S. coin is minted by the Treasury and distributed by the nation's twelve Federal Reserve banks. Coin is carried on the Treasury's books as a liability and on the books of all other institutions as an asset.

Currency

Currency comprised about 30 percent of U.S. money, or $163 billion, in 1984. Like coin, currency is used primarily by individuals for small dollar-value transactions. Today's currency consists almost entirely of Federal Reserve notes, which are issued by each of the nation's twelve Federal Reserve banks. Unlike coin, U.S. currency is not a direct responsibility of the Treasury but of the Federal Reserve, the central bank of the United States. When issued, it is carried as a liability on the Federal Reserve's books and as an asset on the books of all other financial institutions that hold currency, including the Treasury.

From 1914 to 1968, Federal Reserve notes had to be partially backed (collateralized) by gold. Gold backing was seen as a means of tying U.S. currency into the gold standard. It ensured that Reserve banks would not overissue paper money and generated public acceptance of the new currency.

In 1914, the currency issued by the Reserve banks, known then as Federal Reserve bank notes, had to be backed by 40 percent gold and 100 percent eligible paper. Eligible paper consisted of the short-term loan agreements of businesses and farmers that were presented to the Reserve banks by commercial banks as collateral for loans the commercial banks themselves obtained from the Federal Reserve. The eligible paper requirement was reduced to 60 percent in 1917. The Reserve banks obtained the gold they needed from the U.S. Treasury through a bookkeeping purchase arrangement. The Treasury issued gold certificates to the Reserve banks (claims on the U.S. gold stock) in return for credit to their checking account at the Federal Reserve in the amount of the gold certificates issued.

The gold and eligible paper backing requirements were initially designed to regulate automatically the issuance of currency to match the pace of the economy's growth. Economists believed that automatic regulation would be assured because only short-term bank loans made to expand manufacturing or farm output were designated eligible as collateral by the Federal Reserve, and only increased business activity and bank lending could generate the collateral necessary for additional currency issuance.

In the 1930s, the concept of automatic currency regulation gave way as new insights were developed into the workings of the economy and new theories were formulated on how money should be regulated. Backing requirements were liberalized and reduced. Congress allowed Reserve banks to use assets other than eligible paper, such as U.S. government securities, to back currency. By the 1940s, Congress had reduced the gold backing requirement to 25 percent, and in 1968, it eliminated gold backing entirely. Today, Federal Reserve notes are backed by the assets of the Reserve banks. About 90 percent of these assets consist of government securities owned by the Federal Reserve. The remaining 10 percent consist of the gold certificates the Reserve banks purchased from the Treasury in the 1914-68 gold backing era.

Checkable Deposits

Checkable deposits are account balances on banks' books against which checks can be drawn. These deposits comprise about 70 percent of the nation's money and are used to effect more than 90 percent of the dollar value of all commercial and personal payments made in the United States by consumers, businesses, and governments.

The predominant checkable deposit in the U.S. banking system is the demand deposit (checking account), which allows the holder to withdraw funds on demand or transfer funds by check. This account pays no interest, unlike other types of checkable deposits such as negotiable orders of withdrawal (NOW). Because demand deposits are created mainly by the nation's 14,800 commercial banks and are the dominant component of the nation's money supply, the Federal Reserve's attempts to control money focus on regulating banks' ability to create demand deposits.

Since the late 1970s, commercial banks and thrift institutions—savings banks, savings and loan associations, and credit unions—have been allowed to offer depositors other forms of checkable deposits that pay interest. In 1984, Americans held about $125 billion in these other checkable deposits—primarily NOW accounts, automatic transfer service accounts, credit union share drafts, and money market deposit accounts—compared with about $245 billion held in traditional demand deposits.

Credit Cards

More than half of all American families use credit cards to make some payments. However, credit cards are not money. Credit cards are deferred payment devices that allow consumers to acquire goods and services immediately while making payment in cash or check at a later date. In effect, credit cards are prearranged loans.

About one-third of the credit cards used in the United States are the product of bilateral (two-party) arrangements made by department stores and gasoline companies. They allow the credit card user to buy goods and services on credit from only the institution, merchant, or chain that issues the card. The most common form of credit card use is the multilateral (three-party) arrangement entered into by major banks and travel and entertainment companies. In this type arrangement, consumers buy goods and services on credit from thousands of different merchants that participate with the banks and the travel and entertainment companies in offering these predetermined loan arrangements. Most multilateral credit cards allow the user to draw cash itself on credit from banks participating in the arrangements.

THE CIRCULATION OF MONEY

The Federal Reserve determines how much money should circulate as cash and checkable deposits to maintain a growing noninflationary economy. The public, however, through the banking system, freely determines the form in which that money is held.

When people or businesses want more coin or currency, they typically manifest these demands by cashing checks at their banks. That is, they exchange one form of money—checkbook money—for another form of money—cash. Banks, in turn, do the same thing. When banks need more coin or currency than they have on hand to meet growing public demands, they "buy" the cash from Reserve banks with the deposit balances they maintain at the Reserve banks. That is, they exchange an equal amount of deposit money for cash money. Banks that do not have a direct account at a Reserve bank typically rely on a correspondent bank from which they obtain services. They, too, exchange part of their deposit balance at the correspondent bank for cash.

As people and businesses spend their newly obtained cash, it flows back into the banking system in the form of other business and individual deposits. As banks accumulate more cash than needed for day-to-day transactions, they deposit the cash for credit to their own checking accounts at Reserve banks or at correspondent banks where the funds can be more effectively used for business, clearing, or investment purposes.

When cash deposits are received at Reserve banks, currency that is too worn for further circulation is culled from these deposits, destroyed, and replaced. Unfit coin is returned to the Treasury for melting and recasting. As additional coin and currency is needed by the Reserve banks to replace unfit cash or to meet expanding demand, orders are placed with separate Treasury divisions—the Bureau of the Mint for coin and the Bureau of Engraving and Printing for currency.

The total amount of money available in the economy remains the same whether people and businesses convert their checkable deposits into cash or deposit cash for credit to their checking accounts. In controlling the overall money supply, the Federal Reserve monitors cash flows into and out of the banking system but focuses its control only on deposits.

LEGAL TENDER AND CHECKBOOK MONEY

The term *legal tender* refers to money items designated by the government and the courts as acceptable payment for goods, services, or settlement of debt. In effect, the designation of certain items as legal tender leaves sellers of goods and services and creditors with no legal recourse to demand any other form of payment.

In today's economy, the reliance on legal tender status has been supplanted by public confidence in the strength, safety, and prudence of the American banking system. This confidence has been bolstered by ongoing government supervision and inspection of banks as well as government insurance of deposits provided by such agencies as the Federal

Deposit Insurance Corporation (FDIC) and the Federal Savings and Loan Insurance Corporation (FSLIC). The check clearing and collection system of the Federal Reserve has also helped make checkbook money highly acceptable by assuring banks a degree of certainty in knowing when check collection credit will be received and by speeding up the collection process nationwide.

MONEY SUPPLY

The Federal Reserve regulates economic activity primarily by controlling money supply to ensure purchasing power and a growing economy. In the 1970s, economists, bankers, and the press began to pay more attention to money supply as an economic concept because the Federal Reserve's operating strategy for stopping inflation increasingly emphasized control of money supply growth in conformity with long-range targets and objectives. According to economic theory, how well the Federal Reserve controls the nation's money supply over long periods of time ultimately affects the economy's production, employment, income, and price level.

Defining Money Supply

The term *money supply* does not refer to the sum of all the media of exchange in the economy. Rather, money supply is an economist's term for the sum of all the funds that individuals and business firms have immediately available for spending in the domestic economy. It is a measure used by the Federal Reserve to predict and control the pace and direction of U.S. economic activity. As a statistical sum, it includes estimates and adjustments for seasonal variations in the public's holdings of money balances, and it is consistently revised upward or downward to reflect current data. It is not a lateral dollars-and-cents count of the public's monies.

The reason that money supply is not synonymous with the amount of coin, currency, and checkable deposits in the economy is that, while these represent our functioning media of exchange, spending decisions are not based solely on how much of these three money items we hold. Most of the public's financial wealth (assets) is not held in money, but rather in near monies. Near monies are items that may be good standards of value but that are not generally accepted as money. A key characteristic of many near monies is that they are highly "liquid," which means they can be quickly converted into money.

Measuring Money Supply

The conceptual problem of what to count as part of the money supply has been complicated in the 1970s and 1980s by two factors. First, banking innovations and changes in banking law have allowed banks and thrifts to offer new types of deposit accounts that earn interest yet are checkable (subject to claim on demand and to transfer by check). These new types of accounts, such as negotiable order of withdrawal (NOW) accounts and automatic transfer service (ATS) accounts, authorized in 1980, and money market deposit accounts, authorized in 1982, have blurred the distinction between funds being held for spending purposes (transactions) and funds being held for long-term savings.

Second, rising deposit interest rates have induced consumers and business firms to transfer noninterest-earning demand deposit money into interest-earning checkable deposits and a broad range of near monies. Between 1978 and 1982, for example, the public placed about $250 billion in nonbank money market funds. Between December 1982, when banks were authorized to offer a money market deposit account to compete with the money market funds, and December 1983, the public placed $370 billion in these accounts alone. In 1978, individuals and businesses held $280 billion in demand deposits at commercial banks. By 1984, however, that total had declined to $240 billion. Movements of funds such as these have made the task of classifying money and near money all the more difficult. Patterns of individual and business demand for different types of money and near money may no longer be as predictable as they were in the 1960s.

In implementing monetary policy, the Federal Reserve attempts to provide the economy with a rate of money supply growth consistent with long-range economic growth needs and short-range business conditions. It also uses money supply growth rates to measure its own success or failure to achieve operational objectives. And yet, no one knows with certainty what measure of money supply is most accurate in predicting and in controlling the course of the economy.

The most commonly used and narrowest measure of the money the public has immediately available for domestic spending is referred to as M1. This measure counts all media exchange, including checkable deposits, at both banks and thrift institutions.

M1 consists of

- currency and coin outside the Treasury, Federal Reserve banks, and commercial banks;

- demand deposits at all commercial banks *except*—
  —those due to domestic banks, foreign commercial banks, and certain foreign official institutions
  —those due to the U.S. government

  less

  —cash items in the process of collection
  —Federal Reserve float;

- NOW accounts;

- credit union share drafts;

- savings deposits subject to automatic transfers;

- demand deposits at thrift institutions; and
- traveler's checks.

The broad measure of the money the public has immediately available for domestic spending is known as the M2 measure. The M2 measure counts near monies that either are close substitutes for money, have short maturities (the assets quickly mature into cash), or are readily sold or converted into cash.

M2 consists of

- M1;
- time deposits with minimum denominations of less than $100,000 and savings deposits at banks and thrift institutions;
- overnight Eurodollar deposits held by U.S. residents at Caribbean branches of U.S. banks (Eurodollars are broadly defined as any dollar-denominated deposits on the books of banking offices outside the United States, including non-European banks);
- overnight repurchase agreements at commercial banks (A purchase agreement involves the purchase of a security—usually a 3-month Treasury bill—with an agreement that the seller will buy back the security within a specified time—usually a day or two—at an agreed-upon price.); and
- money market mutual fund shares.

A still broader measure of money supply is the M3 measure. This measure includes highly liquid assets that are used primarily by big business firms.

M3 consists of

- M2;
- term repurchase agreements (those longer than overnight); and
- time deposits with minimum denominations of $100,000.

The Federal Reserve also uses a broad liquidity measure—L—that recognizes the importance of several key near-money financial instruments in individual and business money-holding and spending decisions.

L consists of

- M3;
- other Eurodollar holdings of U.S. nonbank residents;
- bankers acceptances (Bankers acceptances are promissory note credit instruments that are drawn on and accepted by a bank to finance the export, import, shipment, or storage

of goods. The term *accepted* means that the bank agrees to pay the money order at its maturity on behalf of its customer, who is obligated to pay the bank the amount being financed);

- savings bonds;

- commercial paper; and

- marketable, liquid Treasury obligations.

All measures of the money supply share several definitional characteristics. Each successive (broader) measure of the money supply includes the measure that preceded it. M2 includes all of M1 plus related near monies, and M3 includes all of M2 plus additional near monies. Also, no measure counts the monies or near monies held by banks or the government for its own use.

APPENDIX II

MONEY CREATION, COMMERCIAL BANKS, AND THE FEDERAL RESERVE

Commercial banks in the United States historically created money by issuing paper currency in the form of their own bank notes. The federal government ended this practice among state-chartered banks in 1863, when it passed the National Banking Act, and ended the practice among nationally chartered banks in 1913, when the newly established Federal Reserve banks were granted the exclusive franchise to issue U.S. currency. Today, commercial banks create money only on their books, through the lending process. The lending process of commercial banks and how it differs from the lending process of other financial intermediaries are examined in this chapter. Components of bank loan portfolios are described to add perspective. The impact of the Federal Reserve on the lending process is discussed to illustrate how banks and bank reserves serve as vehicles for implementing monetary policy.

LENDING AND MONEY CREATION

Financial intermediaries serve an important role in maintaining the economy's balance and stimulating growth in production, employment, and income. They transfer savings from the consumers, businesses, and governments that have an excess of funds to the consumers, businesses, and governments that want additional funds for spending or investment.

Commercial banks act as financial intermediaries but are in a lending class by themselves because they have the power to create demand deposit money when they lend. This money-creating power has distinguished the lending process of commercial banks from that of other financial intermediaries historically. It also is the reason why monetary policy is directed primarily at commercial banks.

THE LOAN PROCESS OF A FINANCIAL INTERMEDIARY

When a financial intermediary, such as a savings bank or a savings and loan association, takes in funds and lends out those funds, it merely exchanges one form of asset—a cash asset—for another form of asset—a loan asset. This exchange can be illustrated using T accounts to trace the process by which a financial intermediary makes a loan. T accounts are abstracts of an institution's balance sheet that show only those changes in the institution's assets and liabilities being examined.

Assume that the First Intermediary Savings and Loan Association receives $100,000 in cash deposits from 10 different depositors for credit to their savings and time accounts. Further, assume that First Intermediary's management feels that the institution needs to hold liquid assets (cash assets or reserves) equal to 10 percent of its deposits at all times to meet customer demands for cash and to pay other banks for check collection. The Monetary Control Act of 1980 subjected all depository institutions, banks and thrift institutions alike, to new Federal Reserve reserve requirements. Although no reserve requirement was imposed on personal time and savings deposits held at banks and thrifts, First Intermediary's liquidity needs serve as a de facto reserve requirement.

If First Intermediary must hold $10,000 in cash assets against its new $100,000 in deposits, it then has $90,000 in funds available for lending. First Intermediary will be able to make a mortgage loan of $90,000 with these funds.

In granting the mortgage, the savings and loan gives the borrower a $90,000 check drawn on itself or on the savings and loan's account at a correspondent bank. In exchange for relinquishing $90,000 of its cash assets to the borrower, the savings and loan obtains a new earning asset in the form of the mortgage loan. This reallocation of First Intermediary's assets has increased the savings and loan's earnings and profit prospects because cash assets, as purely liquid assets, do not earn a return, but earning assets do. The loan has not increased the amount of money in the economy, however. Before the loan, $100,000 in cash had been deposited in the savings and loan by different depositors.

After the mortgage, one new home buyer holds $90,000 of those funds, and the savings and loan holds the remaining $10,000 as necessary liquidity against the claims of its depositors.

First Intermediary Savings and Loan

Before the Loan

Assets		Liabilities	
Cash assets	+ $100,000	Time and savings deposits	+ $100,000

After the Loan

Assets		Liabilities	
Cash assets	+ $10,000	Time and savings deposits	+ $100,000
New mortgage loan	+ $90,000		

APPENDIX

THE LOAN PROCESS OF A COMMERCIAL BANK

Consider how this same loan transaction would work at a commercial bank. Assume similar conditions tailored to a commercial bank, namely that the bank takes in $100,000 in cash deposits from businesses and individuals for credit to their checking accounts. Further assume that under Federal Reserve reserve requirements, the bank must hold $10,000 in required reserves against these new deposits. (This 10 percent reserve requirement is selected only for its mathematical simplicity. Actual reserve requirements in 1984 against transaction accounts were 3 percent for the first $28.9 million of these deposits held by a commercial bank and 12 percent for transaction deposits in excess of that amount.)

Under these conditions, the commercial bank has $90,000 in excess reserves against which it can create $90,000 by making a mortgage loan. Excess reserves are the difference between the total amount of reserves a bank is holding (the sum of its vault cash and deposit balance at the Reserve Bank) and the amount of required reserves it must set aside to meet reserve requirements.

When a commercial bank makes a loan, it monetizes a private debt. It accepts as an asset the debt obligation of the borrower—the borrower's promise to repay—and creates a liability on its books in the form of a demand deposit balance in the amount of the loan. The deposits that banks create when they make loans are backed by financial or physical assets that collateralize the promissory note or loan agreement. Cash received by banks is rarely loaned out in the same form. The receipt of cash from depositors increases banks' assets and deposit liabilities and enables banks to make additional loans and investments. In this respect, banks act as financial intermediaries as well as money creators.

First Commercial Bank

Before the Loan

Assets		Liabilities	
Cash assets	+ $100,000*	Demand deposits	+ $100,000
*Required reserves	$ 10,000		
Excess reserves	$ 90,000		

After the Loan

Assets		Liabilities	
Cash assets	$100,000*	Demand deposits	$100,000
New mortgage loan	+$ 90,000	Demand deposit created for home buyer	+$ 90,000
*Required reserves	$ 10,000		
Excess reserves	$ 90,000		

First Commercial Bank's loan created a sum of money that did not exist before—$90,000—in the form of a demand deposit balance for the home buyer in the amount of the loan. This act of money creation also increased the bank's assets and liabilities to $190,000 each. The loan did not simply bring about a redistribution of assets as occurred at First Intermediary Savings and Loan.

The new $90,000 in demand deposit money does not disappear when the home buyer uses the loan proceeds to buy the house. The $90,000 check received by the house seller is deposited in the seller's bank and forwarded for collection to First Commercial, which pays the check by transferring $90,000 of its cash assets to the seller's bank. Having paid the check, First Commercial also strikes from its books the $90,000 deposit liability previously carried for the home buyer. After the check collection process is completed, the books look like this:

First Commercial Bank

After Check Collection

Assets		Liabilities	
Cash assets	$10,000*	Demand deposits	$100,000
New mortgage loan	+$90,000		
*Required reserves	$10,000		
Excess reserves	0		

The $90,000 that First Commercial created in step 2 still exists. It now resides on the books of the house seller's bank.

RESERVE REQUIREMENT AND LIQUIDITY CONSTRAINTS

First Commercial's ability to create additional money depends on its excess reserves. Since the bank has no excess reserves at the moment, it cannot create any more demand deposits. If First Commercial tried to do so, it would plunge itself into a reserve requirement deficiency (and subject itself to a financial penalty) as soon as the newly created funds were spent. The effects of First Commercial's attempt to increase its earning assets by a $5,000 loan are as follows:

First Commercial Bank

After Second Loan

Assets		Liabilities	
Cash assets	$10,000*	Demand deposits	$100,000
Initial mortgage loan	$90,000	Demand deposit created for consumer borrower	+$ 5,000
New consumer loan	+$ 5,000		
*Required reserves	$10,000		
Excess reserves	0		

After the check collection process is completed, the books look like this:

First Commercial Bank

After Check Collection

Assets		Liabilities	
Cash assets	$ 5,000*	Demand deposits	$100,000
Initial mortgage loan	$90,000		
New consumer loan	+$ 5,000		
*Required reserve deficiency	$ 5,000		

Because the 10 percent reserve requirement has not changed, First Commercial still must hold $10,000 in reserve assets against its $100,000 in demand deposits. In payment for the consumer borrower's check, however, it had to transfer $5,000 of its reserves to another bank. As a result, even though its books balance (assets equal liabilities), it is in a reserve deficiency. Even in the absence of legal reserve requirements, the senior management of First Commercial might feel that $5,000 in cash assets represents too little liquidity to protect the bank against the cash demands of its depositors.

Either case illustrates a key principle of money creation. No one bank can create an amount of money greater than its excess reserves (or excess liquidity) because it will lose a dollar in reserves (cash assets) for every dollar it creates when the proceeds of its new loans are disbursed and the loan funds are transferred through the check collection process. This limitation, however, does not pertain to the banking system which, in its totality, is capable of creating money in a multiple way.

MULTIPLE DEPOSIT CREATION

Multiple deposit creation is the ability of the banking system to create an amount of deposits many times greater than its initial amount of reserves. Multiple deposit creation in the banking system can be demonstrated by using T accounts to trace a commercial bank loan. This time, however, the multiple effect of the loan on other banks as newly created deposits move from bank to bank will be followed. For simplicity of analysis, assume that all of the deposits created by banks stay in the banking system, that demand deposits are the only form in which newly created funds are held, and that each bank creates loans equal to every available excess reserve dollar. Although these assumptions do not reflect reality, they do not distort the fundamental process by which banks collectively create multiple deposits.

Assume Bank One receives a cash deposit of $100,000 from a corporate customer for credit to the customer's transaction account. Assume, too, that the Federal Reserve's reserve requirement on transaction accounts is 10 percent. As in the earlier examples, this means that Bank One, as well as all other depository institutions, must hold an amount of reserves—vault cash or deposit balances at the Reserve bank—equal to 10 percent of its transaction deposits. Thus, Bank One must hold $10,000 in required reserves against its new $100,000 deposit, and it has $90,000 in excess reserves against which it can create $90,000 in additional funds through the act of lending.

Bank One

After Initial Loan

Assets		Liabilities	
Cash assets	$100,000*	Demand deposits	$100,000
New commercial loan	+$ 90,000	Demand deposit created for borrower	+$ 90,000
*Required reserves	$ 10,000		
Excess reserves	$ 90,000		

APPENDIX

When Bank One makes the loan, both its assets and its liabilities temporarily increase to $190,000, reflecting the addition of the loan to its earning assets portfolio and the addition of the newly created demand deposit to its total liabilities. However, as soon as the borrower uses the newly created funds, Bank One's assets and liabilities will decline to their pre-loan level as an inevitable result of the check collection process.

Assume that the borrower, a small business firm, gives the loan proceeds, in the form of a check payment, to a computer manufacturing company that has an account at Bank Two. When the borrower's $90,000 check clears, Bank One will have to transfer $90,000 of its cash assets in payment for the check to the presenting bank, Bank Two. Upon payment, Bank One also will strike from its books the $90,000 demand deposit liability carried for the borrower. Thus, after check clearance, Bank One has $100,000 in assets and $100,000 in liabilities. Note, however, that the composition of its assets has changed. Before the loan, Bank One held $100,000 in cash assets. Now it holds $10,000 in cash assets and $90,000 in loan assets. The $10,000 in cash assets meets the 10 percent reserve requirement against transaction account liabilities assumed in this example.

Bank One

After Check Collection

Assets		Liabilities	
Cash assets	$10,000	Demand deposits	$100,000
Loan	$90,000		

Bank Two

After Check Collection

Assets		Liabilities	
Cash assets*	$90,000*	Demand deposit	$ 90,000
*Required reserves	$ 9,000		
Excess reserves	$81,000		

The $90,000 in deposit dollars created by Bank One now resides as a deposit on the books of Bank Two, increasing that bank's liabilities. However, because of that deposit, Bank Two also received a transfer of $90,000 in cash assets when it received payment for

ECONOMICS FOR BANKERS

the check deposited by the computer manufacturing company. Bank Two, subject to the same 10 percent reserve requirement as Bank One, must keep $9,000 against that new deposit, but can use the remaining $81,000 in excess reserves to support a new loan and the creation of a new $81,000 demand deposit.

When Bank Two makes that loan, its assets and liabilities will increase initially but then decline to their pre-loan level in response to the collection of the borrower's check. Assume that the borrower uses the loan proceeds to pay for data processing services, and the service corporation deposits the check in Bank Three, where it has an account. Bank Two's newly created $81,000 will now reside in Bank Three together with $81,000 in cash assets it had to transfer in payment for the check.

Bank Three will, in turn, now be able to create demand deposits equal to 90 percent of its new reserve assets. When it does so, it will give still another bank the ability to create new deposits.

Bank Two

After Loan

Assets		Liabilities	
Cash assets	$ 9,000	Demand deposit	$90,000
Loan	$81,000		

Bank Three

After Check Collection

Assets		Liabilities	
Cash assets	$81,000*	Demand deposit	$81,000
*Required reserves	$ 8,100		
Excess reserves	$72,900		

In theory, this process of bank deposit creation could continue through thousands of banks and generate, in our example, a total amount of deposits on all banks' books 10 times greater than the $100,000 in cash deposits that initially started the process.

The multiplier, or expansion coefficient, is the reciprocal of the reserve requirement ratio. That is, because the reserve requirement ratio is 10 percent or 1/10, the multiplier is 10. This means that the banking system could generate $1 million in total deposits using the $100,000 initial cash deposit as a base. Of this $1 million, $900,000 would be newly created money. If the reserve requirement had been 20 percent, the expansion coefficient would have been 5, the reciprocal of the 20 percent or 1/5 reserve requirement, and total deposits could increase to only $500,000.

APPENDIX

Multiple Expansion of Bank Deposits

(Reserve Requirement = 10%)

Position of Bank	New Deposits	New Loans and Investments	Required Reserves
Bank One	$ 100,000	$ 90,000	$ 10,000
Bank Two	90,000	81,000	9,000
Bank Three	81,000	72,900	8,100
Bank Four	72,900	66,510	7,290
Bank Five	65,610	59,040	6,560
Bank Six	59,040	53,140	5,900
Bank Seven	53,140	47,830	5,310
Bank Eight	47,830	43,050	4,780
Bank Nine	43,050	38,740	4,300
Bank Ten	38,740	34,970	3,870
Sum of first ten banks' deposit expansion	651,320	586,170	65,130
Sum of remaining banks' deposit expansion	348,680	313,810	34,870
Total for banking system	$1,000,000 (multiple expansion)	$900,000 (net creation)	$100,000 (original deposit)

Multiple expansion equation = $\frac{1}{\text{reserve requirement}} \times$ initial deposit = total deposits

Multiple expansion in above example = $\frac{1}{.10}$ = 10 × $100,000 = $1,000,000

Factors Influencing Multiple Deposit Creation

The mathematical simplicity of multiple expansion is based on a unique set of assumptions that do not hold in the real world of banking. In reality:

- Some deposits created by banks "leak" out of the banking system into nonbank financial institutions and into money market instruments such as U.S. Treasury bills.

- Consumers and businesses typically convert some of their newly acquired demand deposits into both cash and time deposits.

- There is more than one reserve requirement. In 1984, for example, the reserve requirement rules called for the following: 1) a 3 percent requirement on the first $28.9 million of transaction deposits (checkable deposits) and a 12 percent requirement on any transaction deposits above this level; 2) a 3 percent requirement on short-term time deposits held by businesses; and 3) a 3 percent requirement on Eurodollar borrowings.

- Banks do not usually create money equal to every available excess reserve dollar. This is not because they do not want to but because each day's check collections are subject to next-day corrections (adjustments) that can increase or decrease yesterday's deposit balance and reserve totals. Also, the pace of deposits flowing in and out of banks on any given day is often so rapid and the volume is so large that it is only at the end of a day, or perhaps a day or two later, that banks know precisely how much in reserves they have available to support new loans. Thus, there always tend to be excess reserves in the banking system, even when loan demand is very strong.

THE IMPLEMENTATION OF MONETARY POLICY

The monetary policy goal of the Federal Reserve is to ensure that the amount of deposits created by the banking system is appropriate for the needs of the economy—neither too much nor too little. The central bank does this by controlling the amount and cost of reserves available in the banking system. In implementing monetary policy, however, the Federal Reserve does not involve itself with the decisions that an individual bank's management may make on a daily, weekly, or monthly basis to achieve its overall earnings goals in conformity with its lending or investing policies. Banks are free to compete against each other, against other financial intermediaries, and in other markets for a customer's deposit and loan business and, most important, for the reserves that help them achieve their earnings goals. The Federal Reserve's focus is on the total amount of reserves available in the banking system, not the amount available to any individual bank.

In a recession, the Federal Reserve typically seeks to stimulate bank lending to spark needed business and consumer spending. It provides additional reserves to the banking system for expanding loans. With demand for loans low, a characteristic of recession, banks often find interest rates declining as these new reserves expand the base of available reserves. Banks tend to see this monetary policy as consistent with their own goals because an expansion of excess reserves increases banks' earning potential. Indeed, declining interest rates themselves increase the value of the securities held in banks' portfolios—a major component of most banks' earning assets.

In an inflation, however, the intent of monetary policy may directly conflict with banks' lending goals, as the Federal Reserve seeks to restrain banks' lending to hold down credit-induced buying. To counter inflation, the Federal Reserve will typically attempt to hold back reserves, and with demand for bank loans strong, interest rates often rise. Banks tend to see anti-inflationary monetary policy as reducing their earnings prospects. It cuts them off from the reserves they need to meet all customer loan demands and raises their costs of doing business. Moreover, rising interest rates generate paper losses on the securities held in bank portfolios that were purchased at an earlier time when rates were lower.

APPENDIX

Control of Bank Reserves

The Federal Reserve can control bank lending by altering the quantity of reserves available in the banking system. It uses one or more of the following policy tools:

- *Reserve requirements.* The Federal Reserve can change the reserve requirement percentages it specifies against designated liabilities. If it raises reserve requirements, for example, banks have to come up with more required reserves. Excess reserves available in the banking system are immediately reduced as banks earmark some or all of those reserves to meet the new higher requirements. The Federal Reserve also can change the rules on what bank assets constitute legal reserves. Currently, only vault cash and deposits at a Reserve bank are acceptable. (Depository institutions that are not members of the Federal Reserve system can maintain a reserve deposit at a Reserve bank indirectly through a pass-through deposit made at a correspondent bank, which must be redeposited at the Federal Reserve.) If the Federal Reserve allowed other assets such as government securities to be used as reserves, the total amount of reserves available in the banking system would immediately expand. The Federal Reserve also could change the base against which banks must keep reserves by including or excluding liabilities from its list of bank liabilities against which reserves must be maintained.

- *Discount rate.* The Federal Reserve can raise or lower the interest rate it charges depositories that borrow from it, to either encourage or discourage banks from borrowing reserves. It also can change, explicitly or implicitly, the ground rules under which banks can obtain loans of reserves. In doing so, it increases or decreases the amount of reserves available to banks through its lending practices.

- *Open market operations.* The Federal Reserve can buy or sell government securities in the open market. When the Federal Reserve buys, both bank reserves and the nation's money supply increase because the Federal Reserve pays with checks drawn on itself. When those checks are collected, banks' reserve accounts are increased, as are the private demand deposit accounts of the securities sellers. Since these checks are not collected against any other private banks, the Federal Reserve's purchase does not redistribute reserves and money but actually creates new reserves and demand deposits, just as commercial banks create demand deposits for their borrowers.

When the Federal Reserve sells, bank reserves and money supply decline. Private purchasers—government securities dealer firms—pay with checks drawn on their banks. When the Federal Reserve collects these checks, it reduces the reserve accounts of the banks on which the checks were drawn just as the banks reduce the demand deposit balances of their dealer depositors. Since these reserves and deposits are not transferred into other commercial banks, as they would be in a private transaction, but are retained by the central bank, the effect is a reduction in bank reserves and money supply.

An increase in the quantity of reserves available to banks influences bank lending. A bank may obtain additional reserves, for example, through the Federal Reserve's open market purchase of a U.S. Treasury security. Although it then must keep more required reserves against the new deposit of the securities seller, it has a significant margin of excess reserves against which new loans can be made (new demand deposits created).

Banks with excess reserves will seek to turn them into income-generating assets by making loans or investments. As the recipients of these bank loans or investments spend their money in the economy, these funds are deposited by others in banks throughout the country. Total deposits in the banking system increase, which results in still more money creation for the economy and increases in earning assets for banks. The multiple creation of bank deposits expands the nation's money supply by an amount several times greater than the initial expansion generated by the first loan.

Reserve loss also may affect lending. If a bank loses reserves through the Federal Reserve's open market selling of securities from its $160 billion portfolio, for example, the bank's assets and liabilities usually must be adjusted. If the bank had no excess reserves initially, it would be plunged into a temporary reserve deficiency. A bank in that predicament will seek to obtain the reserves it needs to meet reserve requirements by selling secondary reserve assets (government securities it maintains in its portfolio), borrowing from other banks (federal funds), borrowing from the central bank, calling in loans, or making some other balance sheet adjustment.

Banks that simply lose excess reserves may not have to make such extensive adjustments immediately. However, banks that are extensively involved in loan commitments and loan commitment fees may well have to respond quickly. If reserves don't materialize, these banks must go through the same asset and/or liability adjustments as banks with reserve deficiencies so that they can honor their commitments.

An individual bank can meet a reserve deficiency by borrowing from another bank, selling securities to a private dealer firm, or calling in loans. However, it is impossible for the banking system as a whole to meet a reserve deficiency if the total of all reserves available to all banks is less than the amount needed by all banks to meet reserve requirements. No combination of asset and/or liability adjustments by banks will create new reserves. At best, a given bank can transfer its reserve deficiency to another bank, or a group of smaller banks can redistribute their reserve deficiencies to one or two large money market banks. But, on balance, the banking system itself will still hold the same amount of reserves.

If Federal Reserve policy caused or allowed a banking system reserve deficiency to develop as a means to reduce the money supply, then, within days, the money supply would decline as banks' loans were repaid and no new loans were made (demand deposits created). Only when the total deposit base of the banking system declined would available reserves—the same amount as before—equal the amount needed to meet reserve requirements.

Bank Response to Monetary Control

When the Federal Reserve wants to restrain bank lending and money supply growth, it generally implements restraint in a gradual and subtle way, reducing the growth rate at which it supplies reserves to the banking system. As expansion of reserves begins to slow against strong demand for reserves by banks to make loans and increase earning assets, the cost of reserves begins to rise. The cost of reserves usually is reflected almost immediately in the cost of federal funds, the reserves banks sell (lend) to one another. These federal funds transactions are the primary reserve adjustment device used by the nation's biggest banks. The cost of federal funds, known as the federal funds rate, increases because banks are competing against one another for reserves to expand their individual loan and investment portfolios.

The increased cost of reserves means banks must charge more on loans and command more on investments to make any expansion in earning assets profitable. At least some banks will be induced to cut back on loans as their management responds to rising costs or to a decline in loan demand from customers who are unwilling to pay higher loan rates for borrowed funds. Banks that respond in this way typically will allow loans to be repaid without extending new ones (and may sell some securities to convert assets into reserves) to reduce their deposit base and thus their need for maintaining a high level of reserves. These adjustments invariably reduce the amount of demand deposits in the nation's banking system and the amount of required reserves needed to support those deposits.

APPENDIX III

FEDERAL RESERVE POLICY

Open market operations are the primary policy tool used by the Federal Reserve to control the growth of money and credit in accordance with the nation's long-term economic goals. They also are used to defend the banking system against unpredictable day-to-day strains. The Federal Reserve's buying and selling of government securities to counter recession, to contain inflation, or to promote balanced economic growth is characterized as "dynamic" open market operations. The Federal Reserve's buying and selling of government securities to offset or nullify undesired day-to-day changes in bank reserves and money supply is characterized as "defensive" open market operations.

The Federal Reserve's strategy for implementing monetary policy involves both dynamic and defensive applications, and the nature of that strategy is the primary focus of this chapter. Also examined in this chapter are the major nonpolicy factors that cause changes in bank reserves, money supply, and interest rates, and the impact of bank asset-liability management decisions on monetary policy control.

THE MONETARY POLICY DECISION-MAKING PROCESS

The Federal Open Market Committee (FOMC) meets in Washington, D.C., every 4 to 6 weeks to set monetary policy. At these meetings, fundamental decisions are made regarding whether monetary policy should be structured to stimulate, restrain, or maintain the status quo of the economy during the upcoming month. These decisions are embodied in a policy directive sent to the New York trading desk. This directive specifies not only the goals of monetary policy but also the specific interest rate, reserve, and money supply growth targets that the desk should meet to achieve these goals.

At each FOMC meeting, the seven members of the Federal Reserve Board of Governors and the five Reserve bank presidents that comprise the committee review the current status of the economy, examine a range of economic forecasts and projections, and discuss which of the following three policy alternatives to implement:

- *easier monetary policy*—characterized by declining interest rates and a speedup in reserve and money supply growth;

- *tighter monetary policy*—characterized by rising interest rates and a slowing in reserve and money supply growth; or
- *stable monetary policy*—characterized by no change in interest rates or reserve and money supply growth.

Each policy alternative is examined in the context of the precise interest rate, reserve, and money supply growth targets that would be associated with that approach. Economic implications and GNP forecasts linked to each alternative also are reviewed.

Most FOMC directives call for a stable monetary policy. One reason is the complexity of the economy. Monetary policy changes do not begin to affect the economy until months after implementation. A decision to tighten or ease policy 1 month after a policy change was made would not allow sufficient time to see the results of the initial change.

The general approach of the Federal Reserve is to implement monetary policy gradually so that the economy changes without major market disruptions or dislocations. Changing monetary policy each month would not only be destabilizing to the nation's banking system and credit markets but would also be inconsistent with the 18- to 24-month average cyclical pattern of the nation's business activity.

FOMC policy directives and meeting summaries are made public about 1 month after each FOMC meeting. Included in all directives is a general statement of the FOMC's ultimate goals. The arrangement of the goals within the statement indicates the committee's current sense of priority with respect to each economic objective.

The FOMC directive does not tell the New York trading desk what to buy or sell or precisely when to do so. These operational details are left to the discretion of the System Open Market Account manager in New York.

Objectives and Strategies

Monetary policy strategy is designed to achieve economic objectives.

The Full Employment and Balanced Growth Act of 1978 (Humphrey-Hawkins Act) placed a sharp focus on price stability as a national economic goal and provided the Federal Reserve with a new legislative framework for its monetary policy strategy.

Under the 1978 Humphrey-Hawkins Act, the Federal Reserve must develop annual objectives for money supply and credit growth. These objectives must support the national economic objectives. The Federal Reserve also is required to report periodically to Congress on its performance. Each February, the chairman of the Federal Reserve Board must report to the banking committees of the House and Senate on the objectives the FOMC has set for the growth of various money and reserve measures during the current year and the "annual numerical goals for employment, production, real income, productivity, and prices" for each of the next 5 years. Each July, the chairman must report on any revisions to the year's objectives and provide preliminary goals for the next year.

The Federal Reserve operates under a policy strategy that sets long-range (1 year) targets. These targets are specific numerical values for such economic measures as prices and real GNP growth against which monetary policy actions will be structured and assessed. Targets serve as checkpoints in the attainment of objectives.

The reserve measures considered by the Federal Reserve for possible targeting include the following:

- *total reserves*—all banking system assets that are eligible for meeting reserve requirements (reserve account balances plus currency held by banks in their vaults);
- *borrowed reserves*—reserves borrowed by depositories from the Federal Reserve's discount window;
- *nonborrowed reserves*—total reserves minus borrowed reserves;
- *required reserves*—reserves that banks must keep in compliance with reserve requirements against transactions deposits and certain other reservable liabilities;
- *excess reserves*—total reserves minus required reserves;
- *monetary base*—total reserves plus currency in circulation (the foundation for all money growth in the banking system);
- *net free reserves*—excess reserves in the banking system minus borrowings from the Federal Reserve (when borrowings are larger than excess reserves, this measure is referred to as net borrowed reserves); and
- *basic reserve position*—excess reserves minus discount window borrowings from the Federal Reserve and federal funds borrowings.

Setting the Targets

At each of its monthly meetings, the FOMC sets a money supply growth rate target range for the next 3 months. This decision is the first step in the policy implementation process. The second step is to determine the growth of total reserves that would be required to allow for targeted money supply growth. Specific reserve growth paths for the next 3 months are estimated for total reserves, nonborrowed reserves, and the monetary base. In setting these growth paths, the FOMC tries to project the likely effect of nonpolicy factors on bank reserves. These projections are factored into the targeted reserve paths.

As the third step in the policy process, the FOMC determines the reserve growth needed each month to achieve its 3-month target. Because additions to total reserves provide banks with a base for creating new deposits and are more closely related to money supply than nonborrowed reserves, total reserves are considered the primary reserve target objective. Nonborrowed reserves, however, are more directly controllable by the Federal

Reserve through open market operations. For this reason, open market operations initially aim at the nonborrowed reserve target established to guide policy for the 4- to 6-week period until the next FOMC meeting.

EVOLUTION OF THE FEDERAL RESERVE'S OPERATING STRATEGY
Money Market Strategy

In the 1950s and early 1960s, the Federal Reserve used a money market strategy in applying open market operations. Under this strategy, the Federal Reserve's open market purchases and sales were directed at maintaining stability in financial markets by ensuring that interest rates and securities prices changed in a gradual and stable manner.

The money market strategy stemmed in part from concern over the large amount of government securities accumulated in World War II and held by financial institutions. It also stemmed from concern that rapid increases in interest rates would depress securities prices and impair the functioning of the nation's financial institutions and markets. Prevailing economic theory also maintained that monetary policy really couldn't control economic activity because consumer and business spending decisions were largely insensitive to interest rate changes. Moreover, any interest rate changes sufficient to change spending in the short run would have to be so large that the nation's financial markets would be disrupted. Fiscal policy was seen as the primary way to counter recession and inflation. Monetary policy was only supposed to support fiscal policy by supplying the money and credit growth necessary to meet the needs of an expanding economy and by preventing financial crises.

The Federal Reserve's primary operating target for the money market strategy was net free reserves. Open market operations and discount rate changes were used to maintain a predetermined level of net free reserves. An increase in free reserves meant an easing of policy; a decrease (or movement into net borrowed reserves) meant a tightening of policy.

Even Keel Policy

The term *even keel* was applied to the policy followed by the Federal Reserve's trading desk in the 1960s and early 1970s immediately before, during, and after the Treasury borrowed in the market by selling its new notes, bills, and bonds. During this period, the Federal Reserve did not change monetary policy. Rather, it effectively steered the keel of the monetary policy ship on a straight course.

The Federal Reserve's even keel policy was designed to ensure that the Treasury would have a stable market in which to sell the government's new debt instruments. This meant that the Federal Reserve had to ensure that there were sufficient reserves in the banking system so that banks could lend to dealers. This enabled the dealer firms to buy the Treasury issues. The Federal Reserve also had to ensure that interest rates would remain virtually stable during the financing period so that the Treasury issues would be attractive. Even keel didn't mean that the Federal Reserve would peg interest rates or drive rates down so that the Treasury would get a favorable rate. Rather, it meant that interest rates would remain stable during the period, subject only to shifts caused by market forces and not Federal Reserve policy.

In tight money periods, even keel would mean a temporary pause in restraint to pump up reserves and keep interest rates from rising. The Federal Reserve's primary objective was to ensure that no Treasury financial venture would fail—that there would be sufficient reserves to support loans to the Treasury (purchases of new government debt), and that the Treasury would not have to pay excessive interest rates.

As the government debt began to grow during the 1960s and Treasury borrowing began to accelerate, the Federal Reserve used its even keel policy more and more frequently. The policy began to impair control over bank reserves. The Federal Reserve abandoned the even keel policy when it altered its open market operating strategy in the 1970s to orient open market operations toward achieving better control of reserve and money growth.

Reliance on the Federal Funds Rate and the Monetary Aggregates

In the late 1960s and early 1970s, the Federal Reserve adopted a more comprehensive and quantitative strategy, linking short-term targets to intermediate targets and long-term objectives. It dropped net free reserves as an operating target, designated the federal funds rate as the key operating target for open market operations, and began to set intermediate target ranges for key money supply measures. This change in operating strategy was motivated by the Federal Reserve's growing concern over rising inflation rates and money supply growth in the late 1960s.

By 1970, the FOMC began routinely to specify numerical target growth rates for various monetary aggregates in its monthly policy instructions to the desk. It began to place greater emphasis in assessing monetary policy's effectiveness on how well the New York trading desk achieved precise numerical targets. Open market operating strategy gradually changed in the 1970s and became a strategy in which monetary aggregates were viewed as intermediate targets while interest rates were used as operating targets.

Open market operations were directed at keeping the federal funds rate within the target range on a weekly average basis and, at times, on a daily basis. The target range set by the FOMC, sometimes as narrow as one-half of a percentage point but rarely more than one percentage point, was based on the Federal Reserve's judgment of the short-term interest rate level that would be most appropriate for generating targeted growth in money supply. The range was subject to revision between FOMC meetings if money supply growth moved outside its own targeted range of tolerance.

Under this operating strategy, reserves supplied to the banking system by the Federal Reserve became demand determined. That is, the Federal Reserve would invariably add reserves if strong demand threatened to drive the federal funds rate above the tolerance range ceiling. These additional reserves provided fuel for new money creation and money supply growth in excess of targeted ranges.

A Shift to Reserves

In October 1979, the Federal Reserve changed its open market operating strategy. The daily emphasis of open market operations shifted from stabilizing the federal funds rate to controlling the supply of bank reserves. This change in approach was made to give the Federal Reserve better control over money supply and reserve growth, which had exceeded targets in the late 1970s. It also was made to reduce inflationary expectations among businesses and the public, which had been fueled, in part, by the Federal Reserve's inability to control money growth. In addition, the Federal Reserve wanted to change the perception of banks and other lenders that credit could be aggressively marketed under any circumstances because the federal funds rate and other money market rates would always be stabilized by the Federal Reserve within a narrow range.

The 1979–82 operating strategy emphasized reserve paths and targeting, a technique designed to help the Federal Reserve avoid persistent over- or undershooting of its money and reserve growth targets. Under the pre-1979 approach, over- or undershooting of reserve and money growth targets typically occurred because the Federal Reserve's primary response to upward or downward pressure on short-term interest rates was to buy or sell securities from the open market portfolio. These actions constantly expanded or reduced the supply of reserves and banks' ability to create more money. Under the 1979–82 approach, the New York trading desk's purchases and sales of securities were designed not to stabilize the federal funds rate but to provide a volume of nonborrowed reserves consistent with the targeted growth for money supply.

By expanding or contracting the supply of nonborrowed reserves, the Federal Reserve could more effectively control money supply growth. The result, however, was substantially greater variability in the federal funds rate.

Post-1982 Strategy Modifications

In 1982, the Federal Reserve modified its reserve path and targeting approach in an effort to reduce some of the variability in short-term interest rates that had been a product of the nonborrowed reserves targeting strategy. The federal funds rate was reinstated as an operational target although it was not given the degree of priority it had before 1979. Nonborrowed reserves remained the key operating target, but the automatic character of the targeting method that the Federal Reserve had used in 1979–82 was modified. Under the 1979–82 strategy, when the monetary aggregates deviated from their preset targets, the New York trading desk's buying or selling response was automatic. Under the post-1982 strategy, an FOMC policy decision is made on whether to add or reduce bank reserves to bring the aggregates back on track.

Under the post-1982 nonborrowed reserve growth target approach, the federal funds rate level at which the Federal Reserve initiates open market operations does not reflect the particular federal funds rate desired by the Federal Reserve. It is simply the prevailing rate on the day when the trading desk manager at the New York Federal Reserve believes that reserves should be added or taken out of the banking system to achieve the targeted level of nonborrowed reserves for the reserve maintenance period. Such an action reflects the trading desk's assessment of reserve availability rather than a desire to change the federal funds rate. The trading desk's open market actions, of course, typically change the federal funds rate, but bringing about a specific interest rate change is no longer a primary operational consideration in implementing monetary policy.

The FOMC now targets discount window borrowing from one reserve maintenance period to the next in accordance with a targeted nonborrowed reserve path. At each FOMC meeting, an intended discount window borrowing level for the banking system is set as a matter of policy. This level of borrowing is then deducted from the total of reserves that banks would have to hold to achieve the money supply growth target. An initial path for nonborrowed reserves is then derived using this total as a base. If market demand for money and reserves deviates between FOMC meetings from the set trend lines, the trading desk tries to make the banking system adhere to the intended discount window borrowing level by adjusting the nonborrowed reserves path.

MONETARISM

In the 1950s and 1960s, the American economist Milton Friedman, through his writings and his teachings at the University of Chicago, spawned the body of economic theory known today as monetarism. Friedman not only adapted the quantity theory of money and the Fisher equation of exchange to the modern economy but also provided considerable statistical support for the theory that money was the most important determinant of economic activity. He did this by using national income accounts data that had not been developed when Fisher postulated his equation of exchange.

To Friedman, the key relationship in the economy was not the relationship between total income and total spending, as maintained by Keynesian theory, but the relationship between total income and the quantity of money that the public preferred to hold. Friedman contended that the public's preference (demand) for money was relatively stable and predictable. Thus, if the actual amount of money available in the economy differed from what the public wanted to hold, consumers and businesses would adjust their spending until they held money balances in accordance with their preferences.

If the economy had "too much" money, people and businesses would seek to adjust their portfolios by converting excess money holdings into goods and financial assets until they had the balance of money, goods, and financial assets they preferred. If the economy had "too little" money, people and businesses would seek to adjust their portfolios by holding down spending on goods, selling financial assets, and otherwise building up money balances to match their preferences. These portfolio adjustments would lead to a condition in which public preferences for money matched the actual amount available.

The Basic Tenets of Monetarism

Over the last 2 decades, Milton Friedman and other monetarists have developed a broad body of economic theory that has tended to refute Keynesian contentions about how the economy works. Although monetarists themselves disagree about some of the principles and precepts of monetarism, they tend to share the following general views about the workings of the economy and the effects of monetary and fiscal policy on the economy.

- *The money supply is the single most important determinant of the level of GNP.*

Although many factors affect production, employment, and prices, a change in the growth of the money supply is the major determinant of the economy's current level of production and employment and the major determinant of both the current and future level of prices.

Monetarists grant that the economy's GNP growth over very long periods of time will be determined by technology, productivity, and the quantity and quality of the nation's productive resources. However, to assure reasonable stability in employment and prices in the present, monetarists maintain that money supply growth must be properly controlled.

- *The velocity of money is reasonably stable in the short run. Thus, there is a direct relationship between changes in money supply and changes in income and output.*

An examination of M1 velocity from 1910 to 1983 shows three different velocity trends. From 1915 to 1930, velocity was relatively stable. Velocity declined steadily from 1930 to 1945, and then rose sharply and steadily from 1945 to 1980, increasing at an average rate of about 3 percent annually.

Monetarists point to the reasonable predictability of velocity on a year-to-year basis within each of these three periods to support their contentions. They also note the fairly stable cyclical pattern of velocity, which rises during business cycle expansions and falls during contractions. Other economists, however, point to the sharp changes in the velocity trend in 1930, 1945, and 1980 to support their contention that velocity cannot be assumed to be relatively constant.

- *Trends in money supply growth and prices tend to correlate over time.*

Although there is no clear relationship between short-term changes in the money supply and the price level, trends in money supply growth and the price level tend to correlate over time. Trends in wages and interest rates also appear to track with money supply growth trends between 1960 and 1980.

During the 1960–80 period, the inflation rate, as measured by the increase in the GNP price deflator, rose steadily from 1.4 percent in 1960 to 9.7 percent in 1980. A deceleration in inflation occurred in 1971 and 1972, when the government instituted a program of wage and price controls. However, a sharp surge in inflation followed in 1973–75 when the wage-price controls program was ended and world oil prices were quadrupled by OPEC (the oil-producing exporting countries).

From 1980 to 1984, price and wage growth slowed as the Federal Reserve sought to reduce money supply growth gradually to arrest inflation. During these 4 years, annual increases in wages averaged about 1.8 percent. The inflation rate declined from 9.7 percent in 1980 to 4 percent in 1983. However, money supply growth did not slow. Indeed, it accelerated from 5 percent growth in 1981 to 9.2 percent growth in 1983. This trend reversed a 4-year slowing in the money supply growth rate from 7.9 percent in 1977 to only 5 percent in 1981 and suggested to monetarists that inflation would reaccelerate in the mid-1980s.

- *Changes in the money supply change the level of total spending in the economy through the adjustments consumers and businesses make in their holdings of financial and nonfinancial assets.*

Holders of excess money balances attempt, through spending on goods and financial assets, to adjust their personal portfolios to retain a preferred balance among money, financial assets, and goods. As a result, money supply changes affect a broader range of financial assets and interest rates than Keynesian theory suggests. Under Keynesian theory, money supply increases lead to lower interest rates, which reduce borrowing costs and increase bank lending and business investment spending.

- *Fiscal policy will have little, if any, effect on total spending or the level of GNP unless the money supply changes.*

Monetarists contend that an increase in government spending designed to move the economy out of recession will not work if the government finances its spending increase through increased taxes or borrowings from the public. Both of these financing measures simply reallocate existing money from the private sector to the public sector and thus offer little, if any, net stimulation to the economy.

Likewise, a tax reduction designed to raise total spending in the context of a balanced federal budget would be ineffective without a money supply change. Such a tax cut would mean less government revenue and government spending when the public is spending more.

Under Keynesian theory, a tax cut increases consumer spending and increases total income. An increase in total income increases the demand for money, which, in turn, drives up the interest rate. A higher interest rate pulls some of the public's asset money balances into transactions balances where it is spent. A higher interest rate also results in less investment spending, which blunts some of the stimulus caused by the initial tax cut. Monetarists hold that the increase in the interest rate caused in this static money supply environment would likely offset the positive stimulus of the tax cut. Thus, if fiscal policy is to be used as an economic control device, it must be complemented with appropriate money supply changes to have any effect.

Monetarists contend that money supply increases initially cause the interest rate to decline. However, as consumers and businesses begin to spend their excess liquidity and new income is generated for others, the demand for money is forced up and interest rates begin to rise. Moreover, an increase in money supply fuels market expectations of continued inflation. Lenders add an inflationary premium to "real" interest rates as protection against an anticipated loss of purchasing power of the money that will be received as repayments over time. Monetarists contend that when money supply is increased, the upward pressure on the interest rate tends to exceed the downward pressure, resulting in a net increase in the interest rate.

Monetarists further contend that the Federal Reserve's failure to recognize this response of the interest rate to increases in the money supply causes the central bank to structure inappropriate monetary policy. The Federal Reserve relies on the interest rate as an operating target. When the interest rate increases, the central bank perceives this as an indicator of the effect of its tight monetary policies and structures policy accordingly. To monetarists, a rising interest rate fueled by money supply growth indicates an easy monetary policy and suggests further inflation and a lack of Federal Reserve policy control. Monetarists argue that the Federal Reserve should not rely on the interest rate as an operating target but concentrate instead on controlling the money supply.

- *Monetary policy should be structured to generate a constant 3 to 5 percent annual rate of money supply growth.*

Although monetarists contend that changes in money supply cause changes in income and output, they are unsure precisely how long it takes for those changes to affect the economy. Indeed, monetarists themselves are divided in their assessment of the time lags between money supply changes (cause) and changes in income and output (effect). Milton Friedman, for example, maintains that the lag between money supply cause and economic effect may be 12 to 18 months or longer. Most monetarists, however, believe the lag is much shorter; the consensus view is about 6 months. The lack of agreement about the time lag is rooted in the wide time variations that have been found in the data that link money supply changes to GNP changes.

Because the time lags are variable and unpredictable, monetarists contend that monetary policy should be structured to generate a constant 3 to 5 percent annual rate of money supply growth. They believe that the Federal Reserve's attempts at structuring policy to be easy or tight to counter recession or inflation should be ended.

A constant rate of annual money supply growth of 3 to 5 percent would match the long-term annual growth rate of the U.S. economy. By providing the economy with 3 to 5 percent more money each year, just enough new money would be assured for balanced, sustainable real growth. Although a constant rate of money growth wouldn't cure the economy of business cycles, in time the economy would rid itself of the cycles' more volatile inflationary and recessionary swings and would establish a more stable operating environment.

Monetarists contend that the Federal Reserve's discretionary, or countercyclical, approach to monetary policy is wrong because it tends to destabilize the economy. They maintain that the Federal Reserve worsens the economy's inflations and recessions because it fails to appreciate the long and unpredictable time lag between money supply changes and economic change. This lack of appreciation causes the Federal Reserve to overreact when the economy fails to respond to tighter or easier monetary policy. This overreaction invariably provides the economy with too much ease or too much restraint at the wrong time, which exacerbates inflation or recession.

To prevent the Federal Reserve from using its discretionary judgment in implementing policy, which makes conditions worse, monetarists have proposed the constant rate of money growth rule and have supported federal legislation that would require the Federal Reserve to abide by this rule.

INDEX

A

Ability-to-pay theory, 188
Abscissa, 29
Absolute advantage, 91
Absolute concentration ratio, 212–14
Acceleration principle, 289
Acquisitions. *See* Mergers
Adjusted GNP, 271–75, 283
Adjusted income, 355
Administered inflation, 359, 361, 364
Administrative lag, 444
Adult noninstitutional population, 322
AFL-CIO, 245, 253
Aggregate demand
   consumption expenditures, 398–409
   definition, 397
   fiscal theory and, 431, 438–39
   government expenditures, 409
   investment spending, 409
   multiplier effect, 417–19
   national income equilibrium and, 416
   neoclassical model, 381, 383
   net exports, 413
Aggregate supply, 382, 413. *See also* Gross national product
Aging trends, 230, 406
Allocative efficiency, 15, 72
All-urban index (CPI-U), 343, 351
American Federation of Labor (AFL), 242, 244, 245
Annualized growth rate, 57
Annually balanced budget, 446–47
Antitrust laws, 210–11
Arc formula
   demand elasticity, 154, 156
   income elasticity of demand, 170
   supply elasticity, 166–67
Asymptotic relationships, 39
Automatic stabilizers, 439, 441–42, 445
Autonomous change in consumption, 404–6, 409
Autonomous consumption, 399, 404
Availability of resources, 74–75

Availability of substitutes, 164
Average absolute error, 58, 60
Average deviation, 54
Average duration of unemployment in weeks, 302
Average prime rate charged by banks, 303
Average propensity to consume, 401, 404
Average propensity to save, 402, 404
Average workweek, 293

B

Backward vertical mergers, 211
Balanced Budget and Emergency Deficit Control Act of 1985, 470–73, 477–78
Balanced budget multiplier, 438–39
Base year, 347
Benefits-received theory, 186–88
Bentham, Jeremy, 87
Bracket creep, 351, 358
Brand loyalty, 219
Building permits indicator, 294–95
Bureau of Economic Analysis (BEA), 292, 309
Bureau of Labor Statistics (BLS), 321, 346
Burns, Arthur, 291–92
Business
   antitrust issues, 210–11, 225
   concentration measures, 212–14
   failures, 220
   growth, 209–10, 220
   market entry barriers, 219–20
   market share measure, 215–17
   organizational types, 205–9
   profitability factors, 218–19
Business cycles
   automatic fiscal stabilizers, 439, 441–42
   coincidental indicators and, 302
   definition, 283
   econometric forecasts, 309–10
   economic stability and, 15
   lagging indicators and, 303
   leading indicators and, 296–97
   phases, 283–86

theories, 286–91, 315–17
  unemployment and, 325, 329–30
  See also Economic indicators
Business inventory change, 263
Business profits, 218

C

Capital, 70, 71
Capital consumption allowance, 78, 268
Capital finance and balance sheet accounts, 257
Ceteris paribus assumption, 103, 106, 111, 117
Change in business and consumer credit outstanding, 295–96
Change in business inventory, 263
Change in demand, 111–15
Change in quantity demanded, 111–15
Change in quantity supplied, 120
Change in sensitive prices, 295
Change in supply, 120
Circular flow model, 375–77
Civilian labor force participation rate, 234
Civilian noninstitutional population (CNP), 234
Classical theory, 375
  decline of, 384
  Keynesian criticism of, 386–89
  modern, 381–83
  price-wage flexibility, 380–81, 389
  savings and investment, 378–79, 389
  supply and demand, 377–78, 380, 383
Coefficient of elasticity, 151–54. *See also* Elasticity of demand
Coefficients, 27
Coincidental indicators, 297, 300–302
Collective bargaining
  history of, 240–43
  labor laws and, 243–46
  supplemental unemployment benefit clauses, 442
  wages and, 241, 242, 246–48, 371–72
Command systems, 84–86
Commercial and industrial loans outstanding, 303
Comparative advantage, 90–92
Competition, 89, 92, 185, 210–12, 215–18
Complementary goods, 105–6
Composite coincidental index, 300, 302, 306–8
Composite lagging index, 303, 306–8
Composite leading index, 296–97, 306–8

Concentration measures, 212–17
Concessionary bargaining, 245–46
Conglomerate mergers, 211
Congress of Industrial Organizations (CIO), 244, 245, 253
Constant-dollar GNP, 271–75
Constants, 26, 27, 43
Consumer expenditure survey, 346
Consumer price index (CPI)
  calculation of, 347–48
  definition, 343
  guidelines for use, 352–53
  history of, 346
  limitations of, 348–49, 351
  percent change calculation, 353–54
  quality change measures, 349–50
  relative importance of items, 348
  seasonal adjustments, 350
  uses, 350–52
  weights, 348
Consumer sovereignty, 88
Consumption and investment choices
  law of diminishing returns, 81–82
  production possibility theory, 72–81
  production-related questions, 82–84
Consumption curve, 399, 401, 406
Consumption expenditures
  autonomous changes in, 404–6, 409
  consumption curve, 399, 401
  consumption function, 398
  induced changes, 406, 409
  personal, 260–61
  propensity to consume, 401, 404, 406, 418
  propensity to save, 401, 404
Consumption function, 398
Contractionary fiscal policy, 436, 446–47
Contraction phase, 284
Convergence hypothesis, 85–86
Corporations, 205, 208–10
Cost-of-living adjustment clauses (COLAs), 247–48, 357
Cost-of-living measures, 349
Cost of production variable, 116–17
Cost-push inflation, 358–59, 361, 362
Council of Economic Advisers, 181, 284
Credit theory, 287
Cross elasticity of demand, 169
Crowding-out effect, 449, 466–69
Current-dollar GNP, 258–59, 271–72, 283
Current population survey (CPS), 321
Cyclical innovation theory, 289
Cyclically balanced budget, 447
Cyclical unemployment, 329–30

D

Data conversion, 55–58
Debt. *See* Public debt
Debt burden, 463–64
Debt ownership, 464
Deflationary gap, 420–23, 431
Deflation expectation variable, 116
Demand
   changes in, 111–15
   curve, 108–9, 111–13, 141, 154, 157, 159
   determinants of, 103–6, 112
   equation, 103–4
   law of, 103, 107
   market, 109–10
   market equilibrium and, 121–29
   schedule, 106–7
   See also Elasticity of demand; Supply and demand
Demand-pull inflation, 358, 360–62
Demographic trends, 229–33, 406
Dependent variables, 26, 27, 43, 103, 109, 115
Depreciation, 78, 268
Depressions, 284, 285
Determinants of demand, 103–6, 112
Determinants of supply, 115–17, 120
Difference between periods, 57
Diminishing marginal utility, 107
Direct relationship, 29
Discomfort index, 361
Discouraged workers, 327–28
Discretionary fiscal policy, 442–45
Dismal science, 4
Disposable personal income (DPI), 269–70
Dissavings, 399
Division of labor, 89–90
Dollar depreciation, 360
Dormant partners, 207
Dual terminology, 14–15
Durables, 260, 261
Duration of unemployment, 325–27

E

Earnings, 239–40. *See also* Income; Wages and salaries
Econometric forecasts, 309–10
Economic efficiency, 15
Economic indicators
   assessment checklist, 306–9
   coincidental, 297, 300–302
   criticism of, 65–66
   history of, 291–92
   lagging, 302–5
   leading, 292–97
   time series and, 292–93
Economic profits, 218
Economic Recovery Tax Act of 1981, 351, 462, 469
Economics
   maximization of resources, 71–72
   micro- and macroeconomics, 5–6
   misconceptions, 12–15
   outlook of, 4–5
   reasons for studying, 3
   system goals, 15–16
   tools of, 6–12
   world trade, 21–22
Educational attainment, 232–33, 334
Effect lag, 444
Efficiency, 15, 72
Elasticity
   categories, 152–54
   cross elasticity of demand, 169
   definition, 151
   income elasticity of demand, 169–70
   supply, 166–68
   See also Elasticity of demand
Elasticity of demand
   definition, 151–52
   determinants of, 164–65
   labor, 170–71
   measurement of, 154, 156–57, 159
   tax shifting and, 193–96
Elasticity of supply
   arc formula, 166
   determinants of, 167–68
Employed persons category, 322
Employees on nonagricultural payrolls, 300
Employment Act of 1946. *See* Full Employment and Economic Stabilization Act of 1946
Entrepreneurial ability, 70, 71
Equations. *See* Linear equations
Equilibrium national income, 413, 416–17, 420, 423
Equilibrium price, 121–26, 128–29
Equilibrium quantity, 121–26, 128–29
Establishment survey, 300
Expansionary fiscal policy, 436, 446, 449
Expansion phase, 284, 286
Expectation-induced inflation, 359
Expenditure approach, 260–64
Exports, 263–64, 413
Externalities, 181–83

F

Factors of production, 69, 236
Fair Labor Standards Act, 149
Fairness, 16
Fallacy of composition, 12–13, 87
Fallacy of false conclusions, 14
Federal budget, 446–48. *See also* Public debt
Federal income tax, 191. *See also* Taxes
Federal Mediation and Conciliation Service, 245
Federal Reserve
  bank reserve controls, 499–501
  monetary policy decision making, 503
  monetary policy goals, 498
  money supply role, 484–86
  operating strategy, 506–9
Fiscal drag, 445–46
Fiscal policy
  automatic stabilizers, 439, 441–42, 445
  balanced budget multiplier, 438–39
  case example, 439
  criticisms of, 449–52, 457–58
  crowding-out effect, 449
  discretionary, 442–45
  federal budget and, 446–49
  fiscal drag problem, 445–46
  goal, 423
  government spending effects, 435–36, 438
  speedup of, 444–45
  theory, 431, 435
  timing lag problem, 442–45
  See also Public debt
Flow of funds accounts, 257
Flow of funds approach, 260
Flow of income approach, 260
Forecasts, 58, 60, 309–10, 444
Foreign debt ownership, 464–66, 472, 473
Foreign exchange rates, 360
Forward buying, 359
Forward vertical mergers, 211
Four-firm concentration ratio, 212–14
Four-firm relative concentration ratio, 213–14
Frictional unemployment, 332–35
Full Employment and Economic Stabilization Act of 1946, 181, 376
Full-employment cyclically adjusted budget, 447–48
Function, 25–26
Functional distribution of income, 234–36
Functional finance approach, 447

G

Gasoline supply and demand, 145–47
Give-backs, 245–46
Government bankruptcy, 465
Government deficit. *See* Public debt
Government intervention
  antitrust laws, 210–11
  automatic stabilizers, 439, 441–42, 445
  banking regulation, 201–2
  circular flow model role, 376
  competition and, 185
  economic activity promotion, 179–80
  extent of, 179
  Keynesian approach, 389–90
  market failure and, 181–85
  minimum wage laws, 149
  usury laws, 148–49
  wage-price controls, 97–99, 148, 450–51
  See also Fiscal policy; Taxes
Government spending
  aggregate demand and, 409
  balanced budget multiplier effect, 438–39
  effects of, 435–36, 438
  gross national product and, 263
  trends, 185
  See also Public debt
Gramm-Rudman-Hollings Act, 470–73, 477–78
Graphing
  business cycles, 283–84
  consumption, 399
  consumption and investment choices, 74–80
  demand, 108–9, 111–13
  linear equations, 28–29, 39, 43
  market demand, 110
  supply, 118–19
Gross national product (GNP)
  calculation of, 260–64
  definition, 258–60
  fiscal policy and, 435–36
  inflating and deflating, 274–75
  inflation and, 360
  limitations of, 264
  1987 growth, 279–80
  price change adjustments, 270–73
  public debt and, 463, 473
Gross private domestic investment (GPDI), 262–63, 268
Growth, 16
"Guns" and "butter," 72–74, 77–78

H

Herfindahl-Hirschman Index (H-HI), 215–17
Hidden taxes, 192–93
Hobson, John, 287
Horizontal mergers, 210
Household income, 236–37
Human capital, 80–81
Hyperinflation, 365–66

I

Implementation lag, 444
Implicit price deflator, 274
Imports, 263, 264
Income
    aggregate demand and, 401, 402, 406, 409, 418–19
    consumption-savings factors, 270
    demand equation variable, 104
    earnings, 239–240
    fiscal policy and, 431, 435–36, 438–39, 445–46
    functional distribution measure, 234–36
    inflation and, 355, 357
    national income accounts, 269–70
    national income equilibrium and, 416
    personal distribution measure, 236–37
    poverty index, 238
    See also Wage and salaries
Income approach, 260
Income elasticity of demand, 169–70
Income theory, 5
Independent goods, 106, 169
Independent variables, 26, 27, 43, 104, 109, 115–17
Individuals
    collective bargaining, 240–48
    economic roles, 234
    income, 234–40
    labor force, 234
    population trends and, 229–33, 406
Individual welfare measure, 265–66
Induced changes in consumption, 406, 409
Industrial production index, 300
Inelastic demand, 153, 163, 164, 194, 195
Inferior products, 104, 170
Infinitely elastic, 153, 166, 195–96
Inflation
    definition, 343
    effects, 354–58

hyperinflation, 365–66
rate, 354, 363
real output and, 360–61
sources, 358–60
unemployment and, 361–64
See also Consumer price index
Inflationary gap, 423, 431
Inflation expectation variable, 116
Initial unemployment claims, 294
Injections, 376, 378, 379, 417, 442
Input-output accounts, 257
Interest expense, 463–64
Interest income, 70, 71
Interest rate
    classical theory and, 378–79
    control, 148–49
    inflation and, 356–57
    Keynesian theory and, 386–89
    public debt and, 466–69, 472
    supply and demand and, 141–45
International accounts, 257
Inventory changes indicator, 295
Inverse relationship, 29
Investment spending
    aggregate demand and, 409
    business cycle and, 288–89
    classical theory, 378–79
    gross national product and, 262–63
    Keynesian theory, 386–89
    national income equilibrium and, 416, 417
    public debt and, 466–69

J

Jevons, William Stanley, 290
Job leavers, 323
Job losers, 323
Justice Department, 211, 216–17

K

Keynes, John Maynard, 375, 384–86
Keynesian Cross diagram, 413
Keynesian theory, 375, 384, 393–94
    aggregate demand, 398–410
    aggregate supply, 413
    classical critique, 386–89
    multiplier effect, 417–20
    national income equilibrium, 413, 416–17
    paradox of thrift, 420
    recessionary inflationary gap, 420, 423

recommendations of, 389–90
See also Fiscal policy
Klein, Lawrence R., 309
Kondratieff cycles, 289

L

Labor, 70, 71
Labor contracts. *See* Collective bargaining
Labor cost per unit of output, manufacturing, 302
Labor demand elasticity, 170–71
Labor force, 234
Labor force participation rates, 234
Labor laws, 243–46
Labor-Management Relations Act, 244
Labor-Management Reporting and Disclosure Act, 245
Lagging indicators, 302–5
Laissez-faire economics, 85, 92, 180, 181, 381
Land, 70
Landrum-Griffin Act, 245
Law of comparative advantage, 90–92
Law of consumption, 398
Law of demand, 103, 107
Law of diminishing returns, 81–82
Law of increasing costs, 74–81
Law of supply, 115
Leading index, 293, 296–97
Leading indicators, 292–97
Leakages, 376–79, 417, 442
Leisure time measure, 264–65
Limit pricing, 219
Linear equations
 function concept, 25–26
 graph construction, 28–29, 39, 43
 quadrant coordinate system, 28–29, 39
 structure of, 26–28
 time and distance, 25–26
Liquidity preference function, 387–88
Liquidity trap, 388
Loanable funds, 141–45, 378–79
Local government taxes, 192–93

M

McNees, Stephen K., 310
Macroeconomics, 5–6
Malthus, Thomas, 4, 287
Manufacturing and trade sales, 300

Marginal propensity to consume, 401, 404, 406, 418
Marginal propensity to save, 402, 404
Marginal returns, 81
Marginal revenue, 162–63
Marginal utility, 107
Market basket, 347
Market demand, 109–10
Market entry barriers, 219–20
Market equilibrium, 121–29, 141
Market intervention, 147–49
Market share measures, 215–17
Market supply curve, 119
Market system, 85, 86
 comparative advantage, 90–92
 labor specialization, 89–90, 92
 principles of, 87–89
 shortcomings, 92
Marxist theory, 287–88
Mathematics. *See* Linear equations
Mean, 50–51
Measures of central tendency
 mean, 50–51
 median, 48–49
 mode, 46–48
Measures of dispersion
 range, 52
 standard deviation, 54–55
 variance, 52–54
Median, 48–49
Median family income, 237
Mergers, 210–11, 216–17, 225
Microeconomics, 5
Military buildup theory, 289–90
Minimum wage, 149, 175–76
Mixed economy, 179
Mobility trends, 231
Mode, 46–48
Monetarism, 287, 394, 509–13
Monetary policy, 498–501, 503–6
Money
 bimetal standard, 481
 circulation of, 484
 definition, 479–80
 gold standard, 480–81
 legal tender, 484–85
 supply, 485–88
 types, 481–83
Money creation
 lending and, 489–92
 liquidity constraints, 492–94
 multiple deposit creation, 494–98
Money income, 355

Money supply (M2), 295, 487–88
Monopoly, 210
Monthly data, 56
Multiplier effect, 417–20, 423, 436

N

National Bureau of Economic Research (NBER), 283, 284, 291
National debt. *See* Public debt
National income, 235, 269
National income accounting
  components, 257
  disposable personal income, 269–70
  gross national product, 258–67
  methods, 258
  net national product, 268–69
  personal income, 269
  purpose, 257
National Income and Product Accounting (NIPA), 257
National income equilibrium, 413, 416–17, 420, 423
National Industrial Recovery Act (NIRA), 243
National Labor Relations Act (NLRA), 240, 243, 244
National Labor Relations Board (NLRB), 243, 244
Natural unemployment, 380
Negative savings, 399
Neoclassical economics, 378, 381–83, 393–94
Net exports, 263–64, 413
Net national product (NNP), 268–69
Net private domestic investment (NPDI), 269
New contracts and orders for plant equipment, 294
New entrants, 323
New orders of consumer goods, 294
Nominal income, 355
Nominal interest rate, 356
Nonagricultural employment indicator, 300
Nondurables, 260, 261
Nonlinear demand curve, 159
Nonlinear equations, 39
Nonmonetary income, 237
Nonprice variables, 104–6, 111–15
Nonresidential fixed investments, 262, 263
Normal products, 104, 170
Normal profits, 218
Normative economic statements, 14
Norris-LaGuardia Act of 1932, 243

Not in the labor force category, 322
Number of consumers variable, 106
Number of suppliers variable, 117

O

Occupational earnings, 239–40
Occupational privilege taxes, 192
Oligopoly market, 210
Opportunity cost, 6–8, 74, 79, 90–92
Ordered pairs, 25, 26, 28, 39, 43
Ordinate, 29
Origin, 29
Outsourcing, 171, 246

P

Paradox of thrift, 420
Parameters, 27
Partnerships, 205–8
Percentage difference, 57
Perfectly inelastic, 153–54, 166
Personal consumption expenditure (PCE), 260–61
Personal distribution of income, 236–37
Personal income (PI), 269
Personal income less transfer payments, 300
Phillips Curve, 362–64
Planned investment, 417
Planned savings, 417
Pleasure-pain calculus, 87
Population trends
  age, 230, 406
  educational attainment, 232–33, 334
  growth, 229–30
  mobility, 231
Positive economic statements, 14
Positive relationship, 29
Poverty index, 238
Price
  classical theory and, 380
  controls, 97–99, 147–48, 450–51
  demand equation variable, 103, 108, 111–15
  gross national product and, 270–75
  Keynesian theory of, 389
  limiting, 219
  market equilibrium and, 121–26, 128–29, 141
  supply and, 115, 117–20
  supports, 147–49
  See also Consumer price index

Price elasticity of demand. *See* Elasticity of demand
Price expectation variable, 105
Price index, 272–74
Price of related goods variable, 105–6
Price theory, 5
Price-wage flexibility, 380–81, 389
Prime rate, 144–45, 303
Printing money, 365–66, 449, 465
Privatization, 473
Producer-durable equipment, 262
Production frontier, 74
Production possibility theory, 72–81
Production questions, 82–84
Product life cycle, 69
Profitability, 218–19
Profit and loss, 88–89
Progressive taxes, 188, 189, 191, 441
Property taxes, 192
Proportional taxes, 188, 189, 191, 192, 441
Public debt
  bankruptcy issue, 465
  crowding-out effect issue, 466–69
  debt burden, 463–64
  definition, 461
  Gramm-Rudman-Hollings Act and, 470–73, 477–78
  growth of, 461–62, 469
  inflationary pressure, 359–60
  issues, 464–70
  ownership of, 464–66

Q

Quadrant coordinate system, 28–29, 39
Qualitative measures, 264
Quality change measures, 265, 349–50
Quantity demanded, 103, 104, 108, 111–15, 141
Quantity supplied, 115, 117, 119, 120, 141
Quarterly data, 56

R

Railway Labor Act of 1926, 243
Range, 52
Rational expectation theory, 450
Ratio of consumer installment credit outstanding to personal income, 302–3
Ratio of manufacturing and trade inventories to sales, 302

Real business cycle theory, 315–17
Real GNP, 271–75, 283
Real income, 355, 357
Real interest rate, 356–57
Real output. *See* Gross national product
Recessionary gap, 420, 423, 431
Recessions, 284–86, 361
Recognition lag, 443
Rectangular hyperbola, 39, 154
Reentrants, 323, 327
Reference dates, 284
Regeneration of wants, 70
Regional accounts, 257
Regressive taxes, 188, 189, 191, 192
Relative concentration ratio, 213–14
Relative importance of items, 348
Relatively elastic, 152, 166
Rental equivalent estimate, 259
Residential fixed investments, 262
Resource availability, 74–75
Resource payments, 70–71, 235
Resources, 69
Revenue test, 162–63
Ricardo, David, 377
Right-to-work laws, 244
Risk measurement, 54–55

S

Sales taxes, 192
Savings
  classical theory, 378–79
  inflation and, 356
  Keynesian theory, 386–89, 398–99, 401, 402
  national income equilibrium and, 417
  paradox of thrift, 420
Savings function, 399, 400
Say's Law, 377–78, 386
Scarcity, 69
Scarcity-induced inflation, 359
Schumpeter, Joseph, 289
Seasonal unemployment, 323
Secret partners, 207
Self-fulfilling prophecy theory, 290–91
Self-interest, 87
Sensitive price change indicator, 295
Sequestration process, 471–73
Services, 260, 261
Silent partners, 207
Simple 70 formula, 11–12

Slopes, 27, 29, 39, 43
Social Security taxes, 191–92
Sole proprietorships, 205–6
Specialization, 89–90, 92
Spillovers, 181–83
Spread of values, 52
Stability, 15
Stagflation, 361, 452
Standard & Poor's 500 Stock Index, 294
Standard deviation, 54–55
Standard error, 60
State income taxes, 192
Statistics
    data conversions, 55–58
    forecasting and, 58, 60
    measures of central tendency, 46–51
    measures of dispersion, 52–55
    problems of, 46
Stock of wealth, 405
Structural theory, 288
Structural unemployment, 330–32
Study lag, 443
Subchapter S corporations, 209
Subsidies, 97, 98, 117, 148, 183–85
Substitution, 164–65, 169, 171
Sunk costs, 8–10
Sunspot theory, 290
Supplemental unemployment benefit (SUB) clauses, 442
Supply
    changes in, 120
    curve, 118–20, 141, 166–67
    determinants of, 115–17
    elasticity, 166–68
    equation, 115–16
    law of, 115
    market equilibrium and, 121–29
    market supply curve, 119
    schedule, 117–18
    See also Supply and demand
Supply and demand
    classical theory, 377–78, 380, 383
    gasoline price case, 145–47
    loanable funds, 141–45
    market intervention effects, 147–49
    neoclassical theory, 381–83
    oil industry case, 135–37
    tax and subsidy effects, 182–85
    tax shifting, 193–96
    See also Demand; Elasticity; Elasticity of demand; Supply
Supply-side economics, 445, 452, 462

T

Taft-Hartley Act, 244–45
TANSTAAFL, 11
Taste variable, 105
Tax base, 188, 189
Taxes
    classification, 188–91
    consumer price index use, 351
    corporations, 209
    definition, 185–86
    demand variable, 117
    externalities and, 182–83
    federal deficit and, 462, 465, 469, 473
    fiscal policy and, 436, 438, 441, 445, 446
    inflation and, 358
    shifting, 193–96
    theories, 186–88
    types, 191–93
    underground economy and, 266–67
    worldwide characteristics, 196–97
Tax incidence, 193, 195
Tax liability, 188, 189
Tax rate, 188, 189
Tax Recovery Act of 1986, 462
Technical efficiency, 15, 72
Technological advances, 76–78, 117, 350
Time and distance equations, 25–26
Time series, 292–93
TIPS (Tax-Based Income Policies), 451–52
Total aggregate demand, 397
Transfer payments, 263, 269, 300, 441–42, 452
Tufte, Edward, 290
Turning points, 283–84, 296–97
12-month moving average, 58

U

Underconsumption theory, 287
Underemployment, 328–29
Underground economy, 266–67
Unemployment
    adjusting to, 339–40
    classical theory, 380
    current population survey and, 322–23
    cyclical, 329–30
    definition, 321
    discouraged workers, 327–28
    duration of, 325–27
    frictional, 332–35

inflation and, 361–64
natural, 380
rates, 323, 327, 329, 331, 333–35
seasonal adjustment, 323
status categories, 323, 325
structural, 330–32
Unemployment compensation, 294, 441
Unfair labor practices, 244
Union membership, 240, 242–45. *See also* Collective bargaining
Unintended investments in inventory, 416
Unitary elasticity, 153, 166
Unlimited wants, 69–70
Unreported income, 266–67
"User pay," 188
Usury laws, 148–49

V

Value added, 276
Variables, 26, 27, 43
Variance, 52–54
Vendor performance, 295
Vertical mergers, 210–11

W

Wage-earner index (CPI-W), 343
Wage-price spiral, 359
Wages and salaries, 236
classical theory, 380
collective bargaining and, 241, 242, 246–48, 371–72
controls, 97–99, 450–51
differentials, 239–40
inflation and, 358–59, 362
Keynesian theory, 389
minimum, 149, 175–76
Wagner Act, 243, 244
Wealth variable, 104–5
World trade, 21–22

X

x-axis, 29

Y

y-axis, 29
Yellow journalism, 15

Economics for Bankers

Date: _____

This questionnaire is designed to get reader opinions on the adequacy and relevance of the text. Your comments, both positive and negative, will influence the design and content of future AIB textbooks. Thank you for your assistance.

I. Background Information

A. In this course I was a(n): ☐ instructor ☐ student

B. Highest educational attainment:
☐ High School ☐ Some College ☐ BA/BS Degree ☐ Advanced Degree

C. I am a(n): ☐ Officer ☐ Non-Officer ☐ Non-Bank Employee

D. Asset Size of Bank:
☐ $0-100m ☐ $101-500m ☐ $501-1b ☐ Over $1b

E. My major job responsibility is _____

F. I am pursuing an AIB diploma: ☐ Yes ☐ No

II. The Materials

Please rate the text according to the criteria below. Check the box that most closely corresponds with your opinions.

Thoroughness:	☐ covers too little of subject	☐ Covers sufficient content	☐ Covers too much unrelated content
Difficulty Level:	☐ Too basic	☐ Appropriate for level of course	☐ Too difficult
Interest Level:	☐ Dull and uninteresting	☐ Acceptable	☐ Very interesting
Organization:	☐ Sequenced logically	☐ Not in logical sequence	
Timeliness:	☐ Most content was current	☐ Most content was outdated	
Practicality:	☐ Too theoretical	☐ Has sufficient practical application	

Please rate the *overall effectiveness* of the text by circling the number which represents your opinion.

Very effective as a learning aid   Ineffective as a learning aid
5   4   3   2   1

III. Comments

A. Can you make any suggestions for improving the book?
_____
_____
_____

B. Would you recommend this book to someone who needs to know this information?
☐ Yes ☐ No

FOLD IN HALF AND STAPLE

FOLD HERE

BUSINESS REPLY MAIL
First Class   Permit No. 10579   Washington, D.C.

No Postage
Necessary
If Mailed
In The
United States

Postage Will Be Paid by

Educational Planning
Education Policy & Development Group
American Bankers Association
1120 Connecticut Avenue
Washington, D.C. 20036